Favorite Hobbies and Pastimes

A Sourcebook of Leisure Pursuits

ROBERT S. MUNSON

American Library Association

Chicago and London 1994

General Liability Disclaimer

In keeping with the publishing goals and practices of the American Library Association, its authors and editors apply diligence and judgment in locating and using reliable sources for the information published. However, no guarantee or warranty can be given, and all responsibility and liability for loss or damage are hereby disclaimed by the authors, editors, and publisher of this publication with respect to the accuracy, correctness, value and sufficiency of the data, methods, and other information contained herein as applied for any particular purpose or use.

Illustrations

The Curtiss Sparrowhawk drawing on page 206 is reprinted, by permission, from *Model Airplane News Presents the Best of Wylam, Book 4,* page 58. © 1971 by Air Age Inc.

The Mikado locomotive drawing on page 223 is reprinted, by permission, from *Locomotive Cyclopedia Of American Practice,* seventh edition, page 130. © 1925 by Simmons-Boardman Publishing Co.

The communications receiver drawing on page 260 is by the author. Permission is granted courtesy Kenwood Corporation to depict its product.

All other illustrations are by the author.

Managing editor: Kathryn P. Solt

Cover design: Harriett Banner

Text design: Dianne M. Rooney

Composed by Publishing Services, Inc. in Times Roman and Helvetica on Xyvision/Linotype L330

Printed on 50-pound Springhill, a pH-neutral stock, and bound in 10-point C1S cover stock by Braun-Brumfield, Inc.

The paper used in this publication meets the minimum requirements of American National Standard for Information Sciences—Permanence of Paper for Printed Library Materials, ANSI Z39.48-1984.

Library of Congress Cataloging-in-Publication Data

Munson, Robert S.
    Favorite hobbies and pastimes : a sourcebook of leisure pursuits / by Robert S. Munson.
        p.   cm.
    Includes bibliographical references and index.
    ISBN 0-8389-0638-9 (alk. paper)
    1. Hobbies—Handbooks, manuals, etc. 2. Handicraft—Handbooks, manuals, etc. 3. Leisure—United States—Handbooks, manuals, etc. I. Title.
GV1201.5.M86   1994
790.1′3—dc20   94-21907

Printed in the United States of America.

98 97 96 95 94   5 4 3 2 1

Contents

Acknowledgments

It's a long road from the origin of an idea for a book such as this, to the final product. Along the way many have expressed interest, and a few have provided needed support and encouragement. They include my wife Dorothy, my daughters Barbara Blazer and Carol Morganti, and son Robert J. Munson. Charles Faidley and the staff of the Public Library of Cincinnati and Hamilton County have made research a pleasure. Herbert Bloom and the staff of the American Library Association have provided guidance. Others who have helped significantly are Marshall Barnes, Ken Broo, Sarah Elliston, Brian O'Connell, and George Parsons. Thank you all.

Introduction

THIS IS A BOOK about America's favorite pastimes. It contains essays on a variety of spare time activities. Each essay is supplemented with listings that identify sources of additional information.

A hobby is defined as an activity or interest pursued for pleasure or relaxation, and not as a main livelihood occupation. Based on that broad definition, this book covers more than just traditional hobbies and crafts. It also includes animals, the arts, sports, science, and travel. Continuing education and voluntarism are also presented in view of the pleasure many derive from broadening their knowledge and helping others.

What makes this book different from others about pastimes and recreation? Most hobby books deal with a specific hobby, or a narrow grouping of hobbies. *Favorite Hobbies and Pastimes'* scope and diversity is intended to increase the reader's awareness of the variety of spare time activities that people enjoy. Although the book presents diversity, at the same time it reveals links among the subjects covered.

The distinction between a hobby and an occupation is somewhat unclear for some activities. We will see that professional astronomy depends heavily on the visual observations made by amateurs, and that archaeologists are often accompanied on digs by unpaid, talented students and other interested individuals. Radio amateurs and computer hackers are further examples of hobbyists contributing to the advancement of science.

How then, does one decide which activities should be considered favorite pastimes or hobbies, and included in a book such as this? *The Statistical Abstracts of the Census* are a start, but not broad enough. There are several reference directories that provide statistics on magazines. If people pay for and read a magazine on a subject, it suggests their interest in that activity. The number of readers is an indication of the subject's popularity. By summing up the circulation figures for magazines relating to activities fitting the broad description of a hobby, a general picture of

favorite hobbies is obtained. In this book, each activity is provided with an introductory narrative, and a bibliography that identifies books, magazines, and associations that relate to the subject.

So, we have a general idea about people's favorite spare time activities—who needs the information, and why do they need it? Our family life-style is changing and the change is affecting all ages. For some, there is more free time. Unfortunately, many are not making the best use of that time.

It's important that children be involved with constructive after-school activities. It's a time when young bodies can be toughened-up with sports, and friendships are being formed. Some young people may prefer the mental stimulation of science, or the artistic inspiration of photography. But whatever they choose, youngsters benefit from active involvement in wholesome activities. They learn to set goals, make decisions, and solve problems; and they enjoy the sense of accomplishment that comes with success. Hobbies often mature into lifelong careers. Scouting programs offer merit badges for proven knowledge of a variety of subjects. This is a fine way to discover new interests, and broaden the outlook of young people. As students grow more involved with an activity or field of interest, they become more aware of the importance of a thorough understanding of the primary subject matter taught in school. They see that education plays an important role in their future success.

Rapid advances in technology in the working environment have created increased challenges for adults. What is an exciting challenge to some, is unwanted stress to others. A good way to recharge our batteries and relieve stress is to enjoy spare time activity that serves as a counter-balance to job demands.

Some adults mistakenly think that their education is complete when they graduate from school. Successful people continue to build on their educational foundation. Many learn new skills through the enjoyment of hobbies selected from the thousands of different spare time activities available. Besides leading a fuller life, they are laying the groundwork for a satisfying retirement.

Hobby participation enables us to more fully appreciate the performance of experts. If we have struggled to position our fingers correctly on the strings of a guitar, we will be intrigued by the performances of Andres Segovia or Carlos Montoya.

Senior adults are retiring earlier and living longer than before. They need to continue to feel useful and to have a sense of self worth. Some find fulfillment by volunteering to share their wisdom and experience. Others enjoy the fellowship of organizations dedicated to various spare time activities. It's important to maintain an informal network of people like they had while working.

There seems to be general philosophic agreement that engaging in hobbies is in our best interest. Many medical experts find the enthusiasm, anticipation, and enjoyment people experience when participating in hobbies are life extenders. They can promote fitness, relaxation, and a healthy mental attitude. Most of these activities enable us to make new friends through contact with others who have common interests. They build character, entertain, provide excitement and escape. It's not surprising then, that hobbies are recommended by doctors and sociologists for people of all ages.

Albert Einstein wasn't known for his theories about relaxation, but even he felt that both work and play were needed to achieve success. As usual, he expressed his thoughts with a formula. "If A equals success, then the formula is $A = X+Y+Z$. X is work, Y is Play, Z is keep your mouth shut." (Presumably so you can listen and learn.)

When considering a new field of interest the reader is urged to take into account the health and safety aspects of the pastime. For example, in the "Physical Fitness" section discussion you are advised to get a thorough medical checkup before engaging in stressful physical activities such as running or other intensive sports action.

Take the safety precautions included in the instructions provided with tools and equipment. Wear eye protection and appropriate filters or masks when exposed to harmful fumes or flying objects such as wood chips or other debris. Such precautions ensure continued enjoyment of your chosen hobby.

There is a lot of fun to be had out there. Good hobbies and boredom seldom coexist. If this book helps you to identify an exciting new pastime, then it will have served its purpose. Start planning now for what you want to do next. As Benjamin Franklin once said, "Leisure is time for doing something useful."

Antiques and Collectibles

MAN IS A COLLECTOR by nature. Maybe our heritage of foraging for food and collecting it has stuck in our genes. Collections have been found in ancient Egyptian, Chinese, and American Indian sites, buried with their former owners. These collections provide valuable insights to early civilizations. Today almost a third of the population participates in some form of collecting.

The objects people collect are usually classified as either collectible or antiques. Collectibles range from tree leaves to gems costing thousands of dollars. Although older collectibles may cost more, age is not usually the defining factor. One accepted definition of an antique is anything over 100 years old. Before 1966 antiques made prior to 1830 were admitted to the United States duty free. In 1966 the Educational, Scientific, and Cultural Materials Importation Act specified that anything 100 years old or more may be imported duty free. Experts in some fields use other criteria, such as the time a class of objects began to be trademarked. Many states classify twenty-five-year-old cars as antiques. The most liberal definition of an antique is anything no longer made.

Collecting is a flexible pastime. You decide how much time and money you want to spend. The cost, of course, is determined by the items you choose to collect, and how you go about collecting them. Some find the most satisfaction in the ownership of a fine collection. Others are happiest during the hunt and the thrill of discovery.

Collections provide new insight in many ways. Older antiques or collectibles enable us to see and feel the past. We gain an appreciation for the craftsmanship required to produce handmade items. An in-depth understanding of a collectible relic puts us in touch with history and the ingenuity of our forefathers. We can learn much as we search. Nostalgia enters the picture when collected items remind us of our past. Adults often collect things that were not available to them as children.

Finding Collectibles

Collectible items are found almost anywhere. Some experienced people frequent garage or yard sales and buy items at bargain prices. These items are then either traded for wanted items, or sold at a profit. A woman tried unsuccessfully to sell a family heirloom painting at a garage sale for five dollars. She later got $660,000 for it through an auction house. Thrift shops often contain collectibles that have been priced by volunteers who may underestimate the value of an item.

Swap meets or flea markets sometimes contain collectible items, but you may have to get down and get dirty to find them. Look for old paper items such as sheet music, comic books, or post cards buried among the junk. If you have done your homework, you will be able to identify the bargains. Establish price limits for yourself on needed items before attending swap meets or auctions. You will be less likely to overbid in the excitement of the moment.

Tag sales are another source of collectibles. In this type of sale, all items are tagged with a price, and people are admitted to the sale area in groups. They may then purchase an item for the tagged price. This method is often used when a family moves, or when an estate is being liquidated.

While antique shops may be a bit high, bargains can be found. When buying at antique shops, don't be embarrassed to make an offer of 10 to 15 percent less than the quoted price. If the price is firm, the dealer will tell you so. Simply say, "Will you take X dollars for this?" At swap meets it is not out of the question to say, "What's the least you'll take for this?" Don't irritate the seller by pointing out defects in the item. Some annoyed dealers will actually raise the price when provoked.

When browsing for collectibles, your style of dress and the jewelry you wear sends a strong signal to the dealer. Be especially wary if the stock is not price-tagged. These dealers often quote higher prices to customers they perceive to be wealthy.

Specialization

What you collect depends mostly on your interests and activities, both past and present. You are more likely to appreciate an item if it relates to your lifestyle. A doctor may collect antique surgical instruments because of an interest in their early design.

Your choice of collectible is often dictated, or at least restrained, by cost. The cost of most items is influenced by the laws of supply and demand. However, neither antiquity nor scarcity guarantee value. Ancient Roman coins can be purchased for less than many modern coins. Some items such as coins, stamps, and tools are available in a range of prices. Many collect objects with little monetary value, such as matchbook covers or rocks.

One way to avoid high costs is to collect things that are not normally collected by others. Consider the example of a collection of script car wrenches. In the early days of motoring, a small tool kit was furnished with each auto. The small open-end wrenches contained in these kits bore the name (script) of the car manufacturer. Almost every collector has seen a Ford wrench at some time. Some think that they are valuable antiques. What they don't know is that Ford made fifteen million Model Ts, and five million Model As and he included these wrenches with each car. Although original owners sold or junked those cars, they usually kept the tools. When the search for script wrenches goes beyond Ford and Maxwell to Overland and Cadillac, a fascinating hunt through rusty old tools at flea markets begins. This is an example of a hobby (old cars) creating an interest in the establishment of a low cost collection of relatively rare items. The disadvantages of collecting unique things are that established prices are hard to determine, most dealers don't carry them, and research material is scarce.

Creators and sellers of collectible items trade upon the desire of collectors to either obtain every item available, or all of a given series. The U.S. government produces proof coin sets, medals, thousands of commemorative stamps, and first day covers to sell to the public. These items bring in extra income for the treasury. Companies produce limited editions of figurines, plates, and prints. You are assured that the molds have been broken and no more will be produced. Many collectors spend a lifetime collecting one series after another. If you are a creative person, interest wears thin after an extended period of collecting a series of look-alike items.

Collections that can be expanded almost indefinitely may be termed open-ended. Records, sheet music, or paintings of a given time period are examples of open-ended collections. The best approach to a satisfying collection is to narrow the field through specialization without limiting yourself needlessly.

Students of history have interesting options when deciding on a collection. They can collect items related to a historical event such as the American Civil War, or books relating to a given period, such as the use of the canals that preceded railroads. Photos of covered bridges or steam locomotives are of interest to some. Collections of information about past national heroes and sports figures may include everything from books to bubble gum cards. There are collectors of almost anything related to history.

Condition and Care

We've noted the effects of supply and demand upon price. The condition of a collectible item has an even stronger influence on its value. The price guides for coins and antique cars provide two good examples of how price varies with condition. Coin guides quote prices for coins in good through proof condition. You're on your own if the coin is in less than good condition. A car guide such as *The Old Cars Price Guide* is more realistic. It starts at restorable and goes up to excellent with definitions and sketches describing each level of condition.

Consider photographing your collection as it grows and begins to have significant value. Expensive items may require several close-up still photographs. A video camera is useful for larger collections. Pictures are very important in the event of theft or fire, when an insurance claim must be made or stolen items identified.

As collectors, we have an obligation to pass collectibles on to the next generation in the best possible condition. Modification and over-restoration often reduces value and destroys their usefulness for study purposes. For example, it is wrong to polish old coins to a high luster. Coin and antique dealers refer to the film found on old artifacts as desirable patina. Scientists refer to it as oxidation. Over-restoration is the reworking of an item to bring it to a condition better than it was at the time of manufacture. It is, however, perfectly logical to restore the finish or replace a broken leg on an antique chair when necessary.

Science is developing methods to help preserve original antiquities. The United States Constitution and Declaration of Independence are now contained in helium-filled cases to slow their deterioration. Another problem is the aging of paper caused by chemicals used to bleach it during manufacture. Books assembled from such paper are being treated with certain gases in special chambers, slowing the aging process.

Serious collectors should plan for the expense of tools and facilities that relate to the care of their collection. A rock hound may only require an appropriate hammer and eventually some display cases. A car collector may require an expensive storage building and maintenance facilities. Choose equipment carefully until you gain some degree of expertise in your pastime. First impressions often change as you become more knowledgeable.

Authentication

Serious collecting requires the study of history and careful research. After you locate an object you need to identify it and establish its value, especially if you intend to bid for it at an auction. Armed with what you have learned, you are less likely to overbid in the excitement of the moment. Libraries and reference librarians are primary sources for needed information.

Museum collections also help hobbyists to see the diversity, color, shape, and texture of objects first hand. Many museums maintain research libraries that may be available to serious collectors. Museum gift shops often stock useful reference books. Most museum curators will be happy to share their knowledge.

One of the keys to identification of certain classes of antiques is the marking, sometimes called a hallmark, touchmark, or trademark. Markings usually identify the manufacturer, but this is not always the case. Well-known craftsmen sometimes stamped their mark on items made by others in their employ. The McKinley Act of 1891 required that imports to America be marked with the country of origin. The lack of a country identification may help to date some pieces. Collectibles most likely to be trademarked are china, clocks, dolls, glass, pewter, porcelain, pottery, and silver.

When a significant amount of money is involved in the purchase of an antique, it is prudent to hire a competent appraiser to examine the piece. Even prestigious art museums have been deceived by copies of an original painting. If an old item has great value, reproductions will be made. Some fakes, especially copies of antiques, are cleverly distressed to simulate the ravages of time. Other reproductions are made to look as the original did when new. Probably few of us would knowingly buy a good reproduction if we could find a faded and chipped original that costs more money.

Because of the great variety of collectibles, few people are expert in all branches. Antique dealers are usually either generalists or specialists. The general dealer sells almost all types of collectibles. Since it is difficult to have in-depth knowledge of all items, you may find your specialized item slightly cheaper in such a dealer's store. A specialist will generally be more experienced in a specific field. Although the price will be slightly higher, the expert can offer a more complete selection in the specialty and provide more reliable information.

Investment

If you collect primarily with an eye to future sales and profit, you are an investor. If you collect because you enjoy the objects in your collection, you are a collector. If you have a collection that will appreciate in value, you have the best of both worlds.

Collectors are inveterate horse-traders, so you may want to trade an item in the future without financial loss. Be aware that you will often have to sell an item for much less than the original purchase price. To put this in perspective, check the prices that coin shops will pay for your coins against their selling price for those same coins. If you think diamonds are a girl's best friend, try selling one.

The investor must take into account both the state of the economy and the track record of the particular collectible. When inflation is high, investors turn to such tangible items as gold, art, and antiques. During these times prices are driven up for the collector. The track record of a collectible is subject to so many variables, such as fads and media coverage, that it is often hard to predict trends. Collectible investments that usually bring the largest return involve rare, expensive objects. These items are often beyond the reach of the average collector. Investing in such collectibles is a risky business at best.

The Smithsonian Institute was founded by the bequest of an Englishman, James Smithson. This immense collection certainly meets Mr. Smithson's criterion for it—"for the increase and diffusion of knowledge among men." The Henry Ford museum, Sturbridge Village, the city of Williamsburg, Va., and other museums derived from the collections of persons of great means, have benefited us all. Such museums record the past and help us to set new standards for aesthetics and design.

Bibliography

REFERENCE BOOKS

Barber, Edwin. *Marks of American Potters: With Facsimiles of 1000 Marks and Illustrations of Rare Examples of American Wares.* St. Clair Shores, MI: Scholarly, 1976. Illustrated per title.

Bly, John. *The Confident Collector: How to Recognize an Authentic Antique.* New York: Prentice Hall, 1986. Advice by some of the world's leading authorities on how to detect fakes in a wide variety of collectibles.

Brunner, Marguerite Ashworth. *Antiques For Amateurs on a Shoestring Budget.* Indianapolis, IN: Bobbs-Merrill, 1976. Introduction to antiques and collecting. Emphasis on low cost approach.

Burek, Deborah M., ed. *Encyclopedia of Associations.* Detroit, MI: Gale Research, annual. Includes collector associations.

Cole, Ann Kilborn. *How to Sell Your Antiques at a Profit.* New York: McKay, 1969. How to research your antiques and find dealers. The fair practices and pitfalls of selling.

Davidson, Marshall B., ed. *The American Heritage History of Colonial Antiques.* New York: American Heritage, 1967. Historical information about antiques attributed to the period from 1607 to 1785. Well illustrated.

Green, Robert. *Marks of American Silversmiths, 1650–1900.* Rev. ed. Key West, FL: Green, 1984. Illustrated silver marks.

Hughes, Therle, G. et al. *The Country Life Antiques Handbook.* Middlesex, England: Hamlyn, 1986. Comprehensive coverage of furniture, clocks, silver, china, glass, and small collectibles.

Husfloen, Kyle, ed. *The Antique Trader Antiques and Collectibles Price Guide.* Dubuque, IA: Babka, 1990. Comprehensive listing of antique and collectible prices, well illustrated.

The Lyle Official Antiques Review 1991. New York: Perigee, 1990. Broad coverage of antiques and collectibles. Lists auction prices paid for specific items. Includes photographs of listed items.

Macdonald-Taylor, Margaret, ed. *A Dictionary of Marks: The Identification Handbook for Antique Collectors.* New York: Hawthorn, 1962. Profusely illustrated with marks for ceramics, gold, pewter, silver, furniture, and tapestry.

Rinker, Harry L., ed. *Warman's Antiques and Their Prices.* 25th ed. Radnor, PA: Wallace-Homestead, 1991. Comprehensive listing of antique and collectible prices, dealers, and collector associations.

Rontgen, Robert E. *Marks on German, Bohemian and Austrian Porcelain: 1710 to the Present.* Exton, PA: Schiffer, 1981. Illustrated per title.

Rothschild, Sigmund. *Rothschild on Antiques & Collectibles: A Practical Guide to Collecting.* New York: World Almanac, 1986. General philosophy of collecting. Emphasis on appraising, buying, and where to look for antiques.

Stara, D. *Pewter Marks of the World.* London: Hamlyn, 1977. Illustrated per title.

Stillinger, Elizabeth. *The Antiques Guide to Decorative Arts in America: 1600–1875.* New York: Dutton, 1973. Covers historical periods in 25 year increments, and discusses the furniture, silver, ceramics, and glass of each period.

PERIODICALS

Antique Monthly. Trans World Publishers, 2100 Powers Ferry Road, Suite 300, Atlanta GA 30339.

Antique Trader Weekly. Antique Trader, Box 1050, 100 Bryant Street, Dubuque, IA 52004–1050.

Antiques and Auction News. Engle Publishers, Route 230 W., Box 500, Mount Joy, PA 17552.

Antiques & Fine Arts. Fine Arts Publishers, 25200 LaPaz Road, Suite 210, Laguna Hills, CA 92653–5135

Art & Antiques. Trans World Publishers, 2100 Powers Ferry Road, Suite 300, Atlanta, GA 30339.

Collectors Mart. Web Publications, 650 Westdale Drive, Wichita, KS 67209.

Gun List. Krause Publications, 700 E. State Street, Iola, WI 54990.

Handgunning. P J S Publications, News Plaza, Box 1790, Peoria, IL 61656.

The Magazine Antiques. Brant Publications, 575 Broadway, 5th Floor, New York, NY 10012.

Maine Antique Digest. Main Antique Digest, Box 645, Waldoboro, ME 04572.

Petersen's Handguns. Petersen Publishers, 8490 Sunset Boulevard, Los Angeles, CA 90069.

Sporting Classics. Indigo Press, Box 1017, Highway 521 S., Camden, SC 29020.

Treasure Chest. Venture Publishers, 253 W. 72nd Street, Suite 211A, New York, NY 10023.

West Coast Peddler. Box 5134, Whittier, CA 90607.

ASSOCIATIONS

The *Encyclopedia of Associations,* lists over 300 collector organizations. The *Warman's Antiques and Their Prices* book, lists collector clubs associated with listings of each collectible category. Please see these books listed in the "Reference Books" bibliography above for more information.

Archery

ARCHERY, ONE OF THE ARTS of ancient times, is still practiced today. Enthusiasts use modern archery equipment where others choose to use sporting firearms. Archers shoot at conventional targets and take to the field to shoot at simulated animal targets to hone their hunting skills. Bow hunting continues to grow in popularity. It's estimated that there are almost three million wild game bow hunters in North America.

History

The bow and arrow were once used primarily for hunting and warfare. Evidence from cave paintings and relics found in peat bogs dates the use of archery as a means of survival to at least 10,000 years B.C. When firearms became practical, a transition period occurred during the sixteenth-century where the bow was gradually replaced by the gun. Archery practice, encouraged by kings and military leaders, was no longer required, and interest in the use of the bow and crossbow faded. A revival took place in England in 1781 with the founding of the Toxophilite Society to pursue archery as a sport or recreation. The first American target archery group on record was the Bowmen of Philadelphia, founded in 1828. As interest grew, the Grand National Archery Society was founded in England in 1861, and the National Archery Association (NAA) was established in the United States eighteen years later. Archery became an official event in the modern Olympics in 1900 and was also featured in 1904, 1908, and 1920. International archery competition rules became formalized after the International Archery Federation (FITA) was founded in 1931. When enough countries adopted the Federation's rules, the sport was again introduced into the Olympic games in 1972.

Equipment

An archer's equipment consists of bows, arrows, various shooting aids and protective devices.

Use of Conventional Bow Types

As an archer draws a bowstring back to shoot an arrow, the bow stores energy in its upper and lower flexed parts (limbs). When the string is released, the stored energy propels the arrow. The force required to pull the bowstring back to a specific shooting position is called the draw weight of the bow. In a conventional bow, the draw weight increases as the bowstring is drawn back. When the bowstring and arrow are released, the energy must overcome the inertia of the arrow, the bowstring, and the moving part of each limb. If the bowstring is fully drawn and released without an arrow in place (dry firing), the sudden flexing of the limbs can damage the bow.

Prehistoric bows were usually composed of a single piece of wood. Such simple bows (self bows) reached a peak in their development in the longbow used by the Welsh and English armies during the fourteenth to sixteenth centuries. See Figure 1.1. Today the British Long Bow Society perpetuates the use of this classic bow form in traditional target archery contests. Simple bows were sometimes strengthened by North American Indians and Eskimos by applying an animal sinew backing to the limbs. The sinew was either glued or bound in place. In Turkey and northern India efficient composite bows were made of horn and sinew applied to a wooden core. Such laminated and composite construction techniques are widely used with modern materials today. Recent designs often feature three piece bow construction in which the limbs are bolted to the handle (riser) as shown in the recurved bow in Figure 1.2.

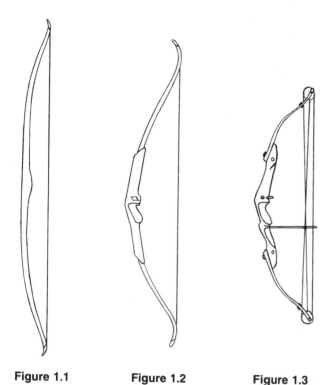

Figure 1.1
Self Bow

Figure 1.2
Three Piece
Recurved Bow

Figure 1.3
Compound
Bow

A recurved bow has a curve built into the tips of the bow. The end curves partially straighten out when the bow is drawn. When the bowstring is released, the tip curves regain their shape, adding to the velocity imparted to the arrow. As the tips regain their shape, the effective length of the bowstring is shortened as it comes to rest against the curve of the bow tips at the instant of discharge of the arrow. This also adds to the discharge velocity. It's customary to loosen the bowstring on a longbow or recurved bow after each shooting session to maintain maximum springiness in the bow.

Compound Bow

In 1969 H. W. Allen was granted a patent for a compound bow system that was destined, in time, to revolutionize the way bows are made. Compound bows employ varying numbers of pulleys to apply a maximum pull weight to the arrow for a greater number of inches. They also reduce the maximum pull weight at the full draw position. See Figure 1.3. With a compound bow, the peak pull-weight poundage is at mid-draw. When the bowstring is released, and moves forward, the pressure increases to a peak before decreasing. This raises the foot-pounds of energy applied to the arrow. We have seen that with a conventional bow the release pressure must overcome the inertia of the inertia of the arrow, the string, and the moving part of each limb. In a

compound, the limb tip travel is greatly reduced, so inertia is reduced. Due to the action of the pulleys reducing the pull weight at full draw, finger strain and muscle fatigue are reduced during the aiming process, and the bow is easier to shoot. The reduced full draw weight also permits the use of lighter arrows, resulting in a flatter flight trajectory. Compound bowstrings are not normally loosened between shooting sessions.

Crossbow

A crossbow is fired from the shoulder like a rifle. The bow is positioned horizontally across the front. The bowstring is drawn back and held in place by a hooked device called a nut. A small arrow called a bolt is placed in a grooved track ahead of the nut. The archer takes aim and releases the bowstring from the nut by means of a trigger like device. The drawing of the bowstring (spanning) is accomplished by hand or mechanical means. With mechanical aides, draw weights of several hundred pounds or more were not uncommon. Crossbows have been in use since Roman times, but never totally replaced the conventional bow. The spanning of the bowstring was such a time consuming procedure, that a good longbowman could release carefully aimed arrows six times as fast as the crossbowman. A typical modern crossbow has a draw weight of about 150 pounds. The use of crossbows is permitted during special hunting seasons in some states.

Arrows

An arrow is composed of an arrow head (point), a shaft, a stabilizing set of vanes near the rear (fletching), and a slot (nock) at the rear to accept the bowstring. It may also include a group of colored bands of paint (crest) forward of the fletching.

Arrowhead designs vary to suit their intended application, as the following examples show. A target point is about the same diameter as the shaft, and has a simple conical point. A field point has a diameter about the same as the shaft, which is stepped down to a smaller diameter, which ends in a simple conical point. Hunting points consist of triangular shaped blades arranged in a traditional "arrow head" shape. Usually three or four blades are used; occasionally two are employed in smaller designs. The blades vary somewhat in shape and length, and often feature lightening holes. All have razor sharp edges to facilitate penetration in game. Blunt or bludgeon points are conical rubber or plastic tips whose diameter increases toward the tip, with a blunt flat face at the very tip. The intent is to stun and kill small game without significant penetration. Fish points feature barbs in the form of blades or wires to hold the fish after penetration. Some feature barb retraction to facilitate arrow removal after capture.

In the past most arrow shafts were made of wood. Straight grained species such as pine, fir, birch, and cedar have been used. Aluminum shafts largely replaced wood in tournament applications in recent years, and although still being produced, are in turn giving way to space age carbon fiber composites. Some are carbon and resin, and others cover a very thin walled aluminum shaft with carbon and resin. Archers who engage in bow fishing often use arrowshafts made of solid fiberglass to withstand the stress encountered when a large fish puts up a fight.

Arrow fletching is also undergoing a transition in material usage. In the past swan and goose feathers have been used, but turkey feathers have been the most popular in recent years. A feather has a naturally curved surface, which imparts lift as it moves through the air. Since feather barbs stand out from the quill from base to end at an angle, feathers differ from the left wing to the right. For this reason all feathers on an arrow must be left wing or right wing feathers. The basic fletching pattern features three feathers set 120 degrees apart. One feather is often colored differently than the other two to assist the archer in correctly positioning the arrow on the bowstring. Those who use bows to hunt birds must be careful when aiming high to see that their arrows don't carry too far and endanger others. For this application, a single large feather is wrapped in a spiral pattern around the arrow shaft and fluffed up to create aerodynamic drag. This is called a flu-flu arrow. Feathers tend to collapse against the shaft and lose their stabilizing effect when wet. As a result target shooters, and especially hunters, are choosing plastic vanes instead. Mylar and soft urethane vanes are gaining rapidly in popularity.

Arrow nocks are applied to the shaft at the rear to interface with the bowstring. The slot in the nock must fit the bowstring correctly. If too tight it will affect arrow movement on release. If too loose, the arrow can fall off the string as you're trying to shoot. Nocks are usually made of flexible plastic.

An arrow crest has the practical function of identifying your arrows when several archers use the same target. FITA tournament rules further require that each arrow be marked with the archer's name or initials.

Arrows must be uniform in construction to enable archers to shoot with consistency. Their weight and physical dimensions are carefully controlled. For reasons that will be explained later, their flexibility (spine) is of prime importance.

Accessories

Manufacturers compete to provide archers with the latest, improved accessories of all types. Arrow rests are applied to a bow to accurately position the shaft and facilitate aiming an arrow. Designs vary from a simple brushlike item to elaborate machined metal devices that permit a short arrow to be drawn so far that its head is behind the bow riser. This is called an overdraw system. Many arrow rests include a plunger on the side, backed by a spring that will yield a prescribed amount when an arrow flexes as it leaves the bow.

Bow sights in the form of a sight pin or crosshairs are attached to a bow to assist in the aiming process. When an arrow leaves a bow it follows a curved path to the ground. To shoot greater distances, the archer aims the arrow higher to compensate. For a given distance the aim should be elevated a consistent amount. Sights are made adjustable and moved on a slide calibrated according to the distance being shot. Bowhunters must often react quickly when sighting game. Since they don't have time to adjust a sight for distance their sights often consist of multiple pins with pointed or spherical tips. Each pin has been previously positioned for accurate aim at a given distance. If the hunter estimates the range of a target at forty yards, aim is taken using the forty-yard pin.

Stabilizers are weights attached to the bow to dampen the effect of twists and torque that occur in the limbs during the discharge of the arrow.

Quivers are used to store arrows to be shot. Target shooters usually strap a quiver around the waist and position it to their side away from the bow. Hunters often attach the quiver directly to the bow.

Many other aids are available such as shooting gloves, arm guards, protective equipment to keep clothing out of the path of the bowstring, and special string release devices.

Shooting Form

The archer's goal is to use the body to provide a stable and unchanging platform from which to launch an arrow. The feet are placed at shoulder width at right angles to the target. To avoid confusion about right or left handedness, the hand holding the bow will be called the bow hand, the other the string hand. Place the bow in the bow hand so that bow pressure is exerted on the meaty part at the base of the thumb. The fingers should hold the bow in a relaxed grip. The fingers on the string hand are hooked about the bowstring to the first joint, with index finger above the arrow and the next two fingers below. The string hand is held in a natural position about one eighth turn off of vertical. The string is drawn back with your string arm elbow raised slightly above the shoulder. With your body and head in an erect position, anchor the string hand against the jaw in a consistent fashion. Some archers insure consistency by establishing anchor points such as the index finger to the corner of the mouth, or the string to the side of the nose. When ready for release, your bow hand, aiming eye, string hand, wrist, and elbow should fall into a straight line. To release the bowstring, relax the string fingers and let the string slip away. In addition to careful aim, the key to accuracy is consistent form.

Logic tells us that if a bowstring is released it would return to a position behind the center of the bow. If that is so, why doesn't the arrow go flying off to one side of the bow as it moves forward. This is called the archer's paradox. High speed photography revealed what is happening: When a right-handed archer releases the string it moves to the left. This causes the front of the arrow to press against the bow and the shaft bends to the left. As the arrow moves forward it straightens and by the time it is halfway past the bow it has vibrated or flexed past straight and has bent to the right. It continues to flex or wobble in this manner so that as the arrow tail passes the bow it has flexed to the left again, causing its tail to swing clear of the bow. This flexure rate is determined by the vibration period of the arrow shaft. This is why the spine of an arrow is controlled during manufacture within thousandths of an inch. It also explains why a spring-backed plunger or button is sometimes used on the side of the bow to control some of the flexure.

Target Shooting

FITA target shooting competitions are subdivided into disciplines, classes, and divisions. Disciplines include: outdoor target, indoor target, field, clout, flight, and ski-arc. Classes include: women, men, junior women, and junior men. Divisions include for outdoor target: freestyle, standard bow, and compound bow; for indoor target: freestyle and compound bow; for field: barebow, freestyle, and compound bow; for clout: freestyle; for flight: target bow and flight bow.

In the target discipline the archers shoot from a line which runs parallel to and is a designated distance from the target faces. Targets are comprised of colored concentric circles which each have point values. A shot in the innermost circle scores the highest point value (usually ten), while a shot in the outermost circle scores the fewest (usually one). Target is the only discipline of archery which is contested in the Olympic Games.

In the field discipline the archer takes on the terrain along with the target. Field archery has widespread participation because it allows the use of three types of bows. A course is set up with twenty-four targets, twelve of which are marked with the distance from the shooting line. The distances to the other twelve targets remain unmarked. Three arrows are shot at each target for a total of seventy-two. The targets are placed with such difficulty that the shots don't resemble target archery. Many of the shots are made uphill or downhill adding to the challenge to aim properly.

The flight discipline involves shooting for distance. Two types of arrows, regular flight and broadhead flight, are used and can be combined with many types of bows. Records are kept for each possible combination of bow and arrow. In a flight tournament, each archer shoots four rounds of broadhead and four rounds of regular flight arrows. Six arrows are shot in each round. The same type of bow must be used for all shots in a round, but a different bow can be used for each round, if desired.

Clout is a rarely practiced discipline. It is a trajectory skill in which the target (fifteen meters in diameter) consists of five concentric circular scoring zones, outlined on the ground. The innermost circle is worth five points, and scores decrease to one point in the outermost circle. Each archer shoots thirty-six arrows at the target, 165 meters away for men, and 125 for women.

Further definition of targets, target placement, and rounds for target shooting is beyond the scope of this work.

There is another form of competition gaining popularity, called 3D, that falls outside of FITA and NAA rules. A course similar to the field discipline is laid out, often in a wooded area. None of the distances to targets are marked. Range finders are not allowed, so archers are required to sharpen distance estimation skills. The targets are full sized replicas of game animals, usually made of Styrofoam. The target animals have circles or other geometric shapes outlined to simulate the location of vital organs. These target outlines are usually not visible from the shooting location. Scoring is determined by hits made in these areas.

Bow Hunting and Fishing

Bow hunting has achieved a level of popularity that far exceeds other archery forms. This is reflected in the predominant manufacture of compound bows that are designed for hunting. Bows have been used successfully to hunt species from rabbits to elephants. In North America bow hunters stalk large game such as deer, moose, elk, and bear. Small game includes chucks, squirrels, rabbits, and turkeys. Predators such as bobcats and coyotes are also hunted. Most states set aside separate hunting seasons for bow hunting.

Bow fishing is done with a line fixed to the arrow for retrieval. Some attach a large drum to the front of the bow around which the fishing line is wrapped. When the arrow is shot, the line is pulled from the face of the drum. The line must be rewound by hand after each shot. A closed face spinning reel can also be used, attached to the bow in a similar manner. Other archers prefer to use a separate fishing pole. Slack line from the pole is coiled on the bottom of the boat and attached to the arrow. Polarized glasses are useful to cut reflected glare so that fish may be seen. Due to the refraction of an image as it passes from water to air, you must learn to aim low when shooting fish under water. Most bow hunting is done for rough fish, such as carp or suckers. Few states have limits on such fish. Check state game regulations in your state for other limitations.

Bibliography

REFERENCE BOOKS

Combs, Roger, ed. *Crossbows.* Northbrook, IL: D B I Books, 1987. In-depth coverage of crossbows. Includes crossbow equipment, techniques, and history.

Constitution and Rules: International Archery Federation. Milano, Italy: Fédération Internationale de Tir à l'Arc, 1992.

Harding, David, ed. *Weapons: An International Encyclopedia From 5000 B.C. to 2000 A.D.* New York: St. Martin's, 1980. Includes historical coverage of bows and arrows.

National Archery Association: 1993 Official Media & Information Guide. Colorado Springs, CO: National Archery Association of the United States, 1993.

Paterson, W. F. *Encyclopedia of Archery.* New York: St. Martin's, 1984. Contains alphabetical listings of archery terms with definitions.

Schuh, Dwight. *Bowhunter's Encyclopedia.* Harrisburg, PA: Stackpole Books, 1987. In-depth coverage of hunting with a bow. Includes information on equipment selection and usage, hunting techniques, and field dressing of the game.

Sparano, Vin T. *Complete Outdoors Encyclopedia.* 2nd ed. New York: Harper & Row, 1980. Contains a section on archery covering equipment for target shooting, bow hunting, and bow fishing.

PERIODICALS

Bow and Arrow Hunting. Gallant-Charger Publishers, 34249 Camino Capistrano, Box HH, Capistrano Beach, CA 92624.

Bow and Arrow Magazine's Bowhunter's Annual. Gallant-Charger Publishers, 34249 Camino Capistrano, Box HH, Capistrano Beach, CA 92624.

Bowhunter. Cowles Magazines, 6405 Flank Drive, Box 8200, Harrisburg, PA 17105–8200.

Bowhunting. Petersen Publishers, 8490 Sunset Boulevard, Los Angeles, CA 90069.

Bowhunting World. Ehlert Publishers, 601 Lakeshore Parkway, Suite 600, Minnetonka, MN 55305–5215.

ASSOCIATIONS

American Crossbow Association. 3245 W. Walnut Street, Springfield, MO 65802. Furthers the knowledge of the crossbow and its safe, legal use both on the target range and in the field. Bestows awards. Publication: *Bolts.*

Bowhunters of America. 1030 W. Central, Bismarck, ND 58501. Works to promote the sport. Seeks to increase the understanding and appreciation of bow hunting. Publications: *The Tab,* and related materials.

Fred Bear Sports Club. RR 4, 4600 SW 41st Boulevard, Gainsville, FL 32608–4999. Bow hunters and others dedicated to protection of outdoor ecology and proper wildlife management. Encourages compliance with state game and fish laws. Maintains museum, and bestows bow hunter and field archery awards. Publications: *Archery Journal,* and related materials.

Junior Bowhunter Program. c/o National Field Archery Association, 31407 Outer Interstate 10, Redlands, CA 92373. Youth compound bow enthusiasts. Provides clubs and programs for youth interested in archery. Sponsors competitions. Publication: *Archery.*

National Archery Association of the United States. 1750 E. Boulder Street, Colorado Springs, CO 80909–5778. For those interested in target archery. Standardizes tournament rules, procedures, and rounds. Maintains official records. Sponsors matches and bestows awards. Publications: *NAA Newsletter, U.S. Archer,* and related materials.

National Bowhunter Education Foundation. PO Box 2007, Fond du Lac, WI 54936. Volunteer bow hunters serve as instructors to educate bow hunters and the public on the use of the bow for hunting legal game. Maintains a program used to teach bow hunters safe hunting and concern for the environment. Publications: *NBEF Newsletter,* and related materials.

National Field Archery Association. 31407 Outer I–10, Redlands, CA 92373. Sponsors field archery schools, and national and sectional tournaments. Works toward conservation of game and its natural habitat. Publications: *Archery Magazine,* and related materials.

Pope and Young Club. PO Box 548, Chatfield, MN 55923–0548. Seeks to enhance the bow hunter image. Maintains the *Bowhunters Big Game Records of North America.* Sponsors photo and art competitions and bestows awards. Publications: Newsletter, and related materials.

Astronomy

THE WORD ASTRONOMY derives from the Greek astron, meaning star and nomos, a system of laws. Modern astronomy goes beyond the study of stars. It includes the entire content of the universe in which we exist.

Our planet Earth rotates on its polar axis once each day. The speed exceeds 1,000 miles per hour at the equator. At the same time the earth travels at 18.5 miles each second during its yearly trip around the Sun. Our Sun is a star located about two thirds of the way out from the center of a huge galaxy of stars called the Milky Way. The Milky Way consists of at least ten billion stars. The Sun orbits the galaxy center, traveling about 155 miles each second, taking 200 million years to make the trip. According to most theories the galaxies move away from one another as the universe expands. The Milky Way galaxy is moving in the direction of the star constellation Leo at a rate of about 335 miles per second. While these are generally accepted facts today, they would have been blasphemous statements in 1530 A.D.

History—The Early Astronomers

Aristotle (384–322 B.C.) believed that the earth was the center of the universe and the Sun and planets orbited around it. Because of his great reputation most astronomers accepted his thinking for more than 1,600 years.

Polish astronomer Nicolaus Copernicus (1473–1543) became convinced that the sun, not the earth, was the center of the universe. He determined that some early Greek philosophers had held the same view. He published his thinking just before his death in 1543. Although this work laid the foundation for planetary astronomy, acceptance came slowly.

Italian Galileo Galilei (1564–1642) built a telescope in 1609, following descriptions of similar Dutch equipment, and became the first person to apply the telescope to a study of the skies. In a 1597 letter to Johannes Kepler he wrote that he believed in the theory proposed by Copernicus, but didn't make his opinion known for fear of ridicule. His telescopic observations, beginning in 1609, strengthened his resolve and confirmed his previous mathematical calculations. His defense of Copernicus' theory resulted in his condemnation by the Catholic Church, and in 1633 he was tried and sentenced to life in prison. The sentence was commuted to house arrest, where he remained for the last eight years of his life. The church officially forgave Galileo in 1992.

Danish nobleman Tycho Brahe (1546–1601) was a meticulous observer of the heavens. His accurate observations enabled him to prove that the stars were located at a great distance, but he failed to grasp the fact that the sun did not revolve around the earth. Tycho was unable to convince Galileo of his (incorrect) belief.

German Johannes Kepler (1571–1630) was a talented mathematician who used Tycho's observations to establish laws of planetary motion. They proved invaluable to him. When he published his theories in 1596, he came to the attention of Brahe and Galileo. They corresponded and compared findings. Prior to Kepler, astronomers held that the planets moved in circular orbits. Kepler was able to show that the planets moved in elliptical orbits.

The Astronomer's Universe

Cosmology—Theory of the Universe

Most cosmologists theorize that the universe began with a tremendous release of energy fifteen billion years ago. According to this Big Bang Theory, all matter was in a condensed state and quickly evolved from complex forces to minute building blocks called quarks, to elementary particles, to nuclei of atoms. This took only three minutes! After 500,000 years the atomic nuclei took on shells of electrons and became atoms, the particles from which all material objects and substances are composed. The Big Bang Theory accounts for the observed rapid expansion of the universe.

During the 1950s and 1960s another theory held that the universe was in a steady state. It was thought that matter was continuously being created to account for the expanding universe. In the late 1960s a primordial background radiation was measured. Its character lent support to the Big Bang Theory and the Steady State Theory was abandoned.

Currently another challenge to the Big Bang is being raised. The Plasma Universe Theory may make the Big Bang look like Aristotle's earth-centered universe. Plasma is the state of matter in which atomic nuclei have not yet acquired their electron shells. A plasma universe is one that is filled with plasma and shaped by electricity and magnetism as much as by gravitation. Plasmas produce prodigious amounts of electromagnetic radiation, which in turn generates electrical currents. Credibility of the Plasma Theory is based on data from space obtained using modern radio telescope dishes and from computer simulations made possible by the huge capacities of the largest super computers. Scientists have run special computer programs based on the Plasma Theory, obtaining images that closely resemble observed star galaxies. In any case, recent findings indicate that the universe has large clumps of matter, or structure, on a very large scale. Such exciting discoveries continue to stimulate interest in astronomy, one of man's earliest sciences.

Galaxies

A nebula is a cloud of gas and dust that may emit, absorb, or reflect light. Galaxies are formed from such localized lumps of matter. The gas and dust are the stuff that coalesces into millions of stars. As galaxies accumulate through gravitational attraction, the mass begins to spin. Some flatten, where centrifugal force exceeds gravity and they become spiral galaxies, great rotating pinwheels of matter in open space. Spiral galaxies are disk-like in form and have spiral arms. They contain gas and dust clouds that support active star formation. Our Milky Way is a spiral galaxy.

Other galaxies have weaker gravity or less initial rotation. They flatten very little and become elliptical galaxies. More than half of all galaxies are elliptical, some five times larger than the Milky Way. They usually contain low levels of gas and dust. This material may have been stripped away by gravitational attraction of adjacent galaxies or by collision with other galaxies. An alternate theory is that almost all the gas and dust have been used up in star building. This is supported by the fact that elliptical gal-axies contain many stars in the later stages of their life cycles.

Large ellipticals are thought to have resulted from accumulations caused by multiple collisions. They have swallowed up and combined with other galaxies. When galaxies collide, they actually pass through each other. The stars are far enough apart that there is usually no direct contact between them. However, the galaxies' gravitational fields do interact with one another, and the gas, dust, and star distribution within the galaxies are influenced by these forces.

Galaxies form in clusters ranging from a few dozens to thousands, all mutually attracted by gravity. The galaxies interact with, and distort one another, forming irregular galaxies. In some cases, streamers of gas and stars are drawn out gravitationally, creating bridges between galaxies. Irregular galaxy shapes can also result from exploding supernovae, or collisions as described above.

Stars

When a small pocket of gas and dust, called a core, reaches a critical density it begins to collapse under its own gravity. As the core shrinks, a dense knot develops at the center. Collapsing from the inside out, the knot grows increasingly dense and attracts more matter. As it does so, it spins more rapidly, like a figure skater pulling in her arms. After enough mass has accumulated, centrifugal force flattens the incoming gas into a disk that surrounds the embryonic star's equator. Within the disk, matter spirals inward until it reaches the surface of the star. Eventually, temperatures and pressures at the center of the star become high enough to trigger the fires of nuclear fusion, consuming hydrogen nuclei and producing helium nuclei in the star's center. Contraction of the core occurs, bringing more hydrogen toward the center and heating it. This causes the star to expand into a giant. The surface cools and turns the star into a red giant as the thermal vibration of its atoms slows. Its enlarged surface area makes it more luminous. As the core runs out of energy, it contracts causing nuclear reactions converting the core to carbon. Further core contractions produce other heavier elements. As the star runs out of fuel, gravity exceeds internal pressure and the star collapses further. Core temperature rises and triggers another round of nuclear reactions, expanding the star's atmosphere some. This contraction-reaction-expansion cycle continues all the while projecting gas out into space, losing star mass in the process. The remaining core reaches the white dwarf stage. At the white dwarf stage, a star has used up its nuclear fuel. Its atoms have shed their electrons and the remaining nuclei and unattached electrons become so tightly jammed together that the star becomes incredibly dense. (A thimble full would weigh many tons.) The high temperatures present at this stage cause the star to burn with a white light. As it burns to a cinder, it no longer glows and becomes a black dwarf.

When our Sun reaches the red giant stage it will have expanded to a ball of hot gas large enough to envelop the planets Mercury, Venus, and probably the Earth.

A larger, more massive star dies in a tremendous explosion, called a supernova, that destroys the star. Supernovae violently eject much of their stellar mass into space. The core collapses to become a neutron star or a black hole. Supernovae are rare. It is interesting that gold, silver, and platinum are some of the heavier elements made only in a supernova. A neutron star has collapsed to a density so high only neutrons can exist. Neutron stars are thought to become pulsars when while spinning rapidly they eject streams of charged particles from their poles, emitting photon beams seen on earth. When large stars continue to collapse past the neutron star stage their gravitational pull attracts adjacent material and even photons of light, creating a black hole.

Giant stars are rare and variable giants called cepheid variables are rarer still. Our north star, Polaris, is a cepheid variable. Such stars pulsate because of unstable energy layers in their outer envelopes. These layers alternately absorb and release energy causing an oscillation of their brightness.

Close pairs of stars that orbit around each other are binary stars. Observing the time required for one orbit, and their average separation, enables calculation of the total mass of the pair. The bright star Sirius is a pair of visible stars called a visual binary. When one star is too faint to be seen, the pair is an astrometric binary. When one star can't be seen, even with a telescope, the pair is a spectroscopic binary. Spectrum analysis reveals the presence of the second star.

The Solar System

We have seen that as stars heat up during their development process, the surrounding cloud of gas and dust forms a spinning disk around the star. Planets form from that material. Our local star, the Sun, is surrounded by nine planets, and some scattered gas, dust and debris.

There are two types of planets in the solar system. Mercury, Venus, Earth and Mars are terrestrial planets. They are small, dense, and rocky. Jupiter, Saturn, Uranus, and Neptune are jovian planets. They are large, gaseous and have low density. Pluto is unique in that it is small but has low density. Its orbit is so far from the Sun that from Pluto, the Sun looks like a very bright star.

Current thinking is that our Moon and the Earth probably formed at the same time, and in the same way, by accretion of the dust around the Sun. Our Earth-Moon combination can be thought of as a double planet. Some other planets have moons or satellites that may be captured

asteroids. Asteroids are small rocky satellites, most of which orbit the Sun between the orbits of Mars and Jupiter.

Comets have a nucleus of ice, composed mainly of water and carbon dioxide. They travel the solar system in a long elliptical orbit. As they near the Sun the ice vaporizes and forms a tail of gas and dust pointing away from the Sun. Because comets come from places in the solar system that are farthest from the Sun, and quite cold, they probably contain matter that is unchanged since the formation of the solar system. Study of the constituents of comets will further understanding of the early stages of solar system formation.

Communications from Space

The universe communicates with astronomers by means of electromagnetic waves radiated from space. These waves can be classified by their frequency, the greater the frequency, the shorter their length. A variety of sensing devices are used to observe the electromagnetic spectrum.

Radio waves repeat their characteristic shape at a low frequency (number of times) each second. They are considered long waves. Radio waves are captured by both massive radio telescope dishes and common transistor radios.

Shorter waves fall into the infrared portion of the spectrum. Shorter still we find the visual portion (light waves), where optical telescopes are used. Shorter still, ultraviolet, then X rays and gamma rays.

Modern astronomic observation is done at all of these frequencies. Complex data is being accumulated faster than it can be evaluated.

Astronomical Distance Measurement

Familiar units of distance measurement such as miles or kilometers prove much too small and cumbersome for astronomical use. Astronomers use the astronomical unit for solar system distance measurement. The average distance from Earth to the Sun is one astronomical unit (AU).

The distances to stars are too large to use AUs. These distances are usually expressed in light years. A light year is the distance light travels in one year, 5.88 trillion miles or 63,000 AUs. The nearest star, other than our Sun, is Proxima Centauri, four light years away.

Equipment

We have seen that communication in the universe takes place by means of electromagnetic waves. Here we'll look at some of the equipment that both professional and amateur astronomers use to collect those waves.

Development of Professional Equipment

In the early 1930s Karl Jansky discovered radio signals originating in the sky. From 1937 to 1944 Grote Reber, an electronics engineer and hobbyist, mapped the sources of radio emissions scattered through the Milky Way using a home-built thirty-one foot parabolic dish antenna. His work was published in professional journals. In 1958 radio astronomers found that the Milky Way had a spiral form, with extended arms delineated by vast fields of hydrogen.

Modern radio astronomers link giant radio telescopes around the world to simulate a receiving antenna as large as the earth to make significant observations and discoveries.

Most large optical telescopes are of the reflector type. Reflecting telescopes usually have a parabolic mirror that reflects gathered light and focuses it on an eyepiece. As mirror size increases, more photons of light are captured. There are variations of this telescope type.

Reflector telescope size appeared to have reached its limits when a 200 inch diameter mirror was made for the Mount Palomar telescope in 1949. Problems include mirror weight, thermal distortion, and proper support. A 236 inch telescope built by the Soviets during the 1970s has not lived up to expectations.

Solutions were found to extend the optical telescope limits using new manufacturing techniques and mirror mounting methods. In the 1960s Frank Low developed a reflector telescope using multiple mirrors based on the work previously done by Frenchman Pierre Connes. The images collected are combined optically to simulate the size of a much larger telescope. Alignment of the mirrors is maintained by computer controlled corrections. This approach continues to be used by others to design ever larger multimirrored telescopes.

Larger single glass mirrors are again being considered based upon experiments by Roger Angel. He uses a giant turntable to spin the molten mirror glass as it cools, forming a parabolic surface. The method saves a great deal of grinding time, making the process economically feasible. It also produces a lighter mirror, reducing stress on mounting equipment.

Today's astronomy requires the collaboration of a large number of scientific disciplines, including cosmologists, astronomers, physicists, mathematicians, computer specialists, and engineers in many fields.

Equipment for Amateur Observation

Binoculars provide excellent wide-field views of the moon and stars. They can be used effectively to familiarize the observer with the patterns of star constellations and their relationship to star charts. They are also useful for hunting comets.

In the common designation of binoculars, the first number is the magnification and the second number is the diameter of the front lens in millimeters (mm). The exit pupil of a 7 × 50 pair is equal to 50 divided by 7 which equals 7.1, which is a close match to the normal millimeter eye pupil dilation found in a person observing under dark rural skies. The value of a 7mm exit pupil is that it provides the widest possible field of view commensurate with the proportions of the front lens. This is desirable for certain kinds of observation, such as comet seeking. A smaller exit pupil is preferred when viewing bright subjects, such as the moon.

Refracting telescopes use a lens as their main light-gathering element. The lens focuses the image on an eyepiece for viewing as shown in Figure 1.1. Refracting telescope lenses are generally much more expensive than an equivalent sized reflector mirror. The light gathering objective lens on good quality refractors is made of two or more elements to enable optimum color transmission.

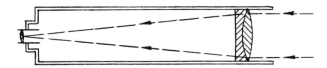

Figure 1.1
Refractor

Reflecting telescopes are popular with amateurs. They use mirrors to focus and reflect images to an eyepiece. Figure 1.2 illustrates the light paths taken by an image through a professional Schmidt camera-type telescope. In this system, the image passes through a corrector lens at the front of the tube. It is focused by a primary mirror at the back and reflected forward to photographic film mounted where the light paths converge.

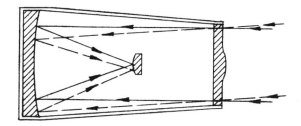

Figure 1.2
Schmidt

Figure 1.3 illustrates another reflector variation called a Cassegrainian telescope. Here the image enters the telescope tube and passes directly to the objective mirror at the rear. It's reflected forward to a secondary mirror which reflects it back, through a hole in the center of the primary mirror, to the eyepiece where it can be viewed by the astronomer. This folding of the light path permits the use of a significantly shorter tube and a more compact instrument.

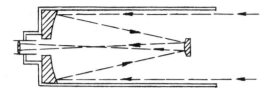

Figure 1.3
Cassegrain

Figure 1.4 illustrates a Schmidt-Cassegrain reflector which incorporates the advantages of both systems. It employs the forward corrector lens found in the Schmidt type and the folded light path of the Cassegrain. The corrector lens feature permits a wider field of view. This system is used in the more sophisticated instruments sold to amateurs.

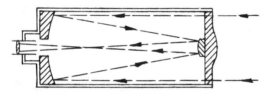

Figure 1.4
Schmidt-Cassegrain

Figure 1.5 illustrates a Newtonian reflector. This type is popular with amateurs who build their own telescopes. Here a flat-surfaced diagonal mirror is used to direct the image out the side of the tube to an eyepiece. Many hobbyists grind their own reflector mirror, even though mirror grinding is a laborious, painstaking process. Grinding kits are available, as well as completed mirrors.

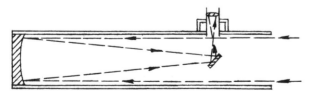

Figure 1.5
Newtonian

As telescope lens or mirror size increases, more photons are captured, so we see objects more clearly. Photography provides another way to capture photons. Using a time exposure, the photons have a cumulative effect, building up a more distinct image of a faint object. A common 35mm camera may be used at the eyepiece. Since we are located on a world that is spinning, it means that you must use a motor drive to continually move the instrument to track the celestial object being viewed or photographed.

New technologies used by professionals are being adopted by some amateurs. Photography is being done by means of a camcorder pointed into the telescope eyepiece. Charge coupled devices (CCDs) are also used to capture images. They are one hundred times as sensitive as the finest photographic plates. When light strikes their surface an electrical charge accumulates which is used to produce an image. CCDs can be made sensitive to X rays or to infrared or ultraviolet light.

Another essential accessory is a good star atlas. An atlas, combined with star charts found in monthly amateur astronomy magazines, enables the viewer to find his or her way about the sky.

Several popular catalogs of celestial nebulous objects provide challenging subjects for the amateur to locate and enjoy. One of the most popular is the *Messier Catalog.* Charles Messier, a French comet hunter, issued a catalog in 1781 of 103 star clusters and nebulae. Another catalog was published in 1888 by John L. E. Dreyer called the *New General Catalog of Nebulae and Clusters* (NGC). Reprinted in 1953, it lists over 7,000 objects. Both catalogs help amateur comet hunters differentiate between comets and nebulae.

Considerations for Visual Observation

Optical instruments capture particles of light called photons. Since stars radiate light and planets reflect light, we see them.

Stars are so distant that they appear as points of light, regardless of magnification. High magnification is needed to observe details on planetary surfaces. However, high magnification reduces the field of view (size of the area), that can be seen. A small field of view makes it difficult to find and track an object. Warm air currents rising from the earth's surface distort the observed image. This is what causes stars to appear to twinkle. Such distortion is called poor seeing. Professional astronomers are attempting to overcome the effects of such atmospheric distortion by using lasers and computers to adjust deformable telescopic mirrors to compensate for the distortion. A laser beam is aimed through the atmosphere toward a celestial object. The distortion experienced by the beam is measured by computer, which in turn adjusts the mirror.

Planets are best viewed on nights affording good seeing, nights having minimal thermal activity.

High light levels in the viewing area, such as city lights, reduce viewing quality.

The entire moon may be viewed at low magnification. High magnification may be chosen to observe surface details.

The Sun *must not* be viewed by looking directly into the eyepiece of a field glass or telescope without an approved sun filter. Severe eye damage may result. The best and safest course of action is to allow the Sun's image to project from the eyepiece onto a piece of white card stock. Make your observation by looking at the image on the card stock.

Role of the Amateur

There are approximately seventy-five amateur astronomers for each professional in the world. The professionals usually work on narrowly defined projects, often unrelated to direct observation. They depend to a large extent on amateurs to discover new visual phenomena. An example occurred in 1975 when amateur Ben Mayer made a sequence of photographs to record a meteor shower. The photographic series also captured a "fast nova" in the act of becoming visible, providing valuable information not previously available to professionals. Another example occurred during September 1990. A predicted outbreak of a storm on Saturn was first discovered by amateurs. It was photographed by the Hubble Space Telescope during November 1990.

When an amateur finds and reports a comet not previously recorded, the comet will bear the name of the amateur throughout history.

A striking example of the value that professional astronomy places on amateur participation is found in the planning of observation time on the Hubble Space Telescope. During preliminary planning seventeen hours were set aside for use on amateur projects during the first year of operation.

The Space Telescope Science Institute (STSI) asked the estimated 300,000 American amateur astronomers to submit proposals for observation projects. Representatives from leading American amateur organizations and STSI narrowed the field from 200 proposals to five lucky amateurs.

Why would NASA consider allowing amateurs to use precious viewing time on this incredibly important and expensive instrument? STSI director Riccardo Giacconi said, "Amateur astronomers were not only the main creators of astronomical knowledge in the past, but they were also the ones best plugged into the public, and they still are today." One of the lucky amateurs said, "It's like being invited to join Christopher Columbus' crew!"[1]

Bibliography

REFERENCE BOOKS

Berry, Richard. *Build Your Own Telescope.* New York: Macmillan, 1985. Detailed coverage of telescope making.

---

1. *Sky and Telescope Magazine,* (January, 1990), 30–32.

Harrington, Philip S. *Touring the Universe Through Binoculars: A Complete Astronomer's Guideboook.* New York: Wiley, 1990. Emphasis on binoculars for astronomical use.

Howard, Neal E. *Standard Handbook for Telescope Making.* New York: Harper & Row, 1984. Detailed coverage of telescope making.

Lerner, Eric. *The Big Bang Never Happened.* New York: Random House, 1991. A startling refutation of the dominant theory of the origin of the universe. The case for the Plasma Universe Theory.

Liller, William, and Ben Mayer. *The Cambridge Astronomy Guide: A Practical Introduction to Astronomy.* New York: Cambridge Univ., 1990. Overview, emphasis on camera use, and amateur involvement.

Maran, Stephen P., ed. *The Astronomy and Astrophysics Encyclopedia.* New York: Van Nostrand Reinhold, 1992. Comprehensive overview.

Muirden, James. *The Amateur Astronomer's Handbook: A Guide to Exploring the Heavens.* New York: Harper & Row, 1987. Overview for amateurs with an introduction to mirror grinding.

Ridpath, Ian, ed. *Norton's 2000.0 Star Atlas and Reference Handbook.* 18th ed. New York: Halsted, 1989. Long established and respected star atlas.

Seeds, Michael A. *Foundations of Astronomy.* 3rd ed. Belmont, CA: Wadsworth, 1992. In-depth textbook on astronomy.

Silk, Joseph. *The Big Bang: The Creation & Evolution of the Universe.* 2nd rev. & updated ed. New York: Freeman, 1988. Big bang overview.

Time-Life. *Computers and the Cosmos.* Rev. ed. Alexandria, VA: Time-Life, 1990. Astronomy overview with emphasis on computer interface.

Trefil, James S. *The Moment of Creation: Big Bang Physics from Before the First Millisecond to the Present Universe.* New York: Macmillan, 1984. Detailed account of big bang physics.

PERIODICALS

Astronomy. Kalmbach Publishers, PO Box 1612, Waukesha, WI 53187–1612.

Griffith Observer. Griffith Observatory, 2800 E. Observatory Road, Los Angeles, CA 90027.

Lunar and Planetary Information Bulletin. Lunar and Planetary Institute, 3600 Bay Area Boulevard, Houston TX 77058–1113.

Mercury. Astronomical Society of the Pacific, 390 Ashton Avenue, San Francisco, CA 94112.

Planetary Report. Planetary Society, 65 N. Catalina, Pasadena, CA 91106–2301.

Sky and Telescope. Sky Publishers, PO Box 9111, Belmont, MA 02178.

Star Date. University of Texas, Austin, McDonald Observatory, Austin, TX 78712.

ASSOCIATIONS

Amateur Astronomers Association. 1010 Park Avenue, New York, NY 10028. Amateur and professional astronomers. Maintains library. Publications: Journal, and brochures.

American Association of Variable Star Observers. 25 Birch Street, Cambridge, MA 02138. Amateur and professional astronomers. Maintains library. Publications: Circulars, monographs, reports, bulletins, and journal.

American Meteor Society. Suny-Genesco, 1 College Circle, Department of Physics and Astronomy, Geneseo, NY 14454. Amateur and professional astronomers interested in meteors. Publications: *Meteor News,* and special reports.

Association of Lunar and Planetary Observers, PO Box 16131, San Francisco, CA 94116. Promotes amateur lunar and planetary astronomy. Publications: Directory, journal, and solar system ephemeris.

Astronomical League. c/o Berton Stevens, 2112 E. Kingfisher Lane, Rolling Meadows, IL 60008. Members of 170 astronomical societies. Coordinates activities, presents awards, and sponsors educational programs. Publications: *Reflector,* booklets, pamphlets, and *Careers in Astronomy.*

Astronomical Society of the Pacific. 390 Ashton Avenue, San Francisco, CA 94112. Professional and amateur astronomers, and educators. Sponsors lectures, conferences, and bestows awards. Publications: *Mercury* magazine, and related material.

Automobiles

A MERICA'S LOVE AFFAIR with the automobile takes many forms. People enjoy the freedom to use their vehicles to travel on roads or off. They explore, go camping, and compete with others.

Automobile Activities

Auto racing is a test of driving skill and design ingenuity. Race cars are built in every conceivable shape and size from go-carts to jet-powered land speed record challengers. Many get their start in racing by modifying recent stock cars and competing in the Sportsman Class of competition. Others enjoy drag racing original or highly modified cars on a straight measured track. Car rallies provide a more relaxed form of driving competition. They may include timed runs where you follow brief instructions and attempt to follow prescribed average speeds between checkpoints. Another variation is the poker run. A playing card is dealt at each check point and the best hand at the conclusion of the run wins.

Other forms of competition emphasize craftsmanship, where older vehicles are restored to original condition. Clubs often sponsor car shows, displaying cars for public enjoyment. Winners of these events may receive trophies for cars judged best in their class. Perhaps the most extreme competition in automobile condition judging occurs in concours meets. At Chevrolet Corvette concours and Antique Automobile Club of America meets some contestants encase each wheel and tire in a special cotton cover after cleaning. They drive to the display area with the covers on, removing them just before judging. Even the underside of the car is polished.

A less restrictive, but still competitive atmosphere prevails at hot rod or custom car meets, where there is much variety to be seen. An example of the tongue-in-cheek attitude is the use of a coffin mounted on wheels as a car trailer.

Other car-related activities include participation in parades and tours. The Glidden Tour of old cars commemorates a reliability run begun in 1905. The original Glidden Tours were used to demonstrate the condition of roads then being used for auto travel. Although the last of the original Glidden Tours occurred in 1913, they have been revived and run by antique auto enthusiasts. The London-Bournemouth run in England commemorates the repeal of oppressive automotive highway regulations imposed in the early days of motoring. As with the Glidden tour, the run is made with antique cars.

Some car clubs sponsor "gymkhana" meets where intricate driving maneuvers are performed in a cleared area. Others take a more relaxed approach where car games such as balloon bursting, stopping closest to a specified spot, and even slow racing—longest time between two points without stopping—are enjoyed.

Automotive pastimes as described above require expenditure of time and money to acquire, maintain, and in some cases, modify or restore a vehicle. Many enjoy the challenge of performing the necessary work themselves.

Working on Cars

Auto mechanic and auto body courses are available in high schools, vocational schools, community colleges, and private technical schools. You can study on your own, but the courses will provide more in-depth knowledge and get you up to speed faster.

The Do-it-yourself Mechanic

The study of a good general book on auto mechanics will help to understand how automobile components are divided into systems. Some mechanics, like doctors, are specialists in one or more systems. Typical automotive systems are engines, electrical, power train, chassis, and brakes. Books are published that specialize in specific systems.

Independent shop manuals are available from publishers such as Chilton, Clymer, Haynes, and Motor. These usually cover more than one car, but the step-by-step instructions are usually specific. Car manufacturer's service manuals can be obtained that cover your car. These will provide almost all the information there is to know about your car. If you are working with an older vehicle, the manufacturer may no longer be able to supply the service manual required. In that case, just refer to a magazine such as *Hemmings Motor News* for listings of book and literature dealers who will provide the shop manual for your 1928 Cadillac at a reasonable price.

As problems are uncovered during any model year, manufacturers provide dealers with service bulletins. Copies of these are also published for some cars. Other useful literature includes parts books that list part numbers for each part of a car, color-upholstery books, and owner's manuals. Interchange manuals are very useful when working with older cars where parts may be scarce. You can select a part from a different car that will fit on your project car.

Most hobbyists will start with light maintenance work such as tire rotation, changing oil and filters, replacing spark plugs, and fan belts. After gaining some confidence in handling tools, one may try brake work, replacing shock absorbers, or rebuilding a carburetor. Just follow the directions in the manual. With more complex work, where engines or drive trains need parts, you will usually find that specialized tools are required.

The "shade tree mechanic" will add tools as the need arises, starting with the usual assortment of quality wrenches and screwdrivers. Buy a sturdy set of jack stands to place under axles when you must work beneath the car. Don't rely on the type of jack intended for use in changing tires. It may tip when side pressures are exerted during the work. Buy inexpensive specialized tools that you expect to use often, such as small bearing pullers. Rent expensive seldom-used specialized tools such as heavy duty engine stands needed for engine removal.

When doing mechanical repair, one disassembles the car or component one piece at a time. Worn or damaged parts that no longer meet the specifications called for in manuals are replaced during reassembly.

New replacement parts for recent model cars are obtained from a dealership. For older cars you may have to resort to reproduction parts from an after-market manufacturer. Such parts may also be used parts that have been rebuilt to as-new condition. Some suppliers specialize in the acquisition of surplus stocks of original parts. They can furnish what is known as "new old stock" (NOS) parts.

Auto Body Work

Some automotive magazines feature articles suggest that repair of dented or rusted sheet metal can be accomplished by simply smearing on plastic body fillers. The proper repair of rusted out areas requires a series of steps. First, remove the paint and grease in the immediate area by applying paint remover or sanding. Cut away thin, weakened metal around the rusted-through area using a saber saw. Obtain a piece of sheet metal of similar thickness to the body part and form it to the original shape of the area. A convenient source of such metal is a scrap body part. Size the metal patch to fit the area removed, leaving a slight gap around the edges. The patch is then brazed or welded in place. Ready-made replacement patch panels for areas subject to rust are available for popular cars. For a high quality repair, a process called hammer welding is sometimes used. A short bead of weld is put in place and while still hot is hammered flat with the surface using a back up piece of metal called a dolly on the underside. The process is repeated until the seam has been completed.

All red rust must be thoroughly removed by repeated applications of products containing inhibited phosphoric acid or equivalent (wear rubber gloves and eye protection). Rub the surface with steel wool between applications. A thin, tightly adhering film of black rust may remain. It is not objectionable as long as it shows no tendency to flake off. When rust removal is complete, treat the area with metal conditioner and rust inhibitor. Add plastic body filler if required, and sand smooth. It is best to start with coarse sandpaper and follow up with smoother grades to obtain an acceptably smooth surface. Apply primer to bare metal to obtain best paint adhesion. Sand away most of the first coat of primer. High spots will be revealed when the bare metal shows through. Rework the high metal surfaces with a hammer and dolly, and reprime. Many hobbyists will drive their cars after priming, but before finish paint has been applied. Moisture can work its way down to the metal surface and cause rust to form under the primer, resulting in paint flaking off in the future.

When metal body panels are merely dented or deformed, body hammers and dollies are used to straighten or recontour the surfaces. During this process, compare the area being worked with the opposite side of the car. The opposite side is usually a mirror image of the side being worked. Over use of the hammering process will thin and stretch the metal creating bulges. Body hammers are available with grooved striking surfaces that will shrink the metal, regaining its original shape.

Good quality spraying equipment, particularly the spray gun, is critical for professional results. Buy the best you can afford and clean it carefully after each use.

Restoration

Restoration is very labor intensive and professional restoration is expensive. You can save by doing at least part of the work yourself. The first step in automobile restoration is research. Obtain service manuals and any other relevant literature available, and become familiar with the entire car. As you disassemble the car, take photographs, make pencil sketches, label parts, and store them in labeled containers. An auto restoration can take years. You will not remember which wire attaches to what, or how parts fit.

Restorations are done in varying degrees of thoroughness. A "cosmetic" restoration might only involve a quick coat of paint and seat covers. A more thorough job would include removal of the finish to bare metal and replacement of the upholstery.

The most thorough restoration is called a "frame-off" or "frame-up" restoration. This requires removal of the car's body from the running gear and a piece by piece reconditioning, cleaning, and repaint before reassembly. Much of this work is semi-skilled at best, and the average person can do it.

Some restoration activities such as welding, upholstery, and plating are more demanding, and you may wish to contract some of this work to the experts. If you decide to do some of the complex work yourself, don't be afraid to ask questions. Experts are more often flattered than offended when you seek their advice.

Custom Cars and Hot Rods

Custom car builders modify original factory built cars to achieve a unique appearance or improve performance. Body sheet metal is recontoured, and sometimes engine or suspension components are interchanged.

Suppliers can provide an entire running gear composed of an underframe and all suspension components intended to be used as the foundation for a custom vehicle. The hobbyist can add the body from an old car, or bolt on a fiberglass copy of one of the more popular body styles now in short supply, such as a 1932 Ford. Building up a custom vehicle from new commercial products such as this can result in a car costing more than a new luxury car.

The less expensive approach involves modification and restoration of old car parts. Popular modifications include "chopping and channeling." Several inches are removed at the window level, lowering the roof line. The suspension is reworked to lower the entire car to within six inches or so from the ground. Chrome ornamentation is removed and radiator grilles, taillights, and wheels from other car models are substituted. Paint schemes vary from subdued single colored flat paint to gaudy multicolored paint jobs sporting simulated flames or pinstriping. The object is to achieve a different look and "improve" the appearance of the car (in the eyes of the owner). It is interesting to note that the emphasis on removing chrome has had some affect on production car styling.

Choosing a Car Project

Regardless of which type of vehicle you select, consider its resale value. In the future you may choose to sell in order to buy another car, or sell out when changing hobbies. Even do-it-yourself restoration costs can easily exceed the resale value of a less popular car model. For older cars the *Old Cars Price Guide* is one place you can start. By studying the current market values, you're less likely to overpay when buying, and can set realistic prices when selling.

Other things to consider are insurance costs and parts availability. Insurance costs are higher for vehicles with high horsepower motors. Parts availability varies considerably. Almost any part for an early Ford such as the Model T (Figure 1) through a 1942 model can be bought by mail from specialist parts houses. In some cases delivery is faster than for a modern car. The same is true for the popular 1955–1957 Chevrolets (Figure 2) and most Corvettes. If you have chosen a less popular orphan car you can often find a needed part in magazines such as *Cars and Parts*.

Automotive Attractions

There are hundreds of automotive attractions that auto buffs look forward to each year. We'll look at a few of the biggest (with apologies to the rest).

Each fall, in early October, the Antique Automobile Club of America hosts the annual Fall Eastern Meet at Hershey, Pa. The meet is known simply as Hershey. Up to 250,000 hobbyists converge on the site from around the world. Approximately 9,500 spots are rented to vendors ranging from your average hobbyist trying to sell off some surplus parts, to high roller professionals selling exotic sports cars. One may buy a London double decker bus, a rusty but restorable classic car, or that elusive part you need to complete your restoration project. It is estimated that you would have to walk twenty miles to see all of the vendor spots located side-by-side in the three huge swap meet fields. The three day event also includes an antique car competition featuring about 2,000 cars. One can stand near the roadway leading to the show area and watch a parade of show cars passing by for several hours. Examples range from a Stanley Steamer or Detroit Electric to a Tucker.

The National Street Rod Association Street Rod National event is held in different locations during midsummer. The event draws up to 12,000 cars from around the country each year. It also includes vendor sales and exhibits. The event is said to be the largest automotive participant event in the world.

The Henry Ford Museum in Dearborn, Michigan houses a collection of about 200 historically significant vehicles. The cars are well displayed, providing easy viewing.

The Indianapolis Motor Speedway not only hosts its spectacular annual Indy 500 mile race annually, but also maintains a museum displaying a collection of more than twenty-five winning race cars and about thirty vintage, antique, and classic cars at any one time. Their entire collection contains over 125 race cars and about the same number of passenger cars.

Figure 1
Model T

Figure 2
A good candidate for restoration, the very popular 1957 Chevrolet.

The Merle Norman Classic Beauty Collection in Slymar, Cal. emphasizes, but is not limited to, classic cars such as Duesenburg, Rolls-Royce, Cadillac, and Packard. The cars are displayed in an opulent showroom setting. About sixty of the 173 cars in the collection are displayed at any one time.

The famous Harrah auto collection in Sparks, Nevada once numbered more than a thousand cars. After the death of William F. Harrah much of the collection has been auctioned off, with the 300 most significant cars retained for a museum to be run by a public foundation.

Bibliography

REFERENCE BOOKS

The American Car Since 1775. New York: Bailey, 1971. A complete survey of the American automobile by the editors of *Automobile Quarterly Magazine.*

Antonick, Michael. *Corvette Black Book.* Powell, OH: Bruce, 1992. Corvette facts and descriptions for each model year.

Crouse, William H. *Automotive Mechanics.* 8th ed. New York: McGraw-Hill, 1980. Complete overview text on auto mechanics. Designed for use as a teaching aid. Includes auto systems, tools, trouble diagnosis, and related materials.

Eves, Edward, and Dan Burger. *Great Car Collections of the World.* New York: Smith, 1986. Describes museums in eighteen countries, listing significant cars in their collections. Well illustrated.

Finch, Richard, and Tom Monroe. *Welder's Handbook.* Los Angeles: HP Books, 1985. Welding processes for automotive, aviation, home workshop, and arts and crafts applications.

Fournier, Ron, and Sue Fournier. *Metal Fabricator's Handbook.* Rev. ed. Los Angeles: HP Books, 1990. Fabrication techniques for race, custom, and restoration use including bodywork, welding tips, and hammer forming.

Gilles, Tim. *Automotive Engines: Diagnosis, Repair, Rebuilding.* 2nd ed. Albany, NY: Delmar, 1991. An introduction to the technology of engine repair. Techniques applicable to all engines are discussed.

Joseph, Matt. *Standard Guide to Automotive Restoration.* Iola, WI: Krause, 1992. A practical approach to car restoration, all makes, models, years. Step-by-step hows and ways arranged by system.

Mitchell International Staff. *Mitchell Automechanics.* 2nd ed. Englewood Cliffs, NJ: Prentice-Hall, 1991. Complete overview text on auto mechanics. Designed for use by auto technology instructors and students of the subject.

Rhone, L. C., and H. David Yates. *Total Auto Body Repair.* 2nd ed. Mission Hills, CA: Glencoe, 1983. A student's text for autobody instruction. Describes the shop, tools, materials, and methods.

Ruiz, Marco. *One Hundred Years of the Automobile 1886–1986.* New York: Smith, 1985. Illustrated automotive history from an international perspective.

Scharff, Robert. *Motor Auto Body Repair.* 2nd ed. Albany, NY: Delmar, 1992. Complete overview of body work tools and techniques. Procedures include disassembly of mechanical components.

Schild, Jim. *Restorer's Classic Car Shop Manual.* Florissant, MO: Auto Review, 1991. Restoration and maintenance guide for all 1925–1948 CCCA classic cars including Cadillac, Duesenberg, and many more. Explains systems and techniques.

Toboldt, Bill. *Auto Body Repairing and Repainting.* Rev. ed. South Holland, IL: Goodheart-Willcox, 1982. Simplified methods of metal straightening, filling dents, repainting, and related material.

Hundreds of manuals are published intended for use in the servicing of automobiles produced by a specific manufacturer. Some of the largest manual publishers are listed below:

Chilton Book Co. Chilton Way, Radnor, PA 19089.

Clymer Publications Intertec Publishing Corp., PO Box 12901, Overland Park, KS 66212

Haynes Publications, Inc. 861 Lawrence Drive, Newbury Park, CA 91320.

Motor. Hearst Books/Business Publishing Group, 5600 Crooks Road, Troy, MI 48098.

PERIODICALS

Antique Automobile. Antique Automobile Club of America, 501 W. Governor Road, Hershey, PA 17033.

Auto Racing Digest. Century Publishers, 990 Grove Street, Evanston, IL 60201–4370.

Automobile Quarterly. Automobile Quarterly, Box 348, Kutztown, PA 19530.

Car and Driver. Hachette Magazines, 1633 Broadway, New York, NY 10009.

Car Collector & Car Classics. Classic Publishers, Box 28571, Atlanta, GA 30328.

Car Craft. Petersen Publishers, 8490 Sunset Boulevard, Los Angeles, CA 90069.

Cars & Parts. Amos Press, 911 Vandemark Road, Box 482, Sidney, OH 45365.

Four Wheeler Magazine. Four Wheeler Publishers, 6728 Eton Ave., Canoga Park, CA 91303

Hemmings Motor News. Watering, Box 256, Bennington, VT 05201.

Hot Rod. Petersen Publishers, 8490 Sunset Boulevard, Los Angeles, CA 90069.

Motor. Hearst Business Publications, 645 Stewart Avenue, Garden City, NY 11530.

Motor Trend. Petersen Publishers, 8490 Sunset Boulevard, Los Angeles, CA 90069.

Off-Road. Argus Publishers, Box 49659, Los Angeles, CA 90049.

Old Cars Price Guide. Krause Publications, 700 E. State Street, Iola, WI 54990.

On Track. O T Publishers, 17165 Newhope, Unit M, Box 8509, Fountain Valley, CA 92708–0509.

Popular Hot Rodding. Argus Publishers, Box 49659, Los Angeles, CA 90049.

Road & Track. Hachette Magazines, Road & Track, 1499 Monrovia Avenue, Newport Beach, CA 92663.

Special Interest Autos. Watering, Special Interest Publications, Box 904, Bennington, VT 05201.

Stock Car Racing. Stock Car Racing Publishers, 27 S. Main Street, Ipswich, MA 01938.

Street Rodder. McMullen Publishers, 2145 W. La Palma Avenue, Anaheim, CA 92801.

ASSOCIATIONS

Antique Automobile Club of America. 501 W. Governor Road, Hershey, PA 17033. Those interested in the preservation, maintenance, and restoration of automobiles, and in their history. Maintains library, bestows awards, and sponsors Glidden Tour. Publication: *Antique Automobile.*

Horseless Carriage Club of America. 128 S. Cypress Street, Orange, CA 92666–1314. Those interested in the preservation of old cars and related items. Sponsors tours and maintains museum. Publications: *Horseless Carriage Gazette,* and related materials.

International Show Car Association. 1520 S. Lapeer Road, Suite 221, Lake Orion, MI 48360. Owners of customized vehicles who exhibit their vehicles in sanctioned events, and interested individuals. Provides judging and classification rules, sanctions shows, organizes competitions, and bestows awards. Publications: *Show Stopper,* and related material.

Kustom Kemps of America. 2548 Glacier Drive, Wichita, KS 67215. Enthusiasts of custom cars and trucks from 1935 to 1964, and a separate division for non-stockcars and trucks from 1965 to the present. Maintains hall of fame and bestows awards. Publications: *KKOA - The Trendsetter,* and related material.

National 4 Wheel Drive Association. 3310 E. Shangrila Road, Phoenix, AZ 85028. Sanctions four-wheel-drive runs. Clearinghouse for information and news concerning subject vehicles. Publications: *Bulletin, News,* and related materials.

National Street Rod Association. 4030 Park Avenue, Memphis, TN 38111. Street rod builders and enthusiasts. Conducts national events. Publication: *StreetScene.*

Sports Car Club of America. 9033 E. Easter Place, Englewood, CO 80112. Competition sports car enthusiasts. Sanctions races, conducts race driver schools, rallies, gymkhanas, and concours events. Publications: *Sports Car,* and related materials.

United Four-Wheel Drive Associations. 4505 W. 700 S, Shelbyville, IN 46176. Purpose is to work with land problems and establish better communication between four-wheelers and the government. Publication: *United Voice.*

Veteran Motor Car Club of America. c/o William E. Donze, M. D., PO Box 360788, Strongsville, OH 44136. Those interested in antique automobiles and related items. Publication: *Bulb Horn.*

There are over 250 active automotive associations primarily interested in a single manufacturer's products. A selection of some of the largest single marque associations follows:

BMW Car Club of America. 2130 Massachusetts Avenue, No. 1A, Cambridge, MA 02140. Bavarian Motor Works.

Classic Chevy Club International. PO Box 607188, Orlando, FL 32860. 1955 to 1957 Chevrolet.

Late Great Chevrolet Association. PO Box 607824, Orlando, FL 32860. 1958 to 1964 Chevrolet.

Mercedes-Benz Club of America. 1907 Lelaray Street, Colorado Springs, CO 80909. Mercedes-Benz.

Model A Ford Club of America. 250 S. Cypress, La Habra, CA 90631. 1928 to 1931 Ford.

National Corvette Owners Association. PO Box 777–A, Falls Church, VA 22046. Chevrolet Corvette.

National Corvette Restorers Society. 6291 Day Road, Cincinnati, OH 45252. 1953 to 1977 Chevrolet Corvette.

National Council of Corvette Clubs. PO Box 813, Adams Basin, NY 14410. Chevrolet Corvette.

Porsche Club of America. PO Box 10402, Alexandria, VA 22310. Porsche.

Studebaker Driver's Club. PO Box 1040, Oswego, IL 60543. Studebaker.

Zcenter. 550 Lexington Avenue, Clifton, NJ 07011. Datsun/Nissan 240Z and 300ZX.

Aviation

THERE ARE OVER 700,000 PILOTS in the United States, and another 100,000 people decide to try flying each year. For every pilot, there are many "armchair" pilots, or aviation buffs, who wish they could fly. This discussion will be limited to the popular heavier-than-air, noncommercial side of general aviation. Few nations make it as easy as the United States does to own and operate an airplane. However, if you choose to take up flying, be prepared for considerable study, practice, and expense. In addition to mastering flight basics, you need a working knowledge of navigation and meteorology if you expect to leave sight of the airport.

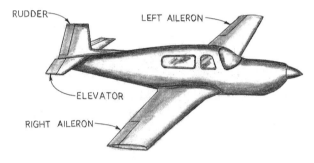

Figure 1

Typical airplane control surfaces.

History

After the Wright Brothers' successful flight in 1903, designers made gradual improvements to aircraft by trial-and-error methods. Development accelerated just before, and during World War I. Postwar surpluses of airplanes and engines slowed the production of new aircraft, but provided some interested individuals with inexpensive planes for private flying. Following Charles A. Lindbergh's solo flight across the Atlantic in 1927, interest in private flying increased and accelerated up to the period of the United States' entrance into World War II. After the war, returning military pilots found they couldn't afford to own and operate their own aircraft. Over the years we have seen the rate of production of aircraft designed for private use dwindle. We will see how private pilots have overcome the costs by cooperative ownership of airplanes, aircraft rental, and the purchase of used equipment.

Airplane Control

Let's refer to Figure 1 and see how a typical airplane is maneuvered. Due to the shape of a wing, air flowing over the convex top must travel farther and faster to reach the trailing edge than air flowing under the bottom. This faster moving air on the upper surface is forced to thin out, creating a lower pressure area on top than that found under the wing, providing an upward force. The lifting force is increased by tipping the leading edge of the wing up causing the air striking the lower surface to deflect the wing upward. It's the job of the elevator, located back on the tail, to position the wing at the angle required. When the elevator is raised (by pulling back on the stick) the wing leading edge will tilt upward. Too much tilt, and the airflow over the upper surface of the wing will be interrupted and most of the lift will be lost. The wing is then said to be stalled. Everything an airplane does in flight depends upon the angle at which the leading edge of the wing meets the air; it's the wing's angle of attack.

In order to make a proper left turn three control actions are coordinated. A control stick (or wheel) is moved to the left by hand, raising the left aileron and lowering the right. This causes the left wing to tilt down, causing the wing lift to be directed upward to the left. The left foot is used to depress the left rudder pedal moving the rudder to the left, turning the plane in that direction. During the turn the control stick is also moved back slightly to maintain altitude. If the stick is moved too far back, the wing will stall. Aircraft are susceptible to stalls in turns, the cause of half of all flying accidents.

To recover from a stall, the pilot must keep the wings level and push the stick forward to drop the nose and regain the proper angle of attack while applying power. If the pilot wishes to enter a tailspin (from sufficient altitude), the plane is intentionally stalled, full rudder is applied, and the stick is pulled straight back. The plane will spin as long as the control positions are held. Although the plane is descending, it is falling in a nose high (stalled) position with respect to its flight path. To recover from a spin apply full rudder against the direction of spin rotation and move the stick forward. As the spin stops, center the rudder, return the wings to a horizontal position, and slowly pull back on the stick to recover from the dive. Aircraft types vary in regard to their ability to withstand aerobatic maneuvers such as spins.

Aircraft Types and Pilot Certificates

We'll look next at a few popular general aviation aircraft types as defined by the Federal Aviation Administration (FAA).

Hang Gliders

Hang gliding reached a peak of activity during the 1980s. While many hang gliding pilots have turned to powered flight, a significant number still enjoy the sport. The father of practical hang gliding is Otto Lilienthal. He built his first glider in Germany in 1891. Today's standard basic hang glider stems from an invention by Francis M. Rogallo. This triangular glider has a tubular framework that supports a fabric sail attached to a frame down the centerline and at the leading edges. The sail is left to billow like a parachute; its trailing edge is not attached to the frame. Other forms of hang glider use a rigid wing. They are more difficult to transport, so are less popular.

Hang gliding requires careful instruction and a gradual approach to more complex flight. Ski slopes are often used for a flying site. Rogallo hang gliders drop about one foot for each four feet they move forward, so a three to one slope is considered about right for the flying site. Hang gliders are as susceptible to stalls as other aircraft. If you fly too fast however, (somewhere between thirty and forty miles per hour) the sail will deflate and you will drop. To soar, you can glide just ahead of the top of a hill, into the prevailing updraft. Too far back, and turbulence can upset you. Soaring in hang gliders is for the experienced.

No pilot certificate is required by the FAA for hang gliding. If the glider is used for recreation or sport and weighs less than 155 pounds, it is considered an ultralight vehicle and requires no certification. Restrictions for operation are specified by the FAA.

Ultralight Aircraft

Ultralight powered aircraft are subject to regulation by the FAA. The aircraft must weigh less than 254 pounds, excluding safety devices intended to be employed in emergencies. Fuel capacity must not exceed five U.S. gallons. Maximum speed is fifty-five knots, power-off stall speed not to exceed twenty-four knots. The craft is intended for recreational or sport use. No aircraft certification is required. No airman or medical certificate is required. The craft must be operated during daylight hours when the ground is visible. Minimum flight visibility and distance from clouds is specified for various altitudes in FAA FAR Part 103 (ultralight vehicles). Operation is not permitted in certain areas, such as over towns or congested areas. You may not operate within an airport traffic area, control zone, airport radar service area, or terminal control area, unless prior authorization has been obtained from the air traffic control facility.

Ultralight powered aircraft continue to become more sophisticated, crowding the 254 pound weight limit, and often resembling fully enclosed light aircraft. Two-place operation is only allowed for instructional purposes.

Soaring Gliders

Soaring gliders, or sailplanes, can be towed aloft by an airplane to about 2,000 feet, and released to glide to the ground or catch an updraft and soar for long periods. Another launch method involves attaching a tow cable to a winch, and pulling the glider aloft like a kite.

Glider flight instruction can start as early as fourteen years of age, after obtaining a medical certificate and a student pilot certificate as specified by the FAA. After twenty-five to fifty flights you may solo, and seventy to 100 flights are normally required to become skilled enough to pass the examination for a glider pilot's certificate.

A typical club charges $300 to join, $30 for monthly dues, and $10.50 for each 2,000 foot tow by the club plane. You have access to the clubs gliders. Some clubs allow you to reduce tow costs by working as a launch crew member. As fliers gain experience they sometimes buy into the ownership of a glider with others to keep the cost of ownership down.

High performance sailplanes travel over forty-five feet for each foot of lost altitude. Glider pilots search out thermal updrafts to offset lost altitude and sustain flight for hours. The current out and return distance record for a glider is over 1,000 miles, and the maximum altitude record is over 42,000 feet.

Light Planes

Piloting a light plane takes coordination, judgment, training and money. To obtain a private pilots certificate you must first obtain a medical certificate, student pilot certificate, pass a written test and a flight test, and be seventeen years of age. The average number of hours of flying time you will spend to obtain your license is sixty-three. The legal minimum is forty hours. It usually takes about eight months. The national average cost to obtain a private pilot's license, including ground school, instructor time, plane rental, and incidentals, is just over $4,000. After you obtain your private pilot's certificate you can carry passengers, but not for hire. Your must pass another test to obtain an instrument rating if you wish to fly in poor visibility conditions (IFR).

Recognizing the growing need for pilots, the FAA established a new certificate level in 1989. The Recreational Pilot Certificate rating requires fewer training hours, but is more restrictive in some areas. It is designed to allow beginners to enjoy the seat of the pants flying done in the past. The minimum flight time requirement is reduced to thirty hours; fifteen hours with an instructor, and fifteen solo (alone). The requirements for study of radio communications, basic instrument flying, and radio navigation were lifted. The student must be at least seventeen, possess a third-class medical certificate, and be able to read, speak, and understand English. Recreational pilots are limited to a fifty-mile radius from where their training took place, to 2,000 feet above ground level (AGL), to having visual reference to the ground while in flight, and to carrying one passenger.

Other Aircraft Types

There are many other types, some requiring additional ratings and study. Examples include helicopters, gyroplanes, experimental craft, aerobatic planes, racers, and restored warplanes. The number of those flying these types of craft is limited, but they are a dedicated lot, and have the finances to match that dedication.

Additional certificates are required for commercial flying. Aviation's equivalent of an educational doctorate is the airline pilot's certificate. You must be at least twenty-three to hold that rating.

Aircraft—Share, Rent, Buy, or Build

General aviation yearly airplane sales have dropped from almost 18,000 to just over 1,000 in the past fourteen years. Just over half of recent deliveries have been single engine piston craft. With today's prices for single engine planes ranging from $50,000 to $100,000 and higher, purchase of a new ship is quite an investment.

Used airplanes are the answer for a growing number of prospective aircraft owners. Forty-five year old lightplanes sell for $8,000 to $20,000 depending on condition and reputation. A twelve- to fourteen-year-old craft in prime condition can cost $40,000 to $50,000.

Many have turned to the purchase of kits to assemble their own airplanes. Kits to build a very light craft start at $6,000 and an average lightplane kit runs from $20,000 to $35,000.

Most kit manufacturers sell sets of plans for their designs; the skilled builder then gathers the necessary materials and hardware on his own. Plans can be had for sixty dollars, but most average $200 or more. If you would like a real challenge, consider plans for a full sized World War II fighter at only $3,000. It is said that more than half of these kit planes are never completed. It takes the determination of people like an eighty-year-old friend who is completing his fifth ultralight. It's a scaled down copy of a 1930s plane crafted from an 8½-by-11 inch drawing of the original.

There are alternatives to the high cost of aircraft ownership. You can enter into a partnership to purchase a plane. As we have seen, considerable money is involved, so have a legal partnership agreement drawn up. Keep the number of partners low enough to minimize problems with scheduling time on the plane.

Flying clubs share the use of a fleet of planes. Make sure the club you join is incorporated to minimize your financial risk if unforeseen claims are made on the club. Nationwide aero clubs exist that give members ready access to a plane at locations across the country.

Airplane rental affords flexibility when you go after a rating in a different type of aircraft, or need a larger craft for a certain cross-country run.

Flight Planning and Navigational Systems

Aircraft are flown in two distinct sets of conditions. Visual flight rules (VFR) apply when the pilot has visual access to the ground and sufficient unobstructed view of the surrounding area to fly safely. Instrument flight rules (IFR) apply when less than visual navigation is possible, as with heavy cloud cover or storm activity.

The FAA regulations covering cross-country flight require that the pilot be familiar with "all available information concerning that flight." The regulations specifically require that the pilot study weather reports and forecasts, calculate fuel requirements, determine alternate courses and landing sites, and be familiar with any known traffic delays.

Weather conditions determine whether a planned flight is even possible for a pilot who does not have an instrument rating, or who does not have a properly equipped IFR aircraft. The legal minimums for VFR flight are three statute miles visibility and a 1,000 foot ceiling (distance from ground to bottom of clouds) for most situations.

For a VFR flight, the pilot will call the local flight service station (FSS) to obtain a weather briefing. The briefing will identify adverse weather conditions, weather along the proposed route, current conditions, forecast, destination forecast, and winds aloft. The weather information is followed by a review of all relevant notices to airmen (NOTAMs). These notices include such information as equipment outages, runway closures, or anything that might affect flight safety. The pilot, officially termed the pilot in command, must make the final decision whether to go or delay the flight. It is wise to request weather information for routes leading to alternate landing sites that have been identified while planning the flight.

For IFR flight, the pilot will file an IFR flight plan with the nearest FSS station. The purpose is to record the basic aspects of the flight to provide search-and-rescue service in the event of trouble. It is also used to generate clearances, the basis for aircraft separation in the clouds. It is the pilot's responsibility to inform the FSS of takeoff, and to report arrival in order to "close" the plan. If the pilot fails to close the plan within one half hour after the estimated time of arrival, a search will be made for the aircraft.

The VFR pilot may navigate by means of "pilotage." This is done by adjusting the course line flown to compensate for the crosswind speed information obtained during the weather briefing. Another adjustment is made for the compass deviation caused by the offset of magnetic north from true north. Headwinds or tailwinds are also considered when calculating the time of arrival and fuel requirements. The pilot will check for accurate calculations by identifying features on the ground. He/she may follow a railroad track or highway and note a check point by means of a racetrack shown on a map. While a standard Rand McNally atlas may suffice, aviation sectional charts are the best choice. Sectionals are drawn at a scale of eight miles to the inch. The U.S. is divided into thirty-seven sections. These charts contain all airports, topographical information, radio navigation aids, and many other features vital to pilots. They are available at most airports. Sectionals are updated every six months.

Well-equipped IFR pilots have a number of navigational aides at their disposal. The FAA has established an extensive very high frequency omni range (VOR) system that can be used by all pilots for route guidance. The pilot simply tunes in the VOR station at his/her destination and observes a course deviation indicator to determine that he/she is on course to the destination. On long range flights, the pilot picks a series of VOR stations along the chosen route and flies from one to the next until the destination is reached. Distance measuring equipment (DME) operates on the UHF radio band. After accessing it, the pilot is given the distance to the station, ground speed toward the station, and time to reach the station.

A more sophisticated system has also become very popular. Loran C receivers have extensive chart capacity stored in their internal computers. You punch in the latitude and longitude of your present location and that of your destination. Loran will direct you via a great circle route, which is the shortest distance between any two points on a globe. Along the way, you have a constant readout of ground speed, distance remaining to your destination, and a visual course deviation indicator to keep you on track. Position accuracy is said to be within sixty feet. Loran was originally established for maritime use. The bulky shipboard equipment has been transistorized into an eight inch high hand-held unit suitable for primary use or backup navigation equipment on a lightplane.

The next advance in radio navigation is the global positioning system (GPS) satellite navigation. The GPS system uses a three-channel sensor to track up to eight satellites. The worldwide database stored in the receiver contains VORs and airports with at least one runway of 2,000 feet or longer. You can enter a series of waypoints along your planned route. In the navigation mode the GPS unit displays ground speed, bearing, distance traveled, time of arrival, and a course deviation indicator. The near mode displays your bearing and distance to the ten nearest airports, VORs, and waypoints closest to your present position, or closest to any waypoint you select. Wouldn't that be nice if you were lost in a storm? Other features include the ability to read out the total distance and time you have traveled, the highest and lowest altitudes you have achieved, current, average and maximum speed, and the time of sunrise and sunset—anywhere. All this in a hand-held unit similar to the Loran above.

A fully equipped IFR capable plane will have a glide-slope and marker beacon receiver that will enable the pilot to land in minimal visual conditions. This system, plus a terminal approach chart for the airport to be used, completes the navigation package.

Spectator Favorites

There are many events and attractions that appeal to the aviation enthusiast. We'll take a look at a few of the best based on variety and sheer size.

The Air Force museum located in Dayton, Ohio houses a very large display of military aircraft both indoors and out. Aircraft displayed include those from the World War I and II periods, experimental craft that explored the sound barrier, jets, and bombers from the B–17 to the B–70. A large selection of aviation books is available in the bookstore and a large collection of aircraft plans can be accessed by the public.

The National Air and Space Museum in Washington, DC displays many historical craft, including spacecraft. Don't overlook their Garber facility in Maryland where many planes awaiting restoration are stored. A tour of this facility includes a look at their restoration shops, with crews busy restoring planes to pristine condition.

Old Rhinebeck Aerodrome in Rhinebeck, New York houses antique aircraft in flyable condition. Many are displayed in hangers built to appear as they would in the early days of aviation. Demonstration dogfights of World War I aircraft are conducted on weekends during the summer months. An extensive collection of civilian antique aircraft is on display in their museum.

The small airport in Oshkosh, Wisconsin becomes the world's busiest airport for eight days in late July when members of the Experimental Aircraft Association fly in more than 15,000 planes to compete with their aircraft in various ways. The planes include antiques, classics, homebuilts, warbirds, ultralights, light planes, and rotorcraft. About 850,000 people attend. Hundreds of educational forums, workshops, and seminars are held. Air shows are continuous, and the museum of general aviation and experimental aircraft is exceptional.

Bibliography

REFERENCE BOOKS

Adkins, Hal. *The Ultralight Accessory Book*. Blue Ridge Summit, PA: TAB Books, 1986. Ultralight accessories—what's available, how they work, and where to get them.

Christy, Joe. *Your Pilot's License*. 4th ed. Blue Ridge Summit, PA: TAB Books, 1987. An introduction to aircraft systems and flight training.

Clausing, Donald J. *The Aviator's Guide to Flight Planning*. Blue Ridge Summit, PA: TAB Books, 1989. A guide to modern flight planning techniques.

Cook, LeRoy. *101 Things to Do With Your Private License*. Blue Ridge Summit, PA: TAB Books, 1985. Emphasis on flying techniques, including navigation.

Dehaan, Warren, and Vici Dehaan. *Moving Through the Ratings: Passing From Private to Professional Pilot*. Blue Ridge Summit, PA: TAB Books, 1987. Coverage of various pilot ratings, basic training, and flight techniques.

Frazier, David. *ABCs of Safe Flying*. 3rd ed. Blue Ridge Summit, PA: TAB Books, 1992. Flying techniques, the federal airspace system, and emergency procedures.

Illman, Paul E. *The Pilot's Handbook of Aeronautical Knowledge*. Rev. ed. Blue Ridge Summit, PA: TAB Books, 1991. The technical knowledge you will need to prepare for private pilot certification.

Markowski, Michael A. *Ultralight Technique: How to Fly and Navigate Ultralight Air Vehicles*. Hummelstown, PA: Ultralight, 1983. Ultralight coverage from the principles of flight to operational technique. Includes applicable FAA rules.

Nelson, John L. *The Beginner's Guide to Flight Instruction*. 2nd ed. Blue Ridge Summit, PA: TAB Books, 1990. Pilot training and the purchase of an aircraft.

Padfield, R. Randall. *Cross-Country Flying*. 3rd ed. Blue Ridge Summit, PA: TAB Books, 1991. The equipment, techniques, and skills you need to master for cross-country flying.

Schweizer, Paul A. *Wings Like Eagles: The Story of Soaring in the United States*. Washington, DC: Smithsonian Institution, 1988. A history of American gliding activity told by a man who made soaring his life work.

TAB-Aero Staff. *AIM/FAR 1992: Airman's Information Manual/Federal Aviation Regulations*. Blue Ridge Summit, PA: TAB Aero, 1992. A compilation of federal aviation regulations.

Welch, John F., ed. *Van Sickle's Modern Airmanship*. 6th ed. Blue Ridge Summit, PA: TAB Books, 1990. A complete manual on flying. Information for improving your piloting skills, abilities, and techniques.

PERIODICALS

Air & Space—Smithsonian. Smithsonian Institution, 370 L'Enfant Promenade, S.W., 10th Floor, Washington, DC 20024–2518.

Air Classics. Challenge Publications, 7950 Deering Avenue, Canoga Park, CA 91324.

Flying. Hachette Magazines, 1633 Broadway, New York, NY 10009.

General Aviation News & Flyer. Northwest Flyer, Box 98786, Tacoma, WA 98498–0786.

Kitplanes. Fancy Publications, Box 6050, Mission Viejo, CA 92690.

Plane and Pilot. Werner Publishers, 12121 Wilshire Boulevard, No. 1220, Los Angeles, CA 90025–1175.

Private Pilot. Fancy Publications, Box 6050, Mission Viejo, CA 92690.

Trade-a-Plane. 410 W. Fourth Street, Crossville, TN 38555.

Ultralight Flying. Glider Rider, Box 6009, Chattanooga, TN 37401.

ASSOCIATIONS

Aircraft Owners and Pilots Association. 421 Aviation Way, Frederick, MD 21701. Sponsors AOPA Air Safety Foundation. Publications: *AOPA Pilot,* and *Aviation U.S.A.*

Antique Airplane Association. Rte. 2, Box 172, Ottumwa, IA 52501. Persons restoring and flying pre World War II aircraft. Publications: *Antique Airplane Digest* and *Antique Airplane News.*

Civil Air Patrol. Bldg. 714, Maxwell AFB, AL 36112–5572. Civilian volunteer auxiliary of the U.S. Air Force. Activities include flying four out of every five hours on search and rescue missions directed by the Air Force Rescue Coordination Center, and operation of a network of 32,000 emergency radio stations. Extensive training courses and opportunities for experience are provided for cadets. Publications: *Membership Directory,* and *Newsletter.*

Confederate Air Force. PO Box 62000, Midland, TX 79711. Persons preserving, in flying condition, World War II aircraft. The organization has a fleet of 143 aircraft which are flown at numerous events.

Experimental Aircraft Association. EAA Aviation Center, PO Box 3086, Oshkosh, WI 54903–3086. Sport and recreational flying. Activities include research programs, educational courses, maintenance of 30,000 volume library, and large museum of private aircraft. Promotes building of aircraft in high school industrial arts classes, sponsors competitions, and bestows awards. Divisions include EAA Antique/Classic, International Aerobatic Club, and Warbirds of America. Publications: *EAA Experimenter, Sport Aerobatics, Sport Aviation, Vintage Airplane, Warbirds,* and related material.

National Aeronautic Association of the U.S.A. 1815 N. Fort Myer Drive, Suite 700, Arlington, VA 22209–1805. Supervises sporting aviation competitions and official world records. Divisions include: Experimental Aircraft Association, Helicopter Club of America, Soaring Society of America, U.S. Hang Gliding Association, U.S. Parachute Association, and U.S. Ultralight Association. Affiliated with the International Aeronautical Federation. Publications: *For the Record: NAA Newsletter,* and *World and USA National and Aviation-Space Records.*

Negro Airmen International. PO Box 1340, Tuskegee, AL 36087. Individuals holding at least a student pilot's license who are active in aviation. Seeks greater participation by blacks in aviation. Maintains Summer Flight Academy for teenagers. Sponsors competitions and bestows awards. Publications: Newsletter and related materials.

Ninety-Nines, International Women Pilots. Will Rogers Airport, PO Box 59965, Oklahoma City, OK 73159. Women pilots united to foster a better understanding of aviation. Multiple programs include consultation, competition, and education. Bestows awards and grants scholarships. Publications: *Ninety-Nine News, Membership Directory,* and related material.

Soaring Society of America. PO Box E, Hobbs, NM 88241–7504. Promotes soaring and gliding. Sanctions contests and bestows awards. Divisions include the National Soaring Museum, Sailplane Homebuilders Association, and Vintage Sailplane Association. Publications: *Soaring, Technical Soaring,* and related material.

U.S. Hang Gliding Association. 559 E. Pikes Peak, Suite 101, PO Box 8300, Colorado Springs, CO 80933. Nonpowered ultralight flight. Sponsors competitions and bestows awards. Conducts educational programs. Publications: *Hang Gliding,* and *Hang Gliding Organization Directory.*

U.S. Ultralight Association. PO Box 557, Mt. Airy, MD 21771. Promotes ultralight aviation. Conducts educational programs, sponsors competitions, and bestows awards. Publications: *Ultralight Flying!,* and related material.

World War I Aeroplanes. 15 Crescent Road, Poughkeepsie, NY 12601. Individuals and institutions in ten countries. Provides documentation, research, and information to restorers, modelers, and historians. Publications: *Skyways* (1920–1940), and *WW I Aero (1900–1919).*

Baseball

A BASEBALL PLAYER ATTEMPTS to complete a run around a prescribed path after hitting a ball with a wooden bat. An opposing team attempts to impede that progress, within the rules of the game.

How the Game is Played

Baseball is played by two teams, each having nine members. The layout of the playing field is shown in Figure 1.

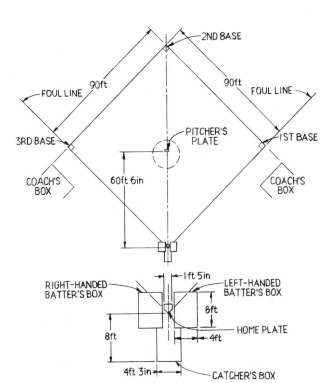

Figure 1

Playing field layout. The area around home plate is shown enlarged in the lower diagram.

Players are positioned according to Figure 2.

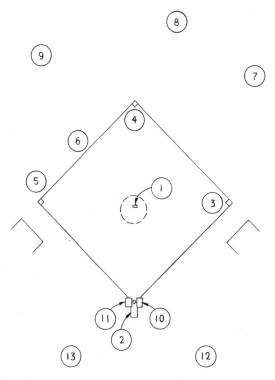

Figure 2

Player positions. The fielding team will move from the positions shown to better defend against the batting or running skills of individual batters.

The Battery	**Outfielders**
1. Pitcher	7. Right Fielder
2. Catcher	8. Center Fielder
Infielders	9. Left Fielder
3. First Baseman	**Batter's Positions**
4. Second Baseman	10. or 11. Batter
5. Third Baseman	12. or 13. Next Batter
6. Shortstop	

Play begins as the pitcher attempts to throw the ball past the batter to the catcher. (Figure 3) The batter tries to hit the ball in such a way as to permit a run to first base or beyond before the ball is recovered by a member of the fielding team. If the fielding team touches the base before the batter (now the runner) arrives, or touches the runner with the ball, the runner is retired from play and said to be out.

Each batter is allowed a number of attempts to hit the ball with a bat. Three misses and the batter is out. A miss is called a strike. The pitcher is required to throw the ball past the batter within an imaginary strike zone, providing the batter with a reasonable chance to hit the ball. The strike zone is the area over home plate. The top of the zone is halfway between the batter's shoulder and belt line. The bottom of the zone is the top of the batter's knees. An official called an umpire stands behind the catcher and rules whether the ball passes through the strike zone. If the baseball passes outside the zone, the umpire calls the pitch a "ball." If the pitcher misses the strike zone four times while pitching to a single batter, the batter is allowed to go to first base.

Lines extending from home plate, through first and third bases and beyond, are called foul lines. When a batter hits a ball along the ground it must travel between these lines. A ground ball must not cross the foul lines unless it passes first or third bases after it hits the ground. If the ball is hit into the air it must travel between the foul lines past foul line markers at the edge of the playing field. If these conditions are not met, it is declared a foul ball and the batter is penalized one strike.

Once on any base, the runner can go to the next base if the next batter hits the ball successfully. The runner can also attempt to steal the next base. This is usually done while the pitched ball is on its way to the batter at home plate. When a runner crosses home plate a run is scored and one point is awarded to the runner's team. If a batter hits the ball well enough to run the 360 feet around the bases and back to home, a home run is scored.

When a batting team has three outs they take to the field and the opposing team's pitcher starts the process again. An inning has been completed when both teams have had their turn in the above manner. Nine innings comprise a game unless the score is tied. In this case additional innings are played until the tie is broken.

History

Baseball has been played for years on sandlots throughout the country with a minimum of rules. In the eighteenth century it might have been called, "one old cat" when only a pitcher, catcher, and batter got together, or "stick ball" in city streets where a parked car might be first base. Young people would, "choose up sides" and have fun. Baseball is similar in some respects to games once played in both the United States and England.

Legend has it that a military preparatory school instructor named Abner Doubleday laid out the first true baseball field in 1839 at Cooperstown, New York. That city became the location of the National Baseball Hall of Fame and Museum in 1939. The rules for present-day baseball have remained relatively unchanged since they were formalized in 1845.

Equipment

The game is played with a ball weighing between 5 and 5¼ ounces, having a circumference of 9 to 9¼ inches. It has a cork and rubber core wound with yarn. The yarn is covered with white horsehide or cowhide.

The bat is a smooth round piece of wood with a maximum length of three feet and six inches. It has a maximum diameter of 2¾ inches at any point along its length.

All team members wear a uniform of the same design and color. It must have a distinctive number to identify the player.

Figure 3
Pitcher's stance during windup before the throw to home plate.

The catcher and home plate umpire wear protective equipment such as chest protectors, face masks, and helmet. The catcher also wears shin guards. The batter wears a batter's helmet. The catcher and each member of the fielding team wear a leather glove.

Strategy

How can such a simple game capture the imagination of millions of players and fans? There are many factors influencing the course of the game that are not readily apparent. In professional baseball, scouts and statisticians have learned much about the opponent's abilities and style well before the game.

When the pitched ball passes home plate at ninety miles per hour, the batter has 1½ seconds to decide whether it is in the strike zone and where it will pass. Coaches have told the batter what the pitcher likes to throw—fast, slow, curved ball, etc. The catcher has signalled the pitcher what kind of pitch to throw based on scouting reports about what this batter's strong and weak points are. A veritable battle of wits and athletic ability takes place.

Game Variations and Related Activity

Not all baseball is played according to the strict regulations imposed on the professionals. Rules are modified to suit conditions and the capabilities of the competitors.

Amateur Baseball

Many amateur baseball organizations operate in the United States catering to ages five through senior citizen level.

There are differences between professional rules and high school or youth league rules. See the bibliography for contacts to obtain information for your league.

Youth league managers and coaches are subjected to many outside influences such as parental pressure to win or to play their child. The manager must remember that the purpose of having a team is to teach fundamental baseball skills. It involves art and science. As Lawrence (Yogi) Berra once said, "90 percent of baseball is 50 percent mental."

Children can be introduced to baseball before they can throw a ball from the pitcher's mound to home plate. The solution is Teeball. In this game the ball is placed upon a suitable stand about three feet high and is batted out to the field. The pitcher is merely another fielder. Games last only about four innings. Since all players are allowed to bat each inning, the game may last an hour and a half.

Managers and coaches must keep their instruction simple and make the game fun. Their actions and attitudes set an example that has a strong impact on the lives of their young team members.

As a child matures there are many options available to develop ball-playing skills. Organizations such as Little League and Babe Ruth League admit members at age six.

All of this youthful activity produces trained candidates for professional baseball teams. A select few will be scouted by minor league teams and may eventually find a career in the major leagues.

Softball

Softball was first played as an indoor version of baseball in Chicago in 1887. It wasn't until 1933 that the Amateur Softball Association of America was formed to standardize the rules. The game has grown to be the largest team sport in the United States with thirty million adults and children playing each year. It is played in over fifty countries.

Softball is played in two ways; fast pitch (FP) and slow pitch (SP). The rules for softball differ from those of baseball as follows:

Bases are sixty feet apart (FP), and sixty-five feet apart (SP). They are fifty-five feet apart (SP) when the larger sixteen inch circumference ball is used. Distances vary for youth divisions to as low as fifty feet.

Pitching distance is forty feet for women, forty-six feet for men (FP); forty-six feet for men and women (SP) and thirty-eight feet for men and women (SP) using the sixteen-inch ball.

The ball is larger and heavier: twelve-inch circumference used for (FP). Either twelve-inch or sixteen-inch circumference may be used for (SP), and eleven-inch circumference is used for certain girl's and women's (SP) competitions.

The bat is shorter and lighter: two feet, ten inches long maximum.

Games consist of seven innings.

The ball is pitched underhand. It is released the first time past the hip (SP) or the pitcher is permitted one revolution of the arm in "windmill" fashion (FP).

Softball pitching has evolved to the point that the speed of a fast pitched ball is close to that achieved in baseball.

Memorabilia and Fantasy

Baseball fans are avid baseball card and memorabilia collectors. Autographs of baseball greats are eagerly sought. A large network of manufacturers, dealers, and periodicals provide services to these fans. Conventions, trade shows, and auctions are found throughout the country.

A growing number of fans engage in an armchair sort of baseball competition called fantasy baseball or rotisserie baseball. The game pits knowledgeable sports enthusiasts against one another using professional player's performance as a determining factor. With as many as two million people involved, this activity has emerged as a major pastime. See the section in this text entitled "Games, Gambling" for more information.

Bibliography

REFERENCE BOOKS

Athletic Institute. *Softball: A Complete Guide for Coaches and Players.* North Palm Beach, FL: Athletic Institute, 1984. Illustrates proper techniques and skills.

——. *Youth League Baseball Coaching and Playing.* North Palm Beach, FL: Athletic Institute, 1984. Outlines techniques, provides guidance.

Daney, Mike. *Coaching Kids Teeball.* Newhall, CA: American Youth Sports, 1985. Written with insight and humor.

Fiffer, Steve. *How to Watch Baseball.* New York: Facts on File, 1989. Reveals the intricacies of baseball.

Lau, Charley, with Alfred Glossbrenner. *The Winning Hitter: How to Play Championship Baseball.* New York: Morrow, 1984. Hitting advice from an expert coach.

McCrory, G. Jacobs. *Softball Rules in Pictures.* New York: Putnam, 1987. Includes Amateur Softball Association Rules.

McFarland, Joe S. *Coaching Pitchers.* Champaign, IL: Leisure Press, 1989. Physical development and strategy.

McIntosh, Ned. *Little League Drills and Strategies.* Chicago: Contemporary Books, 1987. Source of practice drills for all positions.

——. *Managing Little League Baseball.* Chicago: Contemporary Books, 1985. Guidance from an experienced coach.

Meyer, Gladys C. *Softball for Girls and Women.* New York: Scribners, 1982. Drills, training, conditioning.

Official Little League Baseball Rules in Pictures. New York: Putnam, 1988. Includes Little League rules.

Oliva, Tony. *Youth League Hitting Like a Champ.* Palm Beach, FL: Athletic Institute, 1991. Total batting coverage.

PERIODICALS

Baseball America. Baseball America, Box 2089, Durham, NC 27702.

Baseball Cards. Krause Publications, 700 E. State Street, Iola, WI 54990.

Baseball Digest. Century Publishers, 990 Grove Street, Evanston, IL 60201–4370.

Baseball Guide. Kwik-Fax Books, Box 14613, Surfside Beach, SC 29587.

Baseball Hobby News. 4540 Kearny Villa Road, Suite 215, San Diego, CA 92123–1573.

ASSOCIATIONS

Amateur Softball Association of America. 2801 NE 50th Street, Oklahoma City, OK 73111. Governing body of softball in the United States. Regulates 230,000 teams. Maintains Amateur Softball Hall of Fame and Museum. Publications: *Rules,* newspaper.

American Legion Baseball. PO Box 1055, Indianapolis, IN 46206. Teams of teenagers playing baseball financed by individuals, service clubs and commercial firms. Publication: *Baseball Handbook.*

Babe Ruth Baseball/Softball. PO Box 5000, 1770 Brunswick Avenue, Trenton, NJ 08638. Youths aged six through eighteen playing baseball and softball. Conducts World Series annually. Publications: Newsletters, rule manuals.

Cinderella Softball Leagues. PO Box 1411, Corning, NY 14830. Female softball players aged eighteen-years-old and younger. Publications: Newsletter and rulebook.

George Khoury Association of Baseball Leagues. 5400 Meramec Bottom Road, St. Louis, MO 63128. Boys and girls aged seven and older playing baseball and softball in 60,000 leagues organized by local fraternal, church, service or community organizations or individuals. Conducts end-of-season playoffs.

International Softball Congress. c/o village of Kimberly, 515 W. Kimberly, Kimberly, WI 54136. Federation of men's amateur fast pitch softball associations with members in Canada, Mexico, and the United States. Sponsors area tournaments and maintains hall of fame.

International Softball Federation. 321 N. West End Avenue, Lancaster, PA 17603. National softball associations. Fosters Olympic recognition of softball. Publications: Newsletter, and playing rules.

Little League Baseball. PO Box 3485, Williamsport, PA 17701. Organizes baseball and softball programs in every state and thirty-eight foreign countries. Largest youth sports program in the world. Publishes handbooks and rulebooks.

National Wheelchair Softball Association. 1616 Todd Court, Hastings, MN 55033. Enforces rules, compiles statistics, and maintains hall of fame.

Pony Baseball/Softball. PO Box 225, Washington, PA 15301. Sponsors youth leagues from ages seven to eighteen. Publications: Manuals and rulebooks.

United States Baseball Federation. 2160 Greenwood Avenue, Trenton, NJ 08609. Representatives of collegiate, high school, and amateur baseball sports councils and athletic associations. Bestows awards, conducts research, and maintains hall of fame.

United States Slo-pitch Softball Association. 3935 S. Crater Road, Petersburg, VA 23805. Promotes amateur slo-pitch softball. Team categories include: men's, women's, church, industrial, coed, youth, Hispanic, armed forces, and sixteen inch. Maintains museum and hall of fame.

United States Stickball League. PO Box 363, East Rockaway, NY 11518. Organizes stickball leagues and sponsors competitions. Publications: Newsletters, league standings, and scores.

Basketball

A BASKETBALL PLAYER ATTEMPTS to throw a ball through a hoop at one end of a playing area in a prescribed manner. An opposing team attempts to prevent that scoring action within the rules of the game.

How the Game is Played

The game is played by two teams, each having five players; two Forwards, two Guards, and a Center. The layout of the playing court is shown in Figure 1.

At the beginning of the game the ball is put into play by an official called a referee. The two opposing Centers face off at center court and the referee throws the ball up vertically between them. They attempt to tap the ball to deflect it to a player on their team. This is called a jump ball. It is also used when opposing players share possession of the ball or simultaneously cause it to go out-of-bounds. Subsequent periods begin with a throw in from out-of-bounds.

The team taking possession of the ball is required to advance the ball over the division line within ten seconds or give up possession.

Points are scored when a player causes the ball, with an average diameter of about 9½ inches, to pass through the eighteen inch basket hoop. Two points are awarded if this is done during play from any position on the court. This is called a field goal or basket. In professional and some high school and college games three points are scored if the player makes the field goal from a point outside a circular three point line on the court beyond the free throw area. One point is scored if an uncontested free throw is made from the free throw line. Such free throws are allowed as a penalty for various rule infractions by the opposing team.

After a team scores a basket, an opposing team Guard takes possession of the ball behind the end line and throws the ball to a teammate to resume play. A player having the ball must pass or attempt a basket before taking two steps, or must bounce the ball on the floor, before taking a second step on the way down the court. This type of bouncing is called dribbling. The ball may also be tapped or batted with the hands, passed, bounced, or rolled in any direction.

Basketball is called a noncontact game, but there is a lot of physical interaction and inadvertent contact. If an official deems that a player has made contact with an opponent so as to put the opponent at a distinct disadvantage, a foul will be declared. The player who has been fouled is permitted to attempt a basket from the free throw line.

Game length varies. High school games consist of four eight-minute quarters. College games have two twenty-minute halves, and the professionals use four twelve-minute quarters.

History

The history of basketball is colorful and well documented. Dr. Luther Halsey Gulick Jr. asked Dr. James Naismith to invent a game to occupy students at the YMCA school in Springfield, Massachusetts. A game was needed to occupy students between the football and baseball seasons. In December of 1891, working against a fourteen-day deadline, Dr. Naismith needed to come up with a game that could be played indoors without damage to the school gymnasium. He wanted a new game that would combine the basic elements of existing games, but without bruising contact. A game in which a soccer ball was passed from one player to another resulted. Naismith decided to place a goal on the running track that happened to be ten feet above the gym floor. He asked the janitor for two eighteen inch square boxes for the goals, but only a pair of peach baskets could be found. So Naismith nailed up the baskets and went back to his office on the fourteenth day and wrote the original thirteen rules of the game in less than an hour.

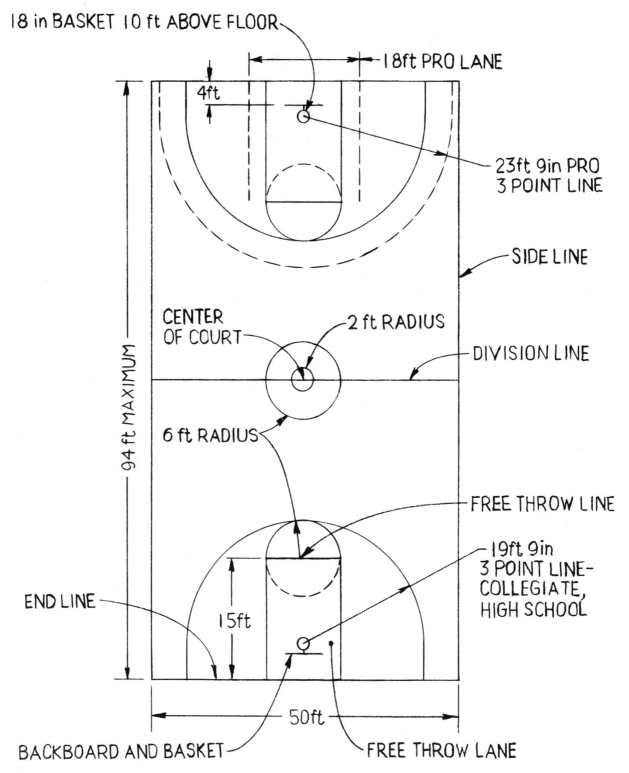

18 in BASKET 10 ft ABOVE FLOOR

18ft PRO LANE

4ft

23ft 9in PRO
3 POINT LINE

SIDE LINE

CENTER
OF COURT

2 ft RADIUS

DIVISION LINE

6 ft RADIUS

FREE THROW LINE

94 ft MAXIMUM

19ft 9in
3 POINT LINE-
COLLEGIATE,
HIGH SCHOOL

END LINE

15ft

50ft

BACKBOARD AND BASKET

FREE THROW LANE

Figure 1

Layout of a Basketball Court.

Equipment

The basketball has a thirty-inch circumference and weighs twenty to twenty-two ounces. The uniform consists of shorts, a sleeveless shirt and rubber soled athletic shoes. The shirt has identifying numbers on front and back.

Strategy

Teams may emphasize speed or ball control under certain conditions. A team may elect to move the ball quickly down the court before the opposition can arrive to set up an adequate defense of their basket. When ball control is used, the ball is moved more deliberately with offensive players positioning themselves to screen defensive players from moving into desired defensive positions. During the course of play, defending players may guard or defend against a specific opponent (man-to-man) or may be assigned a specific area to guard (zone defense). Intricate plays are designed and practiced to enable them to be executed quickly in this fast-paced sport.

Amateur Basketball

High schools and colleges field most of the amateur basketball teams. Faced with small athletic budgets, many of the 19,000 high schools find that basketball is a low-cost and popular sport.

High school courts are limited to eighty-four feet in length. If the court must be less than seventy-four feet long, it is provided with two division lines, each forty feet from the farther end line.

Basketball was first played in Olympic competition in 1936 at Berlin with twenty-one nations participating. Dr. Naismith was present to toss up the first ball. Olympic exposure has created international interest in the game, which is now played in more than 120 nations.

People of all ages can be found practicing and playing informal games of basketball on school grounds, backyards or driveways; anywhere a backboard and basket can be installed.

Netball

Netball is a game similar to basketball, usually played by women. It is played on a court 50-by-100 feet. The 100 foot length is divided into three equal zones. Baskets are provided ten feet above the end lines. There are seven players on each team. The ball is moved by passing, which is limited to a distance of 66⅔ feet (from one zone to the next). Players are restricted to certain areas of the court. A game consists of four quarters of fifteen minutes each.

Bibliography

REFERENCE BOOKS

Athletic Institute. *Youth League Basketball: Coaching and Playing.* Rev. ed. North Palm Beach, FL: Athletic Institute, 1990. Game principles and techniques for young players.

Beard, Butch, with Glenn Popowitz and David Samson. *Butch Beard's Basic Basketball: The Complete Player.* New York: Kesend, 1985. Players at all levels, drills, insights, and techniques.

Cousy, Bob, and Frank G. Power, Jr. *Basketball Concepts and Techniques.* 2nd ed. Boston: Allyn & Bacon, 1983, Offense and defense, techniques, and plays.

Gandolfi, Giorgio, and Gerald Secor Couzens. *Hoops: The Official National Basketball Players Association Guide to Playing Basketball.* New York: McGraw-Hill, 1986. NBA's top players' drills, moves, and insights.

Hill, Bob, and Randall Baron. *The Amazing Basketball Book: The First 100 Years.* Louisville, KY: Devyn, 1991. Insightful history of the game told with humor.

Krause, Jerry, ed. *Coaching Basketball: The Official Centennial Volume of The National Association of Basketball Coaches.* Grand Rapids, MI: Masters, 1990. Definitive reference book for coaches at all levels.

Marcus, Howard. *Basketball Basics: Drills, Techniques and Strategies for Coaches.* Chicago: Contemporary Books, 1991. Coaching youth basketball. Emphasis on drills and safety.

Mikes, Jay. *Basketball Fundamentals: A Complete Mental Training Guide.* Champaign, IL: Leisure, 1987. Mental training and preparation.

Pruitt, Jim. *Coaching Beginning Basketball.* Chicago: Contemporary Books, 1980. Game techniques and strategies for junior- and senior-high school coaches.

———. *Play Better Basketball: An Illustrated Guide to Winning Techniques and Strategies.* Chicago: Contemporary Books, 1982. For youthful players.

Smith, Dean. *Basketball: Multiple Offense and Defense.* Englewood Cliffs, NJ: Prentice Hall, 1981. An analytical overview of each element of the game. Alternative actions are explained. Practice planning is discussed.

Wissel, Hal. *Becoming a Basketball Player: Individual Drills.* Springfield, MA: Basketball World, 1990. Drills and techniques.

Young, Faye, and Wayne Coffey. *Winning Basketball for Girls.* New York: Facts on File, 1984. Getting in shape, drills, and strategy.

PERIODICALS

Basketball Case Book. National Federation of State High School Associations, 11724 NW Plaza Circle, Box 20626, Kansas City, MO 64195–0626.

Basketball Digest. Century Publishers, 990 Grove Street, Evanston, IL 60201–4370.

Basketball Guide. Kwik-Fax Books, Box 14613, Surfside Beach, SC 29587.

ASSOCIATIONS

Eastern College Basketball Association. 1311 Craigville Road, PO Box 3, Centerville, MA 02632. Trains and assigns officials for college basketball games in the eastern U.S.

Naismith Memorial Basketball Hall of Fame. 1150 W. Columbus Avenue, PO Box 179, Springfield, MA 01101. Museum and library.

National Amateur Basketball Association. 6832 W. North Avenue, Suite 4A, Chicago, IL 60635. Promotes amateur basketball and provides high-level competition for former college athletes.

U.S.A. Basketball. 1750 E. Boulder Street, Colorado Springs, CO 80909. Administers the international basketball program for the United States as the U.S. member of the International Basketball Federation. Serves as the national governing body for the U.S. basketball program for the Pan American games and Olympic competition. Publication: *Handbook.*

Bicycles

EACH YEAR ABOUT TEN MILLION bicycles are sold in the United States. About three-fourths of them will be mass-produced units bought in department stores and discount outlets. Many bike styles have been developed to match individual needs, making selection a complex process. Bicycle shops with experienced personnel are equipped to help you pick the right bike that will meet your needs, goals, and fitness level. They will consider the environment in which you intend to ride, and can furnish a bike that is sized to fit you properly.

Of approximately eighty million bikes in use, almost half are ridden by adults. Bicycles offer efficient low-impact exercise for all ages. It has been found that cycling is several times more efficient than walking. When walking, we use energy to raise our bodies with every step; this motion is not required when cycling. If we use our one-tenth horsepower engine—our bodies—efficiently, we can travel with greater ease. More about that later when we discuss gearing.

History

In 1817 German Baron Karl Von Drais introduced a one-hundred pound wooden walking machine. It consisted of two wheels connected by a frame. The front wheel was steered by a sort of tiller. The rider sat on a seat and straddled the frame. There were no pedals; the machine was propelled by pushing with the legs. By 1861, propulsion was refined by adding foot-driven cranks to the front wheel.

Before the advent of the geared bicycle, higher speeds were attained in the late 1860s by making the front wheel larger, since the pedals were still attached to the front wheel. These "penny farthing" or "ordinary" bicycles came to the United States from England about 1876. The front wheels were as large as sixty inches in diameter. Bike club members may sometimes be seen riding these historical vehicles during special events at the Henry Ford Museum, the Mystic Seaport, and at the Indianapolis Motor Speedway. It takes a certain amount of agility and coordination to get started on these bikes. Sudden stops cause the rider to be toppled over the handlebars.

When chains were first used to drive the rear wheel, the oversized front wheel was no longer required, reducing the dangers brought about by stopping. Accordingly, the new designs were called safety bicycles. The chain-drive design caught on about 1885.

The market for bikes went wild after Dr. J. B. Dunlop developed the pneumatic tire in 1888 and bike tire manufacturers began to use the invention. In 1897, two million bikes were sold in the United States by the likes of Henry Ford and the Wright brothers, impacting sales in other businesses and an entire way of life. It wasn't until the next bike craze in 1972 that more units were sold in proportion to the size of the population. At that time more than 13 million were sold in the U.S.

Anatomy of a Bike

Referring to Figure 1 on page 40 we see that the structure of the frame is rather simple.

1. Seat Stays	8. Down Tube
2. Saddle	9. Front Derailleur
3. Top Tube	10. Chainwheels
4. Handlebar Bend	11. Freewheel with Sprockets
5. Head Tube	12. Rear Derailleur
6. Seat Tube	13. Chain Stays
7. Gear Shift Levers	14. Pedal

The head tube houses bearings that permit the steering column to turn freely. The seat tube supports the saddle. The seat stays and chain stays hold the rear wheel in position, and the top tube and down tube bridge the two wheels. Handlebars are made in a variety of shapes to accommodate different riding positions. Some extend

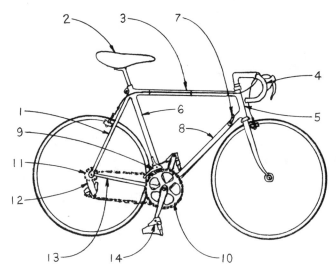

Figure 1
Parts of a Bicycle.

away from the center horizontally for a short distance then curve forward, down and then to the rear. This type permits the rider to sit erect and place the hands on the short horizontal portion. The design also permits adoption of a fully crouched position where the hands are placed on the lower rear-pointing sections. This position is favored by racers or tourers to reduce the wind resistance or drag caused by their upright bodies. In some cases supplementary tubes are attached to the handlebars permitting riders to vary their positions to reduce fatigue. The currently popular mountain bikes are often fitted with handlebars that simply extend straight out horizontally from the center.

Some bikes are fitted with shock absorbing suspensions. These are especially useful for off-road riding for better handling and comfort. Most are applied only to the front wheel, but efforts are underway to improve shock-absorption for rear wheels as well. Some rear suspensions are prone to impart a bobbing motion as the rider alternately presses down on the pedals. There is a trend to adapt motorcycle technology to bicycle design.

The Mechanics of a Bicycle

Most of the mechanical complexity of a bicycle centers around the drive train. A linked chain is used between the front sprocket or chainwheel and the rear sprocket or freewheel. If a large sprocket is used in the front and a small one at the rear, the rear wheel will cover more ground (you will travel farther) for each revolution of the pedals, but it will require more effort on the part of the rider while pedaling. Conversely, if the front sprocket is small and the rear is larger, the rear wheel will cover less ground for each revolution of the pedals, but will require less effort to climb a hill. The best of both worlds is achieved if the sprocket sizes that are employed can be changed as riding conditions change. A device called a derailleur permits the chain

to be shifted from one sized sprocket to another while the bike is in motion. The rider presses a lever to actuate a derailleur on the front or rear sprocket to effect a gear change. Derailleur activation has been made easier with improved designs that automatically shift up or down one sprocket size at the press of a trigger. At one time most bikes that featured gear changes were limited to ten-speeds. Although this limitation was soon overcome, and as many as twenty or more forward speeds were possible, the term ten-speed is often used when referring to a geared bike.

Bicycle Materials

The materials used in bicycle construction have evolved to take advantage of the latest advances in lightweight metals and composite materials. A lightweight bike requires less effort to pedal. Lighter materials are generally more expensive, and this is reflected in the price of the bike. Most low-cost bike frames are made of alloy steels. Lighter units are fabricated from aluminum alloys. Still lighter components are made from titanium. The ultimate light-weight frames are made using carbon fiber and epoxy. Riders who are trying to save every possible ounce will substitute titanium nuts and bolts for the factory supplied steel parts. Aluminum handlebars replace the originals. Special lightweight tires, saddles, and wheels are also considered.

Bicycle Assemblage

Cyclists who want the ultimate in bicycle performance can assemble their own to meet their needs, subject to budget limitations of course. Components, and sets of components, are readily available from many suppliers. After selecting a frame set, the mechanical components are usually obtained as a matched set, or gruppo (from the Italian for group). The primary manufacturers of these specialized gruppos are the Italian firm Compagnolo, and the Japanese firms Shimano and Sun Tour. When components are purchased separately one or more "middle-men" are involved, driving up the cost significantly. Some cyclists upgrade portions of their bikes this way when new technologies make certain components obsolete.

Selecting the Right Bike

Your first consideration must be to obtain a bike that fits properly. If the design features a top tube that is positioned high, as with most touring bikes, be sure the frame allows about one or two inches between the top tube and your crotch when you straddle it with your feet on the ground. The saddle to handlebar distance should permit a comfortable riding position. The saddle height adjustment range should allow the leg to stretch comfortably without completely stretching the knee. When the pedal is at its highest point the knee should not be bent excessively.

Nearly two million people use their bikes to commute to work. A typical city bike has a light frame, straight handlebars, adequate gear change capability for hills, and wide (fat) tires. The straight handlebars permit an upright riding position for better visibility in traffic.

A touring or road bike is used for both short casual rides and long distance touring. It usually has a light frame, downward curved handlebars, gear systems usually featuring fifteen or eighteen speeds, and narrow tires. Accessories often include lights and a sturdy rear rack for attaching travel bags.

Racing bikes have very light frames, and downward curved handlebars set low on a low height head tube to permit a low crouched riding position. Very light thin tires are used. Some performance race bikes provide gear change capability; others use a direct drive without gear change for use in track racing. True racing bikes are often custom-built for specific types of racing. They may feature solid wheels or some form of spoke cover.

Mountain bikes are intended for rough usage on any terrain. The frame tubes are of a larger diameter, making the overall weight from three to five pounds heavier than a touring bike. They employ fat tires, straight handlebars, and a multiple gear change capability adapted to hill climbing. Mountain or all terrain bicycles (ATBs) have been refined to the point that they are the closest thing to an all-purpose bicycle. They represent more than 70 percent of all adult bicycles sold.

Some cycling enthusiasts collect and restore old bicycles. Those who enjoy working with their hands and tinkering with mechanical things are drawn to this hobby as others are attracted to antique cars or motorcycles.

Safety

It is not unusual to attain speeds of thirty miles per hour while riding. A sudden stop at that speed can result in severe injury. Head injuries top the list of serious injuries sustained while cycling. Choose and use a good helmet designed for bike riding.

When riding for sustained periods a cyclist will sweat as much as a quart of water in an hour. It is no accident that one of the most common accessories on bikes is a special holder for a water bottle. If the liquids lost are not replaced on a regular basis while riding, dehydration and early fatigue will result.

Bibliography

REFERENCE BOOKS

Berto, Frank J. *Bicycling Magazine's Complete Guide to Upgrading Your Bike.* Emmaus, PA: Rodale, 1988. Detailed discussion of bicycle components and advice on parts selection to meet your personal requirements.

Coello, Dennis. *Touring on Two Wheels: the Bicycle Traveler's Handbook.* New York: Nick Lyons Books, 1988. Selecting a bike and choosing proper equipment. Planning, riding, and lodging, as they relate to touring.

Doughty, Tom. *The Complete Book of Long Distance Competitive Cycling.* New York: Simon & Schuster, 1983. Covers both touring and racing. Discusses riding techniques, tactics, maintenance, and clothing.

Leccese, Michael, and Arlene Plevin. *The Bicyclist's Sourcebook: The Ultimate Directory of Cycling Information.* Rockville, MD: Woodbine House, 1991. Comprehensive bibliographic information on all aspects of cycling.

LeMond, Greg, and Kent Gordis. *Greg LeMond's Complete Book of Bicycling.* New York: Perigee Books, 1987. What you need to know about buying, riding, and maintaining a bike, whether you are a recreational rider or a serious racer.

Sloane, Eugene A. *The Complete Book of Bicycling.* 4th ed. New York: Simon & Schuster, 1988. A comprehensive overview of bicycling that has stood the test of time.

Van Der Plas, Robert. *Bicycle Technology: Understanding, Selecting and Maintaining the Modern Bicycle and Its Components.* Rev. ed. San Francisco: Bicycle Books, 1991. Emphasis on description of components and their required maintenance.

————. *The Bicycling Touring Manual.* San Francisco: Bicycle Books, 1987. Description of applicable bicycle styles, tour planning, and camping gear. Includes information on handling and safety.

————. *Mountain Bike Magic: The Complete Full-color Book on Mountain Biking.* Mill Valley, CA: Bicycle Books, 1991. Comprehensive coverage of the mountain bike. How to select a bike and equipment. Includes riding techniques and maintenance.

Winning, Robert. *Bicycling Across America: A Guide to the Best Route, Plus a How-to Section for Any Bike Tour.* Berkeley, CA: Wilderness, 1988. Planning for a trip across the United States. Detailed route description is given and related to strip maps.

PERIODICALS

B M X Plus. Hi-Torque Publications, 10600 Sepulveda Boulevard, Mission Hills, CA 91345.

Bicycle Forum. Bikecentennial, 150 E. Pine Street, Missoula, MT 59802–4515.

Bicycle Guide. Winning International, 744 Roble Street, Suite 190, Allentown, PA 18103.

Bicycle U.S.A. League of American Wheelmen, 190 W. Ostend Street, Suite 120, Baltimore, MD 21230.

Bicycling. Rodale Press, 33 E. Minor Street, Emmaus, PA 18098.

California Bicyclist. 490 2nd Street, Suite 304, San Francisco, CA 94107.

Cycling U.S.A. U.S. Cycling Federation, 1750 E. Boulder Street, Colorado Springs, CO 80909.

Dirt Bike. Hi-Torque Publications, 10600 Sepulveda Boulevard, Mission Hills, CA 91345.

Go: The Rider's Manual. Wizard Publications, Box 2806573, Torrance, CA 90503–2806.

Mountain Bike. Rodale Press, 33 E. Minor Street, Emmaus, PA 18098.

Mountain Bike Action. Hi-Torque Publications, 10600 Sepulveda Boulevard, Mission Hills, CA 91345.

Southwest Cycling. Southwest Cycling, 422 S. Pasadena Avenue, Pasadena, CA 91105.

Velonews: The Journal of Competitive Cycling. Inside Communications, 1830 N. 55th Street, Boulder, CO 80301–2700.

Winning Bicycling Illustrated. Winning International, 744 Roble Road, Suite 190, Allentown, PA 18103–9100.

ASSOCIATIONS

American Bicycle Association. PO Box 718, Chandler, AZ 85244. Off-road bicycle enthusiasts. Sanctions races.

Bicycle Federation of America. 1818 R Street NW, Washington, DC 20009. Designs and manages national bicycle promotion campaigns. Maintains library. Publications: *Pro Bike News,* directory, and related material.

Bikecentennial: The Bicycle Travel Association. PO Box 8308, Missoula, MT 59807. Research, maintenance, and mapping of bicycle touring routes. Publications: *Bicycle Forum, BikeReport, Cyclists' Yellow Pages,* and related material.

International Bicycle Touring Society. PO Box 6979, San Diego, CA 92166–0979. Arranges bicycle tours in U.S. and abroad. Publications: Newsletter, tour listings, and related material.

International Randonneurs. Old Engine House No. 2, 727 N. Salina Street, Syracuse, NY 13208. Amateur long-distance bicyclists. Conducts related events. Publications: Newsletter, and journal.

League of American Wheelmen. 190 W. Ostend Street, Suite 120, Baltimore, MD 21230. Bicyclists and bicycle clubs. Sponsors events, bestows awards, and maintains library. Publications: *Bicycle USA,* and *Bicycle USA Almanac.*

National Bicycle League. PO Box 729, Dublin, OH 43017. BMX racers. Establishes rules and regulations, sponsors competitions, and bestows awards. Publications: *Bicycles Today,* and rule book.

Ultra Marathon Cycling Association. 2761 N. Marengo, Altadena, CA 91001. Sanctions ultra marathon (over 200 miles per day) cycling, such as Race Across America. Bestows awards. Publications: Directory, manual, and newsletter.

United States Cycling Federation. c/o USOC, 1750 E. Boulder Street, Colorado Springs, CO 80909. Governing body of amateur cycling in the U.S. Supervises and controls all amateur competitions, sponsors national championships, and bestows awards. Publications: *Cycling USA,* newsletter, rule book, and related material.

Wheelmen. c/o George Garrellson, 216 E. Sedgewick Street, Philadelphia, PA 19117. Those interested in early cycling, and early cycling history. Maintains library and museum. Sponsors events. Publications: *The Wheelmen* magazine, and related materials.

Billiards

THERE ARE TWO BASIC TYPES of billiards. Pocket billiards, or pool, is played on a table having six pockets. The other, simply called billiards, is played on a table without pockets. There are about twenty-three million pool players in the United States.

Pool

In pool, the player uses the tip of a stick called a cue to drive a cueball into other balls (object balls), causing them to drop into holes (pockets) in the surface of a pool table. The competitor earns points for balls dropped according to rules of a specific pool game.

A white cue ball and fifteen colored number balls are used in the game of pool. Balls from one to eight have solid colors, and from nine to fifteen are striped.

Basic pool is played by individuals or two teams. One individual or team tries to pocket eight balls before their opponents do. On all strokes following the opening shot, the individual must call the ball or balls intended to be pocketed. The specific pocket need not be identified.

Rules of the game of rotation require that the fifteen object balls be pocketed in numerical order. Points are scored according to the number on the ball. Since the numbers on the fifteen balls total 120, the winner is the first individual or team to score sixty-one.

In the game of straight pool, the balls need not be played in numerical sequence, but the player must identify the ball in play and the intended pocket.

Only object balls one through nine are used in the game of nine-ball. Any ball that drops counts on the first shot (the break), if the one ball is hit first. Anything that drops on subsequent shots counts if the cueball hits the lowest numbered ball first.

In the popular game of eight-ball you must either pocket all the balls lower than eight or all those higher than eight, followed by the eight ball.

The game of snooker is popular in Great Britain and the former English commonwealth. In snooker, twenty-two balls are used: a white cueball, fifteen red balls, and six numbered balls of other colors. The player must pocket a red ball before any numbered ball, and continue to alternate red and numbered balls. When numbered balls are pocketed, the player returns them to the table until all red balls are pocketed. When this has been done, the numbered balls are pocketed, in numerical order, to complete the game.

The above is only a sampling of the many variations of pocket billiards.

Billiards

Billiard players use only three balls in their game. To score a point, the player must drive his/her cueball into a certain sequence of side cushions and the two object balls. In the game of three-cushion billiards, the player scores a point when the cueball hits three or more cushions and one of the object balls, in any sequence, before it hits the other object ball.

History

The origin of billiards is unknown. Some believe that it evolved from several dissimilar games such as early shuffleboard and croquet. Paintings and the written record establish the existence of billiards during the sixteenth century. Some early forms of billiards included obstacles on the playing surface such as hoops and pegs, similar to the bumper pool tables of today.

The present form of billiards dates from the beginning of the nineteenth century. The first national billiards match in the United States was played in Detroit in 1859.

Equipment

Billiard or pool tables are twice as long as they are wide. Sizes run from 3½ feet by seven feet, to five feet by ten feet. They range from two feet six inches to two feet seven inches high. Better quality tables have a slate bed, covered by a cloth playing surface. Pool tables have six pockets; one on each corner, and one in the middle of each long side. Billiard tables have no pockets. All tables have vulcanized rubber cushions along their rails.

Tables have diamond markers (usually small disks) set into the rails 12½ inches apart on a 4½ foot by nine foot pool table, and fourteen inches apart on a five-by-ten-foot billiard table.

Pool cues are about fifty-seven inches long. They have a leather tip, with a diameter ranging from eleven to thirteen millimeters. The tip is kept slightly rounded, and sufficiently roughened to hold chalk.

Pool chalk increases friction between the cue tip and the cueball. The compressed chalk is usually in the form of a small block. Chalk the cue tip frequently during play.

Billiard and pool balls were once made of ivory. They are now made of composition plastics. Balls used for billiards are $2^{25}/_{64}$ inches in diameter. Pool balls are two and one-fourth inches in diameter. Snooker balls are smaller, measuring 2⅛ inches in diameter.

Strategy

Support the cue close to the cueball using the left hand (for a right-handed person). The left hand supports the cue, and restricts side motion as the cue moves forward. The hand forms a "bridge" for the cue. You can further restrict lateral motion by encircling the cue with a finger of the left hand, forming a "closed bridge."

Hold the cue with the right hand, keeping it as level as possible. Align it carefully so as to drive the cueball toward the intended target. Stroke the cue forward against the cueball, taking care to make contact at the center of the cueball.

When the cueball, targeted ball (object ball), and the pocket are not in line, it's necessary to target the object ball off-center. Draw an imaginary line from the object ball to the pocket and aim the cueball to strike the object ball at a point along that imaginary line.

There are times when obstacles, such as another ball, stand between the cueball and the object ball. In these situations, you can make the cueball follow a curved path toward the object ball. If you hit the cueball off-center, a side-spin (called English) is added to the normal forward roll. The farther from the center you hit the cueball, the more it spins. It is risky to strike it more than halfway from the center. It is possible to cause a cueball to jump over another ball by striking the cueball smartly below center.

Details of the application of the above principles account for a major portion of the instruction given in Byrne's books listed in the bibliography.

When planning a pool shot, consider where the cueball will come to rest after the shot. You receive a penalty if the cueball falls into a pocket. It is desirable to have the cueball lie in a good position to make the next shot in pool, or to have it stop in an awkward spot for your opponent when playing billiards. It follows that the seemingly obvious choice of an object ball is often not the best choice. Experienced players often bank the cueball off a second object ball, or one or more cushions before it drops the object ball in a pocket.

Some billiard players use the diamond markers on the table rails as aiming points when making the multiple cushion shots required in that game. They assign numbers to the markers (diamonds) on the rails and use formulas to determine where the cueball will finally travel.

Bibliography

REFERENCE BOOKS

Byrne, Robert. *Byrne's Advanced Technique in Pool and Billiards: Everything You Need to Know to Reach the Highest Level.* San Diego: Harcourt Brace Jovanovich, 1990. Complement to the standard book by Byrne. Details of making specific shots.

————. *Byrne's Standard Book of Pool and Billiards,* Rev. ed. San Diego: Harcourt Brace Jovanovich, 1987. A definitive guide to pool and billiard playing.

————. *Byrne's Treasury of Trick Shots in Pool and Billiards.* New York: Harcourt Brace Jovanovich, 1982. A book full of illustrated trick shots with instructions to complete them.

Cottingham, Clive, Jr. *The Game of Billiards: Pocket, Carom, Three Cushion.* No. Hollywood, CA: Wilshire, 1964. Fundamentals for learners, instructions for advanced players, and techniques for professionals.

Knuchell, Edward D. *How to Win at Pocket Billiards.* No. Hollywood, CA: Wilshire, 1970. Explains game basics, gives advice for playing specific game situations.

Martin, Ray, and Rosser Reeves. *The 99 Critical Shots in Pool.* New York: Times Books, 1977. Illustrates the proper form, technique, and approach to pool shots. Provides tips on buying and maintaining equipment.

Mizerak, Steve, with Joel H. Cohen. *Steve Mizerak's Pocket Billiards: Tips and Trick Shots.* Chicago: Contemporary Books, 1982. Covers equipment, techniques, practicing, and competition.

Mizerak, Steve, with Michael E. Panozzo. *Steve Mizerak's Complete Book of Pool: Everything You Need to Know to Play and Win.* Chicago: Contemporary Books, 1990. Covers game rules, techniques, drills, and equipment.

PERIODICAL

Billiards Digest. Luby Publishers, 200 S. Michigan Avenue, K, Suite 1430, Chicago, IL 60604–2404.

ASSOCIATIONS

American Poolplayers Association. 1000 Lake St. Louis Boulevard, Suite 325, Lake St. Louis, MO 63367. Sanctioning body for amateur pool leagues. Sponsors competitions and bestows awards. Publications: *American Poolplayer,* and newsletter.

Billiard Congress of America. 1700 S 1st Avenue, No. 25A, Iowa City, IA 52240. Develops rules for billiards and pocket billiards. Maintains hall of fame. Conducts annual championship and presents award. Publications: *BCA Break, Official Rules and Records Book,* and other related materials.

National Pocket Billiard Association. PO Box 340245, Milwaukee, WI 53234–0245. Sanctions league and tournament competition. Standardizes rules and procedures. Bestows awards and maintains hall of fame. Publications: *NPBA News,* reports, and rule manual.

United States Billiard Association. 757 Highland Grove Drive, Buffalo Grove, IL 60089. Promotes the sport of three cushion billiards. Sponsors competitions and bestows awards. Publications: Bulletin, and tournament notices.

Bird Watching

WE ARE SO ACCUSTOMED to wild birds in our surroundings that their presence is often overlooked. When a bird does strike our fancy, and we want to know more about it, we're on our way to becoming a bird-watcher. The pastime has been called a science, sport, excuse for travel, recreation, and certainly a challenge. Then there's the aesthetics of it; you're out enjoying the beauty of nature looking at beautiful birds. Bird-watchers seek out wild birds, identify their species, and usually catalog their presence. Serious bird-watchers keep lists of species they spot, and regularly send their lists to bird organizations. The lists help biologists monitor the decline and rise of certain species, migration and nesting patterns. Most of the ornithological information we have today is the direct result of contributions made by amateur bird-watchers and naturalists.

Estimates vary considerably regarding the number of birdwatchers. A study made for the U.S. Fish and Wildlife service found that there are about two million who watch with some regularity, use a field guide, and record their findings. Over 1,400,000 copies of one particular field guide used to identify birds were sold.

Leonardo da Vinci devoted much of his life to the study of birds. He was fascinated with their flight, and attempted to translate his observations into workable inventions applicable to human flight.

Thomas Jefferson could recognize about 100 birds. While president, a pet mockingbird sometimes followed him around the White House grounds. President Theodore Roosevelt was another dedicated bird-watcher, considered by some to be even more informed than Jefferson. Theodore's cousin, President Franklin D. Roosevelt, collected many bird specimens when he was young. Watching birds was one of his lifetime hobbies.

When merchant John James Audubon's business failed in 1819, he turned to his hobby to start a new career. He had always studied and painted America's birds for pleasure. He produced the masterpiece *Birds of America*. The format was quite large, and therefore unsuitable for field use by bird-watchers. In the 1840s a small edition was published, providing a valuable resource for bird-watchers of the time.

Other notable bird-watchers included Henry Ford and his nature-writer friend, John Burroughs.

History

Various species of birds are pictured in Egyptian hieroglyphics inscribed 3,000 or more years ago. Before Europeans discovered North America, Indians were hanging gourds in trees to attract purple martin colonies. Martins are known to reduce the insect population. Indians were careful observers of nature. They named many bird species, unaware of the pioneering work done by the Swedish botanist Carolus Linnaeus (1707–1778). For example, the Chippewas named the house wren, o-du-na-mis-sug-ud-da-we-shi meaning "making big noise for its size." By the time one bird-watcher called this bird to the attention of another, one would think the bird would have flown.

Bird Evolution and Physiology

Scientists believe that a small dinosaurlike reptile took to the trees and grew scales extending from its arms and legs allowing it to glide like a flying squirrel. The scales evolved into feathers and the arms into wings.

Remains of the earliest known birds have been found in the fossil beds of Bavaria. Scientists named the group "Archaeopteryx," which means ancient wing. It's illustrated in most encyclopedias. Although descended from reptiles, it grew feathers, but still retained teeth, a bony tail vertebrae, and claws on the wings.

Modern birds have scales on their legs some fourteen million years since Archaeopteryx flew prehistoric skies.

Their skeletons are light in weight because many of their bones are hollow. The breastbone is fused to a deep keel that serves as the attach point for the large muscles that provide the powerful downstroke of the wing. These muscles account for up to 25 percent of a bird's total body weight.

Since birds use so much energy while flying, they have a respiratory system that allows air to flow through the lungs and into several adjacent air sacs. This allows for better transfer of oxygen into the blood stream enabling the bird to maintain a higher energy level than mammals.

Bird's brains have developed reaction times twice as fast as humans. This permits them to fly at high speed through dense forests, changing course quickly to avoid colliding with tree branches. They do have one thing in common with humans—they walk on two feet.

Migration

More than 600 of the 800 plus bird species in North America migrate. They move south in the winter when their food supply runs low. They move north in the spring when food is available, and to breed. If they fly north too soon, they starve, if they fly north too late, the good territories already are occupied and their potential mates taken.

Spring and fall migrations present bird-watchers with the opportunity to see species not normally seen by local residents. Since birds habitually follow similar paths or flyways during migration, bird-watchers can visit locations on the flyways to add species to their bird lists.

Most birds migrate by night and rest during the day. This requires them to navigate by the stars or an internal magnetic compass. Experiments have revealed that both of these factors are a possibility.

Activities

Most bird-watching is associated with activities administered by organizations such as the Audubon Society and the American Birding Association. Members cooperate in taking counts of the bird population throughout the country at certain specified times. One of the oldest of these activities is the Christmas bird count. Begun in 1900 with twenty-seven birders, the count is now conducted by over forty thousand people in the United States, Central America, northern portions of South America, and the West Indies. Each volunteer counts all the birds observed, by species, within a fifteen mile diameter circle during one twenty-four hour period.

A Thanksgiving bird count is made by counting the number of birds, by species, that come into a fifteen-foot circle around a bird feeder within one hour. Bird-watchers often use bird feeders, special flower plantings, and tree and shrubbery plantings to attract birds. Cameras can be set up and prefocussed on feeder perches to facilitate close-up photography.

A breeding bird atlas is another form of count in which breeding birds are counted within a ten square mile area. This requires frequent visits to the assigned area throughout the breeding season.

Club activities include not only local tours, but tours to distant locations noted for bird species not found at local sites. Members are kept informed of hot spots, places where high levels of activity can be expected under certain conditions, such as during migratory periods. Birding hotlines are available to members and nonmembers alike. Recorded messages regarding latest unusual bird sightings and locations, club news, and other information useful to a birder can be accessed by simply dialing the telephone number. Hotline numbers can be found when traveling by consulting the phone book for the number of the local Audubon Society, the local nature center, or park personnel.

Some experienced birders enjoy bird banding. This involves trapping birds in a fine net, removing them from the net, and placing a metal band on their leg. The whole process takes only a few minutes. When the bird dies, or is caught in the future, the band is mailed to the Bird Banding Laboratory in Washington, DC. Each band carries an identifying number, which is recorded at the time of banding. This enables the laboratory to determine the migratory habits of the bird and its life span. A special license is required to band birds. Bird lovers enjoy the work, because it gives them close-up access to the birds, and they learn a lot about the various species' habits.

Bird Identification

Until about 1902 bird enthusiasts shot birds for study. The celebrated John James Audubon wrote in his journal "I call birds few when I shoot less than 100 per day." The birds were skinned and sometimes mounted in lifelike poses. This practice enabled close study of physical features and coloring. Bird paintings used to illustrate field guides reflected the observed small marking details. A new era began in the 1900s when shooting specimens and collecting birds eggs were discouraged. Few subtle marking details were visible using the low-powered binoculars available to the average amateur of the day.

Roger Tory Peterson was an active bird-watcher and painter. He became impatient with the lengthy, highly detailed descriptions found in bird guides at the time. He decided to write and illustrate his own guide concentrating on conspicuous differences in marking patterns among similar birds. His illustrations were less detailed and the specific marking patterns peculiar to a bird, and visible at a distance, were highlighted with a line drawn to the area of difference. These patterns are called field marks. Peterson's book, *A Field Guide to the Birds,* first published in 1934 sold out in a few weeks. It eventually sold three million copies, establishing Peterson as the preeminent birder of his time.

Linnaeus devised a system for defining genera and species of plants and animals. It consists of a series of divisions and subdivisions that permit their classification. Each species is given two names. The first is of generic significance, and the second more specific to designate a particular species. Names are given in Latin to achieve commonality in name assignments by scientists who speak different languages. In this system we first find birds at the Class level. They are called Aves. Next below Class comes Order. The Order listing of birds found in most bird guides and checklists roughly follows the evolutionary ladder. The ostrich is considered the most primitive of living birds, so appears first in the Order *Struthioniformes.* At the bottom of the list we find the perching or sparrowlike birds in the Order *Passeriformes.*

Bird identification has gone from the highly detailed approach of the ornithologist, to the use of field marks and song patterns, and now to what birders call the jizz of a bird. It includes the shape, size, color, field marks, behavior, family group, habitat, and song. Bird identification is a process of elimination. The process is speeded up by introducing these additional factors.

The well-prepared birder will do some preliminary study before going out in the field. Review bird guides that illustrate the birds peculiar to the region. Obtain a bird checklist. Most parks and government agencies will provide printed checklists of bird species normally found in the area. Recordings and video cassettes of bird songs are available for preliminary study and comparison to tape recordings you might make in the field.

Birders often record the bird species they have seen on specialized lists. A life list records all the species that a birder has seen to date. Of approximately 8,700 species in the world, the record stands at 7,069 at the end of 1991. Some compete to list the most species seen in North America. In 1991 that record stood at 806. Lists are made during competitions for most species seen during big days, 24 hour listing periods taken at the peak of the spring migration. Other lists may involve state, county, or local club competitions. Programs are available for most personal computers that enable birders to set up efficient checklists and record extensive notes.

Equipment

Many bird-watchers make do with only three pieces of equipment: A field guide, a pair of binoculars and a notebook. Add to that some comfortable clothing and shoes suitable for long walks in rough terrain. The clothing should be rugged enough to withstand rough usage, and of subtle coloring to blend in with your surroundings (unless you are in areas frequented by hunters).

Binoculars or other optical aides extend your range of observation without additional walking. They allow the considerate birder to maintain an adequate distance from birds' nests and reduce any disturbance of their normal activities. The best kinds of binoculars for birding are 7 × 35 or 8 × 40. The first number indicates the magnification. The second number is the diameter of the outer lens in millimeters. A pair 7 × 35 will magnify an image seven times, and have a 35mm front lens. The larger the front lens, the more light will enter the binoculars. A large front lens contributes to the weight, making the binoculars hard to hold steady during prolonged watching. Avoid binoculars in which the second number is less than five times the magnification. The lens would be too small to admit enough light in a shady forest. If more than five times the magnification, too much light will cause eye discomfort in sunlit areas. If possible, try using a friend's binoculars to see what feels best for you.

Serious birders use spotting telescopes mounted on tripods for long distance viewing. The telescope should be lightweight. The tripod is needed to hold the telescope steady. It should be sturdy and allow quick set up.

Photography plays a role in the bird-watching pastime. When using a long telephoto lens, it's necessary to steady the camera, preferably using a tripod. Since bird photographs are frequently made at a distance and against contrasting backgrounds, the chances of getting an accurate light reading on a bird can be improved by using a photographic spot meter.

When photographing rapidly moving subjects in dim light, it is common practice to open the camera shutter briefly and provide an extremely short burst of light for a strobe effect. This results in a stop-action affect on the subject. This method is especially effective for photographing birds in flight.

Experienced watchers can identify many birds without seeing them. They have become familiar with their characteristic calls. Some use tape recording equipment in the field to capture and study the voices of birds; others buy tapes with bird voices recorded.

Benefits

Bird-watchers enjoy fresh air and healthful exercise. They can choose to relax in solitude soaking up the sights and sounds of nature, cement lifelong friendships, and/or compete with fellow birders. They develop a deep awareness of the environmental balance. Some choose careers based on the scientific knowledge gained from this very popular pastime.

Bibliography

REFERENCE BOOKS

Conner, Jack. *The Complete Birder: A Guide to Better Birding.* Boston: Houghton Mifflin, 1988. Covers many aspects of birding. What to expect in different seasons, information on equipment selection, bird migration, and habits of many types of birds.

Dunne, Pete, David Sibley, and Clay Sutton. *Hawks in Flight.* Boston: Houghton Mifflin, 1988. Emphasis on hawk identification using many characteristics of the bird. Roger T. Peterson calls it, "A landmark. The first book dealing with a new aspect of bird-watching—the holistic method."

Farrand, John, Jr. *How to Identify Birds.* New York: McGraw-Hill, 1988. An Audubon handbook featuring the jizz, or overall identification process of bird identification.

Freethy, Ron. *How Birds Work: A Guide to Bird Biology.* Poole, Dorset, England: Blandford, 1982. An introduction to the science of ornithology. Analysis of contributions made to the subject by amateurs and professionals and how each can help the other.

Harrison, Colin. *A Field Guide to the Nests, Eggs and Nestlings of North American Birds.* Cleveland, OH: Collins, 1978. Coverage of birds north of the Mexican border. Lists information on breeding season, eggs, incubation, nestling, and the nestling period.

Harrison, George H. *The Backyard Bird Watcher.* New York: Simon & Schuster, 1988. Emphasis on creating a backyard environment for birds. Feeders, plantings, and photography.

Harrison, Hal H. *A Field Guide to Eastern Birds' Nests.* Boston: Houghton Mifflin, 1975. Covers birds' nests and eggs of 285 species located east of the Mississippi River. Intended to supplement the *Peterson Field Guide* of the area.

Harrison, Kit, and George Harrison. *America's Favorite Backyard Birds.* New York: Simon & Schuster, 1989. Detailed coverage of ten birds that will be found in many American backyards, plus general coverage of many more.

Harrison, Peter. *A Field Guide to Seabirds of the World.* New York: Viking, 1987. Field guide featuring photographs, field marks, habits, and distribution.

Kastner, Joseph. *A World of Watchers.* New York: Knopf, 1986. Emphasis on history and the accomplishments of the major figures in birding.

Kress, Stephen W. *The Audubon Society Guide to Attracting Birds.* New York: Macmillan, 1985. Coverage of landscaping, selecting plants, making pools, nest boxes, and feeding.

Laycock, George. *The Bird Watcher's Bible.* Garden City, NY: Doubleday, 1976. Overview of birding. Covers history, bird characteristics, equipment, and photography.

Lotz, Aileen R. *Birding Around the World: A Guide to Observing Birds Everywhere You Travel.* New York: Dodd, Mead, 1987. Where to find birds and how to get there. Excellent reference section on sources for books, field guides, tours, and other material of interest to birders.

Mace, Alice E., ed. *The Birds Around Us.* San Francisco: Ortho Books, 1986. An overview of birds and birding written by experts in their field. Includes history, behavior, attracting birds, photography, and data on a selection of 125 common birds.

Peterson, Roger Tory. *A Field Guide to the Birds: A Completely New Guide to All the Birds of Eastern and Central North America.* 4th ed. Boston: Houghton Mifflin, 1980. Field guide emphasizing field marks and groups of similar birds. Still a valuable resource.

————. *A Field Guide to Western Birds.* 3rd ed. Boston: Houghton Mifflin, 1990. Field guide emphasizing field marks and groups of similar birds.

Reilly, Edgar M., and Gorton Carruth. *The Birdwatcher's Diary: Designed to Increase the Pleasures of Birding.* New York: Harper & Row, 1987. Broad coverage of activities of interest to bird-watchers. Provision for noting observations. Includes checklist of United States and Canadian birds.

Socha, Laura O'Biso. *A Bird Watcher's Handbook: Field Ornithology for Backyard Naturalists.* New York: Dodd, Mead, 1987. Overview of birding, including field techniques, equipment, bird banding, and useful reference material.

PERIODICALS

American Birds. National Audubon Society, 700 Broadway, New York, NY 10003.

Auk. The American Ornithologists' Union, Museum of Natural History. University of Kansas, Lawrence, KS 66045.

Bird Watcher's Digest. Pardson, 149 Acme Street, Marietta, OH 45750.

Birder's World. Birder's World, 44 E. Eighth Street, Suite 410, Holland, MI 49423–3502.

Birding. American Birding Association, PO Box 6599, Colorado Springs, CO 80934.

Living Bird Quarterly. Cornell Laboratory of Ornithology, 159 Sapsucker Woods Road, Ithaca, NY 14850.

ASSOCIATIONS

American Birding Association. PO Box 6599, Colorado Springs, CO 80934. Promotes birding and the study of birds in their natural habitat. Contributes to the development of improved methods of population studies of birds. Tends to attract the serious birder. Publications: *Birding, Checklist of Birds of North America,* directory, *Winging It* newsletter, and a series of bird guides.

American Ornithologists' Union. National Museum of Natural History, Smithsonian Institution, Washington, DC 20560. Professionals and amateurs interested in birds. Bestows awards. Publications: *The Auk, Checklist of North American Birds,* monographs, and newsletter.

Cornell Laboratory of Ornithology. 159 Sapsucker Woods Road, Ithaca, NY 14850. Center for the study, conservation, and appreciation of birds. Known worldwide as an educational liaison between the professional ornithologist and the public. Encourages volunteer participation in bird observation and data collection. Sponsors home study courses in bird biology and photography. Operates Library of Natural Sounds with over 60,000 taped bird sounds. Bestows awards. Maintains library. Publications: *Birdscope, Feeder-Watch News, Living Bird Quarterly,* and *Birder's Life List and Diary.*

National Audubon Society. 950 Third Avenue, New York, NY 10022. Persons interested in wildlife, wildlife habits, soil, water, and forests. Sponsors camps, clubs, and the Audubon Expedition Institute. Supports a force of thirty-five wardens to patrol wildlife sanctuaries. Bestows awards. Publications: *American Birds,* and *Audubon.*

North American Rare Bird Alert. Suite 6A, 807 S. Friendswood Drive, Friendswood, TX 77546. Provides a telephone forum to members, exchanging information about bird sightings.

Birds, Caged

PET BIRDS MAKE EXCELLENT companions. You can enjoy the soothing warbling of a canary, or watch the comical antics and hold a brief conversation with a member of the parrot family. Be aware that when you purchase your feathered friend you are entering into a demanding long-term relationship. Birds often become very attached to their owners, giving much, and expecting much in return. Take the time to learn about the various characteristics and requirements of birds suitable as pets. Of about 8,600 different bird species, relatively few have the necessary temperament and trainability to be pets. Many wild species are imported from tropical or semi-tropical environments. Despite a quarantine period and inoculations, some diseased birds occasionally enter the country. Birds that have been hand-raised domestically will be healthy and accustomed to handling by humans, shortening the period required to tame the bird.

History

Paleontologists have conclusive evidence that birds evolved from reptiles about 160 million years ago. The earliest known bird fossil, Archaeopteryx, bears a strong resemblance to earlier flying reptiles, and it had feathers. Current thinking is that feathers evolved from scales. Note that bird's legs still contain a scaly appearance. Birds are one of the earliest domesticated animals. The reasons for domestication varied over time. The red jungle fowl of southeast Asia is the ancestor of today's chicken. Pigeons were also kept as a source of food, and in the West Indies Columbus found natives raising macaws for food and as pets. The Incas of South America tamed species such as the Amazon parrot as pets, and the Pueblo indians of the southwest owned macaws and other parrots, acquiring them through trade with Mexican cultures. Early explorers and traders often took exotic tropical birds from Central and South America on their return voyages to Europe. One of the earliest bird fanciers for their aesthetic value was Alexander the Great, who shipped birds to Rome from the Far East. A species of parakeet became the most popular caged bird in the Roman Empire. Parrots and other tropical species became more readily available in Europe after the fifteenth century, and have increased in popularity ever since.

When the Spanish conquered the Canary Islands in 1478 they discovered the canary, a beautiful songbird of the finch family. They sent birds back to Spain for breeding purposes. Canaries were sold all over Europe by both the Spanish and Italians. Today canaries are bred with emphasis on both song and color.

Most Popular Species

Bird species vary considerably in their characteristics and suitability as caged pets. Here, we'll look at some of the most popular species.

Canaries

The domestic canary is kept primarily for its singing ability, although many breeders place great emphasis on the development of color and physical characteristics for competition in bird shows. Although usually thought of as yellow birds, canaries are also bred in red, brown, and other variegated colors. Over twenty-eight varieties are bred. They are primarily seed eaters; but other beneficial supplements to a commercial seed mix may include diced apples, spinach, and ground whole wheat bread. Since birds have no teeth, they grind their food in their gizzard, where strong muscles contract and bring grit in contact with food. The grit remains in the gizzard for a long time and needs to be replaced only occasionally. The bird owner can add a pinch of grit to the food a few times weekly. Clean water should be made available at all times. The average life span is five to fifteen years. Cages should allow for free movement and some flight. Very tall cages are not effective because birds normally don't fly vertically. Rectangular cages offer the most efficient utilization of space. Cages should be a minimum of two cubic feet, 1′ × 1′ × 2′. The cage should be located in a draft-free environment, away from heating and cooling vents, and positioned to avoid direct sunlight. Perches should be positioned within the cage to provide easy access to food and water sources, and to prevent contamination of those sources by droppings. Upper perches shouldn't be placed directly over lower ones to prevent soiling by droppings. Where possible, provide perches with a variety of sizes and shapes to cause different parts of the bird's foot to make contact, providing greater comfort and conditioning. Most canaries enjoy an occasional bath, splashing around in a water container attached to the cage door.

Other Finches

Most other finches are lively colorful birds. Most don't sing, learn to talk, or become tame. They prefer to be caged in pairs with sufficient room to move about. They crack seeds with their hard bills, removing the shell or husk, and swallow the kernel. Food, grit, and water requirements are as for canaries. The average life span is about five to eight years. Cage requirements for a pair should be a minimum of two cubic feet, 1′ × 1′ × 2′.

Budgerigars

The Budgie, a member of the parrot family, is the most popular of all caged birds. It's originally a native of Australia, living in the vast interior in flocks of over a thousand birds. Their presence was reported by Captain James Cook when his exploration carried him there in 1770. First introduced to England in 1840, their popularity soon spread and they were being bred all over Europe by the turn of the century. The native budgerigar is light green in color. The European breeding efforts began to yield birds of other colors, but breeders were unable to follow up and preserve the strains. By 1910, birds with a pure white face and a sky blue body were produced, and this coloration was maintained in subsequent generations. This was followed by a rainbow of other color mutations that continues to expand today. Budgies are easily tamed and can be trained to do simple tricks. Most can also be trained to mimic simple words and phrases; some have been taught to sing songs. Budgies like to occasionally fly freely around a room. Take care to close windows and doors and curtain the windows to prevent the bird from flying into the glass. Average life span is eight to fifteen years. Budgies are primarily seed eaters, but other beneficial supplements to a commercial seed mix may include diced apples, carrots, celery, corn-on-the-cob, raisins, spinach, and whole wheat

bread. Grit and water are made available as with canaries. Budgies enjoy bathing. It encourages them to preen and condition their feathers. Keep water levels less than 1½ inches to avoid drowning. Cages should be a minimum of two cubic feet, 1′ × 1′ × 2′. A suitable branch can be fixed to the top of the cage to provide exercise and a landing site for around-the-room flights.

Cockatiels

The cockatiel is the next step up in the parrot family. It's slightly larger than the Budgie, sports a longer tail and has a jaunty crest on its head that can be held erect or lowered. The cockatiel has a gentle nature and the ability to talk and whistle simple tunes. They show a great deal of affection for their owners. The male bird also produces a cheerful warbling song. The cockatiel is a native of Australia. It was brought to Europe at about the same time as the Budgie, and has been bred around the world. Its life span is about ten to fourteen years, but some have been known to live into their late twenties. Its larger size with a longer tail calls for a larger cage. A minimum size being twelve cubic feet, 2′ × 2′ × 3′. The diet is the same as that of the Budgie.

Lovebirds

Lovebirds, members of the parrot family, are intelligent, curious, and somewhat aggressive in nature despite their name. The name was derived from the fact that pairs tend to preen one another. They tend to single out one owner for affection. Young hand-raised birds are easiest to tame. These natives of Africa are very colorful, with multiple colors appearing on one bird. Examples include red, yellow and green, or black, white, and blue. Nine species are recognized. Their lifespan averages ten to fifteen years. Some can be taught to talk. They are best kept in pairs, so a large cage is required. A minimum size being twelve cubic feet, 2′ × 2′ × 3′. The diet is the same as that of the Budgie.

Conures

Conures are members of the parrot family resembling miniature macaws. Of approximately fifty species only a few are suitable as pets. Some of the smaller species such as dusky conures, halfmoon conures and peach-fronted conures tend to be quieter than the red-faced varieties. They are pretty, sweet and affectionate. They are capable of mimicking speech and make good pets. One should be careful to obtain a domestic hand-raised bird for best results. They will be much more at ease with people, and easier to tame. Conures are originally from Central or South America, or the Caribbean Islands. The life span ranges from ten to as much as thirty years. A small conure diet is similar to that of the Budgie. They can be most easily maintained on a commercially pelleted diet, with fruit and vegetable supplements. A minimum cage size is twelve cubic feet, $2' \times 2' \times 3'$.

Parrots

There are many species of large parrots that may be kept as pets. Here, we'll look at several representative types and their characteristics.

Amazon parrots are native to Central and South America. These are the birds Columbus took back to Spain on his first voyage. They are available as hand reared chicks with a predominately green plumage. Amazons are generally prone to screeching in the morning and evening, a feature that must be taken into account if neighbors live closeby. Ownership is a long-time commitment because they may live fifty or more years. Large parrots must have adequate exercise which requires letting them out of their cages each day. If obtained when young, they will grow tame quickly and learn to talk. Amazons generally have an affectionate temperament, and enjoy human company.

African grey parrots are native to Africa. These parrots are more prone to an uneven temperament than other species. For this reason, it's important to acquire a young bird that has been treated properly. Such parrots tend to have long memories for distasteful experiences and are most unforgiving. Treated properly they become a lovable and tame pet. Greys imitate speech very closely, actually capturing the tone of voice of the trainer. They also have the intelligence to match learned phrases with the appropriate situation. "Good morning" is said only in the morning for example. They mimic sounds very accurately as well, from a creaking door to the ring of a telephone.

Cockatoos are intelligent show-offs. They spread their wings and position their heads with crest extended to get attention. If the display is ignored, they will give a loud scream to attract attention. They are native to Australia and New Zealand. They can mimic speech, but not as well as the African grey. Cockatoos are very curious birds, examining any new object carefully. They can be taught to perform tricks. Their life expectancy is comparable to that of humans. Captain Cook collected a sulphur crested cockatoo on his early voyage to Australia.

Macaws average about thirty-four inches in size. These multicolored birds are native to Central and South America. They are usually gentle giants, becoming very tame, but like cockatoos, readily recall any mistreatment. They tend to limit their affection to one person. They develop a limited vocabulary.

Many types of parrot will resort to feather plucking when they become bored. Once this habit begins, it's very difficult to stop. In extreme cases the bird will almost totally eliminate its feathers.

Cages for large parrots range from $2' \times 3' \times 4'$, often with a play area with perches above its flat top.

In addition to a commercial feed mix, other beneficial supplements may include sliced apples, carrots, celery, corn-on-the-cob, grapes, oranges, papaya, raisins, spinach, sweet potatoes and whole wheat bread.

Related Pastimes

Hobbies related to caged birds include training and breeding. Details of these activities are beyond the scope of this work, but are well covered in books listed in the bibliography below.

Bibliography

REFERENCE BOOKS

Alderton, David. *The Complete Cage and Aviary Bird Handbook.* Neptune, NJ: T. F. H., 1986. Covers history, pet selection, housing, feeding, ailments, breeding, and the various breeds.

Axelson, R. Dean. *Caring For Your Pet Bird.* Rev. ed. New York: Sterling, 1989. Discusses the bird's environment, gives tips on care, feeding, and taming. Identifies diseases, and provides detailed information on selected species.

deGrahl, W. *The Parrot Family.* New York: Arco, 1984. A reference book on keeping and breeding all types of parrots.

Freud, Arthur. *All About the Parrots.* New York: Howell, 1980. Covers the wide variety of parrot species with descriptions, habitats, histories, and breeding habits for each.

Gallerstein, Gary A. *Bird Owner's Home Health and Care Handbook.* New York: Howell, 1984. Covers the purchase, feeding, and caging of pet birds. Provides tips on spotting sickness, treatment at home or at the veterinarian, breeding, and training.

Harper, Don. *The Practical Encyclopedia of Pet Birds for Home & Garden.* New York: Harmony Books, 1987. A selection guide to 200 birds covering choosing, handling, feeding, taming, accommodation, health care, and breeding.

Moizer, Stan, and Barbara Moizer. *The Complete Book of Budgerigars.* New York: Barron's, 1988. A selection of topics related to budgerigar ownership arranged in alphabetic sequence.

Vriends, Matthew M. *Breeding Cage and Aviary Birds.* New York: Howell, 1985. Covers purchasing, housing, and feeding with strong emphasis on breeding.

————. *The New Bird Handbook.* New York: Barron's, 1989. Everything about housing, care, nutrition, breeding, and diseases.

Vriends, T. *Cage Birds in Color.* New York: Arco, 1984. Covers bird history, choosing a pet, care, feeding, and breeding.

PERIODICALS

American Cage-Bird Magazine. American Cage-Bird, One Glamore Court, Smithtown, NY 11787.

Bird Talk. Fancy Publications, Box 6050, Mission Viejo, CA 92690.

ASSOCIATIONS

American Federation of Aviculture. 3118 W. Thomas Road, Suite 713, Phoenix, AZ 85017. Hobbyist groups of aviculturists, professionals, and individuals. Promotes aviculture as a means of conserving bird life through captive breeding programs. Conducts seminars. Publications: *Watchbird,* and related material.

COM-U.S.A. PO Box 122, Elizabeth, NJ 07207. Promotes and educates bird fanciers in the art of genetic cage-bird breeding. Conducts educational meetings to teach the art of identifying, classifying, pairing, and breeding all kinds of cage birds with particular attention to color-breeding.

Society of Parrot Breeders and Exhibitors. PO Box 369, Groton, MA 01450. Aviculturists, parrot breeders, and exhibitors. Seeks to prevent parrot extinction. Maintains show standards, provides sanctioned judges, and bestows awards. Publication: *Journal of the Society of Parrot Breeders and Exhibitors.*

Note: There are additional associations devoted to specific bird species listed in the Encyclopedia of Associations, available in libraries.

Boats

AMERICA'S EARLY DEVELOPMENT and expansion were made possible by travel over the seas and inland waterways. Explorers, colonists, and traders gained access to the interior by means of rivers and lakes. During colonial times America's virgin forests provided the materials for tall, straight masts for foreign sailing vessels. In subsequent years America played a major role in the shipbuilding industry. Howard I. Chapelle's books capture the history of American wooden sailing vessels of the period. They contain detailed accounts and beautiful line drawings useful to historians and model builders.

Some believe man emerged from the sea during his evolution. Maybe those few drops of salt water left in our blood attract us to the water and to boats of all kinds. Our pastimes reflect a variety of interests relating to boats and the water. Armchair sailors may only study maritime history or build ship models. If you intend to actually participate, to deal with the wind and waves, you need to prepare yourself.

Preparing for Boating

There are no visible pathways on the sea, so if you plan to venture far from shore, the art of navigation must be mastered. Modern seafarers learn to use charts, radio systems, buoys, and lighthouses to stay on course. In addition to navigation, a basic knowledge of meteorology and amateur radio is desirable when attempting long voyages. Storms can come up quickly over large bodies of water. For the serious boating enthusiast, the book entitled *Chapman Piloting, Seamanship and Small Boat Handling,* originally written by C. F. Chapman is, and has been for many years, an invaluable source of maritime knowledge. Chapman's book explains the role of the United States Power Squadrons and the United States Coast Guard Auxiliary in teaching courses about boating to the public. Another

useful text is *Dutton's Navigation and Piloting,* by E. S. Maloney. From books such as these you learn the rules of courtesy, and above all, of safety on the water. You will learn to interpret the complex system of color-coded buoys that mark a safe pathway through congested waterways. You will find where to purchase nautical charts and learn how to read and use them. You will be able to judge the Beaufort Scale wind force by observing water surface conditions, telling you when it's safe to sail. In short, you will learn how to be a responsible sailor. See "Radio, Amateur" (for communication); "Aviation" (for navigational aids); and "Weather Forecasting" (for meteorology) elsewhere in this book. In the following discussion we'll look at various classes of boats that are used for recreation and competition.

Boat Classes

Rowboats

Rowboats range in size from the small freshwater pleasure boats rowed by one person, through the salt water fishing dories, up to the surf boats used by life saving squads at beaches. They provide an excellent exercise platform for young and old. With the addition of a sliding seat, you also get leg exercise while rowing.

An average canoe is about seventeen feet long. It's open at the top and most modern examples are made of aluminum or fiberglass. They are used for recreational pleasure paddling, racing, and river travel in medium swift water. Since they have little draft (the depth a boat extends below the water line), they are especially adaptable to shallow rivers where a motorboat would not be able to go. They can carry heavy loads for camping. Kayaks are usually somewhat smaller than canoes. Their covered top keeps splashing water out of the boat making them less likely to become swamped in swift white-water rivers.

Shells are highly specialized rowing craft that are narrow, light in weight, and are the thoroughbreds of rowboats. Sculling is accomplished with two oars per rower, while in sweep events, each person rows with one oar. A good eight-man shell will cover a mile in four and one-half minutes.

Power Boats

Power boats come in all shapes and sizes. They tend to take on certain characteristics depending on their intended use. Small pleasure boats are typically powered with outboard gas motors; however, electric motors are often employed for slow trolling while fishing. Typical fifteen to twenty-one foot pleasure boats often have inboard motors. They are used for cruising, pulling water skiers, fishing, and skin diving. They look simple to operate and innocent. Without proper training in their use they can be deadly. Exploding gas vapors from improper fueling practices, collisions resulting from inadequate knowledge of boat handling practices, and injury to swimmers from the boat's propeller are some of the dangers. There are more than 30,000 miles of improved inland waterways in the United States. Many are interconnected. Boaters can spend relaxing days cruising and exploring.

Power boat racing is done in eleven classes. The speeds attained vary from ninety miles per hour to over 200 miles per hour for unlimited hydroplanes. The American Power Boat Association sets standards for safety equipment and sanctions races. Parachutes are usually worn at speeds over 100 miles per hour. They enable the skipper to enter the water feet first in the event of a spill. Water feels very firm when entered at that speed. Stock racing classifications allow few modifications to the boat, and fuel octane ratings are set at 100 maximum. You can break into the smallest class, the T class, for about $3,000 for a used state-of-the-art boat, which will be about twelve feet long. Race boat drivers have experts modify stock propellers to achieve top performance.

Power boats designed for special applications include bass boats used in bass fishing competitions. They provide a stable platform for high swivel chairs used while fishing. Large motors are used to hurry to choice fishing spots during competition. Salt water boats are also specially outfitted for deep sea fishing. Some sailboats are provided with auxiliary motors. An example is shown in Figure 1. When the motors are operated, the boat is subject to the rules applicable to power boats. Probably the most versatile of specialty boats is the houseboat. Capable of accommodating whole families in complete comfort, houseboats are used on rivers and lakes such as Lake Powell in Arizona, where they may be rented for family outings.

Sailboats

Large sailboats have been described as a hole in the water into which one keeps pouring money. While it is true that

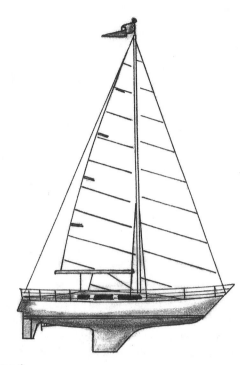

Figure 1
A large sailing vessel of a type likely to be fitted with an auxiliary motor.

any large boat requires expensive maintenance and storage, many weekend sailors pursue their hobby for a lifetime and handle the maintenance themselves.

The dividing line between pleasure and racing craft is not as distinct as with power boats. Many pleasure sailboats are also raced in their respective class. Recreational sailing involves three general classifications. The day sailor is a family boat designed for a day on the water. A cruiser is designed to be sailed for an extended period of time. A racing boat is designed for speed, often at the expense of comfort.

When two or more boats are built the same, they are called one-design boats. They are often raced in that one-design class. There are many such classes, usually sporting a special symbol on their sails for identification. Another approach to sailboat classes is the rating classification in which the boat designs are not identical, but must meet a general set of specifications. One of the most famous rating classes is the twelve meters, used in the America's Cup Races.

Piloting a sailboat requires the study of age-old practices and terms. When sailing toward the wind (upwind or windward), you must sail (beat) a zig-zag course called tacking. You can't sail directly into the wind. The sails wouldn't fill with wind, and would simply flap in the breeze. If you sail as close to upwind as possible, you are sailing close hauled. The sails are set fore and aft, almost over the center of the boat. Sailing at right angles to the wind is called sailing a beam reach. When you sail (run) with the wind the sails may be set almost perpendicular to the length of the boat, where they can fill with wind and propel the boat. See windsurfing under the "Surfing" heading elsewhere in this text for information on wind force and the Beaufort Scale.

The cost of a boat large enough to warrant the title yacht, or ship (over sixty-five feet long), has risen dramatically in recent years. This has limited ownership to the very rich and to the very resourceful. Resourceful yacht owners with minimum funds can rent or charter their boats to others when they don't plan to use them. They can also make their services available as captains. It is not unusual for groups to charter a boat, or rent it outright for their exclusive use for a limited time. Yachts are used for pleasure and racing. Sailing yachts that are fitted with an auxiliary motor are called auxiliary yachts. Sailing yachts are becoming popular, and cruising is replacing racing in popularity.

The Owner Builder

While the vast majority of boat owners buy a new or used boat, there is a hardy group of do-it-yourselfers who enjoy creating their own dreamboat. You can save up to 50 percent of the cost in this way. Modern methods and materials such as marine plywood and fiberglass ensure durable, long lasting construction. Consult your library for books or magazines listing sources of boat kits, plans, materials, and specialized hardware. You may be the type to enjoy your boating hobby before the boat is even launched the first time.

Bibliography

REFERENCE BOOKS

Chapelle, Howard I. *Boatbuilding: A Complete Handbook of Wooden Boat Construction.* New York: Norton, 1969. Detailed descriptions and line drawings of early wooden ships.

———. *The History of American Sailing Ships.* New York: Bonanza Books, 1935. Detailed descriptions and line drawings of American ships including the colonial period, naval craft, privateers, schooners, merchant craft, and sailing yachts.

———. *The History of the American Sailing Navy: The Ships and Their Development.* New York: Bonanza Books, 1949. Detailed descriptions and line drawings of naval ships used during the eighteenth and nineteenth centuries

———. *The Search for Speed Under Sail 1700–1855.* New York: Bonanza Books, 1967. Detailed discussion with line drawings of a selection of ships built in America and abroad.

Cunliffe, Tom. *Easy on the Helm: Boat Handling Under Sail and Power.* New York: Norton, 1992. Boat handling in all weather conditions.

Frisbie, Richard. *Basic Boat Building.* Chicago: Regnery, 1975. How to build your own boat at home on a small budget with minimum experience.

Gerr, Dave. *The Nature of Boats: Insights and Esoterica for the Nautically Obsessed.* Camden, ME: International Marine, 1992. A naval architect explains how boats tick. Covers all types of watercraft.

Maloney, Elbert S. *Chapman Piloting, Seamanship and Small Boat Handling.* 60th ed. New York: Hearst Marine Books, 1991. First written by Charles F. Chapman at the request of Franklin D. Roosevelt in 1922, this book has been continually updated over the years. It provides comprehensive coverage of boating information. More than 200,000 persons take courses in pleasure boat operation each year. Many of them use Chapman's as their textbook and as their keep-aboard book afterwards.

———. *Dutton's Navigation and Piloting.* 14th ed. Annapolis, MD: Naval Institute, 1985. Another important book for boaters who venture far from shore.

Parker, Mark, and Ed McKnew. *Power Boat Guide.* 3rd ed. Camden, ME: International Marine, 1992. Pictures, specifications, and reviews of over 850 current and out-of-production inboard models.

Russell, Charles W. *Basic Sailing.* Washington, DC: The American National Red Cross, 1966. Text developed for the American Red Cross sailing course.

Steward, Robert M. *Boatbuilding Manual.* 3rd ed. Camden, ME: International Marine, 1987. The standard reference for small wooden boat building. Used as a textbook by boat building schools. Covers tools, materials, and building techniques.

Trefethen, Jim. *Wooden Boat Renovation: New Life for Old Boats Using Modern Methods.* Camden, ME: International Marine, 1993. Discusses the practicality of boat renovation. Provides an overview of tools, materials, and techniques required in the process of wooden boat renovation.

Walker, Stuart H. *The Tactics of Small Boat Racing.* New York: Norton, 1966. A detailed technical study of the tactics of sailboat racing for the experienced sailor.

PERIODICALS

Boating. Hachette Magazines, 1633 Broadway, 45th Floor, New York, NY 10009.

Boating World. Trans World Publishers, 2100 Powers Ferry Road, Atlanta, GA 30339.

Cruising World. Cruising World Publications, 5 John Clarke Road, Newport, RI 02840.

Houseboat Magazine. Harris Publications, 520 Park Avenue, Idaho Falls, ID 83402.

Motor Boating & Sailing. Hearst Magazines, 250 W. 55th Street, 4th Floor, New York, NY 10019.

Ocean Navigator. Navigator Publishers, Box 569, Portland, ME 04112–0569.

Paddler. Paddling Group, 4061 Oceanside Boulevard, No. M, Oceanside, CA 92056.

Powerboat. Nordco Publishers, 15917 Strathern Street, Van Nuys, CA 91406.

Sail. Cahners Publishing, 275 Washington Street, Newton, MA 02158–1630.

Sailing World. Cruising World Publications, 5 John Clarke Road, Newport RI 02840.

Woodenboat. Woodenboat Publications, Box 78, Brooklin, ME 04616.

Yachting. Times Mirror Magazines, 2 Park Avenue, New York, NY 10016.

ASSOCIATIONS

American Power Boat Association. P O Box 377, 17640 E. 9 Mile Road, Eastpointe, MI 48021. Governing body for the promotion of power boat racing in the U.S. Sanctions regattas and formulates rules. Publications: *American Power Boat Association Reference Book, Propeller,* and related materials.

American Sailing Association 13922 Marquesas Way, Marina Del Rey, CA 90292. Promotes sailing safety and internationally recognized standards for sail education. Publications: *American Sailing,* and related materials.

Boat Owners Association of the U.S. 880 S. Pickett Street, Alexandria, VA 22304. Owners or prospective owners of recreational boats. Provides related services. Maintains library. Publications: *Boat/U.S. Reports, Boating Equipment Guide,* and related materials.

Inter-Lake Yachting Association. 18291 Glencreek Lane, Strongsville, OH 44136. Clubs in the Great Lakes region. Holds regatta and sponsors races. Bestows awards. Publication: *Inter-Lake Yachting Association Yearbook.*

National Ocean Access Project. Annapolis City Marina, PO Box 3377, Annapolis, MD 21403. Develops and promotes marine recreational opportunities for people with disabilities. Sponsors regatta and conducts model boat races. Publications: *Ocean Access,* and related material.

United States Power Squadrons. PO Box 30423, Raleigh, NC 27622. Pleasure boat owners. Offers free instruction in safe boating to the public. Conducts other boating-related courses. Publication: *The Ensign.*

United States Rowing Association. 201 S. Capitol Avenue, Suite 400, Indianapolis, IN 46225. Rowers and rowing enthusiasts. Promotes and governs amateur rowing in the U.S. Selects crews to represent the U.S. in the World Games, Pan American Games, and the Olympics. Maintains hall of fame, and bestows awards. Publications: *American Rowing,* and *Rowing Directory.*

U.S. Sailing. PO Box 209, Newport, RI 02840. Coordinating and governing body of sailboat racing in the U.S. Conducts educational program and bestows awards. Publications: *American Sailor,* and related materials.

Bowling

A BOWLER ROLLS A BALL weighing no more than sixteen pounds along a sixty foot long wooden lane in an effort to knock down ten pins, each weighing about three and a half pounds. As with many target sports, consistent form is the key to success. Any variation in body or arm movements during ball delivery will cause the ball to vary in its path toward the pins. Pins are set up in a triangular pattern with one point of the triangle facing the bowler. The most effective aiming point is just to the right of the nearest pin for a right-handed bowler or to the left for a left-handed person.

People of all ages and levels of society enjoy bowling. More than sixty million Americans bowl. More than ten million compete in leagues conducted according to rules set by three closely integrated governing bodies in the United States. The American Bowling Congress, established in 1895, regulates male bowling. The Women's International Bowling Congress was formed in 1916, and the Young American Bowling Alliance began to serve the needs of younger bowlers in 1982. More specialized bowling governing bodies, listed in the bibliography, also serve large numbers of enthusiasts.

History

Some form of bowling has existed since early recorded history. Sir Flinders Petrie found bowling implements in a 5200 B.C. Egyptian grave believed to be the burial site of a child. The small balls and slender pins were made of stone. Early European bowling centered in Germany, Belgium, Luxemburg, and the Netherlands before 300 A.D.

In Germany during the early Christian era people carried clubs called kegles. During this time churches set up a kegle to represent Heide, or heathen. The parishioners were given a large round stone to roll at the kegle. If the kegel was hit, the heathen was slain, and the parishioner was cleansed of sin. If the kegle was missed, the parish-

ioner was instructed to lead a better life. Bowling is still sometimes called kegling.

Early ninepin bowling in Germany was done outdoors on clay lanes. Later the Germans added a twelve-inch board down the center, and the ball was rolled on that. Photographs of the first commercial bowling lanes in the United States also show a narrow lane leading to the pins. This would surely make it difficult to knock down remaining pins when attempting to make a spare.

The Dutch brought outdoor bowling to New York in the 1600s. The sport soon became popular in Chicago, still as an outdoor sport.

The game of ninepins was outlawed in some areas during the 1800s due to the gambling that became associated with it. The prohibition against ninepins was circumvented by simply changing the number of pins to ten, resulting in the game of tenpins. The first indoor lanes were built in New York in the 1840s, and bowling began a rapid rise in popularity. In 1952 mechanized pinsetters began to replace pinboys and bowling surged to new levels of popularity. President Abraham Lincoln would envy the present occupants of the White House; there was no bowling alley there when Abe bowled during his presidency.

Equipment

Bowling balls range in weight from six to sixteen pounds. The lightest versions are for junior bowlers. Occasional bowlers will find lighter balls easier to handle, with little sacrifice in performance. For such bowlers, women may want to consider a twelve- or thirteen-pound ball, and a man can do well with a fourteen- or fifteen-pound ball. The ball measures twenty-seven inches in circumference, and a little over eight and a half inches in diameter.

Bowling balls are made of hard rubber or the more popular plastic. In an effort to maintain a uniform density within the ball, a weight block is built-in to compensate for the material removed when drilling finger holes to the specifications of the user. It is possible to affect the ball's action by the placement of the thumb and finger holes relative to the location of the weight block. Finger hole placement can affect the curved path (hook) taken by the ball. The distance from the inner edge of the thumb hole to the inner edge of the finger hole (span) is critical to performance. While balls furnished for public use at bowling alleys may approximate your required span, a ball drilled to your measurements for personal use will improve your consistency.

Bowling pins weigh between three pounds two ounces and three pounds ten ounces. They are usually made of hard wood with a plastic coating. Pins are slightly over four and three-quarters inches in diameter at the height that the ball contacts them, and stand fifteen inches tall.

Bowling shoes should allow a sliding action for your left foot (if you are right handed), and a braking action for your right foot. Accordingly, good bowling shoes have a leather sole on the left shoe, and a rubber sole on the right. The opposite arrangement is available for left handed persons. Both left and right bowling shoes furnished in bowling establishments have leather soles.

Many bowling accessories are available from special leather gloves to coatings for fingers to reduce blister formation. As you gain experience you may want to try some during practice sessions.

Strategy

Bowling lanes have groups of markings used as reference locations and as an aid to targeting. See Figure 1. Numbers given are the distances, in feet, from the foul line. The three rows of locator spots in the approach area are used to position yourself consistently for delivery of the ball. The triangular targeting arrows located at fifteen feet from the foul line are used in spot bowling. The row of spots located seven feet from the foul line are used for additional targeting reference. The bowling pins are set in the triangular pattern shown in Figure 1. They are numbered as shown for identification.

The following discussion applies to a right-handed person. When a bowling ball strikes the pattern of pins between pins one and three, it hits four pins directly (pins 1, 3, 5, and 9). These four knock the rest down. The most efficient target for the first ball rolled is the 1, 3 "pocket."

Pins are targeted in several different ways. In pin bowling, you set yourself in a position you feel will take you to the foul line to release the ball in a way that will bring the ball into the pocket. You aim directly at the pocket. If any part of your technique is flawed, you have no check points along the way to note what you have done wrong.

In spot bowling, you start in the same position and release the ball in the same position as above, but aim at a particular triangular targeting arrow. The method has the

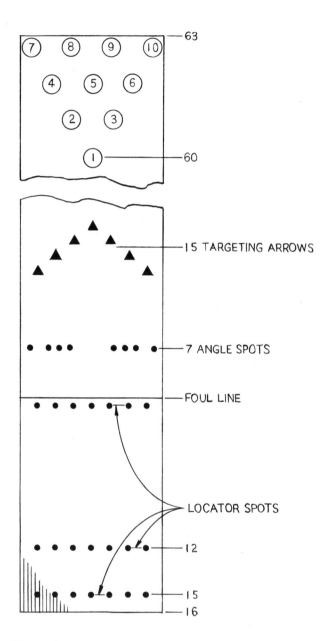

Figure 1

Bowling lane layout. Numbers to the right of the lane are the distances, in feet, from the foul line.

advantage that you have a nearby target to check the path of the ball. The disadvantage is that a near miss at the targeting arrow becomes a greater miss at the pins.

Line bowling makes use of a number of check points. With experience you can follow the path of the ball with your eye, noting the accuracy of location as it passes the foul line, the first set of spots, the targeting arrow, and the pocket.

The above techniques apply to aiming at specific pins when attempting to complete a spare. In such cases, a different set of locator spots is often used to guide your set up before release.

In reaction to the forces imposed when a ball is released, it normally skids, then rolls and turns. The ball travels in a straight path during the skid phase, and begins to hook during the roll and turn phase. For best action of ball against pins, the second phase should begin in the ball's final movement into the pins. If the ball travels too fast, it will skid too far.

The condition of the bowling lane has an effect on ball travel, especially on the amount the ball will hook. Experienced bowlers are quick to adjust for these factors as they move from lane to lane.

Scoring

The first-time bowler may find it hard to believe that the ball is about one and three-eighths inches bigger than the space between any two adjacent pins. However, with sufficient practice, and someone to evaluate your performance and provide instruction, the pins will begin to fall.

When all the pins are knocked down with one ball you have made a strike. When two balls are required, you have made a spare. When some pins remain after rolling two balls, your score is based on the number of pins knocked down. A frame is complete after making a strike, or two balls are rolled as above. There are ten frames in a game.

Score keeping is a somewhat complex process. Each frame is scored separately, and a cumulative score is recorded. Suppose you knocked down seven pins with your first ball, and two with the second. You will record a score of nine for the frame.

If you score a strike with the first ball, you have completed that frame, but the scoring for that frame is not recorded yet because you have a bonus coming. The strike is worth ten points, plus a point for each pin you knock down with the next two balls rolled. So a strike, followed by seven pins on the next roll, and two on the next, has a value of nineteen points.

If you score a spare with the first and second ball, you have completed that frame, but the scoring for that frame is not recorded yet because again, you have a bonus coming. The spare is worth ten points, plus a point for each pin you knock down with the next roll. So a spare, followed by seven pins on the next roll, has a value of seventeen points.

Scoring is much easier if you simply keep recording strikes. Ten strikes in a row is a perfect game, worth 300 points. Take heart, computers are slowly being introduced into bowling establishments to facilitate scoring.

Bibliography

REFERENCE BOOKS

Anthony, Earl, with Dawson Taylor. *Winning Bowling.* Chicago: Contemporary Books, 1977. All aspects of bowling, including how to practice, improve concentration, and increase consistency.

Aulby, Mike, Dave Ferraro, with Dan Herbst. *Bowling 200 Plus: Winning Strategies to Up Your Average and Improve Your Game.* Chicago: Contemporary Books, 1989. Insider tips for analyzing and correcting common bowling mistakes.

Grinfelds, Vesma, and Bonnie Hultstrand. *Right Down Your Alley: the Complete Book of Bowling.* 2nd ed. West Point, NY: Leisure, 1985. Concise, well illustrated book about the significant details of bowling.

Ozio, David, with Dan Herbst. *Bowl Like a Pro: Winning Techniques and Strategies That Will Raise Your Average.* Chicago: Contemporary Books, 1992. Step-by-step instructions detail fundamentals of good shot making.

Pezzano, Chuck. *Professional Bowlers Association Guide to Better Bowling.* New York: Simon & Schuster, 1974. A step-by-step handbook intended to make bowlers understand the game better and score higher.

Salvino, Carmen, with Frederick C. Klein. *Fast Lanes.* Chicago: Bonus Books, 1988. Stories behind the achievements of a professional bowler. Includes tips on exercise, equipment, mechanics and tactics.

Strickland, Robert H. *Bowling: Steps to Success.* Champaign, IL: Leisure, 1989. Describes correct swing, ball dynamics, and targeting.

Taylor, Dawson. *Bowling Strikes.* Chicago: Contemporary Books, 1991. Covers game fundamentals, step-by-step instructions, and techniques.

Weiskopf, Herm, and Chuck Pezzano. *Sports Illustrated Bowling.* New York: Harper & Row, 1981. A comprehensive, illustrated handbook on the fundamentals of bowling.

PERIODICALS

Bowlers Journal. National Bowlers Journal, 200 S Michigan Avenue, Suite 1430, Chicago, IL 60604.

Bowling Digest. Century Publishers, 990 Grove Street, Evanston, IL 60201.

Bowling Magazine. American Bowling Congress, 5301 S. 76th Street, Greendale, WI 53129.

Bowling News. Bowling News, 2606 W. Burbank Boulevard, Burbank, CA 91505.

Woman Bowler. Women's International Bowling Congress, 5301 S. 76th Street, Greendale, WI 53129.

ASSOCIATIONS

American Blind Bowling Association. 411 Sheriff, Mercer, PA 16137. Legally blind men and women, eighteen years of age and older, competing in organized tenpin bowling. Sanctions member leagues and presents awards. Publication: *The Blind Bowler.*

American Bowling Congress. 5301 S. 76th Street, Greendale, WI 53129–1127. Provides standard rules, approves equipment, conducts research, sponsors seminars, operates hall of fame and museum, presents awards, and sponsors annual bowling competition. Sponsors bowling writing competition. Publications: *Bowling Magazine* and related material.

American Lawn Bowls Association. c/o Merton Isaacman, 17 Buckthorn, Irvine, CA 92714. Sponsors competition play-downs at all levels. Presents awards and maintains hall of fame. Publications: *Bowls* magazine, and related materials.

American Wheelchair Bowling Association. 3620 Tamarack Drive, Redding, CA 96003. Promotes wheelchair bowling and regulates rules. Conducts tournaments, presents awards, and maintains hall of fame. Publications: *The 11th Frame,* and the book, *Wheelchair Bowling.*

National Bowling Association. 377 Park Avenue S., 7th Floor, New York, NY 10016. Promotes bowling tournaments and other activities. Sponsors fundraising programs for sickle cell anemia and the United Negro College Fund. Bestows awards and local scholarships. Maintains hall of fame. Publications: *Bowler,* and related materials.

National Deaf Bowling Association. 9244 E. Mansfield Avenue, Denver CO 80237. Hearing impaired bowlers. Conducts tournaments, bestows awards, and maintains hall of fame. Publication: *The Deaf Bowler.*

National Deaf Women's Bowling Association. c/o Kathy M. Darby, 33 August Road, Simsbury, CT 06070. Hearing impaired bowlers. Promotes fellowship among participants. Publication: *NDWBA Constitution and Bylaws.*

National Duckpin Bowling Congress. 4991 Fairview Avenue, Lynthycum, MD 21090. Rule making and governing body for duckpin bowling. Sponsors tournaments, bestows awards, conducts workshops, and operates hall of fame. Publications: *Duckpin News, Duckpin World,* and *Duckpinner.*

Women's International Bowling Congress. 5301 S. 76th Street, Greendale, WI 53129. Sanctions bowling for women in twenty countries. Provides uniform qualifications, rules, and regulations. Sponsors tournaments, bestows awards, and maintains hall of fame. Supports fund to aid persons in Veterans Administration Hospitals. Publications: *Woman Bowler Magazine,* and related materials.

Young American Bowling Alliance. 5301 S. 76th Street, Greendale, WI 53129. Youths, 21 years of age and under. Sanctions leagues, bestows awards, trains instructors, and holds championship competitions. Publications: *New YABA World,* and related materials.

Boxing

NATIONAL ORGANIZATIONS in the United States promote amateur boxing to help young people develop their bodies and build character. Members of groups such as the Police Athletic League, the Boys' Club of America, and various civic organizations see the sport as a way to help youngsters express themselves and develop self-confidence. Although professional boxing gets most of the media coverage, there are far more participants who compete in amateur sport because they enjoy it.

Boxers require hours of training and conditioning before it is safe to commit to the brief period spent in the ring. Calisthenics, roadwork, and training with specialized equipment under the supervision of a qualified instructor, build the strength and stamina needed to compete. A family doctor can help you establish a fitness program that best fits your particular needs.

History

Ancient Greek fighters wore leather thongs bound around their fists and forearms to protect hands and wrists. Things turned ugly when the Greeks and Romans began to use metal studs or spikes on the thongs, resulting in fights to the death. Such practices waned quickly with the fall of the Roman Empire early in the Christian era.

Modern boxing evolved from bare-knuckle fighting done in England during the seventeenth century. A champion fighter would challenge all comers to a fight. A crowd of spectators would form a loose circle by holding a length of rope. If a man wanted to accept the challenge, he would toss his hat into the ring. Bets were placed, and the winner would share in the winnings, or prize money. The rise of London as a major city gave birth to the prize fight. Prize fighters were champions of different sections of the city. Their admirers were willing to bet that the champions could beat one another and arranged fights to settle the issues. At first there were few rules. Wrestling was permitted and it was common practice to hit a man who was down. A champion named James Figg emerged, followed in the 1730s by Jack Broughton. Broughton introduced a set of more civilized rules that governed boxing until 1838 when the London Prize Ring rules took their place. These rules provided for a ring twenty-four feet square and bounded by ropes. When a fighter went down, the round ended. He was helped to his corner. Time was called after thirty seconds and if he could not get unaided to a mark in the center of the ring in eight seconds, he was declared "not up to scratch" and lost the fight. These rules governed fighting in England and America for over fifty years.

In 1867 rules were changed by John Graham Chambers to eliminate bare knuckle fighting by requiring the use of padded gloves. In addition, wrestling was declared illegal, three minute rounds were established, and the ten second knockout count was introduced. John Sholto Douglas, Marquess of Queensberry, lent his name to Chambers' rules so that they would be associated with the nobility.

In America, John L. Sullivan was considered to be the world's heavyweight champion under the old London rules. In 1889 he fought and won his last bare knuckle fight, a seventy-five round match. After the match Sullivan converted to the new Queensberry rules and lost to Jim Corbett in 1892.

Today, amateur boxing is governed by the United States of America Amateur Boxing Federation, established in 1980 through the joint efforts of the Amateur Athletic Union, Golden Gloves, U.S. Armed Forces, and the Police Athletic League. More details are given in the bibliography.

Scoring

In open class amateur boxing, contests consist of three rounds of three minutes duration, with one minute intervals between each round. The length of rounds is reduced to two minutes for younger boxers.

Participants score points for the number of blows landed on the opponent. Each blow to have scoring value must, without being blocked or guarded, land directly with the knuckle part of the closed glove of either hand on any part of the front or sides of the head or body above the belt. Nonscoring blows include blows landing on the arms and those that merely connect, without the weight of the body or shoulder. One point is awarded for three scoring blows. Points are deducted when the boxer commits a foul, such as striking a blow below the belt line. If the winner of the round fouled, the opponent gets one point. If the loser of the round fouled, a point is subtracted from the loser. A contest is marked for each round by five judges. At the end of the bout, each judge totals the points and nominates a winner. The boxer who has been awarded the decision by a majority of the judges is declared the winner.

A boxer may also win if: the opponent is down and fails to box within ten seconds; the opponent retires due to injury or other causes; the referee judges the opponent to be outclassed or receiving excessive punishment; the opponent has been knocked down for a compulsory count of eight on three occasions in one round, or four times in the bout; the opponent has been disqualified or doesn't appear within three minutes of the announced start of the bout.

Rules

Each competitor is entitled to one coach and one assistant coach. Only one coach may enter the ring between rounds, and neither may remain on the ring apron during a round. A coach may retire his boxer by throwing a sponge or towel into the ring, or mounting the ring apron, except when the referee is counting.

The referee enforces rules and maintains control of the contest. He uses three commands: "Stop" when ordering the boxers to stop boxing; "Box" when ordering them to continue; "Break" when boxers have restricted one another by entrapment of their opponent's arms (clinch). Upon the break command, each boxer shall step back before continuing boxing. A referee may caution a boxer or stop the boxing to issue a warning to a boxer against fouls or for any other reason in the interests of fair play, or to ensure compliance with the rules. He has the power to disqualify a competitor and end the bout. Examples of improper actions that constitute a foul include: tripping, kicking, butting with the head, hitting with an open glove, holding an opponent, hitting a downed opponent, and hitting during the break after a clinch. Coaches can contribute fouls to their boxer by actions such as coaching from the corner during progress of a round.

Equipment

In amateur boxing the contestant must wear a sleeveless athletic shirt and a pair of loose fitting trunks. Shoes must be of soft material, without spikes or heels. Safety equipment includes an approved headguard, a foul-proof protection cup, and a fitted mouthpiece.

The hands are protected by an approved cotton gauze wrapping, over which approved gloves are worn. Competition organizers provide boxing gloves. Gloves weigh ten ounces for open category boxers in the 106–156 pound weight class. Open category boxers and junior olympic boxers use twelve-ounce gloves in the 165–201 pound weight class.

The boxing ring is from sixteen to twenty feet square within the ropes. The apron of the ring floor extends beyond the ropes a minimum of two feet. Four ropes define the ring area. They are spaced from eighteen to fifty-four inches above the ring floor. The floor is padded with foam rubber, or equivalent, and covered with canvas or similar material.

Strategy

A boxer attempts to land as many blows on his opponent as possible while minimizing the number received. To that end certain classic offensive and defensive actions have evolved.

When assuming the boxing stance, (for a right-handed person) hold the left hand forward at about shoulder height. Position the right hand to the right of the jaw. Keep both elbows close to the body to protect the ribs. Position the left leg forward, foot flat on the floor. Position the right leg rearward, weight on the ball of the foot. Assume a well-balanced position. The stance provides a starting position from which you may quickly move forward, back, circle or launch a blow.

When throwing a left jab, the boxer steps ahead with the left foot and snaps the left fist out in a straight line. This puts the weight of the body behind the punch. You follow through with the blow, in effect punching through the target and quickly return to the onguard, or stance position.

During the delivery of a straight right, shift the weight to the right foot as the body rotates, again using the weight of the body to increase the force of the blow.

The left hook differs from the left jab in that the boxer pivots on the left foot and moves the left shoulder forward to add force to the punch.

By flexing the knees slightly while delivering a punch in an upward arc an uppercut is delivered. When aiming this punch at an opponent's chin, a boxer is vulnerable to a counterpunch coming under the boxer's raised punching arm.

Boxers use certain techniques to block or avoid an opponents blow. They may lean and step forward, or move back to duck a punch. The head may be moved to the left or right to slip a punch. If a punch to the head can't be slipped, then the head should be moved in the same direction as the punch to roll with the punch.

The defensive position of the stance enables a boxer to deflect oncoming punches with forearms or gloves. Done skillfully, the opponent will have an arm extended and open to a counterpunch. Another ploy is to begin to throw a punch (feint) drawing an opponent out of the defensive position, then follow through with a different punch to an unguarded area. When all else fails, the opponent's arms are restrained in a clinch.

Bibliography

REFERENCE BOOKS

Bernstein, Al. *Boxing for Beginners.* Chicago: Contemporary Books, 1978. A professional boxer's view of boxing techniques and training.

Bodak, Chuck, with Neil Milbert. *Boxing Basics.* Chicago: Contemporary Books, 1979. Outlines the fundamentals of boxing including psychological preparation, physical conditioning, strategies, and ring psychology.

Carson, Julius McClure. *Winning Boxing.* Chicago: Contemporary Books, 1980. A noted professional trainer describes preparation for boxing, techniques, and strategy. Emphasis is on advanced amateur and professional boxing.

Cokes, Curtis, with Hugh Kayser. *The Complete Book of Boxing: For Fighters and Fight Fans.* Palm Springs, CA: ETC, 1980. The training, techniques, strategy, and equipment for boxing. Written by a former welterweight champion.

Gorn, Elliot J. *The Manly Art: Bare-Knuckle Prize Fighting in America.* Ithaca, NY: Cornell University, 1986. The lives and times of the great American bare-knuckle champions, describing not only their fights, but also the street culture that supported the ring.

Oates, Joyce Carol. *On Boxing.* Garden City, NY: Dolphin/Doubleday, 1987. A study of the motivations, attitudes, and skills of boxers. An overview of the sport.

Poliakoff, Michael B. *Combat Sports in the Ancient World: Competition, Violence, and Culture.* New Haven, CT: Yale University, 1987. An in-depth look at the roots of fighting, including boxing and wrestling.

Sullivan, George. *Better Boxing for Boys.* New York: Dodd, Mead, 1966. How boys eight to fourteen can learn to box skillfully and correctly. Well illustrated.

White, Jess R., ed. *Sports Rules Encyclopedia.* 2nd ed. Champaign, IL: Leisure, 1990. Covers boxing rules.

PERIODICAL

Ring. G. C. London Publishing Associates, Box 48, Rockville Center, NY 11571.

ASSOCIATIONS

Golden Gloves Association of America. 3535 Kenilworth Lane, Knoxville, TN 37914. Civic organizations, newspapers, radio and television stations, police groups, church groups, and boys' clubs that conduct amateur boxing matches on local, regional, state, and national levels. Publication: Newspaper.

International Veteran Boxers Association. 35 Brady Avenue, New Rochelle, NY 10805. Former professional and amateur boxers and other interested individuals united to raise funds for former boxers in need. Maintains museum and hall of fame. Bestows awards. Publications: *Boxing Digest, Boxing World, Punch Lines, Reporter, Ring Magazine,* and *Scoop's Corner.*

United States Amateur Boxing. 1750 E. Boulder Street, Colorado Springs, CO 80909. Administers, develops, and promotes Olympic-style boxing at local, regional, and national levels. Sponsors national and international meets, selects teams for international events including the Olympics, World Championships, and Pan American Games. Conducts national training camps for top boxers and sponsors clinics for coaches and other officials. Publications: *At Ringside, Boxing USA, Official Rules,* and related material.

Camping

CAMPING IS THE ULTIMATE PASTIME for lovers of the outdoors. It's often associated with other sports such as hiking, hunting, and fishing. Campsites in the United States range from the primitive to those in commercial trailer campgrounds with hot showers and other amenities. Finding suitable campsites available to the public takes some investigation and planning. Permission must be sought for use of uninhabited private land. Most private land, both primitive and improved for camping, is only available for a fee. Organizations such as The National Campers and Hikers Association provide members with information on such campsites, as well as on routes, equipment, and related issues. Millions of campers turn to another valuable resource—the facilities available in many public parks.

Public Park and Forest Areas

National Parks

The national parks are under the jurisdiction of the U.S. Department of the Interior. There are more than 100 of them, many with facilities that should suit any camper. They range from the wooded campgrounds near the rock-bound coast of Acadia National Park in Maine to those in the Chihuahuan Desert, and the Rio Grande Canyon of Big Bend National Park in Texas. You can camp by the water at Cinnamon Bay in the Virgin Islands or deep in the rugged wilderness of the parks in Alaska.

Most campsites are available on a first-come, first-served basis, but many sites are available by reservation. Depending on the camping area, reservations are made with a park concessionaire, or in some cases with the park directly.

Some parks also provide unimproved regions for your use. Camping in the remote back-country of a park requires more preparation than other camping. Most parks require that you pick up a back-country permit before your trip so rangers will know of your plans and be able to talk them over with you. You will be expected to stay on trails, pack out all trash, and obey fire regulations. Be prepared for sudden and drastic weather changes. Carry a topographic map or nautical chart when necessary, and carry plenty of food and water.

If you aren't into solitude, some national parks offer a wide range of special activities for visitors. In many parks evening programs are given in main camping areas at outdoor amphitheaters or around a campfire.

Most states have some state parks that provide camping facilities. They're usually shown on highway maps. It's a good plan to reserve a site in advance. Other state-run potential camping sites include state forests or wildlife management areas. Availability will vary considerably. Such areas are more difficult to find. Check state headquarters for directions.

National Forests

The National Forest Service is under the jurisdiction of the U.S. Department of Agriculture. The national forests cover 191 million acres of public land in all but seven states throughout America. The system includes 156 national forests and grasslands administered by 630 ranger district offices.

Almost all national forest system lands are available for outdoor recreation, which often occurs along with other uses of the forests. There are minimum restrictions, most of which are necessary to ensure the safety and enjoyment of the user and to protect the environment. Meeting the nation's increasing demands for recreational opportunities such as camping and backpacking in a pleasing forest environment is a major aim of forest land managers. More than forty-one million persons use the developed campgrounds on these public lands each year. Camping accounts for over one-quarter of all recreational activities in the national forests and national grasslands. The national forests have over 106,000 miles of trails, and over 10,000 recreation sites, which include 6,000 campgrounds. Picnic areas, ski areas, and visitor centers are also provided. Although no two campgrounds are identical, you can expect certain basic things at most of them. Privacy is one, if you wish it. Campgrounds are blended into the landscape to preserve the forest atmosphere, and shrubs and trees serve to screen camping units. Each unit has a place to park, a cleared spot for a tent, a fire grate, and table and benches.

Approximately 17 percent of all national forest land, or thirty-two million acres, is congressionally-designated wilderness. These areas offer outstanding opportunities for a more primitive type of recreation experience amid some of the county's most spectacular scenery. If you've never camped, join an experienced camper for your first camping trip into the woods, or study camping magazines and books.

Write to the National Forest Service for a United States map showing the locations of national forests and the addresses of the regional field office headquarters. For further information about national parks or national forests consult your telephone directory. A toll free number for the Federal Information Center is listed under U.S. Government.

Equipment

You will want to consider using a tent unless you're planning to rough it in a sleeping bag without further shelter. Tents vary in size, shape, materials, and weight. Cabin or dome tents are popular with families. Backpackers or camping cyclists prefer light-weight tents such as the various styles of hoop tents or tube tents. Tube tents are light, but they are open at the ends, so they tend to let in rain. Look for a tent made of water-repellent and breathable materials such as taffeta nylon. Breathable fabrics minimize condensation and improve air circulation inside the tent. Examine tent features at sporting goods stores, army surplus stores, and in camping magazines.

Use a ground sheet to minimize dampness when sleeping on the ground. Special sheets are made for the purpose, but the 4-mil plastic used for drop cloths when painting also works. An air mattress placed over the ground sheet provides some insulation from the cold ground and smoothes outs the bumps.

Sleeping bags are used to conserve body heat. Select a bag having insulating qualities appropriate for your intended use. If too well insulated, you will perspire, and the dampness will make you feel cool and uncomfortable. Most bags have strategically placed zippers that enable the user to open a zipper partway to adjust the ventilation to suit changing temperatures. Some mummy-type bags fit the body closely. They are best for backpackers because

less material means less weight. Looser fitting bags are preferred by many, but your body has to warm a larger volume of air in the bag.

The camping environment is a major factor in planning your food and water supplies. In primitive remote areas the emphasis will be on light-weight freeze-dried foods and ample supplies of water. In extreme cases, the prior establishment of caches of food and water may be required. Campfires are prohibited in many forested areas during dry seasons of the year. This calls for pre-cooked or dried foods. Water requirements are dependent on daily temperatures, humidity, and the amount of exercise performed. Just be sure to carry enough to avoid dehydration. Consult books such as *The Complete Walker III,* by Colin Fletcher for more detailed information about camping accessories and supplies.

Campsite

Select your campsite during daylight hours. Look for level ground, without rocks or other debris, that is relatively free of insects. Make sure the site has good drainage, being especially careful not to select a low area in the path of a drainage channel. Avoid camping under trees with dead branches that may fall in a high wind. If a fire is used for warmth or cooking, be sure to surround it with rocks, or start it in a trench, keeping flammable materials well away from the area. Avoid making large fires that can damage the environment, make your campfire just large enough to serve your purpose. Thoroughly water the embers and/or cover them with dirt when leaving camp. Follow proper sanitation procedures, select a spot well away from camp to eliminate bodily wastes. Avoid water sources or drainage channels. Dig or scrape away the soil before use and bury wastes after use. Burn garbage, and carry out refuse that will not burn. During the night, or while away from camp, store food supplies in tightly closed containers that can be hung by a rope from a tree so that they will not attract hungry animals. If no trees are available bury the container or take it with you.

Bibliography

REFERENCE BOOKS

Fishbein, Seymour L., ed. *Wilderness U.S.A.* Washington, DC: National Geographic Society, 1973. An illustrated overview of wilderness areas highlighting national parks and national forests.

Fletcher, Colin. *The Complete Walker III: The Joys and Techniques of Hiking and Backpacking.* 3rd ed. New York: Knopf, 1984. Extensive coverage of equipment and techniques useful to a camper.

Lyttle, Richard B. *The Complete Beginner's Guide to Backpacking.* Garden City, NY: Doubleday, 1975. Covers camp shelter and cooking techniques.

Off the Beaten Path: A Guide to More Than 1,000 Scenic and Interesting Places Still Uncrowded and Inviting. Pleasantville, NY: Reader's Digest, 1987. Identifies the availability of camping facilities for each of the places listed.

Perry, John, and Jane Greverus Perry. *The Sierra Club Guide to the Natural Areas of New England.* San Francisco: Sierra Club Books, 1990. One of a series of guides about natural areas for campers, hikers, and others who enjoy the outdoors. Identifies areas that permit camping.

Robertson, Dave, and Dr. June Francis. *National Parks: The Family Guide.* Pt. Roberts, WA: On Site!, 1991. Focuses on the national parks' exceptional recreational and educational opportunities. Covers national parks by state.

Roth, Wendy, and Michael Tompane. *Easy Access to National Parks.* San Francisco: Sierra Club Books, 1992. A Sierra Club Guide describing park access for people with disabilities.

Wolverton, Ruthe, and Walt Wolverton. *Thirteen National Parks with Room to Roam.* Bedford, MA: Mills & Sanderson, 1990. A selection of national parks that are uncrowded, yet offer a variety of outdoor activities. Describes camping facilities.

Woodall's Campground Directory: 1992 North American Edition. Lake Forest, IL: Woodall, 1992. Provides information by state for the U.S., and by province for Canada. Describes topography, climate, travel information sources, popular attractions, and events. Emphasis is on campground identification and description.

PERIODICALS

Camping and RV Magazine. Box 337, Iola, WI 54945.

National Park Guide. Prentice Hall Travel Directories, 15 Columbus Circle, New York, NY 10023–7706.

ASSOCIATIONS

American Camping Association. 5000 State Road 67 N., Martinsville, IN 46151. Professionals and others interested in organized summer camp. Conducts educational programs, maintains library, and bestows awards. Publications: *Camping Magazine,* and related materials.

National Campers and Hikers Association. 4804 Transit Road, Bldg. 2, Depew, NY 14043. Family campers and hikers. Members exchange information on routes, campsites, equipment, and related issues. Assists in teaching college and YMCA courses in camping and outdoor recreation. Publication: *Camping Today.*

North American Family Campers Association. 16 Evergreen Terrace, North Reading, MA 01864. Families interested in camping. Informs members about camping areas, equipment, and techniques. Sponsors camping shows, clinics, competitions, and workshops. Publication: *Campfire Chatter.*

Carpentry

IF A PERSON CAN READ A BLUEPRINT, understand basic mathematics, and has learned woodworking, he or she has the knowledge and skills required to do basic carpentry. Of course this assumes the necessary physical stamina and tenacity to stick with the job. (See the section in this text on "Woodworking" for further recommendations regarding training and additional reference material.)

Most people get their first exposure to carpentry during minor renovation projects. To do renovation properly the carpenter must know what lies beyond the floor, wall, or ceiling. Once acquainted with standard construction practices the worker will know how to change wall framing to add a window or close off a door.

Basic House Construction

Let's begin at the foundation and describe the construction of a typical residence. See Figure 1. A sill is bolted to the foundation wall. Floor joists are nailed to the sill and to support girders when required. A sub-floor is nailed to the floor joists. It may be one-inch boards or plywood. Wall frames are nailed together on the sub-floor. The sole plate, studs, one top plate, and any rough opening pieces are assembled, raised into position and nailed through the sub-floor into the joists. The second top plate is nailed in place and ceiling joists are added. Rafters are then nailed to the plates and the ridge board. The walls and roof may be sheathed with a variety of materials. Wood boards may be found in older construction. Plywood is the normal choice for roofs; plywood, insulating board, and other composites are choices for the outer walls. Various materials are applied to finish exterior walls ranging from wood or aluminum siding to brick, stone, or cedar shakes.

House framing is done with standardized materials. Framing lumber is specified in inches in its unseasoned rough state. A two-by-four-inch stud will measure 1½-by-3½ inches when it has been dried and surfaced ready to

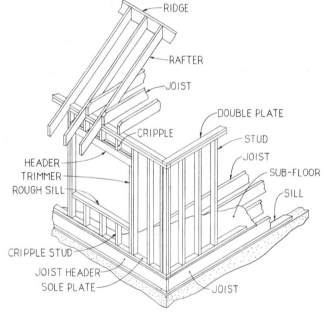

Figure 1
Typical wood frame house construction.

use. A two-by-twelve-inch floor or ceiling joist used for long unsupported spans will actually measure 1½-by-11½ inches ready to use. Nail sizes are specified in penny units. A two penny (2d) nail is one inch long. Nail size increases one penny for each additional ¼ inch. Studs are often fastened with 8d and 10d common nails. Other framing joints may require 10d or 16d lengths.

Planning a Renovation

When renovating a house for your own use, make changes to fulfill family needs. Be sure the needs are of reasonable duration. Many finished basements remain unused because they weren't needed. Add plenty of storage space when remodeling. Older homes often have too little closet or cabinet space.

Start a renovation project by establishing your plan. The least expensive renovation is one in which features are removed. Suppose you wish to eliminate a dark hallway or enlarge a living space by removing a partition. Determine whether the partition is load bearing, whether it supports the structure above. If the ceiling joists are joined above the partition or the joists above it have a particularly long unsupported span, you will probably not be able to remove the partition completely. Seek professional advice at this point. Other considerations that affect partition removal include any heating ducting, plumbing, or electrical lines that may be present in the wall. They may have to be rerouted. If the partition is not load bearing, remove the plaster or plasterboard and the studs and refinish the adjoining walls, floor, and ceiling where the partition was previously attached.

When installing a new partition, proceed as described for exterior walls. Nail the partition together on the floor if possible, providing the rough openings as required for doors or other openings. Normal stud spacing is sixteen inches. This is used to accommodate standard panel dimensions of forty-eight-inch widths. In some construction twenty-four-inch stud spacing may be found.

Door frame units with the door hinged and mounted and window units ready to install are available. The supplier will furnish rough opening dimensions needed when framing the wall or partition.

When planning closet construction consider any built-ins you may wish to add to the adjacent room. A built-in bookcase installed flush with the wall will extend into the next room and can be hidden in a closet. Built-ins of this type are mounted in wall framing much the same as a door. The more precise craftsmanship needed to fabricate the bookcase will draw upon your experience with woodworking jobs.

It follows that the experience gained during renovation jobs can be applied to house construction. If you are like many Americans, you may wish to volunteer your carpentry skills to help others. Contact Habitat for Humanity International for more information. A side benefit from this volunteer activity is that you learn techniques applicable to your own future projects. Knowledge of proper construction methods is also useful when evaluating a house you wish to buy.

Another source of building information known to many is your TV set. Popular network shows include "This Old House," "Home Again," and "Hometime."

Planning House Construction

If the construction of an entire house is contemplated take the time to do exhaustive research. Review relevant litera-ture geared to the owner-builder. A selection of books and periodicals will be found in the bibliography. New titles continue to be released as publishers try to keep up with the needs of the thousands of Americans who design and build their own homes each year. A good, efficient floor plan is difficult for the layman to visualize. Visit open houses and the houses of friends and neighbors and make a sketch of what you like. If you don't mind being obvious, take along a tape measure and measure what you have seen. If you purchase a prefab or precut house package, the architectural work has been done for you. If you design it yourself, you will probably save money by paying an architect to critique it.

Consider the effect of your plan upon the exterior style of the house. Exterior style may be dictated by the surrounding neighborhood. Neither you, nor your neighbors, would want a geodesic dome house built between a pair of Cape Cod houses in New England, for example.

Be sure to check local ordinances and union attitudes. Ask for information on local building codes before starting major projects. You may find that local restrictions prevent the project entirely. For example, location of structures and fences is often specified in some detail and you must comply.

Permits and Inspections

Once you have drawn your renovation plan, you can apply for a building permit. This is required before starting construction or renovation in most communities. The local official will require a description of the work to be done and an estimate of the cost. A drawing of the proposed project will often be needed. You may need to request inspection of the work in progress. This is particularly true of electrical and plumbing work before it is hidden by walls. A final inspection is made when the job is completed.

Doing It Yourself

Large municipalities may require that your work be done by a licensed contractor. In this case you can sometimes make an arrangement with the contractor permitting you to do some of the work. The contractor will then see to the building inspection. Significant savings can be realized with this approach. When dealing with skills you don't care to master, look for ways that you can help, such as boring holes for the electrician.

If you do have the freedom of choice, decide what to do yourself and what to contract to others. Many people prefer to have the house shell put up by a contractor and finish the interior themselves. When the detailing of the interior begins, things slow down. Since over 60 percent of the construction cost of a house is labor, you can put a lot of "sweat equity" into a house to reduce costs. There are additional advantages to building or renovating your house besides the obvious dollar savings. You know that the best materials are being used and that you didn't stint on the insulation thickness or lumber quality. You can add features due to the savings realized on labor costs.

A few final thoughts on do-it-yourself building. Move in as soon as practical. The remaining work will go faster if you live on the site. Whether you are working on a new house or old, the do-it-yourselfer will find that this is a pastime that satisfies the creative urge to a degree that few hobbies can match.

Tools and Materials

Most carpentry work can be accomplished with the tools specified under the "Woodworking" section in this text. There are, however, a few additions that are needed to assure a square and true structure. You will need a framing (or rafter) square, a level (twenty-four-inch size is convenient) and a plumb bob. These tools are available in aluminum which minimizes corrosion and weight.

Consult the yellow pages of your telephone directory for suppliers of materials and special tools that may be needed. Tool rental should be considered for seldom used, high priced tools and equipment. Most dealers will be happy to answer your questions and supply how-to books and literature about their products.

Bibliography

REFERENCE BOOKS

Ball, John E., and John Leeke. *Carpenters and Builders Library.* 4 v. rev. ed. New York: Macmillan, 1991. Hand and power tools, framing, joinery, mathematics, plans, and specifications.

Birchard, John. *Make Your Own Handcrafted Doors and Windows.* New York: Sterling, 1988. Setting up shop, doors, windows, installation, maintenance, and finishing.

Harrison, Henry S. *Houses: The Illustrated Guide to Construction, Design and Systems.* 2nd ed. Chicago: Dearborn Trade, 1991. Basic construction, materials, and house systems.

Lewis, Gaspar J. *Carpentry.* San Bernardino, CA: Borgo, 1991. Tools, materials, rough carpentry, exterior finish, and interior finish carpentry.

Litchfield, Michael W. *Renovation: A Complete Guide.* 2nd rev. ed. New York: Prentice Hall, 1990. Emphasis on renovation.

Reed, Mortimer P. *Residential Carpentry.* 2nd ed. New York: Prentice Hall, 1987. Materials, tools, practices, rough carpentry, exterior and interior finish carpentry.

Roskind, Robert. *Building Your Own House.* Berkeley, CA: Ten Speed, 1984. Detailed construction methods, foundation to roof.

———. *Building Your Own House Vol II, Interiors.* Berkeley, CA: Ten Speed, 1990. Tools, paneling, trim, floors, cabinets, decks, and stairs.

Savage, Craig. *Trim Carpentry Techniques: Installing Doors, Windows, Base & Crown.* Newtown CT: Taunton, 1989. Installation techniques.

Wagner, Willis H. *Modern Carpentry.* Rev. ed. South Holland, IL: Goodheart-Willcox, 1987. General coverage, tools, materials, and construction techniques.

Wing, Charlie. *The Visual Handbook of Building and Remodeling: The Only Guide to Choosing the Right Materials & Systems for Every Part of Your Home.* Emmaus, PA: Rodale, 1991. Design, site, construction methods, and materials.

PERIODICALS

Better Homes and Gardens Building Ideas. Meredith Special Interest Publications, 1716 Locust Street, Des Moines, IA 50336.

Better Homes and Gardens Remodeling Ideas, Meredith Special Interest Publications, 1716 Locust Street, Des Moines, IA 50336.

Family Handyman, Home Service Publications, Inc., 7900 International Drive, Suite 950, Minneapolis, MN 55425.

Fine Homebuilding, Taunton Press, 63 S. Main Street, Box 5506, Newtown, CT 06470.

Home Mechanix. Times Mirror Magazines, 2 Park Avenue, New York, NY 10016–5601.

House Beautiful's Home Remodeling and Decorating, The Hearst Corporation, 1700 Broadway, Suite 2801, New York, NY 10019.

Old-House Journal. Old-House Journal, 2 Main Street, Gloucester, MA 01930–5726.

Owner Builder, Owner Builder Center, Box 11736, Berkeley, CA 94701–2736.

Practical Homeowner Magazine. Westar Media, 656 Bain Island Road, Suite 200, Redwood City, CA 94063.

ASSOCIATIONS

Habitat for Humanity International. 121 Habitat Street, Americus, GA 31709. An ecumenical Christian housing organization that builds low-cost housing for sale at no profit to low-income people throughout the world. Overseas assignments are for two years, but there is plenty of activity sponsored by the organization in the United States.

Log House Builder's Association of North America. 22203 S. R. 203, Monroe, WA 98272. Log house builders, professional and nonprofessional, and interested individuals. Has an apprenticeship program and operates the Museum of Early American Tools. Publications: Journal, newsletter, and apprenticeship brochure.

Cats

A SOFT, WARM, PLAYFUL KITTEN appeals to most of us. Few cat owners use similar adjectives to describe their full grown cats. A delicate, gentle, graceful, exotic, dignified, and independent feline can turn into an intelligent, clever, and infuriating tease at a moments notice. Most cat lovers share a common belief that their cat is the most loving, and delightfully complicated pet to be found, and an excellent mouser as well. (See Figure 1.)

Surveys have shown that the United States cat population, over fifty-five million animals, exceeds that of the dog. That's quite a clowder (group) of cats. Of course, it includes many kindles (groups) of kittens. Let's take a look at where the cat first entered our lives.

Figure 1
A playful kitten. Markings are similar to that of the Maine coon cat breed.

History

About thirteen million years ago a weasel-like creature called Miacis wandered the earth. It's interesting to note that both the dog and the cat descended from that animal. The cat branch evolved by way of the cat-like Ditictis. The wild cat family (*Felidae*) contains thirty-eight species. All domestic cats (*F. catus*) are but one species of the *Felidae* family. Most experts agree that today's cats are related to the African wild cat (*Felis libyca*) and the European wild-cat (*Felis sylvestris*) (no relation to the cartoon character).

As civilized people began to farm and congregate in settlements, excess grains were stored for future use. The grain stores attracted rodents, which in turn lured wildcats from their jungle habitat. The cats were efficient rodent killers, a skill greatly appreciated by mankind. The Egyptians domesticated the cat and honored the animal by creating gods with cat-like heads. They mummified large numbers of cats, some with mummified mice for use in their afterlife. Egyptian art depicting the cat dates domestication at least 4,000 years ago. Evidence now suggests that similar events occurred elsewhere at least 8,000 years ago.

Cats from Africa are known to have been brought to the British Isles by Phoenician traders and the Romans. During the Dark Ages the black cat was thought to be evil and associated with sorcery. Until the seventeenth century the Christian church made a sustained effort to eradicate black cats. Soon after, the medical profession determined that the ashen powder that resulted from the burning of certain parts of a black cat had curative properties. Needless to say, such practices had an adverse impact on the cat population in Europe until the Victorian Age, when the cat regained its reputation as a desirable household pet.

Cats prospered in parts of Asia during the difficult period in Europe. Early records are somewhat vague, but it's thought that longhaired cat breeds common in Turkey and Persia may have originated in Russia. Some very old breeds such as the Japanese bobtail are native to Japan, China, and Korea.

Cats were imported into the American colonies from England during the mid 1700s to help control a growing rat population. The American shorthair breed evolved from these cats and others brought by the colonists as pets and mousers.

Characteristics and Disposition

Many traits found in our domestic cats have been inherited from their ancestors. Cats are flesh eaters. In the wild, they generally hunt alone at night. Their graceful, almost fluid movements result from the practice of silently stalking their prey. Cats will remain motionless to avoid giving away their presence, then pounce suddenly to land close to their victim. They often use their teeth to kill by biting the back of the neck. To catch a bird, the cat will leap to bite it, or knock it to the ground with a paw. Fish are scooped from the water with a paw and killed on shore. These stalking, pouncing, and paw-batting movements are practiced during a kitten's play.

It's interesting to compare the traits of cats and dogs based on their history in the wild. Dogs lived in packs with a degree of social order that included a leader. It was natural for them to accept man as their leader or master. On the other hand, the cat was more of a loner and continues to remain aloof unless it decides to permit you to be its friend. This happens through imprinting—a process where an animal is exposed to a person or other animal very early in life and accepts the individual as an alternative to its parent. During this period, unlikely friendships evolve between cats and dogs or other animals who share the same home. When you have been accepted, cats need your affection. After a brief absence, owners often find that their cat won't allow them out of sight for a time, following them from room to room. However, a cat's independent instinct usually allows an owner to leave it for a time unattended. This makes cats popular these days when family members are often away from home at the same time.

Cats can be taught tricks by exercising patience and a soft-voiced approach. Sharply spoken commands, customarily employed with dogs, are not effective with cats. Cats are sensitive animals. They don't like roughness, noise, or quick movements. As with the dog, they are easiest to train early in life, after about eight weeks of age.

The Cat's Senses

Cats depend on both sight and sound to locate their prey. Their eyes adapt to varying light conditions in several ways. The iris can open to a full circle in subdued light, permitting them to see in lower light situations than hu-

mans. It can also be closed to a narrow slit in bright light. A second eyelid, called a haw, can be drawn upwards across its eye from the inner corner to filter light still further. Cats tend to rest their eyes, with an average of eighteen hours of sleep each day. They can hear a wider range of sounds than humans, particularly in the higher ranges. This enables them to hear the high-pitched squeaks of rodents. They also have the ability to detect the source of a sound with accuracy.

A cat's keen sense of smell also has a back-up system. A small pouch located in the roof of the mouth helps to identify scents. This accounts for the drawing back of the lips in a kind of sneer when the cat wants to check out an unusual smell more closely.

The sense of touch is aided by groups of pressure sensitive hairs. They consist of the whiskers, another set above the eyes, and a third set on the underside of the front paws. Sensitivity is such that even air pressure differences caused by nearby objects can be sensed. Three other types of hair that make up a cat's fur serve to keep the animal warm and dry. Short, thin down hairs are located close to the skin. They provide insulation. A middle coat of bristly hairs, called awn hairs, serves to protect as well as insulate. An outer coat of long, thick hairs called guard hairs protects the fur below from the elements.

Communication

Cats use their eyes, tail, ears, fur, voice, and posture to communicate. Let's look at some of the ways we can read a cat's body language. When a cat is relaxed and content, the eyelids are half-closed, the tail is curved down and then up on the end, and a soft purring may be heard. Purring is caused by air passing over a set of false vocal cords in the larynx called vestibular folds. When alert and interested, the eyes dilate, the eyelids open fully, and the tail becomes erect with tip tilted over. When provoked to anger the eyes dilate, the eyelids open fully, the tail twitches violently from side to side, and the cat attempts to look larger and more of a threat by causing its fur to stand on end with the tail fully bristled. The cat will growl or howl. When anxious or fearful, the tail will be held low and fluffed out, the ears will flatten and twitch, the eyes will dilate, and the cat may crouch low to the ground. A yowl or hiss will be sounded. It's thought the hiss imitates the sound of a snake, frightening an adversary. When a cat becomes totally submissive, the eyes may close to both protect them and shut out the oppressive scene. The tail is lowered, possibly between the legs. When in pain, a cat may produce a loud deep purr or shriek loudly.

Cats enjoy having their owners talk to them. They often respond with murmurs of their own. They don't like to be stared at, and they consider fully opened eyes fixed upon them an aggressive signal.

Standardization of Breeds

The cat "fancy," an interest in breeding and showing cats, resulted in a major cat show in London in 1871. This was followed by a similar show at the Madison Square Garden in New York City in 1895. Organizations were founded to set standards for the various recognized breeds. Judging practices and award categories were also established. Over the years the number of "official" cat associations and show organizers has increased, with minor differences in judging standards and the breeds recognized. Cat shows are usually divided into at least three parts: All breeds, shorthair specialty, and longhair specialty.

A cat's pedigree is the record of its parentage traced back for at least four generations. In the United States, there are at least eight national organizations for the purpose of registering the names and pedigrees of purebred cats. These organizations also sanction shows and record winners at shows conducted by affiliated clubs. Pedigreed cats are the aristocracy of the cat world, but they represent a very small percentage of the cat population. Cat clubs don't require that your cat be pedigreed to participate in many shows.

Ways Breeds Originate

Cat breeds originate in three basic ways. A prolonged period of exposure to a natural environment produces a natural breed. The American shorthair evolved from European cats brought by immigrants. It adapted to the free-roaming life of a rodent hunter. When the cat fancy took hold in America, cat lovers looked to the exotic, rare breeds; there was little interest in the common American shorthair. Eventually standards were established for the ultimate configuration of the American standard, and breeders selectively bred to achieve that ideal shape and color. Another example of a natural breed is the Japanese bobtail. Even though it has a tail similar to that of a rabbit, it's a natural breed that has roamed Japan, Korea, and China for centuries.

The mating of two dissimilar breeds produces a hybrid cat. Many new breeds have originated in the last half of the current century. When sufficient numbers are available to warrant recognition by registering organizations, a new breed is established. Examples include: Bombay (American shorthair and Burmese), Colorpoint shorthair (American shorthair and Siamese), Himalayan (Siamese and Persian), and Tonkinese (Siamese and Burmese).

Mutations due to genetic abnormalities have produced a number of breeds. One of the best known is the Manx cat. These cats have drastically short tails, or no tail at all. Manx cats originated on the Isle of Man where the closed environment perpetuated the breed. Other examples include: Scottish fold—has ears folded forward; Somali—is a longhaired Abyssinian; and American wirehair—has a thick, coarse, resilient coat like a sheep's wool resulting from a change in guard hairs.

Breed Colors and Behavior

Some cat breed descriptions specify particular colors for the fur, nose leather, and paw pads. The most familiar color pattern seen on cats' fur is the irregular striped and blotched pattern most often found on kittens. This is the tabby pattern inherited from the European wildcat. The name is derived from the Attibiya District of Baghdad.

Some cats are a uniform light color with darker colors on their points. Points are considered to be the face mask, legs, and tail. Examples are the Siamese and the colorpoint shorthair. Other possible color patterns include bi-colors, spotted, calico, and tortoise shell combinations.

With all of the interbreeding going on, it seems peculiar that certain breeds have specific behavioral characteristics. For example: The Turkish van cat and the Japanese bobtail love to swim. The Maine coon cat likes to play with water, and the French chartreux cat prefers the company of dogs to cats and acts more like a dog than a cat.

Selecting a Pet

When selecting a cat for a pet you have two basic choices, pedigreed or mixed breed. The pedigreed cat will be more expensive, but the behavior of the parent cats is an indication of what your kitten may become. The mixed breed can have all of the good traits, or bad traits of the parents—if they can be found. You will not know the result until much later. The average life span for a cat is twelve to twenty years, so choose carefully.

Cat behavior demands a certain amount of tolerance on the part of its owner. They like to climb curtains, snack on house plant shoots, and sharpen claws on furniture. If you provide a carpeted scratching post and a warm, safe spot for the cat to sleep, it will be happy. Longhaired cats require daily grooming with a comb and brush.

Bibliography

REFERENCE BOOKS

Anderson, Janice. *The Cat·A·Log.* London: Guinness Books, 1987. A mixture of useful reference material and fun facts about cats.

Loxton, Howard. *A Superguide to Cats.* 2nd ed. New York: Gallery Books, 1989. Covers over one hundred breeds of cats recognized by the Governing Council of the Cat Fancy in Great Britain.

Morris, Desmond. *Catlore.* New York: Crown, 1988. Covers a series of often-asked questions about cats.

Ramsdale, Jeanne. *Persian Cats and Other Longhairs.* Rev. ed. Neptune City, NJ: T. F. H., 1976. Provides information on diet, selecting and buying a longhaired cat, grooming, feline ailments, breeding and selling, and the characteristics of longhair varieties.

Richards, Dorothy Silkstone. *An Illustrated Guide to Cats.* New York: Arco, 1982. A practical guide to help you select and care for a cat. Features over one hundred breeds and colors.

Wilbourn, Carole C. *Cats on the Couch.* New York: Macmillan, 1982. A cat therapist shares her expertise in feline psychology in this book about cat care. Also covers physical health, grooming, and breeding.

Wilson, Meredith D. *Encyclopedia of American Cat Breeds.* Neptune, NJ: T. F. H., 1978. Provides a roundup of the cat breeds recognized by cat associations in the United States and Canada. Well illustrated text covers background and characteristics of each breed.

PERIODICALS

Cat Collectors. 33161 Wendy Drive, Sterling Heights, MI 48310. Cat collectibles.

Cat Companion From Friskies. Quarton Group Publishers, 2155 Butterfield, Suite 200, Troy, MI 48084.

Cat Fancy. Fancy Publications, Box 6050, Mission Viejo, CA 92690.

Cat Lover. Fancy Publications, 2401 Beverly Boulevard, Los Angeles, CA 90057.

Cat World. Cat World International, Box 35635, Phoenix, AZ 85069.

Cats Magazine. Box 290037, Port Orange, FL 32129.

ASSOCIATIONS

American Cat Association. c/o Susie Page, 8101 Katherina Avenue, Panorama City, CA 91402. Cat register. Maintains a stud book registry of cats. Sponsors cat shows.

American Cat Fancier's Association. PO Box 203, Point Lookout, MO 65726. Breeders and exhibitors of purebred cats. Maintains stud book registry and licenses cat shows and cat judges. Registers pedigreed cats. Bestows awards. Publications: Bulletin, *AFCA Parade of Royalty,* and related material.

Cat Collectors. 31311 Blair Drive, Warren, MI 48092. For those who collect cat memorabilia. Facilitates the purchase, trade, and selling of cat items, and reviews cat books. Publications: *Cat Collectors Catalog,* and *Cat Talk.*

Cat Fanciers' Association. 1805 Atlantic Avenue, PO Box 1005, Manasquan, NJ 08736–1005. Federation of all-breed and specialty cat clubs. Registers pedigrees, licenses shows, and bestows annual achievement awards. Publications: *Almanac, Year Book,* and related material.

Cat Fanciers' Federation. PO Box 389, Upton, MA 01568. Federation of local clubs who own, breed, and exhibit cats. Maintains records on the ancestry of cats, trains show judges, creates rules and standards. Publications: *CFF Yearbook, Newsletter,* and related materials.

The International Cat Association. PO Box 2684, Harlingen, TX 78551. Maintains registration records and ancestry information, conducts judging schools, sponsors cat shows and bestows awards. Publications: *TICA Trend, TICA Yearbook,* and related materials.

United Cat Federation. c/o Georgann Chambers, 5510 Ptolemy Way, Mira Loma, CA 91752. Federation of cat clubs. Registers cats, promulgates rules for cat show management, and presents awards. Publication: *UCF-Forts.*

Note: There are additional associations devoted to specific cat breeds listed in the Encyclopedia of Associations, available in libraries.

Ceramics

A PERSON WHO CHOOSES CERAMICS as a pastime can dig clay from the earth and turn it into a beautiful piece of pottery or porcelain. Clay is soft and pliable in the hands of the artisan who creates a bowl or piece of sculpture, but when fired, it becomes a material capable of withstanding corrosive agents and the ravages of time.

Unfired clay has had limited use in some forms of sculpture and architecture. Many civilizations have used it to make sun-dried adobe brick, for example. Early man lined woven hemp baskets with clay to make them waterproof and more durable. Hard clay pots have been found with the imprint of the woven basket on their outside surfaces. This leads potters to believe that discarded lined baskets had been burned, firing the clay lining. Archaeologists believe that pots have been made for about 10,000 years. Human figurines and animals were modeled in clay even earlier.

As with any work of art, the design of a ceramic piece should reflect good proportion, visual balance, and be aesthetically pleasing to the eye. A piece designed for utility should perform its function well. It should be free of excess weight, excessive transmission of heat, or other defects in design creating inconvenience to the user. American astronauts would have found it very inconvenient if the ceramic tiles covering the nose of their space shuttle didn't meet the above criteria.

The beginning potter will find that tools and supplies are readily available, and premixed materials eliminate the need for a knowledge of chemistry or mathematics. However, those who have an interest in the technical aspects of the craft will find enough to keep them satisfied. Personal computer programs are available that perform ceramic calculations. The programs help the user to deal with material incompatibilities and make firing temperature adjustments.

Working in clay makes people more aware of good ceramic practice and critical of manufactured ware. They develop an interest in museum collections and contemporary galleries.

Variations in the Composition of Clay

Silicon accounts for about 58 percent of the earth's crust. Aluminum accounts for another 15 percent. Feldspar rock contains both of these elements. All of our clay is a product of the decomposition of feldspar due to the actions of wind, water, and temperature changes. All types of feldspar contain alumina and silica combined with other elements. During weathering the other elements dissolve and the alumina and silica both remain to form clay. Such pure clay is very rare. Primary or residual clays are those that remain where they were formed. They are the purest clays. Their particle size is large, making them difficult to work (less plastic). They mature (become properly hardened) at high temperatures. Kaolin or China clay is of this type.

When feldspar decomposes, its particles are often carried great distances by wind and water, picking up other minerals and soil debris on its way. The thin layer of earth's soil contains sand, mica, mineral compounds, and organic matter. Secondary or sedimentary clays are those that have been contaminated in this manner. The action of wind and water results in a smaller particle size that makes the clay more plastic. A mixture called a clay body contains added components such as plasticizers, fluxes, or materials to open up the clay body making it more porous so it will dry uniformly. There are numerous formulas for the combinations of materials needed to achieve needed results. The applications of more specific clay types will be covered later as they relate to certain kinds of pottery.

Working with Clay

The first step in the preparation process is called wedging. The wedging action eliminates any trapped air bubbles and thoroughly mixes the various materials present in the batch. You can do this best on a sturdy bench with a wire stretched from the front surface rising to a point several feet higher at the back of the bench. Pass the ball of clay through the wire, cutting it in half. Slam each half to the bench surface and knead it. Apply the weight of your upper body while imparting a twisting motion with your hands to wring the two halves together. Repeat this sequence until examination of the cut surfaces reveals an even texture with no air holes. Production workers use pug mills to mix their clay bodies. These mechanical devices accomplish the mixing process very efficiently.

When satisfied with the mixing process, allow the clay to age. The aging process uses bacteria to break down any organic material present. Bacteria growth produces acid residues and gels that increase plasticity. This type of aging is especially important when a potter uses clay from a less controlled environment as when digging local clay for use. The ancient Chinese placed great stock in aging, often passing raw clay materials from one generation to the next before putting it to use. Some modern potters begin the aging process by mixing old bacteria-laden clay with a new batch. Some go so far as to add compost bacterial tablets to the mix.

Hand Building

You can create pottery using only your hands. Employing the pinch method you can shape a simple bowl by inserting your thumb into a ball of clay and pinch with the thumb and fingers while rotating the ball. Larger and more complex shapes are entirely possible by increasing the size of the ball or by joining shapes made separately from several balls.

The coil method enables one to produce larger bowls, bottles, or vases. Place a flat circular piece of clay on a wood or plaster slab. This will be the base for the bowl. A long rope of clay is squeezed out and rolled on the bench using both the fingers and palms of your hands. Place the rolled clay on top of the edge of the base and press it firmly onto the base, following the edge around until the roll overlaps the starting point. Continue in this fashion, smoothing and sealing the seams between coils by pressing with fingers or a wooden tool.

As clay begins to dry it becomes stiffer, gradually becoming leather-hard. At this point you can still join it to other clay pieces, or carve it. These characteristics permit the construction of large projects by the coil method, provided that you allow sufficient time for the lower coils to harden in order to support the weight of the coils above.

You can modify the shape or thin the walls using a paddle and anvil technique. Hold a curved piece of wood on the inside and beat the clay with a flat wooden paddle on the outside while turning the bowl. Once you achieve the desired size and shape, smooth the surface by scraping.

Some projects are easier to make using a method called slab construction. The clay is first formed into uniformly flat sheets. You do this by rolling or cutting it with a wire. Trim the sheets to a pattern outline and form them into any

necessary shape. Boxes are popular, but even curved shapes are possible.

When joining separate pieces of clay be sure that the pieces have a similar moisture content. Roughen the mating surfaces and join the parts together firmly.

Other techniques include shaping a slab in a mold, either by pressure or simply draping the clay over a mold of the desired shape.

You can cast clay in plaster molds. By adding water, clay becomes a creamy liquid called a slip. Such a mixture results in a large amount of shrinkage when the water evaporates. The addition of alkaline material allows the slip to flow with a lower water content. It permits the mixture to arrive at a liquid state using only about 40 percent water. When you pour the slip through a mold, it will adhere only to the mold surface. This will produce a hollow cast part.

Another approach is to use a solid cast mold. In this method the part cast is solid but usually has thin walls. When casting large pieces with thick walls, add grog (clay that has been fired then ground and screened) to the slip to provide openings through which moisture can escape, preventing cracking.

Throwing

Throwing is the process of turning clay on a potter's wheel to shape a piece. The potter's wheel has existed for over 4,000 years. In its simplest form, it is a disk (wheel head) mounted on top of a shaft free to turn on bearings. There is another disk attached to the lower end of the shaft. The potter uses it to push, or kick, with the foot to cause the wheel head to turn. Electric motors power most modern wheels.

Before placing the wheel in motion, the potter throws a lump of clay onto a flat plaster disk called a bat placed on top of the wheel head. The bat provides a convenient way to lift the finished piece from the wheel head. The potter's hands then shape the rotating lump of clay.

Suppose you want to form a cylinder, since it's the starting point for making more complex shapes. Press your thumbs into the center of the clay and allow the fingers to trail on the outside to round the surface. Draw up the cylinder walls by coordinating the action of your hands. Place one hand on the inside of the part opposite the other on the outside. You will be squeezing the wall to thin it and cause it to elongate. You manipulate a cylinder by hand or tool pressure to arrive at the elegant and graceful shapes found in vases, bottles, pitchers, and other pottery.

If you want to make a pitcher, shape its body on the wheel. Then stop the wheel and work with your hands. Using your fingers or a wooden tool, form a spout shape while the clay is still plastic. Form a handle from a separate piece of clay and attach it firmly to the pitcher body.

A bottle or teapot requires a lid. Make the lid separately, and take care to get a good fit with the pot. Special calipers are available to transfer your measurement from body to lid. They serve as your guide while forming the lid on the wheel.

Very large pieces may collapse under their own weight. To avoid this, make the top and bottom halves separately, and join them when they are hard enough to support their combined weight.

Pottery books will help you understand the workings of the pottery wheel, but it takes hands-on training from an expert, and considerable practice to master the wheel.

Decorating

Pottery is decorated by surface carving or deforming the surface by pressing a design into it. You can pierce the surface, removing parts of it entirely to create a design. Conversely, elaborate cast clay patterns are sometimes joined to the surface. This is called sprigging, a decorating technique often found on English Wedgwood ware.

You can add colored clay slip designs to a leather-dry surface by painting or trailing the slip from a rubber bulb fitted with a nozzle. These colored slips are called engobes. Their shrinkage rate must match that of the pot, or they will flake off. You can dip the entire piece into colored slips.

In a method called sgraffito, a design is scribed through the slip, exposing the color of the clay pot below. Still another approach involves the application of a wax pattern to the pot to mask the surface. The wax prevents the slip from adhering to the pot, producing the desired colored pattern.

The silkscreen process is extensively used to deposit glaze patterns before firing. Practically every piece of commercial ceramic ware is decorated by silkscreen. The screening of glazing materials is done directly, where possible, or by using silkscreened decals on complicated surfaces.

Glaze

A glaze is fundamentally a thin coating fused to the surface of the clay by the high temperature made possible by firing it in a kiln. It is sometimes accomplished during initial firing, but often as a second firing operation. The glaze process may be used to impart color patterns and/or a shiny, lustrous finish. The practice of glazing pottery is a very complex subject. Results are subject to many variables such as application conditions, oxides used, and colorants in the formulas. The particular color that develops from an oxide depends upon the type of flux used, the proportions of alumina or silica, and the firing temperature.

Before selecting or handling glazing oxides, consult a reputable text to determine whether they are toxic. Some require very careful handling.

Firing

Clays are heated to high temperatures in a kiln to harden and glaze them. The clay matures at the appropriate hardening temperature. There are several ways to determine operating temperatures. Pyrometers are available, but a bit expensive for the hobbyist. The most common temperature measuring device is the pyrometric cone. A cone is a little pyramid made of clay with fluxes added so it will melt at a known temperature. Each cone is stamped with a number indicating the melting temperature.

Cone marking ranges from 022 (1,121 degrees F.) to 15 (2,615 degrees F.). The numbers decrease as temperatures rise (022, 021, 020), then increase as they pass through midrange (02, 01, 1, 2, 3). A typical set-up used to attain a cone 8 temperature would include three cones set in a pat of clay (cones 7, 8, 9). When the temperature reaches cone 7, the cone will melt. When cone 8 melts but before cone 9 melts, you have reached the desired temperature.

Maximum temperature ratings of kilns are often given as cone numbers (fire to cone 10). The cone rating is used to relate to the firing range of various types of ware, such as cone 02 for earthenware or cone 13 for a type of porcelain.

Kilns are fired by wood, gas, and electricity. The electric being the most often used by amateurs. A typical kiln for the hobbyist complete with shelves, vent, and assorted accessories (called furniture) will cost nearly $1,000. For this reason, many amateurs depend on the use of the equipment available at ceramic classes.

Pottery Materials and Processes

Earthenware is usually made from natural clay with a high iron content, rather than from a clay body composed of several materials. It's soft and porous, requiring a glaze in order to hold liquids. Firing temperatures range from cone 08 to cone 2.

Stoneware may be made from some high-firing natural clays having a fairly plastic composition. Some stoneware clay bodies are prepared to cope with firing ranges as high as cone 8. It's hard and vitreous.

China is made from a clay body containing kaolin, ball clay, feldspar, flint, and a flux. Ball clay is usually found contaminated by organic matter, making it quite plastic. It has a high shrink rate. When used with other clays, it imparts improved plasticity, dry strength, and vitrification. China is fired to about cone 10, glazed, and refired in the cone 2 range. When decorated, further lower temperature firing is required.

Porcelain is prepared from a material mix nearly the same as china, although the flux ingredients will vary. Porcelain is glazed and fired only once to about cone 13. The result is very hard and vitreous.

Most of the above types of pottery clays can be formulated to be used for throwing on the wheel, slip casting, and hand-building sculpture.

Raku is made from a clay body similar to stoneware, with the addition of grog to enable it to withstand the thermal shock used in the process. A piece is glazed and raised to firing temperature. It is then transferred to a chamber filled with combustible materials such as sawdust, straw, or dry leaves. After a few minutes it is plunged into water.

Egyptian paste is a low-firing mixture that has minimum plasticity. The material mix causes it to become self-glazing during firing.

Safety Considerations

Ceramics can be a relaxing, creative, and thoroughly enjoyable hobby, as long as you take certain precautions. If at all possible, attend a class with a competent instructor to learn the potential safety risks. Avoid breathing dust when handling dry clay mixes. Be certain that kilns are adequately vented. Use caution when handling glaze mixes containing lead and other toxic oxides. Avoid disturbing or handling asbestos used for thermal insulation.

Bibliography

REFERENCE BOOKS

Birks, Tony. *The New Potter's Companion.* Englewood Cliffs, NJ: Prentice Hall, 1982. General coverage, emphasis on pottery wheel techniques. Well illustrated.

Casson, Michael. *The Craft of the Potter.* First U.S. ed. Woodbury, NY: Barron's Educational Series, 1979. Overview of techniques. Good illustrations.

Chappell, James. *The Potter's Complete Book of Clay and Glazes.* New York: Watson-Guptill, 1977. Emphasis on clay body preparation. Extensive coverage of formulas for clay and glazes.

Dedera, Don. *Artistry in Clay: Contemporary Pottery of the Southwest.* Flagstaff, AZ: Northland, 1985. The native potters and pottery of the Southwest.

Dickerson, John. *Pottery Making: A Complete Guide.* New York: Viking, 1974. Good brief general overview of techniques.

Kenny, John B. *The Complete Book of Pottery Making.* Radnor, PA: Chilton Books, 1949. Slightly dated, but better than most

books on the subject. Detailed step-by-step illustrations of clay handling.

McNerney, Kathryn. *Collectible Blue and White Stoneware.* Rev. ed. Paducah, KY: Collector Books, 1989. Photographs and prices for collectors.

Nelson, Glenn C. *Ceramics: A Potter's Handbook.* 5th ed. New York: Holt, Rinehart & Winston, 1984. General techniques. Heavily illustrated.

Nigrosh, Leon I. *Claywork: Form and Idea in Ceramic Design.* 2nd ed. Worcester, MA: Davis, 1986. Overview of ceramics. Well illustrated coverage of clay-handling techniques.

Rada, Pravoslav. *Book of Ceramics.* London: Spring Books, 1962. General overview. Good introductory text.

Schwartz, Marvin D. *Collector's Guide to Antique American Ceramics.* Garden City, NY: Doubleday, 1969. Discussion and photographs of antique pottery.

PERIODICALS

Ceramic Arts and Crafts. Scott Advertising and Publishers, 30595 Eight Mile Road, Livonia, MI 48152–1798.

Ceramics. Duncan Enterprises, 5661 E. Shields Avenue, Fresno, CA 93727.

Ceramics. Scott Advertising and Publishers, 30595 Eight Mile Road, Livonia, MI 48152–1798.

Ceramics Monthly. Professional Publications, Box 12448, 1609 Northwest Boulevard, Columbus, OH 43212.

ASSOCIATIONS

International Association of Duncan Certified Ceramic Teachers. 4901 W. Seldon Lane, Glendale, AZ 85302. Ceramic teachers interested in promoting ceramics as a hobby. Bestows award. Publication: Newsletter.

International Ceramic Association. PO Box 39, Glen Burnie, MD 21061. Ceramists in seven countries. Promotes standardization of entries and judging at shows, organizes competitions, encourages improved teaching methods, conducts pilot programs for the handicapped, and maintains an educational foundation. Presents awards and operates a hall of fame. Publications: *Blue Book, Trade Journal, Judging Manual,* and *Teachers' Manual.*

National Council on Education for the Ceramic Arts. c/o Regina Brown, PO Box 1677, Bandon, OR 97411. Ceramists at all levels. Gathers and disseminates information and ideas among members. Conducts lectures, workshops, traveling exhibitions, and seminars. Bestows awards. Publications: Journal, and *NCECA News.*

Coins, Collecting

A COIN IS A STAMPED OR CAST piece of metal issued by an authority that guarantees its value. The surface of a coin is usually decorated with the likeness of an important person, place, or thing. Most coins also bear inscriptions and the date of coinage. These features enable collectors to fix the coin's geographic origin and determine its historical significance; we can see and feel the past. The coin collector enjoys the excitement of discovering a rare find, the nostalgia and joy of collecting, and the satisfaction of preserving historically significant pieces. We are temporary custodians of these relics, and must properly care for them while in our possession.

How Coins Are Made

A coin is made from a metal blank that is placed between engraved dies. The design is pressed into the blank by hammering the die or exerting some other means of pressure. Some early coins were made by casting. A design was pressed into a mold of fine sand and a metal casting was made. Early artists had to engrave the fine details into a die or cast pattern that was the same size as the coin. Since about 1839 dies have been prepared by first fashioning a larger scale design in plaster of paris or wax. An exact duplicate is made in metal called an electrotype. An electrotype is a copperplated lead piece. A reducing lathe is used to create a reduced sized die of the design. A reducing lathe is a machine, working on the principle of the pantograph, that uses a point to trace the contours of the electrotype design and a fine cutter to cut away the steel and produce the reduced size die. After an engraver touches up any irregularities, the master die is used to make duplicates in soft steel that are then hardened and used to make coins.

Great care is taken during the manufacture of special proof coins popular with collectors. The coin blanks are polished before stamping, selected dies are highly polished and cleaned periodically, and extra pressure is used when stamping to ensure high quality.

Coin collectors call the front or "heads" side of a coin the obverse side. The back side is called the reverse. The obverse usually features a person or significant object. The design of both sides of the coin constitute the coin type. In the past, the value of the metal contained in a coin has often approximated the face value. Some unethical individuals would scrape or pare metal from the edges of coins to sell as scrap. Grooved or reeded coin edges discouraged that practice. United States dimes and quarters are now made with an outer cladding of copper-nickel (75 percent copper and 25 percent nickel) bonded to a copper core.

History

The first metal currency consisted of copper, iron, gold, or silver bars, ingots, or rings. Some were cast to a given size standard, but many had to be weighed to determine their value during a transaction. True coinage began about 650 B.C. Early Greek coins were made from an alloy of gold and silver called electrum. Some Greek coins are very beautiful, comparatively rare, and expensive. Roman coins are numerous, and despite their age, somewhat less costly. Roman coinage began about 300 B.C. and continued until 476 A.D. During this long time span coins were used throughout the vast Roman empire. It was not unusual for people to bury hoards of coins for safekeeping. Even today these hoards are being unearthed by bulldozers and farmer's plows.

Coins have been collected since the beginning of their manufacture. Many significant collections begun by rulers and other noted individuals have found their way into national collections. Examples include emperor Maximilian's collection in Austria, and Louis XIV's collection in France. With time, the number of countries producing coins has made it impossible to assemble a complete coin collection, so king and commoner are forced to specialize.

Getting Started

The beginning collector usually starts to collect from circulation. A United States collection will be influenced by several factors. Silver coins made prior to the beginning of clad coinage have long since disappeared from circulation. For a time, the value of their silver exceeded their face value. The most popular kind of collecting in America is to obtain all the coins of a given type by date. Most such series include a date when the number of coins produced was small. This drives the cost up significantly. For example the 1909 Lincoln penny produced at the San Francisco mint that includes the initials of the designer, VDB, in almost uncirculated condition, sells for about $440. Coin costs are a product of supply and demand, so since Americans prefer to collect U.S. coins, they are worth more in the United States. A collector can expand the search for coins beyond those received in change. You can purchase rolls of coins from banks on a periodic basis. If you have a friend in city hall, or at the local police precinct, you can go through the take from parking meters. Church collection plates are another source. When all else fails, visit a local coin shop and purchase a needed coin.

If you are interested in collecting foreign coins you can broaden your search to include a foreign currency exchange. Buy coins there as you would at a bank. Also try antique shops and coin dealers who specialize in foreign coins. Various correspondence, or pen-pal associations, match up people with common interests. Several coin collecting pen pals around the world could help one another significantly.

Specialization

Coin collectors have many options regarding the contents of their collection. When all of the dates and mint marks of a given type are collected, it is called a series collection. In a typical type collection, coins of a given denomination are collected, with each representing a series having a different face. For example, a one cent type collection might include a flying eagle cent, an Indian head cent, and a Lincoln cent. Some type collections reflect even very minor changes to the type, such as variations in the height of numbers used in the date. Another type collection approach can be applied to foreign coins. Students of history would enjoy collecting a type set of Roman emperors or English kings.

Proof Coins

Proof quality (excellent condition) coins are currently minted and sold in sets to collectors. Before 1956 fewer than 400,000 sets were produced by the U.S. Mint. The value of these early sets has escalated in recent years. After 1956 the number of sets rose to over one million, and currently stands at approximately three million. Except for sets containing minor variations in their content, these later sets appreciate very little. However, for those planning to retain their coins over a long period of time, proof coins will appreciate more than regular issue coinage. Although proof coins were struck for collectors from 1858 on, the early proofs are very rare and costly. The current value of a 1936 proof set is $4,500, since only 3,837 sets were minted.

Colonial Period Coins

During the colonial period in America business was conducted with a strange collection of foreign coins. Old worn English and Irish copper coins were shipped to America to be used, and the gold Spanish doubloon served for large transactions, supplemented by silver one-through-eight reales coins of Spanish America. The Massachusetts Bay colony had silver shillings, sixpences, and threepences made in 1652. They were struck for thirty years, always using the 1652 date to conceal continuing mintage from the British. It wasn't until after the Revolution that coins were struck in the colonies in any appreciable quantities.

Trade Coins

From about 1750 to 1940 some nations minted trade coins. These were intended to be used to facilitate trade with foreign countries. Examples include the silver trade dollars of Great Britain, Japan, and the United States. Of significant interest to American collectors were the Spanish colonial reales, mentioned earlier. A collection of trade coins would mirror the colonial expansion of the eighteenth and nineteenth centuries.

Taler and Crown Coins

A large coin called a thaler or taler was struck in Bohemia in 1486. Its great size enabled fine detail to be incorporated in the design. Its size has also caused it to be especially durable. A similarly large five-shilling coin was issued in England in 1551. It was called a crown, the name given to the fine silver used in its production. The name crown was applied to subsequent coins of a like size produced by other European nations. Today collectors refer to any large-sized coin as a crown. Beautiful crowns and talers have been made by many countries, especially since 1900, so they form the basis for an attractive and diversified collection.

Commemorative Coins

Commemorative coins display some of the great people and events of the past. The first United States commemorative was the Columbian Exposition half dollar issued in

1892. Such coins are issued in small numbers for a short time, so they appreciate accordingly. Noncirculating legal tender sounds like a contradiction of terms, but it's used to describe a group of coins issued by a sovereign government expressly for collectors. They are primarily individual coins and sets of commemorative nature, marketed at prices in excess of face value, and most often do not have counterparts released for circulation.

Unique Coins, Gold Coins, and Defective Coins

Unique coins often result from the effects of siege or war. Relatively recent examples include the Civil War stamp coins and the U.S. steel cents issued during 1943 at the height of World War II. For a brief period during the Civil War postage stamps were substituted for coins due to metal shortages. After some circulation the stamps began to deteriorate. Enterprising merchants had small coin-sized holders made to house the stamps. They featured mica windows to cover the stamp, and the merchant's advertising was applied to the back of the case.

Gold coins have a special appeal to collectors. During periods when the value of their contents exceeds their face value, they tend to be hoarded and flow in the direction of speculators, both domestic and foreign. During the unsettled conditions brought about by the depression of 1929–1933 hoarding became so common it threatened the nation's financial structure so the government ordered all gold coins to be turned in. Since the Hoarding Act of 1933, interest in gold coin collecting has increased. Today there are no restrictions on collecting gold coins.

Mints occasionally have defective coins slip by their inspection process and enter circulation. These mint errors are eagerly sought by collectors. They become especially valuable if the number of defective coins is small. Examples include double strikes, off-center strikes, or raised lines due to a cracked die. An intentional type of "error" is committed when coins are restruck to change the date, leaving a vestige of the previous date visible.

Condition and Authentication

The condition of a coin is dependent on the extent of its wear, disfiguration, corrosion, or discoloration. Condition impacts a coin's value. The American Numismatic Association (ANA) has set up a grading system to define the condition of coins:

> *Proof.* The choicest of all coins. It will have a mint luster and no "bag marks" will show. During normal mintage, coins are deposited and stored loose in bags. Slight scuffing of the coins may occur. The special handling of proof coins prevents such marking.

> *Mint State* (MS). Mint state coins are also referred to as uncirculated coins (Unc.). They are subdivided to segregate minor differences in quality. Uncirculated (MS–70) are in perfect new condition. Uncirculated (MS–65) may have very few bag marks. Uncirculated (MS–60) have no trace of wear, but may show a number of bag marks, and the surface may be spotted or lack some luster.

> *About Uncirculated.* About uncirculated coins are subdivided as follows: Choice about uncirculated (AU–55). Slight evidence of wear on only the high points of the design. About uncirculated (AU–50). Has traces of wear on many of the high points.

> *Extremely Fine.* Extremely fine coins are subdivided as follows: Choice extremely fine (EF–45). Light overall wear shows on highest points. Extremely fine (EF–40). Design is lightly worn throughout.

> *Very Fine.* Very fine coins are subdivided as follows: Choice very fine (VF–30). Light even wear on the surface and highest parts of the design. Very fine (VF–20). Moderate wear on high points, all major details are clear.

> *Fine* (F–12). Moderate to considerable even wear.

> *Very Good* (VG–8). Well worn with main features clear but rather flat.

> *Good* (G–4). Heavily worn with design visible but faint in areas. Many details are flat.

> *About Good* (AG–3). Very heavily worn with portions of lettering, date and legends worn smooth.

The above definitions are provided to describe the grading system. They are too general to be used in the actual grading process. For more detail see books such as the *Official A.N.A. Grading Standards for U.S. Coins,* by the American Numismatic Association. A reasonably priced authentication and grading service is also available from the ANA. These meticulous grading criteria may seem somewhat overdone to the uninitiated, until one looks at a coin price catalog and notes the wide variation in values determined by condition.

Collectors retain coins in the lower grades as "space fillers" until better specimens are found. As coins are replaced, the rejects may be retained for trading purposes if their condition warrants.

Investment

We have seen that coins usually appreciate in value over time. Coin values given in the various books and magazines are usually the prices you are likely to have to pay for a given coin when buying from a dealer. You will receive about one-half of that price when selling your coins to a dealer. The dealer's selling price includes overhead costs and profit. If coins are to be used as a profitable investment, you must select coins that will appreciate in a timely manner. This requires a thorough knowledge of market trends.

Bibliography

REFERENCE BOOKS

French, Charles F. *American Guide to U.S. Coins, 1992*. Rev. ed. New York: Simon & Schuster, 1991. Provides basic information about the hobby and includes illustrated price lists.

Hobson, Burton H. *Coin Collecting as a Hobby*. Rev. ed. New York: Sterling, 1986. Emphasis on analysis of the hobby. Includes ways coins are collected, ancient coins, gold coins, and listings of the most popular coins for general collections that are readily available.

Krause, Chester L., and Clifford Mishler. *Standard Catalog of World Coins*. 20th ed. Iola, WI: Krause, 1992. Comprehensive coverage of world coins. Includes numerous aides to identification, mints, associations, prices, and much more.

Stevenson, Seth William, et al. *Dictionary of Roman Coins: Republican and Imperial*. London: Seaby, 1964. An in-depth historical review of Roman coins.

Yeoman, R. S. *A Guidebook of United States Coins*. 45th ed. Racine, WI: Western, 1992. Provides history of U.S. coins, condition descriptions, and an illustrated price guide to early American coins, commemoratives, and privately minted coins.

———. *Handbook of United States Coins, 1992*. 48th ed. Racine, WI: Western, 1991. Basic information includes distinguishing marks on coins, early American coins, commemoratives, and privately minted coins.

Zimmerman, Walter J. *The Coin Collector's Fact Book*. New York: Arco, 1974. Numismatic straight talk to the beginning collector—how and what to collect, rarity, demand, condition, care, and mint marks.

PERIODICALS

Coin Prices. Krause Publications, 700 E. State Street, Iola, WI 54990.

Coin World. Amos Press, Box 4315, Sidney, OH 45365.

Coinage. Miller Magazines, 4880 Market Street, Ventura, CA 93003–2888.

Coins. Krause Publications, 700 E. State Street, Iola, WI 54990.

Edmunds United States Coin Prices. Edmund Publications, 300 N. Sepulveda Boulevard, Suite 2050, El Segundo, CA 90245–4469.

Fell's U.S. Coins Quarterly Investment Guide. Blockbuster Periodicals, 2131 Hollywood Boulevard, Hollywood, CA 33020.

Numismatic News. Krause Publications, 700 E. State Street, Iola, WI 54990.

The Numismatist. American Numismatic Association, 818 N. Cascade Avenue, Colorado Springs, CO 80903–3279.

ASSOCIATIONS

American Numismatic Association. 818 N. Cascade Avenue, Colorado Springs, CO 80903–3279. Collectors of coins, medals, tokens, and paper money. Sponsors correspondence courses, maintains museum, library, and hall of fame. Provides an authentication and grading service for coins. Publications: *ANA Communiqué, ANA Resource Directory, First Strike Supplement: Emerging Collectors, The Numismatist,* and related materials.

American Numismatic Society. Broadway—between 155th & 156th Streets, New York, NY 10032. Collectors and others interested in coins, medals, and related materials. Seeks to advance numismatic knowledge. Maintains museum and library. Bestows awards. Publications: *American Journal of Numismatics, ANS Newsletter, Numismatic Literature,* and related material.

Early American Coppers. PO Box 15782, Cincinnati, OH 45215. Collectors and dealers of early American copper coinage. Seeks to promote sharing of information and trading among members. Maintains library. Publication: *Penny-Wise*.

International Pen Friends. PO Box 290065, Brooklyn, NY 11229. Individuals in 188 countries who wish to correspond with people from different nations or cultures. Correspondents are matched by age, sex, and language. Publication: *People and Places*.

Society of Paper Money Collectors. PO Box 1085, Florissant, MO 63031. Collectors of paper money, checks, stocks, and bonds. Maintains library and bestows awards. Publication: *Paper Money*.

World Pen Pals. 1694 Como Avenue, St. Paul, MN 55108. Individuals in 150 countries aged twelve to twenty. Promotes international understanding and friendship through correspondence.

World Proof Numismatic Association. PO Box 4094, Pittsburgh, PA 15201. Individuals dedicated to the study and collection of proof coins in all metals. Information exchange for members. Bestows awards. Publications: *Proof Collectors Corner,* and *How to Order Foreign Coins*.

Worldwide Friendship International. 3749 Brice Run Road, Suite A, Randallstown, MD 21133. Individuals in 110 countries aged four to eighty-five. Goal is to assist those who wish to have pen friends at home and abroad.

Computers, Personal

A PERSONAL COMPUTER (PC) is an electronic device that accepts information, processes it in a manner we have selected, and returns it in a form that is more organized, refined, and usable than before. PCs manipulate, speed up, and extend our thinking. Computers have undergone an explosive period of development and worldwide acceptance, creating a computer generation. They are being introduced into our daily lives at every turn. They dole out money at the bank teller machine, take it back at the supermarket checkout, and tell us what's left when we receive our bank statement. They are found in homes, schools, and at the office. Let's see how all this started.

History

Man has used some form of computer for thousands of years. A significant step was taken when the Chinese and Romans developed the abacus to speed business calculations. Another benchmark event occurred when Scotsman John Napier devised a simplified method to divide and multiply. Calculations were reduced to addition and subtraction by substituting equivalent numbers he called logarithms. This development led to the slide rule, a device having numbers spaced at distances relative to their logarithms.

Mechanical devices using gears and numbered wheels followed. English inventor Charles Babbage used punched cards to operate his mechanical computer. Although his machine was not completed in a practical sense, his device had features that were reinvented a century later.

Computer technology accelerated rapidly in the twentieth century with the invention of the electronic computer. Work began in 1943 on an electronic computer that contained radio tubes and electrical components common to the period. The computer was 100 feet long, ten feet high and three feet deep. It weighed thirty tons. It required 17,468 vacuum (radio) tubes. Called the Electronic Numerical Integrator and Computer (ENIAC), it was the first general-purpose electronic computer. Although simpler single-purpose units had been developed previously, the ENIAC could be programmed with flexibility. Computers using vacuum tubes are called first-generation computers.

In 1950 John Bardeen, Walter Brattain, and William Shockley of AT&T's Bell Laboratories developed the first practical transistor. The transistor, and the miniaturized integrated circuits that followed, revolutionized electronics and the computer. Multiple circuits were combined on small silicon chips to produce microprocessor units. By the mid-1970s a hand held calculator could out-perform the thirty-ton ENIAC. Computers using transistors are called second generation computers and those using integrated circuits, third generation. Today's fourth generation computers use very large scale integrated (VLSI) circuits containing as many as 100,000 to a million transistors. Not very many when compared to the human brain which contains about ten trillion circuits.

How Computers Work

Let's define some computer terms. Hardware consists of the computer, and the input devices that drive it, such as a typewriter-like keyboard. It also includes the output equipment that the computer uses to communicate with us, such as a TV-like monitor and/or a printer. Software "tells" the hardware what to do. It consists of programs written in computer language that can be stored on floppy disks. The disks are inserted into disk drives in the computer, enabling it to perform specific tasks.

Computers contain a built-in operating memory called read only memory (ROM) that stores the instructions a computer needs to translate a computer language into it's own internal language. They also have separate random access memory (RAM) storage. This RAM storage area is used for temporary program and document storage during each operating session. A central processing unit (CPU) contains a logic unit to do the calculations, and a control unit to route the data from an input device to the memory and take processed information back out of memory and send it to an output device.

Blank floppy disks or diskettes may be used to capture the processed information for future use. They are very thin vinyl disks encased in plastic or cardboard containers. Floppy disks can be removed from their drive unit. Hard disks have much greater information storage capacity. They are operated within a special drive unit and are usually not removable.

Applications and Interfaces

Relatively few personal computers are used by hobbyists to perform mathematical calculations. The name is somewhat misleading. PCs are being used in a growing number of ways not even imagined by their far-sighted inventors. Let's look at some examples.

Word processing programs offer great convenience to the user. There is no carriage to return; you just keep typing. After viewing your completed work on the monitor, you may want to add or delete text. You type in the change you want and the previous text rearranges itself between margins automatically. You can bring blocks of text in from other documents and move portions of existing text to another location. Many word processing programs contain a dictionary used to check and correct spelling. Some contain a thesaurus for reference and a grammar checker to catch errors. Most provide automatic hyphenation.

Word processing programs are used in the preparation of letters, themes, articles, essays, books, and to address mailing labels. The quality of word processing programs and printers has increased to the point that the name "desk top publishing" has been given to the practice of preparing pages ready to be photographed and used for flyers, newsletters, and book printing.

Illustrations are prepared on the PC using drawing programs that enable the user to input lines, simulated brush strokes, and simulated spray paint.

The lines can be drawn with a hand-held pointing device called a mouse, or with a special pen applied to a graphics tablet that is connected to the PC.

Existing drawings or photographs can be captured by a scanning device, fed into the PC, and modified using the drawing program. Thousands of commercial illustrations, called clip-art, are available on computer disks. They are intended to be used to enhance your documents.

Drafting programs compatible with PCs are used to make mechanical and architectural drawings. Drafting programs use a lot of computer memory. Large drafting sheets may be printed on special plotters.

Music is processed by PCs using several accessory devices. A musical piano-like keyboard can be used to play notes that are processed by a musical instrument digital interface (MIDI) unit and fed to the computer by way of an audio circuit board. The notes can be stored in a hard disk and/or sent along to speakers to be heard. Composers find the system useful since the musical data can be manipulated by the computer or combined with other musical data. More about this later.

The computer's capability to deal with text, pictures and sounds is fully exploited in entertainment programs. Hundreds of computer games are available. Categories include: strategy, adventure, mystery, luck and skill, those involving dexterity, space, war simulation, flight simulation, and auto racing simulation. Programs construct crossword puzzles; simulate a slot machine, pinball machine or the throw of dice.

PCs have been found valuable for classroom instruction. By interacting with the PC instead of listening to prolonged lectures from the teacher, students become more involved. An interesting example teaches children to identify animals. When a picture of the animal is shown, players must select it's correct name. If successful, they are rewarded with the sound of it's voice. When tests are administered on the PC a student gets immediate feedback regarding the answers given. Normally the student would not see a corrected paper until the following day. Experience has shown that students learn best from programs that require them to deal with a simulated problem. Programs that take a drill and practice approach have not been as effective.

Some computer hobbyists enjoy working with their equipment to explore the many ways it can be used. They may look for ways to streamline existing methods or invent new ones. These users are called hackers. They sometimes make major contributions to computer technology.

When PC users input data into their computer storage disks they are creating their own small database. They can enjoy access to a world of information by connecting their PC to about 1,000 commercial databases. By subscribing to information services such as CompuServe and installing a modem unit between the PC and a telephone, the user can contact commercial databases. A communications software program will also be required.

Databases are compilations of information about a subject or a group of subjects. Examples include an encyclopedia, the Associated Press news service, library information systems, language translation, and sports information.

Examples of other information service features include the following:

Electronic mail, or E-mail, is a system that accepts a message from your computer and stores it in a "mailbox" in a central computer. The "addressee" checks his or her electronic mailbox periodically and prints any messages that have been received.

Forums or roundtables are set up for subscribers with a common interest. Members exchange views and information.

Bulletin boards are provided for specific subjects. A subscriber may place an ad to sell an item. The boards are viewed by thousands of subscribers, especially collectors.

Subscribers can also shop, trade stocks, and make reservations of all types.

Selecting Equipment and Getting Started

Visit one or more reputable dealers of different brands and ask about user groups in your area. User groups are formed by enthusiasts who have similar equipment. They enjoy keeping up-to-date on their computer brand and usually are glad to help newcomers. Read the popular computer magazines to determine the advantages and disadvantages of different models. Note the availability of repair and service facilities at the dealer's location, and the length of guarantees on the equipment. There are dozens of firms in the field, some of which import the same computer from the Orient and add their nameplate to it. Computers that are copies of equipment produced by established manufacturers are called clones.

You will find a wide price range on PCs, influenced primarily by the memory capacity and special features provided. If possible, try to establish what programs you will be using on the PC. User groups can help with this. Program sizes will determine required memory capacity.

Most printers are of three general types. Dot-matrix printers use a print head containing small pins that impact a typewriter-like ribbon. These are the least expensive units. They are also the noisiest. Print quality varies with the number of pins used. Ink jet printers deposit ink on the paper. No ribbon is used. Print quality is superior to dot-matrix. Laser printers are considerably more expensive, but print quality is outstanding.

A PC and a printer make a typical start-up combination. Software programs will also be required for the type of work you will be doing. As experience is gained, you may want to add a hard disk drive to increase memory capacity. A modem will enable you to access database vendors. A scanner will allow copying and inserting graphics in your copy. There are many other pieces of specialized equipment and they get better all the time.

Computer software is distributed in three ways: Through normal commercial channels, as Shareware, and as public domain software.

Commercial programs are purchased from retail outlets, mail order houses, or directly from the manufacturer. Shareware and public domain programs can be acquired at minimal cost by mail order or from computer clubs. With Shareware, the user tests the program before purchasing. If it is acceptable, the author is paid a specified price. Public domain programs may be distributed free by their authors, or by manufacturers as some form of incentive promotion. They may be obsolescent material no longer protected by copyright.

A typical mail order house has over 7,000 Shareware and public domain programs available. With a single commercial word processing program selling at $260 and a business program as high as $500, the low-cost alternatives are attractive to hobbyists. However, there is no free lunch.

Unscrupulous computer hackers enjoy inserting spurious computer commands into programs from sources such as Shareware and other uncontrolled sources. When these contaminated programs are inserted into your computer's memory, they scramble or wipe out your stored data. Your computer is said to have a virus. Special programs are available to detect and eliminate viruses, but new strains continue to be invented.

Advanced Systems and the Fifth Generation

Computers can be programmed using a method known as an expert system. One or more experts in a narrow field of interest supply all the lore and rules-of-thumb known on the subject. Information, such as all rules that apply to decision-making regarding the subject, is fed into a computer program, working out the logical consequences of all the rules taken together.

Rules may take the form of "if this and that happens, the result will be that." Probability can even become involved when the rules are stated "if this is above (a certain amount) when that is below (a certain level) then the result will probably be (percent likely). In a typical logic matrix many such rule statements are entered. Examples of applications for such programs include fields as diverse as medical diagnosis, computer fault-finding, engineering stress analysis, and political risk. Expert programs are usually specific and narrow in scope to keep program size and complexity within practical limits. When properly programmed, they can isolate problems and provide answers in a timely manner.

Developments such as the expert systems cause some to believe that computers can be made to think. The popular designation for this ability is artificial intelligence. In practice, computer memory capacity is unlikely to approach that of the human brain. We must tell a computer what to do; we can't tell it what we want it to do. As researchers work toward the goal of artificial intelligence, they are developing useful computer applications.

We have seen that computers can receive sound inputs from a musical keyboard. They can also accept it from a microphone, a tape recorder, or a compact disk. Practical results are now being realized with the computer's ability to convert spoken words to typed text, adapting itself to the accent and voice pitch of the speaker. Computers can accept visual inputs from camcorders, VCRs, and video disks.

There is an international effort in progress to develop a fifth generation of computers. Expert systems will be expanded and refined. The goal is to have computer memories capable of storing tens of thousands of logical inference rules and be able to make 1,000 million logical inferences per second. Additional goals of automatic language translation and improved image processing are being pursued. Although true artificial intelligence is likely to be an unattainable goal, the multi-faceted aspects of computer development are sure to continue to capture the imagination of both hobbyists and the public.

Bibliography

REFERENCE BOOKS

Covington, Phillip. *Computers: The Plain English Guide.* 3rd ed. Jackson, MI: QNS, 1991. General reference on computers and their use.

Dvorak, John C. et al. *Dvorak's Inside Track to the Mac.* Berkeley, CA: Osborne/McGraw-Hill, 1992. Broad coverage on the Macintosh computer for users from beginners to programmers.

Ferrarini, Elizabeth M. *Infomania: The Guide to Essential Electronic Services.* Boston: Houghton Mifflin, 1985. A guide to electronic information services.

Forester, Tom. *High-Tech Society: The Story of the Information Technology Revolution.* Cambridge, MA: MIT Press, 1987. PC history, Silicon Valley, and the future of the computer.

Gassee, Jean-Louis. *The Third Apple: Personal Computers and the Cultural Revolution.* Rev. ed. San Diego: Harcourt Brace Jovanovich, 1987. Overview of personal computers with emphasis on Apple Computer Inc.

Glossbrenner, Alfred. *Alfred Glossbrenner's Master Guide to Free Software for IBMs and Compatible Computers.* New York: St. Martin's, 1989. Available software, where to get it, and what to get.

Michie, Donald, and Rory Johnson. *The Knowledge Machine: Artificial Intelligence and the Future of Man.* New York: Morrow, 1985. Expert systems, artificial intelligence, and fifth generation computers.

Murray, Katherine. *Introduction to Personal Computers.* 2nd ed. Carmel, IN: Que, 1991. Guide to IBM, Apple, Macintosh, and Amiga computers. Hardware and software advice.

Stephenson, Peter. *Introduction to Personal Computers: Self Teaching Guide.* New York: Wiley, 1991. Coverage of hardware, and an overview of software. Tips on using programs.

Stoler, Peter. *The Computer Generation.* New York: Facts on File, 1984. Emphasis on the use of the computer as a teaching tool.

PERIODICALS

AmigaWorld. TechMedia Publishers, 80 Elm Street, Peterborough, NH 03458.

Atari Explorer. Jainschigg Communications, 1196 Borregas Avenue, Sunnyvale, CA 94089–1302.

CompuServe. CompuServe, 5000 Arlington Centre Boulevard, Columbus, OH 43220. (Information Service.)

Compute. Compute Publications, 324 W. Wendover Avenue, Suite 200, Greensboro, NC 27408. (IBM and compatible)

Incider-A Plus. I D G Communications, 80 Elm Street, Peterborough, NH 03458. (Apple II—Macintosh.)

MacUser, Ziff-Davis Publishers, 950 Tower Lane, 18th Floor, Foster City, CA 94404. (Macintosh.)

Macworld. Macworld Communications, 501 Second Street, San Francisco, CA 94107. (Macintosh.)

Nibble. Mindcraft Publishers, Box 256, Lincoln, MA 01773–0002. (Apple II.)

PC Magazine. Ziff-Davis Publishers, One Park Avenue, New York, NY 10016. (IBM)

PC Today. Peed, 120 W. Harvest Drive, Box 85380, Lincoln, NE 68501–5380.

PC World. PC World Communications, 501 Second Street, Suite 600, San Francisco, CA 94107. (IBM)

Shareware Magazine. PC-SIG, 1030 E. Duane Avenue, Suite D, Sunnyvale, CA 94086.

ASSOCIATIONS

Berkeley Macintosh User's Group. 1442-A Walnut Street, No. 62, Berkeley, CA 94709. Can provide information if you are interested in starting your own user group.

Boston Computer Society. 1 Kendall Square, Cambridge, MA 02139. National organization of individuals, institutions, corporations, and others interested in learning about computers. Maintains twenty-five user groups for specific personal computers and twenty-nine special interest groups on computers in music, artificial intelligence, and publishing. Makes available over 3,000 software programs. Publications: *BCS Update* magazine, and newsletters.

Capital PC User Group. 51 Monroe Street, Plaza E., No. 2, Rockville, MD 20850. An educational and support group for users of IBM personal computers and compatible computers. Encourages experimentation and research on PC use. Maintains library and collection of diskettes containing public domain software. Operates in Washington, DC area, membership is international. Publications: *Capital PC Monitor,* and membership directory.

Computer Virus Industry Association. PO Box 391703, Mountain View, CA 94039–1703. Provides information on how to identify and eradicate computer viruses. Publication: *Computer Virus Newsletter.*

Fog International Computer User Group. PO Box 1030, Dixon, CA 95620. Users of PCs united to increase the effectiveness of microcomputer operation. Provides a forum for communicating ideas and solving problems. Encourages the creation, modification, maintenance, duplication, and distribution of public domain software. Publication: *Foghorn/Foglight.*

National Appleworks Users Group. PO Box 87453, Canton, MI 48187. Acts as technical support group for users of Apple-

Works software. Maintains collection of over 1,000 Apple-Works templates. Publication: *AppleWorks Forum.*

PC-SIG. 1030 E. Duane Avenue, Suite D, Sunnyvale, CA 94086. Promotes knowledge, public awareness, and sales of share-ware software for IBM personal computers and compatible systems. Maintains library of software. Publications: *PC-SIG Encyclopedia of Shareware,* and *Shareware Magazine.*

Special Interest Group for Computers and the Physically Handi-capped. c/o Association for Computing Machinery, 1515 Broadway, 17th Floor, New York, NY 10036. Physically disabled computer professionals. Persons involved in the ap-plication of computers to aid the disabled and others interested in aiding the disabled. Publication: Newsletter.

FURTHER INFORMATION

Apple Macintosh User Groups. For the name of the Macintosh users group nearest you call 800–538–9696.

IBM User Groups. Information about IBM computer users groups can be obtained from: Gene Barlow, IBM Corporation (27–03–01), 1501 LBJ Freeway, Dallas, TX 75234.

Cooking

MANY FOODS ARE HEATED before eating to improve their flavor and kill harmful bacteria. Over the years we have developed a range of cooking techniques that work best for certain types of foods. These methods have been passed along from generation to generation. Cooking techniques have been modified though interaction between ethnic groups and benefited from the availability of improved equipment. High school classes introduce students to current culinary trends. Vocational schools teach the subject in greater depth, and offer evening classes to a growing number of adults who want to broaden their cooking skills.

History

From Plants to Animals

Mankind consumed food raw for hundreds of thousands of years. Cooking appears to have come upon the scene before 75,000 B.C. Our early ancestors ground grain, mixed it with water and ate the paste. American Indians did the same thing using corn, and it was a large part of the diet of American colonists during the seventeenth century. They called it hasty pudding. In some cultures the paste was baked, producing a flat bread. This simple method is still used in many countries.

As people began to depend upon the fields of wild grain that supplied their source of food, they grew concerned about wild animals feeding on those fields. This led to domestication of the animals both to save the crops and provide a ready source of meat. We find that pigs were domesticated about 7000 B.C., cows around 6000 B.C., and chickens, brought out of the jungles of India, soon after. As the number of potential entrees increased, mankind developed a variety of ways to prepare and cook food.

Menus from Home and Abroad

In America the Indians were cultivating crops before the colonists arrived. They showed the settlers how to grow various beans, corn, pumpkins, sweet potatoes, and squash. The settlers in turn brought native dishes with them. Examples include: sauerkraut from Germany; cookies, coleslaw and waffles from the Netherlands; chowder from France; meatballs from Sweden; and apple pie from England. Such diverse influences have formed the basis of American cuisine.

As immigrants to America tended to settle in areas with others from their native land, their former cooking styles began to predominate in those areas. The resulting patchwork of foreign influences has generated an enormous variety of cooking styles and food content in America, from the Mexican hot sauces on Texas barbecues to the seafood and chowders of the northeast coast.

Common Cooking Methods

Boiling is cooking food immersed in fluid, usually water, kept at boiling temperature (Figure 1). Bubbles will rise continually and break at the surface. Water boils at 212° F at sea level, but at a lower temperature at higher altitudes. If sugar or salt is added, the boiling point is raised. When cooking is done just below the boiling point, the process is called simmering. Meat is stewed by simmering. When meat is cut into pieces and stewed, the term fricasseeing may be used.

Steaming is done when applied heat generates steam from water within the food, or from added water. Vegetables or other foods are steamed in a covered saucepan. The food is usually kept in a perforated steamer basket placed above the boiling water. When steaming is confined within a special pressure cooker, the temperature of the

Figure 1
Boiling in water is but one method of cooking vegetables.

boiling water, and the resulting steam, rises above 212° F, speeding the cooking process.

Broiling, or grilling, is cooking by direct dry heat, usually at about 500° F. The process is usually applied to meat, fish, and poultry.

Baking is cooking by dry heat, as in an oven. Cooking temperatures will range from 250° to 500° F.

Roasting of meat can be done by dry heat or by a process called pot roasting in which a small amount of water is added to a large piece of meat and a cover is placed on the pot. Both methods require about a 325° F temperature. When water is added and a lower temperature is employed, the method is often called braising.

Slow cooking of meat and/or vegetables is also done in liquid using an electric slow crockery cooker (crockpot). Cooking times may range up to eight or ten hours.

Fried foods are heated in fat. In deep-fat frying, the food is placed in a saucepan or deep-fat fryer and immersed in shortening or cooking oil at about 375° F. In oven frying, butter or margarine is brushed on the food. The food is

placed in a shallow baking pan and cooked at about 375° F. When pan-frying, the food is placed in a skillet with a small amount of shortening or cooking oil at medium heat. Stir-frying may be done at high heat in a wok or skillet. A small amount of cooking oil is used. The food is stirred continually while cooking for about five minutes.

Microwave cooking uses very short, high-frequency radio waves to agitate food molecules. The air in the oven is at room temperature, but the energy turns to heat in the food. Because the heat is produced within the food itself, rather than being transferred from a warmer source, interior heating is complete before exterior browning and crust formation occur.

Some other heating processes are employed in the partial processing of food:

Blanching involves heating with boiling water or steam followed by plunging in cold water. It preserves color of vegetables and is used as an aid in removal of skins from nuts and fruit. Blanching is also done before freezing vegetables for storage.

In parboiling, a food is boiled until partially cooked. The completion of cooking is done by another method.

When steeping, a substance is allowed to stand in a liquid below the boiling point to extract flavor or color.

The average American family uses only about ten recipes, day after day. It's estimated that to find a better balanced and more healthful diet, you would have to sample as many as 600 new recipes to identify ten new ones that would satisfy your taste and still provide proper balance. Sounds like a pleasant hobby. If you are interested in broadening your cooking horizons, take a trip to your library. A few hours there with pad and pencil will provide recipes that will take months to try out.

In recent years Americans have become increasingly conscious of the ingredients in their food. In addition to counting calories to reduce weight, people want to decrease their intake of cholesterol and saturated fat to prevent heart disease.

In the past, man's diet was dependent upon what was available locally. Today, with modern food preservation methods and rapid transportation, we can enjoy unprecedented variety and the necessary food for a balanced diet if we know how to select the right foods and prepare them.

Cooking Hobbies

Cookbooks written before 1900 didn't contain exact measurements and cooking times. As people have become better educated, but more poorly trained on-the-job in the kitchen, cookbooks have had to stand alone to provide more information to the user. Cookbooks such as *Better Homes and Gardens Complete Step-by-Step Cookbook* explain cooking terms and illustrate equipment needed to prepare food.

If you have only been popping a TV dinner into the microwave oven, a cooking hobby can open a new field of interest and provide the added benefit of a more healthful diet. Cooking is not only the way to a man's or woman's heart, it is also the joy of the barbecue buff and an excellent hobby for a young person contemplating a career as a chef or restaurateur. Cooking hobbies include menu planning, collecting regional or ethnic recipes and cookbooks, cooking, baking, food preservation, and candy making. While many have learned how to turn out passable fudge, few have ventured into the variations available in the medium of chocolate.

Food preparation and tasting can be fun for the entire family. For example, a PTA sponsors a "dessert out." In this affair, parents bake all types of cakes, pies, and cookies. The desserts are displayed, sold and consumed in the school gym or cafeteria. Money is raised for the PTA, neighborhood fellowship is promoted, and everyone has a chance to sample each other's cooking.

Another group took an interesting approach to preparing a cookbook. Each family provided a copy of its favorite recipe. The recipes were then typed up, copied, bound and sold to group members and others as a fund-raising method.

Many prefer a less organized approach. A return to the customs of exchanging dining invitations with friends, the backyard barbecue, and family picnics all bring people closer. You also get a chance to show off your new recipes.

Bibliography

REFERENCE BOOKS

Better Homes and Gardens: Complete Step-By-Step Cook Book. Des Moines, IA: Meredith, 1978. Comprehensive illustrated coverage of cooking practices.

Child, Julia. *The Way to Cook.* New York: Knopf, 1989. A well illustrated cookbook with chapters structured around master recipes, providing detailed instruction. Recipes are grouped according to method. It blends classic techniques with free-style American cooking.

Claiborne, Craig. *The Original New York Times Cookbook.* New York: Harper & Row, 1961. Contains traditional American recipes and selected recipes from twenty different countries. It's intended for daily use in the home kitchen.

Hertzberg, Ruth, Beatrice Vaughan, and Janet Greene. *Putting Food By.* 3rd ed. Brattleboro, VT: Greene, 1982. Preparing food for storage. Covers canning, freezing, curing, and drying foods.

Hupping, Carol. *Stocking Up III.* Rev. ed. Emmaus, PA: Rodale, 1986. Preparing food for storage. Covers canning, freezing, drying, and root cellaring of foods.

McGee, Harold. *On Food and Cooking: The Science and Lore of the Kitchen.* New York: Scribner's, 1984. A treatise on the science and history of food and cooking. It covers all major food categories, providing easy-to-understand scientific explanations of the principles involved.

Tannahill, Reay. *Food in History.* Rev. ed. New York: Crown, 1988. A world history of food from prehistoric times to the present. It traces the way in which food has influenced the entire course of human development.

PERIODICALS

American Cookery. American Taste, c/o Jean Frey, 7 Park Avenue, New York, NY 10016–4330.

Best Recipes. Grit Publishers, 208 W. Third Street, Williamsport, PA 17701.

Better Homes and Gardens Holiday Appetizers. Meredith, 1716 Locust Street, Des Moines, IA 50336.

Bon Appetit. Bon Appetit Publishers, 5900 Wilshire Boulevard, Los Angeles, CA 90036.

Chile Pepper. Out West Publishers, 5106 Grand Avenue, NE, Box 4278, Albuquerque, NM 87110.

Christmas Helps & Holiday Baking. New York Times Magazine Group, 110 Fifth Avenue, New York, NY 10011.

Cookbook Digest. Grass Roots Publishing, 950 Third Avenue, 16th Floor, New York, NY 10022.

Cooking Edge. Cuisinart Cooking Club, Box 120067, Stamford, CT 06912–0067.

Cooking Light. Southern Progress, 2100 Lakeshore Drive, Birmingham, AL 35282–9558.

Land O'Lakes Collection of Classic Recipes Cookbook. Russ Moore and Associates, 4151 Knob Drive, Suite 200, St. Paul, MN 55122.

Microwave Times. Recipes Unlimited, Box 1271, Burnville, MN 55337.

Rodale's Food & Nutrition Letter. Rodale Press, 33 E. Minor Street, Emmaus, PA 18049–4113.

Simply Seafood. Waterfront Press, 1115 NW 46th Street, Seattle, WA 98107.

Specialty Cooking. Blockbuster Periodicals, 2131 Hollywood Boulevard, Hollywood, FL 33020.

Tufts University Diet and Nutrition Letter. 53 Park Place, 8th Floor, New York, NY 10007.

ASSOCIATIONS

American Institute of Wine and Food. 1550 Bryant Street, 7th Floor, San Francisco, CA 94103. Professionals and others interested in the art of wine and fine cuisine. Promotes a broad exchange of information and ideas to benefit all who care about wine and food. Publications: *Journal of Gastronomy, American Wine and Food,* and *Directory.*

Confrerie de la Chaine des Rotisseurs, Bailliage des U.S.A. (Brotherhood of the Chain of Roasters). 980 Madison Avenue, Suite 202, New York, NY 10021. International wine and food society of professionals and laymen. Stresses the interrelation between the amateur and professional. Promotes participation in related activities sponsored abroad by similar organizations. Bestows awards. Publication: *Gastronome.*

Feingold Association of the United States. PO Box 6550, Alexandria, VA 22306. Promotes the elimination of synthetic colors and flavors in food in the interest of a healthy diet. Publications: *Pure Facts,* and related materials.

International Chili Society. PO Box 2966, Newport Beach, CA 92663. Chili enthusiasts. Sponsors chili cook-offs, holding competitions at the local level, leading to state and national eliminations. Publications: Magazine, newsletter, and an *Official Chili Cookbook.*

James Beard Foundation. 167 W. 12th Street, New York, NY 10011. Seeks to honor great cook James Beard, and advance the recognition and appreciation of the culinary arts in the United States. Maintains library and bestows awards. Publications: *Food Professional's Guide, News from the Beard House,* and *Professional Reviews.*

Lovers of the Stinking Rose. 1563 Solano, No. 201, Berkeley, CA 94707. Professionals and others interested in the applications of garlic. Sponsors festivals and contests, bestows awards, and maintains hall of fame. Publications: *Garlic Times,* and related materials.

Vegetarian Resource Group. PO Box 1463, Baltimore, MD 21203. Those interested in any aspect of vegetarianism. Acts as referral and information service for members and nonmembers. Publications: *Vegetarian Journal,* and related material.

Dance

DANCE AND THE MEASURED BEAT found in music are inseparable. Some of us, like music lovers, prefer to enjoy the performance of others. Many however, would rather participate in order to experience this active, but relaxing, pastime. Dancing has been a part of the culture of all recorded civilizations.

History

Twentieth-century dance owes its diversity to the customs of many nations. Many current dance styles originated over a century ago and have remained relatively unchanged. Let's examine some of these dances and their sources.

English Country Dance

In seventeenth century England, country dancing consisted of circle dances, couple dances, and longways dances. Longways dances are performed by two parallel lines of dancers. The interactions between the two lines follow set patterns of movement developed over the centuries. In the past, dance masters each taught their own techniques and variations, making it difficult for dancers to participate beyond their own communities. Some standardization was finally achieved through the writings of John Playford. Longways dances accounted for about a third of the dances described in Playford's 1650 book, *The English Dancing Master.* Subsequent editions of the book record a continual rise in popularity of longways dancing. The final edition, in 1721, prepared by John Young, was almost entirely devoted to the longways format. As a result, many English country, or contra, dances consist of variations in the longways format.

English colonists brought contra dancing to New England. The Puritan work ethic discouraged frequent participation, but the contra open-couple style of dance was generally permitted on special occasions.

French Influence

Although the English experimented with four-couple variations of the contra during the 1600s, it was the French who developed a popular version called the quadrille. The English further refined the quadrille adding a set of figures they called the lancers. Note that these quadrilles were performed in a prescribed pattern, or set, without the benefit of a caller.

Several other dances originated in Europe, became popular in France, then made their way to America. The waltz began in Vienna, Austria in the seventeenth century. Although popular in France by the 1750s, it wasn't until 1834 that it was first danced in the United States. The polka came from Bohemia, was demonstrated in Paris about 1840, and reached the United States ten years later.

Italian Influence

The ballet began as part of the entertainment that accompanied elaborate feasts given by Italian nobility in the fifteenth century. It spread to France and then to England by way of their royal courts. Ballet was performed for the first time before the general public in 1632. The Royal Academy of Dancing was established in Paris during 1661 to train professional dancers for ballet performances.

Ballet was introduced to the American colonies in 1735. Foreign ballet companies were well received in the United States for the next hundred years. Some small scale presentations were made by American groups during this period, and local ballet training schools were in operation. Between 1885 and 1887 the American Opera Company presented fine ballet performances. It wasn't until the twentieth century that America began to play a prominent part in international ballet.

Classical ballet technique requires years of arduous training, usually beginning before the pupil reaches ten years of age. Daily practice is required to attain and maintain proficiency. A turned-out position of the legs is developed to increase the range of movement by means of added mobility in the hip joint. The training is designed to enable the body to move with agility, control, speed, lightness, and grace.

Spanish Influence

Spanish colonists introduced music to Mexico in the sixteenth century. Subsequently, performances of lyric theater throughout America included songs and dances from Spain. Development of Spanish music in South America and the West Indies was also influenced by the cultures of Africa, Portugal, France, and to a lesser degree, the local Indian culture.

The original Spanish tango is an exhibition dance performed by one person. It blends the flamenco and classical Spanish dance forms.

The Argentine tango is a couple dance in closed position. The music has a moderately slow tempo. The Argentine version has undergone considerable change since its origin in the 1880s. Different styles were developed after its introduction into France, England, and the United States. The current American version features rapid tempo changes and gliding movements made with the feet remaining close to the floor.

Nineteenth Century Expansion

The 1800s witnessed increasing popularity of the polka and waltz, replacing most contra dances. One contra-style dance that retains its popularity is the Sir Roger de Coverly, commonly known as the Virginia reel. The reel is performed by six couples arranged in two straight lines. The couples respond to the directions of a caller who directs them through various interactions somewhat like square dance movements.

Contra dance also survives to a limited extent in rural New England and the southern Appalachian region. Circle dances are performed in these areas, often in connection with square dance gatherings. Dancing couples are arranged in large circles. A caller directs their movements in much the same manner as with the Virginia reel.

Many Irish immigrants came to America during the middle of the century, bringing their native dances with them. Black Americans enjoyed the jigs, clogs, and reels performed by the Irish, and they were quick to transform them into tap and the beginnings of jazz dance.

The century saw the emergence and rapid expansion of the square dance. Elements of the seventeenth century English contra squares, the French quadrille, and cotillion came together in the American west. The new dance was called the cotillion at first. A caller was used to direct and vary the movements of four couples. The lively music used included jigs, reels, and contemporary music. A more detailed description of the square dance appears later.

Twentieth Century—Old Favorites and Newcomers

In 1900 the waltz accounted for three fourths of all ballroom dance programs. While its popularity has dropped considerably since, it continues as an important element of ballroom dancing. Other survivors are the polka, tango, jazz dance, and square dance. They have been joined by Latin-American newcomers bossanova, cha-cha, mambo, merengue, rumba, and samba.

The fox trot was introduced in 1914 by Harry Fox. It is performed to a four-beat rhythm with accents on counts one and three. The steps may be taken quick (one step per beat), or slow (one step lasting two beats). Slow steps and quick steps are combined in endless variety, but the quick steps must be combined in any multiple of two. Any combination of slow and quick (in multiples of two) steps may be made.

The lindy hop was named in honor of Charles Lindbergh's 1927 solo Atlantic flight. The dance is performed to syncopated jazz music that accents the second and fourth beats of four-beat rhythm. Although short-lived, it set precedents for the acrobatic jitterbug dances performed during World War II years, and the hustle dance of the 1970s.

The lindy, jitterbug, and other similar dances are called swing dances. Swing is a versatile dance that can be fitted to the music of the fox trot, swing rhythm, or the rock and roll sound. Jazz dance is performed to any of the popular syncopated jazz rhythms.

Dance Positions

In the closed position, both partners stand facing one another, with the lady slightly to the man's right. They place their body weight over the balls of the feet. The man places his right hand on the lady's back above her waistline and below her left shoulder blade. The lady places her right hand in the man's left hand, which is extended to his left at shoulder level. Elbows are turned downward. The lady places her left hand on the man's right shoulder. The exact distance between partners depends upon the dance and a particular figure in that dance.

In the promenade position, the partners turn toward their clasped hands so that they are side by side, still maintaining the closed hand hold.

The open position is the same as the promenade, except the clasped hands are released.

In the challenge position, partners face one another. They may hold one or both hands, or eliminate contact.

The polka may require the varsovienne position in which the man stands behind the lady to her left. Both arms are extended and hands are clasped.

In the shoulder-waist position, dancers face one another. The man's hands are placed on the lady's waist; and she places her hands on his shoulders.

Leading

The man communicates his next move to his partner using subtle pressure slightly before the move is to take place. In the closed position, the man's right hand gently pulls the lady forward, pushes her back, or turns her to one side. This may be done with pressure from the fingertips or the heel of the hand. Occasionally the hand and the arm will signal movement. The man's left hand is used in a similar manner to gently push or pull to indicate direction.

Square Dance

The square dance will be used here to illustrate some dancing procedures and terms.

Square dancing is done with four-couple sets or squares. Couples form a square, facing toward the center, about ten feet apart. The lady is positioned to the man's right. Dancers are identified by the following scheme: Couple one stands with their backs to the source of the music. Couple two stands to the right of couple one. Couple three faces couple one, and couple four faces couple two. Facing couples are called opposites. Couples one and three are head couples. Couples two and four are side couples. The person to the man's left, or the lady's right is their corner.

The above positions are home positions. Dancers leave and return to their home positions in response to the instructions sung by a caller. The caller may instruct gent two, or lady three to move according to the dance figure (pattern or set of steps) required.

Examples of typical calls follow:

Head couples forward and back. Couples one and three dance four steps forward and four steps backward.

Circle left all the way. All dancers step forward and join hands. Beginning on left feet, they step in unison to the left, facing to the left for sixteen steps to arrive at home position.

Face corners and do-si-dos. Couples face their corners and loop in a smooth continuous motion all the way around each other without changing the direction faced. They move forward and to the left of each other, pass back to back, and end facing one another.

All promenade. Partners face counterclockwise, side by side, with the man on the inside of the ring. The man places both hands in front of the lady. She places both of her hands in his, left to left, and right to right (skating position). Both walk around the set to sixteen beats, if all the way.

The caller cues the dancers with such calls, then fills in the time between calls with patter, sung in time with the beat of the music.

Some square dance teachers/callers have an experienced couple assume the number one position. They perform each figure first, then each of the other couples perform the figure in turn. This repetition enables the inexperienced couples to learn quickly.

Bibliography

REFERENCE BOOKS

Audy, Robert. *The Robert Audy Method Tap Dancing: How to Teach Yourself to Tap.* New York: Vintage Books, 1976. Step-by-step instruction, well illustrated. Includes warm up routine.

Casey, Betty. *The Complete Book of Square Dancing (and Round Dancing).* Garden City, NY: Doubleday, 1976. Illustrated instruction for square dance, round dance, and selected contras. Includes information on costumes and equipment.

———. *Dance Across Texas.* Austin, TX: University of Texas Press, 1985. History of early Texas dancing, and instructions for twenty dances.

Greene, Hank. *Square and Folk Dancing: A Complete Guide for Students, Teachers and Callers.* New York: Harper & Row, 1984. More than ninety square and folk dances are presented, with all the terms defined, calls explained, and steps illustrated.

Keller, Kate Van Winkle, and Genevieve Shimer. *The Playford Ball: 103 Early Country Dances 1651–1820.* Pennington, NJ: A Cappella Books, 1990. A selection of early English country dances. Provides instruction and music. This historical work is copublished by The Country Dance and Song Society.

Kraus, Richard. *Folk Dancing: A Guide for Schools, Colleges, and Recreation Groups.* New York: Macmillan, 1962. Detailed instruction for a group of international folk dances.

Lustgarten, Karen. *The Complete Guide to Disco Dancing.* New York: Warner Books, 1978. Well illustrated guide to selected disco steps.

Morton, Virgil L. *The Teaching of Popular Dance.* New York: Pratt, 1966. Detailed instruction for a selection of ballroom dances.

Schurman, Nona, and Sharon Leigh Clark. *Modern Dance Fundamentals.* New York: Macmillan, 1972. Warm-up, exercises, and movement. Emphasis on symbols used by dance teacher and choreographer Rudolf Laban to communicate dance movement.

Stephenson, Richard M., and Joseph Iaccarino. *The Complete Book of Ballroom Dancing.* Garden City, NY: Doubleday, 1980. Well illustrated instruction for selected ballroom dances. Includes information on history, techniques, and terminology.

Traguth, Fred, and Otto Handtke. *Modern Jazz Dance.* Englewood Cliffs, NJ: Prentice-Hall, 1983. Jazz dance warm-ups, steps, and combinations. Techniques for improving strength, flexibility, and style.

Weikart, Phyllis S. *Teaching Movement & Dance: Intermediate Folk Dance*. Ypsilanti, MI: High/Scope, 1984. Detailed instruction for folk dances from around the world, with emphasis on Europe.

PERIODICALS

American Squaredance. Sanborn Enterprises, 661 Middlefield Road, Salinas, CA 93906–1004.

Dance Magazine. 33 W 60th Street, New York, NY 10023.

Dancing U S A. Dot Publishing, 10600 University Avenue, NW, Minneapolis, MN 55488–6166. (Ballroom.)

ASSOCIATIONS

Ballet Theatre Foundation. 890 Broadway, New York, NY 10003. Parent organization of the American Ballet Theatre. Offers special events, open rehearsals, and priority ticket buying for members.

Callerlab—International Association of Square Dance Callers. 829 3rd Avenue SE, Suite 215, Rochester, MN 55904. Square dance callers in fifteen countries. Has a caller training curriculum and a program of caller school accreditation. Bestows awards. Publications: Newsletter and related materials.

Committee For Handicapable Dancers. PO Box 280, Gulf Breeze, FL 32562. Square dance clubs and callers specializing in calling for handicapable dancers. Acts as a network and referral system of local square dance organizations for the disabled. Publications: Newsletter and directory.

Country Dance and Song Society of America. 17 New South Street, Northampton, MA 01060. Promotes modern use of English and American folk dances, songs, and music. Maintains library. Publications: Newsletter and related materials.

Dance Masters of America. PO Box 438, Independence, MO 64051–0438. Sponsors Performing Arts Competition Scholarship auditions, dances, and competitions. Bestows awards. Publications: Magazine, and newsletter.

United Square Dancers of America. c/o Jim Segraves, 8913 Seaton Drive, Huntsville, AL 35802. Square dancers united to provide integration between dancers and leaders. Prepares educational literature and conducts a charitable program. Maintains museum, library, and hall of fame. Publications: *USDA News* and related materials.

United States Amateur Ballroom Dancers Association. PO Box 817, Sparks, MD 21152. Individuals interested in competing in, or observing amateur ballroom dancing. Sponsors competitions, bestows awards, and conducts educational programs. Publication: *Amateur Dancers*.

Dogs

A PLAYFUL PUPPY, devoted companion, mankind's best friend—that's *Canis familiaris* for you, no matter how large or small. Dogs have adapted to their master's needs and desires for thousands of years. Just having their friendship reduces our stress, loneliness, and depression.

Early History

It is generally thought that dogs are descended from wolves. The process was initiated by man during prehistoric times, about twenty thousand years ago. Selective breeding resulted in the development of animals best suited for a particular job: large, strong bodies for pulling heavy loads; a keen sense of hearing and smell for hunting. Although evolving rapidly at first, there is evidence that some breeds have not changed in 6,000 years. The afghan hound, greyhound, and saluki remain the same today as they looked when drawn or sculptured by ancient Egyptian artists in 4000 B.C.

Once dogs became domesticated, they accompanied migrating civilizations around the world. The ancestors of the dog are believed to have migrated from America across the Bering Strait, and settled in Asia. Domestication matured there and the dogs migrated in all directions, including back across the Bering Strait to America. They were well established in American Indian cultures before the arrival of European settlers. The Indians used dogs for hunting, guarding, and pulling toboggan-like sleds.

Characteristics

Dogs are descended from pack animals. They instinctively retain the desire to socialize with a group. When a puppy is weaned from its mother and joins a family, it considers the family to be its pack.

Canine pack members are part of a hierarchy, or pecking-order. There is one dominant member who commands the respect of the others. The other members show their respect by greeting the leader warmly and imitating its actions. A puppy sees the head of a household as the pack leader. The young dog may try to assert dominance at some point. It must be firmly, but not brutally, reprimanded at the time of the challenge. If not, the dog may assume it has dominance and be a problem to control in the future.

Territorial instincts are strong. Dogs mark their territory by leaving their scent daily. This instinct to mark and defend territory causes a dog to perform well as a guard or watch dog.

Dogs communicate by their tone and type of bark or howl. They are sensitive to the tone of voice we use when talking to them. Dogs have the ability to understand as many as fifty words. They don't understand sentences, so instructions are most effective if given as clear, brief commands, spoken in a consistent manner. They also make their feelings known through physical contact and posturing.

Breeding and Showing

During the past century kennel clubs have standardized their specifications for the various breeds, and breeders take great care to meet these criteria. Dog breeding is a hobby that can also provide income. It can be done on any scale, local ordinances permitting. The investment and profit will depend upon the quality of the animals and the breed selected. As with any pet, dogs depend upon you twenty-four hours a day, so your freedom will be somewhat limited.

Proper veterinary care and grooming are essential for a healthy dog—especially a show dog. It is a good idea to establish contact with a veterinary clinic while your dog is young. They will usually notify you when necessary shots are due, and you will know where to go without delay during an emergency. Dogs often display an air of pride after grooming—head held high as in Figure 1, and a little more spring in the step.

The first dog show in the United States was organized in 1874, just five years after the first show in England. Today, several thousand shows are held in the United States annually, and hundreds of thousands of people attend. What better way to learn about the many breeds available when you wish to choose a family pet?

Dogs are compared to breed standards established by the organization sanctioning the show. In the United States this is most likely to be the American Kennel Club (AKC). The criteria for physical shape, condition and color of the coat, movement, and attitude are very specific for each breed. Over 145 breeds are officially registered. This poses quite a challenge to judges, especially when judging Best of Show, where various breeds are compared to one another.

Championship dog shows operate under AKC license. To be certified as a champion, a dog must win fifteen points at championship shows. The points are awarded by the AKC in a complex system that involves type of win, number of dogs competing, and other factors. Two of the wins must have been scored in the winners class (against other winners). The AKC issues the championship certificates. Once received, the word champion is used in the dog's title. Owners of champions gain prestige for their kennels and receive higher prices for the sale of puppies, not to mention higher stud fees.

For championship shows it is common practice for the owner to hire a professional handler to put the dog through it paces for the judges.

Training

Dog training schools provide a high level of obedience training. They can sometimes correct a dog's bad habits that owners have not been able to deal with. Some schools start training when the pup is seven or eight weeks old, others prefer to start at sixteen weeks. Training may be delayed until the dog develops sufficiently physically. For example, trainers of retrievers prefer to wait until the puppy has its second teeth.

Dogs can be trained by owners who understand that they must communicate clearly by voice and example. Keep training sessions short to avoid stress. Frequent brief sessions that incorporate lots of play and praise will ease the tension. Useful training tips will be found in books such as those listed in the bibliography.

Hunting Dogs

The training of a good hunting dog is a lengthy process. Consider the demands that are placed on a retriever. The dog must remain quiet at the hunter's side so that game will not be warned of their presence. Retrievers are trained to look in the direction that the gun is pointed so the location of fallen game can be marked. They must not react when the gun goes off. The dog starts to retrieve on command, tracking wounded game when necessary. Retrievers are often required to jump into cold water and swim to fallen game. They are taught to minimize damage to game during retrieval, to have a "soft mouth." Retrieval is done quickly and the game is surrendered to the hunter's hand willingly. These actions require an intelligent, disciplined animal.

Competitions are held to evaluate the retrieving skills of dogs. These tests, or field trials, are conducted by organizations such as the Hunting Retriever Club, the North American Hunting Retriever Association, and the AKC. Interested readers can write to the AKC for single copies of the latest rules for retriever trials.

Every variety of hunting dog—pointer, hound, retriever, or terrier—receives different, specialized training. But the basic education, which includes all the obedience exercises, is the same for all.

Other Working Dogs

Working dogs of the world help man in many ways. For years they herded flocks of domestic animals. This trait becomes so inbred that their offspring appear to do it instinctively.

Eskimos use teams of dogs to pull their sleds. The use of dog teams to pull sleds has received publicity through the annual press coverage of the Alaskan Iditarod race. In this race, teams of up to eighteen dogs travel over one thousand miles from Anchorage to Nome.

The superiority of sled dogs for polar travel was illustrated again dramatically in the daring trans-Antarctica trip completed in 1990.

Figure 1

A miniature schnauzer. Note that the ears have been trimmed so they stand erect. Such trimming is not allowed in some countries.

The influence of northern-wolf ancestry is seen in dogs especially suited for this kind of work. The Eskimo dog emerged from mixed breeds interbred with wolves. The samoyed is named after Iranian nomads who migrated to Siberia. The Siberian husky originated in northeast Siberia. It is noted for blue eyes. The Alaskan malamute was bred by eskimos. It is a large powerful dog possessing great endurance. It always has brown eyes.

The military has used dogs for sentry, scouting, pulling sleds, and messenger work. Large mastiff-type dogs were used in combat by the early Greeks and Chinese.

The police have used dogs for guard work, to accompany officers in the K9 divisions, and for tracking. Police rely on a dog's keen sense of smell to detect the presence of drugs, bombs, and to locate victims buried during earthquakes or avalanches.

Dalmatian dogs take to horses (who are also gregarious), becoming companions and protectors. The dogs were often used to guard the horse teams used to pull stagecoaches and fire apparatus. The presence of dogs at firehouses today is a continuation of that tradition.

Service Dogs

The service dog group reflects an even deeper bond between man and animal. The selfless dedication of the pilot dog, or leader dog, as it guides a blind person through potentially dangerous situations is heartwarming.

Signal dogs are trained to aid those with hearing problems. They alert the deaf when a doorbell rings. Dogs are trained to protect their masters or warn them of intruders.

A recent innovation is to train dogs for therapy. Mental patients, the aged, and prisoners have been helped significantly by association with dogs and other animals. At least one dog was trained to sense its master's hand temperature and warn of an impending attack of convulsions. This is a real tribute to the skill of the dog trainer.

Racing Dogs

Competition involving dogs has taken many forms over the years. Dog racing with breeds such as the magnificent greyhounds and whippets is still practiced today. Commercial operators have put many of these dogs to sleep when their racing careers began to fade. Growing public awareness of this practice has resulted in the adoption of these animals as pets.

Pet Dogs

Although we train dogs to serve us in many ways, few require training to play one of their most important roles. The majority of dogs act as loyal, loving, companions.

Researchers tell us that sharing our lives with such animals reduces stress and even lowers blood pressure. Pet dogs need not have a fancy pedigree. Most owners will assure you that their mixed-breed dog has the best characteristics of each of its ancestors. It is the friendliest, most loyal mix to be found.

Considering the many ways that dogs serve us and make our lives more pleasant, it is not surprising that the dog is one of the most popular of pets.

Bibliography

REFERENCE BOOKS

Bauman, Diane L. *Beyond Basic Dog Training.* New York: Howell Book House, 1986. Detailed instruction in dog obedience training.

Brown, William F. *Field Trials: History, Management, and Judging Standards.* San Diego, CA: Barnes, 1975. For people involved with trials, and selecting a bird dog.

Bruette, Dr. William A., and Kerry V. Donnelly. *The Complete Dog Buyers' Guide.* Rev. ed. Neptune City, NJ: TFH, 1984. Detailed description of physical characteristics and disposition of dog breeds. Care, training, and breeding information.

Casey, Brigid, and Wendy Haugh. *Sled Dogs.* New York: Dodd, Mead, 1983. History of dogs, and dog sled racing.

Cross, Jeannette W. *The New Standard Book of Dog Care and Training.* New York: Hawthorn Books, 1962. Selecting a dog, care, training, breeding, shows and trials, and characteristics of breeds.

Fraser, Jacqueline, and Amy Ammen. *Dual Ring Dog: Successful Training for Both Conformation and Obedience Competition.* New York: Macmillan, 1991. Training and exercise leading to participation in shows when dogs are judged on the basis of physical perfection and their performance of tasks to illustrate their obedience.

Free, James Lamb. *Training Your Retriever.* Rev. ed. New York: Putnam's, 1991. Selecting the right breed and dog. Coverage of field trials.

Heacox, Kim. *Iditarod Spirit.* Portland, OR: Graphic Arts Center, 1991. Story of the Iditarod race, maps, and numerous photos.

Howe, John. *Choosing the Right Dog: A Buyer's Guide to All the AKC Breeds Plus.* Rev. ed. New York: Harper & Row, 1980. A review of dog breed characteristics useful in pet selection.

Koehler, William. *The Koehler Method of Dog Training.* New York: Howell Book House, 1962. General dog training by a man who has trained dogs for the Walt Disney Studios and the U.S. Army K-9 Corps.

Schwartz, Charlotte. *The Howell Book of Puppy Raising.* New York: Howell Book House, 1987. Dog breeding and care. Emphasis on puppy care during all critical periods.

Sylvester, Patricia, ed. *The Reader's Digest Illustrated Book of Dogs.* Rev. ed. Pleasantville, NY: Reader's Digest, 1989. Extensive coverage of history, dog identification, care, and education. Very well illustrated.

Tarrant, Bill. *Training the Hunting Retriever.* New York: Macmillan, 1991. Choosing a dog, training, exercises, and hunting retriever clubs.

Wolters, Richard A. *Family Dog.* Rev. ed. New York: Dutton, 1975. The family pet. Care and training, showing how even a child can do it.

PERIODICALS

Dog Fancy. Fancy Publications, Box 6050, Mission Viejo, CA 92690.

Dog Sports. DSM Publishers, Box 1000, Glenrock, NY 82637–1000.

Dogs USA. Fancy Publications, Box 6050, Mission Viejo, CA 92690.

Dog World. Maclean Hunter Publishers, 29 N. Wacker Drive, Chicago, IL 60606.

ASSOCIATIONS

Amateur Field Trial Clubs of America. 360 Winchester Lane, Stanton, TN 38069. Field trial clubs of dogs used in hunting upland game birds. Promotes, regulates, controls, and conducts field trials. Sponsors national amateur championships. Publishes handbook of rules and regulations.

American Kennel Club. 51 Madison Avenue, New York, NY 10010. All-breed, specialty breed, obedience, and field trial clubs. Maintains stud book registry, approves judging standards, adopts and enforces show and trial rules, and maintains library. Publications: *Complete Dog Book, Hunter's Whistle,* and *Pure-Bred Dogs-American Kennel Gazette.*

Hunting Retriever Club. c/o United Kennel Club, 100 E. Kilgore Road, Kalamazoo, MI 49001. Trains and tests hunting retrievers. Awards title of Hunting Retriever Champion to dogs passing testing program. Publication: *Hunting Retriever.*

National Amateur Retriever Club. PO Box 828, Carlisle, MA 01741. Amateurs who run retrievers in field trials. Sponsors national championship, establishes qualifications, and bestows awards.

Owner Handler Association of America. c/o Mrs Mildred Mesh, 6 Michaels Lane, Old Brookville, NY 11545. Those involved in the breeding, training, and showing of purebred dogs. Conducts handling and obedience classes, and presents awards. Publications: *Advocate* and newsletters.

United Kennel Club. 100 E. Kilgore Road, Kalamazoo, MI 49001–5598. Registry for purebred dogs. Establishes rules for events, sponsors events, bestows awards, conducts seminars, and maintains library. Publications: *Coonhound Bloodlines,* and *Hunting Retriever.*

SERVICE DOG ASSOCIATIONS

Canine Companions for Independence. PO Box 446, Santa Rosa, CA 95402–0446. Signal dogs for the deaf, social dogs for pet therapy, Service dogs to perform assistance tasks (pull wheelchair, turn on switches), and specialty dogs for those with multiple disabilities.

Dogs for the Deaf. 10175 Wheeler Road, Central Point, OR 97502. Signal dogs.

Guide Dog Foundation for the Blind. 371 E. Jericho Turnpike, Smithtown, NY 11787. Guide dogs.

Guide Dogs for the Blind. PO Box 151200, San Rafael, CA 94915–1200. Guide dogs.

Guiding Eyes for the Blind. 611 Granite Springs Road, Yorktown Heights, NY 10598. Guide dogs.

Hearing Dog Resource Center. PO Box 1080, Renton, WA 98057–1080. Signal dogs.

International Hearing Dog. 5901 E. 89th Avenue, Henderson, CO 80640. Signal dogs.

New England Assistance Dog Service. PO Box 213, West Boylston, MA 01583. Signal dogs, and service dogs to perform assistance tasks.

Pilot Guide Dog Foundation. 625 W. Town Street, Columbus, OH 43215. Guide dogs.

Therapy Dogs International. c/o Ursula Kempe, 260 Fox Chase Road, Chester, NJ 07930. Social dogs for therapy.

Note: There are over ninety additional associations devoted to specific dog breeds listed in the *Encyclopedia of Associations,* available in libraries.

Drawing and Sketching

ALL ARTISTS' MEDIA have some limitations. A balance occurs between a picture having a photographic quality and one in which the artist has carried the chosen medium to its limits. These limitations stimulate creativity. The artist searches for ways to exploit the advantages of the medium selected. When the work is done skillfully, the human brain has the capacity to fill in the blanks, to see what may be merely suggested. Artists tend to reflect the techniques that they have been taught, but eventually develop distinctive styles. Occasionally a unique approach is used and the art world is taken by storm.

Sketching

Sketching is a preliminary step in planning most art work, regardless of which medium is chosen to complete the work. A sketch is a simple, rough drawing done rapidly and without much detail. When an artist or hobbyist develops a sketch beyond a simple outline of a given subject, the resulting drawing may itself be considered a finished work of art. Over the years many have come to enjoy sketching as a means of creative self-expression.

Sketches are often used to supplement other means of communication. Naturalists, botanists, and bird watchers supplement their field notes with sketches. Engineers and draftsmen communicate their ideas to one another using sketches before committing their designs to working drawings. Architects also convey their suggestions to prospective customers by the use of such drawings.

Composition

Our eyes view a scene with great flexibility. They constantly change focus as objects are noted both near and far. Scientific studies have shown that our eyes dart from one object to another, the direction of sight often tracing a path around the perimeter of an object of interest. We observe a scene in a dynamic way. Our drawing is static, frozen in time. We choose the lighting, the point of view, and the portion of the scene we wish to sketch. The elements of a scene should be positioned on the paper with proper consideration given to balance and good composition.

It has been found useful to divide the drawing into thirds, both horizontally and vertically. The primary subject is then positioned at one of the four points where the lines dividing the thirds intersect. Where there is only one subject such as a person located in an otherwise vacant setting, the subject may be moved toward the center a little. In this case it is often advisable to have the person face slightly toward the center. The area to be featured should generally be defined in greater detail and strength of tone to emphasize it. We are free to include details that a casual observer may miss.

The eye can be drawn toward an area you wish to emphasize by framing the subject with dissimilar shapes. For example, a beautiful lake framed between trees with overhanging limbs. Or the eye can be led to a distant farmhouse along a road or path running from the foreground to the house. In Figure 1 we see the objects that catch our eye located at the intersections of thirds, and the pathway leads our eye to the main feature, the large tree.

When working from small photographs or preliminary sketches it is convenient to enlarge them on the final drawing by means of a grid system. Divide the small picture into small squares. Divide the larger drawing into an equal number of squares large enough to fill the drawing space. Transfer the image a square at a time in light pencil as an outline for your drawing.

During the planning of a drawing, the artist may wish to substitute a different background or add a new feature that wasn't in the original scene. At times like this a picture file is useful. When you see a picture of an attractive scene or object of interest clip it and save for future use. Such files

Figure 1
A simple sketch with the eye-catching objects located at, or near, the intersections of thirds. The pathway leads the eye to the main feature, the large tree.

can also be expanded to include examples of pleasing or unusual techniques used by others.

An artist must illustrate the effect that light has on the subject. Light produces highlights and shadows that bring life to the scene. When drawing a portrait, the simple addition of a white dot can bring sparkle to a subject's eyes. When working outdoors, the artist may have to wait for the sun to reach a position that lights the subject best. If you work from a combination of photos be sure to compensate for any differences in lighting.

If your work is done in color you need to consider color balance. It contributes to the overall composition. Bright colors can command attention; subdued shades can deemphasize backgrounds or produce the illusion of shadows.

Contrast, texture, shape, perspective, and pattern are other factors that are to be considered when choosing a subject and planning a drawing.

Tools and Materials

The first graphite pencil was made in 1662. Before that time artists such as Leonardo da Vinci and Rembrandt used silverpoint. This was a stylus of silver metal that was used to scribe silver-gray lines on a specially prepared drawing surface.

Modern graphite art and drafting pencils have a wide range of hardness. The softest designation is 8B. As hardness increases the number decreases until midrange is reached, at this point designations read 2B, B, HB, F, H, and 2H through 10H. Writing pencils range from 1 to 4, where a 1 is about the hardness of a 3B and 4 is close to a 3H. Various drafting lead holders provide a convenient way to handle leads, affording easy sharpening.

Ink is applied by a wide variety of specialized pens and brushes. Technical pens have a reservoir to contain the ink supply. Their tips are comprised of a hollow tube with a wire, weighted internally, contained in the tube. They are sized from 0.13 mm (designated 6x0) to 2mm (designated 7) in width. The midrange sizes of 00 and 1 are most used.

Dip pens come in a variety of sizes and shapes, from the common crow quill nib, to a five-pointed pen designed to cross-hatch five lines at once. Dip pens are designed for writing, drawing, or calligraphy.

Other special pens include, fountain pens, ballpoint pens, fibertipped pens, and marking pens. Be sure the ink in such pens is fade-resistant and compatible with the surface to be used.

On occasion a brush may be used to apply ink to large areas. Thin sable brushes are preferred.

Other drawing media include colored pencils, charcoal, pastels, and crayons.

Erasers must be selected with care to avoid destroying the texture of the drawing surface. Soft vinyl plastic erasers are best for use with graphite pencil and drawing paper. Use pink rubber erasers with care for colored pencils. Kneaded erasers are much less abrasive when used with charcoal, pencil, or to clean up an ink drawing. Abrasive ink erasers must be used with caution. Non-abrasive vinyl types are available for ink removal. Common drafting erasing shields are useful accessories.

Stomps are compressed rolled paper cylinders used to blend dry drawing materials such as pencil or charcoal. They are pointed on both ends. Another variety, generally smaller, is pointed on one end. It is called a tortillon.

There are many types of drawing paper and artist board available. Bristol is a good all-purpose choice. Bristol plate finish has a slick surface good for ink. Bristol vellum finish has a surface generally preferred for use with pencil, colored pencil, and pastels. Common drawing papers in small sized pads are useful for field sketching.

Spray fixatives are used on charcoal and pencil drawings to prevent smudging. Modern types permit work to continue even after spraying.

When traveling outdoors, take a portfolio to contain your sketch pad and pencils. When ready to set up, the portfolio can serve as a drawing board. Bring a folding stool and you can sketch in relative comfort.

Pencil Techniques

When preparing a pencil sketch try to stay relaxed and loose. Draw with flowing lines rather than short, choppy strokes. It's not important if you make a mistake; you're just trying to capture the essence of the subject. If you'll be using the sketch as the basis of a more formal drawing, feel free to add notes relative to image elements not included in the sketch, such as size, color, or texture.

When working on a formal drawing, many prefer to do preliminary composition planning on a separate sheet of paper. The major shapes or volumes are sketched and larger details are outlined. Once satisfied with the overall format, the outlines are transferred to the final sheet very lightly. This may be done by rubbing the back of the sketch with a soft pencil. The sketch is then placed on the final sheet and the sketch lines are traced, transferring the lines to the final sheet. This method avoids exposing the final sheet to the multiple erasures made while composing the sketch.

After the light outlines have been added to the final sheet, the artist fills in dark areas with a broad, soft pencil. A sharp pencil is then used to bring the dark areas closer

to their final shape. Subtle medium density tones are then added to bring the picture close to its final appearance. Stomps are used to blend areas and a kneaded eraser may be used to accentuate highlights and clean up expanses of white areas.

Ink Techniques

Many who work with ink prepare a preliminary sketch or drawing in pencil in order to identify the areas requiring the representation of medium tones. In some forms of pen and ink drawing a diluted ink or watercolor wash can be used to obtain medium tones. In most cases the medium tones are represented by a form of textured cross-hatching or a pattern of dots called stippling.

The quality of ink lines is reduced when drawing over areas that have been erased or exposed to oils and moisture from the hands. Some use white cotton gloves to avoid contact with the drawing surface. A clean white piece of bond paper placed under the hand can also be used.

There is no substitute for practice while developing your technique with pen and ink. Many books are available that outline practice drills to familiarize the artist with pen handling practices; but you will learn most from close study of the work of professionals. Note how they emphasize certain features, omit some detail entirely, or handle the presentation of shaded areas.

Working Space

The ideal working space would be one in which your work could be left set up and undisturbed. There should be plenty of light on both work surface and subject being drawn. Light sources should be positioned to minimize glare. The drawing table, or easel, and seat should provide comfort during prolonged work sessions.

Other Media to Explore

The world of art is ever-changing. The following examples offer exciting new challenges.

In the past, illustrators engraved pictures in wood. Around 1880 an improved method was introduced which today is called scratchboard. A black surface is coated with hard white chalk or china clay about six thousandths of an inch thick. The design is scratched or engraved into the clay surface, exposing the black surface beneath, creating a line. Touch-ups can be done with India ink. Black coating on a white subsurface is also available. Once widely used for printing, scratchboard has been replaced by halftone techniques. It remains a fine form of artistic expression for its own sake. You may have to do some digging to obtain supplies.

Watercolor is a demanding medium. Mistakes are difficult or impossible to correct, and usually mean starting over. The artist starts by making a very light pencil sketch to which the watercolor is added. The traditional watercolor technique allows the color to build up in the painting by successive applications of thin washes of dilute, transparent color, leaving bare patches of paper for white highlights. The watercolor painter must work dark over light colors.

Pastels are sticks of powdered pigment bound together by weak gum or resin. They produce an opaque color on a textured surface. The texture scrubs the pigment off of the stick. The pigments cannot be mixed like oils or watercolors to achieve other shades. Each stick stands alone, so a number of sticks of varying colors are required. The final picture is more fragile than most other media, since the chalk-like surface is easily damaged. Despite their shortcomings, pastels offer a wide range of creativity and style. Many famous artists have used pastels for over two hundred years.

Oil paints have been with us for centuries. They have the advantage that colors can be mixed to achieve a wide range of color values. Another advantage is that light colors can be successfully applied over dark. The beginner can correct errors with ease.

The airbrush is a painting tool that can produce effects ranging from pencil-thin lines to smooth uniform areas of color. With experience, remarkable lifelike paintings are possible. The airbrush cannot be mastered quickly. It takes patient practice and study. One of the advantages of the medium is the speed with which work can be accomplished.

In recent years personal computer graphics programs have been commonly available. They continue to improve at a remarkable rate. The user can simulate spray painting or drawing with a pencil. Unwanted areas can be erased and various patterns can be inserted into areas bounded by lines. They have become sophisticated enough to warrant use in commercial applications such as brochures and newsletters. Commercial programs are being used to simulate the human form in almost photographic quality. This is a medium that is certain to attract many as it continues to develop.

Bibliography

REFERENCE BOOKS

Calle, Paul. *The Pencil.* Cincinnati, OH: North Light Books, 1974. Overview of pencil drawing. Covers history, materials, tools, techniques, and numerous excellent illustrations by a nationally recognized artist.

Curtis, Cecile. *The Art of Scratchboard.* Cincinnati, OH: North Light Books, 1988. History of engraving techniques. Step-by-step instruction in the art of scratchboard engraving, including coverage of tools and materials.

Franks, Gene. *Pencil Drawing.* Tustin, CA: Foster, 1984. Materials and practices used by the artist. Step-by-step illustrations showing the development of a group of formal drawings.

Glassford, Carl. *Pen and Ink: Line, Texture, Color.* Tustin, CA: Foster, 1985. Materials and practices used by the artist. Well illustrated with many examples of advanced pen and ink drawings.

Guptill, Arthur L. *Rendering in Pen and Ink.* New York: Watson-Guptill, 1976. Overview of pen and ink drawing covering equipment, exercises, and techniques. Emphasis on basics and architectural presentation.

————. *Rendering in Pencil.* New York: Watson-Guptill, 1977. Overview of pencil drawing covering equipment, exercises, and techniques. Emphasis on basics and architectural presentation.

Johnson, Cathy. *The Sierra Club Guide to Sketching in Nature.* San Francisco: Sierra Club Books, 1990. Coverage of pencil, pen and ink, and watercolor presentation. Emphasis on sketching in the field. Good introduction to a variety of media.

Lloyd, Christopher. *1,773 Milestones of Art.* New York: Harrison House, 1985. Profusely illustrated historical analysis of art.

Lohan, Frank J. *Countryside Sketching: Pen and Pencil Techniques for Drawing Covered Bridges, Barns, Old Mills, and Other Rustic Settings.* Chicago: Contemporary Books, 1989. Pencil and pen techniques. Coverage of tools, illustrations of how to draw scenes and specific objects.

Loomis, Andrew. *Figure Drawing: For All Its Worth.* New York: Viking, 1971. Detailed presentation of the art of drawing the human figure emphasizing proportion, techniques, and figure in action. Well illustrated.

Parramon, Jose M. *Painting Landscapes and Figures in Pastel.* New York: Watson-Guptill, 1990. Stage-by-stage illustrations of the development of a selection of pastel drawings. Notes on materials used.

Saitzyk, Steven L. *Art Hardware: The Definitive Guide to Artists' Materials.* New York: Watson-Guptill, 1987. Detailed overview of drawing tools and materials. Includes framing, storage, and safety hazards.

Smith, Stan, and H. F. Ten Holt, eds. *The Artist's Manual.* New York: Gallery Books, 1988. Comprehensive overview of art, graphic design, and sculpture. History, equipment, and techniques of a wide variety of media. Useful as an introduction to the subject. A beginner may require more detailed coverage of media selected.

Vero, Radu. *Airbrush: The Complete Studio Handbook.* New York: Watson-Guptill, 1983. Introduction to airbrush technique. Description of equipment, techniques, and fields of specialization. Well illustrated.

Watson, Ernest W. *The Art of Pencil Drawing.* New York: Watson-Guptill, 1985. Overview of pencil drawing techniques. Covers tools, materials, composition, and sketching. Emphasis on trees and architecture.

PERIODICALS

Airbrush Action. Airbrush Action, 1985 Swarthmore Avenue, Box 2052, Lakewood, NJ 08701.

American Artist. BPI Communications, 1515 Broadway, New York, NY 10036.

American Artist Directory of Art Schools and Workshops. American Artist Magazine, 1515 Broadway, New York, NY 10036.

Art in America. Brant Publications, 575 Broadway, 5th Floor, New York, NY 10021.

Artist's Magazine. F&W Publications, 1507 Dana Ave., Cincinnati, OH 45207. (Each year the March workshop issue provides information on workshops and art teachers.)

U S Art. Adams Publishers, 12 S. 6th Street, Suite. 400, Minneapolis, MN 55402. (For collectors of print art.)

ASSOCIATIONS

American Watercolor Society. 47 Fifth Avenue, New York, NY 10003. Members interested in the advancement of watercolor painting. Bestows awards, maintains scholarships, and supports exhibition. Publication: Newsletter.

Deaf Artists of America. 87 N. Clinton Avenue, Suite 408, Rochester, NY 14604. Primary goal is to make the arts more accessible to hearing impaired artists. Operates speakers bureau, library, and art gallery. Conducts workshops, sponsors competitions, and bestows awards. Publications: *Uncharted: Exploring the World of Deaf Artists,* and related materials.

Drawing Center. 35 Wooster Street, New York, NY 10013. Seeks to display the drawing as a major art form. Critiques examples of art work for any artist. Sponsors work-study program, offers conservation workshops, and presents exhibitions. Publications: Art books and catalogs.

Drawing Society. 15 Penn Plaza, Box 66, 415 Seventh Avenue, New York, NY 10001. Those interested in drawing and the drawings of all periods and cultures. Publications: *Drawing,* books, and related materials.

National Watercolor Society. 18220 S. Hoffman Ave., Cerritos, CA 90701. Encourages interest in water medium painting. Provides exhibitions, operates the NWS Artists Referral Program which provides demonstrations and workshops. Awards grants and bestows awards. Publication: *National Watercolor Society Annual Exhibition Catalog.*

Pastel Society of America. 15 Grammercy Park S., New York, NY 10003. Focuses attention on the renaissance of pastel. Conducts exhibits, workshops, lectures, and classes. Offers scholarships, bestows awards, and operates hall of fame. Publications: *Pastel Info, Pastelagram,* and newsletter.

Education, Continuing

MANY AMERICANS CHOOSE TO APPLY their spare time to a program of self-improvement. It is not unusual for people to become expert in a field other than their daily occupation.

There is an interdependent relationship between education, interesting pastimes, and the workplace. Consider the student aircraft pilot. To obtain a private pilot's license the student will take courses in aerodynamics, meteorology, and navigation. Advanced pilot's licenses require knowledge of aircraft engines and airframes. Professional astronomers spend little time stargazing. Most of their time is devoted to analysis of data and the development of theory. Amateur astronomers study the subject and observe the skies, providing professionals with needed information concerning unusual sightings. Birdwatchers provide a similar service to ornithologists, conducting bird counts and providing requested data. Archaeologists also depend upon knowledgeable amateurs to assist in their digs. In these pastimes and many others like them, there is always the potential that the hobby will turn into a lifetime career.

Students often discover interesting pastimes through the study of elective courses taken while attending high school or college. Well-rounded students participate in activities such as school clubs, scouting, community involvement, and volunteer work. These programs expose the student to new information, possible career paths, and rewarding pastimes. They also develop social skills and leadership experience. Students who have been exposed to some of the above activities are better equipped to ask the right questions of school counselors regarding schooling options and career choices.

Continuing Education Sources

When selecting sources for courses on specific subjects, a part-time student has many options. Many universities offer correspondence courses. The National University Continuing Education Association publishes a guide to the institutions involved and the courses offered. Some institutions may require previous educational experience for specific courses. Check before attempting to enroll. Another source involving a group of colleges is The University Without Walls. Correspondence study is demanding. Without the discipline afforded by the classroom, the student must have the initiative and self-reliance to develop good study habits and maintain a regular schedule of study.

In keeping with advances in communications technology some universities have developed unique home study programs. The Colorado State University uses cable TV to instruct students in certain courses. It also offers courses on video tape. Students take their examinations for such courses at an accredited university. The University of Phoenix uses its computer bulletin board to conduct a class for students located at several locations. Classes in both examples above lead to college degrees.

Proprietary trade or vocational schools are usually established to teach one type of subject, such as auto mechanics, refrigeration, or television repair. They are somewhat expensive because they receive little or no income besides your tuition. Check the school's accreditation, equipment, reputation with local industry, and instructor qualifications before you invest. These schools can be located through your state employment office.

Adult education classes are available from a variety of sources in most communities. Examples of institutions that offer courses include: The American Red Cross, Community Chest, Park District, Public Schools—Vocational/ Continuing Education Branch, Recreation Commission, Travelers Aid, YMCA, YWCA, and of course a university evening college. Be sure to look beyond the obvious places in your community when searching for specialized training.

Benjamin Franklin recognized the value of bringing together individuals with divergent knowledge and points of view. In 1727 he formed the Junto Society, which consisted of a number of citizens who were mostly tradesmen. This discussion group used a format in which several questions read at each meeting were debated at the following meeting. Members researched the subjects between meetings and came the following week prepared to discuss them in depth. Franklin considered the club to be an excellent school of philosophy, morals, and politics. The Junto Society was responsible for the establishment of a circulating library for its members and for other citizens of Philadelphia.

Today, The Great Books Foundation is active in the United States. It is similar to the Junto Society in that material is researched and discussed by a group. The foundation supplies books, training, and study outlines leading to adult liberal education. A junior program is also available. Thousands of groups are currently involved.

Scientists have found that when the mind is continually used and its capacities expanded, there is minimal effect due to aging. Recall, and ability to understand and learn new areas of knowledge sometimes surpasses younger minds.

There is an almost unlimited body of knowledge that you can tap into without the one-on-one help of others. Good books enable you to share the thoughts of the best minds of the ages. Columnist Abby Van Buren said, "The person who does not read is no better off than the person who cannot read."

The largest and most under-used sources of such material are the public and university library systems with their books, films, and recordings. Abraham Lincoln said, "The things I want to know are in books; my best friend is the man who'll get me a book I ain't read."

Education and the Workplace

It is useful to broaden your knowledge base and outlook by studying subjects other than those directly relating to your work. It enables one to view the work experience from a different perspective, and the knowledge may provide a safety net if your job is lost.

The time spent gaining proficiency in the pursuit of such pastimes can have a significant pay-off in today's volatile job market where second careers have become common. Prospective employers are often impressed when a job-related spare-time activity appears on your resume.

Most of us know an expert who has worked at a job for thirty years and has had one year of experience thirty times. The well-rounded expert, who keeps up with the latest state-of-the-art developments is the most valued employee, and the one who will be promoted and well-compensated.

Education for Seniors

The retiree who has been freed of the demands of the working world is often heard to say, "I've always wanted to know more about this, but I never had time." Or worse, "If I had only known about this years ago."

Two of the best learning experiences are combined in an educational program called Elderhostel—education and travel. Prospective students sign up for courses at a college of their choice, selecting one or more noncredit courses per day. Since over 1,600 institutions are involved, a broad range of subject matter is available. The program is designed for people over sixty, but they may bring a partner fifty or older. Most of the programs run for a week beginning on Sunday. In the United States students make arrangements and pay for travel to the university. When traveling to locations in about forty-seven foreign countries, travel arrangements and costs are usually included in the trip package. Participants sometimes use student facilities such as dormitories and cafeterias. Classes, rooms, and meals average about $315 a week in the United States. About 250,000 people enroll in Elderhostel programs each year.

Programs such as Elderhostel motivate and expand the interests of seniors. Many of these benefits can be found by taking advantage of educational opportunities locally. Don't overlook the alternative programs mentioned earlier. There is a growing trend for local evening colleges to offer seniors very attractive rates for their courses. They may not offer credit, but if your goal is simply to be informed, just relax and enjoy the learning experience; you won't even have to sweat the test.

Picking Up Where You Left Off

The educational path to a productive life is cut short when students drop out before completing high school. Their earning capacity is reduced and their future access to many educational opportunities and pleasurable pastimes is limited. A student still has options if it is necessary to drop out before graduation.

The General Educational Development Tests (GED) are a series of examinations that are designed to determine whether the person taking them has the literacy and computational skills equivalent to those of the upper two-thirds of the students currently graduating from high schools in the United States. Before taking the GED test, a student should review the information and sample tests included in a book such as, *GED High School Equivalency Test Examination*. This will identify areas needing additional study. If further study is required, call a nearby school district office or local library for information about availability of needed books and classes. Nationally, during 1991, 763,000 GED tests were administered to applicants from sixteen to ninety-six years old. There are even some who go on to finish college and earn Ph.Ds. When studying for the GED, it is worth noting that many correspondence schools offer high school courses.

When planning to transfer from one college to another now, or at a later time, ask the college from which you expect to receive your degree which course credits can be transferred. In some instances, even credit obtained from an evening college is not transferable to a daytime degree in the same institution. The question of transferable credits is especially important when considering one of the many correspondence course options.

Students, particularly older students, often fail to realize the value of their own skills and abilities acquired through work and other activities. Be sure to make a conscious effort to list these skills and discuss them with appropriate personnel when applying for entrance to learning institutions. At the college level, a student is often given the opportunity to get credit for past study or experience. In most such instances a test is given to prove proficiency in the subject. The best known program of this type is The College-Level Examination Program (CLEP). Ask the college you are attending which tests and subjects it honors.

Bibliography

REFERENCE BOOKS

Barasch, Seymour et al. *GED High School Equivalency Test Examination.* 12th ed. New York: Arco, 1990. Information about GED, study tips, and sample tests.

Bird, Caroline. *The Case Against College.* New York: McKay, 1975. Author discusses the limitations of college education. Emphasis on alternative education.

Buzan, Tony. *Use Both Sides of Your Brain.* Rev. ed. New York: Dutton, 1983. Understanding how the mind works and how to use it to the best advantage. Study techniques.

Dubrovin, Vivian. *Guide to Alternative Education and Training.* New York: Watts, 1988. Explains educational opportunities with emphasis on programs other than college. Useful advice and contact information.

Haponski, William C., and Charles E. McCabe. *New Horizons: The Education and Career Planning Guide for Adults.* 2nd ed. Princeton, NJ: Peterson's Guides, 1985. Assessing your career goals and educational options. Financing and getting accepted into college. Coping with college and looking at alternatives.

Hegener, Mark, and Helen Hegener. *Alternatives in Education: Family Choices in Learning.* Tonasket, WA: Home Education, 1987. Overview of educational options from elementary school through university level.

Hyman, Mildred. *Elderhostels: The Students' Choice.* 2nd ed. Santa Fe, NM: Muir, 1991. Provides information about a broad selection of Elderhostel locations. Lists information on courses, environment, housing, food, attributes, and shortcomings.

Illich, Ivan. *Deschooling Society.* New York: Harper & Row, 1971. Author provides an alternative view to traditional educational methods. Emphasis on learning outside the confines of school buildings.

Ready, Barbara C., and Raymond D. Sacchetti, eds. *The Independent Study Catalog: NUCEA's Guide to Independent Study Through Correspondence Instruction.* 4th ed. Princeton, NJ: Peterson's Guides, 1989. Advice on correspondence study. Participating institutions and courses offered with emphasis on university participation.

Smith, Peter. *Your Hidden Credentials.* Washington, DC: Acropolis Books, 1986. Covers the importance of personal learning from experience and its relationship to college credit and the workplace.

Unger, Harlow G. *But What If I Don't Want to Go to College?* New York: Facts on File, 1992. Alternative education and career selection. Useful reference material such as school accreditation agencies.

PERIODICALS

Adult Learning. American Association for Adult and Continuing Education, 2101 Wilson Boulevard, Suite 925, Arlington, VA 22201.

For Seniors Only: A Magazine for High School Seniors. Campus Communications, 339 N. Main Street, Suite 4, New City, NY 10956.

Need A Lift? American Legion, Need a Lift, Box 1055, Indianapolis, IN 46206. Career and scholarship information.

ASSOCIATIONS

Colorado State University. Fort Collins, CO 80523. Uses cable TV and video tape to instruct students in certain courses.

Earthwatch. 680 Mt. Auburn Street, Box 403, Watertown, MA 02272. Research and educational organization that allows individuals to become working members of research teams led by qualified scientists. Provides career training scholarship program for students. Publications: *Earthcorps-Our Daily Planet,* and *Earthwatch.*

Elderhostel, Inc. 75 Federal St., 3rd Floor, Boston, MA 02110. A network of over 1600 educational institutions in forty countries. Offers special, low-cost, short-term residential academic programs for adults over sixty. Publications: *Elderhostel Catalogs* listing current educational programs.

General Educational Development Institute. 16211 6th Avenue, NE, Seattle, WA 98155. High school dropouts, GED candidates, and adults seeking academic and job skills. Provides motivation, encouragement, and information. Maintains library and bestows awards. Publications: *The Adult Learner* magazine, and *GED Predictive Tests.*

Great Books Foundation. 35 E. Wacker Drive, Chicago, IL 60601–2298. Fosters education of children and adults through reading and group discussion of acclaimed literary works. Conducts courses on discussion methods for volunteers and teachers. Publications: *Leader Notes,* curriculum materials, and handbook.

Interhostel. University of New Hampshire, 6 Garrison Avenue, Durham, NH 03824. Provides opportunities for adults fifty and older to travel to foreign countries and to study a particular region of the world in detail under the auspices of the

University of New Hampshire and participating institutions overseas. Publications: Catalog and a brochure.

The National University Continuing Education Association. 1 Dupont Circle, Suite 615, Washington, DC 20036. Institutions of higher learning, both public and private, with active extension and continuing education programs. Publications: *Continuing Higher Education Review, Guide to Independent Study Through Correspondence Instruction, Innovations in Continuing Education,* and related materials.

Outward Bound. 384 Field Point Road, Greenwich, CT 06830. Operates five wilderness schools and six urban centers in the United States to help young people and adults discover and extend their own resources and abilities. Has assisted in establishing a training program for Peace Corps Volunteers. Publications: *OB Newsletter,* a catalog, and the book, *Outward Bound USA.*

University of Phoenix. 4615 E. Elwood Street, Phoenix, AZ 85040. Uses its computer bulletin board to conduct a class for students at several locations.

University Without Walls. Union for Experimental Colleges and Universities, Antioch College, Yellow Springs, OH 45387. Uses a flexible system of bringing the campus to the student. In some cases the professor travels to the student, in others, various means of communication are employed.

Embroidery and Quilting

EMBROIDERY IS DEFINED as the application of decoration to a base or ground material. The decorative material may be pieces of fabric or one of several types of needlework. These variations, together with their historical background, are discussed below.

History

When pieces of fabric are used to form a design on a ground, the process is called appliqué. The method has been practiced for centuries. Appliqué was used by the Egyptians to apply leather pieces to a ground in the seventh century B.C. Siberians used felt for sophisticated pictures in the fourth century B.C., and battle flags of the Middle Ages featured applied symbols.

Thread or yarn may be stitched onto a ground to form a decorative design. The method, called crewel embroidery, dates back to the fifth century A.D. in Egypt. One surviving example was made in the eleventh century.

When thread or yarn is stitched onto a ground based on a counted number of warp and weft threads in the canvas ground, the process is called needlepoint. It's interesting to take note of the prominent people whose designs influenced needlepoint and other types of embroidery:

Architect Robert Adam (1728–1792) produced a pattern book.

Furniture designer Thomas Chippendale (1718–1779) offered suggestions in his book, *The Gentleman and Cabinet Maker's Director.*

Furniture designer George Hepplewhite (d. 1786) covered the craft in his book, *The Cabinet-maker and Upholsterer's Guide.*

William Morris (1834–1896) created designs and prepared kits for customers to embroider in 1855.

Furniture designer Thomas Sheraton (1751–1806) produced designs.

Stained glass designer Louis Comfort Tiffany (1848–1933) designed murals, tapestries, and needlework.

When two layers of material separated by a layer of padding are stitched together, the method is called quilting. The Crusaders took quilting to Europe when they returned from Asia wearing quilted undergarments. Bedcovers have long been associated with the technique. Quilted bedcovers, or quilts, became popular in Europe during the fourteenth century.

During colonial times cloth was in short supply. Old garments were saved for any scraps that could be used to patch clothing. The scraps also found use as part of the patchwork pieced together for quilts. Many of these early quilts, called crazy quilts, had no particular pattern or design. In later years, cloth became readily available and new, brightly colored materials were used by early homemakers in quiltmaking.

During the nineteenth century many young women made quilts in preparation for marriage. A young woman's hope chest may have contained as many as a dozen examples demonstrating various fine needlecraft skills. Antique dealers travel across the country seeking to purchase quilts handmade during this period. They are sold at prices befitting their quality and antiquity.

Embroidery Processes

Appliqué

If you wish to create an appliqué design, start by selecting harmonizing fabric scraps. Rough out the design on paper, trace it onto colored paper, and cut it out. Pin the colored paper patterns to the ground and revise or adjust the pattern until satisfied. If the pattern is to be repeated, make the final pattern of cardboard. Trace the final pattern on the fabric to be sewn to the ground, allowing additional material for the seam. Sew the appliqué to the ground by hand, using fine or ornamental stitching. If the appliqué is to be machine-sewn, it is usually glued to the ground and a zigzag machine is used for sewing. When thicker pieces are applied or several layers of material or stitches are used to create a three dimensional effect, the result is called raised work.

Needlepoint

Today, needlepoint is a general term for all varieties of counted thread embroidery that entirely cover the ground. It's a method of stitching where stitches are worked over a counted number of warp and weft threads that comprise a canvas. A threaded needle is taken in and out of the ground in a prescribed manner forming a stitch. Two methods commonly used are the cross-stitch and the tent stitch.

The threads that make up the cotton canvas ground are treated as a grid upon which a design can be duplicated from another source of information. The size or gauge of needlepoint canvas is designated by the number of meshes per inch. A mesh is one intersection of horizontal and vertical threads. A ten-mesh canvas, for example, has ten mesh to the inch, hence ten stitches to the inch. If the work is based on more than sixteen stitches per inch it is called petit point. Gros point contains eight or fewer stitches per inch.

The design may be a geometrical figure or an elaborate picture. You can create or copy a design on graph paper, which is then used as a guide for stitching. Each square on the graph equals one stitch on the canvas. This method works best for geometrical designs. For more intricate designs, such as pictures, place the canvas over the picture and paint the canvas with a colored medium such as a waterproof marker. When the work is completed, the canvas will be dampened to smooth and straighten it in a process called blocking. If the paint or markers used on the canvas are not waterproof, they will stain the yarn used to create the designs.

As in the past, one of the first embroidered projects attempted by people is the sampler. Needlework samplers today include pictorial scenes, alphabets, numerals, verses, and borders of flowers done mostly in cross-stitch on even-weave fabric. In earlier times young ladies made samplers as part of their course of study in needlecraft. An early use of the sampler was the trial of a design on a special piece of cloth before pattern books were available.

Crewel

The name is sometimes applied to a type of thread, a fine wool two-ply yarn. Crewel embroidery is stitching without relation to the count of threads in the ground, but rather to a design printed or drawn on the surface of the ground. A wide variety of stitches are employed to obtain the desired texture in the design.

The Quilting Process

Quilting is a unique form of needlework. A soft material is placed between two layers of fabric and stitching is applied through all thicknesses. The stitching, usually applied in an ornamental manner, keeps the filling material from shifting. Some quilt designs are achieved solely by the use of stitched patterns. Most designs feature an upper layer of colorful patchwork in combination with a stitched pattern.

Since the early 1970s quilting has achieved the status of an art form with contemporary examples hanging in art galleries. The best quilts command prices as high as 20,000 dollars. Interest in quilting has increased in recent years, fueled by the nation's bicentennial in 1976.

Bibliography

REFERENCE BOOKS

Boling, Gary, ed. *America's Best Cross-Stitch*. Des Moines, IA: Better Homes & Gardens Books, 1988. Provides patterns, instructions, and suggests materials for a variety of cross-stitch designs.

Christensen, Jo Ippolito. *The Needlepoint Book: 303 Stitches With Patterns and Projects*. Englewood Cliffs, NJ: Prentice-Hall, 1976. Detailed, illustrated how-to instructions for performing needlepoint stitches.

Enthoven, Jacqueline. *The Stitches of Creative Embroidery*. Rev. ed. West Chester, PA: Schiffer, 1987. Detailed illustrated instructions for creating 241 stitches.

Fox, Sandi. *Wrapped in Glory: Figurative Quilts and Bedcovers 1700–1900*. New York: Thames and Hudson, 1990. Illustrations and descriptive text of a selection of quilts displayed by the Los Angeles County Museum of Art in 1990.

Gammell, Alice. *Polly Prindle's Book of American Patchwork Quilts*. Rev. ed. New York: Putnam, 1976. How to make fifty patchwork patterns from America's past.

Grauel, Zoe A. ed. *Quilting By Machine*. Minnetonka, MN: Cy DeCosse, 1990. Techniques used by the experts to quilt by machine.

Nadelstern, Paula, and LynNell Hancock. *Quilting Together: How to Organize, Design and Make Group Quilts*. New York: Crown, 1988. Colorful illustrations of notable quilts. Step-by-step instructions for making quilts. Problems and benefits of a group quilt project.

Rehmel, Judy. *The Quilt I. D. Book*. New York: Prentice Hall, 1986. Illustrations of 4,000 quilt designs. Presents a quilt identification system.

Stiles, Phyllis, ed. *Not Just Another Embroidery Book*. Ashville, NC: Lark Books, 1986. Step-by-step instructions for making a variety of stitches. Includes a selection of designs.

Whiteaker, Stafford. *English Garden Embroidery: 80 Original Needlepoint Designs of Flowers, Fruit and Animals.* New York: Ballantine Books, 1987. Colorful illustrations, many shown on a background grid for the convenience of the reader craftsperson.

PERIODICALS

Needlepoint Plus. E G W Publishers, 1041 Shary Circle, Concord, CA 94518.

Plastic Canvas! Magazine. Jerry Gentry, 206 West Street, Big Sandy, TX 75755.

Quick & Easy Quilting. House of White Birches Publishers, 306 E. Parr Road, Berne, IN 46711.

Quilt. Harris Publications, 1115 Broadway, 8th Floor, New York, NY 10010.

Quilt Craft. Lopez Publications, 152 Madison Avenue, Suite 905, New York, NY 10016.

Quilt World. House of White Birches Publishers, 306 E. Parr Road, Berne, IN 46711.

Quilter's Newsletter Magazine. Leman Publications, 6700 W. 44th Avenue, Wheatridge, CO 80033.

Quilting International. All American Crafts, 243 Newton-Sparta Road, Newton, NJ 07860-2848.

Quiltmaker. Leman Publications, 6700 W. 44th Avenue, Wheatridge, CO 80033.

Sew Beautiful. Martha Pullen, 518 Madison Street, Huntsville, AL 35801.

Simply Cross Stitch. Jerry Gentry, 206 West Street, Big Sandy, TX 75755.

ASSOCIATIONS

American Needlepoint Guild. PO Box 3525, Rock Hill, SC 29732-3525. People of all ages who enjoy needlepoint. Sponsors exhibits and offers correspondence courses. Sponsors awards. Publication: *Needle Pointers.*

American Quilter's Society. PO Box 3290, Paducah, KY 42001. Promotes quilting and assists in the sale of quilts. Sponsors competitions and bestows awards. Publications: *American Quilter,* and related materials.

Continental Quilting Congress. PO Box 561, Vienna, VA 22183 Promotes quilting and organizes quilting tours of foreign countries to exchange ideas and techniques. Maintains hall of fame.

Council of American Embroiderers. PO Box 700768, Plymouth, MI 48170-0953 Promotes high standards in embroidery, needlework, and stitchery. Sponsors exhibitions of quality work for professionals and amateurs. Maintains correspondence school and library. Publication: *Flying Needle.*

Counted Thread Society of America. 1285 S. Jason Street, Denver, CO 80223. Promotes counted thread embroidery through its publications and slide rental program. Publications: *Counted Thread,* and books on related material.

Embroiderer's Guild of America. 335 W. Broadway, Suite 100, Louisville, KY 40202. Promotes high standards in all kinds of embroidery and canvaswork. Sponsors exhibitions, competitions, and field trips. Conducts classes and maintains library. Publication: *Needle Arts.*

National Quilting Association. PO Box 393, Ellicott City, MD 21041-0393. Persons interested in quilts. Recognizes outstanding quilters, and registers quilts for future historians. Maintains quilt block collection and library. Sponsors competitions and bestows awards. Publication: *Patchwork Patter.*

Fish, Aquarium

MANY OF US HAVE ADMIRED the tranquil beauty of a school of multicolored fish swimming lazily in tropical waters. For most of us the scene was played out on the Discovery channel of our television set, but some have been there, snorkeling and scuba diving to enjoy it all. Whether the experience was real or vicariously enjoyed in a favorite armchair, it has left the desire to take a living portion of that beautiful, restful scene and place it in our homes. Keeping fish as pets presents a different set of circumstances than we encounter with other members of the animal kingdom. Once the necessary equipment is in place, fish are cheap to keep and feed. They don't take up much room, need to be taken for a walk, or need to be groomed. But they can be very demanding when it comes to proper and timely care and feeding. As with caring for any living thing, you take on a responsibility that lasts as long as they live.

History

Some forms of fish having a bony skeleton have been swimming the earth's waters for over 230 million years. Fish were one of the first animals kept by mankind for pure enjoyment. There are references to goldfish in Chinese documents dating back almost 2,500 years. Goldfish hatcheries are known to have existed in China in the tenth century. The term goldfish is somewhat misleading relative to these creatures, because following domestication they were also bred in black, red, and mottled colors. Goldfish were welcomed to Japan in the sixteenth century. The Chinese, Japanese, and Koreans bred goldfish and carp for hundreds of years, developing colors and characteristics that reflected their ideas of the ideal form. The Chinese favored exaggerated features such as bulging eyes. The Japanese liked the more graceful features such as long filmy tails. These features are still found in fish today. One must remember that large glass bowls and aquariums were not available in those early days. Ornamental fish were kept it pools, tubs, and crockery. As a result fish were bred to be viewed from above. The ancient Romans also built huge ponds which they stocked with rare and valued specimens. Goldfish were brought to Europe in the seventeenth century by travelers as oriental curios, but it wasn't until the middle of the nineteenth century that they were imported into the United States.

Fish Anatomy

A basic understanding of fish anatomy is necessary in order to identify the various classifications. The mouth opening may be directed forward, up, or down. If forward, the mouth is located at the tip of the snout, and is said to be terminal. If downward, the upper jaw is prolonged, and the mouth is said to be subterminal. If upward, the lower jaw is prolonged, and the mouth is said to be supraterminal.

The fish's body is covered by several skin layers. The outer layer is covered by a fine membrane. Beneath the membrane a large number of mucus cells produce a secretion that keeps the body surface slippery and protected. Disturbance or removal of the surface mucus leaves the fish vulnerable to infection. The next layer beneath (dermis) contains pigment-bearing cells that, when stimulated, change the color of the fish. The scales are formed in the dermis and form a protective coat. Most fish have a lateral line running along their sides. It consists of sensory buds used to sense water pressure variations, to feel water current direction, and to feel pressure variations caused by sound and by moving objects such as other fish.

The fins provide stabilization and movement. Some fins occur in pairs, others singly. The pectoral pair are located on each body side just behind the gills. The ventral pair are located on each side about half way back on the lower body. The single dorsal fin is located along the forward top center of the body. Some species have two separate dorsal fins with one located behind the other. A small adipose fin is sometimes found aft of the dorsal fin at the top center. A single anal fin is located on the lower aft center of the body. The aft tail is called the caudal fin. In a few fancy species, the caudal fin may be divided into two.

In addition to the digestive and reproductive systems, the body contains a swim-bladder. This gas-filled bladder enables the fish to obtain neutral buoyancy and to stay at a desired level without sinking to the bottom. Some fish lacking this organ dwell primarily on the bottom.

Fish Classification

Many kinds of fish have more than one common name, but each kind should have only one scientific name. If you know the scientific name you can place an order for a fish or discuss it with fellow ichthyologists (fish lovers) with confidence. Since there are over eight thousand species of freshwater fish and well over eleven thousand sea fish species, you can see the value of proper identification. During the eighteenth century, Carolus Linnaeus improved and formalized some existing systems of naming plants and animals. Since scientists spoke many languages, his system used Latin names to achieve universal acceptance and understanding. His system is still found useful in modern times because of its suitability for continued correction and expansion. It's flexible. The system is based on a descending series of layers (taxonomic categories) that start at the top with the most general classification, the kingdom, and descend to the most specific classification, the species. A fish would be placed in the kingdom *animalia,* for example. The categories below kingdom, in descending order are: phylum, class, order, family, genus, and species. Taxonomists have subdivided the above categories into subcategories until there are about twenty categories at present. For practical purposes, you will most often encounter fish family, genus and species names. A species has been defined as an evolved or evolving, genetically distinctive, reproductively isolated natural population. Since the acceptance of the principle of evolutionary change, species have been considered to be dynamic entities, not fixed or static as once believed. So as science makes new discoveries of evolutionary pathways, fish will be moved from one genus to another. Add to this the genetic research currently being done, and you will understand the comment at the opening of this section that one "kind" of fish "should" have only one scientific name.

Let's see how all this works for a goldfish. The wild ancestor of the domestic goldfish is the carp species *Carassius auratus gibelio.* The genus *Carassius* belongs to the carp family (*Cyprinidae*), which is classified in the suborder of carplike fish (*Cyprinoidei*) in the order of cyprinid fish (*Cypriniformes*) in the superorder of bony fishes (*Teleostei*). The goldfish species is closely related to the crucian carp (*Carassius carassius*), cataloged there by none other than Linnaeus himself in 1758. So we turn to the family *Cyprinidea* in an illustrated fish reference book, and find that *Carassius auratus—xanthoristic* is, sure enough, a goldfish.

Native Environment

In order for fish to survive and remain healthy in captivity, we must create conditions in an aquarium similar to those found in nature. In general terms, fish come from either a freshwater or saltwater (marine) habitat. Freshwater fish come from cool waters (coldwater fish) and from tropical waters. Marine fish come from temperate waters and tropical waters. A clear-cut distinction can't be drawn between coldwater fish and tropical fish because individual fish species' temperature requirements vary within each category. However, books such as Simon & Schuster's *Guide to Freshwater and Marine Aquarium Fishes* list temperature ranges associated with each species. This information allows the hobbyist to keep in an aquarium more than one species whose native temperature ranges overlap.

Many freshwater fish come from waters with elevated acidity. Some originate in waters with high alkaline content. As with temperature, note the pH range tolerance of fish selected to be kept in the same aquarium. Alkalinity is expressed in pH units, where seven is a neutral level, with alkalinity above and acidity below. Natural sea water has a pH value between 7.9 and 8.5, which is slightly alkaline.

Setting Up Your Aquarium

The first step is to decide what kind of environment you want to create for your pets. A tropical freshwater environment is easiest for the beginner. Many plants are available that thrive in fresh water. Normal temperatures encountered in most homes come close to meeting the temperature requirements for many tropical species. If cold water species are chosen, the water will have to be cooled in summer, which can be expensive. Marine (saltwater) fish require more exacting conditions than freshwater species. Few tropical marine fish are bred in captivity, so most fish you purchase have recently come from the sea where temperature, salinity, alkalinity, sunlight, and other factors remain relatively constant. Seawater currents also provide a constant supply of fresh water. To successfully keep marine fish the hobbyist must be careful to create a similar environment. Commercially prepared chemicals added to simulate sea water contain trace elements that are consumed, resulting in the need to change at least portions of the aquarium water periodically.

The exchange of oxygen and carbon dioxide between aquarium water and the atmosphere takes place mainly at the water's surface. The larger the surface area the more fish can be stocked. A tall thin tank may hold more water, but with less surface area it can't support more fish. For this reason, a globular fish bowl should be filled only half way to maximize water surface area. Formulas have been derived to calculate the surface area required for a given fish length. A typical example for a two-inch fish in a tropical fresh water aquarium: six square inches of water surface for each inch of fish length. The area doubles for a cold freshwater aquarium and nearly triples for a tropical marine aquarium.

Set up a typical freshwater aquarium by placing several inches of substrate material on the bottom. This may consist of sand and/or pebbles. Fill halfway with water and add insoluble stones and clean wooden items to allow the fish to hide when they feel stressed. Add plants that will draw nutrients from food particles and waste products released by the fish. Finally, add water to an appropriate level.

Certain accessories are required to create and maintain the proper environment:

A pump to circulate and add oxygen to (aerate) the water.

A filter to remove unwanted solids.

Illumination that will not produce heat. Fluorescent lighting is usually recommended. Artificial lighting enables more accurate control of the light-dark cycle, important to the health of the fish.

A thermostatically controlled electrical heating unit to control temperature for certain tropical species.

An accurate thermometer to monitor proper temperature control.

Indicator papers to check pH level. These papers are available commercially and should be used to make occasional alkalinity checks.

A scraper or other device to clean algae from glass surfaces.

A siphon to collect unwanted debris from the bottom of the aquarium.

A small supplementary aquarium should be kept to hold newly purchased fish in quarantine. Your entire stock can be lost if a diseased new arrival is introduced directly into the aquarium. Such separate containers are also useful to isolate breeding fish. Some hobbyists breed fish to increase their stock and observe the varied and fascinating methods used in the propagation and rearing of the young.

Manufacturer's instructions should be carefully followed when using electrically operated equipment in the wet aquarium environment. Pull electrical plugs from their sockets while handling any electrical appliances.

Fish food for all species and sizes of fish is commercially available. Occasional feeding of live foods has proven beneficial in certain circumstances. These too, are commercially available. Some are frozen, and some are freeze-dried.

Bibliography

REFERENCE BOOKS

Dawes, John A. *A Practical Guide to Keeping Freshwater Aquarium Fishes.* New York: Exeter Books, 1987. Covers biology, aquariums, and a well illustrated selection of aquarium plants and freshwater fishes.

Levine, Joseph S. *The Complete Fishkeeper: Everything Aquarium Fishes Need to Stay Happy, Healthy, and Alive.* New York: Morrow, 1991. Covers biology, fish care, aquariums and equipment, and a selection of freshwater and saltwater fishes.

Mills, Dick, and Gwynne Vevers. *The Encyclopedia of Aquarium Fish.* New York: Crescent Books, 1986. Details the setting up of a freshwater aquarium and describes a selection of tropical freshwater species.

Pénzes, Bethen, and István Tölg. *Goldfish and Ornamental Carp.* Woodbury, NY: Barron's, 1986. Covers biology, behavior, varieties, requirements, and breeding of goldfish and ornamental carp.

Petrovicky, Ivan. *Aquarium Fish of the World.* New York: Crown, 1989. Brief coverage of fish anatomy, environments, and breeding. Well illustrated, detailed coverage of a wide variety of freshwater species.

Simon & Schuster's Guide to Freshwater and Marine Aquarium Fishes. New York: Simon & Schuster, 1977. Provides an introduction to aquarium equipment, followed by a well illustrated and detailed description of aquarium plants, freshwater fishes, and marine fishes.

Vierke, Jörg. *Vierke's Aquarium Book: The Way the Germans Do It.* Neptune city, NJ: T. F. H., 1986. Covers setting up an aquarium, equipment, and provides well illustrated descriptions of aquarium plants, and a selection of freshwater fishes.

Note: Additional current specialized aquarium books are available from: T. F. H. Publications, PO Box 427, Neptune, NJ 07753–0427.

PERIODICALS

Aquarium Fish Magazine. Fancy Publications, Box 6050, Mission Viejo, CA 92690.

Fish Culturist. Pennsylvania Fish Culturists Association, 16 Wexford Road, Gibbsboro, NJ 08026.

Freshwater and Marine Aquarium. R-C Modeler, 144 W. Sierra Madre Boulevard, Sierra Madre, CA 91024.

Tropical Fish Hobbyist. T. F. H. Publications, One T. F. H. Plaza, Third and Union Aves., Neptune City, NJ 07753.

ASSOCIATIONS

American Killifish Association. 903 Merrifield Place, Mishawaka, IN 46544. Those wishing to propagate and study the killifish tropical fish family. Publications: Newsletter, journal, and related material.

Associated Koi Clubs of America. PO Box 1, Midway City, CA 92655. Clubs interested in the ornamental variety of the Japanese carp. Conducts seminars, advises interested individuals on keeping koi fish. Bestows awards. Publications: *Koi U.S.A.,* and related materials.

Goldfish Society of America. PO Box 851282, Richardson, TX 75085–1282. Disseminates information on breeding and care of goldfish. Sponsors competitions and bestows awards. Publications: *Goldfish Report,* and related materials.

International Betta Congress. c/o Sally Van Camp, 923 Wadsworth Street, Syracuse, NY 13208. Those interested in the betta fish genus, particularly the betta splendens. Seeks to train and certify show judges, and establish judging standards. Sponsors research, and offers technical assistance in the breeding of bettas. Organizes competitions and bestows awards. Publications: *FLARE,* journal, and membership handbook.

International Fancy Guppy Association. c/o Dorothy Arms, 3933 Bush Avenue, Cleveland, OH 44109. Guppy clubs and interested individuals. Establishes standards for shows and judging. Conducts seminars, sponsors competitions, and bestows awards. Maintains hall of fame. Publications: *IFGA Official Publication,* and *Official Rules and Judging Standards.*

Fishing, Freshwater

TO SOME, THE SUBJECT OF FISHING brings back pleasant memories of going barefoot on a warm summer's day and taking a bamboo fishing pole down to the pond. Many of today's anglers pull on their wading boots, reach for their composite graphite fly-casting rod, and head for their favorite trout stream. For pure relaxation and as a way to get back to nature, freshwater fishing is hard to beat. For those willing to investigate, the good old days are still with us. In his book *The Traveling Angler*, Ernest Schwiebert tells us that fifty miles from Times Square in New York City there are still trout streams worth fishing. Schwiebert tells you where they are, how to get there, and where to spend the night. Robert Gartner tells you everything you need to know to fish in 125 national parks throughout the United States and its territories in his book, *The National Parks Fishing Guide*. Local fishing clubs control some other fishing streams and lakes around the country. Inquire at fishing tackle or bait shops for contact information. The International Game Fish Association has formulated rules to promote sporting angling practices, and that organization has served as keeper of marine game fish world records for sportfishermen and women since 1939. The location, date, fish weight, and angler's name are recorded for world record catches for over a hundred different species using various forms of tackle.

Two of the most popular game fish are bass and trout. Bass are found in all but a few states, and trout are fished in over forty states. Other freshwater fish having a wide distribution across the country include bluegills, catfish (or bullheads), crappie, perch, and pike (in the north). You will excuse me if I don't join you in fishing for gar in Missouri or Texas. These armor-plated beasts can weigh over 200 pounds and have to be shot with a .38 to kill them.

The Fish's Senses

Let's take a look at the physical characteristics of a fish. With eyes located on each side of the head, the fish's field of view covers all but a narrow sector at the rear. Some can see a narrow sector in front with both eyes at once, creating binocular view. Experiments reveal at least some can distinguish colors. Trout and probably other species can see objects above the water's surface, although the field of view is somewhat limited. Sound is sensed by means of an inner ear and a lateral line. The inner ear, located beneath the surface on the head, senses high pitched sounds. Extending the length of the fish, the lateral line senses low frequency sounds. Sounds originating above the surface in the air are not readily transmitted through the water's surface to the fish. Anglers talking in normal tones would not be sensed. Sounds originating in the water are easily detected by fish. The scraping together of stones caused by a wading angler's feet, or the splash of an oar or of a fishing lure onto the surface will be detected. The sounds made by a rushing brook sometimes mask some of these man-made sounds. Some fish are known to have a sense of smell and taste, causing them to reject certain baits and lures. They also have sensitive nerve endings on the surface of their bodies that sense temperatures and provide the ability to feel.

Habitat

Fish are said to hold or lie in certain areas of the water. Such a home location is selected for a number of reasons: It provides cover to hide from predators and affords cooling shade. The fish's preferred food is also found in or near the cover. The location provides an ambush point from which to attack prey, or to which prey are drawn by water currents. The depth level provides a water temperature to the liking of the particular species. Anglers find the best locations remain productive as replacement fish take over positions where former fish were caught.

The water temperatures near the surface of lakes become warmed due to a warming climate and longer periods of sunlight. The level of warmed water gradually drops until it reaches equilibrium with the cool water below. It tends to stratify, to create a level where warm and cool waters meet. This level is called the thermocline. Certain fish species prefer to hold near or below the thermocline. Experienced anglers know the temperatures their quarry prefer. Temperature measurements are taken and the bait is positioned accordingly.

Equipment

Fishing equipment is selected according to the weight of the species being fished, the techniques used to present the bait to the fish, and in some cases, the angler's preference in materials and design of the rod and reel.

Rods and Reels

A reel is attached to a fishing rod near the rod's handle. Fishing line is stored on a spool within the reel, and the line is threaded out along the rod through guides. The bait or lure is attached to the end of the line. A modern bait-casting reel is mounted just forward of the aft handle on the rod. It has a spool that can turn freely when the line is let out when a cast is made. The axis on which the spool turns is at right angles to the rod. When the lure and line strike the water's surface the spool has a tendency to continue turning. If this motion is not controlled the line will tangle or backlash on the reel. The angler can stop the turning at the proper moment by applying a thumb to the spool. Various braking devices, including a magnetic spool, have been used to minimize backlash. Most baitcasting reels are provided with a drag mechanism that permits line to be drawn out by a hooked fish at a predetermined level of pull. The idea is to prevent damage to the rod or line breakage in the event of a sudden forceful pull. The angler rewinds the line as the pull lessens.

A spinning reel has a stationary spool mounted with its axis parallel with the rod. It is mounted just forward of the aft handle on the rod. When a cast is made the weight of the lure uncoils the line from the end of the spool until the lure stops. Since there is no turning spool to stop, line tangling is minimized. A special wire bail turns during rewinding to reposition the line onto the spool.

Fly-casting reels are mounted at the very end of the rod with their axis at right angles to the rod. In use, the fly-casting angler pulls the line from the spool by hand during the cast so the reel's main function is to store line not in use.

Most bait-casting rods are made of fiberglass, graphite, or other composites such as Kevlar or boron. Rod lengths vary from about four to seven feet. Five and one half feet length is most popular. Rods are classified according to the lure weights they can handle effectively. Fly-casting rods are made of fiberglass, graphite, or bamboo. They are designed to be most flexible at the tip for light dry fly casting (fast-action), or flexible half their length for wet fly

work (medium-action), or fully flexible for lures that are positioned deeply in the water (slow action). A good all-purpose rod will be a medium action rod about eight feet long, weighing about five ounces.

Lures

Fishing lures are designed to look like a live baitfish, insect, or other animal when drawn over, or through the water. The angler usually imparts some motion to the lure to simulate living bait. When bait casting or trolling, the illusion of a swimming minnow is created in many ways. A *jointed plug* that wiggles in a swimming action can be used. A *stickbait* is a rigid minnow shaped device, weighted at the tail so the head rises just above the surface. The angler imparts an irregular darting motion to the stickbait by reeling at varying rates. A *crankbait* is a form of plug that features a thin sheet plastic or metal angled lip at the front that causes it to move erratically, even when cranked in at a constant rate (hence the name crankbait). A *spinnerbait* features two mounting points—one has small free-moving bright metal tear-drop-shaped pieces that reflect light as the scales of a minnow would; another point mounts a small mop-like patch of plastic strips, possibly simulating the action of a tail. A *spinner* features a freely rotating blade mounted on a single shaft. Behind the blade a body of some sort is placed, and this may be supplemented by a skirt of feather or strip plastic. A *spoon* is a form of lure that looks like a teaspoon without a handle. Although the outline may vary somewhat, the idea is to cause it to flip and reflect light as a light colored minnow would when swimming. All of the above types of lure trail a hook at the rear, having from one to three barbs.

Fly-casting lures are usually designed to represent the appearance of insects at various stages of their development. For example, a female winged Mayfly deposits her eggs on the water. The eggs sink to the bottom, and in about thirty days hatch into nymphs—an underwater bug that clings to underwater rocks and vegetation. In one year the nymphs hatch and rise to the surface, emerging as winged flies called duns. The duns fly away, change into a spinner, and eventually return to the stream to mate, lay eggs, and die on the surface. Anglers refer to insect emergence tables that indicate the approximate date that a variety of insect species will emerge from the water's surface in various parts of the country. Fly-casting lures fall into several levels of imitation of the live insect. A *suggestive fly* is a rough suggestion of the kinds of insect fish eat most often. An *impressionistic fly* is a closer copy of a specific order of insects. An *imitative fly* is made to look as close as possible to the insects emerging at the time. Fly-casting lures also fall into the several levels of development of the live insect. *Dry flies* are floated on the surface to reflect the emerged dun or the egg laying spinner. *Wet flies* are basically versions of dry flies tied sparsely to allow them to sink. They are used to simulate a drowned dun or spinner. *Nymphs* simulate the underwater nymph stage of the insect. As such, they are cast out to sink to the bottom from their own slightly heavier construction, or in faster moving water they are sunk by use of lead weights. You can see that fly lure construction can be a very challenging activity.

Various forms of plastic worms, crawdads, and lizards are used as lures. Worms are used for all species of game-fish, and are especially effective for bass. Although the first rubber worm was patented in 1860, it wasn't until modern soft plastics were perfected that fish began to take them readily. In use, they are usually cast out and allowed to sink to the bottom. They are reeled in a short distance at a time to cause them to appear to be crawling along the bottom.

Fishing Techniques

Fishing techniques vary to suit the species of fish and its habitat, the type of lure, and local conditions.

Jigging and Flipping

A jig is a piece of lead with a hook molded into it. Various dressings are added to cover the lead. Other forms include the addition of a spoon or spinner. Jigging is performed by casting out and allowing the jig to fall to the bottom, then retrieved in short hops much as you would with a plastic worm. Other approaches are to lower the jig to a level where the fish are thought to be and twitch the rod tip. Jigs can also be slowly trolled along the bottom retaining the skipping movement forward.

When flipping, the angler holds the rod nearly vertical, extends the line five feet or so, and pulls an additional length of slack line from the reel with the other hand. The lure is swung forward and slack line is released at the same time resulting in flipping the lure well away from the angler to a predetermined spot. When the lure is in the water the technique can be used to jig the lure up and down or crawl it along the bottom.

Trolling

The various plug and spoon lures used for bait casting can be moved through the water by pulling them along behind a boat. The practice is called trolling. When flat line trolling, the line with lure attached is let out to a length that will cause it to travel a desired distance below the surface. Variations in boat speed sometimes make depth control difficult. To solve the problem a technique called down-rigging was developed. A heavy weight is suspended on a cable at the desired depth. A fishing rod is held in a suitable bracket and the fishing line is run down to the weight, through a quick release mechanism, and allowed to trail along behind the weight as the boat moves along. A

suitable lure is attached to the trailing line. The idea is to maintain a constant depth for the lure. When a fish strikes the lure, the line comes free from the quick release and the fish is played by the angler as under normal circumstances. Trailing lines being trolled can be diverted from their normal paths with various planing devices. A device on a cable featuring a flat plate positioned to deflect the path of the device to one side of the path of the boat is used, and a fishing line is run to the device and trails to one side of the boat. Two or more such planing devices can be used to trail several fishing lines at the same time.

Bait Casting

Before artificial lures were developed anglers used their rods to cast live bait out away from the shore. After artificial lures became common, both artificial and live bait casting were referred to as bait casting to distinguish them from fly casting. We have seen the variety of lures, rods, and reels that can be used. Here we'll look at bait casting technique. The three types of casting used are the overhead, sidearm, and underhand casts. The wrist and the forearm do the work to cause the top of the rod to provide thrust. Start with the rod low and pointed at the target. Bring the rod up swiftly to just past vertical, where flex of the rod tip will cause it to carry back. Without hesitating, start forward motion sharply, releasing the line halfway between the rod's vertical and horizontal positions. The whipping motion will carry the lure out away from the angler. Accuracy in placing the lure at the desired location can only be improved with practice. Some anglers practice at home on a lawn using a large basket for a target. Don't forget to take the hook off of the lure.

Fly Casting

The ancient art of fly fishing is unique in that the weight of the line itself is cast. Other forms of casting depend upon the weight of the lure to carry the line; fly lures contribute minimal weight. A fly cast is begun with about twenty feet of line extended in front of the rod. The rod is held firmly in one hand and the line between the reel and the rod is held with the free hand. Consider a horizontal line through your hands to be the nine o'clock position, and a line directly over your head to be the twelve o'clock position. Raise the rod slowly to a ten o'clock position, then swiftly raise the rod tip throwing the line high and to the rear. As the line straightens out behind you, pull some line down with your free hand. Stop the backward motion of the rod just past vertical at one o'clock. Look back to see that the line is extended behind you. When the line is fully extended, pause briefly, and start moving the rod forward to about ten o'clock, releasing the line held slack in your free hand. As the rod moves forward the line will move forward in a loop and straighten out in front of you. Releasing the slack in the free hand will cause the slack line to run out through the rod line guides, extending the distance. The line will settle to the water surface. Anglers sometimes repeat the above whipping action forward and back one or more times, keeping the line in the air. This is called a false cast, often used to shake excess water off of dry flies. The basic overhead cast described above doesn't require significant strength or effort once the technique is mastered. Precise fly placement takes time and practice. Placement, or presentation, is critical when fly fishing. The fish will not strike the lure if it isn't close enough to see. The cast should place the fly in front of the fish, but without allowing the line to lie over the fish. When a fly lands, it should float with the water current freely and naturally—not deflected by a pull on the line. This requires that there is line slack between the rod and the floating fly.

Accessories

Topographic maps are very useful to fishermen, especially when traveling to unfamiliar areas, or when you would like to record good fishing spots you have discovered. They can also be used in conjunction with Loran, described below. Some maps are available that show lake bottom contours, another valuable resource. Topographic maps are available at some sporting goods stores, marinas, and large city map stores.

Loran C is a low-frequency land-based navigation system that can be used to allow boaters to locate and return to specific places. It was originally established for maritime use. Modern portable Loran Cs have been transistorized into an eight inch high hand-held unit. Position accuracy is said to be within sixty feet. See the section in this text on "Aviation" and the heading on navigational systems for more detail on Loran C and the next generation navigation system, the global positioning system (GPS).

Sonar is an electronic system that sends pulsed signals through the water and records their return when they bounce off solid objects such as a lake bottom or a fish. An image of the solid surface can be viewed on a screen or on a graph recorder that produces a permanent paper image.

Temperature sensors are used to obtain water temperatures at various depths. These are useful when searching for the thermocline. Some units combine temperature indication and trolling speed readouts.

Electric trolling motors are often attached to the bow of a boat to be used for quiet trolling for fish. The units actually pull the boat rather than push it, affording better forward visibility in congested areas.

Bibliography

REFERENCE BOOKS

Bashline, Jim. *The Trout and Salmon Fisherman's Bible.* New York: Doubleday, 1991. A practical guide for trout. Covers equipment, techniques, fish characteristics, and cooking fish.

Gartner, Robert. *The National Parks Fishing Guide.* Chester, CT: Globe Pequot, 1990. A fishing book that tells everything you need to know to fish in 125 national parks. Identifies park location, maps available, contact addresses, licenses and permits required, fish to be found, and suggested lures.

Hughes, Dave. *Tactics for Trout.* Harrisburg, PA: Stackpole Books, 1990. Covers trout foods, fly pattern selection, tackle, and casting techniques.

Rogers, E. L. *The World's Best Fishing Holes.* New York: Prentice Hall, 1986. More than seventy fishing destinations are described in detail including well known American gamefish and little known Arctic and South American species.

Rosenbauer, Tom. *Reading Trout Streams: An Orvis Guide.* New York: Nick Lyons Books, 1988. Describes in detail how to identify the best locations to fish for trout.

Schultz, Ken. *The Art of Trolling.* Lexington, MA: Stephen Greene, 1987. The latest freshwater methods and tackle, plus techniques for major game fish. How to rig lines, select lures, and find fish.

———. *Bass Fishing Fundamentals.* 2nd ed. Lexington, MA: Stephen Greene, 1986. A bass fishing primer for beginner or expert. Broad coverage of techniques and equipment.

Schwiebert, Ernest. *The Traveling Angler: 20 Five-Star Angling Vacations.* New York: Doubleday, 1991. A unique book about fishing locations, interesting experiences, and good eating. Identifies special fishing sites around the world, how to get there, and where to stay when you do. Includes contact information.

Sparano, Vin T. *Complete Outdoors Encyclopedia.* 2nd ed. New York: Harper & Row, 1980. A wide-ranging book about the outdoors with extensive coverage of fishing. Includes coverage of equipment, techniques, and such detailed subjects as knot tying, International Game Fish Association Records, and fly tying.

Sternberg, Dick. *Fishing with Artificial Lures.* Minnetonka, MN: DeCosse, 1985. Well illustrated coverage of fishing equipment with emphasis on artificial lures of all types.

———. *Northern Pike and Muskie.* Minnetonka, MN: DeCosse, 1992. Well illustrated coverage of fishing equipment with emphasis on techniques for pike and muskellunge fishing. Includes information on habitat and fish characteristics.

Walton, Izaak. *The Compleat Angler.* New York: Everyman's Library, Dutton, 1965. Probably the most read book about fishing has been reprinted 300 times. Readers who enjoy a bit of philosophy with their fishing will like this classic.

PERIODICALS

Field & Stream Fishing Annual. Times Mirror Magazines, 2 Park Avenue, New York, NY 10016–5675.

Fish and Game Finder. 1233 W. Jackson Street, Orlando, FL 32805.

The Fish Sniffer. Northern California Angler Publications, Box 994, Elk Grove, CA 95759–0994.

Fisherman. L I F Publishers, 14 Ramsey Road, Shirley, NY 11967.

Fishermen's News. W. Wall Building, Room 110, Fisherman's Terminal, Seattle, WA 98119.

Fishing and Hunting News. Outdoor Empire Publishers, 511 Eastlake Avenue E., Box C 19000, Seattle, WA 98109.

Fishing Annual. Prentice Hall Press, One Gulf & Western Plaza, New York, NY 10023.

Fishing Facts. 312 E. Buffalo Street, Milwaukee, WI 53202.

Fishing Smart. Aqua-Field Publishers, 66 W. Gilbert Street, Shrewsbury, NJ 07702.

Fishing World. Allsport Publishers, 51 Atlantic Avenue, Floral Park, NY 11001.

Fly Fisherman. Cowles Magazines, 6405 Flank Drive, Box 8200, Harrisburg, PA 17105–8200.

Fly Fishing Made Easy. Aqua-Field Publishers, 66 W. Gilbert Street, Shrewsbury, NJ 07702.

ASSOCIATIONS

American Bass Association. 886 Trotters Trail, Wetumpka, AL 36092. Promotes bass fishing events. Sponsors competitions and bestows awards. Publication: *American Bass News.*

American Casting Association. c/o Dale Lanser, 1739 Praise Boulevard, Fenton, MO 63026. Federation of amateur tournament fly and bait casters. Establishes rules for sanctioned tournaments. Sponsors competitions. Maintains hall of fame and bestows awards.

Association of Northwest Steelheaders. PO Box 22065, Milwaukie, OR 97222. Seeks protection of salmon, trout and steelhead, and promotes recreational angling. Publication: *Northwest Steelheader.*

Bass Inc. c/o Wayne Goble, PO Box 17900, Montgomery, AL 36141–0900. Individuals who enjoy the sport of bass fishing. Produces weekly TV program, "The Bassmasters." Sponsors competitions and bestows awards. Publications: *BASS on Tour Newsletter, BASS Times Newspaper, Bassmaster Magazine, Fishing Tackle Retailer, Southern Outdoors,* and *Southern Saltwater.*

Bass'n Gal. PO Box 13925, 2007 Roosevelt, Arlington, TX 76013. To bring together women anglers of the U.S. and help improve members' skills as anglers through the exchange of techniques and ideas. Conducts youth fishing projects through affiliated club programs and local level seminars by affiliated clubs. Bestows scholarship. Publication: *Bass'n Gal Magazine.*

Federation of Fly Fishers. PO Box 1088, West Yellowstone, MT 59758. Promotes fly fishing. Conducts water quality, specialized education, and fly fishing instruction programs. Sponsors competitions and bestows awards. Maintains library and museum. Publications: *The Flyfisher,* and related materials.

Great Lakes Sport Fishing Council. c/o Dan Thomas, 293 Berteau, Elmhurst, IL 60126. Disseminates information and provides educational programs on conservation and sport fishing in the Great Lakes. Publication: *Inland Seas Angler.*

International Game Fish Association. 1301 E. Atlantic Boulevard, Pompano Beach, FL 33060–6744. Federation of freshwater and saltwater anglers and angling clubs. Promotes the study of game fish and game fish angling. Compiles and maintains fishing records. Maintains library. Publications: *International Angler, International Tournament Calendar, World Record Game Fishes,* and related material.

National Fishing Lure Collectors Club. PO Box 0184, Chicago, IL 60690. Promotes tackle collecting and classifying. Assists members with their appraisal and identification efforts. Maintains small library and museum. Publications: *NFLCC Gazette,* and related material.

North American Fishing Club. 12301 Whitewater Drive, Suite 260, Minnetonka, MN 55343. Seeks to improve the fishing skills of members and promotes enjoyment of the sport. Provides information about fishing guides/outfitters. Publication: *Fishing Club Journal.*

United Fly Tyers. PO Box 220, Maynard, MA 01754. Serves individuals who develop, practice, and carry on the craft of fly tying. Offers educational programs, and bestows awards. Publication: *United Fly Tyers Roundtable.*

Football

A FOOTBALL TEAM ATTEMPTS to move a ball the length of a field and across a goal line in a prescribed manner. An opposing team attempts to prevent that scoring action within the rules of the game.

The field is laid out as shown in Figure 1.

Each team fields eleven players positioned in a pattern similar to Figure 2.

Offensive players

1. Center
2. Guard
3. Tackle
4. Tight End
5. Wide Receiver or Split End
6. Wide Receiver
7. Quarterback
8. Fullback or Running Back
9. Half Back or Running Back

Defensive Players

10. Defensive Tackle
11. Defensive End
12. Nose Guard
13. Linebacker
14. Cornerback
15. Safety

Player substitutions are permitted and it's common practice to substitute the whole team when changing from offensive to defensive play.

Before the game begins, an official will determine which team will be first to receive the ball. This is usually done by the toss of a coin.

Play is initiated when the defensive team kicks the ball, from the thirty yard line in professional play, to a point as far down the field as possible to the offensive team. A player from the offense catches the ball and runs toward the defense's goal until tackled or forced out of bounds by a defending player. The ball is dead when a ball carrier is forced outside of the sidelines. The next attempt to move the ball (a down) is begun on a line passing through the point the ball carrier crossed the sideline, and toward the center of the field beyond the inbound line nearest the sideline that was crossed. A tackle is made by causing the ball carrier to touch the ground by applying forceful contact or by using the arms to grasp or encircle the ball carrier's legs or body. The ball is dead when the ball carrier is tackled and touches the ground with any part of the body except hands or feet. In professional play, if the ball carrier slips to the ground without being tackled he can continue to run.

The offense has four downs to advance ten yards. If ten yards are gained, another four downs are allowed. If ten yards are not gained, the ball reverts to the opposition. If far from the goal line the offensive team often elects to kick the ball to the opposition on the fourth down. Each down is initiated when the center passes the ball back to a player behind the line of scrimmage, usually to the quarterback.

The ball may be advanced by kicking, carrying or throwing (passing) the ball. When passing the ball, the passer must do so from a location behind the line of scrimmage. The line of scrimmage for each team is defined as a line passing through the tip of the football nearest the team when the football is at rest after the preceding down. After catching the ball the offensive receiver may run until tackled or forced out of bounds. If the defense catches the ball it is called an interception and they take possession of the ball.

A touchdown is scored when the ball is either carried over the the opponent's goal or passed over the goal and caught in the opponent's end zone. Six points are awarded. An extra point can be made after a touchdown by kicking the ball over the crossbar and between the goal posts, or two points can be made by carrying or passing the ball over the goal line from a point two yards from the goal line.

A field goal is scored when a player kicks the ball over the crossbar and between the goal posts from a point behind the line of scrimmage. Three points are awarded.

A safety is scored when an offensive player is tackled in his own end zone. The defensive team is awarded two points.

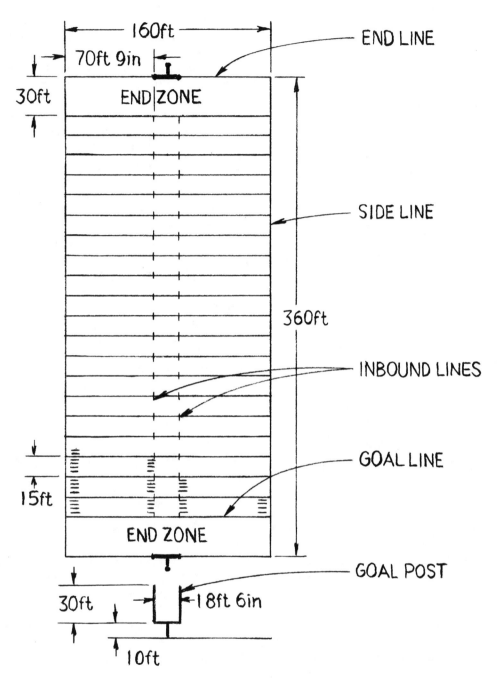

Figure 1
Professional football field layout.

A game consists of four fifteen-minute quarters. If the game ends in a tied score, an additional fifteen-minute period is played, terminated when either team scores and breaks the tie. If neither team scores during the fifteen-minute overtime period, the game ends in a tie.

History

The name football has been given to other similar games. In fourteenth century England a large number of players representing two neighboring towns played a game with an inflated animal bladder. Starting at a midpoint they used their town limits as goals and kicked, punched, and carried the ball as many as three or four miles. King Richard II banned the game in 1389 because it interfered with archery practice. Eventually rugby and soccer emerged from these large-scale beginnings.

The American game of football, as it is known today, evolved from a soccer-like game played in colleges early in the nineteenth century. In the early days the game was rough, frequently resulting in the injury, even death of players.

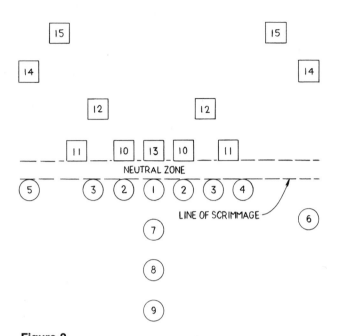

Figure 2

Nominal player positions. During play, the quarterback will signal instructions to position players as required for a planned play action.

At the urging of President Theodore Roosevelt an American Inter-Collegiate Football Rules Committee was formed in 1906 to promote a safer and more interesting game. New rules were established and continued to evolve significantly. By 1912 many features had been added that are part of the modern game. They include the addition of a fourth down, raising the points awarded for a touchdown to six and establishing the field length at 100 yards. One 1907 rule change that present day quarterbacks certainly appreciate was the elimination of a fifteen-yard penalty for failure to complete a forward pass.

Equipment

The game is played with a ball weighing fourteen to fifteen ounces. It is 11-to-11¼ inches long, has a circumference of 21¼-to-21½ inches around the middle and 28-to-28½ inches over the ends.

A special padded helmet is worn that also provides face protection and an attach point for a mouthpiece. Various pads are worn from the shoulders to the ankles. All team members wear a similar colored uniform with a conspicuous number to identify the player. Specific number series are reserved for each player position.

Strategy

Football plays are diagrammed and codified so the quarterback can call out or signal instructions and the team will know what action is to take place. During these plays the positions of players are specified and they will vary from the normal set-up shown in Figure 2 to accommodate planned action. In any case the offense must have seven players on the line of scrimmage.

When a forward pass is made, only the players on the ends of the scrimmage line or those standing at least one yard behind the line are eligible to receive the ball.

There are many potential plays using the linemen or backs to deflect or check opposing tacklers. It's like a game of chess with highly trained and conditioned athletes. Each threat by the offense is countered by a specialist in defense. When a wide receiver sprints down the field to catch a pass from the quarterback, the defending cornerback is there trying to deflect the ball or, with luck, catch it. The offensive line will try to separate the defensive line according to a planned play to provide a path for a running back to advance, only to be tackled by a linebacker from the opponent's defense.

In professional football, game strategy is planned using information from scouting reports and a study of previous game films of the opposing team. A game plan is then established. Spotters located in the stadium maintain telephone contact with coaches, who modify plans as the game unfolds.

Game Variations and Related Activity

Amateur Football

College football is played on a field similar to professional football with the exception that the inbound lines are 53 feet 4 inches from the sidelines. Significant differences in the game include the following: The football is slightly shorter. In college ball a game can end in a tie. In college ball a pass receiver need only have one foot inbounds when catching as opposed to both feet in bounds for the professionals. In college ball a ball carrier can't advance after slipping to the ground if any part of the body except hands and feet touch the ground.

High school and youth league football rules differ from college and professional rules. See the bibliography for contacts to obtain information for your league.

Touch or flag football can be played with little or no equipment except the football. Body contact is minimized since the tackle is replaced by touching the ball carrier, usually with both hands. Another variation has the player carry a handkerchief or flag in a back pocket. When the opposing team captures the flag the play is ended. National touch football leagues establish the rules. Touch football is also played on sand lots throughout the country with a minimum of rules. It provides exercise with a minimum of bruises.

Memorabilia and Fantasy

Football fans are avid football card and memorabilia collectors. Autographs of football greats are eagerly sought. A large network of manufacturers, dealers and periodicals provide services to these fans. Conventions, trade shows, and auctions are found throughout the country.

Fantasy Football is gaining popularity. This is an armchair hobby pitting knowledgeable sports enthusiasts against one another using a professional player's performance as a determining factor. See the section "Games, Gambling" for more information.

Bibliography

REFERENCE BOOKS

Allen, George. *Strategies for Winning.* New York: McGraw-Hill, 1990. Philosophy and motivation.

Athletic Institute. *Youth League Football, Coaching and Playing.* North Palm Beach, FL: Athletic Institute, 1980. Conditioning, safety, and techniques.

Bass, Tom. *Play Football the NFL Way.* New York: St. Martin's, 1990. Techniques and drills for the offense, defense, and special teams.

Jennings, Dave, Matt Bahr, and Rick Danmeier. *The Art of Place-Kicking and Punting.* New York: Simon & Schuster, 1985. Mechanics of kicking and punting, and mental demands.

Johnson, John L. *How to Watch Football.* 2nd ed. San Marcos, CA: Slawson Communications, 1991. Understanding the game.

Namath, Joe. *Football for Young Players and Parents.* New York: Simon and Schuster, 1986. How to play your best at every position.

Schiffer, Don, and Lud Duroska, eds. *Football Rules in Pictures.* New York: Perigee Books, 1988. Illustrated rules.

Wilkinson, Bud. *Sports Illustrated Football: Winning Offense.* Rev. ed. New York: Sports Illustrated Winner's Circle Books, 1987. Offensive techniques.

PERIODICALS

Football Digest. Century Publications, 990 Grove Street, Evanston, IL 60201–4370.

Football Guide. Kwik-Fax Books, Box 14613, Surfside Beach, SC 29587.

Football News. Football News, 17820 E. Warren, Detroit, MI 48224.

ASSOCIATIONS

National Football Foundation and Hall of Fame. Bell Tower Building, 1865 Palmer Avenue, Larchmont, NY 10538. Elects great ex-players and coaches of college football to The College Football Hall of Fame. Publication: Newsletter.

National Touch Football Leagues. 1039 Coffey Court, Crestwood, MO 63126. Men's and women's touch and flag football. Maintains hall of fame. Publication: Newsletter.

Pop Warner Football. 920 Town Center Drive, Suite I–25, Langhorne, PA 19047. Youths aged seven to sixteen organized into 4,000 teams. Presents awards and maintains hall of fame. Publications: Magazine, and rules and regulations.

United States Flag Football League. c/o John D. Carrigan, 5834 Pine Tree Drive, Sanibel, FL 33957. Flag football for men eighteen and over on an amateur basis. Publication: Rule book.

Fossils, Rocks, and Artifacts

ASTRONOMERS TELL US that during the formation of a star, the gas and dust surrounding it form into a flat disk that surround the star's equator. When our star, the Sun, evolved in this manner, the materials in the disk formed the planets, probably by the process of accretion, where bits of matter collide and stick together. They gradually grow large enough to exert a gravitational pull on surrounding material, and the process speeds up, forming a planet such as our Earth. Some elements, such as gold and silver, were created when distant stars were formed and died in supernovae, contributing their dust to the formation of the earth.

The Earth

The force of gravity on the Earth's surface creates sufficient pressure to raise the core temperature enough that the core remains in a molten condition. The Earth's crust is made up of a group of massive continental plates. When molten material rises to the surface between plates, it cools and forms new land surface area. The action causes the existing land to move away from the source of the rising material. This movement is called continental drift. When plates move toward one another and collide, one slides under the other, raising it to form mountain ranges. The abrasive action of wind and water wears the mountains away and the material is redistributed, and the cycle of continental building and eradication continues. Lines of volcanic action are found at the edges of plates where the upwelling of molten material takes place. Only 200 million years ago most of the continents familiar to us today fitted together like a jigsaw puzzle. The land mass that was to become the North American continent slowly drifted from the equator to its present position.

When molten material hardens, igneous rock is formed. Any trace of life-forms has been burned away. Mineral compounds and some gemstones are found in such rock.

Sedimentary rock forms when silt and material worn from other rocks are deposited in layers and become compressed. Fossilized plant and animal remains are found in this type of rock.

Metamorphic rock is any rock that has been changed from its original form. Mineral compounds are more likely to be found than gemstones or fossils.

The Earth formed by accretion from about 5,000 to 4,500 million years (M.y.) ago. Bacteria and blue-green algae appeared 3,200 M.y. ago. Trilobites were first found on the sea floor about 590 M.y. ago. Land plants appeared about 450 M.y. ago. Dinosaurs lasted from 240 to 70 M.y. ago. Primates appeared 30 M.y. ago. Hominids, the ancestors of man, appeared about 13 M.y. ago in the form of a long-armed, ape-like individual scientists call Ramapithecus. *Homo erectus,* a more modern form of man lived from 1.5 M.y. to half a million years ago. He was gradually replaced over a period from 400 thousand and 100 thousand years ago by *Homo sapiens sapiens,* who by twenty thousand years ago looked much the way we do today.

Rocks and Minerals

Rocks are usually composed of several minerals, making exact identification a laboratory process. There are approximately thirty-five hundred known mineral species. Minerals are naturally occurring chemical elements and compounds. For general classification purposes the hobbyist can note the following characteristics.

Hardness is expressed by a number on the Mohs Scale. Friedrich Mohs set up a scale from one to ten. He selected minerals having a hardness equal to each number to provide a basis for comparison. The following are the numbers and their respective minerals: 1. talc (softest), 2. gypsum, 3. calcite, 4. fluorite, 5. apatite, 6. feldspar, 7. quartz, 8.

topaz, 9. corundum, 10. diamond. Actually a diamond is much harder than corundum; its true value would be about forty-two. You can estimate a mineral's hardness by determining whether it will scratch or be scratched by other minerals in the Mohs hardness scale. Common objects of known hardness can be substituted. Items and their Mohs hardness include: fingernail 2.5, copper coin 3.5, steel nail 4.5, penknife blade or window glass 5.5, steel file 6.5–7.

Streak is the color of the fine powder obtained by rubbing a mineral against unglazed porcelain, such as the reverse side of a white tile. This is the most useful color-based test. This characteristic applies almost exclusively to opaque, metallic minerals because the powder of most transparent minerals is colorless.

Luster is the amount of light reflected, absorbed, or transmitted by the specimen. It is primarily divided into metallic or nonmetallic. Nonmetallic minerals may appear vitreous (luster of glass), pearly, resinous (luster of resin), greasy, adamantine (like the reflection from a diamond), silky, or dull. Luster is often cited for identification purposes, but it may vary within a single specimen.

Other tests include the way a mineral breaks when struck, the specific gravity (weight compared to water), and chemical composition.

Many hobbyists specialize in the collection of crystals. Their beautiful colors and structure make an attractive display.

The most difficult minerals to find and collect are gemstones. This is not surprising because the characteristics that set gem minerals apart from the rest are beauty, durability and rarity. A gem can be described as any mineral cut and polished for ornamental purposes. This broad definition encompasses many minerals that are not traditionally included as gems. The following sixteen minerals have achieved importance as gems: beryl, chrysoberyl, corundum, diamond, feldspar, garnet, jade, lazurite, olivine, opal, quartz, spinel, topaz, tourmaline, turquoise, and zircon. Other names are sometimes applied to variations of the above when impurities change their color. An emerald is green corundum, and an aquamarine is blue corundum. The art of cutting, polishing, and engraving precious stones is called lapidary.

Fossils

Life-forms that have inhabited the earth are preserved in the form of fossils when they are covered by sediment and encased. Over the years minerals often replace most of the original specimen forming a cast of the plant or animal. Since we have learned which types of specimens lived during certain time periods, geologists can use fossils to date a given earth layer. This is useful knowledge when prospecting for minerals and oil. The branch of geology

that deals with prehistoric forms of life through the study of plant and animal fossils is called paleontology.

Fossils can be found in most states. Check your library, university, or museum of natural history to determine which geologic time periods lie exposed in your area. Most hobbyists will never be able to collect giant dinosaur bones or have access to California's famous La Brea tar pits. But they do have an almost unlimited opportunity to collect the fossilized remains of sea creatures that inhabited the shallow seas covering much of North America many millions of years ago. Figure 1 illustrates a selection of brachiopods from Ohio sea bottoms whose ages range from 250 to 400 million years. The most easily found invertebrates that are known to have left fossils are: Porifera (sponges), Coelenterata (corals, hydroids, jelly fishes, sea anemones, and allied forms), Bryozoa (moss animals), Chaetognatha (arrow worms), Brachiopoda (lampshells), Annelida (segmented worms), Echinodermata (crinoids, starfish, and sea urchins), Mollusca (mollusks), and Arthropoda (trilobites, crustaceans, horseshoe crabs, insects, and spiders). These life-forms are divided into classes, orders, genera, and species providing an interesting classification challenge to the serious collector.

When plants such as ancient ferns were suddenly buried in fine sediment, they produced a gas bubble as they decayed. The hollow in the sediment formed by the bubble gradually filled with minerals, encasing the fragile fern outline. Fossil hunters discover resulting elliptical stone nodules that easily can be split to reveal the beautiful outlines of the original foliage.

Artifacts

Anthropology is the total study of mankind. It includes man's origins, physical and cultural development, racial characteristics, social customs, and beliefs. Archaeology involves the scientific study of ancient peoples and their cultures by searching for and analyzing physical remains and artifacts. While most hobbyists will engage only in the hands-on aspects of archaeology, they will be more successful in finding and understanding collected material if they study the basics of anthropology.

There is evidence that before 8000 B.C., our ancestors had begun to develop language, society, shelter, clothing, and religion. They had also begun to use fire. Between 8000 and 7000 B.C., man started rudimentary farming and domesticated the dog. Between 7000 and 3000 B.C. he had domesticated other animals for food, made pottery, and polished stone tools. Between 3000 and 1200 B.C. he learned the use of bronze, and after 1200 B.C. he mastered the use of iron.

The relative position of artifacts at a site is important to the archaeologist. Usually, the deeper the object is found, the older it is. Artifacts found at the same level tell the story

Figure 1
Fossils

Dating Artifacts

of the cultural development of the period. When archaeologists carefully dig and record data from a site, they destroy the site for future use. Only their records remain.

When amateur archaeologists or treasure hunters dig for artifacts, they disturb the position of specimens, making the site less useful for scientific study. Would-be amateur archaeologists are urged to volunteer their aid to established archaeological groups to learn and make useful contributions. Opportunities can be found in the classified section of *Archaeology Magazine* and through organizations listed in the following bibliography.

Dating Artifacts

The depth at which artifacts are found gives an idea of relative age, but modern science has developed techniques that are more precise. Living things have a certain carbon content. Science makes use of this fact in a system of radio carbon dating. Normal carbon has an atomic weight of 12. Radioactive carbon has an atomic weight of 14. Carbon 14 is produced in the upper atmosphere and is absorbed by living things. These living things reach a level of combined carbon 12 and 14 equal to the atmosphere. At death the atomic weight of the carbon in their remains drops back toward twelve at a uniform rate. In 5,730 years, it reaches one-half of its former level. Knowing the normal ratio during life, we measure the radioactivity in the artifact now and we can calculate the time since death.

A similar form of dating is the potassium-argon method. A radioactive isotope of potassium present in rocks and volcanic ash decays into the gas argon at a known rate. Half of a given amount will change to argon in about 1.3 billion years. When molten rock solidifies, argon is trapped inside. By measuring the ratio of potassium to argon, it is possible to estimate the time since the rock or ash cooled and solidified. Because of the long half-life of potassium this method is useful to date materials many millions of years old.

Recent wooden artifacts can be accurately dated by study of the growth rings visible in their end grain. Most trees add a single ring each year to their circumference. Trees grow more rapidly during years with above average rainfall. Their growth rings are further apart. In times of drought, the rings are close together. Over a period of time a recognizable growth pattern develops. The ring pattern on a wooden article will reflect the time when a tree was cut to make the article. By comparing trees whose lifetimes overlapped, it is possible to trace the growth patterns back from the present to earlier times. The method is called dendrochronology.

Modern Aids to Anthropology and Archaeology

Recent findings in the study and interpretation of deoxyribonucleic acid (DNA) are providing important new insights to the genealogy and migration paths of man. Startling discoveries are being made, such as the fact that chimpanzees and man share more than 98 percent of the same genes.

The modern archaeologist receives assistance from many scientific disciplines. Sites may first be identified by study of photographs taken from satellites or aircraft. A well-staffed expedition may include geologists, ecologists, plant-geneticists, botanists, and zoologists.

Modern computers get into the old-age business in many ways. One example is analysis of the distribution of types of artifacts and their patterning. This improves and speeds the analysis of data.

The professional archaeologist studies, records, and photographs finds and usually doesn't expect to keep them, especially in foreign countries where they become the property of the state by law. Amateurs take note.

Underwater Artifacts

While we usually expect to find artifacts by digging, we may also find them by diving. The examination of ancient shipwrecks in the Mediterranean Sea has caused the rewriting of many historical pages. Plans of ancient boats are both rare and vague, so much is learned of ancient shipbuilding practices by study of the remains found in the sea.

During prehistoric times, the level of lakes and rivers changed substantially. Dwellings built near lakes during periods of low water became submerged when the water rose. These well-preserved sites yield artifacts from the early Stone Age through the Bronze Age. They include stone implements, bronze weapons, swords, pottery, and even gold and jewelry. Such sites are found throughout Europe.

Catastrophic events like the volcanic eruption that buried Pompeii, or shipwrecks, capture a moment in time that enables the archaeologist to see the relationship between implements, art, and the culture of the period.

Amateur Activity

Research the area you plan to visit and the material you can expect to find. This will save wasting time looking in the wrong places and overlooking the obvious. A fossil collector was told that there were abundant fossils at a location in Indiana. All that was found was some coarse sand. After some time searching, a closer look revealed that the sand grains were tiny gastropods (snails), pelecypods (clams), and bits of coral from an ancient seashore.

Proper clothing made of durable materials should be worn on collecting trips. Shoes should cover your ankles and have tough soles. If you plan to be out of touch with people, let someone know where you will be, and take along clothing appropriate for weather changes, food, water, and a first aid kit.

Other related equipment will vary some with the material you are collecting. A typical rock or fossil collecting kit will include a rock hammer whose head is blunt on one end and chisel-shaped on the other. A small chisel will also be useful. Small containers, plastic bags, and labels keep collected items separated and organized. A notebook can be used to record details of the site and specimen locations. Toilet paper will be found useful to wrap and pack fragile specimens (and for emergency use). These items can be carried conveniently in a small canvas shoulder bag or backpack.

Some rules of conduct should be observed. If you haven't prearranged a visit with the site owner, ask for permission before trespassing. Leave gates and fences as you find them. Don't litter, do refill holes you have dug before leaving. Plan the necessary time to have a pleasant, relaxing day. It is a healthful and educational way for a family to enjoy the great out-of-doors.

Collections should be cleaned and cataloged in a timely manner. Specimens that cannot be linked to their place of origin lose much of their value to both ourselves and other interested individuals.

Rock and mineral collectors process their finds in a variety of ways. Some tumble them with abrasives to make them smooth, shiny, and colorful. Attractive specimens are mounted as jewelry. Gem quality specimens may be ground to create facets that reflect light. There are many ways that mineral collections are used for ornamentation, both indoors and out. Collectors who wish to process their finds for study purposes sometimes mount small samples in plastic boxes. Thumbnail collections feature one-inch square specimens. Smaller one-sixteenth inch square micromount collections are also prepared. Data about the specimen is written on the box.

Bibliography

REFERENCE BOOKS

Arem, Joel. *Rocks and Minerals.* Rev. ed. Phoenix, AZ: Geoscience, 1991. Illustrated identification guide including useful tables listing characteristics.

Arem, Joel E. *Color Encyclopedia of Gem Stones.* 2nd ed. New York: Van Nostrand Reinhold, 1987. Comprehensive coverage of gems including physical properties, occurrence, chemistry, and rarity.

Calvin William H. *The Ascent of Mind: Ice Age Climates and the Evolution of Intelligence.* New York: Bantam Books, 1990. Looks at the rapid evolutionary drives that transformed the ape brain into a human mind.

Casanova, Richard, and Donald P. Ratkevich. *An Illustrated Guide to Fossil Collecting.* 3rd ed. Happy Camp, CA: Naturegraph, 1981. An overview of fossils with emphasis on collecting.

Case, Gerard R. *A Pictorial Guide to Fossils.* New York: Van Nostrand Reinhold, 1982. An illustrated presentation of past lifeforms, from one celled animal to the mammal.

Chesterman, Charles W. *The Audubon Society Field Guide to North American Rocks and Minerals.* New York: Knopf, 1979. Illustrated identification guide with detailed information on rock and mineral types.

Diamond, Jared. *The Third Chimpanzee: The Evolution and Future of the Human Animal.* New York: Harper Collins, 1992. Discussion of what makes us human. Explores our unique sexuality and behavioral patterns, and what makes us different.

Eckert, Allan W. *Earth Treasures: Where to Collect Minerals, Rocks, and Fossils in the U.S.* 4 v. New York: Harper & Row, 1987. Specific locations in which to collect in four quadrants of the continental U.S.

Fenton, Carroll Lane, and Mildred Adams Fenton. *The Fossil Book: A Record of Prehistoric Life.* Rev. ed. New York: Doubleday, 1989. A survey of fossils from the earliest traces of Precambrian life to beasts and birds that lived only a few centuries ago.

Gowlett, John. *Ascent to Civilization: The Archaeology of Early Man.* New York: Knopf, 1984. The world of prehistoric man from the time the first human walked the earth to the beginnings of civilization.

Hadingham, Evan. *Early Man and the Cosmos.* New York: Walker, 1984. A study of man's perception of the universe with emphasis on ancient astronomy.

Harris, Marvin. *Our Kind: Who We Are, Where We Came From, Where We Are Going.* New York: Harper & Row, 1989. The origins and evolution of man. Explores the various elements of our culture.

Holden, Raymond. *Secrets in the Dust: The Story of Archaeology.* New York: Dodd, Mead, 1960. Anecdotes of significant archaeological finds.

Leakey, Richard E. *Human Origins.* New York: Dutton, 1982. What our human and prehuman ancestors were like. How they lived and evolved.

MacFall, Russell P. *Rock Hunter's Guide.* New York: Crowell, 1980. Guide to collecting, identifying, and displaying rocks and minerals.

Pough, Frederick H. *Peterson First Guides: Rocks and Minerals.* Boston: Houghton Mifflin, 1991. A basic illustrated guide to the origins and appearance of common gems, ores, and rocks.

Shapiro, Robert. *The Human Blueprint: The Race to Unlock the Secrets of Our Genetic Script.* New York: St. Martin's, 1991. Discussion of the implications of the Human Genome Project, the effort to read human genetic information. Traces the development of genetic theory.

Thompson, Ida. *The Audubon Society Field Guide to North American Fossils.* New York: Knopf, 1981. Well illustrated guide to fossils, with maps showing the location and geological age of fossil bearing rocks.

Throckmorton, Peter. *Shipwrecks and Archaeology: The Unharvested Sea.* Boston: Little, Brown, 1970. Emphasis on the value of underwater archaeology. Explains techniques.

Turek, Vojtiech, J. Marek, and J. Benes. *Fossils of the World.* New York: Arch Cape, 1989. A comprehensive guide to collecting and studying fossils.

Wenke, Robert J. *Patterns in Prehistory: Humankind's First Million Years.* 3rd ed. New York: Oxford University, 1990. A comprehensive review of world prehistory with emphasis on cultural development.

PERIODICALS

American Mineralogist. Mineralogical Society of America, 1130 17th Street, NW, Suite 330, Washington, DC 20036.

Archaeoastronomy. Center for Archaeoastronomy, Box X, College Park, MD 20740–1024.

Archaeology. Archaeological Institute of America, 135 William Street, New York, NY 10038.

Earth. Kalmbach Publishers, PO Box 1612, Waukesha, WI 53187–1612.

Gems and Gemology. Gemological Institute of America, 1660 Stewart Street, Santa Monica, CA: 90404.

Geotimes. American Geological Institute, 4220 King Street, Alexandria, VA 22302–1507.

Lapidary Journal. Lapidary Journal, 60 Chestnut Avenue, Suite 201, Devon, PA 19333.

Mineralogical Record. Mineralogical Record, 4631 Paseo Tubutama, Tucson, AZ 85740.

Rocks and Minerals. Heldref Publications, 1319 Eighteenth Street, NW Washington, DC 20036–1802.

ASSOCIATIONS

Alliance for Maritime Heritage Conservation. PO Box 27272, Central Station, Washington, DC 20038. Individuals and organizations interested in sea exploration. Seeks to assist underwater archaeologists in the survey and excavation of historic shipwrecks. Publications: Newsletter, and journal.

American Anthropological Association. 1703 New Hampshire Avenue, NW, Washington, DC 20009. Professionals, students, and interested individuals. Numerous units covering all aspects of anthropology. Publications: *American Anthropologist, American Ethnologist, Cultural Anthropology,* and much related material.

American Federation of Mineralogical Societies. PO Box 26523, Oklahoma City, OK 73126–0523. Hobbyists, collectors of minerals, and amateur lapidaries. Promotes interest in geology, mineralogy, paleontology, and lapidary. Publications: *American Federation Newsletter,* and related materials.

American Institute for Archaeological Research. 24 Cross Road, Mt. Vernon, NH 03057. Professionals, students, and interested individuals. Promotes research and conducts digs with colleges and universities. Publications: Newsletter, and *On Site* magazine.

Archaeological Institute of America. 675 Commonwealth Avenue, Boston, MA 02215. Professionals and interested individuals. Numerous groups covering all aspects of archaeology. Publications: *American Journal of Archaeology, Archaeology* magazine, and related material.

Center for American Archaeology. PO Box 366, Kampsville, IL 62053. Professionals, organizations, students, and interested individuals. Conducts research, excavates and conserves sites and artifacts. Publications: Reports, newsletter, and related material.

Dinosaur Society. PO Box 2098, New Bedford, MA 02741. Promotes research and education in the study of dinosaurs. Publications: *Dino Times,* and related materials.

Institute for American Indian Studies. 38 Curtis Road, PO Box 1260, Washington, CT 06793–0260. Individuals and institutions. Seeks to discover, preserve, and interpret information about Native Americans. Conducts surveys and excavations. Sponsors archaeological training sessions. Publications: *Artifacts,* and related material.

Institute of Nautical Archaeology. PO Drawer HG, College Station, TX 77841. Individuals interested in nautical archaeology. Studies ship remains spanning 3,300 years. Supports related research. Publication: *INA Newsletter.*

Mineralogical Society of America. 1130 17th Street, NW Suite 330, Washington, DC 20036. Professionals, students, and interested individuals. Encourages the preservation of mineral collections, displays, mineral localities, and type minerals. Publications: *American Mineralogist,* and related materials.

Paleontological Research Institution. 1259 Trumansburg Road, Ithaca, NY 14850. Professional and amateur paleontologists, and others interested in natural history. Receives, collects, preserves, and makes accessible paleontological type specimens. Conducts explorations and research. Maintains a 50,000 volume library. Publications: Bulletins, newsletter, and related material.

Paleontological Society. c/o Donald L. Wolberg, New Mexico Bureau of Mines and Mineral Resources, Socorro, NM 87801. Professionals and amateurs interested in the study of paleontology. Publications: *Journal of Paleontology,* and related materials.

Society for American Archaeology. 808 17th Street, NW, Suite 200, Washington, DC 20006. Professionals, students, and interested individuals. Stimulates scientific research. Guides, on request, the research work of amateurs. Publications: *American Antiquity,* bulletins, and related material.

World Archaeological Society. HCR 1, Box 445, Hollister, MO 65672. Professional and amateur archaeologists, anthropologists, and art historians in thirty-two countries. Promotes scientific study and maintains information center. Publications: *WAS Newsletter,* and related materials.

Games, Board and Table

BOARD GAMES ARE GAMES OF SKILL and chance played with pieces on a board or restricted field. Board games have been played for thousands of years. Early boards have been found in Egyptian tombs and game diagrams have been found engraved in stone in many parts of the world. Board games imitate the activities of mankind—a race, a battle, and territorial conquest.

Games Involving a Race

Modern Parcheesi is derived from the game of pachisi played extensively in India. Earlier Indian versions include games called ashtapada, and thaayam. In the game of Parcheesi a player attempts to be the first to advance all of his/her pieces, space by space, around a board, making moves in accordance with a throw of dice. Various rules are designed to slow an opponents progress around the board. If a player lands on a space occupied by an opponent, the opponent must return to the starting point and begin again.

Backgammon appears to be one of the oldest games in the world. Its most probable origin seems to be in Mesopotamia or China and India where many modern games had their origin. The early Chinese, Egyptians, Greeks, and Romans played the game. The goals are similar to Parcheesi, but obstacles to race completion are more involved. Each of the two players has fifteen pieces that must be moved on a prescribed path around a board containing twenty-four triangular spaces. Moves are made based on a throw of dice. The number of spaces moved is based on the numbers that come up on each die. If a four and a three come up, the player can move one piece four spaces and another piece three spaces, or one piece can be moved seven spaces. A player cannot move a piece to occupy a space containing two or more of the opponent's pieces. The pieces constitute a door. If any optional moves indicated by the throw of dice would result in arrival at an opponent's door, the player loses a turn. If a player arrives at a space occupied by only one of an opponent's pieces, it is called

a hit. The opponent's piece is removed and placed in a space called a bar. On the opponent's next play, any pieces located in the bar must be removed first. When either player has completed the prescribed path with all fifteen pieces that player begins to bear them off. This is accomplished by removing them according to the throw of dice. The player whose pieces are removed first wins the game.

Monopoly is a modern game from the 1930s. The journey around the board's spaces is continuous, instead of racing to a finish. Each player is furnished with an equal bankroll of play money. The first player to land on a space may purchase property there, and even improve it with houses or hotels. Opponents who subsequently land on the space must pay rent to the owner using play money. The goal is to acquire property along the way and bankrupt your opponents by charging rent.

Games Involving War Simulation

Go is one of many early board games that imitate battle strategy. Go was first mentioned in Chinese writings as Wei-Ch'i about 625 B.C. The game was introduced to Japanese royalty about 500 A.D. By the thirteenth century it was very popular with Japanese samurai warriors. Go is played on a square board inscribed with nineteen vertical and nineteen horizontal lines. Play is on the intersections instead of within squares. Play begins when a player places one piece on any point of the board. Play then alternates, only one piece being placed at each turn. Once played the piece cannot be moved and remains in position until the end of the game, unless it is captured. When a piece is captured it is removed from the board. A piece is considered captured when it is surrounded by an opponent's pieces, or by an opponent's pieces and the edge or corner of the board.

Stone slabs have been found in Egypt that have been engraved with a grid of horizontal and vertical lines. The pattern is consistent with that used for an Arabic game called quirkat, played in the tenth century. The Moors carried the game with them when they invaded Spain where the name became alquerque. Alquerque was played with pieces moved from intersection to intersection instead of using spaces. The player was permitted to move sideways, diagonally forward to left or right, and straight forward. A player could jump over an opponent's adjacent piece if the space beyond the piece was empty. This constituted a capture and the piece was removed from the board. When one player's pieces were all lost or couldn't be moved, the game was over. The modern game of checkers uses the same capture feature and pieces are moved forward, but only diagonally on spaces. Checkers also allows rearward movement of a piece once it has reached the opponent's edge of the board and been declared a king. A form of checkers existed in Europe in the twelfth century.

Chess was probably invented in northwest India about the sixth century A.D. Archeological evidence suggests the game existed in both India and China about the same time. Chess is played on a board composed of sixty-four equal squares alternately light and dark in color. The eight vertical rows of squares are called files. The eight horizontal rows of squares are called ranks. The lines of squares of the same color, touching corner to corner are called diagonals. The game is played with sixteen dark colored pieces and sixteen light ones. The pieces have unique shapes to indicate their rank. Each player starts the game with the following pieces: One king, one queen, two rooks, two bishops, two knights, and eight pawns. Based on their rank, the pieces are allowed varying degrees of mobility. Ignoring, for the moment, a unique situation called castling, the pieces may be moved as follows:

King. Moves to any adjoining square that is not attacked by an opponent's piece.

Queen. Moves to any square on the file, rank, or diagonals on which it stands.

Rook. Moves to any square on the file or rank on which it stands.

Bishop. Moves to any square on the diagonals on which it stands.

Knight. Moves in two steps; first, one step of one single square along its rank or file and then, still moving away from the square of departure, one step of one single square on a diagonal. It doesn't matter if the square of the first step is occupied.

Pawn. Moves only forward. Except when making a capture, it may move only one or two squares forward along the file on which it is placed. On subsequent moves, it may move only one vacant square along the file. When capturing, it advances one square along either of the diagonals on which it

stands. When it reaches the last rank, it must be exchanged immediately for the player's choice of a queen, rook, bishop, or knight of the same color.

Castling is a move of the king and either rook, counting as a single move of the king and executed as follows: the king is transferred from its original square two squares toward either rook on the same rank; then that rook is transferred over the king to the square immediately adjacent to the king and on the same rank.

A piece played to a square occupied by an opponent's piece captures it as part of the same move. The captured piece must be removed immediately from the chessboard by the player making the capture.

The king is in check when the square it occupies is attacked by one or two of the opponent's pieces; in this case the latter is or are said to be checking the king. The check must be parried by the move immediately following. If the check can't be parried the king is said to be checkmated or mated. The game is won by the player who has mated his opponent's king. The game ends in a draw when the king of the player who has the move is not in check and the player can't make any legal move. The king is then said to be stalemated.

Games Involving the Matching of Numbers

The popular game of bingo is played with cards having twenty-five squares placed in a five by five grid. The center square is usually designated as a free square. The vertical rows are labeled B I N G O. The remaining squares are randomly numbered using numbers from one to seventy-five. Each card will be numbered differently. A caller pulls numbered balls from a revolving drum, or equivalent, and announces the row letter and the number. Players mark any card squares that match any numbers called. The first player to match five numbers in a row horizontally or vertically, or four numbers and the center free square, calls out "bingo" and wins the prize. In some games the caller may instruct the players that the winning combination must be a diagonal five squares, or all squares around the edge of the card.

The casino game of keno is played with tickets bearing numbers one through eighty. Players are supplied with ink and brushes or a black crayon. The player marks the ticket with the numbers chosen to be played and the sum to be waged. The player presents the cash and the marked ticket at the keno counter where the dealer furnishes the player with a copy of the chosen numbers. Players may choose anywhere from one to fifteen numbers. A blower device contains eighty numbered ping-pong balls and twenty of these are drawn. A great number of different bets can be made because the players can select various combinations of numbers. If one number is bet and it's one of the twenty drawn, the player wins. If two numbers are bet both must be drawn to win. If ten numbers are bet the player wins if five or more are drawn. Payoffs are based on the odds set by how many numbers are bet. Typically, a successful one number bet of one dollar would pay only $3.20.

Dominos are small rectangular tiles with dots on the face representing the appearance of two dice. A line is often used across the center to divide the two groupings of dots, each group ranging from one to six. Some sets utilize dot groupings from one to nine. Dominos appear to be a Chinese invention. The game was slow to catch on in Europe until about the eighteenth century. Although a relatively simple game, many variations have evolved. In a typical game the players take turns progressively matching tiles. A player places a domino and the next player matches one end if possible. If this can't be done a turn is lost, and the next player tries. If no one can play, the game is blocked and each player counts the spots on the tiles still held in hand. The player with the lowest number of spots scores the total number of spots held in the opponent's hand in addition to those in his/her own. The first player to reach 121 wins the game.

Game Matching Figures

Mah-jongg is a western version of a Chinese game in which tiles substitute for playing cards. The play strongly resembles the card game of rummy. The tiles are identified by Chinese characters and symbols. The game was very popular in the United States in the 1920s and 1930s, and still retains a small, loyal following. The game is played with 136 or 144 tiles divided into suits and honors. Suits bear names such as bamboos, circles, characters, honors (colored dragons), and winds. The usual game is for four players. The object of the game is to obtain sets of tiles. There are three kinds of sets:

Chow. A run or consecutive sequence of three tiles in the same suit.

Pung. A sequence of three like tiles of the same suit and rank, three dragons of the same color or three identical winds.

Kong. A pung plus a fourth matching tile.

The winner is the first player to hold a complete hand, composed of four sets and a pair of like tiles.

Bibliography

REFERENCE BOOKS

Bell, R. C. *Board and Table Games From Many Civilizations.* Rev. ed. New York: Dover, 1979. A basic reference to board and table games from around the world. Contains rules and methods of play for 182 games.

Kazic, Bozidar, et al. eds. *The Official Laws of Chess.* New York: Macmillan, 1986. Chess laws as revised by the World Chess Federation at the Thessalonika Olympiad.

Pachman, Ludek. *Modern Chess Tactics: Pieces and Pawns in Action.* New York: McKay, 1979. Covers the field of chess tactics, in both the offensive and defensive mode. Discusses moves, maneuvers, and combinations.

Reinfeld, Fred. *The Complete Chess Course.* Garden City, NY: Doubleday, 1959. A comprehensive book on chess instruction, with over 1,000 diagrams illustrating the principles of the game.

Scarne, John. *Scarne's New Complete Guide to Gambling.* Rev. ed. New York: Simon & Schuster, 1986. Includes coverage of keno.

Tzannes, Nicolaos, and Basil Tzannes. *Backgammon Games and Strategies.* Cranbury, NJ: Barnes, 1977. An overview of backgammon. Covers the play of a number of variations, plus the role of probability theory in the playing of the game.

PERIODICALS

Bingo Bugle. Bingo Bugle, Box 527, Vashon, WA 98070.

Chess Correspondent. C C L A, Box 3481, Barrington, IL 60011–3481.

Chess Horizons. Massachusetts Chess Association, c/o Steve Frymer, 64 Asbury Street, Lexington, MA 02173–6521.

ASSOCIATIONS

All Service Postal Chess Club. 1805 S. Van Buren Street, Amarillo, TX 79102. Individuals united to promote postal chess activity in the U.S. Armed Services. Holds competitions and sponsors educational programs. Publications: *King's Korner,* and related materials.

American Association of Backgammon Clubs. PO Box 12359, Las Vegas, NV 89121. Provides forum for the exchange of information, conducts tournaments. Maintains library. Publication: *Backgammon Magazine.*

American Checker Federation. PO Drawer 365, Petal, MS 39465. International supporters of the game. Stages world title match and encourages competition by mail. Maintains museum and hall of fame. Publication: *ACF Bulletin.*

American Chess Foundation. 353 W 46th Street, New York, NY 10036. Conducts activities to promote chess among schoolchildren, senior citizens, and the public. Sponsors competitions and bestows awards.

American Go Association. c/o Roy Laird, PO Box 397, Old Chelsea Station, New York, NY 10113–0397. Individuals united to conduct Go tournaments. Bestows awards and conducts an education program. Publications: *American Go Journal,* newsletter, and related materials.

American Postal Chess Tournaments. Box 305, Western Springs, IL 60558. Conducts postal chess tournaments and bestows awards. Publication: *APCT News Bulletin.*

Chess Collectors International. c/o Floyd Sarisohn, PO Box 166, Commack, NY 11725. Collectors of chess related items in thirty-two countries. Publication: *Chess Collector.*

International Backgammon Association. 1300 Citrus Isle, Fort Lauderdale, FL 33315–1324. Promotes the game of backgammon. Publication: *Backgammon Tournament Notices.*

National Mah-Jongg League. 250 W. 57th Street, New York, NY 10107. Promotes the game of mah-jongg. Publications: Newsbulletin, *Official Standard Rules,* and related materials.

United States Chess Federation. 186 Route 9W, New Windsor, NY 12553. Governing body of U.S. chess players unit of the World Chess Federation. Conducts all championship events. Works to promote chess in schools, communities, and the Armed Forces. Operates hall of fame and maintains library. Publications: *Chess Life, School Mates,* and *USCF Rating List.*

USMA. 26097 Hendrie, Huntington Woods, MI 48070. Persons interested in developing competitive skills in the game of Monopoly. Conducts an annual tournament and bestows awards. Publication: *Tourney Notes.*

Games, Card

THE EARLY HISTORY of playing cards is uncertain. The Chinese appear to have had numbered cards similar in appearance to their paper money during the tenth century. The Italians had tarot cards in the fourteenth century that were divided into suits and numbered. The tarots were picture cards used primarily for fortune telling. The tenth century Chinese cards and the fourteenth century Italian cards evolved into a combined deck of seventy-eight cards. They were used to play tarok, or tarot, which is a form of "trick-taking" game. In modern times these seventy-eight card tarot decks are used primarily for fortune telling. Over time, the size of card decks varied to meet the requirements of games being devised. The French adopted a fifty-two card deck, and the current symbols that identify suits, that became standard in English speaking countries.

In 1742 an English barrister named Edmund Hoyle wrote a game book called *A Short Treatise on Whist,* a popular card game of the time. Fourteen editions were published during his lifetime adding the card games piquet and quadrille. The games of backgammon and chess were also included in this work. Although Hoyle died in 1769, modern writers continue to capitalize on his fame by including his name in their book titles.

Some card games quickly rise in popularity and then fall into obscurity. The following represent a few of those that have stood the test of time.

Baccarat

Baccarat is a gambling game played with cards. The variation of the game most popular in the United States is called baccarat-chemin de fer, or simply shimmy. It is played using six or eight decks of cards shuffled together. The object of the game is to win a coup by holding a combination of two or three cards totaling nine or as close as possible to nine, or to a two-digit number ending in nine.

When the total of the cards is a two-digit number, only the later digit has any value. A count of nineteen has a value of nine. An ace has a point value of one. Kings, queens, and jacks are each worth ten, and all other cards have their numerical face value. Although the number of players is only limited by the spaces around a table, only two players are active at a time. One player acts as the banker. The banker places a bet, within house limits, that the banker will win. The other players have the option to cover the entire amount of the bet. If they choose to do so they call banco. The first player to the right of the banker-dealer has the first option to call banco, the option continuing to the right if players choose not to cover the entire bet. If no one bancos the same procedure is followed to place partial bets. Any uncovered portion of the bet is withdrawn by the banker. Anyone who bancos becomes the active player. If no one bancos, the player who bets the highest amount against the banker becomes the active player. The banker deals one card to the active player, one to him-/herself, a second to the active player and the fourth card to him-/herself. After examining the cards, the active player turns them face up if they total eight or nine. If eight they are la petite; if nine they are la grande. The banker's cards are now turned face up. If the active player's count is highest, the banker pays off the active player. If more than one player faded the bet, they get their share of the winnings. If the banker wins the banker collects all the bets. When played in a casino several people are involved in running the game. In this case, the casino gets a percentage of the banker's winnings. The rules of the game are quite complicated beyond this basic description. In many casinos the players are supplied with a card describing the rules. As an example, if the active player doesn't make eight or nine the active player says pass and the banker wins providing that the banker has eight or nine. If the banker doesn't have eight or nine either, play reverts to the active player. The process continues with additional cards being dealt based upon the point values held by the two players.

Blackjack

Blackjack, sometimes called 21, is a gambling game played with cards using four decks shuffled together. In casinos, the game is played with one house employee who is both dealer and banker, and from one to seven active players. The ace has a count of either one or eleven depending on house rules. Kings, queens and jacks have a count of ten, and all other cards have their numerical face value. The object of the game is to have a higher total card count than the dealer by reaching 21, or as close to 21 as possible without going over 21. If the player's count exceeds 21 the bet is lost. The dealer begins play by discarding the top card. This is called burning the card. The dealer gives one card face up to each player and to him-/herself. A second card is then dealt face up to each player and face down to the dealer. If the dealer's face up card is a 10 count or an ace, the dealer must look at the face down (hole) card. If the hole card and face card make 21 (a natural 21), the dealer must say so. In this case the dealer collects all bets made by players who don't have 21. If a player also has 21 the player neither wins nor pays the dealer on his/her bet.

If the dealer does not hold a natural 21, the player on the dealer's left plays first. If the player has 21 the player wins at three-to-two odds. If the player does not have 21, he/she may elect to not request additional cards (stay). Optionally the player may request additional cards until the count is 21 or as close to it as the player cares to risk. When a player's count goes over 21 (busts), it must be declared and the cards are "burned" in the discard pile. Play moves to the players remaining and each player either stays or requests additional cards. If all players bust, the dealer's cards are placed in the discard pile. If any active players are left the dealer's hole card is turned up. If the count is 17 through 20 the dealer must stay. If the dealer's count is 16 or less the dealer must draw a card and continue to do so until 17 or more is reached, at which point the dealer must stay. At the end of his/her play the dealer pays off players having a higher count than the dealer's with an amount equal to the bet they placed, and collecting from players with a lesser amount. If a player and the dealer have an equal count, no money changes hands.

Bridge

The most popular variant of bridge, contract bridge, will be described. The game is played by four, two against two as partners. A fifty-two-card deck is used with the ace ranking high. The suits rank downward in order of spades, hearts, diamonds, clubs. The first dealer is determined by drawing cards. The player drawing the highest ranking card deals thirteen cards to each player. Player's evaluate their cards and each makes a call of pass, bid, double, or redouble. If all four pass, the deal goes to the next dealer. If any player makes a bid in the first round, the bidding is opened. A bid consists of the number of tricks (called odd tricks) in excess of six that the bidder proposes to win, and a suit that will become the trump suit if the bid becomes the contract. As the players bid or pass in turn, each bid must be for a higher number of tricks or, if for the same number of tricks, in a higher-ranking suit, or no-trump. No-trump is the highest ranking bid, outranking spades. To double the value of odd tricks, overtricks, and undertrick penalties on an opponent, a player may call double. In turn, the first bidder's partner may now offer support by calling redouble, which increases the scoring values still further.

The bidding process sets up the challenge of the game. The bids predict what will be accomplished, but almost as important, the bidding technique communicates the contents of your hand to your partner. You can signal that you are able to support the suit the partner has chosen for trump, or possibly suggest an alternative.

When a bid, double, or redouble is followed by three consecutive passes the auction is closed. The highest bid becomes the contract. The suit named in the contract becomes trump. The player who first named the suit becomes the declarer. A play consists of placing a card, face up, in the center of the table. Four cards played in this manner constitute a trick. The first card played is a lead. The opponent on the declarer's left makes the first lead. The declarer's partner is called the dummy. The dummy's cards are then placed in front of the dummy on the table, face up. Both the declarer's and the dummy's cards, each in proper turn are played by the declarer. Subsequent players must follow suit, or if unable, may play any card including a trump if they wish. A trick containing any trump is won by the highest trump. If the trick contains no trump, the trick is won by the highest card of the suit led. The winner of each trick leads to the next. When all thirteen tricks have been played the result is scored. Scoring is done by a complex process beyond the scope of this work. It involves whether the contract was made, the tricks taken over six, what was trump, whether doubling or redoubling was called, and other factors.

Euchre

The game is played by four, two against two as partners. The deck is composed of twenty-four cards. The cards nine through ace are used. The ace ranks highest except in the case of the trump suit where the jack of trumps is highest, followed by the other jack of the same color, then A, K, Q, 10, 9 of trumps. After dealing five cards to each player the dealer places the remaining four cards face down on the table and turns the top card face up. This card establishes the trump suit for the deal. Each player in turn, beginning with the player to the dealer's left, has the right to accept or reject the turned card as trump. If any player accepts, the dealer discards one card, and takes the turned card instead. If all four players reject the turned card as trump, it's turned face down, and the player to the dealer's left may name a trump suit or pass. If all four players pass again, the hands are thrown in.

The player who makes the trump has the right to play it alone. In this case, the partner doesn't participate, and the player to the left of the person making the trump leads, otherwise the player to the left of the dealer leads. Each player must follow suit if able. If unable to follow suit, any card may be played. A trick containing any trump is won by the highest trump. If the trick contains no trump, the trick is won by the highest card of the suit led. The winner of each trick leads to the next.

The object of play is to take at least three tricks. If the making side fails to do so, it is euchered. If all five tricks are taken by the making side, it's called march. Makers' side scores one point for winning three or four tricks; two points for march; four points for march won when playing alone. For euchre, opponents score two points. Four-hand euchre is usually played to ten points.

Hearts

The game may be played with from two to seven players. The deck is composed of fifty-two cards with aces ranking high. The cards are dealt as far as they will go equally, with remaining cards left on the table face down. They are taken by the player who takes the first trick.

Players evaluate their hands and select three cards to pass to their right-hand opponent. Only after passing the three cards may they look at the three received from their left-hand opponent. The player to the left of the dealer leads. Each player, clockwise, must follow suit. If unable to follow suit, any card may be played, except that the holder of the queen of spades must discard it at the first legal opportunity. A trick is won by the highest card of the suit led. The winner of each trick leads to the next. The object of the game is to avoid winning any trick containing any hearts or the queen of spades, or to win all of them.

When scoring, each heart counts one point. The queen of spades counts thirteen. Points count against you, and the lowest score wins. If you win all the tricks containing hearts, and the queen of spades, twenty-six points are added to each of the opponents' scores.

The game may be played for an agreed time, or number of hands, or to an agreed score.

Pinochle

The game played with two players is called two-hand pinochle. A three-hand variant is called auction pinochle,

and a four-hand variant is called partnership auction pinochle. The deck is composed of forty-eight cards. There are duplicates in each suit of the ace, ten, king, queen, jack, nine, which rank downward in that order. There are three different methods of scoring the cards:

	Original Count	Simplified Count	Streamlined Count
Ace	11	10	10
Ten	10	10	10
King	4	5	10
Queen	3	5	0
Jack	2	0	0
Nine	0	0	0

The total count for each method adds up to 240 in cards plus ten for the last trick won for an overall total of 250 points for any system.

Combinations of cards, called melds, score additional point values:

Sequence or Flush (A, K, Q, J, 10 in trumps)	150
Royal Marriage (K, Q in trumps)	40
Marriage (K, Q in any other suit)	20
Four Aces, one in each suit (100 Aces)	100
Four Kings, one in each suit (80 Kings)	80
Four Queens, one in each suit (60 Queens)	60
Four Jacks, one in each suit (40 Jacks)	40
Pinochle—Queen of Hearts and Jack of Diamonds	40
Nine of Trumps (Deece)	10
King and Queen of each suit (Roundhouse)	240

If a player holds duplicates of the above melds, each meld itself has the value shown above.

In the game of two-handed pinochle twelve cards are dealt to each player, three at a time. The next card is turned up. This card establishes the trump suit for the deal. The undealt cards are placed over the trump card to partly cover it and become the stockpile.

The nondealer leads first to begin play. A card led by one player and the card played in response constitute a trick. The trick is won by the card led unless the opponent plays a higher card of the same suit or a trump on a plain-suit lead. Any card may be led and any card played. Until the stockpile is exhausted it isn't necessary to follow suit.

After winning a trick, a player may lay meld on the table, scoring points. Only one meld is allowed per turn. Each meld must contain at least one card from the hand. The same meld may be repeated using different cards. A king and queen melded in a sequence can't be used later in a marriage. The winner of a trick may exchange a nine of trumps (deece) for the trump card, or show the deece and score ten.

Melded cards are used in play as though they were in the player's hand. After the winner of a trick melds, each player draws a card from the stockpile, the winner drawing first, then leading off the next trick.

When only one card remains in the stockpile, plus the trump card, melding stops. The winner of the next trick takes the last stockpile card and the opponent takes the trump card. Melds on the table are picked up.

As the last twelve tricks are played, players follow suit if able. If unable to follow suit a trump must be played if able. If a trump is led the opponent must win the trick if able. The winner of the last trick scores ten. The cards in the tricks are counted and added to the player's score in even tens. The game is won by the first player to reach 1,000 points. If both players pass 1,000, the game is played to 1,500.

The game of auction pinochle retains most of the features described for two-hand. Exceptions include the dealing of four hands and a bidding process. After the deal, players bid based on their estimate of the point count they expect to make. The winning bidder either collects or pays out chips or money depending on whether the final point count exceeds the bid. When play begins, the winning bidder adds the cards from the fourth hand (the widow) to his own.

Partnership auction pinochle is similar to auction pinochle. The bid system is retained, with the highest bidder naming the trump. In partnership pinochle the partners score jointly, but a player may not combine any card with a card from the partner's hand to form a meld.

Poker

The game is played with from two to ten players. A regular fifty-two-card deck is used with aces ranking high. But the ace may be used at either end of the suit, as the highest card in a straight or royal flush and as the lowest in a straight or straight flush.

The object of the game is to win the accumulated chips in the pot after showing a hand of higher rank than that of other players. An alternative win occurs when all other players are forced to drop out of the competition.

The following card combinations have value in poker. They are listed from the highest to the lowest:

Royal Flush. A, K, Q, J, 10 of any one suit. Suits have equal rank.

Straight Flush. Any five cards in the same suit in numerical sequence. If two straight flushes occur, the one with the highest top card wins.

Four of a Kind. Any four cards of the same denomination.

Full House. Three of one kind and two of another. Between full houses the one with the highest three-of-a-kind wins.

Flush. Any five cards of the same suit but not in sequence. Between two flushes the one containing the highest card wins. If both hands contain the same highest card, the second highest cards are compared, and so on.

Straight. Five cards in sequence but not in the same suit. Between two straights the one containing the highest card wins.

Three of a Kind. Three cards of the same numerical value plus two unmatching cards. Between two such hands of three of a kind, the one containing the highest three matching cards wins.

Two Pairs. Two sets of two matching cards plus an unmatched card. Between two such hands, the one containing the highest pair wins. If the highest pairs are tied, the highest second pair wins.

One Pair. Two cards of the same numerical value plus three unmatched cards. Between two such hands, the one containing the highest pair wins. If the pairs are tie, the highest unmatched card wins.

High Card. A hand containing five unmatched cards that falls into none of the above combinations. Between two such hands, the one containing the highest card wins. If the highest cards tie, the second highest are compared, and so on.

When two or more players hold hands of equal rank, they divide the pot equally.

In all forms of poker (and there are many), after the deck has been shuffled and cut by the player on the dealer's right, the cards are dealt, one at a time, beginning with the player on the dealer's left. Each player usually receives five cards.

Depending on the game being played, all or only a portion of the cards will be dealt face down. Players bet as to which player holds the best hand. Bets are placed by putting chips into the pot. Betting occurs during periods of the game called betting intervals. In draw poker the first interval occurs when all players have been dealt the original five cards. In stud poker the first interval occurs when each player has received the first two cards. When the first player has bet, succeeding players must pass, call, or raise. To pass is to drop out and discard the hand. A call means the player adds enough chips to the pot to match the greatest number of chips that any previous player has bet. To raise means to match the previous player as with call, plus an added amount. Betting continues until it becomes the turn to bet of the last player who raised, and all others have either passed or called. After betting is completed, the pot is won by the player holding the winning combination of cards as described above.

Rummy

The game is played with from two to six players playing independently. A regular fifty-two-card deck is used with aces ranking lowest. The king, queen, and jack count ten points each. All other cards have their numerical face value.

For two players, ten cards are dealt to each. This number is reduced to seven cards for three or four players, and to six cards for five or six players. The remaining cards, placed face down, form the stockpile. The top card from the stockpile is taken and placed face up to form a discard pile.

The common goal of all rummy games is to build sets or melds such as three or four of a kind, or sequences of three or more cards of the same suit. A joker may be used to represent any needed card.

The player to the left of the dealer plays first. Each player, in turn, first draws one card from either the stockpile or discard pile. If a player chooses to play, and thereby expose, any meld this may be done. The player may also play any cards that match melds previously made by either himself or other players. A player's turn ends when placing a card in the discard pile, except that no discard need be made if all a player's cards have been melded. A player who has melded all cards has won the hand and the deal. The hand is then scored. If the stockpile is exhausted during play, the discard pile is turned face down and play resumes.

In the gin rummy variant, two players are dealt ten cards. When the stockpile and discard pile have been formed, the nondealer may take the discard pile card or refuse it. If refused the dealer has the same option. If both refuse, play begins with the nondealer drawing from the stockpile. Object of the game is to form melds as in rummy. Cards that don't form a meld are called unmatched. After drawing, a player may knock (go down) if his unmatched cards, less one discard, total ten or less. If all cards are matched, the player has gone gin. The opponent of the knocker may lay off any unmatched cards on the knocker's sets.

The game of canasta, a form of rummy, can be played by two or four players playing in two partnerships. Two fifty-two-card decks are used. Sequences are not used in melding. All jokers and deuces are wild cards. A meld may be three or more cards of the same rank, including at least two natural cards and not more than three wild cards. Players can lay off on partner's melds, but not on those of an opponent. Players may add a red three or a wild card to the discard pile to prevent an opponent from using the pile. The discard can then only be taken if a player has two natural cards in the hand that match the top card on the discard pile. If the top card of the discard pile is taken, the remaining cards in the pile must also be taken. Card point values also differ from rummy.

Bibliography

REFERENCE BOOKS

Gibson, Walter B. *Hoyle's Modern Encyclopedia of Card Games.* New York: Doubleday, 1974. Rules to all the basic games and popular variations.

Goren, Charles H. *Goren's New Bridge Complete.* Rev. ed. Garden City, NY: Doubleday, 1985. Goren presents an authoritative and detailed description of how to play a five-card major system of bridge.

Jacoby, Oswald, and James Jacoby. *Jacoby on Card Games.* Rev. ed. New York: Pharos Books, 1989. Instructions, strategies, examples, and rules and regulations for 125 different card games.

Parlett, David. *The Penguin Book of Card Games.* New York: Crescent Books, 1987. Covers 300 card games from around the world.

Scarne, John. *Scarne's Guide to Modern Poker.* Rev. ed. New York: Simon & Schuster, 1984. A thorough analysis of how best to play the most popular of all card games—poker.

———. *Scarne on Cards.* Rev. ed. New York: Dutton, 1989. A fundamental reference and rule book. Includes advice on how to avoid being victimized by cheating.

PERIODICALS

Bridge Today. Granovetter Books, 18 Village View Bluff, Ballston, Lake, NY 12019.

Bridge World. Bridge World Magazine, 39 W. 94th Street, New York, NY 10025.

Card Player. 1455 E. Tropicana Avenue, No. 450, Las Vegas, NV 89119.

ASSOCIATIONS

American Contract Bridge League. 2990 Airways Boulevard, Memphis, TN 38116–3847. Establishes, interprets, and enforces the rules and regulations governing the game of contract bridge. Holds competitions and bestows awards. Maintains library. Publications: Bulletin, directory, and related material.

International Home and Private Poker Players Association. Route 2, Box 2845, Manistique, MI 49854. Conducts poker lessons, registers clubs, and trains tournament directors. Publications: Newsletter, *Poker Tips,* and related material.

National Euchre Players Association. 811 Pike Street, Etna, OH 43018. Sponsors competitions and bestows awards. Publications: Newsletter, and *The Official Laws of Euchre.*

National Poker Association. 2460 Juniper Avenue, Boulder, CO 80304. Individuals interested in the formal game of poker as played in casinos. Sponsors tournaments. Publication: *NPA Newsletter.*

Games, Gambling

GAMBLING HAS EXISTED in every known society, from the most primitive to the most complex, and the United States is no exception. Gambling is the leading industry in the country by far, both in participation and the amount of money involved. While people can, and will, bet on almost anything, this discussion will center primarily on gambling activities associated with casinos. Casino card games such as baccarat, blackjack, and poker can be found in the section on "Card Games." Keno, a bingo-like game is discussed in the section on "Board Games."

Early gamblers thought that a streak of luck when playing with dice was controlled by the gods, but by the sixteenth century scientists knew that all games of chance have a mathematical basis. The great astronomer Galileo was asked why the combination 10 showed up more often than 9 when three dice were thrown. After some deliberation Galileo responded that of 216 combinations possible with three dice, twenty-seven form the number 10 and twenty-five the number 9. The mathematician and physicist Blaise Pascal answered a similar question regarding the likelihood of certain results occurring when the dice are rolled. The principles formulated by Galileo, Pascal, Newton, and others formed the groundwork of probability mathematics. Probability theory supplies mathematical methods for discovering what can be expected when the results depend upon chance.

Pure games of chance involve no element of skill. Examples include lotteries, slot machines, and bingo. Games of skill involve little or no chance. Examples are bowling, chess, and golf. Games in which both skill and chance play a part include most card games, and betting on certain sports. Knowing what odds apply when chance is involved is a great advantage to a gambler. However, in the controlled gambling environment of a casino, the casino operators know the odds, expressed to several decimal places, and their profit as well as your opportunity to win, are established well in advance.

Craps

The game of craps is played with dice. While primitive dice have been made from any material at hand for over 2,000 years, today's die is usually made of some type of plastic. The standard die is marked on each face with a number of dots from one to six. The dots on opposite sides always total seven: one opposite six, two opposite five, and three opposite four. Casino dice are manufactured to much closer specifications than those purchased through most commercial outlets. Most casinos standardize on a die measuring three-quarters of an inch.

The game of craps is played with two dice by any number of players. The player throwing the dice is the shooter. With closed hand, the shooter shakes the dice and throws them so that both die hit and rebound from a backboard. If neither die hits the backboard or one or both dice falls off an elevated surface, the roll is no-dice. The dice must be thrown again. When the dice are thrown the two numbers, added together, that face skyward when the dice come to rest are the deciding numbers. The shooter's first roll is a come-out. If the shooter throws a 7 or 11 it's a winning decision called a pass. If a 2, 3, or 12 is thrown it's a losing decision called a miss-out. If any other number is thrown, that number becomes the shooter's point and throwing is continued until the point is repeated producing a winning decision, or until a seven is thrown, which is a miss-out. After any miss-out the dice are passed to the next player on the shooter's left.

Bets are made before the dice are thrown. There are a number of ways that bets can be made by the shooter or other players in the game. A few examples follow: *A right bet*—that the dice will pass. *A wrong bet*—that the dice won't pass. *Center bet*—the shooter may bet he/she will pass. When a player covers the shooter's bet by betting an equal amount against the shooter, the player is fading the shooter. *Side bet*—any bet not a center bet. The shooter may make any side bet. *Point bet*—After the shooter throws a point on the come-out, side bets may be made for or against the shooter's success in making the point. Usually odds are given for or against that likelihood.

We have seen earlier that the odds of a given point being thrown are dependent upon the number of ways that the point can be made. There are six ways that will produce a point of seven using two dice. A four can be made in three ways: 1–3, 3–1, 2–2. To figure the odds of a shooter making a point of four versus making a pass (shooting 7), the correct odds would be six against three, or two to one.

The game of craps as played in casinos is called bank craps. In this game a design is printed on the table cover, divided into spaces of different shapes and sizes representing different bets. Players place chips on the space representing the bet they wish to make. The principle difference between bank craps and the private craps game described above, is that in bank craps players can't bet among themselves. All bets must be placed on the spaces of the craps layout and made against the bank. Another difference is that each bet made at bank craps has odds in favor of the bank. The layouts are clever exercises in probability designed to give the player an exciting game, but at the same time give the bank a mathematical edge on every bet on the layout.

Roulette

A roulette table consists of a table having a bowl-shaped recess, called the bowl. The bowl contains the wheel, called a wheel head. The bowl has a spindle at its center with a single ball bearing at the top. The wheel head is balanced on top of the bearing. The bowl has a grooved track running around its circumference. The croupier spins the wheel in a counterclockwise direction, then flips a ball in the bowl's track so that it travels clockwise. As the ball loses speed it drops down on the spinning wheel head, bounces over several partitions, and settles into one of thirty-eight pockets designated by the numbers 1 through 36, 0, and 00. The pockets are painted alternately red and black, except for 0 and 00 which are painted green. On either one or both ends of the table a design is printed on the table's surface that forms the betting section. The design is comprised of thirty-six numbered spaces arranged in three long columns. The numbers read from one to three across the top of the three columns, and continue below as four through six, the numbering continuing in sequence to the bottom of the three rows. Provision is made

to bet twelve numbers at a time from top to bottom of a single row. Another provision is made to bet twelve numbers at a time in the other direction—numbers one to twelve, or thirteen through twenty-four, or twenty-five through thirty-six. The player may bet that the ball will fall into either a red or black pocket. Another optional bet is that an odd or even number will win.

The player places a bet by judiciously placing a chip or chips on the betting surface. If the chip is placed within a numbered space, the bet is made on that number. If it is placed on the line between two spaces, both spaces' numbers are being bet. If the chip is on the intersection of four spaces all four numbers are being bet. Similar careful placement will bet a three space street, or twelve space column, and there are special spaces for odd or even, and black or red.

If the ball falls into the 0 or 00 pocket the bank wins all bets placed, except those placed on the 0 or 00 betting spaces. The odds on winning at roulette are determined by the number of pockets on the wheel head. Since there are thirty-six numbers on the wheel, plus the 0 and 00, making a total of thirty-eight, the correct odds would be thirty-seven to one when a single number bet is made. However, the bank pays off at only thirty-five to one on a single number bet, having the advantage of the 0 and 00. As a percentage, this is $2/38$ of 100, or $5\frac{5}{19}$ percent, which is about twenty-six cents on a five dollar bet. The odds specified for all of the betting options described above favor the bank in a similar manner, ensuring that in the long run the casino will make its profit.

Slot Machines

Slot machines have come a long way since inventor Charles Fey placed his first machine in San Francisco in 1887. A typical machine has three or more narrow wheel-like reels, placed side by side, and encased in a cabinet. The reels have symbols marked on their rims. The player uses a handle or button to set the reels in motion. The machine automatically pays the player if like symbols are positioned along a horizontal pay line when the reels come to rest. The payoff varies according to a schedule posted on the machine. The alignment of certain symbols, such as bars, constitute a jackpot, the largest payout available from the machine.

Some machines have as many as five pay lines. The number of active pay lines is determined by the number of coins deposited before pulling the handle.

The percentage of coins returned to the player in the form of payoffs is determined by the number of reels, the number of symbols on each reel, and the number of possible payoff combinations. The payoff combinations are set by the distribution of symbols on the reels. The percentage of coins returned varies significantly, depending on the location of the machine. It is lowest where machines are illegal, and highest in legally operated casinos where competition is provided by other adjacent casinos.

Sports Betting

The sports betting done in casinos and elsewhere can't be discussed within the limits of this work. However, there is a fast-growing sports competition called fantasy baseball, usually played by nonprofessionals, that does fit the description of a gambling game. Although the following discussion is limited to fantasy baseball, very similar games are becoming popular based on football and hockey.

In fantasy baseball a group of people assume the role of a baseball league. Each person is a team owner. At the beginning of the baseball season, owner's select baseball players for their fantasy teams from the ranks of a real baseball league or leagues. The performance statistics of the real players are used to earn points for the owner's fantasy team. The fantasy team earning the most points at the end of the season wins the pennant, and some money if the fantasy game players established a franchise fee at the outset.

Fantasy baseball capitalizes on the competitive instincts of fans and their interest in sports. Owners take a new interest in the performance of real baseball players belonging to teams they have never followed in the past. They can't wait to read the sports page statistics to see how "their team" is doing. Fantasy league operating rules are somewhat flexible at the local level, but the rules agreed to must be recorded to prevent future disputes.

The following are some typical approaches to the game:

The number of team owners should be at least six, with a maximum of ten or twelve owners if players are picked from one real league, or twenty or more owners if two leagues are used to supply players. The number of players on each team will average about sixteen to eighteen. It's good practice to pick a roster of real players that fit all of a real team's positions, such as pitchers, fielders, and good hitters. The most popular time for owners to select real players for their team is the weekend after opening day. If money has been put up by owners for a franchise, the amount may be used as a basis for an owner to bid on real players, simulating the problems real owners have in conserving their money. If the fantasy owner has $100 to work with and bids $20 on a skilled player, there is only $80 left with which to bid for the rest of the team. Most fantasy leagues have a franchise fee from about $25 on up. An alternative player selection method is to use the draft. Owners pick numbers out of a hat. The owner who picks number one gets the first pick, and on down the line. Some fantasy leagues have owners who live in other cities who travel significant distances to be on hand for the annual fantasy draft.

Most leagues keep score in four or five categories in both hitting and pitching. Hitting categories may include: batting average, hits, runs, home runs, runs batted in, and stolen bases. Pitching categories include: wins, win-loss percentage, losses, earned-run average, strikeouts, and saves. Points are assigned to each category used. It is well to remember that the more categories chosen, the more laborious will be the job of recording, calculating, and record keeping. An owner with a personal computer becomes very popular. An alternative is to have the statistics done professionally. There are dozens of persons and firms coast-to-coast who provide this service. These services typically charge $40 per team on up, and give you weekly standings—by mail or fax.

To maintain interest near the end of the season, it's good practice to spread the payoff money around. Perhaps 50 percent for first place, 25 percent for second, and on down.

Bibliography

REFERENCE BOOKS

Ainslie, Tom. *Tom Ainslie's How to Gamble in a Casino.* New York: Simon & Schuster, 1987. Detailed discussion of casino games with recommendations of bets to avoid.

Clark, Thomas L. *The Dictionary of Gambling and Gaming.* Cold Spring, NY: Lexik, 1987. A dictionary of the language of gambling.

McQuaid, Clement. *Gambler's Digest.* 2nd ed. Northfield, IL: DBI Books, 1981. Comprehensive coverage of gambling games with tips on how to play them.

Revere, Lawrence. *Playing Blackjack as a Business: A Textbook on Blackjack.* Rev. ed. Secaucus, NJ: Lyle Stuart, 1977. Comprehensive overview of blackjack from an insider's viewpoint.

Riddle, Major A. *The Weekend Gambler's Handbook.* New York: Random House, 1963. Advice for casino gambling. Playing to win, and good games to stay away from.

Scarne, John. *Scarne's New Complete Guide to Gambling.* Rev. ed. New York: Simon & Schuster, 1986. A comprehensive guide to all types of gambling from one of the world's foremost gambling authorities.

Stuart, Lyle. *Casino Gambling for the Winner.* Rev. ed. New York: Ballantine, 1984. A philosophical overview of techniques regarding casino gambling games and practices.

PERIODICALS

Card Player. 1455 E. Tropicana Avenue, No. 450, Las Vegas, NV 89119.

Casino Digest. Casino Digest, 1901–G Ashwood Court, Suite 123, Greensboro, NC 27455.

Fantasy Baseball. Krause Publications., 700 E. State Street, Iola, WI 54990.

Fantasy Football. Preview Publishers, 17962 Midvale Avenue N., Suite 204, Seattle, WA 98133–4922.

ASSOCIATIONS

Mathematical Association of America. 1529 18th Street NW, Washington, DC 20036. Individuals using mathematics as a tool in a business or profession. Sponsors competitions and bestows awards. (Literature applicable due to the probability mathematics involved in gambling.) Publications: *American Mathematical Monthly, Mathematics Magazine,* and related materials.

National Poker Association. 2460 Juniper Avenue, Boulder, CO 80304. Individuals interested in the formal game of poker as played in casinos and cardrooms. sponsors tournaments. Publication: *NPA Newsletter.*

Games, Mental

MENTAL GAMES USUALLY INVOLVE the manipulation of words, mathematics, or the application of logic. Some games employ various combinations of all three. The origins of many of these games predate the ancient Greek and Roman civilizations.

Word Games

An acrostic is a verse or arrangement of words in which certain letters in each line, such as the first or last, when taken in order spell out a word, or words. Fourth century Greeks, monks of the Middle Ages, and poets of the Italian Renaissance were fond of acrostics. Still popular in Victorian England, the game became somewhat more complex. The player had to guess words or phrases from clues given, and then use the words or phrases in the method described above to find the hidden word or words.

Word squares are another form of play that extends back into ancient history. In this game, a square made of letters is arranged so that they spell the same words in the same order horizontally and vertically. See Figure 1.

```
D A T E
A C I D
T I N G
E D G E
```

Figure 1
Word square.

An elaborate Egyptian word square dating from about 300 A.D., is known as the "Stele of Moschion." It is thirty-nine Greek letters wide, and thirty-nine high. Archaeologists like examples of this type because when part of an inscription is missing, it can still be read.

An extension of acrostics and word squares was presented in the magazine section of Sunday's *New York World* newspaper on December 21, 1913. Arthur Wynne called his creation a word-cross. This first crossword puzzle was very popular and the public wanted more. The newspaper made the puzzle a regular feature. About ten years later two young men decided to publish the first crossword puzzle book. Intimidated by the doubts of well-meaning friends in the publishing business, they published the book under the alias Plaza Publishing. The resounding success of the crossword book helped to put the struggling pair on a firm financial footing and Dick Simon and Lincoln Schuster became the well-known publishers, Simon & Schuster.

As most readers know, a crossword puzzle is a word game composed of an arrangement of numbered squares to be filled in with words, a letter to each square, so that a letter appearing in a word placed horizontally is usually also a part of a word placed vertically. Numbered definitions are given as clues to enable the player to enter the words in corresponding squares. Most fans of crossword puzzles have to seek help from a dictionary at one time or another. A good, specialized, crossword puzzle dictionary combines the features of a standard dictionary, an almanac, and an encyclopedia.

The game of Scrabble consists of forming interlocking words in crossword fashion on a playing board using letter tiles with various score values. Words are scored by counting up the points of letters used, adding in the count of any premium squares. Players compete for high score by using their letters in combinations and locations that take best advantage of letter values and premium squares on the board. Play passes from person to person until all tiles are used or until no more words can be formed.

Other word games often found in the newspaper puzzle section are variations on anagrams. They include making words and sentences from scrambled letters, or making as many words as possible from the letters in a given word. Playing word games is an enjoyable way to increase your vocabulary.

Logic Games

Logic games provide a minimum of information and the player must manipulate known facts to arrive at a conclusion. In some games, such as twenty questions, the player is allowed to ask a limited number of questions that can only be answered yes or no. Other logic games can be simple but tricky such as the classic: If an electric train is traveling north at sixty miles per hour, and the wind is blowing east at thirty miles per hour, which way is the smoke blowing?

Charades is a game in which a word or phrase to be guessed is acted out in pantomime, syllable by syllable or as a whole. In this case the players must use logic to interpret the pantomimed movements.

People make competitive games out of everyday activities. In one example each player is given a mythical $500,000 and challenged to simulate investments in the stock market for maximum profit. Players call their deals into a central location that keeps track of their earnings. Whoever ends up with the most mythical earnings at the end of a prescribed period wins. In one such case, sponsored by a newspaper, a radio network, and a TV network, the winner received 25,000 real dollars.

An international competition involving a variety of word and picture puzzles was sponsored by *Games Magazine* and Random House publishers. Competitors from over a dozen countries entered the competition. The puzzles were created for the contest by an international team of puzzle experts.

Consider the case of Phillip Jourdain's liar paradox. One side of a card contains the sentence, "The sentence on the other side of this card is true." On the opposite side the card reads, "The sentence on the other side of this card is false."

The Möbius band is a strip that has no other side. Take a long strip of paper and mark one long edge with an *A* in the left corner and a *B* in the right corner. Then mark the parallel edge *B* in the left corner and *A* in the right corner. Tape the short edges together so that one *A* is above the other *A,* and one *B* is over the other *B*. Make a mark on the surface and trace around the band. Half way around you will be on the opposite side of the paper, but when you continue to the mark you will be where you started. Other puzzles challenge the player to dissect a given geometric figure into either a number of similar shapes, or into a group of specified shapes—such as dividing a hexagon into pieces that will fit together to create a square.

Puzzles involving scenarios with characters that either consistently tell the truth or lie are popular. These are sometimes called knights and knaves puzzles. We find many variations of this theme in the popular computer games. See the section in this text on "Computers, Personal" for a further listing of computer game types.

Additional challenges are found in folding paper to achieve a required result, and in explaining the seemingly impossible behavior of interacting geometrical shapes.

The bibliography identifies several books that describe a wide variety of challenges to logic.

Mathematical Games

The field of recreational mathematics is featured in periodicals such as *Scientific American,* and *The American Mathematical Monthly.* Most of us have sweated over word problems while studying elementary school arithmetic, or high school algebra, but most of the problems posed in this pastime take mathematics to an entirely new level. Educators are finding that the introduction of mathematical games stimulates math students and makes the learning process more enjoyable. Mathematics is often a factor in the solution of logic games. It has even found its way into crossword puzzles when the squares have to be filled with the solutions to math problems posed as clues. We also see in the section of this text, "Games, Gambling," that mathematical probability theory can play a useful role in the analysis of games of chance.

Bibliography

REFERENCE BOOKS

Gardner, Martin. *The Unexpected Hanging and Other Mathematical Diversions.* Rev. ed. Chicago: University of Chicago, 1991. A classic collection of puzzles and games from *Scientific American.*

———. *Wheels, Life and Other Mathematical Amusements.* New York: Freeman, 1985. A collection of problems, classical paradoxes, geometric fallacies, and games.

Lawrence, Michael, and John Ozag. *The Ultimate Guide to Winning Scrabble.* New York: Bantam, 1987. A detailed strategy for playing the game to win.

Lewis, David B. *Eureka! : Math Fun From Many Angles.* New York: Perigee, 1983. Puzzles involving words, mathematics, and logic.

Millington, Roger. *Crossword Puzzles: Their History and Their Cult.* New York: Nelson, 1984. An overview of the subject including the evolution of the game, and numerous examples of various types of puzzles.

Pulliam, Tom, and Clare Grundman. *The New York Times Crossword Puzzle Dictionary.* 2nd ed. New York: Times Books, 1984. Comprehensive dictionary tailored to the needs of the crossword puzzle enthusiast.

The Random House Cross-Word Puzzle Dictionary. New York: Random House, 1989. Well suited to the needs of the cross-word puzzle enthusiast.

Smullyan, Raymond. *To Mock a Mockingbird: and Other Logic Puzzles.* New York: Knopf, 1985. A book of logic puzzles culminating in an exercise in combinatory logic.

PERIODICALS

Games. B & P Publishing, 575 Boylston Street, Boston, MA 02116–3607.

Scientific American. Scientific American, 415 Madison Avenue, New York, NY 10017.

ASSOCIATIONS

American Crossword Federation. PO Box 69, Massapequa Park, NY 11762. Crossword enthusiasts. Creates puzzles for businesses and the media. Sponsors competitions. Publications: *Tough Puzzles,* and related books.

Mathematical Association of America. 1529 18th Street, NW, Washington, DC 20036. Teachers and individuals using mathematics as a tool in a business or profession. Sponsors high school mathematics contests and bestows awards. Publications: *American Mathematical Monthly, College Mathematics Journal,* and related materials.

National Puzzlers' League. c/o Judith Bagai, Box 82289, Portland, OR 97282. Hobbyists interested in word puzzles. Publications: *The Enigma,* and *NPL Directory.*

National Scrabble Association. c/o Williams & Co., PO Box 700, Greenport, NY 11944. Sanctions Scrabble crossword game tournaments in the U.S. and Canada and bestows awards. Publication: *Scrabble* News.

Puzzle Buffs International. 1772 State Road, Cuyahoga Falls, OH 44223. Individuals interested in word puzzles and word games. Provides puzzles to patients in various institutions. Sponsors competitions and bestows awards. Publications: *GIANTS—The World's Largest Crosswords, Puzzle Buffs Newsletter,* and *See the USA.*

Gardening and Landscaping

THERE ARE FEW PASTIMES that return so many benefits for the time invested as gardening. You get healthful outdoor exercise while producing fresh, wholesome food, without additives or preservatives, and beautiful, fragrant flowers. Gardeners experience the pride and satisfaction of improving the appearance of their property with trees, shrubs, and plants that reflect their personality and imagination. Then there is the excitement of finding the first vegetable or flower blossom each spring that results from your efforts.

History

For at least 12,000 years people have been farmers, gardeners, and landscapers. Once they learned how to produce enough food to satisfy their needs, they collected and raised plants that furnished sensory pleasure. The early Greeks, Romans, and Egyptians enjoyed the sights and smells of beautiful flowers such as the iris, crocus, and lily.

The spread of various plants through the world parallels the history of travel. Botanist/explorers from Europe collected seeds, bulbs, and plants from Africa, China, Japan, Burma, India, and Russia. The Himalayan mountain areas are noted as the source of many beautiful species of rhododendrons. Early Chinese civilizations developed roses, azaleas, peonies, and camellias in the eighteenth century. Shipment of plants from such remote areas was made practical by use of a glass case devised by English physician Nathaniel B. Ward. Using the Wardian case, plants could be shipped successfully all over the world.

Landscape Planning

Drawing a Layout

Proper landscape planning must take all plant life into consideration. Make a dimensioned layout of your property showing buildings, driveway, and walks. Use symbols and simplified sketches as shown in Figure 1 to make the job easier. Add tree locations first. They are the largest and longest lived element in the overall plan. Be sure to show them at the size they will reach at maturity. Many people plant trees too close to their house, or under a power line. If too near a drive or sidewalk, their roots can lift heavy concrete out of alignment. Trees and large shrubs can be positioned to provide shade, shield a vegetable garden from prevailing winds, or direct cooling breezes toward a patio in summer.

Shrubbery is a semi-permanent consideration, and should be added to the plan next. Use it as a backdrop for flowers, to divide an area or to anchor a corner of the lawn or the house.

Perennial flowers have a life cycle of more than two years. Since they reproduce themselves naturally, they will be around for some time and their locations should be chosen carefully. Draw them in next. Annual flowers last only one season so you can experiment freely with differing approaches to their locations in the overall design. Try to achieve a sense of physical balance in your landscape. When selecting flowers try to achieve a balance of color. Balance colors by picking hues that complement one another. When colors clash, plant some white flowers in between.

Good flower gardening practice requires proper timing. Whether the flowers are perennials, annuals, or grow from bulbs, they bloom at certain times of the season. Select early bloomers and plant them according to your plan. These should then be replaced by another such group that blooms midseason, and so on. Don't overlook flowering trees and shrubs in your overall color scheme. Information about plant coloring, blooming time, and compatibility can be found in many gardening books and seed or nursery catalogs.

Rock gardens often feature dwarf plants intermingled with stones that simulate the conditions found at high

Figure 1
A simple sketch used for landscape planning.

altitudes in the mountains. An alpine plant is dwarfed by the cold, well-drained environment. It must send roots between rocks and deep into the soil to obtain sufficient water. Many alpines have adjusted to short growing seasons by using their brightly colored flowers to achieve swift pollination. This is a plus for an attractive rock garden.

Preseason Planning

The flower gardener will start to select the next season's annuals in January or February. Working with seed and nursery catalogs and a piece of graph paper, the design of colored borders will be established. Some prefer to order seeds and start them indoors. There are many advantages. They can be started earlier—free from wind, cold, and insects; light can be controlled more closely, and the seedlings need not compete with larger established plants. When ready to be introduced to the outdoors, they are placed in a glass-topped cold frame for about five days to harden off and become accustomed to the harsher outdoor conditions. The seedlings are then placed in the garden.

If the gardener elects to purchase seedlings from a nursery, the preseason activity will consist of planning which species to plant and conditioning the soil.

The vegetable gardener will follow a similar procedure except that the starting dates for various vegetables must be closely adhered to if more than one planting is planned for a given area of the garden. When planning a vegetable garden it's best to take account of the crops planted the previous year, and rearrange the positions of vegetables so as to rotate the crops. Another consideration is to position tall crops on the north side of smaller crops in order to afford maximum sunlight to the smaller crops.

Site Preparation

A garden should be located in an area that has adequate drainage. If plants are to grow, water should drain off in no more than three or four hours. When plant roots are subjected to prolonged soaking, the plant will die. One popular way to control moderate moisture problems is to use raised beds. The garden plot soil is raised eight inches or so above the surrounding grade level, permitting better drainage.

The acidity or alkalinity of soil is measured on the pH scale by a number from 0 to 14. Zero is completely acid, and 14 is completely alkaline. Most plants thrive best in soil having a neutral 6.0 to 7.0 pH. For a reasonable fee, your county extension service will analyze your soil sample and determine the pH level, as well as levels of other important ingredients important to plant growth such as nitrogen, phosphorus, and potash. If the soil is acidic, add ground limestone; if it is too alkaline, add agricultural sulfur.

The structure of most garden soils may be classified as sandy, loamy, or clayey. Sandy soil is made up of comparatively large pieces. It feels gritty. Its open structure allows beneficial air to reach the roots, but permits too rapid drainage of water and other nutrients. Clayey soil has very fine particles, packed tightly, which slow the penetration of water, air, and root growth. It has a slippery feel. Loam provides the desirable compromise. There are enough air spaces between soil particles to allow air, water, and roots to penetrate. Loam also holds moisture and nutrients long enough to permit plant roots to absorb them.

Both clayey and sandy soils can be improved by the addition of organic matter, or humus. Humus acts to retain moisture as it fills the spaces in sand, and acts to create spaces in clay, loosening the soil and allowing root growth. Humus decomposes in time and must be replenished periodically. Humus in the form of compost or peat moss, fertilizer, and materials to adjust pH, are worked into the soil by forking or rototilling. Avoid compacting the soil by walking on it after tilling. When greater water holding capability is required, consider adding vermiculite. Vermiculite is mica expanded by heat treatment. We'll discuss composting and appropriate fertilizers below.

Planting

Few experts agree completely on the best shape of garden beds and the way plants should be arranged. When arranged in long rows, plants are accessible from pathways between the rows. Space is conserved if the plants are spaced in wide, long rows with pathways between. If plants are closely spaced in this arrangement, it is argued that they shade the soil and moisture will be retained longer. Close spacing also is claimed to discourage weed growth. When plants are arranged in four foot squares, they are accessible from all sides. However, the square arrangement requires added pathways. Probably the most popular arrangement for home gardeners is the raised bed about four feet wide and eight feet long. Two foot wide pathways permit comfortable kneeling when required.

Probably the most common mistake is overplanting. It's common practice to plant seeds closely, then thin the seedlings to achieve proper spacing. Pulling out healthy closely-spaced seedlings is a traumatic experience for many beginning gardeners. It takes more time to thin overcrowded seedlings than to painstakingly plant one seed at a time. When you must thin, it's easier to cut seedlings with a scissors than to pull them. Adhere to instructions on the seed packet regarding seed planting depth.

Add mulch during the planting process. Mulch is a covering that holds moisture, prevents weeds from getting started, and retains some heat. Black plastic sheeting is popular. Cut out about a four inch square hole where you want to install a seedling or seeds. Damp newspaper will work, but requires more maintenance. Organic materials are also used such as grass clippings. Avoid excessive thickness of grass clippings in hot weather since they may generate too much heat.

Container gardens include window boxes and various forms of tubs or large pots. Container gardening is an excellent way to isolate crops or flowers for special treatment. A special plant may require more or less water, or a different pH than its neighbors. It is wise to avoid metal or plastic containers since they retain the heat of the sun and will dry out plant roots. The soil in containers should be replaced each year or two. Choose containers with adequate space and soil depth of as much as two feet to retain sufficient moisture. Containers of less than one gallon capacity will have to be watered daily. Provide adequate drainage to prevent root rot.

Plant Growth Process

When light strikes a leaf, some of it enters the leaf and is captured by chlorophyll, the pigment that gives leaves their green color. Carbon dioxide is part of air. Air enters leaves through microscopic pores called stomates. Usually stomates are located on the bottom surfaces of leaves. Roots absorb water, which is drawn upward to the leaves, but most of it is lost when its evaporates through the open stomates to keep the leaves from overheating in the sun.

Photosynthesis takes place when chlorophyll molecules trap energy from light and use the energy to split water molecules into hydrogen and oxygen. The oxygen flows out through the stomates; the hydrogen combines with carbon dioxide to make glucose and other sugars. Glucose molecules are later joined together to make starch and cellulose. In combination with nitrogen and other nutrients, sugars are also the primary ingredients from which plants make proteins, oils, vitamins, pigments, and other compounds.

Maintenance

One way to revitalize your garden soil is to plant a cover crop that matures over the winter months. Wheat, barley, clover, and soybean plants enrich the soil when tilled into the garden bed in the spring. It is best to till at least two weeks before spring planting to allow the cover crop to decompose. The tilling process can be laborious if done by hand. Consider renting or buying a gas-powered tiller.

Compost is decomposed organic material. It is made by laying down a six-inch layer of organic material composed of leaves, garden refuse, and kitchen waste such as vegetables, fruits, eggshells, and coffee grounds. Avoid meat, bones, grease, lawn clippings containing weed killers, and diseased garden clippings. Add two inches of soil, then two handfuls of lime, and two handfuls of any garden fertilizer.

Repeat the above process with subsequent layers of organic material, and so on. Leave a depression in the center of the pile to collect water that will speed decomposition. Avoid overwatering. The compost is ready for use when there is no longer any heat in the pile, and when the compost is dark brown and crumbly.

All chemical fertilizers carry a three-number designation. The first number indicates the percentage of nitrogen. It helps plant protein formation and the creation of chlorophyll. The second number indicates the percentage of phosphorus. It promotes strong root development, disease resistance, and fruit formation. The third number indicates the percentage of potash. It promotes growth and disease resistance. Different formulations are useful for different plants. For example 5–10–5 is best for squash and tomatoes, while 10–10–10 is better for lettuce, spinach, cabbage, and annual flowers.

When plants are watered, the water fills all the air spaces in the soil and drives out the air. These are the same air spaces occupied by the plant's roots. As the water drains down through the soil the air follows it and replenishes the roots of the plant with oxygen. Plant roots stop growing when they are submerged. When a plant has too little water, growth is also suspended.

Bibliography

REFERENCE BOOKS

Adams, James. *Landscaping with Herbs.* Portland, OR: Timber, 1987. An examination of the methods used to create an ornamental garden with herbs.

Alexander, Rosemary, and Anthony du Gard Pasley. *The English Gardening School: The Complete Master Course on Garden Planning and Landscape Design for the American Gardener.* New York: Weidenfeld & Nicolson, 1987. How to deal with site, soil, climatic conditions and how to choose and design with plants.

Allen, Oliver E. *Gardening with the New Small Plants.* Boston: Houghton Mifflin, 1987. A complete guide to growing dwarf and miniature shrubs, flowers, trees, and vegetables.

Baker, Jerry. *Jerry Baker's Fast, Easy Vegetable Garden.* New York: Plume, 1985. Gardening advice, shortcuts, strategies, and tips. Covers the subject from the first stages of planning to storing the produce.

Bartholomew, Mel. *Square Foot Gardening.* Emmaus, PA: Rodale, 1981. Emphasis on a square foot system to make the most of garden space, conserve the amounts of water, soil conditioners, and labor required.

Bradley, Fern M., and Barbara W. Ellis, eds. *Rodale's All-New Encyclopedia of Gardening: The Indispensable Resource for Every Gardener.* Emmaus, PA: Rodale, 1992. A mixture of brief essays on a variety of gardening topics such as individual vegetables, trees, flowers, gardening practices, and folklore.

Brookes, John. *The Book of Garden Design.* New York: Macmillan, 1991. Step-by-step instruction on how to conceive, lay out, and realize a design. Design solutions for many types of gardens.

Coughlin, Roberta M. *The Gardener's Companion: A Book of Lists and Lore.* New York: Harper Collins, 1991. Practical information about flowers, vegetables, trees, shrubs, and soils. Covers what, where, and when to plant and much more.

Hunt, Marjorie B., and Brenda Bortz. *High-Yield Gardening: How To Get More From Your Garden Space and More From Your Gardening Season.* Emmaus, PA: Rodale, 1986. Comprehensive coverage of gardening techniques. Emphasis on increasing yields by methods such as extending the gardening season, interplanting different crops, and more.

Logan, William Bryant. *The Gardener's Book of Sources.* New York: Viking, 1988. A comprehensive bibliography of gardening.

Murray, Elizabeth. *Essential Annuals: The 100 Best for Design and Cultivation.* New York: Crescent Books, 1989. Emphasis on annual flowers. Covers growing from seed, identification of species, and garden design.

Phillips, Roger, and Martyn Rix. *Shrubs.* New York: Random House, 1989. A guide to more than 1,900 shrubs arranged according to their flowering season. Describes plant's origin, important characteristics, and required growing conditions.

Raymond, Dick. *Dick Raymond's Gardening Year.* New York: Simon & Schuster, 1985. A full year—month by month, step by step—guide to everything to grow in a vegetable garden.

Taylor's Guide to Bulbs. Boston: Houghton Mifflin, 1986. An encyclopedia of 300 bulbs. Tips on selecting the right plant for the right place. Covers planting and growing bulbs.

Thomson, Bob. *The New Victory Garden.* Boston: Little, Brown, 1987. Practical time-tested techniques for the backyard gardener. A companion to the television show, "The Victory Garden." Describes month-by-month activity in a backyard garden.

Toogood, Alan. *The Flower Garden: Summer Flowers From Seed.* New York: Crescent Books, 1987. Includes plans for using color, creating special effects, and a color catalog of annuals and biennials.

PERIODICALS

American Fruit Grower. Meister Publishers, 37733 Euclid Avenue, Willoughby, OH 44094.

American Horticulturist. American Horticultural Society, 7931 E. Boulevard Drive, Alexandria, VA 22308.

Better Homes and Gardens Garden, Deck and Landscape Planner. Meredith Corp., Special Interest Publications, 1716 Locust Street, Des Moines, IA 50309.

Better Homes and Gardens Garden Ideas and Outdoor Living. Meredith Corp., Special Interest Publications, 1716 Locust Street, Des Moines, IA 50309.

Fine Gardening. Taunton Press, 63 S. Main Street, Box 5506, Newton, CT 06470–5506.

Flower and Garden. K C Publishers, 700 47th Street, Suite 310, Kansas City, MO 64112.

The Herb Companion. Interweave Press, 201 E. Fourth Street, Loveland, CO 80537.

Herb Quarterly. Long Mountain Press, Box 548, Boiling Springs, PA 17007.

Horticulture. Horticulture Limited Partnership, 98 N. Washington Street, Boston, MA 02114–1913.

Landscaping Homes & Gardens. Arden Communications, 340 E. 93rd Street, Suite 14C, New York, NY 10128–5552.

Rodale's Organic Gardening. Rodale Press, 33 E. Minor Street, Emmaus, PA 18098.

Seed Savers Exchange. RR 3, Box 239, Decorah, IA 52101.

ASSOCIATIONS

American Horticultural Society. 7931 E. Boulevard Drive, Alexandria, VA 22308. Amateur and professional gardeners. Operates free seed exchange and gardener's information service for members. Maintains library and bestows awards. Publications: *American Horticulturist, American Horticulturist: News Edition,* and related materials.

American Rock Garden Society. c/o Jacques Mommeais, PO Box 67, Millwood, NY 10546. Persons interested in cultivation of wild or native species of alpine and saxicolous plants. Members in thirty-two countries. Maintains seed exchange, operates library, sponsors competitions, and bestows awards. Publications: *Bulletin of the American Rock Garden Society,* seed list, and related material.

Dynamics International Gardening Association. Drawer 1165, Asheboro, NC 27204–1165. Professionals, hobbyists, and youth groups. Promotes gardening in elementary schools. Maintains library and plant locator service. Sponsors competitions and bestows awards. Publications: *Garden Today News, Tips,* and related material.

Garden Club of America. 598 Madison Avenue, New York, NY 10022. Amateur gardeners. Seeks to promote gardening among amateurs and encourage civic planting. Maintains library, bestows awards. Publication: Bulletin.

The Gardeners of America. 5560 Merle Hay Road, PO Box 241, Johnston, IA 50131. Professional and home gardeners. Sponsors local beautification programs and offers consultation services on horticulture. Sponsors gardening programs. Maintains library and bestows awards. Publications: *Gardener,* directory, and newsletter.

National Council of State Garden Clubs. 4401 Magnolia Avenue, St. Louis, MO 63110. Federation of garden clubs. Conducts landscape design schools. Grants scholarships in horticultural education, conservation, and landscape design. Maintains library. Publication: *National Gardener.*

National Gardening Association. 180 Flynn Avenue, Burlington, VT 05401. Amateur gardeners. Seeks to help individuals be successful gardeners at home, in community groups, and in institutions. Conducts programs providing technical assistance, materials, and grants to children's gardens nationwide. Maintains library. Publications: *National Gardening, National Gardening Survey, New England Gardener,* and related materials.

National Junior Horticultural Association. 441 E. Pine Street, Fremont, MI 49412. Conducts educational programs for young people interested in horticulture. Sponsors projects and contests in horticulturally related fields. Publication: *Going and Growing.*

Seed Savers Exchange. RR 3, Box 239, Decorah, IA 52101. Vegetable gardeners dedicated to finding, multiplying, and spreading heirloom vegetable and fruit varieties before they are lost. Members trade seeds through the mail. Interested in locating vegetable varieties that have been in families for generations. Maintains growers network. Publications: *Harvest Edition, Summer Edition, Winter Yearbook,* and related material.

Genealogy

GENEALOGY IS THE STUDY of family descent. As hobbyists do research to accumulate knowledge of family history they are rewarded with a greater understanding of the part their families played in our nation's history. In our discussion of genealogy we will see that the pastime also promotes increased knowledge of geography, immigration patterns, research techniques, and the evolution of language.

Who, When, and Where

Consider the name Samuel Powell, Esquire. Powell is derived from Ap Howell, a Welsh name signifying the son of Howell. In Britain a person with esquire placed at the end of his name was able to bear arms and was next in social precedence to a knight. A gentleman was considered a person of gentle birth, one step below esquire. If Samuel had been the head of a household he would be termed a goodman. His first name may be referred to as his Christian name, after early Christians who converted their pagan first names to Christian ones after baptism.

Mrs. Elizabeth Smith born in seventeenth-century England or the American colonies may not have been married. At that time the term Mrs. was a title for a woman of gentle birth, married or single. She probably had an ancestor who was a blacksmith, since some last names (surnames) were based upon a person's occupation.

During the investigation of early ancestors, we attempt to learn as much as possible about them. Often we are limited to the minimum information required to establish the linkage or lineage between family members. This would include an accurate name, date of birth, date of marriage, and date of death.

When we look closer at naming practices, we find some interesting trends. Almost five thousand years ago the Chinese had three names. The middle and surname were chosen from the words of certain poems. Most western civilizations were content with one name until about the twelfth century. At that time western surnames generally originated in similar ways: according to place, occupation, patronymics (son of), or nicknames. One of the difficulties facing genealogists concerns the spelling of names. Since many people couldn't write, and spoke with an accent, their communication to those who wrote their names often resulted in a variety of spellings. To overcome this problem genealogists often group similar sounding names together using a system called soundex indexing. Many European immigrants were given new surnames by immigration officials who couldn't understand their foreign names. They selected the nearest English sounding name.

Written records of the colonial period require careful interpretation. Little or no punctuation was used. Capital letters are difficult to distinguish, especially *I* and *J*, or *U* and *V*. Words are often capitalized indiscriminately in midsentence. Extensive abbreviations are used. Most abbreviations are formed by shortening the word, then putting the last letter, or even two or three letters, of the word above the line. For example "according" would be abbreviated as accord^g, or receipt as rec^t.

Chronology is important to genealogy. The proper sequencing of individual family members depends on accurate dating. Individual information sources must often be verified and correlated with other sources by comparing dates. Genealogists have to be careful when using information dated close to 1752. At that time Britain and her colonies changed from the Julian to the Gregorian calendar. The Julian calendar had New Year's Day fall on March 25. This means that whenever a date falls between January 1 and March 24 before 1752 it's recorded to reflect both calendars (March 4, 1718/9).

Knowing the chronology of major immigration patterns helps genealogists narrow their searches. The first immigrants who arrived during the seventeenth century were primarily English. Even today as many as 82 percent of Americans can trace at least one line of their ancestors to

England. Early in the eighteenth century Germans and Scotch-Irish settlers began to arrive. In the middle of the nineteenth century a flood of immigrants came from many countries, including southern and eastern Europeans. Chinese and some Japanese also arrived on the west coast at this time.

In addition to knowing who and when, genealogists need to know where. Since towns, even counties rise, fall, and change, maps of the time period under study are very useful. Old records are often organized under political subdivisions that no longer exist. Also, the location of such records may be inferred by identifying major municipalities that existed at the time.

Research

The quality of genealogical study is dependent upon the sources of information. Original, or primary, sources are best. They are created at the time of the event by someone who knew. Your birth certificate is a primary source of information about you. If your birth certificate includes birth date information about your parents, this is secondary information because it's recorded long after the event occurred. Secondary sources are the easiest to obtain. Various directories and indexes are secondary sources that guide us to the location of further information and speed our search. Often secondary sources provide the only information available. In this case, accuracy of information can sometimes be checked by comparing data from several secondary sources.

Review all family records as the first step when compiling a family history. Work from the known back to the unknown. Then determine what research has previously been done by others that relates to your family. Make detailed records of all information. Seemingly insignificant facts often help solve problems found later.

Information Sources

Local Library. As your research carries you to different localities where ancestors once lived, check the local library for copies of local histories and other documents that may contain references to your family.

Libraries specializing in genealogy. Most libraries of this type have indexes that identify family genealogies in their collection. Your search should extend beyond your family to genealogies of other families with which yours is connected. Such libraries may be located in the reference book, *Subject Directory of Special Libraries and Information Centers,* under the genealogy heading.

The Genealogy Library of The Church of Jesus Christ of Latter-day Saints (LDS). This is the largest genealogical library in existence. It has more than 600 branch genealogical libraries located throughout the world. The LDS library publishes *Genealogical Research Papers and Research Outlines,* the *International Genealogical Index (IGI),* and a comprehensive *Genealogical Library Catalog (GLC)* that describes each record in its vast collection. LDS branch libraries are often located in local LDS meeting houses, and are available to the general public. Check your phone book for their location. The LDS has an ongoing program for microfilming additional records and expanding their collections.

The National Archives. The archives contain information on population, immigration, military records, and records relating to particular groups such as Native Americans and Afro-Americans. These records, on microfilm, are available through interlibrary loan or direct through a rental program. The National Archives has branches in eleven major cities. An important guide to this source is *Guide to Genealogical Research in the National Archives.*

Vital Records. Records of births, marriages, and deaths are important sources of genealogical evidence. When the English Church separated from the Church of Rome in the sixteenth century, vital records were required to be kept in parish church records. The practice was continued in America in the seventeenth century. Vital record keeping by the states didn't become universal until the mid-nineteenth century.

Some Useful Records

Immigration Records. Ships' passenger arrival lists provide a useful checkpoint in the life of an ancestor. Knowing the date of arrival, we can concentrate our search in America after that date. The National Archives has most of the American passenger lists that are in existence. Books such as William P. Filby's, *Passenger and Immigration Lists Index* help guide a search.

Military Records. The Continental Congress authorized each private and noncommissioned officer to receive fifty dollars, fifty acres of land, and a new suit of clothes for his service in the War for Independence. The records of this bounty land are in the National Archives together with the service records of the soldiers who served. If your ancestors lived at a time when they could have served in a war check the Archives because the information is often of such a nature that it facilitates the use of other sources and suggests new avenues of research.

Census Data. The first U.S. Census was taken in 1790. The data was limited to the names of heads of families, the number of free white males in the family, free white females in the family, number of other free persons, number of slaves, and the civil division of place of residence. The census was taken every ten years thereafter, but it wasn't until 1850 that the names of all persons in the household were included, together with other information of use to genealogy. It's interesting to note that census information less than seventy-two years old is restricted, to protect the privacy of the living. The 1920 census is available at the time of writing. Copies of census data are available in many libraries throughout the United States.

Evolution of Data Formats

As original documents deteriorate due to age and handling, it has been necessary to photograph them to make them available to researchers. The process also reduces the storage space required for the originals. The two most common formats are continuous rolls of documents on microfilm and multiple documents photographed on rectangular sheets of film. The latter are called microfiche.

The rapid evolution of the computer has had a major impact on genealogy. Vast amounts of data are being captured on computer disk files, enabling researchers using home computers to access centralized databanks. The introduction of compact disk computer storage enables the transfer of, and access to, very large record files. This is a major breakthrough for genealogical research. See the section in this text on "Computers, Personal" for more information.

Some experts estimate as many as twenty million Americans are involved to some degree in researching their family trees. An entire industry has emerged to serve all those amateur genealogists, so let them help you.

Organizing and Recording Your Findings

Pedigree Chart. Forms are readily available from genealogical societies and many libraries. You fill in the blanks for the subject of the genealogical search: Date born, location of birth, date of marriage, date died, location of death, and name of spouse. At this point the chart splits in two. The upper half provides spaces for the above information for the father, the lower half for the mother. The chart splits again, this time into quarters to record the data regarding the four grandparents. And on to eighths to record the great grandparents. Where the family lineage can be traced many generations, additional pedigree charts may be started for a person located, for example, at the great grandparent level.

Family Group Form. The pedigree chart makes no provision for multiple brothers and sisters who may be part of a given marriage. The family group form is limited to information specific to one generation. The parents are listed together with the names of their parents. Any previous spouses of the parents are listed. The data on all children is included. Space is also provided for the researcher to record the sources of information.

Search Control Record. As a researcher works back through genealogical lineage, the number of surnames involved grows rapidly. The geographical area also expands as family members are found to have lived in many states or countries. Some researchers have found it useful to prepare a listing in which vertical columns are headed by surnames and horizontal rows are made to identify sources of information such as court houses, libraries, or specific record books. A symbol is recorded where the columns and rows intersect to indicate completion of that check, review, or other activity. The idea is to show status, avoid repeating work, and have a reminder of work to be done.

Bibliography

REFERENCE BOOKS

Crandall, Dr. Ralph. *Shaking Your Family Tree: A Basic Guide to Tracing Your Family's Genealogy.* Emmaus, PA: Yankee Books, 1988. An overview of the subject. Guidance in the way to proceed with the research of your family tree.

Darnay, Brigitte T., ed. *Subject Directory of Special Libraries.* 14th ed. Detroit: Gale Research, 1990. Useful for locating genealogy libraries.

Doane, Gilbert H., and James B. Bell. *Searching For Your Ancestors: The How and Why of Genealogy.* 6th ed. Minneapolis: University of Minnesota, 1992. Step-by-step guidance to help you use research techniques.

Filby, William P., with Mary K. Meyer, eds. *Passenger and Immigration Lists Index: A Guide to Published Arrival Records of About 500,000 Passengers Who Came to the U.S. and Canada in the 17th, 18th, and 19th Centuries.* Detroit: Gale Research, 1983. Passenger names are provided in alphabetical order followed by passenger's age, place and year of arrival, and a notation regarding the source book in which the information was originally recorded.

Greenwood, Val D. *The Researcher's Guide to American Genealogy.* 2nd ed. Baltimore: Genealogical, 1990. A genealogical textbook covering all aspects of the subject. Extensive coverage of sources and bibliographic information.

The Handy Book for Genealogists. 8th ed. Logan, UT: Everton, 1992. A sourcebook for genealogical research. Includes county record locations, maps, migration trails, waterways, and more.

Helmbold, F. Wilbur. *Tracing Your Ancestry: A Step-by-Step Guide to Researching Your Family History.* Birmingham, AL: Oxmoor, 1978. A book designed to allow a complete beginner to research and compile a family history.

National Archives & Records Administration Staff. *Guide to Genealogical Research in the National Archives.* Rev. ed. Washington, DC: National Archives, 1985. A guide to a systematic review among the wide range of federal records in the National Archives.

Nichols, Elizabeth L. *Genealogy: Boy Scouts of America Merit Badge Series.* Irving, TX: Boy Scouts of America, 1988. A condensed overview of the subject for the scouts, but useful to any beginner.

Westin, Jeane Eddy. *Finding Your Roots: The Official Handbook for Heritage Hunters.* Rev. ed. New York: Ballantine Books, 1989. Comprehensive coverage of the subject. Emphasis on finding roots abroad.

PERIODICALS

American Genealogist. Box 398, Demorest, GA 30535–0398.

Ancestry Newsletter. Ancestry, Box 476, Salt Lake City, UT 84110–0476.

Family History World, Research News. Family History World, Box 22045, Salt Lake City, UT 84122.

Genealogical Computer Pioneer. Posey International, 635 S. 560 E., Orem, UT 84058–6327.

Genealogical Computing. Ancestry, Box 476, Salt Lake City, UT 84110–0476.

Genealogical Helper. Everton Publishers, Box 368, Logan UT 84323–6368.

Genealogical Societies & Historical Societies in the United States. Summit Publications, Box 222, Munroe Falls, OH 44262.

Genealogy America. Press America, Box 1076, Provo, UT 84603.

Genealogy Bulletin. Dollarhide Systems, 203 W. Holly Street, Suite M1, Bellingham, WA 98225.

Heritage Quest. Box 329, Bountiful, UT 84011–0329.

People Searching News. Box 22611, Ft. Lauderdale, Fl 33335–2611.

Reminisce. Reiman Publications, 5400 S. 60th Street, Greendale WI 53129.

Second Boat. Pentref Press, Box 398, Machias, ME 04654.

ASSOCIATIONS

Daughters of Union Veterans of the Civil War, 1861–1865. 503 S. Walnut Street, Springfield, IL 62704. Lineal descendants of Union veterans of the U.S. Civil War. Conducts genealogical projects, maintains museum and library. Publications: *General Orders,* and related materials.

Family History Department of the Church of Jesus Christ of Latter-Day Saints. 50 E. North Temple, Salt Lake City, UT 84150. A department of the Mormon Church. Promotes local and family history research. Maintains worldwide genealogical library system. Publications: *News of the Family History Library,* and *Research Outlines.*

General Society of Colonial Wars. 1316 7th Street, New Orleans, LA 70115. Male descendants of men who rendered military or civil service to the colonies between 1607 (settlement of Jamestown, Va.) and 1775 (battle of Lexington). Conducts research and educational programs. Publications: *Gazette,* and related materials.

General Society, Sons of the Revolution. Fraunces Tavern Museum, 54 Pearl Street, New York, NY 10004. Descendants, on either parent's side, of veterans of the American forces who served in the Revolution of 1776, or of American officials whose activities made them liable to charges of treason under British law. Publications: *Drumbeat, and Flintlock and Powderhorn.*

National Genealogical Society. 4527 17th Street, N., Arlington, VA 22207–2399. Promotes genealogical research. Maintains library, operates Hall of Fame, and bestows awards. Publications: *National Genealogical Society Newsletter, National Genealogical Society Quarterly,* and related materials.

National Society of the Children of the American Revolution. 1776 D Street NW, Washington, DC 20006. Lineal descendants of patriots of the American Revolution from birth to twenty-two years of age. Publication: *CAR Magazine.*

National Society Colonial Dames XVII Century. 1300 New Hampshire Avenue NW, Washington, DC 20036. American women who are lineal descendants of persons who rendered civil or military service and lived in one of the British colonies in the U.S. before 1701 as a colonist or a descendant of one. Maintains museum and bestows awards. Publication: *Seventeenth Century Review.*

National Society, Daughters of the American Colonists. 2205 Massachusetts Avenue NW, Washington, DC 20008. Women descended from men and women who gave civil or military service to the colonies prior to the Revolutionary War. Maintains library and awards scholarships. Publications: *Colonial Courier,* and related materials.

National Society, Daughters of the American Revolution. 1776 D Street, NW, Washington, DC 20006–5392. Women descendants of Revolutionary War patriots. Maintains library and museum. Bestows awards. Publications: *Daughters of the American Revolution Magazine,* and related materials.

National Society, Sons of the American Revolution. 1000 S. 4th Street, Louisville, KY 40203. Descendants of men and women who served the patriot cause in the Revolutionary War. Operates museum and maintains library. Bestows awards. Publication: *SAR Magazine.*

New England Historic Genealogical Society. 99–101 Newbury Street, Boston, MA 02116. Collects and preserves materials relating to family and local history. Maintains library. Publications: *New England Historical and Genealogical Register, Nexus, Genealogists Handbook for New England Research,* and related materials.

Sons of Confederate Veterans. Box 5164, Southern Station, Hattiesburg, MS 39406. Lineal and collateral descendants of Confederate Civil War veterans. Maintains library. Publication: *Confederate Veteran.*

United Daughters of the Confederacy. 328 N. Boulevard, Richmond, VA 23220–4057. Women descendants of Confederate veterans of the Civil War. Maintains library. Publication: *Magazine.*

Golf

A GOLFER USES A CLUB to hit a ball from a teeing ground. The objective is to cause the ball to drop into a hole in as few additional strokes as possible.

Golf courses are laid out in a way that provides a challenge to the player. They contain hazards in the form of sand traps, bodies of water, trees and tall grass. Skillful players negotiate their way between these hazards along grassy fairways leading to a 4¼ inch diameter hole surrounded by a closely cropped grassy area called a green.

A round of golf consists of eighteen holes. Some courses have only nine holes that are played twice for a round. The two most popular forms of the game are stroke and match play. In stroke play the golfer who completes a round in the fewest strokes wins. In match play the game is played by holes; the lowest score for each hole wins the hole. Match play can be played by two individuals or as four ball, in which two players play their better ball against the better ball of two other partners. Another form of match play is the foursome. In this game the partners on each side take alternate shots at the same ball.

During the course of the game the golfer drives the ball forcefully, using one or more strokes to get from the tee to the green. Then more gentle and precise effort is required to drop the ball into the hole. The latter is called putting. Golf can be described as two games in one.

Golf courses are designed with holes presenting varying degrees of challenge. The number of strokes a first-class player should take for a particular hole is called par for the hole. Par is usually determined as the length in yards from the teeing ground to the hole. For men: par 3—up to 250; par 4—251 to 470; par 5—471 and over. For women: par 3—up to 210; par 4—211 to 400; par 5—401 to 575; par 6—576 and over. Most courses have a total 18-hole par of 72 made up of par 3, 4 and 5 holes.

When a golfer takes one stroke more than par on a hole the player is said to have made a bogey. Scoring two over constitutes a double bogey. One under par is called a birdie, two under an eagle, three under a double eagle or an albatross. Under par you fly with the birds.

The game of golf features a handicap system that allows players of varying degrees of skill to compete against one another. The handicap is the number of strokes it would take to reduce the golfer's average score to par. If the average score is 92, the handicap would be 20 on a par 72 course. A scratch player is one who plays par golf with no handicap.

History

Man has enjoyed games similar to golf for centuries. The Dutch played a game called het kolven. Its influence on golf terminology is evident. The Dutch word for club is *kolf,* the hole was called a *put* and the equivalent of today's teeing ground was a *tuitje,* pronounced toytee.

There is evidence that the Dutch brought their game to the American colonies. In 1657 a Fort Orange (later called Albany), New York sheriff filed a complaint against three men playing het kolven on the ice on Sunday. It seems that these pregolfers were quite devoted to the game even then.

Although games somewhat similar to golf were played in other countries, it is likely that golf as we know it originated in Scotland, much to the consternation of King James II. The popularity of golf was causing his loyal subjects to neglect their archery practice, which was bad for the defense of the kingdom. In 1457 he issued a decree that "Fute-ball and Golfe be utterly cryed downe and not be used." However, Scotland's King James IV authorized payments for his own, "golf clubbis and ballis."

The Scots played golf for 300 years before the game was taken up in England. From there it gradually spread around the world. The first documentation of a golf club in the United States records the founding of the St. Andrews club at Yonkers, New York in 1888. That was quite some time after the het kolven incident in Fort Orange. Today's Royal and Ancient Golf Club of St. Andrews, Scotland (R and A) was formed under the name of The Society of St. Andrews in 1754. The United States Golf Association (USGA) was founded in 1894. The rules or laws of golf are administered by the rules committees of the R and A and the USGA, and are jointly revised every four years.

Equipment

Golf equipment has evolved over the centuries, taking advantage of new materials and manufacturing processes.

The original ball had a leather cover which was tightly stuffed with boiled goose feathers. Not surprisingly it was called a feathery.

The interior of today's golf ball may be a solid rubber core wound with a rubber thread and covered with a composition material. An alternate design calls for a solid rubber center extending out to the composition cover. Ball exterior covers are usually made of balata or surlyn material. The balata is softer and more prone to damage. It is preferred by professionals who feel it allows them greater control of the spin placed on the ball. The surlyn cover is tougher and holds its shape longer. Its durability appeals to amateurs.

A golf ball cover has a pattern of small depressions or dimples on its surface. Dimple size varies the aerodynamic effect on ball flight. Larger dimples provide greater lift. The ball is 1.68 inches in diameter.

Golfers should be fitted with golf clubs suited to their individual stature, strength and hand size. This is done best by a very knowledgeable sales person or golf professional. When the player assumes the correct position prior to the swing (known as addressing the ball), the bottom of the club head should rest squarely on the ground. The club grip should be sized to fit the hand. If the grip is too small a right-handed player will tend to hook the ball to the left. If too large, the ball will tend to slice to the right.

Because of the wide selection of clubs available it is advisable to rent clubs first. In view of the high cost of a new set, a prudent step would be to buy used clubs next. Later you can buy the latest professional choice of clubs with confidence.

Golf club shaft materials have evolved from wood to steel, then aluminum, fiberglass, stainless steel, graphite, graphite/boron, and titanium. The lighter materials allow the golfer to swing faster, driving the ball farther. Stainless steel shafts are best for amateurs due to lower cost with little performance loss when compared to the graphites that can cost considerably more.

A player is allowed to use only fourteen clubs during a game. The clubs are classified as woods and irons. The clubs have varying degrees of loft. Loft is the angle a club face is set back from the perpendicular. A larger degree of loft causes the ball to fly higher when struck. An average amateur's golf bag may contain as many as five woods, six irons, a pitching wedge, sand wedge and a putter.

It should be noted that metal is sometimes substituted for the wood used in the large heads of the clubs called woods. This gives them the odd name of metal woods, or simply metals.

A golf bag and a pair of spiked golf shoes together with appropriate clothing and gloves round out your equipment needs.

Strategy

When a person hits a golf ball, a number of links are in motion. They extend from the feet, up through the body, out the arms, down the club to the ball. If any of these links with their connecting joints move in an inconsistent pattern, the ball will not travel as expected. Accordingly, much emphasis is placed on the stance when addressing the ball, the backswing, and the downswing. In addition to consistent movement, the player must view the ball from the same position for consistent aim.

Care must be taken to align the club face carefully with the hole during the swing. In 100 yards, a variation of just one degree will cause about a 5¼ foot miss of the desired aiming point. Remember, the hole is only 4¼ inches in diameter.

The angle the club face makes with the perpendicular (its loft) is one factor that determines how far it will drive a ball. The greater the angle, the higher the ball will fly and it will cover a shorter distance. So when the the distance to the front of the green can be achieved with one club, the distance to the middle of the green may be achieved by a club with less loft even though each club is swung roughly the same way.

The best course of action for an unskilled golfer is to play conservatively. When teeing off, aim to the side of the fairway away from hazards. When approaching the green, try to place the ball on the green in a position that will afford the easiest putt. When long putts are required you have two choices, aim for the hole or just short of the hole. If you aim for the hole, miss and run beyond it, you may still have a long putt back. If you aim just short of the hole you have a better chance of sinking the next short putt.

When aiming your putt on the green you must consider the slope of the surface and the grain of the grass. Grass will tend to lean toward the sun. The direction of the lean can deflect or slow the ball.

Mental control is an important part of golf. If you continue to fret over the last bad shot you will not concentrate sufficiently on the requirements of the next. If you allow an excellent shot to get your adrenalin flowing too fast, you may easily stroke the next shot too hard.

Safety

Players often encounter sudden thunderstorms while on the golf course. Lightning can be very hazardous. Remember that trees attract lightning and golf clubs and umbrellas can act as lightning rods.

Players can also encounter other golfers' flying golf balls. Yelling out "fore" warns golfers they may be in harm's way.

Bibliography

REFERENCE BOOKS

Dobereiner, Peter. *Golf Rules Explained.* New York: Sterling; Devon, England: David and Gareth, 1988. Detailed presentation of the rules of golf.

Gallwey, W. Timothy. *The Inner Game of Golf.* New York: Random House, 1981. Mental strategies and conditioning.

Hay, Alex, and Julian Worthington. *Golf School.* Secaucus, NJ: Chartwell Books, 1986. Instruction, detailed illustrations of golf techniques.

Kite, Tom, and Larry Dennis. *How to Play Consistent Golf.* Trumbull, CT: Golf Digest/Tennis, 1990. Techniques, well illustrated.

Lopez, Nancy, with Don Wade. *Nancy Lopez's, The Complete Golfer.* Chicago: Contemporary Books, 1987. Advice, techniques, the woman's perspective.

Mulvoy, Mark. *Golf: Play Like a Pro.* New York: NAL/Dutton, 1988. Advice on equipment selection, instruction, and drills.

Olman, John M., and Morton W. Olman. *The Encyclopedia of Golf Collectibles.* Florence, AL: Books Americana, 1985. A collector's identification and value guide, bibliography of historical books.

Pelz, Dave, with Nick Mastroni. *Putt Like the Pros: Dave Pelz's Scientific Way to Improving Your Stroke, Reading Greens, & Lowering Your Score.* New York: Harper & Row, 1989. Techniques and fundamentals.

Stirk, David. *Golf: The History of an Obsession.* Los Angeles: Price, Stern, Sloan; Oxford, England: Phaidon, 1987. Colorful history of the sport and equipment.

Strange, Curtis, with Kenneth Van Kampen. *Win and Win Again: Technique for Playing Consistently Great Golf.* Chicago: Contemporary Books, 1991. Techniques and instructions. Illustrated.

United States Golf Association. *Golf Rules in Pictures.* Rev. ed. New York: Putnam, 1984. Rules of golf, illustrated.

Watson, Tom, with Frank Hannigan. *The Rules of Golf: Explained and Illustrated.* New York: Random House, 1984. Illustrated rules.

Wiren, Gary. *The PGA Manual of Golf: The Professional Way to Play Better Golf.* New York: Macmillan, 1991. Broad coverage of golf, golf science, techniques, and drills.

PERIODICALS

Golf Digest. 5520 Park Avenue, Box 395, Trumbull, CT 06611–0395.

Golf Illustrated. VP International, 5050 N. 40th Street, Suite 400, Phoenix. AZ 85018.

Golf International Magazine. Golf International, 2796 Quail Street, Lakewood, CO 80215–7138.

Golf Journal. United States Golf Association, Golf House, Box 708, Far Hills, NJ 07931.

Golf Tips. Werner Publishing, 12121 Wilshire Boulevard, No. 1220, Los Angeles, CA 90025–1175.

Golf Traveler. Golf Card International, 1137 E. 2100 South, Box 526439, Salt Lake City, UT 84152–6439.

Golf World. 5520 Park Avenue, Box 395, Trumbull, CT 06611–0395.

ASSOCIATIONS

American Junior Golf Association. 2415 Steeplechase Lane, Roswell, GA 30076. Golfers aged 13–18. Sponsors AJGA tour. Publication: Newsletter.

Golf Collector's Society. PO Box 491, Shawnee Mission, KS 66201. Golf artifact collectors. Publication: Bulletin.

Ladies Professional Golf Association. 2570 Vousia Street, Suite B, Daytona, FL 32114. Maintains hall of fame. Publications: *Fairway Magazine,* and *Player Guide.*

National Amputee Golf Association. PO Box 1228, Amherst, NH 03031. Promotes rehabilitation of amputees through golf. Offers college scholarships. Publication: *Amputee Golfer Magazine.*

Professional Golfer's Association of America. 100 Avenue of Champions, Palm Beach Gardens, FL 33418. Sponsors several championship events, maintains PGA World Golf Hall of Fame, and maintains golf library. Publication: *PGA Magazine.*

United States Golf Association. PO Box 708, Far Hills, NJ 07931. Conducts championships, sponsors teams for international competitions, and maintains library. Publications: *Golf Journal, Rules of Golf,* and *Decisions on The Rules of Golf.*

World Amateur Golf Council. Golf House, PO Box 708, Far Hills NJ 07931. National organizations for amateur golf. Organizes men's and women's World Amateur Championships. Publication: Record book.

Guns—Marksmanship and Hunting

YOU CAN BECOME FAMILIAR with guns and shooting practices through the study of literature available from organizations such as The National Rifle Association of America (NRA). Read and carefully follow the rules relating to the safe operation of firearms. This should be followed by hands-on instruction at local shooting ranges using targets. Ask your local sporting goods store or police department about shooting range locations.

Target Shooting

Target shooting is an international sport with more than twenty-five million participants worldwide. You don't have to be a highly conditioned athlete to participate, but steady hands help. Friendly competition is keen and readily available. Target shooting also serves as a way to sharpen your shooting skills for hunting, but most shooters prefer to concentrate on bettering their scores than on going hunting. There are National Rifle Association sponsored local shooting events, state championships, regional affairs, and an annual national championship.

A nostalgic branch of target shooting makes use of muzzle loading rifles. While some of the guns used are antiques, many participants make their own rifles, following the designs of the Civil War period. Some cast their own bullets. The accuracy attained with such antiquated weapons is amazing. These hobbyists often travel to distant locations to compete with fellow enthusiasts. On occasion, they dress in appropriate uniforms and appear in events that reenact Civil War battles. Contact the National Muzzle Loading Rifle Association for more information.

A sophisticated type of target shooting utilizes bench rest rifles. These "shooting machines" are rigidly mounted on a bench and are usually assembled from finely machined parts obtained from suppliers who specialize in such components. At 100 yards they shoot at a target measuring only 3.50 inches by 4.75 inches. The object of the competition is to attain the smallest shot group. Special .22 caliber long rifle match ammunition is often used. Ammunition of .22 caliber is $22/100$ of an inch in diameter. Contact the National Bench Rest Shooters Association for more information.

Shooters often practice with a .22-caliber rifle equipped with .22 short ammunition to keep target shooting costs down. A still cheaper approach is to use an air rifle. This type of air rifle propels a special skirted pellet at high speeds with great accuracy. It is definitely not your toy BB gun. Some are capable of extremely small shot groups on a target whose official bull's-eye, at ten meters, is a ring one millimeter in diameter.

Trap shooting is done at a moving target. Participation in this sport helps sharpen skills and improve reaction time, both so important for successful hunting. The trap shooter stands sixteen yards behind a catapult that sends a clay disk flying about fifty yards in random directions. The disk is called a clay pigeon, reflecting the fact that live pigeons were once used for this purpose. The shooter uses a 20-gauge shotgun to fire at each of five target disks. Five sets of five targets comprise a round. Another variation is the use of two targets fired at once. Both must be hit for a perfect score. In this case a round consists of fifty shots. Amateur Trapshooting Association members take part in about 4,000 registered competitions each year.

In skeet competition participants shoot from eight different locations at clay pigeons catapulted from two different locations. This comes even closer to simulating skills needed for hunting wild fowl. The National Skeet Shooting Association is the governing body of this sport.

Trap and skeet shooting require considerable practice and concentration to become competitive. As with golf, you must forget about the shot you just missed and concentrate on the one you are about to make.

Shotguns

Modern shotguns use a smooth bore with special techniques to improve accuracy. The shotgun uses a cartridge called a shell which houses either a cluster of small shot or a single slug. When used to shoot small game the small pellets are guided into a small shot-pattern by a device called a choke. This simply makes the gun barrel smaller near its end to squeeze the pellets into a smaller stream. An adaptation of the Kentucky rifle patch system is used, whereby the pellets are wrapped in a thin plastic cylinder that exits the barrel with the pellets, reducing their tendency to fan out. When hunting large game such as deer, the pellets are replaced by a single lead slug. Shotguns lose their effectiveness over 100 yards. This feature has safety advantages in wooded areas close to residences. The shot will not carry far enough to endanger property or other people not visible to the shooter.

The size of a shotgun barrel is given as a gauge number. A 12-gauge barrel bore would equal the diameter of one of twelve lead balls of equal size weighing a total of one pound. Therefore the lower the gauge number, the bigger the bore of the barrel.

The diameter of the lead shot used in shotgun shells can be found by subtracting the shot size number from seventeen and you'll get the pellet diameter in hundredths of an inch. A number six shot would be .11 inches in diameter (17−6=11).

History

It has required almost 700 years of evolution for firearms to reach their present state of development. The Chinese invented gunpowder about the eleventh century. By the thirteenth century crude bullets were fired through bamboo tubes. During fourteenth century Europe, a smoldering cord was touched to gunpowder to fire matchlock rifles. Soldiers were at a disadvantage during rainstorms using this method, but they continued to use the system until about 1700. Americans started using wheel lock guns around 1625. This approach, originating in Germany, consisted of a rough-edged wheel that spun on a flint when the trigger was pulled, throwing sparks into a pan containing powder and setting off the charge. Concurrent with the wheel lock, the Scandinavians and the Dutch used a flint-lock system in which the powder is exploded by a spark produced by the striking of a flint in the hammer against a steel plate. An improved flintlock system invented in France in the early 1600s became the standard after 1700.

The slow, steady advance of firearms technology took a leap forward with the invention of a compound that would explode when struck sharply. This discovery by a Scottish clergyman led to the percussion cap, making possible the present-day cartridge. A cartridge is simply a combination of the percussion cap, propellant powder, and the bullet, wrapped in a brass casing. It evolved into a practical device in 1856 when Smith and Wesson produced a rim-fire cartridge.

Firearms developed along specialized lines from their beginning. American colonists wanted to take advantage of the plentiful small game found in their new land, so they required a rifle that shot accurately at long range. This led to the development of the Kentucky rifle in Pennsylvania by German and Swiss immigrants. The breakthrough involved the use of a greased cloth patch. After the shooter rammed powder into the gun barrel, a lead ball was placed on the patch and knocked down the barrel. The patch sealed the gap between the ball and the rifled interior of the gun barrel so that maximum pressure would develop when the powder exploded. Rifling is a spiral grooving of the barrel interior. It is used to impart a spin on the bullet to achieve a straight flight path. A small group of marksmen used these rifles in the Revolutionary War for sniping activities, taking a heavy toll of British officers. It is said that the Kentucky rifle may have provided an advantage that led to eventual victory. During the Revolution most soldiers on both sides used muskets with smooth bores. While not as accurate as rifled firearms, they were adequate at short range. Modern rifles and handguns usually feature the spiral grooved rifling.

Hunting

About twenty-two million people enjoy hunting, many choosing to concentrate on small game. The uninitiated might think that this level of activity would decimate the animal population. Strangely enough, the opposite in usually true. The sale of hunting licenses funds the various governmental game departments, who in turn promote wildlife welfare. These departments set limits on the taking of game that assures a continued appropriate animal population level. In temperate zones animal life expands during summertime to the limit that the environment can support. In winter, lack of food, the cold, and disease serve to thin excess animal populations to a level that the winter environment can support.

Upland hunting includes small and large game, both birds and animals. The cottontail rabbit is the most hunted game animal in North America. Rabbits have survived fifty million years due to their prolific breeding habits. One female will have four or five litters of two to eight young in one season. Hunting rabbits is a lot easier with a good hunting dog to flush them out of hiding. Rabbits dislike leaving their home grounds, so when chased they will circle around its perimeter and right back to you. Some hunters use a .22 rifle to hunt rabbits in sparsely populated areas where the longer range of the rifle is not a safety factor. Most rabbit hunters use a 12-gauge shotgun with number six shot in their shells.

Squirrel hunting requires patience. A quiet wait in a wooded area will often result in their appearance as they scurry around the trees. Hunters use a shotgun or .22 rifle. Squirrel meat is good both fried or stewed; but bag several, because a gray squirrel weighs less than two pounds.

Successful hunters spend considerable time in prospective hunting areas studying game distribution and actions. They also learn the habits of the quarry. It's useful to know that a duck flies in a straight line, but a dove has a swerving, erratic flight path. A wild turkey has excellent eyesight and hearing and will require practice with a turkey call to bring it into view. Pheasants may be flushed out of cover by a number of hunters called drivers who sweep across a field toward another group called blockers. Retriever dogs are very useful. The dogs benefit from practice prior to the hunting season. Additional examples of challenging small game are woodcock, quail, grouse, and partridge.

Farmers are generally glad to see hunters. When hunters kill animal pests classed as varmints, they reduce damage done to crops and fields. Varmints include woodchuck, rockchuck, prairie dog, raccoon, fox, coyote, bobcat, lynx, and puma. Be sure to practice safe hunting and get the farmer's permission. Once again, rifle bullets carry great distances.

The most popular upland big game animal in America is the deer. Carefully controlled hunting seasons assure an appropriate deer population. The hunter will find deer active and feeding early in the morning and late evening. Bright colored clothing helps prevent accidental shooting by other hunters. Deer are sensitive to movement, but not color. They have excellent hearing and sense of smell. For these reasons, your best chance of taking a deer is to post yourself quiet and motionless, and wait for a deer to approach. Preseason scouting will determine the locations most frequented by the deer. An alternative is the driving method described for pheasants. It's said that a hunter has about one chance in five of bagging a deer, so a cooperative drive and sharing of the resulting bag can be advantageous.

Big game also includes elk, moose, pronghorn antelope, goat, sheep, bear, boar, cougar, and peccary. The national forests are home to one third of the big game animals in the United States. They aren't posted so hunting is permitted during hunting season, conditions permitting.

Another broad category of hunting involves waterfowl. This is an activity where your trapshooting practice pays off. In contrast to upland hunting where you go after the game, in waterfowl hunting you wait for ducks and geese to come to you. Once again, prior scouting of the bird's habitat tells you where to position yourself. In most cases the hunter will seek the camouflage of a thicket or a specially prepared blind. The birds are enticed to come within firing range by the use of decoys and duck or goose calls. Proper clothing is a must in these wet areas during chilly fall hunting seasons.

The wild goose is a particularly crafty quarry, possibly prompting the familiar reference to a "wild goose chase."

Most goose hunting is done from pits dug into fields with an appropriate camouflaged cover. These are located along the migratory flyways where the geese drop down to feed and rest.

Bibliography

REFERENCE BOOKS

Anderson, Luther A. *How to Hunt American Small Game.* New York: Funk & Wagnalls, 1969. Discusses appropriate guns for small game. Also covers the habits, life cycles, and hunting techniqes required to bag the most popular four-footed and winged game.

Dalrymple, Byron. *Fresh Looks at Deer Hunting.* Clinton, NJ: New Win, 1992. Tips and techniques for deer hunting. A study of the animal's habits and the ways to take advantage of that knowledge.

————. *North American Game Animals.* New York: Crown, 1978. A comprehensive study of the game animals of North America. Each chapter presents important data about the animal including where and how they live, their daily and seasonal routines, and much more.

Fadala, Sam. *The Complete Black Powder Handbook.* Rev. ed. Northbrook, IL: D B I Books, 1990. All about muzzle-loading rifles, handguns, and shotguns. Includes proper handling and maintenance.

————. *The Rifleman's Bible.* New York: Doubleday, 1987. Information on rifle handling, ammunition, ballistics, and shooting accessories.

Flayderman, Norm. *Flayderman's Guide to Antique American Firearms and Their Values.* 5th ed. Northbrook, IL: D B I Books, 1990. Comprehensive coverage of guns with valuable advice on collecting.

Lewis, Jack, ed. *Shotgun Digest.* 3rd ed. Northbrook, IL: D B I Books, 1986. General discussion of shotgun usage with emphasis on hunting techniques.

McIntyre, Thomas. *The Way of the Hunter: The Art and the Spirit of Modern Hunting.* New York: Dutton, 1988. The methods and equipment used by experts in hunting game from rabbits to lions.

Rees, Clair. *Be an Expert Shot: With Rifle, Handgun, or Shotgun.* Piscataway, NJ: New Century, 1984. An illustrated self-coaching method to improve shooting skills.

Rees, Clair F. *Beginner's Guide to Guns and Shooting.* Rev. ed. Northbrook, IL: D B I Books, 1988. Understanding firearms, how they work, and how to safely use them. Covers shotguns, rifles, hand guns, and air guns.

Smith, Richard P. *Deer Hunting.* 2nd ed. Harrisburg, PA: Stackpole Books, 1991. Deer habits and habitat. Hunting techniques for firearm, bow, and camera.

Smith, Steve. *Hunting Upland Game Birds.* Harrisburg, PA: Stackpole Books, 1987. Covers shooting techniques and provides advice on gun selection.

Walter, John. *The Rifle Book.* London: Arms & Armour, 1990. A guide to the world's shoulder guns. Includes a directory of the performance and availability of the products of over fifty manufacturers.

PERIODICALS

American Handgunner. Publishers' Development, 591 Camino de la Reina, Suite 200, San Diego, CA 92108.

Dixie Gun Works Blackpowder Annual. Dixie Gun Works, Box 684, Union City, TN 38261.

Field & Stream. Times Mirror Magazines, 2 Park Avenue, New York, NY 10016.

Gun World. Gallant-Charger Publishers, 34249 Camino Capistrono, Box HH, Capistrono Beach, CA 92624.

Guns. Publishers' Development, 591 Camino de la Reina, Suite 200, San Diego, CA 92108.

Guns and Ammo. Petersen Publishers, 8490 Sunset Boulevard, Los Angeles, CA 90069.

Handloader. Wolfe Publishers, 6471 Airpark Drive, Prescott, AZ 86301.

Petersen's Handguns. Petersen Publishers, 8490 Sunset Boulevard, Los Angeles, CA 90069.

Petersen's Hunting. Petersen Publishers, 8490 Sunset Boulevard, Los Angeles, CA 90069.

Pheasants Forever. Pheasants Forever, Box 75473, St. Paul, MN 55175.

Precision Shooting. Precision Shooting, 37 Burnham Street, E. Hartford, CT 06108.

Safari. Safari Club International, 4800 W. Gates Pass Road, Tucson, AZ 85745.

Shooter's Bible. Stoeger Publishers, 55 Ruta Court, S. Hackensack, NJ 07606.

Shooting Times. P J S Publications, News Plaza, Box 1790, Peoria, IL 61656.

Shotgun News. Snell Publishers, Box 669, Hastings, NE 68901.

Shotgun Sports. Box 6810, Auburn, CA 95604.

Skeet Shooting Review. National Skeet Shooting Association, Box 680007, San Antonio, TX 78268.

ASSOCIATIONS

Amateur Trapshooting Association. 601 W. National Road, Vandalia, OH 45377. Sanctions and determines rules governing trapshoots held by local, state, provincial, and worldwide trapshooting associations. Maintains Hall of Fame, museum, and library. Publications: *Trap and Field Magazine, Rules,* and related material.

Association of American Rod and Gun Clubs, Europe. USAREUR/7A, DCSPER, CFSD, APOAE, New York, NY 09014. Federation of rod and gun clubs connected with American military forces in Europe, North Africa, and the Near East. Promotes hunting and fishing trips throughout Europe for members. Sponsors skeet shooting team, sponsors competitions, and bestows awards. Publications: *Hunting and Fishing Event Newsletter,* and *Rod and Gun Club Location Guide.*

Deer Unlimited of America. PO Box 1129, Abbeville, SC 29620. Hunting and conservation clubs. Seeks to provide a place for members to hunt by leasing land. Sponsors competitions and bestows awards. Publications: *Deer Unlimited,* and periodical.

International Bench Rest Shooters. c/o Joan Borden, RD 1, Box 244A, Tunkhannock, PA 18657. Those interested in developing the ultimate of rifle accuracy. Sponsors tournaments with demonstrations, and seminars. Publication: *Precision Shooting Magazine.*

National Bench Rest Shooters Association. 2027 Buffalo, Levelland, TX 79336. Those interested in precision shooting. Conducts shoots, certifies records, and bestows awards. Maintains Hall of Fame. Publication: *NBRSA News.*

National Hunters Association. PO Box 820, Knightdale, NC 27545. Provides hunting information service, tours, and training courses.

National Muzzle Loading Rifle Association. Friendship, IN 47021. Persons interested in black powder shooting. Maintains national range at Friendship, Ind. Offers educational program in hunter safety. Publications: *Muzzle Blasts,* and range rules.

National Rifle Association of America. 1600 Rhode Island Avenue, NW, Washington, DC 20036. Those interested in firearms. Promotes shooting, hunting, gun collecting, home firearm safety, and wildlife conservation. Educates police firearms instructors, and sponsors teams to compete in world championships. Bestows awards, maintains museum and library. Lobbies on firearms issues. Publications: *American Hunter, American Rifleman, Badge, Insights,* and *Shooting Sports USA.*

National Skeet Shooting Association. PO Box 680007, San Antonio, TX 78268. Amateur Skeet Shooters. Registers competitive shoots. Honors outstanding contributors to the sport and bestows awards. Publications: *Skeet Shooting Review, Sporting Clays: The Shotgun Hunters Magazine,* and *Record.*

North American Hunting Club. 12301 Whitewater Drive, PO Box 3401, Minnetonka, MN 55343. Hunters of North America. Leases hunting lands and maintains Big Game Awards Program. Publications: *Keeping Track, North American Hunter,* and related materials.

North-South Skirmish Association. 9700 Royerton Drive, Richmond, VA 23228. To pay tribute to the soldier on both sides in the War Between the States. To display arms and equipment of the period for the entertainment and education of the spectators. Sponsors marksmanship matches using arms of the period. Publication: *Skirmish Line.*

Wildlife Legislative Fund of America. 801 Kingsmill Parkway, Columbus, OH 43229–1137. Sportsmen, lobbyists, and others seeking to protect the sportsman's legal right to hunt, fish, and trap. Publications: Reports, update, and related materials.

Gymnastics

GYMNASTICS ARE PERFORMED to promote physical development or as a sport. The ancient Greeks saw it as a systematic training of the body to develop strong, agile warriors. The Greek system of gymnastics has since developed as separate sports such as track and field athletics, boxing, and wrestling.

History

The modern development of gymnastics started with the founding of gymnastic societies in Germany and spread throughout Europe. Children's classes started youngsters as early as the age of five. The German gymnastic system made use of apparatus stressing muscular development. In Sweden a system of free exercises on the ground was developed in mid-nineteenth century, with the objective of developing rhythm of movement. Both systems were introduced to the United States during the 1880s as immigrants brought the ideas of their societies with them and founded gymnastic societies wherever they settled.

In the 1920s the Federation Internationale de Gymnastique (F.I.G.) established a system that blended the rhythmic, flowing movements of the Swedish system with the precision and developmental emphasis of the German system.

Modern gymnastics is recreational and good for developing discipline of both mind and body. As a competitive sport in the United States, amateur gymnastics is administered by the United States Gymnastics Federation (USGF). Separate events take place for males and females. In most cases, particularly for major competitions, each event is composed of a compulsory series of moves and an optional, or free-style series. Gymnastic events are performed using a variety of specialized equipment. A brief description of the individual events and equipment follows.

Women's Artistic Gymnastics

Women gymnasts compete and earn points in four events. The points are totaled and recognition is given to the overall champion of the competition. The four events are: asymmetric bars, balance beam, floor exercises, and the vault. The elements of the various compulsory events are revised periodically.

Asymmetric Bars

The apparatus consists of two horizontal bars, spaced 60 to 110 cm apart. One is about 155 cm from the floor and the other at about 235 cm.

The compulsory series rules are specific regarding the method of mounting the bars and movement between them. Elements of the series include: swings into handstands or between bars; releasing the grasp and "flight" between bars or to the ground; various pirouettes and turns. The movements are judged for execution and continuity.

The optional series allows the gymnast to choose the elements to be performed, within certain constraints. Only four consecutive elements may be performed on the same bar. Ten elements must be included. The dismount, or return to the floor, should be compatible with the level of difficulty of the rest of the series.

Balance Beam

The 10 cm wide wooden beam is about 500 cm long. It is raised 120 cm above the floor.

The gymnast performs a compulsory series of acrobatic movements along the beam. The elements include handstands, somersaults, running, leaping, and acrobatic dismounts.

The optional series must include: acrobatic elements, acrobatic strength elements, gymnastic elements, dance steps. Judges will deduct points for repetitive or monotonous movements, more than three pauses, falls from the beam, using the side of the beam for support.

Floor Exercises

The women's floor exercises are performed to music. As with balance beam, the series includes elements of acrobatics, display of strength, gymnastics, and dance. The gymnast must avoid a monotonous performance, but not place too much emphasis on theatrics. Specific movements include flips, cartwheels, handsprings, graceful steps and turns, handstands, leaps and spins—all confined to the surface of a 12 m square mat.

Vault

The vaults are performed using a springboard and a horse, which is a leather covered form 160 cm long and 35 cm wide, raised about 120 cm from the runway surface.

The 120 cm long springboard (Reuther board) is positioned to the side of the horse. The gymnast takes a running start, jumps on the springboard and "flies" to the horse, making contact with the hands and flipping over it to perform a variety of turns in flight. She then lands firmly on her feet, without further movement.

The rules for the vault specify both vault types and their degree of difficulty. The gymnast must identify the vault to be performed before making the attempt.

Rhythmic Gymnastics

Rhythmic gymnastics is all floor work performed to music with or without small hand apparatus. It is a separate competition from the women's artistic competition group of events described above.

Gymnasts use ropes, hoops, balls, clubs, and ribbons to complement and enhance body movement. The performer bounces, tosses, or rolls a ball, while interacting with graceful body movements. A pair of wooden clubs are swung, tossed, and tapped during performance. Hoops are rolled, tossed, and passed over the body. Ropes are used for skipping, jumping, and swinging. A ribbon attached to a stick is whirled about in different planes forming circles, figure eights and snake-like shapes.

Gymnasts are judged on their performance of body movements and their interaction with each specific item of apparatus.

Men's Artistic Gymnastics

Men gymnasts compete and earn points in six events. The points are totaled and recognition is given to the overall champion of the competition. The six events are: floor exercises, horizontal or high bar, parallel bars, rings, side or pommel horse, and vault. The elements of the various compulsory events are revised periodically.

Floor Exercises

The exercises are performed without music. The performance must be smooth and rhythmic. Exercises consist of acrobatic movements and displays of flexibility, strength and balance. The performance must include three different acrobatic elements, one strength feature, and one static element of balance on one arm or one leg. All available floor space must be used. The performance takes place on a 12 m square mat.

Horizontal Bar

The apparatus is a 240 cm long bar raised about 235 cm from the floor. The exercise consists of swinging movements smoothly flowing into "flying" elements when the bar is released and recaught. The body is turned in pirouette fashion during swings, and somersaults are included during the "flight" portion of the dismount.

Parallel Bars

The apparatus consists of two horizontal bars, 350 cm long, spaced 42 to 52 cm apart. They are both raised the same height, 165 cm from the floor. The exercise consists of movements combining swings, vaults, strength, and balances. There may not be more than three balances, such as handstands, in an exercise. Required elements include one movement of strength, motion above and below bars, and the release and recatching of the bars.

Rings

The apparatus consists of a pair of rings with a diameter of 18 cm, located about 275 cm from the floor. The rings are suspended by straps from a structure about 575 cm high. The exercise should be composed of strength, swing, and held elements. Specific requirements include: a minimum of two handstands—one pressed into by strength from a support above the rings, and one swung up from a hanging position below the rings; a strength movement such as a cross—holding the body vertical with arms stretched horizontally; various swinging and hanging movements. The above movements must be accomplished while holding the rings stationary; they must not swing.

Pommel Horse

The apparatus consists of a horse, which is a leather covered form 160 cm long and 35 cm wide, raised about 115 cm from the floor. It has two half loops of wood, called pommels, inserted into the top. They are spaced 40 to 45 cm apart, and equidistant from the center of the horse. The gymnast supports himself on the pommels over the horse and performs continuous movements of the body and legs. Various turns, swings, and changes of hand support are accomplished with emphasis on the use of all parts of the horse. One or both hands are used for support during the various movements.

The pommel horse evolved from a wooden horse introduced by the Romans and used to teach mounting and dismounting. They added it to the ancient Olympic Games.

Vault

The apparatus consists of a horse, which is a leather covered form 160 cm long and 35 cm wide, raised 135 cm from the runway surface. A 120 cm long springboard is positioned at one end of the horse. The gymnast takes a running start, jumps on the springboard and "flies" to the horse, making contact with the hands and flipping over it to perform a variety of turns in flight. He then lands firmly on his feet, without further movement. Note that the male gymnast passes over the length of the horse.

The rules for the vault assign a degree of difficulty to the various acrobatic maneuvers. The gymnast must identify the vault to be performed before making an attempt.

It should be noted that the dimensional specifications for all gymnastic equipment are subject to change.

Preparation

Gymnastics requires extensive conditioning to achieve needed strength and coordination. Years of dedicated training and conditioning are required to compete effectively at the national level. Most successful gymnasts start at an early age and stick with a program that begins with general exercises such as running, windsprints, calisthenics, and resistance training. Specific exercises that will enhance later development of specific skills come next. They include exercises such as handstand push-ups, leg lifts, and kips (pulling oneself up onto an overhead horizontal bar). At the point when the gymnast is performing a large number of competitive routines to gain consistency, the routines provide a good deal of general conditioning. Look for an experienced coach to provide proper, safe, development guidance.

Bibliography

REFERENCE BOOKS

Conner, Bart, with Paul Ziert. *Winning the Gold.* New York: Warner Books, 1985. Autobiographical coverage of a champion gymnast.

Cooper, Phyllis. *Feminine Gymnastics.* 3rd ed. Minneapolis, MN: Burgess, 1980. Provides the instructor with methods of teaching, skill analysis, and spotting techniques.

Grumeza, Ion. *Nadia: The Success Secrets of the Amazing Romanian Gymnast.* New York: Giniger, 1977. The story of a 14-year-old east European gymnast.

Hunn, David. *The Complete Book of Gymnastics.* Secaucus, NJ: Chartwell Books, 1979. An overview of men's and women's gymnastics.

Maddux, Gordon, and Arthur Shay. *40 Common Errors in Women's Gymnastics and How to Correct Them.* Chicago: Contemporary Books, 1979. Illustrates mistakes made during individual elements of programs, together with corrective action required.

Progressive Gymnastics. Rev. ed. Champaign, IL: YMCA, 1987. National YMCA Progressive Gymnastics Program for youth. A multilevel development program for beginners.

Retton, Mary Lou, and Bela Karolyi, with John Powers. *Mary Lou: Creating an Olympic Champion.* New York: McGraw-Hill, 1986. Provides insight into the coaching and development of an Olympic athlete.

Sands, Bill. *Coaching Women's Gymnastics.* Champaign, IL: Human Kinetics, 1984. Covers the preparation and training of a gymnast from the coaches point of view.

Sands, William A. *Modern Women's Gymnastics.* North Palm Beach, FL: Athletic Institute, 1982. A well-illustrated book for training women gymnasts.

Stuart, Nik. *Gymnastics for Men.* London: Stanley Paul, 1978. Step-by-step training methods for gymnastic competition.

Taylor, Bryce, Boris Bajin, and Tom Zivic. *Olympic Gymnastics for Men and Women.* Englewood Cliffs, NJ: Prentice-Hall, 1972. Discussion of individual elements of gymnastics programs, with typical faults, method of teaching, and spotting techniques.

Wettstone, Eugene, ed. *Gymnastics Safety Manual.* 2nd ed. University Park, PA: Pennsylvania State University, 1979. The official manual of the United States Gymnastics Safety Association. Covers physical preparation, safety, apparatus dimensions, and areas of concern for use of each type of apparatus.

PERIODICALS

International Gymnast Magazine. Sundby Sports, 225 Brooks, Box 2450, Oceanside, CA 92051.

USA Gymnastics. U.S. Gymnastics Federation, Pan American Plaza, Suite 300, 201 S. Capitol Avenue, Indianapolis, IN 46225.

ASSOCIATIONS

Amateur Athletic Union of the United States. 3400 W. 86th Street, P. O. Box 68207, Indianapolis, IN 46268. Sports associations. Sponsors AAU/ USA Junior Olympic Games, which includes competition in fifteen sports, AAU Youth Sports Program, and the Presidential Sports Award. Maintains library and hall of fame. Publications: *Info AAU, Newsmagazine,* and related materials.

American Turners. 1127 E. Kentucky Street, PO Box 4216, Louisville, KY 40204. Promotes health and physical education for the family through gymnastics and other sports. Also supports cultural education through classes in music, painting, and handicrafts. Holds annual national tournament in gymnastics. Publication: *American Turner Topics.*

United States Gymnastics Federation. 201 S. Capitol, Suite 300, Indianapolis, IN 46225. National associations concerned with amateur sports, particularly gymnastics. Conducts national program in gymnastics for Junior Olympics and junior, senior, and elite international level gymnasts. Selects teams for World Championships, World Cup, Pan American Games, Olympic Games, and other international events. Bestows awards. Publications: *Technical Journal, USA Gymnastics,* and related materials.

Hiking and Backpacking

WHEN PEOPLE CHOOSE WALKING as a pastime, their goals are usually to promote physical fitness and enjoy the scenery. Hiking is defined as a long, vigorous walk through country or woods. When hiking for an extended period of time in remote locations, it becomes necessary to carry provisions and shelter. Backpacking challenges us because it requires strength and stamina; but the rewards are worth the effort. As we hike, far removed from our complex civilized life, we are exposed to the simple, more basic, elements of nature and survival. It's a time of renewal as we get time to think and sort things out. The activity promotes independence, self esteem, and an appreciation of nature's beauty. We return to civilization with a new appreciation for everyday conveniences.

Public Trails

As a result of the foresight of the founding fathers, we have vast areas of the country reserved for public use. The national parks and national forests provide extensive opportunities and facilities for hiking. The Bureau of Land Management (BLM), under the jurisdiction of the U.S. Department of Interior, has almost 6,000 miles of hiking trails. The BLM controls one-eighth of the land of the United States.

Two of the country's largest and most famous, hiking trails are located along mountain ranges. The Appalachian National Scenic Trail extends 2,135 miles from Maine to Georgia. It's composed of a network of trails and camps along the ridges of the Appalachian Mountains. Hikers may choose to travel any portion of the trail as time and endurance allows. Each season thousands of hikers enjoy it; some complete the trail after several years of hiking segments of it. In an average year about 100 thru-hikers walk all 2,135 miles. Volunteers work to keep the trail cleared, blazed, and protected.

The Pacific Crest Trail extends 2,500 miles from Canada to Mexico along mountain crests. It crosses twenty-four national forests and seven national parks. It's a high mountain trail for hikers and horsemen. No vehicles are allowed. Of 109 mountains, forty-seven are glacier peaks and difficult to climb. Its highest point is 13,200 feet at Forester Pass in the Sierra Nevada Range in California.

The organizations and periodicals listed in the bibliography provide more information on the many smaller trails open to public use. There now are more than 500 rail-to-trail conversions and hundreds more wagon, horse, and canal tow paths that provide historical perspective. For further information on related governmental agencies consult your telephone directory. A toll free number for the Federal Information Center is listed under "U.S. Government."

Planning

Factors affecting your plan for an extended hike will depend upon where you are going, the season of the year, and the duration of the trip. First obtain maps and literature relating to the area to be traveled. A careful review may uncover dangers to be avoided or points of interest to be included. It's better to learn beforehand about streams that rise and become impassable during certain times of the year. If your pastimes include the study of botany or birdwatching, it would be disheartening to learn after your trip that a nearby area featured specimens you wish to see. A good example of preplanning is employed along the Appalachian Trail. Thru-hikers mail packages of food and clothing to themselves to be picked up at post offices along the route.

Most backpackers will drive to the starting point (road head) of a planned hike. The distance to be traveled from the road head, or to the planned destination, will determine the amount of food, equipment, and survival gear to be carried. For example, if you will be only two days away from either the beginning or end of a trip during a dry, hot season, you may elect not to carry any rain gear. It's a good plan to prepare a complete checklist of items to be carried under the most severe conditions. You can then review the list, choosing items that are appropriate for less extensive trips. The terrain, temperature, and weight carried will determine how far you can travel in a day. Take these factors into consideration when planning the above equipment load.

Preparation

Preparation for an extensive hike, or hiking season, should begin months beforehand. One of the first considerations is physical fitness. Hiking or backpacking should not be attempted by those in poor health. In his book, *The Outdoor Athlete,* Steve Ilg describes an off-season regimen of calisthenics, weightlifting, flexibility exercises, and sprints to strengthen muscles and build endurance. Increase the levels of stress applied during this training gradually. See the "Physical Fitness" section in this text for more detail. Your first hiking trips should be day trips, starting at about one hour and working up to longer trips as you gain strength.

A backpack places added weight above your beltline. This tends to make you top-heavy. To balance and stabilize this load, muscles must be maintained in constant tension. As you assume different positions while walking or climbing, more stress will be placed on some muscles, but opposing muscles must still maintain tension to keep you erect. The amount of weight that a hiker can carry will vary with the person's size and physical condition; but for a healthy, well conditioned person, some experts recommend a maximum pack weight of one fourth of your body weight. Even this may be high when hiking up steep inclines. Learn your limits by taking short hikes. If you become short of breath, stop and rest. Your first overnight trip with backpack should be limited to one night and taken during reasonably mild weather. If the weather is changeable, especially at high altitudes, anticipate the worst and pack warm clothing. Increase trip lengths as you gather strength and experience.

On the Trail

Before you set off on the trail, let some responsible person know where you're going and when you'll be back. In remote areas, it's best to stay on the trail to avoid getting lost in wooded areas, or sustaining injuries where you won't be discovered. These precautions are especially important if you are traveling alone. If you are beginning your hike at altitudes above which you're accustomed, you may experience shortness of breath. Acclimate yourself by breathing oftener and more deeply. Pay attention to warning signs such as headaches as you make your ascent, and pause occasionally to give your body time to adjust.

If you become lost, stop and take time to think logically. Gain high ground so you can look for landmarks on your map. Trails, roads, and power lines lead to civilization. Note the direction of the sun. If lost for an extended period, and you find your way out, notify the person you left word with, so others will not continue to look for you.

Equipment

Clothing should be selected that can be worn in layers so that as temperature conditions change you can add or subtract layers as required. Although somewhat dictated by the seasons, your outfit consists of: Seasonal underwear. A warm layer or layers of clothing that trap dry air to insulate, but will also allow water vapor from perspiration to pass through and escape. A wind and waterproof outer layer. In hot, dry conditions hikers wear shorts and other light garments.

As with jogging and running, good shoes are of primary importance. Hiking boots must meet certain criteria to be effective: The upper must yield under pressure but provide support. It must protect the foot and repel water. The sole must cushion the foot, provide traction with the trail surface, provide support, be waterproof, and still be flexible enough to respond to movements of the foot. Boots that meet the above requirements should be durable and at the same time be as light as possible. Boot manufacturers work to meet these seemingly conflicting requirements using fabrics, leather, and plastics in various combinations.

Backpacks are made in a variety of styles, sizes, and materials. They vary from fanny packs that strap around your hips for an afternoon in the country, to large external-frame packs with special suspension systems.

An external-frame pack usually consists of: A rectangular frame made of light weight tubing. The frame is contoured to follow the curvature of the back in order to hold the load close to the body, creating the least leverage or pull on muscles. The frame has several broad straps or a wide piece of fabric mesh running across horizontally. These contact the back when a harness pulls the frame toward the body. The harness consists of a pair of padded shoulder belts and a wide, padded, hip belt. The hip belt transfers the pack's weight to the muscular structure of the hips and legs. The shoulder belts function primarily to hold the pack in close to the body. The pack bag is attached to the back of the frame. The pack bag is usually divided into compartments with access provided by means of zippers.

Internal-frame packs have the support structure built into the pack bag, allowing the bag to ride close to the body. The shoulder and hip straps and other stabilizing straps afford additional opportunity for adjustment.

It's beyond the scope of this work to provide a complete checklist of items useful to the hiker. Items such as a flashlight, compass, knife, a water filter, matches, first aid and snake bite kits, are near the top of the list, but are only a start. Consult knowledgeable hiking club members and a reliable mountain shop or other outdoor outfitter for guidance. Also see the section in this text entitled "Camping."

Bibliography

REFERENCE BOOKS

Bridge, Raymond. *High Peaks & Clear Roads: A Safe & Easy Guide to Outdoor Skills.* Englewood Cliffs, NJ: Prentice-Hall, 1978. Covers trip planning, campsites, equipment, clothing, cooking, and related activities such as cycling, canoeing, and mountaineering.

Fisher, Ronald M. *Mountain Adventure: Exploring the Appalachian Trail.* Washington, DC: National Geographic, 1988. Well illustrated coverage of the Appalachian Trail with emphasis on its fiftieth anniversary in 1987.

Fletcher, Colin. *The Complete Walker III: The Joys and Techniques of Hiking and Backpacking.* 3rd ed. New York: Knopf, 1984. A practical and comprehensive guide to walking, written with insight and humor.

Ilg, Steve. *The Outdoor Athlete: Total Training for Outdoor Performance.* Evergreen, CO: Cordillera, 1987. Describes an off-season regimen of exercises to strengthen muscles and build endurance for hiking and backpacking.

Lyttle, Richard B. *The Complete Beginner's Guide to Backpacking.* Garden City, NY: Doubleday, 1975. The techniques and equipment of hiking and backpacking.

Rudner, Ruth. *Off and Walking: A Hiker's Guide to American Places.* New York: Holt, Rinehart and Winston, 1977. Covers the planning of a trip, needed equipment, and describes a selection of back country hiking tours.

Schreiber, Lee. *Backpacking: A Complete Guide to Why, How, and Where for Hikers and Backpackers.* New York: Stein and Day, 1978. Covers equipment, clothing, conditioning, backpacking in various weather conditions and terrains, navigating, cooking, and first aid.

Wood, Robert S. *Pleasure Packing.* Berkeley, CA: Ten Speed, 1991. A comprehensive guide to backpacking basics, food, clothing, equipment, camping, navigation, and first aid.

PERIODICALS

Appalachia Journal. Appalachian Mountain Club, 5 Joy Street, Boston, MA 02108.

Appalachian Trailway News. Appalachian Trail Conference, Box 807, Harpers Ferry. WV 25425.

Backpacker. Rodale Press, 33 E. Minor Street, Emmaus, PA 18098.

Fodor's Sports: Hiking. Fodor's Travel Publications, 201 E. 50th St., New York, NY 10022.

Trail Walker. New York-New Jersey Trail Conference, 232 Madison Ave., New York, NY 10016.

ASSOCIATIONS

Adirondack Mountain Club. RR 3, Box 3055, Lake George, NY 12845–9523. Persons interested in mountains, trails, and camping. Maintains trails, operates two lodges, sponsors mountaineering schools, and maintains library. Publications: *Adirondack,* and related materials.

American Hiking Society. PO Box 20160, Washington, DC 20041–2160. Seeks to educate the public in the appreciation of walking, and encourage hikers to build and maintain footpaths. Bestows awards. Publications: *American Hiker, Pathways Across America,* and related material.

Appalachian Mountain Club. 5 Joy Street, Boston, MA 02108. Maintains 1,400 miles of trails, twenty trail shelters, and an eight unit alpine hut system. Conducts educational workshops and maintains a large library that includes photographic maps. Publications: *Appalachia Bulletin, Appalachia Journal,* and related material.

Appalachian Trail Conference. Corner, Washington and Jackson Streets, PO Box 807, Harpers Ferry, WV 25425. Federation of clubs and individuals interested in walking. Manages the Appalachian Trail. Maintains museum. Publications: *Appalachian Trailway News, Register, Trail Lands,* and related materials.

Florida Trail Association. PO Box 13708, Gainsville, FL 32604. Conservationists, hikers, and canoeists interested in Florida wilderness and scenic areas. Maintains and develops the Florida Trail. Holds seminars and workshops and sponsors hikes. Publications: *Footprint, Walking the Florida Trail,* and related material.

The Mountaineers. 300 Third Avenue W., Seattle, WA 98119. Those interested in exploring the northwest. Conducts short hiking, skiing, camping, and mountain climbing trips for members. Maintains museum and library, and bestows awards. Publication: *The Mountaineer.*

New England Trail Conference. c/o Forrest E. House, 33 Knollwood Drive, East Longmeadow, MA 01028. Coalition of organizations interested in hiking, trail clearing, and maintenance. Information clearinghouse on hiking trails in New England. Publications: *Hiking Trails of New England,* and *New England Trails.*

Potomac Appalachian Trail Club. 1718 N Street, NW, Washington, DC 20036. Maintains 230 miles of Appalachian Trail. Maintains locked cabins and open shelters for use of the hiking public. Maintains courtesy patrol along trail in summer. Publications: *Potomac Appalachian,* and related materials.

Rails-To-Trails Conservancy. 1400 16th Street, NW, Suite 300, Washington, DC 20036. Hikers, bicyclists, cross-country skiers, and others interested in the conversion of abandoned railways into trails for public use. Seeks to build a transcontinental network. Publications: *Guide to America's Rail-Trails, Trailblazer,* and related materials.

History and Research

HISTORY IS THE BRANCH of knowledge dealing with past events. Everything and everyone around us has a history. Many of us have been turned-off on the subject when we were required to memorize textbooks full of political events and dates. In the broadest sense, our entire educational curriculum is a chronicle of past discoveries and events—it's all history. History comes to life when presented by a skillful teacher, providing clear mental images of the past.

Although most hobbies relate to history in one way or another, for some, history is the hobby.

Historical Pastimes

Some pastimes that are closely related to history are covered in detail elsewhere is this book:

In "Genealogy," we see how one goes about tracing a family history. In "Antiques and Collecting," the acquisition of antiques and historical artifacts is discussed. In "Fossils, Rocks, and Artifacts," the emphasis is on earth history. In "Travel," we find that many select travel destinations to enjoy the ambiance of historical locations and significant museums. Getting in touch with the actual locations where history was made can be a moving experience, as anyone who has visited the Holy Lands will tell you. In "Voluntarism," we note that many volunteer their skills to perform preservation activities on artifacts or entire buildings. Some serve as guides (docents) for historical sites. In model building, hobbyists recreate miniatures of all sorts of historically significant vehicles and other objects. In "Guns, Marksmanship and Hunting," we find Civil War buffs reenacting battles and other activities. Some people create reproductions of early furniture to decorate their homes, or reproduce early costumes for amateur theater productions or various historical functions. Others restore historical cars, airplanes, and boats for their personal enjoyment.

Probably the most popular historical activity is reading. Many enjoy the study of a particular branch or era of history. There are thousands of history books that relate to specific locations or time periods. Some are claimed to include the history of the world. (The author's world perhaps, but certainly not all of civilization.) Two excellent books in the bibliography, *The Timetables of History,* and *The People's Chronology,* provide a framework of history that the reader can build upon in areas of particular interest.

As you become expert in a field of study you find that usual sources of information don't provide answers to your questions. You perceive a need to enhance your research skills.

Historical Research

A historian must select appropriate material from the mountains of data available. It's this selection process that places a slant on the reporting of historical events. Each historian's output is a product of that person's own education, experience, research, interests, and bias. It follows that if a researcher is to obtain a true picture of an event, more than one source should be consulted. Furthermore, original or primary sources are less likely to be slanted than those that have been retold by a series of historians.

A practical example of the value of historical research involves the purchase of a house built more than a century ago. By conducting some research at the local library, the new homeowner found the life history of the original, locally prominent, owner. Photographs of the house taken when it was first built were also found. These photos helped in the accurate restoration of the building.

Under the heading "Computers, Personal," we see that by using a modem and a telephone one can tap into information systems. These information system data bases are a storehouse of the world's knowledge. No matter how specialized your interests become, needed information is usually there. If no answers can be found, you can access the roundtables and forums sponsored by the information services. There, you will be put in touch with experts in a wide variety of fields.

Libraries

Some libraries will access information services for a small fee. In cases where your inquiry requires an extensive or complex search, this service can be well worth the fee. Modern libraries are information centers. Their services extend far beyond being merely a depository for books. The contents of a typical library are tailored to the needs of its patrons, who may number in the thousands or millions.

So what can a full service library do for you? First, be aware that the library staff wants to help you. Without your taxes and use of their facilities, they wouldn't have a job. If you have a specific question, need to know where to begin your research, or just settle a bet, call them on the phone.

When visiting an unfamiliar library to research a subject, you may want to stop first at the information desk to determine which department is responsible for the subject. The information desk is sometimes part of the general reference department. This department has a collection of reference books and librarians having knowledge of many fields.

Armed with preliminary information your next step is to consult the card catalog file or computer file. These library files are designed to accept inquiries by author, subject, or both. Most computer files can respond to inquiries containing only key words. When you have identified a needed book, or other item such as an audio or video cassette, note the call, or class, number.

A call numbering system was organized by a library assistant named Melvil Dewey back in 1872. It's composed only of numbers. By 1898 the Library of Congress grew so large and complex that it was found necessary to add letters to the class number to accommodate the variety of subjects. The first system is called the Dewey Decimal Classification. The second, the Library of Congress Classification System. You may find either system in use. Whole books have been written about the significance of the numbers and letters in these systems.

All you need to know at this point is that the class numbers are usually displayed on the ends of the bookshelves, thus leading you to your book—usually. In larger libraries, only a portion of the books are displayed on shelves accessible to the public. Many additional books are filed in remote areas called stacks.

If your book is not found on the shelves available to the public, ask the librarian to check the stacks. If the book has been taken out by another patron, ask the librarian to reserve the book for you when it returns. Larger books are sometimes filed in separate book shelves that will accommodate their size. A hint that this may be the case will be found in the book identification numbering system. The letter *Q,* for quarto, is sometimes applied to identify any book measuring about nine by twelve inches. In addition to the size consideration, librarians sometimes maintain a separate set of shelves for new book arrivals. In these cases, the librarian can advise you where to look.

You will find encyclopedias, dictionaries, quotation books, bibliographies of books by subject, even bibliographies of bibliographies in certain library departments. Several types of readers guides also aid the researcher in finding needed material. Much information isn't contained in bound books.

Microfilm or microfiche copies of books, newspapers, and pamphlets are sometimes available. Material that would occupy a large volume of valuable shelf space, or is brittle with age, is sometimes photographed by these methods. This facilitates public access. Imagine reading American newspapers dating back to 1704 when *The Boston News-Letter* began, or to 1719 for *The Boston Gazette,* or the Philadelphia paper, *The American.* You can sometimes arrange to borrow microfilms of early newspapers for viewing by means of interlibrary loan.

Most libraries provide interlibrary loan service. After you have identified a needed item in the reference section and find that it's not available at your library, you can have it sent to your library for your use. You will be expected to pay postage for the book to be sent to your library and returned to the original library. The librarian uses a computer network to locate the book after determining how far you wish the search to extend, which of course, affects the cost. It's not unusual to search the entire country, sometimes even foreign countries. Since fourth class mail is used to ship the books, the costs are surprisingly low. Determine what the costs will be before ordering.

University Libraries

To be effective for the greatest number of people, a public library must contain material of general interest. If you need information of a specialized nature, consider a university library. Academic or university libraries are designed to meet the specific needs of their students. Many university libraries have a central library and branches in each college. A check of the courses offered by the school will give an indication of its library's contents. You will find little duplication between public and academic libraries. University libraries are surprisingly accessible to the general public. Some charge a small yearly fee for a nonstudent library card and others provide free library service to area residents. Library procedures and practices generally parallel those found at public libraries.

It is worth noting that an interlibrary loan search done by your public library usually extends into academic libraries. It would be interesting to see what early material could be found in the libraries of Harvard, founded in 1636, or the College of William and Mary, founded in 1693.

Historical Society Libraries

Historical Society libraries vary in scope from the large presidential establishments holding the papers of past Presidents, to the small local society libraries containing material of local interest. You may find unique material in these libraries if their specialty matches your needs. Accessibility will vary with library size and funding available.

National Libraries

The Library of Congress (LC) may well be called the national library. Located in Washington, DC, it serves a standardizing function for library cataloging. When a book is copyrighted, the LC receives a copy and prepares catalog information, assigning call, or class numbers in the process. The LC provides reading rooms open to the public and special facilities for scholars. Founded in 1800, it has grown to contain 270 miles of shelving. Among its many features is a national service for the blind that provides for the lending of books in braille, talking books, and books in large type. The LC is one of 250 libraries in Washington, DC. Washington is second only to New York City for collections available to the American public.

The National Archives and Records Service (NA) holds federal records, making most of them available to the public. NA publishes information to simplify use of their material. Microfilms are available for some of the records.

Other Sources of Historical Information

If you want to research original sources for historical information, you can start at the public library reference department. Catalogs and indexes found there give locations of archives, collections of personal papers, and public records. Don't overlook court houses, churches or synagogues, schools, and social or fraternal organizations. Used book stores are also a good source of out-dated material that provides historical perspective.

Bibliography

REFERENCE BOOKS

Barzun, Jacques, and Henry F. Graff. *The Modern Researcher.* 4th ed. New York: Harcourt Brace Jovanovich, 1985. A manual on research and writing. Detailed analysis of how to find the facts, select and verify data, organize material, and present the work effectively.

Boorstin, Daniel J. *The Discoverers: A History of Man's Search to Know His World and Himself.* New York: Random House, 1983. This book focuses on discoveries and beginnings. It covers exploration of lands, science, and nature.

Deuel, Leo. *Testaments of Time: The Search for Lost Manuscripts and Records.* New York: Knopf, 1985. The story of the scholar-adventurers who gave us vast new knowledge of the ancient civilizations of Egypt, Mesopotamia, Mexico, and Central Asia, and of the origins of the Bible.

Grun, Bernard. *The Timetables of History: A Horizontal Linkage of People and Events.* 3rd ed. New York: Simon & Schuster, 1991. This book provides a concurrent overview of civilization from ancient to modern times. It highlights 30,000 significant moments in history, politics, literature, theater, religion, philosophy, learning, the visual arts, music, science, and daily life.

Horowitz, Lois. *Knowing Where to Look: The Ultimate Guide to Research.* Cincinnati, OH: Writer's Digest Books, 1984. Techniques for efficient researching written by a reference librarian.

Langdon, William Chauncy. *Everyday Things in American Life (1607–1776).* New York: Scribner's, 1965. A description of the way of life during the American colonial period. The houses, activities, equipment, and methods of travel of immigrants from many countries.

Trager, James, ed. *The People's Chronology: A Year-by-Year Record of Human Events From Prehistory to the Present.* New York: Holt, Rinehart and Winston, 1979. A concurrent overview of man from prehistory to the 1970s. Symbols are applied to each entry to identify its relationship to one of thirty different categories.

PERIODICALS

American Heritage. American Heritage, 60 Fifth Avenue, New York, NY 10011.

American Heritage of Invention & Technology. Forbes, 60 Fifth Avenue, New York, NY 10011.

American History Illustrated. Cowles Magazines, 6405 Flank Drive, Box 8200, Harrisburg, PA 17105–8200.

America's Civil War. Empire Press, 602 S. King Street, Suite 300, Leesburg, VA 22075.

Civil War Times Illustrated. Cowles Magazines, 6405 Flank Drive, Box 8200, Harrisburg, PA 17105–8200.

The Historian. Phi Alpha Theta International Honor Society in History, c/o Roger Adelson, Editor, History Department, Arizona State University, Tempe, AZ 85287–2501.

Historic Preservation. National Trust for Historic Preservation, 1785 Massachusetts Avenue, NW, Washington, DC 20036.

Military History. Empire Press, 602 S. King Street, Suite 300, Leesburg, VA 22075.

Smithsonian Studies in History and Technology. Smithsonian Institution Press, 470 L'Enfant Plaza, Suite 7100, Washington, DC 20560.

ASSOCIATIONS

American Antiquarian Society. 185 Salisbury St., Worcester, MA 01609–1634. Gathers, preserves, and promotes serious study of the materials of early American history and life. Maintains research library of nearly five million books, pamphlets, broadsides, and related materials. Publications: *American Antiquarian Society Proceedings, The Book: Newsletter of the Program in the History of the Book in American Culture,* and related materials.

American Association For State and Local History. 530 Church Street, Suite 600, Nashville, TN 37219. Professionals and others interested in the study of state and local history in the U.S. and Canada. Conducts workshops and bestows awards. Publications: Directory, *History News, History News Dispatch,* and related materials.

American Historical Association. 400 A Street SE, Washington, DC 20003. Professionals and others interested in promoting historical studies and collecting and preserving historical manuscripts. Sponsors competitions and bestows awards. Publications: *American Historical Association—Perspectives, American Historical Review,* and related material.

American Institute For Conservation of Historic and Artistic Works. 1400 16th Street, NW, Suite 340, Washington, DC 20036. Professionals and individuals interested in the field of art conservation. Seeks to preserve and maintain objects or structures of historic value. Publications: Journal, newsletter, and related materials.

Mystic Seaport Museum. 50 Greenmanville Avenue, PO Box 6000, Mystic, CT 06355–0990. Persons interested in furthering the study of American maritime history. Restores historic vessels and small craft. Maintains maritime historic library and displays historic small boats. Publications: *Log of Mystic Seaport, The Windrose,* and related materials.

National Society, Daughters of the American Revolution. 1776 D Street, NW, Washington, DC 20006–5392. Women descendants of Revolutionary War patriots. Maintains genealogical/ historical research library, and a museum. Bestows awards. Publications: *Daughters of the American Revolution Magazine,* and related materials.

National Society, Sons of the American Revolution. 1000 S. 4th Street, Louisville, KY 40203. Descendants of men and women who served the patriot cause in the Revolutionary War. Maintains genealogical and historical library, and operates a museum. Sponsors competitions and bestows awards. Publication: *SAR Magazine.*

National Trust for Historic Preservation. 1785 Massachusetts Avenue, NW, Washington, DC 20036. Private organization chartered by the U.S. Congress to facilitate public participation in the preservation of significant historical buildings, sites, and objects. Maintains historic properties and bestows awards. Publications: *Historic Preservation,* and related materials.

Oral History Association. 1093 Broxton Avenue, No. 720, Los Angeles, CA 90024. Persons who work to foster the growth of oral history and improve techniques. Involves the recording and preserving of conversations of those who have participated in important developments in modern times for use by future historians. Publications: *Oral History Review, Annual Report,* newsletter, and related material.

Organization of American Historians. 112 N. Bryan Street, Bloomington, IN 47408. Primarily professionals involved with history. Sponsors programs for historical writing and bestows awards. Publications: *Journal of American History, OAH Magazine of History,* and *OAH Newsletter.*

Society For Historical Archaeology. PO Box 30446, Tucson, AZ 85751–0446. Professionals and those with an interest in historical archaeology. Brings together persons interested in studying specific historic sites, manuscripts, and published sources. Publications: *Historical Archaeology, Guides to the Archaeological Literature of the Immigrant Experience in America, Society for Historical Archaeology Conference: Underwater Proceedings,* and related material.

Yarns of Yesteryear Project. University of Wisconsin-Madison, Continuing Education in the Arts Dept., 610 Langdon Street, Room 727, Madison, WI 53706. Offers assistance to seniors who wish to write their memoirs and thereby make a cultural contribution to society. Conducts correspondence course.

Hockey, Ice

THE OBJECT OF THE GAME is to use a hockey stick to hit a small, disk-shaped puck, to drive it into an opponent's goal. A goal is worth one point. A goal can be made as a result of a deflection of the puck off of a skate, stick or the body, but a player is not allowed to kick or throw the puck into the goal.

Ice hockey is played on an ice rink laid out as shown in Figure 1. Each team starts a game with six players on the ice. They are a goalkeeper, a left and right defenseman, and three forwards playing left wing, center and right wing. The goalkeeper does not stray far from in front of the goal. In the modern game the remaining team members will often participate in prearranged plays that carry them far from the locations their titles imply.

An ice hockey game is sixty minutes long, divided into three twenty-minute periods with a rest intermission between periods. Use of overtime to decide ties is at the discretion of the league. Players are substituted frequently due to the fast pace of the game. Players other than the goaltender are usually replaced after play intervals of less than two minutes. This is done on-the-fly with the game in process.

The playing surface is divided by two blue lines into three zones. The line between the two blue lines is the red center line. When viewed from the perspective of the team controlling the puck: the zone behind them containing their goal is the defending zone, the central zone is the neutral zone, and the zone containing the goal of their opponents is the attacking zone.

Certain restrictions impede the free flow of the puck toward an opponent's goal. A player can't pass the puck across two lines (blue and red). An attacking player can't precede the puck across the blue line into the attacking zone. Either of these actions results in an offside penalty call. When a defending team shoots the puck from its half of the ice down to the other end and across the red goal line and an opponent touches the puck first, an icing penalty call is made.

Play is resumed after an offside or icing call by means of a face-off. The referee will drop the puck between two opposing players. Face-off after offside occurs at a spot in the neutral zone. Face-off after icing occurs at a spot in the offender's defending zone. Face-offs occur at center ice at the start of each period and after a goal has been scored.

The penalty for some offenses is spending time on the penalty bench. Time spent depends on the severity of the offense. A minor offense such as delay of game, holding, or unnecessary roughness merits two minutes on the bench. The offender's team plays shorthanded. If the opposing team scores a goal during the two minutes the penalty is terminated. A major offense such as initiating fisticuffs, injuring an opponent by slashing, or grabbing or holding a face mask, draws five minutes, and the offender's team plays short handed. A misconduct offense such as fighting off of the playing surface, obscene language or gestures gets ten minutes, but a substitute can play during the penalty. A match offense such as kicking another player, injuring, or attempting to injure another player calls for removal for the balance of the game. Depending upon severity, a substitute can replace the offender, but only after a five- or ten-minute period. Bench penalties play a major role in the conduct of the game. Teams develop special plays called power plays to be used to take advantage of the loss of a player by the opposition.

History

Ice hockey evolved in Canada during the nineteenth century. The strongest influences appear to be a similar game played in Nova Scotia by the Micmac Indians combined with English field hockey. Early games were played with as many as sixty skaters; thirty on a team. While the Micmacs favored knocking around a wooden block, subsequent players used a ball, until the puck was introduced by Canadians around 1860.

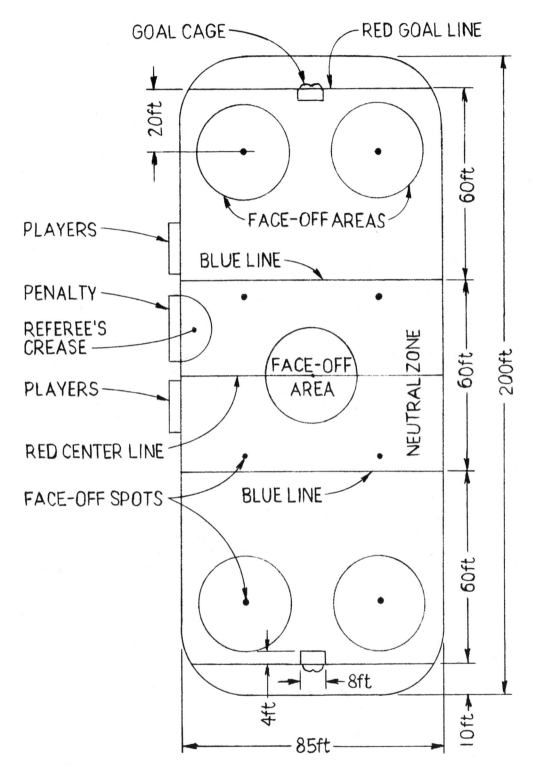

Figure 1
Hockey playing rink layout.

Michigan dentist J. L. Gibson hired Canadian players to form the first professional hockey team in 1903. Needing teams to compete with, he formed the first professional league in 1904.

The National Hockey League was formed in 1917. It grew from six to twelve teams in 1967 and merged with the World Hockey Association in 1979 to form a league with twenty-one teams. It now has twenty-four franchises.

Equipment

The hockey puck is made of vulcanized rubber. It is three inches in diameter, one inch thick, and weighs between 5½ and six ounces.

The stick has a maximum length of sixty inches from heel to end of shaft. The blade length from heel to end of blade is a maximum of 12½ inches. Blade width is two to three inches. A goalkeeper's stick has a 3½ inch maximum width blade and a 3½ inch maximum wide shaft extending up twenty-six inches from the heel. It can also have a maximum blade width of 4½ inches at the heel.

The lie of the stick is the angle between the blade and shaft. The higher the lie number, the smaller the angle, permitting puck control close to the skates. Most players use lies of five or six.

Players use tape to improve the grip at the top of the shaft. Tape, usually black in color, is used to protect the blade. It also serves to aid in control of the puck.

Skates must be of an approved design with a safety heel. Speed or other fancy skates are prohibited.

Players are outfitted with padding from neck to skate top. Protective helmets and gloves are worn. Goalkeepers wear additional leg guards, masks and oversize arm guards. All uniforms must display an identifying number.

Strategy

The puck may be moved by using the stick to hit the puck from side to side as you advance, causing it to move in a zig-zag pattern. The stick blade should lean forward over the puck during impact to cover it, offering some protection from an opponent's efforts to take it away. A similar move can be made forward and backward to outmaneuver an attacker. Prolonged stickhandling of the above types is difficult.

The puck can be passed from one player to the next, mixing up the pattern of play to increase the likelihood that one teammate will be unguarded. Passing pattern plays are designed and practiced. Passing is done along the ice with a forehand or backhand pass, or lofted over an opponents stick blade or other obstruction with a flip pass.

Shooting the puck toward or into the goal can be done with a forehand or flip shot as above. Other techniques include the snapshot, done with a quick wrist movement,

and the slap shot. The slap shot utilizes some windup and a powerful stroke.

The defensive player also uses some well-developed techniques. One of the most versatile is checking. Checking is the act of slowing the progress of a player with the puck. Body checking techniques underscore the fact that hockey is a contact sport. A player can run into an opponent, making contact with the shoulder or hip, providing certain rules are followed. No more than two approaching strides may be taken, your stick and elbows must not be raised, and you should not lead with your leg or you may be accused of tripping.

Checking is also accomplished in various ways with the stick, the primary object being to take possession of the puck. Restrictions include no cross-checking. Cross-checking is the use of two hands on the stick with no part of it on the ice. The player may not check by prodding with the butt-end or blade of the stick. Other stick violations include slashing or tripping, throwing it or carrying it above shoulder height.

Checking a stick-handling opponent toward the boards that surround the rink restricts the opponent's movement and increases the possibility of gaining control of the puck for one's team.

Defensemen also occasionally assist the goalkeeper by blocking shots taken at the goal.

Amateur Hockey and Related Activity

The Amateur Hockey Association of the United States (AHAUS) together with the U.S. Olympic Committee chooses players for Olympic competition. AHAUS chooses the national team for the World Championships. The National Collegiate Athletic Association conducts a championship tournament.

Fantasy hockey is gaining popularity. This is an armchair hobby pitting knowledgeable sports enthusiasts against one another using a professional player's performance as a determining factor. See the section in this text entitled "Games, Gambling" for more information.

Bibliography

REFERENCE BOOKS

Falla, Jack. *Hockey: Learn to Play the Modern Way.* New York: Sports Illustrated Winners Circle Books, 1987. Broad coverage, techniques, drills, and advice for youth league coaches.

Francis, Emile, with Tim Moriarty. *The Secrets of Winning Hockey.* Garden City, NY: Doubleday, 1972. Covers the basic moves on offense and defense, and the methods of play for each position.

Fullerton, James H. *Ice Hockey: Playing and Coaching.* New York: Hastings House, 1978. Covers hockey history, roles of individual player positions, special play techniques, role of the coach, and conditioning.

Gilbert, Rod, and Brad Park. *Playing Hockey the Professional Way.* New York: Harper & Row, 1972. Covers equipment, skating technique, game basics, and conditioning.

MacLean, Norman. *Hockey Basics.* Englewood Cliffs, NJ: Prentice-Hall, 1983. A brief overview of the game, covering equipment and playing techniques.

National Hockey League. *Hockey Rules in Pictures.* Rev. ed. New York: Putnam, 1988. Rules of the game with many illustrations.

Stamm, Laura. *Laura Stamm's Power Skating.* 2nd ed. Champaign, IL: Leisure, 1989. Emphasis on skating techniques and drills.

PERIODICALS

Hockey Digest. Century Publishers, 990 Grove Street, Evanston, IL 60201–4370.

Hockey Magazine. Publishers Group, 1022 W. 80th Street, Bloomington, MN 55420.

Ice Hockey Rule Book. National Federation of State High School Associations, 11724 NW Plaza Circle, Box 20626, Kansas City, MO 64195–0626.

ASSOCIATIONS

U.S.A. Hockey. 4965 N. 30th Street, Colorado Springs, CO 80919. Governing body for amateur ice hockey in the United States, arranges tournaments and awards trophies. Affiliated with the International Ice Hockey Federation and the U.S. Olympic Committee. Publications: *American Hockey Magazine, Official Playing Rules Book,* and instructional materials.

American Hearing Impaired Hockey Association. 1143 W. Lake Street, Chicago, IL 60607. Hearing impaired boys and men aged eleven to twenty-six who wish to play ice hockey.

National Hockey League. 1800 McGill College Avenue, Suite 2600, Montreal, PQ, Canada H3A 3J6. Promotes professional hockey in the U.S. and Canada. Presents the Stanley Cup and maintains hall of fame. Publications: *Goal,* Rulebook, and related material.

Homes, Style and Decor

ONE OF OUR MOST BASIC NEEDS is shelter. It's probably only natural that so many of our spare-time interests center around the home; it's the source of our most popular hobbies.

Much of our spare time is taken up by a never-ending effort to improve our housing environment. Let's look at man's early attempts to do the same.

History

The First Homes

Archaeologists have found evidence of ancient stone walls extending from the mouth of a cave, probably supporting a roof. The evolution of housing has been influenced by many factors since the caveman built the first front porch. Climate, the availability of materials, and security head the list.

In early Egypt and Mesopotamia mud brick houses were built around a central patio or courtyard. Use of windows on the exterior walls was minimized to reduce the effects of solar heating. This plan continued to be used by the Greeks and Romans. Similar courtyards are sometimes found in modern homes.

Man used materials at hand to build early dwellings. Mud, tree branches, animal hides, and stone have been used for centuries. American colonists were forced to resort to crude shelters made from these materials during their first years in this country. As tools and processes developed, mud became brick, stones were shaped, and lumber was milled.

Southwestern American Indians provided for security by building on the face of cliffs. They pulled access ladders up to prevent surprise attack. Some of their adobe structures were entered by means of a trap door in the roof. English castles of the eleventh century featured high, narrow windows to provide a smaller target for arrows and stones. The castle became obsolete with the appearance of accurate firearms. The lords dropped their fortifications, and the grand manor house evolved.

During the next few centuries, English trade with other countries increased and a middle class of merchants and traders emerged. They copied the lord's manor on a smaller scale. The result was an exposed heavy timber structure with the areas between filled with stone and covered with plaster. This style became very popular in England and was copied by English colonists in America. It is referred to as the Elizabethan, or half-timbered style. The Elizabethan style featured large groups of rectangular windows, some in the form of bay windows. Interior style included extensive use of wood paneling and molded plasterwork for ceilings, cornices and walls.

Evolution of American Architectural Style

As colonists, missionaries, and immigrants came to America they built houses in the styles found in their native lands. Their influence can be seen today in areas they occupied. Perhaps the most noticeable are English and Dutch styles found in the northeast, Spanish styles in the south, and French and Spanish styles in the south central areas of the United States.

A study of American architectural history reveals a relationship between house styles and certain periods of our past. During colonial times the saltbox style was built, starting in the 1600s. It is a two-story house with a gabled roof that slopes to the first floor in the rear. The saltbox was accompanied by the Cape Cod style in the late 1600s. The Cape Cod is a small 1½ story house having a gable roof and a central entrance. Interiors featured paneled or painted walls and exposed ceiling beams. The style, and larger versions of it, is still popular today.

In North Carolina, the Swedes introduced the log cabin about 1638. It became popular in Pennsylvania and other newly settled areas. The Pennsylvania Quakers and Germans favored fieldstone construction as a more permanent structure. Many are still standing today.

In the Southwest, Spanish missionaries built adobe buildings of the Spanish villa, mission, or Indian pueblo style during the 1600s and 1700s.

As America matured, people wanted up-to-date styles like those found in England. They turned to English architectural handbooks to learn how to build houses in the Georgian style. Two examples of handbooks of the period are *The Builders Jewel,* and *A Treasury of Designs.* The Georgian style featured large two or three story brick houses of a formal style that included Greek columns at the entrance and sliding sash windows. Interior floor plans included central halls and staircases with intricately turned balusters. Interiors featured paneled walls in warm colors and white plaster ceilings. The Georgian period lasted from about 1725–1820.

The Greek Revival period began about 1820 and lasted thirty years. The war of 1812 with England was over and America became fascinated with classical Europe. Buildings featuring Greek columns and accents became popular. The tall columns and open verandas were especially favored in the South. Interiors sometimes carried the external theme indoors with central domed halls and column-like accents.

The Victorian Age began about 1837, gaining popularity after the Civil War. The highly ornate houses of this period are known by many names, such as Gingerbread houses, High Victorian Gothic, Stick style or Carpenter Gothic. They were often made of wood, sometimes brick. Victorian houses featured bandsawn ornamentation and complex shapes. The interiors were very ornate and cluttered. Heavy curtains and dark muted colors were common. Wallpapers were set off with ornate woodwork, moldings and castings. Closets and built-in cupboards were featured. The style continued through 1901. During this period a champion of country living and the Gothic cottage wrote two books. Andrew Jackson Downing published *Cottage Residences* in 1842, and *The Architecture of Country Houses* in 1850. Both were very popular in their time.

About 1900 the public started to become more independent about style selection. They chose the styles that appealed to them, from Colonial to Italian. It became known as an Eclectic Period. The philosophy seems to continue to this day. About 1930, an International, or modern, style made a few waves. These were smooth white concrete "modern" box-like structures with long horizontal windows. Interiors were plain, simple, and geometric in form.

Another new era of architectural thinking began in 1910 with the first work of Frank Lloyd Wright. Wright believed that a house should blend with its environment. His houses featured horizontal lines, low roofs angled to the ground and few interior walls. His designs were unique and years ahead of their time.

The most recent architectural period followed World War II. Called the Contemporary period, it featured an open room plan, warm colors and materials, efficiency through science and technology, more glass, and less frills. Mr. Wright would have approved.

It is likely that half of our houses today do not match the styles described above. We tend to borrow features that appeal to us from various styles. Perhaps it's appropriate that our houses are like us—a melting pot of inputs from many sources.

We view our landscape differently after reading a few books on architecture. The new undersanding developed adds spice to travel and affords the traveler interesting subjects to photograph. Some people become so involved with historic buildings and sites that they volunteer their time as guides or docents to share their knowledge with others.

Many of the house styles discussed can be seen in restored communities around the country. Examples include:

Cooperstown, New York.
> Early nineteenth-century village.

Elfreth's Alley, Philadelphia, Pennsylvania.
> Row houses, 1713–1811.

Greenfield Village, Dearborn, Michigan.
> Henry Ford collection of historic buildings.

Mystic, Connecticut.
> New England seaport, 1700s.

Old Sturbridge Village, Massachusetts.
> New England town, 1790–1840.

Plymouth, Massachusetts.
> Pilgrim village.

Williamsburg, Virginia.
> Colonial houses before 1800.

Interior Decoration

Interior decoration involves the decorating and furnishing of the inside of a house to make it a home. Decorating requires making difficult choices about considerations such as color, balance, harmony, and style. The resulting design should complement the owner's personality and life-style.

Preliminary Planning

Do some research to develop a sensitivity for interior decoration and furnishings. Visit your library and read about the styles of furniture and architecture. Identify the architectural style of your house, and learn how it relates to furniture and color selection. Browse through period furniture display rooms in museums and stores. Other excellent sources of ideas are model homes, where interior decorators are challenged to demonstrate their best work.

Consider your life-style while planning furniture layout. How will the rooms be used, and how often? Do you entertain frequently, requiring space for dining facilities? Will you need to accommodate overnight guests? Arrange for areas that allow an element of privacy for work or study.

Make a scale drawing of your rooms on graph paper. Draw the outlines of your present and proposed furniture on a separate sheet, and cut them out. Try out various furniture arrangements using the paper furniture templates. Consider the following factors:

1. Traffic patterns through and around the room.
2. Positions of windows, doors, fireplaces, or other features that prevent the placement of furniture along walls.
3. Heating, cooling, and electrical outlet locations.
4. Available lighting, both natural and artificial.

Some rooms have more specific requirements. Arrange living room seating for comfort and ease of conversation. Don't face seating toward a bathroom or a cluttered kitchen. In kitchens, the locations of stove, refrigerator, and sink are important. Keep the pathway short from one appliance to another.

Now that furniture requirements and location have been established, take a closer look at style. It affects the selection of furniture, fabrics, color, and accessories.

Furniture Style

Furniture design has evolved over the years in stages. In rural areas, early handmade furniture had to withstand hard usage. With little room in the small houses of the period, furniture often had to serve more than one purpose. The result was plain, rugged furniture with little ornamentation.

In urban areas, the ruling and merchant classes felt a need to demonstrate their status by displaying elaborate furniture. It was made of the best materials by skilled craftsmen. Such furniture was often guilded and upholstered with fine fabrics, with more attention to appearance than comfort.

Some furniture designers or craftsmen achieved such fame that their names became associated with a style of furniture. A few designers published books that reflected the styles of the period. Thomas Chippendale published the *Gentleman and Cabinet Maker's Director* in 1754. George Hepplewhite wrote the *Cabinet-Maker and Upholsterers' Guide* in 1788, and Thomas Sheraton is credited with *The Cabinet-Maker and Upholsterers' Drawing Book,* circa 1791. These books were often used by early American craftsmen who made furniture for wealthy clients.

Furniture styles are sometimes identified with the ruler of the country in which the style evolved—a Louis XVI chair, for example.

To further complicate things, furniture styles differed from one country to another during a given time period. Let's look at some important periods in the evolution of interior decoration.

The Rococo Period (1700–1770). French furniture was light with gracefully curved legs. Parquet floors were often covered by oriental rugs. Wallpaper began to gain popularity. During this time the English favored the designs of Italian Andrea Palladio that featured dark fabric wall hangings, coved ceilings, and light painted, massive woodwork.

The Neoclassical Period (1750–1800). Inspired by the excavations of Pompeii, it featured classic decorative effects such as fluting, and ribbon-like decorations that were added to furniture. Walls were painted to simulate graining, marbling, and the out-of-doors. Delicate French furniture styles gave way to more solidly built English designs, which combined the French and Roman styles. The last twenty years of the period witnessed the emergence of a greater refinement, lightness and delicacy of design. As noted above, the influence of Hepplewhite and others was felt in America at this time.

The Empire Period (1800–1830). The period was characterized by further incorporation of classical style. Direct copying of Roman, Greek, and Egyptian furniture resulted in heavier, more elaborate designs. American manufacturer Duncan Phyfe was influenced by the designs of this period.

The Victorian Period (1837–1901). Named for the English queen, it saw American living rooms feature overstuffed furniture with highly patterned upholstery, heavy draperies, and flower patterned wallpaper. Rooms contained many accessories. Plants and ornaments were everywhere. Kerosene lamps, introduced in the 1860s, did little to dispel the gloom caused by dark wall colors and heavy drapes.

The Modernist Movement. The overindulgence of the Victorian period was replaced for a time by a series of modern movements that featured simple geometric shapes and little ornamentation. American architect Frank Lloyd Wright introduced original ideas in the modernist school with houses that integrated exterior and interior design. Another popular modernist style of the 1920s and 1930s was art deco, characterized by the use of brilliant colors, simple geometrical shapes, and liberal use of glass, plastic, and metal ornamentation.

Eclecticism. This practice of combining various styles in interior decoration became popular as far back as the Victorian period when a home might contain a rococo bedroom and a Gothic dining room. People carry eclectic mixing even further today with furniture from more than one period placed in a single room. It is not unusual to incorporate an accent piece of a different style to produce a desired effect.

Older houses usually reflect their original architectural style. When the interior decoration of such a house is being renovated, consider keeping the interior style somewhat compatible with the exterior. An ultra modern interior would not work well with a Victorian house loaded with exterior ornamentation.

Choosing an Interior Style and Related Materials

While still in the planning stage, clip pictures of interiors that interest you from magazines and sales catalogs. Save a dozen or more for each room in the house. Next, analyze the collected material, looking for your preferences in style, texture, color, and pattern. Compare your present stock of furniture and accessories to these findings. List usable items, and those that must be purchased. Budget restraints often affect these decisions.

Americans spend over ninety billion dollars each year on home furnishings. If you plan furniture additions wisely, you will not waste your contribution to that total. Choose pieces whose styles are compatible, or will serve in a different room in the future. Don't overlook antique shops. Quality antique furniture and accessories are often found at prices comparable to new pieces. Craftsmen make reproduction pieces in the style of the original. Accordingly, it is proper to list a reproduction Queen Anne piece as a Queen Anne style piece.

You can estimate the age of antique furniture by noting the type of hardware used, character of the marks left by tools used in manufacture, width and thickness of wooden pieces, and the overall design. When buying early American furniture, note the species of wood used in its manufacture. Most early American furniture was made of native pine, walnut, cherry, or poplar. Only the very wealthy could afford imported woods during colonial times.

Wall and Floor Treatment

Wall surface treatments include the use of paint, printed fabrics, wallpapers, decorative plaster work, and the display of rugs or quilts.

Painters sometimes use illusion to achieve special decorative effects. In the *Trompe L'oeil* (deceiving the eye) method, the painter can create fake panels and moldings by simulating shadows and perspective with paint. Blank walls often feature imaginary vases of flowers or entire outdoor scenes.

Stenciling is regaining popularity, especially in homes featuring country decor. A mask is made by cutting the pattern out of a piece of paper or thin mylar. Apply paint through the pattern by dabbing the surface to be painted with the ends of the bristles of a special brush. Entire wooden walls were decorated in this manner in some colonial homes.

Inexpensive grooved paneling is made to appear as early solid wood tongue and groove sheathing by simply painting it a solid color.

An effect called color washing simulates an antique finish on walls. Apply a very thin coat of color over a white base coat in random brush strokes. When partially dry, go over the surface with a dampened brush. After the surface is dry, a third paler coat, of another color, may be applied for added depth and texture. This process is especially effective on textured walls.

Simulated wood graining is done by working paint while it's still wet. You can draw a patterned rubber tool, called a rocker, over the surface, or use a brush or feather to rearrange the paint. Good results are surprisingly easy to achieve.

Turning our attention to floors, we find that their color and texture have a considerable impact on the overall decorative scheme of a room. Large, dark floor areas tend to make rooms appear smaller. A wide variety of flooring materials are available to complement every style and decor.

Hard floor surfaces are often used in areas exposed to tough usage and moisture. Materials such as ceramic tile, slate, terrazzo, or marble wear well, and provide a decorative surface. Although vinyl flooring has a softer surface, it can simulate the appearance of the harder materials above.

Carpeting and rugs serve as floor coverings in most rooms. Consider the relationship of their color, pattern, and texture to wall treatments and furniture upholstery. Choose high wear resistant grades for areas such as family rooms.

Exposed wooden floors require sealing with polyurethane or similar coatings to withstand normal wear. Decorative effects can be achieved by laying the flooring in patterns, as with parquet flooring, or by stenciling.

Light and Color

Light sets the mood, tone, and vitality of a room. Windows admit both bright sunlight and soft, colorful sunsets. Artificial lighting can, and should, be used to create a similar wide range of intensity and focus. The lighting required for any room is determined by the activities of the occupants. A bright diffused light, without shadow, is best for reading; soft, indirect lighting creates a relaxed atmosphere in a bedroom.

Although the main function of lighting is general illumination, the system also must provide visual comfort. Lighting also is used to enhance the color and texture of fabrics and wall surfaces, and highlight areas to be emphasized.

Lamps are the generally preferred light source, but there are many exceptions. Ceiling or wall fixtures are effective in dining rooms and bathrooms. Kitchens benefit from a combination of sources, including installation under cabinets to illuminate counters.

Color is affected by everything around it. Light affects the tone, warmth, and clarity or color. Color sets the mood in a room, so consider the lighting conditions at the time of day you use the room and what you will do there. Colors can absorb, conflict with, or blend with one another. Any conflict between colors can be reduced by separating them with an area of white.

Light colors reflect more light and create a feeling of space. White or off-white has become the color of choice for walls. Off-white walls blend easily with other color schemes. Paintings and other artwork are emphasized when displayed on white walls. Many different tints are added to pure white to achieve off-white, so choose your paint with care. Other colors that contribute to the illusion of space include light pastel colors, and medium blues or greens. Warm reds and oranges, or dark colors tend to make rooms seem smaller. These effects also apply to floor coverings.

The right shade of a color is the one with which you are comfortable. Your response to particular colors must be the basis of your selection.

Accessories

Mirrors are used to create the illusion of increased space, and reflect light and beauty. Place mirrors to reflect artwork, decorative objects, and plants. Check tentative mirror placement carefully to avoid unwanted views of steam pipes or bathroom fixtures.

Artwork gives a home personality. Color combinations featured in pictures should be compatible with other decor. Try to arrange pictures so the viewer tends to look at the picture, not at the arrangement of frames. When two equally sized pictures are hung side by side, the eye is led between them. Hang a larger picture between the two smaller ones to capture the viewer's eye. When a vertical row of pictures is hung, it is best to place the larger above the smaller.

House plants bring life and a touch of the outdoors into your home. One large healthy plant adds more style than a group of small struggling ones. Small potted flowering plants are effective when grouped in a basket for display on a table. Pots of flowers or herbs look right at home on a kitchen window sill.

Collections provide interesting focal points when displayed with flair. Choose a suitable stage setting and accentuate the collection with lighting. Collectibles can be tastefully displayed on tables, housed in shadow boxes, or used as creative wall displays. Select good off-beat locations such as entryways, halls, and bathrooms. Antique cooking utensils make attractive accents for a kitchen. To avoid overkill, and maintain interest, a collector can rotate the items shown, storing the rest.

Bringing It All Together

Once you have weighed your options and finalized the selection of individual colors and materials, it's time to see how the combination looks for a given room. One of the best tools for gaining this perspective is the swatchboard. Collect samples of all the colors, fabrics, and other prominent materials to be used in the room, and attach them to a piece of cardboard or the inside of a manila folder. Try to size the samples to reflect their percentage of presence in the room. Arrange the materials as they are positioned in the room so color compatibility can be noted. If problems are uncovered, take the swatchboard along while searching for replacements.

Bibliography

REFERENCE BOOKS

Anderson, George. *Interior Decorating: A Reflection of the Creator's Design.* Minneapolis, MN: Bethany, 1983. Decorating principles presented in a step-by-step plan.

Braschler, Von, ed. *The Essential Guide to Contemporary Home Plans.* Farmington Hills, MI: Home Planners, 1987. A selection of over 335 modern and functional contemporary house designs.

Brumstead, Elaine. *The Home Sewing Library: Soft Furnishings.* New York: Ballantine Books, 1987. Sewing equipment, techniques, and projects such as curtains, bed linen, and furniture slipcovers.

Conran, Terence. *Terence Conran's New House Book: The Complete Guide to Home Design.* New York: Villard Books, 1985. A step-by-step guide to the entire home decoration process. From planning to execution, a very complete text.

Dean, Barry. *Bathroom Design.* New York: Simon & Schuster, 1985. Covers design and describes features of various types of fixture. Lists sources of all types of bathroom equipment.

Dickson, Elizabeth, et al. *The Laura Ashley Book of Home Decorating.* Rev. ed. New York: Harmony Books, 1985. Planning techniques for interior decorating. Emphasis on sewing and decorating with fabrics.

Encyclopedia of Home Designs. Rev. ed. Farmington Hills, MI: Home Planners, 1992. A selection of 500 house designs with emphasis on larger houses.

Franks, Beth. *Very Small Living Spaces: Design and Decorating Strategies to Make the Most of What You Have.* New York: Holt, 1988. Interior decorating for an apartment, condominium, or small house. Emphasis on efficient use of small areas, and techniques to make rooms appear larger.

Gilliatt, Mary. *Period Style.* Boston: Little, Brown, 1990. A survey of period decorating style. Identifies furniture and decorating styles used during each period.

Harrison, Henry S. *Houses: The Illustrated Guide to Construction, Design and Systems.* 2nd ed. Chicago: Dearborn Trade, 1991. Basic construction, materials, and house systems. Illustrations of fifty-seven house styles.

Hoag, Edwin. *American Houses: Colonial, Classic and Contemporary.* Philadelphia: Lippincott, 1964. An illustrated history of America's houses.

Kemp, Jim. *Victorian Revival in Interior Design.* New York: Simon & Schuster, 1988. Describes the blending of Victorian era touches with other styles. Provides sources for materials and objects of the era.

Kostof, Spiro. *America by Design.* New York: Oxford University, 1987. Houses, factories, and skyscrapers. A portrait of America's structures.

McCloud, Kevin. *Decorative Style: The Most Original and Comprehensive Sourcebook of Styles, Treatments, Techniques, and Materials.* New York: Simon & Schuster, 1990. The book title says it all. A valuable resource.

Niles, Bo, ed. *Country Living: Country Decorating.* New York: Hearst Books, 1988. How to create a country look in any home. Advice on collections and instructions for selected handicrafts.

Rees, Yvonne. *Floor Style: A Source Book of Ideas for Transforming the World Beneath Your Feet.* New York: Van Nostrand Reinhold, 1989. Inspiration from some of the world's classic floors, from Imperial Rome to the present day.

Stillinger, Elizabeth. *The Antiques Guide to Decorative Arts in America: 1600–1875.* New York: Dutton, 1973. Covers historical periods in twenty-five-year increments, and discusses the furniture, silver, ceramics, and glass of each period.

PERIODICALS

American Classic House Plans. 380 Lexington Avenue, New York, NY 10017.

Architectural Digest. Knapp Communications, 5900 Wilshire Boulevard, Los Angeles, CA 90036.

Colonial Homes. Hearst Magazines, 1790 Broadway, New York, NY 10019.

Country Living. Hearst Magazines, Country Living, 224 W. 57th Street, New York, NY 10019.

Good Housekeeping. Hearst Corporation, Good Housekeeping, 959 Eighth Avenue, New York, NY 10019.

Home. Hachette Magazines, 1633 Broadway, New York, NY 10019.

Home Planner. Home Planners, 3275 W. Ina Road, Suite 110, Tucson, AZ 85741.

Home Plans. New York Times, Magazine Group, 110 Fifth Avenue, New York, NY 10011.

House Beautiful. Hearst Magazines, House Beautiful, 1700 Broadway, New York, NY 10019–5970.

House Plan Favorites. Archway Press, 19 W. 44th Street, New York, NY 10036.

Interior Design. Cahners Publishing, Interior Design Group, 249 W. 17th Street, New York, NY 10011.

Metropolitan Home. Meredith Corp., Special Interest Publications, 750 Third Avenue, 11th Floor, New York, NY 10017.

Old-House Journal. Old-House Journal, 2 Main Street, Gloucester, MA 01930–5726.

Practical Homeowner Magazine. Westar Media, 656 Bair Island Road, Suite 200, Redwood City, CA 94063.

Southern Living. Southern Progress, 2100 Lake Shore Drive, Birmingham, AL 35209.

ASSOCIATIONS

American Society of Interior Designers. 608 Massachusetts Avenue, NE, Washington, DC 20002. Practicing professional interior designers and affiliate members in allied design fields. Sponsors scholarship competitions and awards special grants. Publication: *Interior Design Career Guide.* Booklet of information on the profession that lists design programs with ASID student chapters.

Decorators Club. 41 E. 65th Street, New York, NY 10021. Professional organization of women interior designers in the New York City area. Holds seminars for students enrolled in various schools of design in the New York City area. Grants scholarships and bestows awards. Publication: *Club Newsletter.*

Home Fashions Products Association. 355 Lexington Avenue, New York, NY 10017–6603. Manufacturers of curtains, draperies, and related products. Sponsors annual design contest for students attending accredited art schools.

Interior Plantscape Division. 405 N. Washington Street, Suite 104, Falls Church, VA 22046. A division of Associated Landscape Contractors of America. Interior plantscape business owners, suppliers, growers, manufacturers of related materials, students, and educators. Sponsors competitions and annual awards program and presentation.

International Association of Lighting Designers. 18 E. 16th Street, Suite 208, New York, NY 10003. Professionals, educators, students and others working in the field of lighting design. Sponsors summer intern program for qualified college students interested in lighting design as a profession. Bestows awards.

International Furnishings and Design Association. 107 World Trade Center, PO Box 58045, Dallas, TX 75258. Executives engaged in design, production, education, and related activities in the interior furnishings industry. Awards Student Design Competition grants annually.

Horses

HORSES ROAMED THE EARTH before man. They have served him for centuries as powerful and devoted helpmates. Although most working horses have been replaced by smog-belching machines, their numbers have not decreased significantly. About 3.4 million people keep horses. Most horse owners enjoy riding and caring for them. Others delight in various forms of horse competition: dressage, racing, jumping, rodeo, and polo. For some it may be nostalgia for the days of the old west, or a desire to enjoy a close relationship with such a noble beast of the animal kingdom. Whatever the motivation, horse lovers are a dedicated lot.

History

Paleontologists tell us that the ancestors of the horse can be traced back some sixty million years. Little *Eohippus* was only as large as a fox terrier. Evolution continued, and an animal more like our modern horse called merychippus grew to the size of a small pony, sharing the plains with mastodons, camels, and prong-horned antelopes. Development continued, and during the Glacial Epoch the last in the ancestral series, *Equus,* came on the scene. Sometime during the period of development of the horse in America, the animal migrated to the Eastern Hemisphere. It subsequently became extinct in America.

We pick up the history of the horse next in the year 634 A.D. when Mohammedan Arabs began the conquest of North Africa. In 711 Moor cavalry entered Spain riding tough, fast, small, and light barb horses. They overpowered the Spanish armored knights riding the larger, slower mounts needed to support the heavy equipment. During the next 700 years the Spaniards learned horsemanship from the invaders and raided their camps to obtain the fine Barb horses used by the Moors. The barb had been the product of the best that Egypt, Syria, and Arabia had before the invasion. The barb horse was bred with local stock and multiplied in middle and southern Spain. Some were taken to England to improve the Norman breed found there. And some found their way to the West on Columbus' second voyage in 1493. Horses were bred on the islands of Hispaniola and Cuba to supply the conquistadores with the mounts they required to explore and conquer the New World. As the island breeders grew rich from the horse trade, they could afford to purchase the best breeding stock that Spain had to offer. Thus, the horses introduced onto the North and South American continents were of superior quality. The horse had found its way back to the North American continent.

Spanish horses were transported to Florida beginning about 1565. A second migration passed through Mexico about the same time, making its way to California missions by 1775. Still others arrived in Texas during the 1600s. By 1770 territories east of the Mississippi were supplied and some had crossed into Canada.

Most of the wild horses that became prolific in the West resulted from Indian attacks on outlying missions and ranches. Stolen roping horses made good buffalo hunting horses.

Due to a lack of race tracks and straight roads in the East, the colonists used to run horse races along the main street in town. The distance chosen was one-quarter mile. English horses were imported about 1620 and selectively bred to produce a horse that was especially fast over the quarter-mile distance. The speedy quarter horse was bred with the tough Spanish horse to produce a cow horse that had the speed, stamina, and endurance desired by the ranchers. Both horses had some Spanish Arab and barb ancestors.

Selective Breeding

Horses have been matched to a wide variety of tasks by selective breeding. Heavy horses carried knights in suits of armor and pulled plows and coaches. Light horses carried

Figure 1
Thoroughbred colt.

riders, herded cattle, and were raced in competition. Let's take a closer look at some of the more popular breeds.

The Arabian is a small spirited horse well suited for racing. They are intelligent, have stamina, and the ability to carry weight. Because of their ancestry, reputation, and value, the best examples are carefully recorded in stud books. Current imports from Arabia are listed as desert bred. This important breed is found in the ancestry of many other breeds of light horses.

The Thoroughbred is a horse used for flat track racing throughout the world. Although horse racing was popular in England in the twelfth century, it wasn't until the eighteenth century that the English established a proper listing of race horse genealogy, called a stud book. The magnificently evolved "purebreds" at the time were a product of Arabian, barb, and some domestic breeds. The American Thoroughbred descended from the numerous ancestors imported from England before there was a stud book. It is intelligent, willing to learn, and has stamina. As with the Arabian, the Thoroughbred is found in the lineage of other improved breeds (Figure 1).

The Standardbred is a harness racehorse. It is bred from Thoroughbred and local stock, including the Norfolk trotter and the Arabian. Trained to achieve speed and endurance at the trot or pace gait, they were once required to trot a mile in a standard time, hence the name. Their stamina makes them useful as an all-purpose horse.

Two other all-purpose riding horses are the Morgan and the Tennessee walking horse. The Morgan descended from one horse, Justin Morgan. It is thought to have been bred from a Colonial Thoroughbred and a quarter horse. It is energetic and strong. The Tennessee walking horse is noted for its smooth running walk. It is a mixture of Standardbred and Morgan breeding.

The American saddle horse breed is a mixture of the Thoroughbred, Morgan, and the trotter. Breed selection resulted in a horse that is easy to ride, and has style and beauty. It does well in horse show competition in the United States.

The American quarter horse, once noted in the East for its speed in quarter-mile races, is a mixture of Thoroughbred and western breeds of Spanish origin. The modern breed has a higher percentage of Thoroughbred blood. Quarter horses are very popular because they are so versatile. Nearly three million are registered in the United States. They are used for pleasure riding, jumping, cutting, roping, and racing.

Beginning in the 1930s, horse breeding organizations were established that classify horses by color. Examples include the palomino, albino, pinto, and the Appaloosa. These horses are bred from a varied ancestry. Their use reflects this heritage.

Training

Horses have keen senses of sight, hearing, and touch. The following are a number of other horse traits that a trainer should remember when working with the animal.

They react quickly to any sudden or unusual sight or sound and depend upon their speed to flee from danger.

They have average intelligence and excellent memories, particularly of unpleasant experiences. They enjoy familiar circumstances; they love routine. Since new experiences break their routine, they can sometimes be slow to accept them. Care must be taken during the training process due to the sensitive nature of the animal.

They are social animals, fond of the company of others. They dislike being shut up in a stall without a view of the outside.

When horses understand what is wanted, and realize they will not be harmed, they tend to be docile and respond to commands.

Horses mature at six years of age and have a life expectancy of twenty to thirty years. Training is a slow process that begins at age two for both saddle and race horses. It is interesting to note that when cowboys "broke" wild horses in the Old West, they chose four-year-olds to ride.

Veterinarians say that some parts of the bone structure of a mature horse are still cartilage until the animal is past five. It is understandable that breeders of fine Arabian horses wish to wait until their horses are four-year-olds before racing them. This explains why Thoroughbred racehorses, usually raced much earlier, are considered past their prime and ready for retirement at five or six. They are raced before coming of age. The best age range of a horse for casual riding is from seven to seventeen years.

A young colt learns to obey the trainer's first basic commands while circling around the trainer at the end of a rope called a longe line. The colt is later trained to accept a bit in the mouth. Long reins are attached to the bit and extend to the trainer, still working from the center of the circle. The colt learns to answer to the commands communicated by a slight pull on the reins. When the young horse is capable of supporting the rider's weight, training begins with the rider in the saddle. Detailed description of training steps is beyond the scope of this book; however, some comment should be made concerning overall methods. If training sessions have been conducted properly, the horse has developed confidence in the instructor. Understanding the trainer's wishes, the horse will want to obey. By exercising patience and a consistent approach the horse will understand and respond to even subtle commands. Leg pressure against the horse's side can be substituted for a pull on the reins. Even a shift of body weight, or voice signals, can be used as a means of communication to execute a maneuver. This becomes very important to a rodeo rider racing to overtake and rope a calf. Remember, once trained, horses have a good memory.

Facilities, Equipment and Maintenance

Horse ownership takes some research and planning. You will need about two acres of land, an appropriate shelter and assorted equipment. Don't forget to check local ordinances during this planning stage. As with the responsibility for any living thing, you must be there, or arrange for someone else to be there, to provide food and care.

During a recent survey in the state of Michigan it was found that 45,000 households maintain 63,000 pleasure/trail horses. They spent $61,000,000 in the process. That works out to an average of about $81 per horse per month. To board a horse averages $250 to $350 per month. Costs are generally lower in the Midwest and higher on both coasts.

In the Midwest an average riding horse will cost from $500 up. A good one will cost $2,000. The following equipment is required at the start:

Saddle, leather or synthetic materials

Saddle blanket

Headstall

Reins

Halter

Lead rope

Brushes, Curry combs, Grooming supplies

Bucket

Feed tub

Manure fork or Pitchfork

This basic equipment will cost between $500 and $1,000, depending on quality selected. Don't overlook used saddles. Good leather ones last for years.

Riding for Pleasure and Competition

Most horse lovers ride for pleasure and exercise. They may rent a horse at a local stable or visit a dude ranch to try and capture the flavor of the Old West. Many such ranches conduct tours and even cattle drives for the enjoyment of their visitors.

Organized long distance riding competitions are held. The horse and rider must cover a set distance against the clock or at a set speed.

Other competitors engage in racing at various levels or demonstrate the classical training routines required in dressage. A relative few compete in the demanding sports of fox hunting, show jumping, and the game of polo.

Rodeo competition highlights the skills of a rider and the cutting horse trained to separate cattle, or the roping horse trained to cooperate in roping and tying a calf or steer in the shortest possible time. Rodeos also feature the agility of the horse during barrel racing, of a rider during bronco riding, and the pageantry of the parade with the participants dressed in their finery.

Olympic competition features a three-day event. It is an all-around competition consisting of dressage, an endurance test in which road, cross-country, and steeplechase performance is judged, and a jumping competition. Also featured is the Grand Prix de Dressage, a competition for individuals, and Prix des Nations, a stadium jumping competition. Horseback riding is also included in the multisport pentathlon event.

Bibliography

REFERENCE BOOKS

Bradwell, Judy. *Eventing: Preparation, Training and Competition.* New York: Howell Book House, 1988. Covers three phases of eventing: dressage, show jumping, and cross country. Horse selection, training, and equipment.

Denhardt, Robert M. *The Horse of the Americas.* Rev. ed. Norman, OK: University of Oklahoma Press, 1975. Extensive history of the horse. Description of the various breeds and their development.

Drummond, Marcy. *Long Distance Riding.* New York: Howell Book House, 1987. Overview of long distance competition riding. Horse selection, care, training, and equipment.

Ensminger, M. E. *Horses and Tack: A Complete One-Volume Reference on Horses and Their Care.* Rev. ed. Boston: Houghton Mifflin, 1991. Comprehensive coverage including:

breeds, training, breeding, care, equipment, vehicles, riding and showing.

Hamilton, Kate. *Dressage: An Approach to Competition.* New York: Howell Book House, 1987. Choosing a horse. Training and how to approach the competition world. Horse and rider fitness.

Hinton, Phyllis, ed. *The Rider's Treasury.* New York: Barnes, 1965. Contents of the *Riding Annuals* released in 1964, 1965, and 1966 by the English periodical *Riding.*

Holderness-Roddam, Jane. *Competitive Riding: An Illustrated Manual of Dressage, Show Jumping and Eventing.* New York: Prentice Hall, 1988. History of equestrian sport. Horse care and training. Hints and advice regarding competition.

Kellon, Eleanor M. *The Older Horse: A Complete Guide to Care and Conditioning for Horses 10 and Up.* Millwood, NY: Breakthrough, 1986. What to look for when buying an aged horse. How to control chronic illnesses.

Kinnish, Mary Kay, ed. *50 Urgent Questions Horsemen Ask: With Answers Provided by Leading Equine Health-Care Authorities.* Gaithersburg, MD: Fleet Street, 1990. Consultants for *EQUUS* magazine answer questions regarding horse health care.

Loriston-Clarke, Jennie. *The Complete Guide to Dressage.* Philadelphia: Running, 1987. Overview of Dressage. History, choosing the horse, training, step-by-step illustration of the movements.

Pervier, Evelyn. *Horsemanship: Basics for Beginners.* New York: Messner, 1984. The physical characteristics of a horse, how to choose and care for one, and techniques of the beginning rider.

Podhajsky, Alois. *The Complete Training of Horse and Rider: In the Principles of Classical Horsemanship.* New York: Doubleday, 1967. Step-by-step methods of training used in the Spanish Riding School in Vienna.

Price, Steven D. *Get a Horse: Basics of Back-Yard Horsekeeping.* New York: Viking, 1974. Coverage of facilities and equipment required. Describes characteristics of breeds and age considerations. Advice on horse care.

Senic, T. L. *Owning Your First Horse: Practical Instruction for the Novice.* New York: Viking Penguin, 1990. General coverage of the care and boarding of a horse. Advice on handling and training.

Taylor, Louis. *Ride Western.* New York: Harper & Row, 1968. Western horsemanship. Training, techniques, and equipment. Covers roping, cutting, and barrel racing.

Walrond, Sallie. *A Guide to Driving Horses.* N. Hollywood CA: Wilshire, 1971. Driving horses. Training, showing, care of vehicles.

Young, John Richard. *The Schooling of the Horse.* Rev. ed. Norman, OK: University of Oklahoma Press, 1982. Overall training of a horse. An introduction to horses and horsemanship.

PERIODICALS

Equus. Fleet Street, Publishers, 656 Quince Orchard Road, Gaithersburg, MD 20878.

Horse and Horseman. Gallant-Charger Publishers, 34249 Camino Capistrano, Box HH, Capistrano Beach, CA 92624.

Horse & Rider. Rich Publications, 1060 Calle Cordillera, Suite 103, San Clemente, CA 92672–6241.

Horse Illustrated. Fancy Publications, Box 6050, Mission Viejo, CA 92690.

Quarter Horse Journal. American Quarter Horse Association, 2701 I40 East, PO Box 200, Amarillo, TX 79168.

Western Horse. Frontier Publishers, Box FF, Sun City, CA 92381.

Western Horseman. Western Horseman, Box 7980, Colorado Springs, CO 80933–7980.

ASSOCIATIONS

Adopt-a-horse Program. Bureau of Land Management, U.S. Department of the Interior, WO–200, Washington, DC 20240. Primary means of disposing of excess wild horses from public lands. Qualified individuals may adopt a limited number of such horses.

American Horse Council. 1700 K Street NW, No. 300, Washington, DC 20006. Breed registries, organizations, and individuals interested in the horse industry. Maintains liaison with government agencies and advises members of current developments. Sponsors public affairs program. Publications: *Business Quarterly,* various bulletins and newsletter.

American Junior Quarter Horse Association. 1600 Quarter Horse Drive, PO Box 200, Amarillo, TX 79168. Youth division of the American Quarter Horse Association. Sponsors shows, bestows awards, operates library, and awards college scholarships. Maintains museum and hall of fame. Publications: *Junior Journal,* and *Quarter Horse Journal.*

American Morgan Horse Association. PO Box 960, Shelburne, VT 05482. Maintains registry, conducts shows, bestows awards, maintains museum, hall of fame, and library. Publications: *Morgan Horse Magazine,* and a newsletter.

American Mustang and Burro Association. PO Box 7, Benton City, WA 99320–0007. Owners of adopted wild horses and burros. Conducts educational programs on such programs as the adopt-a-horse program. Sponsors its own such program. Sponsors competitions, bestows awards, operates hall of fame. Publication: *American Mustang and Burro Association Journal.*

American Paint Horse Association. PO Box 961023, Ft. Worth, TX 76161. Conducts genetic research. Stimulates and regulates matters pertaining to the history, breeding, exhibition, publicity, sale, racing, and improvement of the breed. Publications: *National Show Program, Paint Horse Journal, Stud Book and Registry,* and a newsletter.

American Quarter Horse Association. 2701 I40 E., PO Box 200, Amarillo, TX 79168. Registers pedigrees and maintains records. Approves shows, contests, and races. Publications: *Quarter Horse Journal, Quarter Horse Racing Journal,* books and brochures.

American Saddlebred Horse Association. c/o Kentucky Horse Park, 4093 Iron Works Pike, Lexington, KY 40511. Maintains registry and pedigree records. Maintains library, sponsors museum and hall of fame. Sponsors competitions, bestows awards. Publications: *American Saddlebred Horse registry,* and *American Saddlebred Magazine.*

Appaloosa Horse Club. Box 8403, Moscow, ID 83843. Serves as registry, sets breed standards, maintains breed records, bestows awards, and awards scholarships. Publication: *Appaloosa Journal.*

Arabian Horse Registry of America. 12000 Zuni Street, Westminister, CO 80234. Maintains purebred Arabian registry. Publications: *Arabian Stud Book,* and *Registry News.*

Endurance Horse Registry of America. PO Box 63, Agoura Hills, CA 91301. Registers horses that have completed 300 successful miles of endurance competition in one year, have won races, or have placed in the top ten. Researches bloodlines, sponsors competitions, and bestows awards.

International Arabian Horse Association. PO Box 33696, Denver, CO 80233. Maintains registries and show records. Bestows awards. Publications: *IAHA Handbook,* and *Inside International Newsletter.*

National Cutting Horse Association. 4704 Highway 377 S., Ft. Worth, TX 76116. Promotes exhibition and breeding activities. Prepares rules and regulations for showing. Sponsors competitions and Cutting Horse Hall of Fame.

National Show Horse Registry. 11700 Commonwealth Drive, Suite 200, Louisville, KY 40299. Promotes amateur and open competitions. Publication: *National Show Horse.*

Tennessee Walking Horse Breeders' and Exhibitors' Association. PO Box 286, Lewisburg, TN 37091. Maintains registry, operates speakers bureau. Publication: *The Voice of the Tennessee Walking Horse.*

Invention and Patents

PREHISTORIC MAN MANAGED to survive by inventing tools and the ways to make them. There was no patent office to record the methods first invented to start fires or plant seeds. The invention process requires a pool of knowledge and someone to select ideas from that pool and combine or use the ideas in a new way. Early inventions came slowly because knowledge was limited. Anthropologists have found that isolated cultures progress slowly, but when diverse cultures come in contact, they benefit from their combined knowledge, and more rapid innovation results. We continue to see more rapid evolution in the modern world as communications become more sophisticated. Anthropologists call this process of knowledge integration diffusion.

When America's founding fathers wrote the Constitution, they had the foresight to include the following provision giving citizens certain rights to profit from their ideas: "Congress shall have the power to promote the progress of science and useful arts by securing for limited times to authors and inventors the exclusive right to their respective writings and discoveries." The rights were soon granted—the United States patent records date back to 1790.

Most of us have two kinds of specialized knowledge. One is related to our work. Based on formal schooling and work experience, our thinking often reflects the rigid positions and assumptions taught at school, which are further channeled by our employer's rules and needs. The other kind of specialized knowledge is related to our pastimes. Because they are experienced in a more leisurely manner, the pursuit of hobbies allows time for more innovative thought—invention.

Those with a variety of interests and pastimes can better merge the two cultures mentioned above. The resulting diffusion of interests produces more opportunity to create innovative ideas, which is an advantage for both the employer and oneself. Other qualities useful to inventors are curiosity, creativity, originality, the ability to improvise, and the ability to see things from a unique perspective.

Some people are tinkerers. They take pleasure in coming up with original devices and new ways to do things. Often the satisfaction they get from solving a problem is the only reward they require. But sooner or later, in a flash of inspiration, the big idea hits. This idea should provide some financial reward, and perhaps it should be secured with a patent. Let's take a look at the process of getting a patent.

From Idea to Patent

Hobbyists, or anyone who engages in activities that are a bit outside the mainstream, should keep a diary of daily projects. When a promising idea comes along, put it in writing. Record everything having to do with the idea, from concept through development. Number, sign, and date each diary page. Include sketches and modifications as they occur. Periodically, have a reliable person read and sign the diary. The signature should be placed after a notation such as, "Witnessed and understood by me." If the idea shows promise, have the witness sign the diary in the presence of a notary public. When development of the idea reaches a stage that makes conclusions possible, write a preliminary summary (disclosure) of the idea in the diary. The disclosure should include: Background, purpose, general description, detailed description, and alternative ways to achieve the result of the idea. The date of the conception of an invention can be very important when you are ready to file for a patent. Witnessed files such as those described are taken into consideration in solving disputes when others apply to patent a similar idea during the same period. For those who don't have ready access to appropriate witnesses, the U.S. Patent Office has a "Disclosure Document Program." The inventor mails the preliminary disclosure to the patent office together with a modest fee.

As work continues on the invention, the inventor will continue development, perhaps make a working model, and conduct tests to determine product practicality. The fabrication of a working model also helps the inventor to learn about production costs and problems. This information will be useful if a decision is made to market the invention.

At some time during the above process you should determine what has been done, or is being done, of a similar nature. Visit the nearest patent depository at a large public or university library to make a preliminary search. The largest libraries have records of patents dating back to the nineteenth century, or earlier. An index to the *U.S. Patent Classification* lists product-related subjects together with an identifying number for their classes and subclasses. Look for the class, or classes that most closely match your invention. Since existing patents contain class number(s), you have narrowed your patent search considerably. The patent depository also has a file of the weekly issues of the *Official Gazette of the United States Patent and Trademark Office.* Each gazette lists the patents issued during the previous week, with as abstract, a representative drawing, and other related material about each patent. The main U.S. Patent Office Library is located in Arlington, Virginia, where all U.S. patent records are kept. You're permitted to make your preliminary search there, if convenient. Another search should be conducted using nonpatent media. Most of these sources are located in libraries. They can be found through the registers, indexes, and indexes of indexes, with the help of a reference librarian. Before you spend the money to obtain a patent, you will want to research the market for your invention, production costs, and available financing.

Now, at last, you are ready to apply for a patent. You can prepare the paperwork yourself or hire a patent practitioner. It will take some study to properly prepare a patent application yourself. The language used must by chosen carefully in order to stand up to any future court challenge. A patent practitioner may be a patent agent or a patent attorney. Either can represent you at the patent office; only the attorney can represent you in court.

The usual patent content includes: The title. A list of related patents. An abstract, which is a brief description of the idea. Drawings that may show an object's shape, relationship of parts, a schematic diagram, or other illustration to define the idea. Claims made for the invention—important because they set out exactly what the inventor says the invention will do. A detailed summary description and background of the invention.

The patent is submitted to the patent office where an examiner makes a detailed search of existing patents for similar patented ideas. The examiner will list, on your patent, the applicable classes and subclasses that relate to your invention, that have been searched. When the search has been completed, the examiner may: Approve all claims. Object to all or part of your claims. Reject all or part of your claims. An objection relates to the form of the claim. It may be unclear or improperly worded. Rejections can be made for any number of reasons that the idea isn't patentable. You, or your patent practitioner, may respond with amendments as required.

The usual time required, from patent submission to the granting of the patent, is one to two years. The patent office booklet, *General Information Concerning Patents* covers fees. But expect to pay a filing fee of $170, an issuance fee of $280, and maintenance fees of $225 to $670 at certain intervals of time. If you have hired a patent practitioner, there will also be charges for that service to consider.

Once a patent is received by the patent office and has been numbered and dated, the patent is pending, and you may so state on any items sold. Once a patent is granted you have a seventeen year monopoly on the invention. You can produce the item invented, sell the rights to the idea, or license others to produce the product. If someone infringes on your patent by improper use of your idea, you have the right to sue that person or company, but such suits can be expensive.

The above partial description of the patent process is quite general, and only intended to illustrate where the creative pastime of inventing things can lead. See the books listed in the following bibliography for more specific information and the guidance required to comply with the sign located over the entrance to the patent public search room in Arlington, Virginia. It admonishes, "Don't just stand there. Invent!"

Bibliography

REFERENCE BOOKS

Baldwin, Gordon C. *Inventors and Inventions of the Ancient World.* New York: Four Winds, 1973. Lends historical perspective to the fields of creativity and invention.

General Information Concerning Patents. Superintendent of Documents, U.S. Government Printing Office, Washington, DC 20402.

MacCracken, Calvin D. *A Handbook for Inventors.* New York: Scribner's, 1983. Describes how to evaluate inventions and chronicle their progress. The preparation of a patent application is discussed in detail.

McCormack, Alan J. *Inventors Workshop.* Belmont, CA: Lake, 1981. Features projects to stimulate curiosity and inventiveness in juveniles through Junior High School age.

Olsen, Frank H. *Inventors Who Left Their Brands on America.* New York: Bantam Books, 1991. Brief biographies of a broad selection of famous inventor/entrepreneurs.

Park, Robert. *The Inventor's Handbook: How to Develop, Protect, and Market Your Invention.* 2nd ed. White Hall, VA: Betterway, 1990. Detailed overview of the invention and patent process. Extensive appendix featuring important bibliographic material.

Seemann, Robert A. *Patent Smart: A Complete Guide to Developing, Protecting, and Selling Your Invention.* Englewood Cliffs, NJ: Prentice Hall, 1987. A detailed overview of the invention and patent process.

PERIODICALS

Invent! MM Association, 3201 Corte Malpaso, Suite 304, Camarillo, CA 93012.

Inventing and Patenting Sourcebook. Gale Research, 835 Penobscot Building, Detroit, MI 48226.

Inventor's Gazette. Inventors Association of America, Box 1531, Rancho Cucamonga, CA 91729–1531.

ASSOCIATIONS

Invent America! 510 King Street, Suite 420, Alexandria, VA 22314. Foundation established to stimulate inventiveness and productivity. Works to recover patent models of the nineteenth century to be donated to the Smithsonian Institution. Sponsors an educational program and bestows awards. Publications: Newsletter, and related material.

Inventors Clubs of America. PO Box 450261, Atlanta, GA 30345. Clubs of inventors, and others involved in problem solving. Helps inventors in the patenting through marketing process. Conducts educational programs and competitions. Maintains museum, and hall of fame. Publications: *Inventors News,* and related materials.

Inventors Workshop International Education Foundation. 3201 Corte Malpaso, Suite 304–A, Camarillo, CA 93012. Amateur and professional inventors in eight countries. Provides instruction in patent search and assistance with other elements of the patent process. Operates library, sponsors competitions, and bestows awards. Publications: *Invent,* and related materials.

National Congress of Inventors Organizations. PO Box 6158, Rheem Valley, CA 94570. Coordinates information among inventors' groups. Conducts National Innovation Workshops in cooperation with the National Bureau of Standards. Maintains library. Publications: *America's Inventor,* and related material.

National Inventors Foundation. 345 W. Cypress Street, Glendale, CA 91204. Independent inventors. Educates inventors about patent laws. Maintains museum and hall of fame.

Knitting and Crochet

KNITTING AND CROCHET are forms of needle-work in which a fabric is created by forming loops out of thread or yarn and drawing them through each other. Knitting has two basic stitch forms—knitting and purling, and purling is simply the reverse of knitting. Combinations and derivatives of these two forms account for the diversity of knit products. Crocheting has a wide variety of stitch forms, allowing the worker free design expression.

Knitted fabrics are more elastic and pliable than crocheted ones, so they are favored for close fitting stockings, dresses, and sweaters. Crocheted fabrics are often used for decorative projects such as pillows, tablecloths, and bedspreads due to their stitch design versatility.

History

Fabrics that appear to be knitted have been found in Egyptian burial sites dating from the fourth century. Many such early fabrics were actually made by other techniques using a sewing needle. Knitted fabrics dating from the thirteenth century are more common. The first illustration of a person using knitting needles is the painting entitled *The Visitation of the Angeles to Maria,* dating from about 1400 A.D.

Hand knitted products were commercially produced in Europe starting in about the thirteenth century. Although the earliest mechanical knitting machine was invented in the sixteenth century, better quality hand knitting needles introduced soon after ensured the continuation of commercial hand knitting. By 1900 the knitting machine had taken over and commercial hand knitting was virtually nonexistent.

As commercial hand knitting declined during the nineteenth century, the hobby of hand knitting became popular. Entrepreneurs were quick to introduce knitting books and manufacture yarns for amateur hand knitters.

There is not much of a written record about the history of crochet. Early pieces were examined and copied by succeeding generations. The French were instrumental in recording crochet patterns. French influence is apparent by the name crochet—the French word for hook.

Tools and Materials

Knitting Needles. Straight needles are used for flat knitting. Pieces are later sewn together to form a completed project. Single-pointed straight needles have a point on one end and a knob on the other. Double-pointed needles are straight needles with two pointed working ends. They are often used in combinations of four or more to produce circular, or tubular garments. Circular needles have two pointed ends and a flexible center. That makes them especially adaptable to tubular knitted work, although flat work can also be produced with them.

Stitch Gauge. A small flat metal or plastic piece having a scale to measure the number of knitted rows and stitches, the gauge of a knitted sample. Most units also have a series of holes used to determine needle size.

Crochet Hook. A straight needle-like rod with a hook at one end. They are available in a variety of sizes.

Stitch Markers. Used to mark the place in a row of knitting where a change occurs, such as the beginning of a pattern change or the end of a row in circular knitting. Markers are available as rings that fit on the needle or as split coils that may be easily inserted and removed.

Row Counters. Small devices, sometimes attached to the end of a needle, to keep track of the number of rows knitted. They are advanced manually as each row is completed.

In addition to the above items described in some detail, you will need miscellaneous equipment common to a sewing basket such as needles, pins, bobbins, tape measure, and scissors.

Yarns. All yarns are spun from fiber. The fibers may be continuous (filament), or short lengths less than 6½ inches long (staple). Silk is the only natural filament yarn. In addition to silk, natural fibers include: alpaca, angora, camel, cashmere, cotton, mohair, and wool. Synthetic fibers may be used in their original filament form, or cut into staple lengths. Acrylic, nylon, polyester, polypropylene, and rayon are some of the synthetic fibers. Spinning twists yarn fibers together. A single is a strand of spun yarn. Plied yarn is formed from singles twisted together. Many combinations of fiber materials and spinning techniques are employed in yarn manufacture.

Knitting

Knitting is the process of forming fabric by interlocking loops from a continuous strand or strands of yarn using two or more needles. Each loop is called a stitch. A horizontal series of stitches becomes a row.

The basic stitch is called a knit stitch. A fabric composed of knit stitches will appear as shown in Figure 1.1. This elastic dense fabric stretches more lengthwise than crosswise.

The second basic stitch is called a purl stitch. It's the reverse of the knit stitch. Its fabric will appear as shown in Figure 1.2.

When a row of knit stitches is alternated with a row of purl stitches, it's called stockinette stitch. Stockinette stitch has more crosswise than lengthwise stretch.

The Process

The work begins with casting on, placing the first row of stitches on the needle. A simple method of casting on is shown in Figure 2. Hold the needle with the right hand with the left hand positioned as shown, keeping a slight tension on the yarn with the last three fingers. Insert the needle under the yarn against the outside of the thumb. As you pick up the yarn on the needle, release it from the thumb. Tighten the yarn around the needle with a downward movement of the left hand. Bring the hand up to the starting position, picking the yarn up around your thumb again and repeat until you have cast on enough stitches to establish the required width of your fabric.

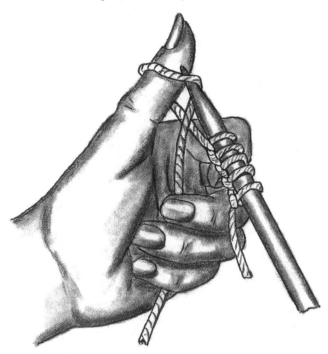

Figure 2
Casting on to begin the knitting process.

The knit stitch is shown in Figures 3.1 through 3.3. See Figure 3.1. Hold the needle with stitches in your left hand and the other in the right (assuming you are right-handed). Put the right needle through a stitch on the left needle as shown, from front to back. Take the yarn around the point of the right needle to make a loop.

Figure 1.1
Knitted fabric.

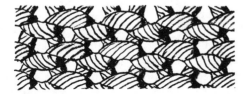

Figure 1.2
Purled fabric.

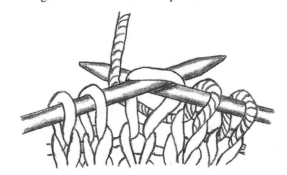

Figure 3.1
The knit stitch, step one.

Figure 3.2 shows the new loop being drawn through the stitch on the left needle, moving it to the right needle. Figure 3.3 shows the stitch moved completely off the left needle. Repeat for all remaining stitches on the left needle.

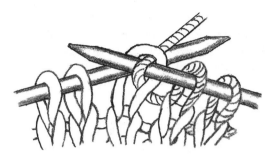

Figure 3.2
The knit stitch, step two.

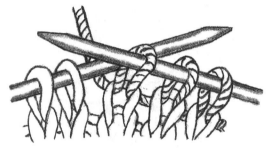

Figure 3.3
The knit stitch, step three.

The purl stitch is shown in Figures 4.1 through 4.3. As shown in Figure 4.1, hold the needle with stitches in the left hand and the other in the right. Put the right needle through the stitch on the left needle from back to front. Take the yarn around the point of the right needle as shown, to make a loop. As shown in Figure 4.2, pull the new loop through the stitch on the left needle, moving it to the right needle. As shown in Figure 4.3, slip the stitch completely off the left needle. Repeat for all remaining stitches on the left needle.

Figure 4.1
The purl stitch, step one.

Figure 4.2
The purl stitch, step two.

Figure 4.3
The purl stitch, step three.

These two stitches, the knit and the purl, are the basis of all knitting and can be worked in unending combinations.

When working with a garment pattern you must knit the fabric to match the size of the pattern. The pattern will specify the number of stitches and rows per a given unit of length, as used by the designer. This is called the stitch gauge. You must knit to the gauge specified for the garment in order to match the pattern. Knitting needle size has a dramatic effect on the gauge. The larger the needle, the fewer stitches and rows per inch. If you are tense you will pull the stitches tighter and increase the number of stitches per inch. Other factors affecting gauge include yarn and stitch pattern selection. Because of the above variables the recommended practice is to prepare a test knitted swatch about six inches square. Compare your gauge numbers to those specified on the pattern and make necessary adjustments to comply with the pattern gauge specification.

Knitting with Colors

Special techniques are employed when knitting in more than one color. The choice of technique depends upon the complexity of the color pattern. A traditional type of color knitting called "fair isle" once specified a limit of two colors to a row. The term as used today refers to a design having frequent color changes in a row. In this case, working in stockinette stitch, the yarn not being featured on the front is carried along the back, or inside. When necessary to carry it for more than, say four inches between color changes, the yarn not in use can be woven over and under the stitches on the back side.

Another color technique called "intarsia" employs separate balls of yarn for each individual area of color. No colors are carried at the back as with fair isle. The yarn being worked is suspended in bobbins at the back of the fabric. A length of yarn is left at the beginning and end of each color change that will be used to form a secure end. Thread the end on a pointed needle. Go back through a couple of the stitches, then double back through the stitches just formed, each time splitting the yarn it is passing through, to ensure a permanent fastening.

Crocheting

Crocheting is begun by making a series of chain stitches whose overall length defines the required width of the fabric. Make a slip knot and slide it on a crochet hook. If you are right handed, hold the crochet hook with the right index finger and thumb. Wrap the yarn through fingers of the left hand to provide tension, and guide the yarn with your left index finger. As Figure 5.1 demonstrates, to make a chain stitch rest the yarn from the skein over the hook as shown and draw through the loop. Repeat until you have a chain of proper length, as shown in Figure 5.2.

A single crochet is made as shown in Figures 6.1 through 6.3. As shown in Figure 6.1, insert hook under two top threads of yarn of the second chain stitch from the hook. Loop yarn from the skein over the hook. As shown in Figure 6.2, draw yarn through the stitch. You now have two loops on the hook. Loop yarn from the skein over the hook. As shown in Figure 6.3, draw the yarn through the two loops on the hook. One loop remains on the hook. Repeat for the length of the chain.

Figure 6.1
A single crochet stitch, step one.

Figure 5.1
Crocheting, step one in chain stitch.

Figure 6.2
A single crochet stitch, step two.

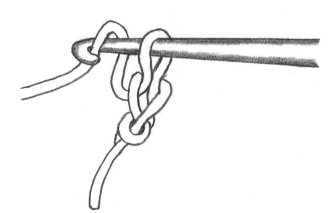

Figure 5.2
Crocheting, step two in chain stitch.

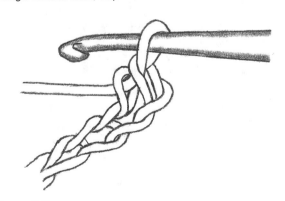

Figure 6.3
A single crochet stitch, step three.

The above single crochet is one of the simplest stitches in crochet work. Literally dozens of stitch variations and combinations are used. An international code of crochet symbols has been devised to circumvent language barriers for enthusiasts around the world. See books such as Linda P. Schapper's *Complete Book of Crochet-Stitch Designs* for information on designs and their symbols.

The seemingly complex techniques touched upon in the above discussion become a pleasant, relaxing activity once the basics have been mastered. The tools and materials are relatively inexpensive, and knitting projects require minimum space while traveling or vacationing. It's a challenging, creative, and satisfying pastime.

Bibliography

REFERENCE BOOKS

Better Homes and Gardens Knitting and Crocheting. Des Moines, IA: Meredith, 1986. Instructions for 100 knitting and crochet projects of all types. Not for the beginner.

Compton, Rae. *The Illustrated Dictionary of Knitting.* Loveland, CO: Interweave, 1988. More than 700 entries describing tips, patterns, stitches, knitting styles, yarn and design features, and more.

Hiatt, June H. *The Principles of Knitting: Methods and Techniques of Hand Knitting.* New York: Simon & Schuster, 1988. A comprehensive and instructive book on knitting. It includes material for the beginner and for the experienced knitter.

Robinson, Debby. *The Encyclopedia of Knitting Techniques.* Emmaus, PA: Rodale, 1987. Tips and techniques, how to work with a purchased pattern or make your own, and more.

Schapper, Linda P. *Complete Book of Crochet Border Designs.* New York: Sterling, 1987. Over 340 border patterns with diagrams of every stitch based on the international symbol system.

———. *Complete Book of Crochet-Stitch Designs.* New York: Sterling, 1985. 500 crochet stitch designs. Each stitch design is described with a photo of the design, written instructions for creating the design, and a diagram showing each stitch and its placement.

———. *300 Classic Blocks for Crochet Projects.* New York: Sterling, 1987. Block designs applicable to such projects as afghans, tablecloths, shawls, and bedspreads. Each block is described with a photo of the design, written instructions for creating the design, and a diagram, based on the international crochet symbol system.

Vogue Knitting: The Ultimate Knitting Book. New York: Pantheon Books, 1989. Comprehensive coverage of supplies, techniques, color knitting, blocking, assembling, and proper care of the finished product. Also explains how to plan and execute an original design garment.

PERIODICALS

All Time Favorite Crochet. Harris Publications, 1115 Broadway, 8th Floor, New York, NY 10010.

Crochet. Harris Publications, 1115 Broadway, 8th Floor, New York, NY 10010.

Crochet Fantasy. All American Crafts, 243 Newton-Sparta Road, Newton, NJ 07860–2748.

Crochet Home. Jerry Gentry, 206 West Street, Big Sandy, TX 75755.

Crochet Patterns. P J S Publications, News Plaza, Box 1790, Peoria, IL 61656.

Crochet World. House of White Birches Publishers, 306 E. Parr Road, Berne, IN 46711.

Crochet World Special. House of White Birches Publishers, 306 E. Parr Road, Berne, IN 46711.

Fashion Knitting. All American Crafts, 243 Newton-Sparta Road, Newton, NJ 07860–2748.

Hooked on Crochet! Jerry Gentry, 206 West Street, Big Sandy, TX 75755.

Knitters. Golden Fleece Publications, Box 1525, Sioux Falls, SD 57101.

Knitting World. House of White Birches Publishers, 306 E. Parr Road, Berne IN 46711.

McCall's Needlework & Crafts. P J S Publications, News Plaza, Box 1790, Peoria, IL 61656.

ASSOCIATIONS

Crochet Association International. PO Box 131, Dallas, GA 30132. Crocheters and professionals whose goals are to promote creation of useful heirlooms and to assist those interested in crocheting. Publication: *Elmore Method of Crochet.*

The Knitting Guild of America. PO Box 1606, Knoxville, TN 37901. Shop owners and individuals interested in knitting. Conducts seminars, sponsors competitions, and bestows awards. Publications: *Cast On,* and related materials.

Martial Arts

MOST OF THIS GROUP of early hand-to-hand fighting techniques originated before the invention of firearms. Some employ arms such as swords, spears and other specialized equipment.

Almost all martial arts training includes the teaching of inner peace and tranquillity. This may be partly due to an early association with religious orders. It may also be that the founders of the more lethal styles saw the wisdom of teaching a balanced attitude to their students. Expert karate practitioners can walk away from a confrontation, secure in the knowledge that they are in control. Interest in the martial arts is increasing. Schools are opening in most populated areas and a number of books are available on the subject.

History

It is noteworthy that many martial arts styles were developed and became widespread as a result of the prohibition of the ownership of arms. This choreographed mayhem has been known by countless exotic names over the years. Many countries can lay claim to part of its development. The ancient Greeks enjoyed two types of wrestling. Upright wrestling was similar to the modern sport. The other variety, called pankration, permitted hitting, kicking, twisting arms or legs and strangling. Biting and gouging were not permitted. Pankration was introduced at the 652 B.C. Olympic games. Historical records are vague regarding the spread of pankration-like fighting. It is likely that it reached Asia when Alexander the Great invaded India, (327–323 B.C.) It is known however, that unarmed fighting systems were practiced in India. Unarmed fighters were taught to compete against armed opponents.

Most combat systems emphasize physical conditioning with some form of bodily contact. Some, called soft systems, require neither bodily contact, nor the use of other combat equipment. As fighting systems passed from one country to another they were combined with local systems. The following will trace the evolution of the systems most popular at this time.

Karate

Karate is the generic term for many of the martial arts that use hand and foot blows as their primary techniques. To avoid injuries, all punches, blows, strikes, and kicks are controlled and pulled back before contact.

In competition, a fighter scores by using a recognized karate technique in good form on the opponents body. This is determined by a judge. When a score is made, a referee stops the match. The opponents take their original positions and the match resumes. An ippon is a blow struck with good form, correct attitude, strong vigor, proper timing and correct distancing. One point is awarded. A waza-ari is a blow that is less correct, but still effective. It's worth a half-point. The first contestant to score three ippons or six waza-ari's or a combination of them totalling three points, wins the bout.

Karate students practice for years to perfect their form. Karate routines can be practiced in several ways. When done alone, the prearranged movements are called katas. When prearranged movements are done with a partner, they are called wazas. Partners take turns being the attacker. When done by two in a freestyle it is called kumite. Needless to say, karate wasn't always this civilized. Ancient karate usage resulted in injury to the participants.

According to legend, a great Indian Buddhist, Bodhidharma, came to China in 520 A.D. to teach and propagate Zen. He took up residence at the Shaolin Temple in the Songshan Mountains of Central China. Before his arrival, Chinese martial artists trained primarily to fight. Bodhidharma taught the Buddhist monks at Shaolin a system of meditation, breathing techniques, and exercises that were designed to help them withstand the rigors of their religeous lives. That training is thought to be the basis of the modern martial arts. Some of the monks were further trained in the fighting arts. About 690 A.D. 500 of the 1,500 in residence at Shaolin were fighting monks. On several occasions they responded to calls for help from the Chinese emperors in times of danger.

There is little doubt that the Shaolin Temple monks played a major role in the development of Chinese martial arts. A series of exercises called I-Chin-Ching was developed that later came to be called Shaolin kung-fu.

An Okinawan fighting system known as Te existed for centuries. In 1429 the island was united under one king who reduced any threat to his sovereignty by prohibiting all weapons. In 1477 the prohibition was extended by another king. During this period the natives improved their ancient Te system for self-defense. It included the hardening of hands and feet as weapons, and the modification of farm implements into weapons. In 1609 Okinawa was invaded by Japan, and again arms were confiscated. At about this time Chinese troops visited and the Okinawans were exposed to Chinese martial arts. These were incorporated into their Te system.

The Japanese emperor invited an Okinawan teacher to demonstrate the Te fighting system in Japan. Gichin Funakoshi set up a school in Tokyo which became a large karate school. The Japanese called his art karate-do (the way of the empty hand). The Japanese continued to develop karate. In 1955 Master Peter Urban brought the Goju style of karate to the United States.

Tai-Chi-Chuan

Tai-chi-chuan existed in China before Bodhidharma's time. It was used to promote the agility of kung-fu fighters. It is descended from early Taoist practices and so is part of a much wider and deeper world view. Tai-chi was divided into hard and soft styles. In the hard styles the karate-like rapid gestures were emphasized. The soft styles consist of slow, graceful movements that provide beneficial stretching, joint manipulation, and some cardiovascular benefits.

It is the soft styles that are growing in popularity in the United States today. The best known style is the yang form. Others include the wu, ng, chen, and sun. There is no competition involved with tai-chi-chuan. Relaxation is attained through concentration upon the slow movements involved. It produces a feeling of peace and calm. It has been called meditation in movement. This is far removed from the interpretation of the name tai-chi-chuan. It means "supreme ultimate martial art way or fist."

Millions of Chinese practice tai chi each morning in parks or other open areas. It is the most practiced of all the fighting arts of the world.

Taekwon-Do

The kingdom of Silla defeated two adversary kingdoms on the Korean peninsula in 337 A.D. The superior fighting corps of Silla had developed soldiers by severe physical and mental conditioning. It is believed the art of empty-hand fighting, which was later to be called taekwon-do, came under popular and enthusiastic study during the period 337–935 A.D. The Koryo dynasty defeated Silla in 935 A.D. and encouraged an unarmed combat style called tae kyon, which was possibly influenced by Chinese martial arts. The Koryo dynasty fell about 1435, replaced by the Yi dynasty. Martial arts were banned. Japan occupied Korea in 1909 and extended the ban. The system of tae kyon went underground during this period. Natives trained in tae kyon fled Korea and learned new fighting techniques in Japan and China. They returned in 1945 when Korea was liberated and improved the tae kyon system. In 1955 the name taekwon-do was chosen for the modified system.

In literal translation taekwon-do means, "to kick or smash with the feet" (tae), "to punch or destroy with the hand or fist" (kwon), and "method or way" (do). The system is similar to karate.

American soldiers learned taekwon-do in Korea during the war and brought the system to the United States. This has resulted in a strong Korean influence on American martial arts activity.

Jiujitsu

The ancient Japanese practiced a form of wrestling, later called sumai. It evolved into sumo wrestling, jiujitsu, and judo. It was a combat form that demanded unconditional surrender. There was an age of almost continuous warfare between clans throughout Japan from the middle of the twelfth century to about 1600. The colorful Bushi, or samurai warrior class, mastered and further developed the many forms of sumai fighting with sword, knife, spear, and bow and arrows. They were also taught to fight with bare hands, in case there were no weapons. This hired warrior fought for pay. Fighting techniques were taught in secret so that a samurai's opponents would not learn of his methods and be prepared for them.

During the mid 1500s Takenouchi Hisamori developed the foundation for modern jiujitsu. Chinese tactics were included. In all, over 700 jiujitsu systems were developed against the sword, spear, knife or another barehanded fighter. Jiujitsu employs throwing arts, as in judo. It also includes many more violent responses such as striking, kicking, locking the joints, dislocating and bone-breaking arts, tying and escaping, and strangulation techniques. This form of jiujitsu peaked in the seventeenth and eighteenth centuries. Nowadays violence is only resorted to when attacked and all else fails. It is discontinued when an attacker is subdued.

Jiujitsu can be dangerous if taught as a technique without emphasis on the mental aspect. The student is trained to have a calm, confident, and positive attitude.

Most competition today is less violent than in the past. There are several types or systems of jiujitsu.

In nage-waza competition, the opponents face one another. They attempt to break one another's balance and achieve a throw. A successful controlled throw is awarded a win (ippon). An almost successful throw is called a wazari. An ippon is scored when the opponent has been thrown with both feet having left the floor and judged to have landed with at least 50 percent of the back on the mat. A wazari is scored if only one foot leaves the floor and at least 50 percent of the back lands on the mat, or both feet leave the floor and less than 50 percent of the back hits the mat.

In ne-waza competition the opponents begin sitting back-to-back. They turn and attempt to pin the opponent on his/her back for thirty seconds. As an alternative, an arm lock or stranglehold may be applied to cause an opponent to submit. An ippon is scored when an opponent is pinned for thirty seconds, or signals submission.

Other competitions involve demonstrations of form against attack by punches, kicks, or simulated weaponry. Points are awarded for style and skill.

Jiujitsu is spelled ju-jutsu in Japan. It means soft combat arts and skills.

Judo

In the 1870s a Japanese law was passed banning the wearing of swords unless a person was in the military. The samurai's sun had set.

In an effort to keep the fighting arts alive, Jigoro Kano took those techniques of jiujitsu that could be safely used and created the sport of judo. In 1882, he supplemented the jiujitsu techniques with physical training and moral, character-building instruction. Judo is more like wrestling than boxing in that it incorporates throws, holds, and pinning to the mat for thirty seconds.

In 1902 Kodokan judo was introduced to the United States by invitation of President Theodore Roosevelt, who studied the art.

Modern competition begins with the opponents standing and facing each other. Contestants are judged on throwing and holding techniques. A competitor wins by scoring an ippon.

An ippon is scored for the following: Throwing an opponent largely on the back with considerable force. When an opponent gives up and signals submission. When one contestant holds the other, unable to get away, for

thirty seconds. When the effect of a strangle or joint-lock is sufficiently apparent.

If the contestant just fails to make an ippon, a waza-ari may be given. Two waza-ari's constitute a win. Rule violations are also considered in scoring. A contestant is penalized one waza-ari for a serious violation.

After World War II interest in judo became widespread. By the 1960s almost every country in the world was involved. In 1964 judo was made an Olympic sport.

Aikido

Originally introduced in Japan by Morihei Ueshiba in 1938, aikido was further developed after World War II into the sport known today. It is a judo-like system in which the attacker's energy is redirected against him/her. Instead of forcefully pushing back when pushed, aikido teaches one to step aside and pull in the same direction as the attacker is pushing.

Although aikido is an excellent means of self-defense, the ultimate goal is to develop a total discipline for spiritual, moral, mental and physical advancement. It is called the gentle way.

Aikido competitions are based upon performance of techniques called katas. One or more opponents assume the role of attacker (Uke), another the role of defender (tori). Kata elements that are judged include avoidance, breaking of balance, correct positioning, performance of throw or control, and the finish. Judges note posture, movement, coordination between tori and uke, pace, and purpose. Judges award a maximum of ten points based on the quality of performance.

Aikido may be performed with three participants, using one defender and two attackers. There are also two systems in which two participants fight in freestyle; one with weapons, the other without.

Benefits of Martial Arts Training

Martial arts training goes beyond physical exercise and sport. It builds self-confidence. Those who work with disadvantaged children find significant improvement in attitude and outlook after martial arts classes. Women seeking a means of self-defense have gained greater confidence and peace of mind after their training. Martial arts training teaches concentration and relaxation techniques that are applicable to our daily lives.

This pastime has had a difficult time shedding the *Kung Fu* movie image, but increasing numbers of people have become involved, obtaining greater respect for themselves and others.

Bibliography

REFERENCE BOOKS

Clark, Robert. *Jiu Jitsu: the Official World Jiu Jitsu Federation Training Manual.* London: Black, 1991. Step-by-step instruction, well illustrated.

Crompton, Paul. *The T'ai Chi Workbook.* Boston: Shambhala, 1987. Broad coverage emphasizing the techniques and diversity of T'ai Chi.

Funakoshi, Gichin. *Karate-do: My Way of Life.* Tokyo: Kodansha International, 1975. Autobiography of a great karate master.

Hancock, H. Irving, and Katsukuma Higashi. *The Complete Kano Jiu-Jitsu.* New York: Dover, 1905. Original tricks of the early judo kano system.

Hatsumi, Dr. Masaaki, and Stephen K. Hayes. *Ninja Secrets from the Grandmaster.* Chicago: Contemporary Books, 1987. Reflections on the past and present status of ninjutsu.

Hoare, Syd. *Judo.* New York: Random House, 1980. Broad coverage of judo techniques, philosophy, and history.

Homma, Gaku. *Aikido for Life.* Berkeley, CA: North Atlantic Books, 1990. A teacher's guide for instructing beginners in aikido.

James, Stuart. *The Complete Beginner's Guide to Judo.* Garden City, NY: Doubleday, 1978. Illustrated throws, safety rules, and finding a school.

Lee, Bruce, and M. Uyehara. *Bruce Lee's Fighting Method: Self Defense Techniques.* Santa Clara, CA: Ohara, 1976. Emphasis on responses to various modes of attack.

McCarthy, Mark, with George Parulski Jr. *Taekwon-Do: A Guide to the Theories of Defensive Movement.* Chicago: Contemporary Books, 1984. General coverage of taekwon-do.

Mitchell, David. *The Young Martial Artist.* Woodstock, NY: Overlook, 1992. Fitness programs and defense techniques for children.

Nakabayashi, Sadaki. *Judo.* New York: Sterling, 1968. Step-by-step text, well illustrated.

Nakayama, N. *Best Karate: Bassai, Kanku.* Tokyo: Kodansha International, 1979. Techniques, well illustrated.

Neff, Fred. *Lessons from the Samurai.* Minneapolis: Lerner, 1987. History, philosophy, and techniques.

Ochiai, Hidy. *Hidy Ochiai's Complete Book of Self Defense.* Chicago: Contemporary Books, 1991. Essential karate basics through advanced moves. Includes kata exercises, well illustrated.

———. *Hidy Ochiai's Living Karate.* Chicago: Contemporary Books, 1986. Philosophy, history, values, and illustrated techniques.

Reid, Howard, and Michael Croucher. *The Way of the Warrior.* New York: Simon & Schuster, 1987. (Supersedes *The Fighting Arts.* London: Eddison/Sadd, 1983.) Comprehensive overview of the fighting arts with historical coverage of Chinese and Japanese styles.

Roth, Jordan. *Black Belt Karate.* Cedar Knolls, NJ: Wehman, 1974. A comprehensive handbook of fundamentals, well illustrated.

Stewart, Paul. *Sports Illustrated Judo.* Philadelphia: Lippincott, 1976. Step-by-step instruction, well illustrated.

Sutton, Nigel. *Applied Tai Chi Chuan.* London: Black, 1991. Emphasis on hard style tai chi.

Suzuki, Tatsuo. *Karate-Do.* New York: Putnam, 1984. History, step-by-step instruction, well illustrated.

Tegner, Bruce. *Karate: Beginner to Black Belt.* Ventura CA: Thor, 1982. Features details of Tegner's karate system. Well illustrated.

———. *Kung Fu & Tai Chi: Chinese Karate and Classical Exercises.* 2nd rev. ed. Ventura, CA: Thor, 1981. Step-by-step directions and illustrations for kung fu and tai chi moves.

Tegner, Bruce, and Alice McGrath. *Solo Forms of Karate, Tai Chi, Aikido & Kung Fu.* Ventura CA: Thor, 1981. Step-by-step text, well illustrated.

Turner, Karyn, with Mark Van Schuyver. *Secrets of Championship Karate.* Chicago: Contemporary Books, 1991. How to fight and win a karate tournament.

Ueshiba, Kisshomaru. *Aikido.* Tokyo: Hozansha, 1985. Authoritative, illustrated, introduction to aikido. Written by the son of its founder.

Urban, Peter. *The Karate Dojo: Traditions and Tales of a Martial Art.* Rutland, VT: Tuttle, 1991. Karate as a sport and philosophy. Describes belt system.

PERIODICALS

Aiki News/Aiki Nyusu. Aiki News, Lions Mansion No. 204, Tamagawa Gakuen 5–11–25, Machida-shi, Tokyo 194, Japan. (Aikido, jujutsu, and related sports. Text in English).

Black Belt Magazine. Rainbow Publications, 24715 Avenue Rockefeller, Box 918, Santa Clarita, CA 91380–9018.

Inside Karate. CFW Enterprises, 4201 W. Van Owen Place, Burbank, CA 91505.

Inside Kung-Fu. CFW Enterprises, 4201 W. Van Owen Place, Burbank, CA 91505.

Inside Taekwon-Do. CFW Enterprises, 4201 W. Van Owen Place, Burbank, CA 91505.

Judo. Judo Ltd., Candem House, 717 Manchester Old Road, Rhodes, Middleton, Manchester M24 4GF, England.

Karate/Kungfu Illustrated. Rainbow Publications, 24715 Avenue Rockefeller, Box 918, Santa Clarita, CA 91380–9018.

M. A. Training. Rainbow Publications, 24715 Avenue Rockefeller, Box 918, Santa Clarita, CA 91380–9018.

ASSOCIATIONS

American Amateur Karate Federation. 1930 Wilshire Boulevard, Suite 1208, Los Angeles, CA 90057. Serves as national governing body of karate. Establishes competition standards. Sanctions and conducts national competitions. Sponsors U.S. team development camp, and other programs. Publications: Directory, *Ranking and Examination Guide,* and *Times Newsletter.*

Feminist Karate Union. 5429 Russell Avenue, NW, Seattle, WA 98107. Teaches self-protection, self-defense, and karate to women, children, seniors and the disabled. Offers demonstrations and training to community and educational groups and social service agencies. Publications: *Fear Into Anger,* and *Acquaintance Rape.*

International Traditional Karate Federation. 1930 Wilshire Boulevard, Suite 1208, Los Angeles, CA 90057. Provides international rules, regulations, and competition standards for traditional karate. Sanctions international competitions. Affiliated with American Amateur Karate Federation. Publication: *Official Circular.*

Patience Tai Chi Association. PO Box 350532, Brooklyn, NY 11235. Offers classes in tai chi chuan and I ching. Offers correspondence courses, sponsors competitions, and bestows awards. Produces instructional videotapes.

Tai Chi Chuan/Shaolin Chuan Association. 33 W. 624 Roosevelt Road, PO Box 430, Geneva, IL 60134. Promotes and offers instruction in Chinese martial arts. Offers educational programs in Chinese philosophy and the art of health. Bestows awards. Publications: *Tai Chi Chuan/Shaolin Chuan Association,* and newsletter.

United States Aikido Federation. 98 State Street, Northampton, MA 01060. Aikido clubs and schools. Provides instruction, represents its members in the International Aikido Federation. Distributes films and instruction manuals. Publication: *New Aikido Complete Book.*

United States Judo. PO Box 10013, El Paso TX 79991. National governing body of judo in the United States. Sanctions competitions, bestows awards. Affiliated with International Judo Federation, International Olympic Committee, and U.S. Olympic Committee. Publications: *United States Judo Times,* and newsletter.

United States Judo Association. 19 N. Union Boulevard, Colorado Springs, CO 80909. Promotes judo. Maintains the National Judo Institute serving as a national training center. Maintains hall of fame. Sponsors and sanctions tournaments. Publications: *American Judo, USJA Coach, USJA Referee,* and handbooks.

U.S.A. Karate Federation. 1300 Kenmore Boulevard, Akron, OH 44314. Serves as the national governing body for karate in the U.S. Certifies instructors. Organizes competitions, including the Junior Olympic Championship. Selects U.S. national karate team. Maintains hall of fame. Conducts classes, bestows awards. Affiliated with World Union of Karatedo Organizations. Publications: Newsletter, rule book, and manuals.

U.S.A.- Korean Karate Association. PO Box 1401, Great Falls, MT 59403–1401. Promotes all Korean-style martial arts. Sponsors seminars, bestows awards. Maintains branches in twenty-five countries. Publications: *The Dragon's Tale,* and newsletter.

U.S. Taekwon-Do Union. 1750 E. Boulder Street, Suite 405, Colorado Springs, CO 80909. Member of the United States Olympic committee and Sport Supervising Committee of the Amateur Athletic Union of the United States. Represents the U.S. in world championships and other international competitions under sanction of the World Taekwon-Do Federation, an organization of the International Olympic Committee. Sponsors competitions, maintains hall of fame, bestows awards. Publications: Handbook, newsletter, and competition rules and regulations.

Zen-do Kai Martial Arts Association International. PO Box 186, Johnstown, NY 12095. Martial arts clubs. Sponsors tournaments, and antirape and police training seminars. Bestows awards, maintains hall of fame, and library. Sponsors competitions. Publications: *The Warrior,* and newsletter.

Model Aviation

AN ESTIMATED ONE MILLION PEOPLE engage in model aviation activity in the United States. The participants are people of all ages and walks of life. Modeling leads to an interest in aviation and space. This often results in career choices that will meet the needs of the industry. Critical shortages are forecast for pilots and aircraft mechanics in coming years. Many pilots, mechanics, aircraft designers and astronauts were model builders. A surprising number still are.

Most people participate in model aviation for the sheer creative fun of it. You needn't be an experienced craftsman to assemble an attractive snap-together plastic kit. Opportunities are plentiful for challenge and competition if you want it. Model building is often a lifetime hobby providing increased pleasure as you accumulate experience.

During the past thirty years rapid development has occurred in aviation, electronics, communications, and the availability of exotic materials. Model aviation has kept pace with this expansion. As the hobby diversified, modelers began to specialize in one or more of the dozens of directions the hobby has taken. Newcomers are faced with a bewildering number of hobbies within the hobby. The Academy of Model Aeronautics and model airplane magazines will help you sort it out and find the aspects that appeal to you.

History

Model airplanes were flown long before their man-carrying counterparts. Alphonse Penaud twisted some rubber bands to successfully power a model in 1872. Others powered their models with steam engines or clockwork mechanisms. Samuel Pierpont Langley came in second to the Wright brothers when it came to a controllable piloted airplane, but he flew a gasoline powered free-flight model successfully in 1901.

In 1915 the Detroit Society of Automotive Engineers asked William B. Stout to speak on aviation at its annual banquet. To enliven his talk, he took four boys with him from the Chicago Model Club. They flew their model airplanes out over the audience. The last model, a flying boat, took off from a big meat platter filled with water that had been placed on the speaker's table, and flew the length of the room. Just twelve years after the Wright brothers flew at Kitty Hawk an established model airplane club had entertained the prestigious Society of Automotive Engineers.[1]

Leaders in the aviation industry inspired young people to participate in the modeling hobby in the 1920s and 1930s through the Airplane Model League of America (AMLA). The AMLA was founded by airplane manufacturer William B. Stout. The AMLA received backing from explorer Admiral Richard E. Byrd, aircraft manufacturer Eddie Stinson, flying ace Eddie Rickenbacher and automaker Edsel Ford. The period is known as the golden age of aviation. As many as 400,000 young people participated in the AMLA. Many of those AMLA members went on to serve their country in the Air Forces during World War II. The scenario has been repeated in the 1990s where hobbyists experienced in building and guiding radio controlled models contributed to the training of ground based pilots of radio controlled reconnaissance drones found so effective in Operation Desert Storm.

When the AMLA conducted its first national contest in June 1928, competition was held inside at the Olympia Stadium and outside at the Ford airport in Detroit. The winners of the competition were sent to Europe to compete in an international contest.

---

1. Frank Zaic, *Model Airplanes and the American Boy* (Northridge, CA: Model Aeronautic Publications, 1982), 158.

Development of an Aeromodeler

A beginner in model aviation is faced with two challenges. The techniques and skills required to construct a light, straight, well-built craft must be mastered. Secondly, the basics of aerodynamics should be understood in order to trim the model for flight. That's a tall order to get started, but with some research and trial and error, it has been done by many. Start your research by reading a few modeling magazines available at your local hobby shop or bookstore. Try to locate a hobby shop with experienced personnel. Join a local flying club if one is available. Members can answer your questions and provide flight instruction, shortening your learning period considerably.

Models respect the laws of physics in that a light weight plane receives much less damage upon unplanned impact than a heavy one. Since the learning process involves an occasional unplanned impact, a simple, lightweight, rubber-powered model is an excellent first choice. Test glide your model over tall grass. This is one of the most often repeated instructions involving the initial trimming and balancing of a model. It has become an inside joke among modelers as such ideal flying sites become harder to find. Fluctuating air currents have little respect for the best flying model. As a result, a modeler should anticipate the need to repair models as well as build them.

Having mastered flight basics, a larger craft may be next on the modeler's agenda. A four to six foot wingspan glider might be considered. The builder will gain experience with larger structures, but still enjoy the minimal damage encountered when flying light weight models. Gliders may be flown from high ground, towed aloft or hi-start launched. The latter can be compared with a five hundred foot slingshot with the far end staked to the ground. More about this later.

Gliders make an ideal transition to radio-controlled flight (RC). They move slowly enough to give the pilot enough reaction time at the controls. An RC flier must develop what is called spatial visualization. Since the pilot is on the ground and not in a seat in the aircraft, certain relationships must become second nature. If the plane is coming toward you, left becomes right. If it is coming toward you upside down, right is right again. You must visualize yourself in the pilot's seat of the model. Most control systems continually respond to control stick movement, so it is possible for the plane to get ahead of your ability to preplan control movements.

Reputable manufacturers design and test the models they sell in kit form. They provide kits with a good set of plans and instructions, and quality materials.

After a few kit projects the modeler may wish to purchase model plans for a favorite airplane from one of the many plan services. In this approach the builder purchases all needed materials separately. This is called scratch-building.

Some hobbyists concentrate their efforts on making exact miniature copies of full-sized aircraft. These scale modelers may work from engineering drawings of the full-sized airplane, modifying the full-sized structure to meet the requirements of the model. Figure 1 illustrates a scale drawing published by hobby industry publisher Air Age Inc. Prints of scale drawings of full-sized aircraft are also available from aircraft museums such as the Air Force Museum and the Smithsonian Institution.

Experienced modelers may design and build their own competitive models. They enjoy testing and redesigning in an effort to gain a competitive edge or improve the state of the art. Noted full-scale aircraft designer Burt Rutan enjoyed such activity with model planes as a youth.

As modelers progress they tend to favor either competitive flying or sport flying.

Activities

Competitive flying is done at many levels. Fliers compete with club members, between clubs, and at national and international levels. Most competitions above club level are sanctioned through the Academy of Model Aeronautics (AMA). Over 2,000 occur each year. The AMA represents the United States to the Federation Aeronautique Internationale (FAI), the world governing body for aviation. National contests are conducted within various classes of models according to AMA rules. International contests are conducted according to FAI rules. It is not unusual for International Model Aviation contests to include teams from as many as thirty-two nations, similar to Olympic competition. AMA selects and helps finance World Championship teams from the United States. In 1928 our top national winners were treated to a trip to Europe, feted in London, Paris and Switzerland, given an official reception home by the mayor of New York, and made newspaper headlines. Today our international winners in model aviation are our best kept secret.

Postal contests are another form of international competition. Modelers box and mail their aircraft to the host country. Proxy fliers are assigned by the host country to fly the model in competition. This is especially popular in Japan and Europe.

Most modelers fly for personal enjoyment, shunning competitive events. This is called sport flying. Model aviation organizations are becoming increasingly aware of this and are providing fun-flys where fliers enjoy each other's company and experiences without the pressures of competition.

Fun-flys are particularly popular with members of the Society of Antique Modelers (SAM). As the hobby of model aviation matures and increases in complexity, many become nostalgic for the good old days when things were

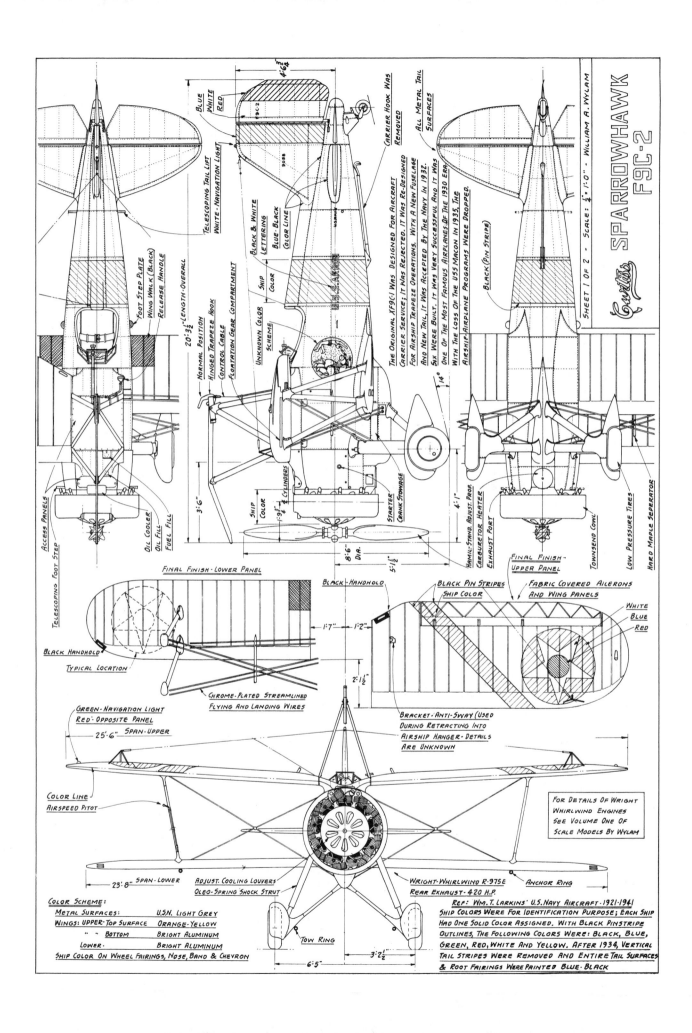

SPARROWHAWK F9C-2

Curtiss

Sheet 1 of 2 · Scale: ½"=1'-0" · William A. Wylam

The Original XF9C-1 Was Designed For Aircraft Carrier Service; It Was Rejected For Airship Trapeze Operations. It Was Re-Designed With A New Fuselage And New Tail. It Was Accepted By The Navy In 1932. Six Were Built. It Was Very Successful And It Was One Of The Most Famous Airplanes Of The 1930 Era. With The Loss Of The USS Macon In 1935, The Airship-Airplane Programs Were Dropped.

Carrier Hook Was Removed

All Metal Tail Surfaces

Blue
White
Red

Black (Pin Stripe)

Telescoping Tail Lift
White - Navigation Light

Black & White Lettering
Blue - Black Color Line

Ship Color

Unknown Color Scheme

Normal Position
Hinged Trapeze Hook
Control Cable

Floatation Gear Compartment

20'-3½" · Length - Overall

Foot Step Plate
Wing Walk (Black)
Release Handle

Access Panels
Oil Cooler
Oil Fill
Fuel Fill
Telescoping Foot Step

3'-6"

Ship Color
9 Cylinders
Propeller
Starter Crank Stowage

Hamil - Stand. Adjust. Prop.
Carburetor Heater
Exhaust Port

Final Finish - Upper Panel

Townend Cowl
Low Pressure Tires
Hard Maple Seperator

Final Finish - Upper Panel

8'-6" Dia.
5'-1½"
4'-1"
1'-4°

Final Finish - Lower Panel

Black - Handhold

Black Pin Stripes
Ship Color

Fabric Covered Ailerons
And Wing Panels

White
Blue
Red

Black Handhold
Typical Location

Chrome - Plated Streamlined
Flying And Landing Wires

1'-7"   1'-2"

2'-1½"

Bracket - Anti-Sway (Used
During Retracting Into
Airship Hanger - Details
Are Unknown)

Green - Navigation Light
Red - Opposite Panel
25'-6" · Span - Upper

Color Line
Airspeed Pitot

23'-8" Span - Lower

Adjust. Cooling Louvers
Oleo - Spring Shock Strut

Tow Ring

6'-5"   3'-2½"

Wright - Whirlwind R-975E
Rear Exhaust - 420 H.P.

Anchor Ring

For Details Of Wright
Whirlwind Engines
See Volume One Of
Scale Models By Wylam

Color Scheme:
  Metal Surfaces: U.S.N. Light Grey
  Wings: Upper - Top Surface   Orange - Yellow
      "   Bottom   Bright Aluminum
  Lower -   Bright Aluminum
  Ship Color On Wheel Fairings, Nose, Band & Chevron

Ref: Wm. T. Larkins' U.S. Navy Aircraft - 1921-1941
Ship Colors Were For Identification Purpose; Each Ship
Had One Solid Color Assigned, With Black Pinstripe
Outlines. The Following Colors Were: Black, Blue,
Green, Red, White And Yellow. After 1934, Vertical
Tail Stripes Were Removed And Entire Tail Surfaces
& Root Fairings Were Painted Blue - Black

simpler. SAM was formed to promote the building and flying of model designs existing before December 31, 1942. An example is shown in Figure 2. The organization has members in all fifty states and chapters in eight other countries around the world.

Materials

Structures. Balsa wood has been a primary model aircraft material for many years. It is light and easy to work. Spruce or pine may be substituted in structures that are heavily loaded and where the added weight is not a problem. Very thin, good quality plywoods are available that also serve highly stressed areas, especially in medium to large sized models.

Modelers have been quick to take advantage of developments in new materials. Fiberglass is commonly used, carbon fiber and Kevlar may be added to increase strength with little added weight. Wings are sometimes designed with plastic foam cores sheeted with wood.

Adhesives. Most model structures are assembled with glue. Old favorite model cements such as Ambroid have been joined by families of cyanoacrylates (instant glues). Some instant glues are thin and fast drying. Others are thick and slower drying. Some are odorless to minimize

allergic reactions. Handle model cements and cyanoacrylates with extreme care and keep them out of children's reach. Use them in a well ventilated work area and follow manufacturer's instructions.

Other strong, slow drying glues that may be used with a slight weight penalty include white casein glues such as Elmer's and aliphatic glues such as Titebond. RC-56 glue made by Wilhold dries clear making it useful for attaching clear canopies. Epoxy glues are used on highly stressed joints where weight is not critical or where the deterioration of joint strength by fuels is a factor.

Covering materials. Extremely lightweight indoor competition models are covered with a special thin transparent microfilm, often prepared by the modeler. Japanese tissue is used for rubber powered models and other small models such as gliders. Silkspan is a heavier material used on intermediate sized models of all types.

Lightweight silk has been used on moderately large models for years. It presents an attractive finish and although often replaced by modern plastic coverings, is still preferred by many.

Nylon and other synthetics are often used on the largest models for their superior puncture resistance.

Some iron-on plastic films have an adhesive coating that permits attachment to airframe structure by the application of heat and pressure from a special small iron. Others require that a special adhesive be applied to the structure before heat is applied.

Dopes and Paints. Dope is used as an adhesive to attach tissues and cloth materials to structures. It is also used to fill pores in these materials. Nitrate dope has been replaced for many applications by Butyrate dope. However, nitrate is still favored for small, lightweight models. Where their weight can be tolerated, acrylic and epoxy based paints often are used for large models with good effect.

Tools

Model building can be done with relatively few tools, but most hobbyists add special ones to make the job easier. Work is done on a building board; preferably one that will accept the pins used to hold parts during assembly. Homasote board works well. The following starter set of tools will be found useful:

Xacto knife with a supply of number 11 blades.

Single edge razor blades.

Razor saw with very fine teeth.

Set of small files.

Figure 2
A reproduction of a free-flying model originally designed in 1940, during the "golden age" of aviation.

Assortment of small pliers and screwdrivers.

Small hammer.

Small vise.

Medium sized (100 watt) soldering iron for brass and music wire.

Small soldering iron or gun for electrical wiring.

Rosin core solder for electrical work.

Acid core solder for brass or music wire.

Small hand drill (cordless rechargeable power drills are handy).

Pin vise for small diameter drills.

Assorted sanding blocks and fingernail sanding boards.

Garnet sandpaper.

T-pins.

Masking tape.

Types of Models

Indoor models are flown inside of a building. Most are very lightweight, fragile and slow flying. The best of these rubber powered endurance models have stayed aloft for as long as fifty-two minutes. Indoor fliers also compete with model helicopters, autogiros, ornithopters (flapping wing powered), and scale models of full-sized craft.

Free-flight models are flown both indoors and outdoors. They are designed to be flown with no "piloted" means of control. They can be powered by rubber band motors, carbon dioxide motors, electric motors, internal combustion motors or no motors at all. Once airborne, the free-flight model takes its direction from subtle angles built into the airframe during its construction. Usually these angles will cause the model to fly in a circular path to keep it from flying out of sight.

In competition, free-flight fliers try to release their models in updrafts called thermals to prolong their flight. Most events don't award extra credit for time aloft beyond a specified limit. For this reason the fliers incorporate dethermalizing devices to the airplane to return it to earth after the limit has been exceeded. Without such devices record times aloft have reached ninety-three minutes for a model powered by an internal combustion engine. Over eighty-eight minutes has been reached using rubber power and over fifty-seven minutes for a glider. Helicopters, autogiros, ornithopters, and scale models are also flown outdoors.

Control line models are designed to be flown on a line or lines in a circular path around the pilot. They are only controlled around the up and down (pitch) axis. The pilot holds a handle with the lines from the aircraft attached to it, and by moving the arm or wrist upwards or downwards, controls the altitude of the plane. Control line competition includes aerobatic, simulated combat, scale and speed. Speeds of 218 miles per hour have been reached with internal combustion engines and almost 213 miles per hour with pulse jet propulsion.

Radio controlled (RC) models can be divided into two categories—powered aircraft and nonpowered gliders. Both are guided by electronic equipment inside the aircraft that responds to signals the pilot sends from a hand-held device called a transmitter. Because the RC airplane flies by the same principles of flight as a full scale airplane, it is more complex in design and operation.

Powered RC models utilize an engine, or motor if it is electric powered, usually on the front of the airplane. It will turn a propeller that pulls the airplane through the air while the pilot controls the craft's direction, and sometimes the engine speed, from the hand-held transmitter. Some powered models feature an engine powered bladed fan mounted internally to propel the craft. These ducted fan models simulate full scale jet aircraft. Speeds of almost 200 miles per hour have been attained with ducted fan models.

RC powered fliers compete in aerobatics, pylon racing, helicopter, combat, scale, and endurance with pre-World War II designs.

An unlimited form of model pylon racing has become popular. Giant scale models, some weighing fifty pounds, are flown around pylons at speeds approaching 200 miles per hour. The competition is patterned after full-scale aircraft racing. It takes a five person team of experts, a budget of over $5,000, and a lot of practice and determination to be competitive. More than sixty-five teams entered a national competition in 1991.

In RC soaring the control systems operate the same as with a powered model. Only the absence of an engine makes them different. As previously explained they may be launched with a hi-start or towed aloft. The towing may be done by hand as one would tow a kite aloft. It may also be done with an electric winch. Still another approach is to utilize the updrafts found along land ridges to maintain flight. By gliding to and fro along a ridge in this manner fliers have attained slope soaring durations exceeding twelve hours. Fliers also employ the radio control to seek and stay in thermal updrafts. This has enabled flights of over nine hours, distances of over 140 miles, altitudes of over 6,000 feet, and measured gliding speed records of up to 86 miles per hour. These are decidedly not your father's model airplanes.

Nonflying scale models are made for display purposes. Most modelers build display models from plastic kits, but occasionally solid or built-up wooden construction is employed. Builders attempt to duplicate the original aircraft as completely as possible. They incorporate the smallest details and apply accurate paint schemes. Some flying scale builders use commercial plastic kits as a reference source when adding fine detailing to their planes.

Bibliography

REFERENCE BOOKS

Berliner, Don. *Flying-Model Airplanes.* Minneapolis, MN: Lerner, 1982. A brief overview of the sport. Juvenile literature.

Boddington, David. *Building and Flying Radio Controlled Model Aircraft.* rev. ed. London, England: Argus Books, 1982. Tools, equipment, materials, and techniques.

———. *Scale Model Airplanes.* Hemel Hempstead, England: Argus Books, 1990. Prototype selection and an introduction to scale modeling.

Pratt, Douglas R. *The Advanced Guide to Radio Control Sport Flying.* Blue Ridge Summit, PA: Tab Books, 1988. Tips on scratch-building, radio systems, and advanced projects.

———. *The Beginner's Guide to Radio Control Sport Flying.* Blue Ridge Summit, PA: Tab Books, 1988. Emphasis on information sources.

Pratt, Douglas R., and Chip K. Smith. *How to Choose RC Ready-to-Fly Airplane Kits.* Osceola, WI: Motorbooks International, 1988. All about factory assembled models.

Ross, Don. *Rubber Powered Model Airplanes.* Osceola, WI: Motorbooks International, 1988. Design, building, and flying basics.

Schleicher, Robert, and James R. Barr. *Building and Flying Model Aircraft.* New York: Dover, 1988. General coverage of model aircraft.

Troy, Jeff. *The Sportflier's Guide to RC Soaring.* Blue Ridge Summit, PA: Tab Books, 1991. Overview of model gliders.

Whitehead, Gordon. *Radio Control Scale Aircraft: Models for Everyday Flying.* Littlehampton, England: RM Books, 1980. Construction techniques and design tips.

Winter, William J. *The World of Model Airplanes.* New York: Scribner's, 1983. Broad coverage of basics, good introduction to the hobby.

Zaic, Frank. *Model Airplanes and the American Boy 1927–1934.* Northridge, CA: Model Aeronautic, 1982. Collection of model airplane articles from the *American Boy* magazine. Covers AMLA activity.

Note: Additional current model aviation books are available from: Historic Aviation, 1401 Kingswood Road, Eagen, MN 55122, and Motorbooks International Publishers and Wholesalers Inc., PO Box 2, 729 Prospect Ave., Osceola, WI 54020.

PERIODICALS

Flying Models. Carstens Publications, Box 700, Newton, NJ 07860.

Model Airplane News. Air Age Publications, Rt. 7, 251 Danbury Road, Wilton, CT 06897.

Model Aviation. Academy of Model Aeronautics, 5151 E. Memorial Drive, Muncie, IN 47302.

Model Builder Magazine. Gallant Models, 34249 Camino Capistrano, Capistrano Beach, CA 92624–1156.

R-C Modeler. R-C Modeler, 144 W Sierra Madre Boulevard, Sierra Madre, CA 91024.

Scale Modeler. Challenge Publications, 7950 Deering Avenue, Canoga Park, CA 91304.

Scale RC Modeler. Challenge Publications, 7950 Deering Avenue, Canoga Park, CA 91304.

ASSOCIATIONS

Academy of Model Aeronautics. 5151 E. Memorial Drive, Muncie, IN 47302–9252. Governing body of model aviation in the United States. It is a division of the National Aeronautic Association (NAA). Through the NAA the AMA is recognized by the Federation Aeronautique Internationale (FAI), the world governing body for all aviation activity, as the only organization that may direct U.S. participation in international aeromodeling activities. The AMA charters clubs, sanctions contests, provides liaison with the Federal Aviation Administration, Federal Communications Commission, and works with local governments and others to promote the interests of local chartered clubs. The AMA recognizes a number of special interest groups that can provide information about specific areas of interest within the hobby. Since officers and addresses change, write to AMA for current contact information about the following groups: International Miniature Aerobatic Association, International Miniature Aircraft Association (Large RC Models), International Radio Control Helicopter Association, National Association of Scale Aeromodelers, National Free Flight Society, National Miniature Pylon Racing Association (RC), National Soaring Society, National Society of RC Aerobatics, Navy Carrier Society (Control Line), North American Speed Society, Precision Aerobatics Model Pilots Association, Society of Antique Modelers, and United Scale and Pattern Judge Association.

Other related associations include the Electric Aeromodeling Association, Flying Aces Club (Rubber Powered), Jet Pilot's Organization, and the Miniature Aircraft Combat Association (Control Line). Addresses for these organizations are also available from AMA.

Model Boats and Ships

IN THE PAST, only professional craftsmen and salty old sailors built high quality ship models. Today, thousands of hobbyists of all ages, who may have begun modeling plastic cars or airplanes, have been attracted to nautical models. They find a wide range of model types and activities available. The image of museum quality models of sailing vessels on a mantelpiece still applies, but new applications have entered the picture such as powerful model racing boats and graceful sailing yachts guided by radio control. Prefabricated kits of parts have reduced the skills and craftsmanship required to produce a model. However, the addition of power and guidance systems has created new challenges. Craftsmanship isn't a thing of the past though, current models prepared for scale competition have raised the state of the art to unprecedented levels.

Since models are built of full-sized craft of all sizes, it's useful to define a few terms. A boat is usually considered to be a small, open vessel propelled by oars, sails, or an engine. A ship is a vessel of considerable size that navigates in deep water. A scale model is one built to a specific size smaller than the prototype craft. Each dimension that defines the model's shape is determined by the same ratio of size difference from the original. For example, if the model is built to a scale of ¼ inch equals one foot, each foot of the subject being modeled is represented on the model as ¼ inch of length. The model would be ¹⁄₄₈ the size of the original subject.

History

The ancient Egyptians buried high ranking individuals with many possessions that were intended to assist them in the afterlife. Sometimes full-sized boats were included for the voyage. Often the objects were merely symbolic. Boat models over 5,500 years old have been found that provide insights into Egyptian boat construction techniques of the period.

The Greeks introduced a fully developed keel, ribs, and outside planking fastened with wooden pegs (treenails) in their boat construction. The planks were made flush at the seams (carvel-built) as compared with the overlapping construction (clinker-built) used by the northern Vikings.

Early builders constructed ships using verbal instructions from an experienced shipwright. Models began to be used, together with scale drawings, after the fifteenth century. The dockside, or Admiralty, models were used to communicate a proposed design to naval Admirals for their approval, and to builders during the construction phase. Parts were drawn (lofted) full size on the floor, and templates were made from the lofted lines. The outlines were then transferred to the wood. Early dockside models have been preserved and are found in many maritime museums. One form of model used for such communication was the half-hull model. Since ships are the same shape each side of the keel or centerline, the shape of a ship's hull can be shown with a model of only one side. Hull contours for the full-sized ship were lifted from the half-hull model and lofted as above. Half-hull models are popular with today's model builders. They are often built up using contrasting-color laminations of wood, and mounted on plaques.

Development of Skills

The beginning ship modeler is advised to build his/her first project from a commercial kit that is available from a hobby shop or mail-order catalog. Select a subject that is within your modeling capabilities. Model clubs, experienced hobby shop personnel, periodicals, and books will help you understand the nautical terms and instructions furnished with the kit.

As experience is gained, you will want to add details to a kit to improve its appearance. Poring over parts catalogs, you select finely crafted castings and other pieces to upgrade your model. Be careful to pick pieces appropriate to the era your model represents. Some items may not be available, so you will gain the experience of fabricating them yourself. This process requires research. Visits to maritime museums take on a new level of interest. You will discover the location of additional museums and other sources of information through your local library, and find that you can borrow needed nautical books by means of interlibrary loan.

When you have upgraded your building and research skills, you are ready to scratch-build some little-known ship that everyone else hasn't built. Plans and specifications for many ships are available to modelers for a fee from the Army and Navy Divisions of the United States National Archives. The Naval History Division of the Department of Transportation of the Smithsonian Institution is another valuable source. For an extensive list of plans, kits, and materials see Milton Roth's book, *Ship Modeling from Stem to Stern*. If a plastic model has been marketed of your proposed scratch-built subject, buy it to use as a guide, taking advantage of the manufacturer's research.

Construction Techniques

Ship hulls can be carved from a single solid block of wood, or for larger models, a solid block laminated from more than one piece. This technique has several disadvantages in the larger sizes: The model will be heavy and difficult to handle during construction. The wood will be less able to expand and contract to accommodate changes in moisture levels, resulting in cracking. The solid hull can be hollowed out as a unit or individual laminations of a laminated hull can have their centers cut out to the inside outline of the hull contour. The laminations are then glued together and final shaping and smoothing is done.

A solid, or hollow, hull can be provided with a fiberglass surface, or planked with strips of wood to achieve the final contour.

A wooden hull can be used as a pattern. A fiberglass mold is made over the wooden pattern and a fiberglass hull is then made by laying up fiberglass inside the mold. This technique can be used for very large models.

A method that is especially appropriate for older sailing vessels involves planking over frames. The internal structure is built up by attaching a number of frames at right angles to the keel. The outline of the frames determines the contour of the hull. Planking is then attached to the frames in carvel or clinker fashion. Some builders omit portions of the planking to expose the attractive internal structure of the ship.

Other partial construction techniques include the half-hull discussed earlier and the waterline model where the ship is mounted on a plaque representing the water surface, and the hull is omitted below the water line.

Tools

A skillful modeler can build a boat using only a pocket knife. Until skills are developed through practice, a complete (if there is such a thing) toolbox will contribute little to quality workmanship. As you specialize in a given area of ship modeling you will find that certain tools are most often required. Tool selection will vary with the materials used in construction. In any case, you will need tools for measuring, cutting, bending, clamping, holding, fastening, and driving. Buy tools as you determine the need. See the section in this text entitled "Model Aviation" for the listing of a starter set of modeling tools.

Model Types and Activities

Static display models are made of all types of nautical crafts. They are used for movie props and museum or home display. Static working models include those used in test tanks to evaluate hull shapes, and intricate models used as training devices in maritime schools. One special category incorporates a sailing ship displayed inside a bottle. The hull is sized to afford a snug fit as it passes through the bottle neck. The masts are hinged at their base and laid back toward the stern of the ship. All sails and masts have threads attached such as you would find on a marionette. The ship is inserted into the bottle stern-first with the threads hanging out of the bottle neck. When the threads are pulled, the masts rise into position. Glue is applied to the rigging by means of a long probe, to fix the masts and sails in position. Once the glue has dried, a long dowel with a cutting edge attached is used to cut off the threads previously used for mast erection.

Before radio control (RC) of models attained its present state of development, modelers raced boats in a circle, tethered to a central pylon. Current RC boats are raced around courses marked by buoys. Competition includes classes for combustion engine and electric power. Further subdivisions for combustion engines are based on engine displacement and hull types, such as deep V, catamaran, and outrigger. Electric boats are divided into classes by hull design and the number of battery cells used. Combustion and electric powered boats are raced in separate stock (as purchased) and modified power plant classes.

Other types of radio controlled powered boats include: Working ships such as fishing boats and tugs; pleasure boats and ocean liners; and warships of all eras. The warships are often animated to a remarkable degree—cranes move, anchors drop, and guns swivel. They are used for sport or competition.

An unique form of RC competition involves combat with models of naval ships of all types. The models are constructed with fragile balsa wood hulls. Working guns shoot projectiles ranging from BB shot to ball bearings, the size depending on the armament of the prototype ship. The shot is propelled by CO_2 gas. The ships are made to maneuver and attack, the object being to shoot holes through an opponent's hull. All ships are required to have a flotation device with a line attached to the hull. If a ship is sunk, the hobbyist rows out to the bubbling water and pulls the ship up. Repairs are quickly made, and the ship is returned to further competition. Safety rules have been established, and they are strictly enforced.

RC submarines provide additional challenges to modelers. In order to run consistently at a desired depth, tanks must be flooded to achieve neutral buoyancy. Pumping and valving systems are used to force water out of the tanks when it's time to surface. Some use fail safe systems to actuate the pumps if radio contact is lost.

Early model sailboats often employed a vane system to achieve controlled operation in varying wind conditions. A weathervane-like vane is positioned at the rear of the boat. It's connected to the water rudder through a pair of gears. As the wind moves the vane, the rudder steers a course predetermined by the modeler.

Today's RC sailboat employs servomotors to steer the boat and play lines in and out to position sails for maximum performance. As with power boat competition, classes have been established using a variety of criteria. There is even a model America's Cup eagerly sought by a dedicated international group of modelers.

Bibliography

REFERENCE BOOKS

Davis, Charles G. *Ship Model Builder's Assistant.* New York, Dover, 1988. Useful information for a boat modeler.

DeMarco, Guy. *Ships in Bottles.* West Chester, PA: Schiffer, 1985. A well-illustrated book covering the techniques used to construct ships in bottles.

Dressel, Donald. *Planking Techniques for Model Ship Builders.* Blue Ridge Summit, PA: TAB Books, 1988. Describes the construction of built-up ship model hulls.

Edson, Merritt, ed. *Ship Modeler's Shop Notes.* Bethesda, MD: Nautical Research Guild, 1986. A compilation of contributions by members of the Nautical Research Guild.

Jackson, Albert, and David Day. *The Modelmaker's Handbook.* New York: Knopf, 1981. General modelmaking information on airplanes, boats, cars, and railroads. Basic tools, techniques and materials are well covered.

Johnson, Gene. *Ship Model Building.* 3rd ed. Centreville, MD: Cornell Maritime, 1961. Describes methods of hull construction.

Mansir, A. Richard. *How to Build Ship Models: A Beginner's Guide.* Blue Ridge Summit, PA: TAB Books, 1984. General text for beginning modelers.

Mastini, Frank. *Ship Modeling Simplified: Tips and Techniques for Ship Model Construction from Kits.* Camden, ME: International Marine, 1990. Overview of kit model building.

Payson, Harold. *Boat Modeling the Easy Way: A Scratch Builder's Guide.* Camden, ME: International Marine, 1993. Tips and techniques for building ship models inexpensively.

Rogers, John G. *Origins of Sea Terms.* Mystic, CT: Mystic Seaport, 1984. An introduction to maritime terminology. Helps interpret plans and instructions.

Roth, Milton. *Ship Modeling from Stem to Stern.* Blue Ridge Summit, PA: TAB Books, 1988. Overview of ship modeling with emphasis on scale display models. Includes useful advice on construction techniques, and extensive bibliographic information on books and other sources of information and materials.

Roush, Ronald C. *Bottling Ships and Houses.* Blue Ridge Summit, PA: TAB Books, 1985. Describes building model ships in bottles piece by piece.

Takakjian, Portia. *Ship Modeling Techniques.* Cedarburg, WI: Phoenix, 1990. Overview of ship modeling.

Underhill, Harold A. *Plank-on-Frame Models and Scale Masting and Rigging,* 2 vols. Glasgow, Scotland: Brown, Son & Ferguson, 1987. Describes the construction of built-up ship model hulls.

PERIODICALS

Model Ship Builder. Phoenix Publications, Box 128, Cedarburg, WI 53012.

Radio Control Boat Modeler. Air Age Publishers, Rt. 7, 251 Danbury Road, Wilton, CT 06897.

U.S. Boat & Ship Modeler. Gallant Models, 34249 Camino Capistrano, Capistrano Beach, CA 92624.

ASSOCIATIONS

American Model Yachting Association. c/o Harry Robertson, 2793 Shellwick Court, Columbus, OH 43235. Those interested in radio-controlled model yacht sailing. Aims to standardize racing classes and establish rules. Schedules competitive events. Bestows awards. Publication: *Model Yachting.*

NAMBA International. 1815 Halley Street, San Diego, CA 92154. Those interested in radio-controlled model boats. Sanctions races, presents awards, and maintains hall of fame. Publications: *Propwash,* and a rulebook.

Nautical Research Guild. 62 Marlboro Street, Newburyport, MA 01950. Ship model builders and others interested in the collection and dissemination of nautical information. Includes illustrations, plans, modeling techniques, and related material for ships.

Ships-in-Bottles Association of America. PO Box 180550, Coronado, CA 92178. Promotes the art of building ships-in-bottles. Publication: *Bottle Shipwright.*

Smithsonian Institution, Department of Transportation, Division of Naval History. Room 5010 HTB, Washington, DC 20560. Source of ship plans.

Steamship Historical Society of America. 300 Ray Drive, Suite 4, Providence, RI 02906. Professionals and amateurs interested in steam or other power-driven vessels. Maintains library and photo collection. Publications: *Steamboat Bill,* and related material.

United States National Archives, Army and Navy Division. 7th and Pennsylvania Avenues, NW, Washington, DC 20408. Assists modelers by providing copies of plans and specifications of ships for a fee.

Model Cars

MODELERS BUILD MINIATURE CARS for many of the same reasons others build model airplanes or boats. For some it's the challenge and fascination of creating an accurate model of a full-scale car they once had or would like to have. Others enjoy the various forms of competition associated with models, from static display models to high speed radio controlled racers. Whatever their motivation, car modeling is a pastime enjoyed by millions.

History

Toy cars followed closely after full-sized automobiles became part of the American scene in the early 1900s. American manufacturers found that they could keep toy car production costs low by using iron castings. Cast iron toy cars sold for pennies. Today's collectors pay hundreds of dollars for some examples. In the 1920s, pressed sheet steel became the material of choice for some toy makers. Brand names such as Buddy L made extensive use of the material. In the 1930s Tootsietoy produced the die cast metal toy car. The process allowed much greater detail to be incorporated into the toy. It was a milestone along the pathway leading from toy car to model car. Tootsietoy sold some kits containing the painted cast parts for several cars. Fascinated youngsters spent hours building up various color combinations. Some other brand names that still employ die castings are Matchbox and Dinky Toys.

Today, complete die cast scale models, in a variety of scale sizes, are produced for collectors. Many manufacturers, both domestic and foreign, produce limited quantities of a particular model, keeping prices high.

Full scale car manufacturers took note of the trend toward more accurate toy cars and decided to commission replicas of their upcoming car models. They were given to potential customers to promote sales. These "promo" models were common through the seventies, but the practice is limited now. Promos are collectible items; some rare examples are sold at three figure prices.

Accurate model car kits that contain either plastic or die cast metal parts are now sold to hobbyists. Plastic kits are less expensive and therefore predominate the market. Almost twelve million plastic car kits are sold each year by the industry.

Development of a Car Modeler

Most beginning car modelers will simply glue a plastic kit together following the manufacturer's instructions. They may do some research on the full-sized car's color scheme and blend some paints to achieve accuracy in the model's paint job.

After a few models, the urge to improve is spurred by pictures in model magazines or by seeing the work of fellow modelers in a club. Details such as electrical wiring and fuel and brake line tubing are added. The cottage industry in after-market special parts is discovered and parts are bought to upgrade some of the parts supplied with the kit. Some modelers build a small diorama to display the car or truck, possibly mastering the art of weathering the vehicle to match the theme of the diorama. Dust and rust are simulated with powdered pastels and other materials. They are adhered to surfaces with flat, clear paints compatible with the plastic. The appearance of grease may require graphite dust or shiny black paint.

As skills are developed, the modeler may wish to modify a kit to create a different version of the full-sized car—a deluxe model made from the kit of a standard model, or a convertible from a two door hardtop kit. This often requires the purchase of sheet plastic to cut and form into place. The work requires the use of a fine toothed modeler's saw to supplement the usual model knife. With practice, a hot knife device called an autocutter simplifies some of this work. Joints are spot puttied and smoothed as with full-scale practice.

Some modelers modify toy cars to either upgrade their accuracy to scale or to serve as part of an entirely different vehicle. For example: building a fire truck body on a toy dump truck chassis. Another excellent source for scale vehicle components is the fine die cast car and truck kits made for the various scales used in model railroading.

Full scale car magazines, repair manuals, and other support literature can be used as sources for photographs and drawings that serve as guides to authentically detail a model car.

Advanced car modelers modify kit parts to simulate the full-scale car practice of lowering roof lines and the suspension. This requires the cutting away of portions of the body and reforming remaining parts to fit together. Some radical custom cars are built up with parts from several kits (cross-kitting), or from their own or a friend's scrap box.

As building skills improve, modelers will also want to upgrade the finish on their models. Many invest in an air brush with a small compressor. This equipment affords more precise control of paint spray placement, and the consistency of spray pattern and density.

Advanced Modeling

Scratch-built cars are usually made from scale plans and raw materials. In 1930 General Motors established the Fisher Body Craftsman's Guild. The Guild was a competition for young people in the design and construction of model automobiles. Awards and scholarships were given to winners for their innovative design and excellence in craftsmanship. The model cars were built to specifications that took into account the requirements for a full-scale car. Contestants were required to originate the design and construct a durable model on their own. The program provided an opportunity for young people to exercise imagination, display their craftsmanship, and demonstrate their ability to see a challenging project through to the end. Winners were chosen for each state and at the national level. Some went on to careers in automotive design. Regrettably, the program was discontinued in 1968.

Relatively few people build model cars completely from scratch today. Perhaps it's because kits of parts and aftermarket components are so readily available. Scratch building presents interesting challenges, a great deal of satisfaction, and a strong sense of accomplishment.

Fewer still construct unique model cars on commission. Master modelers require as much as a year to complete such a project and must charge prices that run into the thousands of dollars. In his book, The *Model Car Handbook*, Bob Cutter reviews the accomplishments of

Guiseppe DaCorte of Rome, Michele Conti of Turin, and a group of masters from England. The English temperament must be compatible with this work because that country has produced Rex Hays, Cyril Posthumus, Harold Pratley, Henri Baigent, and Gerald Wingrove. We can see Wingrove's beautiful work and learn some of his techniques through his two books listed in the bibliography at the end of this section.

Several master builders are creating unique scale cars in the United States. Ron Phillips specializes in one-fourth scale models of classic racing machines, such as those made by Ferrari, Maserati, and Mercedes. His limited-run production is typically terminated at twenty-five cars and the tooling is destroyed. The cars are radio controlled and powered by internal combustion engines. Some models are powered by V12 engines that feature dual overhead cams, forty-eight valves, and an electronic fuel injection system. Most customers of Phillips Quarter Classics, Ltd., in Detroit, Michigan prefer to treat their cars as pieces of art. They are seldom run.

Gary L. Conley also specializes in one-fourth scale RC models of cars, but with emphasis on engines. He produces engines from V2s to V12s. His V8 is the result of ten years of development. It can be purchased as a kit or fully assembled, complete with a working supercharger, if desired. Conley Precision Engines, Inc. is located in Glen Ellyn, Illinois.

Slot Cars

In slot car events, small electric-powered cars are raced on a winding track defined by a slot cut into its surface. The car is fitted with a pin or key that fits into the slot that guides the car along the track. Electric current is fed to two thin copper strips positioned each side of the slot. The car's motor receives power through electrical contact with the copper strips. The driver is provided with a hand held "throttle" that varies the power received by the car's motor. Most commercial tracks have multiple lanes, allowing several drivers to race one another. The popularity of slot car racing reached a peak in the 1960s before radio controlled car racing evolved to its present state. As radio controlled (RC) racing becomes more competitive and technically advanced, related equipment costs have risen, causing some renewed interest in slot cars.

Radio Controlled Cars

RC cars have become very popular, accounting for a large proportion of RC equipment usage. Most cars are operated by young people as toys for personal amusement. Many people of all ages use the equipment for competitive racing.

With no slot to steer the car as in slot car racing, the driver steers and adjusts power to the car to guide it around the track. The result is that cars spin out when overpowered in turns such as full scale race cars do. The driver must develop racing techniques to be competitive. Specially equipped cars are also used for simulated off road racing. Competition takes place in various classes using either electric motors or internal combustion engines for power.

Electric Motors

Most RC cars are powered by electric motors. Enthusiasts go to great lengths to achieve maximum performance from their equipment. A real or imagined edge gained with specially prepared equipment is often negated by an opponent with superior driving skills. Let's take a look at two critical components of the electric powered model car—the motor and batteries.

Electric motors used in model cars have two outer, stationary, permanent magnets. The inner, rotating armature has three stacks of wires that create a magnetic field when electrical current is applied to them. When current is applied, the inner and outer magnets repel one another, causing the inner armature to turn around. Each armature stack is composed of wires wrapped around a central core. The characteristics of a motor are dependent upon the number of times (turns) a wire is wrapped around the stack, and the number of wires (winds) used for each turn on the stack. Generally speaking, the more turns, the slower a motor will be. The fewer the wires used per turn the greater the punch (torque), whereas adding wires per turn increases top speed, but provides less torque. Cross sectional area of the wire on the armature is also a factor. Motor winding is a job for professionals. Model motor manufacturer's advertising claims are often based on only part of the many trade-offs to be considered when buying a motor to be used under certain conditions.

Electric cars are raced with stock or modified motors. A stock motor's case is not meant to be opened. If it is, the car is disqualified. The cases on modified motors can be opened to adjust the motor's timing. Advancing the timing increases speed, but also increases the current required. Timing is usually set at the point where maximum speed coincides with minimum current requirements. If current draw is too great, you can drain the battery and the car will stop before the end of the race.

Batteries

Electric cars are powered by nickel cadmium rechargeable batteries (nicads). This type of battery is found in many portable appliances from electric shavers to power drills. Most such appliances are furnished with an inexpensive slow charger. Normally you can expect a typical slow recharge to be completed overnight. A battery is composed of a number of separate cells. A typical RC car battery used to power the motor uses six 1.2 volt cells. When a cell is charged the current passing through it promotes a chemical reaction resulting in electrons being transferred from nickel atoms to cadmium atoms. As long as charging current is applied, the process continues until the reaction runs out of nickel or cadmium to convert. This occurs at the time the cell is fully charged. If charging current continues to be applied at this point, pressure will build up within the cell and the temperature of the cell will increase. If this continues, gases will vent from the cell and cell damage can result.

When a battery is discharged as it powers the motor, the electrons flow though the circuit from the cadmium atoms back to the nickel atoms. This action continues until the circuit is intentionally broken or until the free atoms are used up and the battery becomes discharged. Modelers often speed the process of charging nicads by charging them at high rates for typically less than one-half hour. The cells can accept such abuse unless the high rate continues beyond the point when a full charge has been reached. Peak chargers have been developed that monitor the charge of the cells. When the cells peak (become fully charged), the charge is cut off. RC model motors draw high currents and discharge the battery more quickly than it was originally designed to withstand. This causes a build up of heat within the cells. This heat should be allowed to dissipate before the battery is recharged.

Since all six cells operated "as a team" in a battery, they work best if they discharge at the same rate. If their discharge rates vary, the slow dischargers will still be producing a limited current while others are dead. The battery will not be as effective as it would have been if the cells selected had similar discharge rates. Hobbyists place great emphasis on their requirement for batteries with matched nicad cells. Nicad cells are usually color coded to signify their degree of acceptance of rapid discharge, recharge when warm, and other characteristics. Higher capacity nicads are continually being sought by modelers and the industry. Using a modified electric motor, a speed exceeding eighty-five miles per hour has been reached by an RC car in competition.

Internal Combustion Engines

Internal combustion engine powered RC race cars usually use engines similar to those in model airplanes. Such engines are air-cooled rather than water-cooled. RC car engine air cooling is often enhanced by increasing the surface area of the engine head. This is done by increasing head size and the number of grooves in the surface, creating an increase in the number of raised cooling fins between the grooves. Although internal combustion engines are much more powerful than electric motors, they usually produce less torque at low speeds (rpm). The gears that transmit the power from the high speed engine to the slower turning drive shaft have to be selected to balance speed versus acceleration. This problem is being solved by incorporating a two-speed transmission that supplies the needed torque in the low range and speed in the high range. Internal combustion engine powered RC cars are raced in various scales and engine displacement classes.

Motive power represents only part of the increasingly complex equipment used by the RC car racers. Tires, suspensions, and chassis configurations have all received their share of scrutiny and careful development.

Model car racing associations are often identified in model car related magazine editorials and advertisements. Since association officers and addresses often change annually, write to the magazine for current contact information.

Bibliography

REFERENCE BOOKS

Angle, Burr, ed. *Hints and Tips for Plastic Modeling.* Waukesha, WI: Kalmbach, 1980. Techniques described include gluing, filling seams, painting, weathering, and super-detailing.

Carter, Robert, and Eddy Rubinstein. *Yesterday's Yesteryears: Lesney "Matchbox" Series.* Newbury Park, CA: Haynes, 1987. Covers colors, construction and detail changes for the subject models.

————.*Yesteryear Companion: Matchbox Models.* Osceola, WI: Motorbooks International, 1989. As companion to *Yesterday's Yesteryears,* this book covers additional information on colors, construction, detail changes, specials, unusual experimental models, and presentation sets.

Cutter, Bob. *The Model Car Handbook.* Blue Ridge Summit, PA: TAB Books, 1979. Covers the collecting of model cars with emphasis on accurate models intended for the serious collector.

Doty, Dennis. *Model Car Building: Advanced Techniques.* Blue Ridge Summit, PA: TAB Books, 1989. Covers restyling, customizing, detailing, and other modifications to car kits.

————. *Model Car Building: Getting Started.* Blue Ridge Summit, PA: TAB Books, 1988. The basics of model car building are thoroughly covered in this guide to model car building and collecting. Includes information on tool selection, materials, and painting for both plastic and metal car assembly.

Force, Edward. *Dinky Toys.* West Chester, PA: Schiffer, 1988. A concise history of Dinky Toys for toy car collectors. Provides a chronological list and price guide that includes Dinky Toys that were made worldwide.

Schiffer, Nancy. *Matchbox Toys.* West Chester, PA: Schiffer, 1983. A history of the Matchbox Company and a description of toys made from 1947 to 1982.

Schleicher, Robert. *Building Plastic Models.* Waukesha, WI: Kalmbach, 1976. The basics of plastic modeling including tool selection, assembly techniques, and painting.

Weiland, James, and Edward Force. *Tootsietoys: World's First Diecast Models.* Osceola, WI: Motorbooks International, 1980. The history of Tootsietoys. Thoroughly covers the development of the various models.

Wingrove, Gerald A. *The Complete Car Modeler.* New York: Crown, 1979. Master modeler Wingrove discusses his approach to the techniques of building model cars from scratch. Specific techniques are discussed and illustrated for creating model bodywork, engines, wheels, and much more.

————. *The Complete Car Modeler No. 2.* Newbury Park, CA: Haynes, 1991. Additional tips and techniques for expert scratch car modeling. Covers workbenches, lighting, tools, materials, and the step-by-step process of construction for a Bugatti Royale model.

PERIODICALS

Model and Toy Collector. Cap'n Penny Productions, 137 Casterton Avenue, Akron, OH 44303.

Radio Control Car Action. Air Age, 251 Danbury Road, Wilton, CT 06897.

Radio Control Model Cars and Trucks. Gallant Models, 34249 Cainino Capistrano, Capistrano Beach, CA 92624.

Scale Auto Enthusiast. Highland Productions, 5918 W. North Avenue, Milwaukee, WI 53208.

ASSOCIATIONS

Antique Toy Collectors of America. c/o Robert R. Grew, Carter, Ledyard and Milburn, 2 Wall Street, 13th Floor, New York, NY 10005. Conducts research, study, and documentation of antique toys. Presents awards. Publications: *Toy Chest,* and related materials.

Ertl Collectors Club. PO Box 500, Dyersville, IA 52040. Collectors of die cast toys. Serves as information clearinghouse on Ertl products. Publication: *Collector's Handbook.*

Kit Collectors International. PO Box 38, Stanton, CA 90680. Those involved in the collection of scale model kits. Encourages and facilitates trading, buying, and selling of model kits among members. Maintains reference library and museum. Bestows awards. Publications: *Vintage Plastic,* and related material.

Model Car Collectors Association. 5113 Sugar Loaf Drive SW, Roanoke, VA 24018. Builders and collectors of model and toy cars. Sponsors competitions and bestows awards. Publication: Journal.

Western Associated Modelers. c/o Myrtle B. Coad, 6073 Sunrise Drive, Lower Lake, CA 95457. Individuals and clubs interested in model planes, cars, and boats. Sanctions competitions. Publication: *Propwash.*

Model Miniatures

THE VALUE OF A SCALE MINIATURE in various professions and industries, as well as its attraction as a hobby, lies in its ability to communicate the visual aspects of something planned or already existing. Miniatures have been used as educational aids, for museum presentations, to demonstrate unique ideas (patent models), and as three-dimensional art. Miniatures can be reminders of a time gone by, an expression of your favorite decorating style, or just an outlet for your creativity. In recent years, scale model building has benefited from increased availability of resources and information. Modelers have more choices, and are challenged to produce more accurate and realistic models. They enjoy researching and planning a project, then employing a variety of skills to produce a model they are proud to show their friends. People who are most attracted to scale models often include those whose professions relate to miniaturization of the full sized environment, such as artists, photographers, draftsmen, architects, engineers, and pattern makers. More importantly, young people who engage in modeling activities develop skills and spatial visualization capabilities they may use in future careers.

History

The early Chinese and Egyptians placed realistic models of items of personal property in tombs to serve the deceased in the afterlife. These items included miniature furniture, weapons, and boats. Models of clothing and architecture have been made since the sixteenth century. Well-to-do families have built child-sized play houses for their children for years. A fine example can be seen on the Edsel Ford property in Detroit, Michigan.

Apprentice cabinetmakers were often required to construct a piece of miniature furniture to demonstrate their skills. These items served a purpose when the newly-graduated apprentice traveled from town-to-town seeking a likely location to set up shop. He had a sample of his work that was portable, and could be used to show prospective customers the quality of his work. Some of these miniature furniture pieces were purchased by parents for their children, and eventually found their way into museums as examples of period furniture design.

Sellers of large or heavy products such as cast iron kitchen stoves or anvils also used miniature copies of their wares to point out the product's valuable features to customers. These miniature pieces are actively sought by collectors.

Many sizes of miniature models are used today during the planning and developing of new products and facilities. The motion picture and television industries also rely heavily on the use of scale models as part of their sets to save the cost of using full-scale items.

Military miniatures have been used during the planning of full scale battles, as well as by hobbyists interested in recreating battles from the past. Modern enthusiasts build miniature tanks and other military equipment, often displaying them in dioramas depicting typical surroundings. Model railroads are often displayed as extended dioramas using houses, foliage, and other items to complete a scene.

Returning to the subject of miniature furniture and related items, we find that there is a rapidly growing interest in dollhouses and their furnishings. Accordingly, the emphasis will be on dollhouses and room boxes in the following discussion.

Development of a Miniature Modeler

In recent years, dollhouse furniture has evolved from somewhat crude representations to accurately scaled reproductions of period pieces. These items are readily available at reasonable prices, considering the amount of painstaking work employed in their construction. As quality went up, the furniture found a ready market among collectors.

The Beginning Modeler

If miniature furniture is to become part of a dollhouse display, the first thing a beginner must decide upon is the scale that will be used for the display. The most common scale employed for dollhouse furniture is one inch of the model representing one foot of the full-sized piece. In the United States it's usually referred to as "one-inch scale." Almost all other countries use the metric system of measurement, so they usually refer to this scale as $\frac{1}{12}$ scale. The second most common scale is one-half inch, or $\frac{1}{24}$ scale. Other scales will be encountered, but the collector will find the widest selection of ready-made items in these scales. Some hobbyists who make all or part of their houses and furnishings, and wish to adopt a smaller scale, will choose a scale similar to a standard model railroad size. This allows the use of accessories and other pieces intended for model railroaders.

When smaller scales are used, the available choices of manufactured components affect design, construction, and modeling techniques. Building designs tend to develop out of available components. Plastics often replace wood in smaller scales to control costs. Only a few manufactured furniture items are offered in one-quarter inch scale; others must be built from basic materials (built from scratch). When building to any scale, but especially small scales, precise adherence to scale sizes can create problems. For example, in $\frac{1}{4}$ inch scale ($\frac{1}{48}$ size), a $\frac{3}{4}$ inch thick shelf would be .0156 inches thick. Sometimes one must rely on proper appearance or feel when working with what would otherwise be overly fragile parts. However, the builder should not revert to the toy-like, primitive appearance common to early pieces.

As a collection of furniture grows, the hobbyist will want a space to display it. Most choose either a dollhouse or a room box. A typical dollhouse kit will include materials to construct a basic house with an open back that provides access to the interior. It will serve as a structure to which additional details and accessories may be added to create a realistic model. A room box is an enclosure, with one or more transparent walls, that serves as a setting for the display of all of the items that go into the furnishing of a particular room. Some research should be done before accumulating the pieces for a room box or dollhouse to ensure that the pieces complement one another and represent a chosen era. Although the term dollhouse is commonly used when referring to multi-room kits, it doesn't mean that they are primarily intended for use with primitive toy dolls. Many are true scale replicas of period houses.

The Experienced Modeler

As experience accumulates, the modeler may choose to modify the basic kit structure. This is called kit-bashing. The experienced modeler not only kit-bashes dollhouses, but furniture as well. The modeler will kit-bash furniture, using pieces from various kits to create a unique piece of furniture. Kit builders save left over pieces from past projects for such activity. Full scale furniture books provide ideas, plans, and guidance for miniature projects of this type. Those who scratch-build furniture can often incorporate factory-made components in their design. Items such as ornate chair or table legs, and other machined wooden parts, are available. The resulting furniture pieces are usually true scale reproductions of full-sized furnishings. Advanced manufacturing techniques have made intricate detailing possible: Wooden pieces may be precisely cut by laser. Small metal parts may be created by lost-wax casting or photo-etching methods. The injection molding process has made intricate plastic parts commonplace.

Many factory-processed materials and manufactured accessories are available. Examples include: Machined wooden flooring, siding, and moldings. Prebuilt window and door units. Kits for producing miniature needlework. Scale china, glassware, canning jars, rugs, bricks, and decals for decorating furniture. When building miniatures of wood, select close-grained woods such as basswood to achieve a realistic scale grain effect.

As you become an experienced builder, you learn a little about a lot of things. You become a jack-of-all-trades. In addition to fine woodworking, you will learn to paint, stain and age pieces. If you develop needlework skills, you can sew miniature curtains, knit afghans, or crochet a blanket. This type of work requires a magnifier and small needles and thread, but hobbyists are doing it. Some learn to bake special clays to make miniature ceramic items, or work with electrical components to create special lighting effects for rooms.

Experienced modelers may wish to enter their work in the many contests associated with trade shows held across the country. Photo contests for various categories of miniature displays are also held, sponsored by magazines.

Tools

In view of the many types of materials and processes used in the miniatures hobby, it's not practical to list all the tools you may need. See the "Model Aviation" section in this text for a starter set of tools, and add others as you attempt additional techniques. You will find that the how-to articles in periodicals listed in the following bibliography contain useful tips regarding tool selection and usage.

Bibliography

REFERENCE BOOKS

Beals, Judy. *How to Build Miniature Furniture and Room Settings*. Milwaukee, WI: Kalmbach, 1983. Techniques for building and modifying furniture kits, and scratch-building and upholstering furniture.

Boulton, Vivienne. *The Doll House Decorator.* New York: Dorling Kindersley, 1992. Creating dollhouse furnishings and accessories from scratch using found items and other widely available materials.

Davenport, John. *How to Make Miniature Furniture.* New York: Wynwood, 1988. Overview of miniature furniture making. Covers material sources, tools, techniques, and several well-illustrated projects.

Eaton, Faith. *The Miniature House.* New York: Abrams, 1991. Coverage of a selection of the finest miniature houses from across Europe and the United States. Most were commissioned by adult connoisseurs as displays for exquisite miniature craftsmanship.

King, Patricia. *Making Dolls' House Furniture.* Rev. ed. East Sussex, England: Guild of Master Craftsman, 1991. How-to book featuring construction techniques for a variety of scale miniature items for dollhouses.

Raymond, Kathleen Zimmer. *Workshop Wisdom: Dollhouse Crafting Tips from Nutshell News.* Sykesville, MD.: Greenberg, 1992. Using and modifying found items in the construction of dollhouse furnishings. Well illustrated construction tips.

Rowbottom, Derek. *Making Georgian Dolls' Houses.* East Sussex, England: Guild of Master Craftsman, 1992. Comprehensive coverage of scale dollhouse and room box making. Includes designing your own house, tools, methods, materials, and several projects.

Rowbottom, Derek, and Sheila Rowbottom. *Making Period Dolls' House Furniture.* East Sussex, England: Guild of Master Craftsman, 1992. Twenty-nine modeling projects for furniture of every description, covering five centuries and a variety of styles.

Stadtman, Shep. *Doll House Furnishings For the Bedroom and Bath.* New York: Dover, 1984. Emphasis on sewing miniature accessories such as bedding and curtains for dollhouses.

Theiss, Nola. *The Complete Guide to Remodeling and Expanding Your Dollhouse.* New York: Sterling, 1993. Comprehensive introduction to dollhouse construction. Covers tools, construction techniques, electrical wiring, and kit construction.

PERIODICALS

Miniature Collector. Scott Publishing, 30595 W. Eight Mile Road, Livonia, MI 48152–1798.

Miniature Gazette. National Association of Miniature Enthusiasts, Box 69, Carmel, IN 46032.

Miniatures Catalog. Kalmbach Miniatures, 21027 Crossroads Circle, Box 1612, Waukesha, WI 53187.

Miniatures Showcase. Kalmbach Publishers. Box 1612, Waukesha, WI 53187–1612.

Nutshell News. Kalmbach Publishers, Box 1612, Waukesha, WI 53187–1612.

Scale Cabinetmaker. Dorsett Publications, 630 Depot Street, Box 2038, Christiansburg, VA 24073.

ASSOCIATIONS

International Guild of Miniature Artisans. PO Box 71, Bridgeport, NY 13030. Those interested in promoting miniatures as an art form. Promotes the placement of miniatures in museum and gallery exhibits and collections. Conducts workshops and Guild School. Bestows awards. Publications: *The Cube,* and *Guild Hotline.*

Miniatures Industry Association of America. 1100-H Brandywine Boulevard, PO Box 2188, Zanesville, OH 43702. Industry professionals and enthusiasts of dollhouse miniatures and dolls. Sponsors seminars and workshops at trade shows. Conducts competitions and bestows awards. Publications: Newsletter, and related materials.

National Association of Miniature Enthusiasts. PO Box 69, Carmel, IN 46032. Collectors and builders of miniatures, and interested individuals. Holds workshops, exhibits and sales. Publication: *Miniature Gazette.*

Model Railroads

History

MOST MODEL RAILROADERS recall the childhood experience of seeing a massive, powerful, locomotive for the first time. These thrilling childhood memories created a desire to own a tangible piece of that awesome source of power. For over a hundred years, railroads have had that dramatic effect on people, and for some it has resulted in a lifelong hobby of collecting, building, and operating miniature replicas of railroad equipment.

History

John Stevens ran his first full-sized steam locomotive on a circle of track in Hoboken, New Jersey in 1825. It began to look as if steam would replace the horses that had been used to pull carriages along rail lines since before the eighteenth century. In 1830 the Baltimore and Ohio Railroad began operations from Baltimore to Ellicott's Mills, just five years after the first successful English steam railway began public service. German toymakers started making trackless trains as early as 1826 in Nuremberg. These early trains were simply pushed or pulled around the floor. Later designs employed clockworks to power the locomotives. In the meantime, the British were producing brass toy locomotives powered by steam. They were affectionately called dribblers due to their habit of leaking water from their steam cylinders as they rolled along the floor. Electric powered toys featuring the outline appearance of steam locomotives first appeared in the 1890s. The acceptance of electric power came slowly at first and both clockwork and steam powered toys continued to be produced through 1910 and beyond. During these early years there was a tendency to make toy designs reflect full-sized equipment of earlier years. This nostalgic practice has continued through the years. Even today children who have never seen such full-scale equipment in action play with steam outline trains.

Early German toy manufacturers such as Bing and Märklin were soon joined by Britain's Stevens's Model Dockyard, and Newton & Co. The French firms of Rossignol and Favre were major manufacturers beginning in the 1860s. In the United States the firm of Carlisle and Finch was making electric powered trains by 1900. Other major American producers were Ives, Voltamp, American Flyer, and Lionel. Many of these early firms are still well-known to collectors; but only Märklin and Lionel have withstood the ravages of war and hard economic times. They continue to claim a large segment of the market.

In the late 1920s the character of toy trains began to evolve. Manufacturers began to capture the details of the full scale prototype more closely. The toys were beginning to look more like scale models. This trend didn't go unnoticed by adults, who appreciated the more lifelike appearance. As trackwork improved with the addition of switches (turnouts) and crossovers, users began to feel that the large size (scale) of the equipment was limiting its usefulness. The track layout took up too much room. Märklin responded in 1935 with their OO gage scale in which one inch of the model train equaled eighty-seven inches of the full-scale prototype (1:87). The 1:87 scale would later become the HO scale so popular today. American Flyer soon introduced their scale-like 1:87 line. Lionel decided to produce an accurately scaled train set in the currently popular O gauge (1:48), and a similar set in their version of OO gauge that was a nonstandard 1:76. Unfortunately, Word War II put an end to the production of the American ventures and they were not resumed after the war. Examples of these train sets are collector's items today.

Tin Plate

Early toy trains were often crafted from thin sheet metal with lithographed color, scrollwork, and simulated detail. In the early 1930s, Lionel used heavy steel stampings, brass trim and durable bright colored paint to capture a large share of the market. These train sets are still so popular with collectors that many are being reproduced today and even some of the reproductions bring very high prices. Although modern toys are made from die cast metal and plastics, the name tin plate is still used when referring to trains designed primarily for use as toys. The distinction between toys and scale models is somewhat blurred today. Each faction has its own associations and favorite magazines and both factions enjoy high levels of activity. The three primary activities pursued in the model railroading hobby are construction, operation, and collecting. Toy train hobbyists deal with ready-built equipment and are most likely to favor the operating and collecting of equipment.

Scale Models

The wheel arrangement of American and British steam locomotives is described by specifying the number of wheels on the leading truck, the number of driving wheels, and the number of wheels on the trailing truck. Interesting names are given to classes of locomotives featuring a given wheel combination. For instance a 2–8–0 is called a Consolidation, and a 4–6–2 is a Pacific. A 2–8–2 Mikado is illustrated in Figure 1. When very large locomotives were required, more than one independent group of driving wheels were employed to allow the locomotive to negotiate tight curves. Such locomotives are called articulateds. A typical wheel arrangement is 4–8–8–2.

Model railroaders take the 4'8½" standard track gauge, which is the distance between rails on a full size railroad, and scale it down to various sizes for modeling purposes. Z gauge is a mere one-fourth inch between rails and the scale is 1:220. Other popular scales include: N 1:160, HO 1:87, S 1:64, O 1:48, LGB 1:32. Some hobbyists choose to model prototypes that didn't have the standard 4'8½" gauge. Narrow gauged track was used extensively for logging and mining railroads. So an HO scale model for a thirty-inch prototype track gauge would have a body at HO size with the wheel gauge set at HO scale thirty inches apart. Hobbyists would identify the scale as HOn30. In some cases, the modeler will use the wheels and running gear from the next smaller scale—for example, mount a HO body on a N scale running gear.

There are a number of factors that enter into the selection of what size scale to use. The larger sizes permit a builder to introduce more detail, promoting realistic appearance. They will weigh more, resulting in smoothr, more stable

operation. However, larger size means more material, resulting in higher cost. Track layouts require more space. At the other extreme, very small sizes are difficult to detail and when well detailed, much of the work is to small to see and appreciate. Cost also rises in very small sizes owing to the watch-like precision required for motors and running gear. But, layouts can be made in restricted spaces. Generally speaking, O gauge is about the limit in size for indoor use, Larger sizes are usually found outdoors in garden railroads powered by electricity or live steam. The currently popular compromise is HO gauge. Because of its popularity a large variety of equipment is available and competition in the marketplace keeps cost down. Both N gauge and S gauge are slowly gaining in popularity. Some modelers use several gauges on a single layout. They position the smaller gauge tracks and equipment to the rear of the layout to create the illusion of distance.

Model railroad components are manufactured in nations around the world. In order for parts to fit and function interchangeably in the wide array of gauges listed above, precise standards must be written and conformance to standards monitored. Consider the following: Model railroad cars cannot be joined together if their coupling devices are not at the same height above the rails; wheel shapes must fit properly with standardized rail shapes. Interfaces such as these are researched, recommended standards and practices are established, and the results are published. Organizations such as the National Model Railroad Association perform these services for manufacturers, dealers, and amateur model railroad hobbyists.

Locomotives and railroad cars can be assembled from kits or purchased ready-to-run. The latter vary considerably in quality and price. Jewel-like scale brass units are imported, mostly from the Orient, that command high prices. Locomotive costs run into hundreds of dollars. Low-cost die cast and plastic units are available that can be upgraded by means of "super detailing" kits of parts that are sold to enhance the scale-like appearance of the model. Many hobbyists enjoy assembling kits. Slight changes are often made during assembly to make the equipment conform more closely to the full scale railroad being modeled. To achieve the desired accuracy, or to create a model that is not available in kit form, modelers combine parts from several kits. These modifications are called kit bashing or cross-kitting. This type of activity is common practice among narrow gauge modelers.

Some experienced enthusiasts build locomotives, rolling stock, and structures from plans or photographs, working with raw materials and scrapbox parts. This scratch-building

Figure 1

A 2–8–2 Mikado locomotive as it appeared in the 1925 Locomotive Cyclopedia of American Practice. The pair of small wheels located at the front of the locomotive support a frame that carries part of the weight of the locomotive. The assembly is called a forward truck. The eight large wheels are called driving wheels. They provide the tractive effort to move the locomotive. The pair of small wheels located at the rear support the trailing truck, which also carries part of the locomotive's weight. Both the forward and trailing trucks are able to turn about a central pivot to enable the locomotive to round sharp curves.

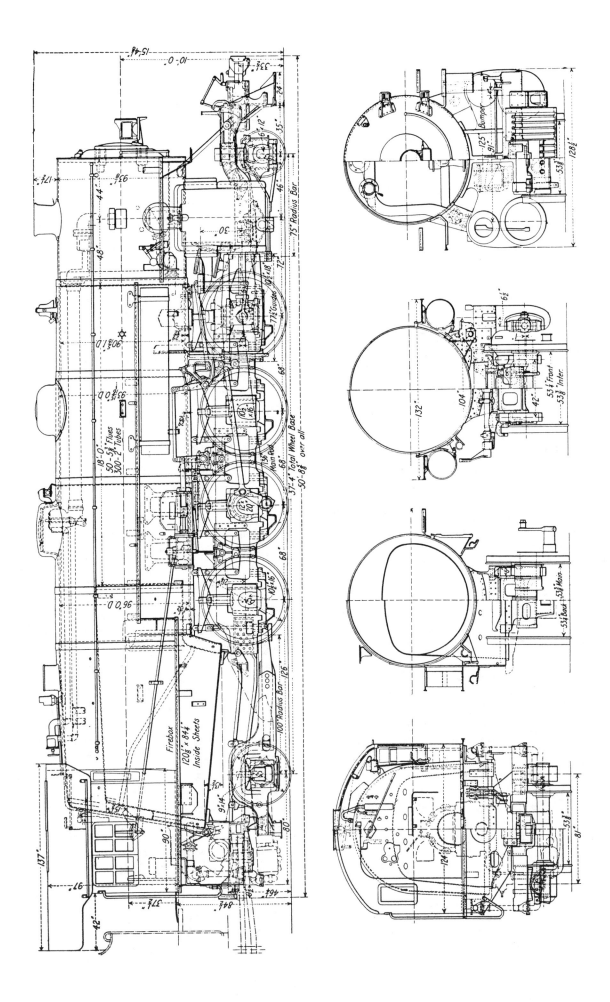

activity is an element of the hobby that is challenging, and rewards the hobbyist with a feeling of accomplishment. Scratch-builders make rubber molds in order to cast parts of resin. They use the lost wax casting method to make precise metal castings, and they vacuum form thin sheets of plastic into useful shapes. These techniques are described in hobby magazines and books such as Brick Price's book, *Modeling Narrow-Gauge Railroads.*

Expert scale modelers often treat the finish on a completed model to simulate the effects of age and weather. Weathered structures and rolling stock will appear to have aged wood, weather-beaten paint, and rusty metal. Tank cars will show liquid spills on their sides and older components will show a buildup of soot.

Layouts

An ideal completed train layout is composed of trackwork realistically positioned in an appropriate scenic diorama. Few modelers will admit that their layout is complete. There is always one more structure to be added, or change to be made. The first steps in layout construction involve research and planning. Decide how to get the most use out of a restricted space. If you are to achieve a realistic miniature replica of a full-sized railroad, your research will begin with historical societies and books that relate to the subject railroad. A few examples of railroad societies are listed in the bibliography, but a comprehensive list of over fifty-five such societies will be found as a monthly feature of *Mainline Modeler* magazine. Other sources of information include clubs, magazines, and field trips to the railroad site. Take plenty of pictures.

Planning and Assembling

Plan your electrical circuitry to permit maximum operating flexibility. Electrical current is usually supplied through the two rails. Sections of a layout are isolated from one another by making gaps in the rails. Current is supplied to the individual track sections by means of separate feeder wires. Electrical switches are used to turn sections on or off allowing a locomotive on one section to be stopped while another train can continue to move on another section. Electrical wiring becomes more involved when turnouts, crossovers, and other complex track patterns are used. Books on such wiring techniques are available at hobby stores that feature model railroad equipment.

Systems are available that control trains by means of coded pulsed signals sent along the rails. Separate channels are employed to control the speed and direction of more than one locomotive independently. Other systems use radio control, allowing additional control of accessories such as turnout motors, signals, and animation devices.

When your layout plan has been firmed up, the wooden substructure (benchwork) is assembled. The benchwork is an open grid that supports the trackwork at various levels. Materials such as plywood, homosote, and cork roadbed are installed between the benchwork and the track. Track is available in long flexible sections or as short rigid lengths that are either straight or curved. Some prefer to lay individual ties and spike the rails to them. A moveable track section called a switch or turnout is installed where a train is to be run off the main line onto a siding. Turnouts are numbered to signify how abrupt the turn will be. A number four turnout will require four inches of running track to displace the siding one inch to the side. A more gradual turn would occur using a number eight turnout where a one to eight ratio would be experienced. Restricted layout spaces require the lower numbered turnouts to make efficient use of space. The use of such turnouts sacrifices realism because full sized railroads use more gradual turns. A low numbered turnout and small radius curved track also restrict the length of a locomotive and rolling stock that can be used on the layout.

Managing the Job

The construction of permanent benchwork and associated scenery requires a long-term commitment. A way has been found to break the job up into more manageable pieces. Using modular construction, a layout is built in sections. One section may be two by six feet for example. All construction, including lightweight benchwork, scenery, structures, and track is completed on that module. The trackwork is laid to rigid specifications that permit the module to be assembled to another module made by a fellow modeler. There are many advantages to this approach: The construction of a module gets your layout in operation sooner. The portable module can be taken to a club location or train show and assembled with others to increase operating possibilities and create an impressive display. If you decide to change a section of your layout you can temporarily remove that portion without disturbing the use of the rest. Complex modules such as switching yards can be worked on comfortably at your workbench.

Some modelers with home computers make use of commercial computer programs that have been created to design layouts, customize railroad cars, and run simulated operational activities including coupling cars, and multiple train control. Other programs are available for those interested in simulating the operations of a full-scale railroad. For example, one program simulates activities at engine terminals, generates waybills, routes freight cars, and assigns locomotives to service various industries. It produces up to sixteen reports during the simulated operation. All of the above activities are paced by a special fast-running clock where perhaps five minutes of actual time represents an hour of full-scale operation, sort of a "scale" time.

The model railroading hobby exposes the modeler to a number of arts and crafts. We have seen the modeling required for the rolling stock, the carpentry required for the benchwork, and the electrical work required for powering the equipment. The simulated terrain that becomes part of the layout is accomplished by using plastic and plaster casting techniques to form hills and waterways. The resulting forms are airbrushed and dry-brushed to achieve realistic coloring. Commercial buildings and residential structures are modeled. Miniature trees and other vegetation are positioned to achieve realistic results. Many of these items are made from scrap materials at hand using photographs as a guide. Modelers find that they look at their surroundings differently after this activity. They see things they never noticed before—how the sun reflects off the landscape, and the picturesque shapes and shadows of old buildings. There's a lot to be learned by "playing with toy trains."

Tools

As you specialize in a given area of model railroading, you will find that certain tools are required. Tool selection will vary with the materials used in construction. In any case, you will need tools for measuring, cutting, bending, holding, fastening, and driving. Buy tools as you determine the need. See the sections in this text entitled "Model Aviation" for the listing of a starter set of modeling tools, and "Woodworking" for a listing of tools applicable to benchwork construction.

Bibliography

REFERENCE BOOKS

Carlson, Pierce. *Toy Trains: A History.* New York: Harper & Row, 1986. Covers toy train manufacture in Europe and America from trackless pull toys of the 1840s to the realistic trains of the 1950s. Useful, but dated, price guide for collectors.

The Complete Atlas Wiring Book. Atlas Model Railroad Co., 378 Florence Ave., Hillside, NJ 07205, 1992. Well illustrated text on electrical wiring for model rairoads.

Fraley, Donald S., ed. *Lionel Trains: Standard of the World, 1900–1943.* 2nd ed. Strasburg, PA: Train Collectors Association, 1989. Detailed catalog of Lionel products.

Garrison, Paul. *All About N Gauge Model Railroading.* Blue Ridge Summit, PA: TAB Books, 1982. Covers N scale model railroading. Discusses trackwork, structures, rolling stock, and electrical wiring.

Greenberg, Bruce C. *Greenberg's Guide to Lionel Trains: 1945–1969.* 2 vols. Sykesville, MD: Greenberg, 1987. Detailed catalog of Lionel products.

Griffin, Jeff W. *Modular Model Railroading.* Blue Ridge Summit, PA: TAB Books, 1986. Discusses the advantages of building layouts in portable sections. Good overview of track planning.

Kalmbach Editorial Staff. *The ABC's of Model Railroading: Model Railroad Handbook No. 11.* Waukesha, WI: Kalmbach, 1978. Includes planning, construction, wiring, structures, and operation.

Kalmbach Editorial Staff. *The Practical Guide to HO Model Railroading: Model Railroad Handbook No. 21.* Waukesha, WI: Kalmbach, 1986. A how-to book for beginners.

Kimball, Steven H., ed. *Greenberg's Guide to American Flyer Prewar O Gauge.* Sykesville, MD: Greenberg, 1987. Detailed catalog of American Flyer O gauge locomotives and rolling stock from 1907 to 1942, and 1945, 1946.

McComas, Tom, and James Tuohy. *Great Toy Train Layouts of America.* Wilmette, IL: TM Books, 1987. Well-illustrated coverage of selected toy train layouts owned by individuals, a museum, and the Lionel showroom in New York City.

Patterson, James, and Bruce C. Greenberg. *Greenberg's Guide to American Flyer S Gauge.* 3rd ed. Sykesville, MD: Greenberg, 1988. Detailed catalog of American Flyer S gauge products.

Price, Brick. *Modeling Narrow-Gauge Railroads.* Radnor, PA: Chilton, 1984. An overview of narrow-gauge railroad model designing, building, and operation. Covers tools, materials, trackwork, and building techniques.

Rohlfing, Christian F., ed. *Greenberg's Guide to Lionel Trains: 1901–1942,* 2 vols. Sykesville. MD: Greenberg, 1988. Detailed catalog of Lionel products.

Sorensen, Albert A. *Model Railroad Scenery and Detailing.* Blue Ridge Summit, PA: TAB Books, 1990. The techniques, materials, and tools required to build railroad dioramas. Also covers trackwork and detailing of rolling stock.

Westcott, Linn H. *How to Build Model Railroad Benchwork: Model Railroad Handbook No. 14.* Waukesha, WI: Kalmbach, 1979. Building benchwork and laying roadbed.

PERIODICALS

Classic Toy Trains. Kalmbach Publishers, Box 1612, Waukesha, WI 53187–1612.

Mainline Modeler. Hundman Publishers, 5115 Monticello Drive, Edmonds, WA 98020.

Model Railroader. Kalmbach Publishers, Box 1612, Waukesha, WI 53187–1612.

Narrow Gauge and Short Line Gazette. Benchmark Publications, Box 26, Los Altos, CA 94023.

O Gauge Railroading. PO Box 239, Nazareth, PA 18064–0239.

Railroad Model Craftsman. Carstens Publications, Box 700, Newton, NJ 07860.

ASSOCIATIONS

Anthracite Railroads Historical Society. PO Box 519, Lansdale, PA 19446–0519. Those interested in the history of the railroads serving the coal-mining regions of the northeastern United States. Publication: *Flags, Diamonds, and Statues* magazine.

Baltimore and Ohio Railroad Historical Society. PO Box 13578, Baltimore, MD 21203–3578. Those interested in railroad history, photography, and model trains. Publication: *Sentinel* magazine.

Chesapeake and Ohio Historical Society. PO Box 79, Clifton Forge, VA 24422. Railroad enthusiasts and model railroaders. Collects and preserves relative artifacts, engineering drawings, and photographs. Researches questions on C & O history upon request. Bestows awards. Publications: *Chesapeake and Ohio Historical Magazine,* and related material.

Lionel Collectors Club of America. PO Box 479, La Salle, IL 61301. Those interested in electric trains manufactured by Lionel. Provides for exchange of trains and train parts among members. Publication: *Interchange Track.*

Lionel Railroader Club. PO Box 748, New Baltimore, MI 48047–0748. Those interested in electric trains manufactured by Lionel. Acts as supply resource for members. Publication: *Inside Track from Lionel.*

National Model Railroad Association. 4121 Cromwell Road, Chattanooga, TN 37421. Amateur model railroad hobbyists, and others interested in scale model railroads and equipment. Conducts research and educational programs. Sponsors contests and bestows awards. Maintains library. Publications: *NMRA Bulletin, Official NMRA Standards and Recommended Practices,* and related material.

Toy Train Operating Society. 25 W. Walnut Street, Suite 308, Pasadena, CA 91103. Collectors and operators of toy trains. Sponsors competitions and bestows awards. Maintains library and museum. Conducts shows and swap meets. Publications: Directory, *TTOS Bulletin,* and related material.

Train Collectors Association. PO Box 248, Strasburg, PA 17579. Collectors of tin-plate toy trains. Operates public museum. Publication: *Train Collectors Quarterly.*

Motorcycles

MOTORCYCLES AND THEIR RIDERS enjoy unprecedented acceptance in today's world. The pastime is no longer limited to the young. Four "full dress" touring bikes were seen in the parking lot of a restaurant along the interstate highway. They had license plates from a state one thousand miles away. Two had feminine names painted on them, and all had a full complement of chromed accessories. Inside, two white-haired senior citizen couples in black leathers were enjoying their meal. Long may they ride! If there is one common characteristic among motorcycle riders, it's their passion for the sport and their equipment. Motorcycle activities and events parallel those that relate to the automobile. Some enthusiasts restore vintage bikes for pleasure or racing. Others enjoy collecting antique bikes and memorabilia. Almost all enjoy the company of fellow enthusiasts at rallies, tours, swap meets, and major events such as the Daytona Motorcycle Speed Week held in Florida each year in early March.

History

Motorcycles have a history that parallels the development of the motorcar. In 1885 Gottlieb Daimler built his Otto cycle engine and needed a test bed to try it out. He constructed a two-wheel vehicle, powered by his new engine, added a couple of training wheels to the sides to keep it from tipping over, and the world was presented with its first motorcycle.

The commercial manufacture and sale of motorcycles was soon to follow. In 1901 E. R. Thomas became the first American motorcycle maker to begin production. In 1903 William Davidson and William Harley, with assistance from Arthur and Walter Davidson, and advice from Ole Evinrude, produced the first Harley-Davidson motorcycle.

The 1950s saw powerful British machines imported, tuned, and raced. But in the late 1950s, and through the 1960s, the Japanese took over the market. Many manufacturers went out of business. Even Japanese manufacturers engaged in a sort of intramural competition that resulted in the relatively few big names active today emerging as the winners. Harley-Davidson is the sole remaining major United States motorcycle manufacturer.

Motorcycle Selection

To the uninitiated a motorcycle, or bike, is a bike. It has two wheels, an engine, and makes a lot of noise when the kid down the street lays rubber on the pavement. However, motorized bikes have become more sophisticated and adapted to specific uses. If you are contemplating the purchase of a bike, consider how you intend use it and look for a bike whose features match your needs. Sit on the saddle and take note of how well the relative positions of the handlebars, seat, and footrests match your bone structure. Compatibility with this so-called ergonomic triangle assures a comfortable ride.

While good low-powered machines are quite affordable, high-powered sport racers can cost more than a car. Insurance costs go up in direct relation to the horsepower of the bike, just as with cars, so check with your insurance agent before you buy. When selecting a dealer and brand name, check the availability of reliable service and spare parts. A big, shiny inexpensive bike may prove to be a lemon if you can't get proper service.

Street Bikes

The most popular bikes are called street bikes. They are designed for use on the road. Street bike features vary to suit specific applications:

Economy bikes are small and lightweight with low displacement engines. They are often chosen as a first bike by beginners, attracted by their low purchase price and economical operation.

Cruisers are stylish boulevard machines with low seats, sweeping handlebars, and forward foot pegs, or rests. Costs and engine displacements vary over a wide range.

Sport Bikes are fast, streamlined, and fitted with engines that provide power at high speeds. They usually have stable, firm suspensions, big brakes, and body fairings to smooth air flow. Engine displacements are in the 500 to 600cc range, and average fuel consumption is 40 to 50 mpg. Top speeds on the track reach as high as 122 mph. Open class sports bikes average over 1,000 cc engine displacement, and can reach almost 180 mph.

Touring bikes are built for comfort for long hours on the road. They have large displacement engines and many touring accessories including luggage storage. A typical example has a 1340cc engine, gets about 40 mpg, and can reach 90 mph. These bikes are usually expensive.

Off-the-Road Bikes

Dirt bikes are designed for use off-the-road on irregular terrain. This group of motorcycles has engines ranging from small to large displacements in incremental sizes to be raced in specific classes. They are designed to accelerate and stop quickly, have a tight turning radius, and have a maximum low speed throttle response. They have maximum ground clearance so the rider sits rather high. Fenders are placed well above the wheels to allow maximum wheel travel to absorb shock on uneven ground.

Dirt bikes are used for motocross racing. This type of racing is done on a dirt course designed by the sponsor, but approved for safety by the American Motorcyclist Association. It requires riding skill and special safety clothing and equipment. Dirt bikes are also used to explore undeveloped areas, with appropriate permission, and for just plain fun while negotiating irregular terrain.

Dual Purpose Bikes

Dual purpose bikes have some of the characteristics of both street and dirt bikes. They have the high saddle and maximum wheel travel of the dirt bike with some of the creature comforts of the street bike. Since they are a compromise design, they are used mainly for fun.

Other specialized designs such as four-wheel bikes are available. Though some of them are used for sport and racing, they are generally put to more utilitarian tasks around farms and industry. There is a three-wheel type that is less stable and is being phased out for some applications.

Safety

Safe operation of motorcycles requires wearing protective clothing and proper training in riding techniques. This is especially true for off-road riding. When a bike goes on its side, serious skin abrasions will result if tough clothing, boots, and helmet are not worn. Leather has been found to have unique properties that make it ideally suited for abrasion resistance. It is made up of irregular interconnected fibers that resist tearing and puncture. Its structure also lets moisture through, allowing leather garments to breathe. Seams are vulnerable to tear apart unless stitched with tough threads such as Kevlar. The best suits use fewer pieces in the construction to minimize seams. Suits made of synthetic materials such as Kevlar-blends and Cordura-blends are being introduced. Some include integral plastic body armor placed in areas most vulnerable to injury, such as at the knees, elbows, hips, and shoulders.

The Motorcycle Safety Foundation states that 30 percent of all bike accidents happen to riders in their first twelve months of operation. Check your local motorcycle dealer for a riding course in your area. Proper riding instruction will get you off to a good start on a lifetime of biking pleasure.

Bibliography

REFERENCE BOOKS

Clarke, Massimo. ed. *100 Years of Motorcycles: A Century of Development.* New York: Portland, 1988. Notable motorcycles from around the world. Well illustrated with photographs and drawings. Includes specifications and manufacturer's data.

Code, Keith. *A Twist of the Wrist II: The Basics of High-Performance Motorcycle Riding.* Venice, CA: Acrobat Books, 1993. Advanced motorcycle riding for both street and race riders.

Johns, Bruce A., and David D. Edmundson. *Motorcycles: Fundamentals, Service, Repair.* South Holland, IL: Goodheart-Willcox, 1987. A book for the novice mechanic to learn the basics to prepare you to work on motorcycles.

Reid, Peter C. *Well Made in America: Lessons From Harley-Davidson on Being the Best.* New York: McGraw-Hill, 1990. The story of Harley-Davidson's comeback. How a pioneering group of owner-managers pumped new life into the ailing motorcycle company.

Sucher, Harry V. *Harley-Davidson: The Milwaukee Marvel.* 4th ed. Newbury Park, CA: Haynes, 1990. Definitive history of Harley-Davidson motorcycles.

Wright, David K. *The Harley-Davidson Motor Company: An Official Eighty-Year History.* 2nd ed. Osceola, WI: Motorbooks International, 1983. Well-illustrated history of the company. Includes model designations for each year of production.

Wright, Owen. *BSA: The Complete Story.* Marlborough, Wiltshire, England: Crowood, 1992. The history of the BSA motorcycle. Well illustrated with significant examples.

PERIODICALS

American Motorcyclist. American Motorcyclist Association, Box 6114, Westerville, OH 43081–6114.

Cycle News. C N Publications, 2201 Cherry Avenue, Box 498, Long Beach, CA 90801.

Cycle World. Hachette Magazines, 1499 Monrovia Avenue, Newport Beach, CA 92663.

Dirt Rider Magazine. Petersen Publishers, 8490 Sunset Boulevard, Los Angeles, CA 90069.

Easyriders. Paisano Publications, 28210 Dorothy Drive, Box 3075, Agoura Hills, CA 91301.

Harley Women. Asphalt Angels Publications, Box 374, Streamwood, IL 60107.

Hot Bike. McMullen Publishers, 2145 W. La Palma Avenue, Anaheim, CA 92801.

Motorcycle Road Racer Illustrated. C N Publishers, 2201 Cherry Avenue, Long Beach, CA 90806.

Motorcyclist. Petersen Publications, 8490 Sunset Boulevard, Los Angeles, CA 90069.

Outlaw Biker. Outlaw Biker, 450 Seventh Avenue, Suite 2305, New York, NY 10001.

Road Rider. Fancy Publications, Box 6050, Mission Viejo, CA 92690.

ASSOCIATIONS

American Historic Racing Motorcycle Association. 4000 Mountain Lane, PO Box 882, Wausau, WI 54402–0882. Those interested in vintage racing motorcycles. Sponsors races and related activities. Publications: *AHRMA Competition Rulebook, Vintage Views,* and related materials.

American Motorcyclist Association. PO Box 6114, Westerville, OH 43081. Rulemaking body for motorcyle competition. Promotes highway safety, maintains museum and hall of fame. Publications: *AMA Pro Report, American Motorcycle Association—Action,* and *American Motorcyclist Magazine.*

Antique Motorcycle Club of America. c/o D. K. Wood, 14943 York Road, Sparks, MD 21152. Those interested in collecting and restoring antique motorcycles. Maintains library and bestows awards. Publications: *Antique Motorcycle,* and related materials.

Bikers Against Manslaughter. 5455 Wilshire Boulevard, Room 1600, Los Angeles, CA 90036. Those united to reduce motorcycle accidents. Conducts educational and research programs. Maintains library and bestows awards. Publications: *BAM News Service.*

BMW Motorcycle Owners of America. PO Box 489, Chesterfield, MO 63006. BMW owners organized for mutual benefit, such as recreation, safety, and information exchange. Publication: *BMW News.*

Christian Motorcyclists Association. PO Box 1265, Levelland, TX 79336. Promotes Christian fellowship among motorcyclists. Conducts rallies, tours, and religious events. Publication: *CMA Newsletter.*

Gold Wing Road Riders Association. PO Box 14350, Phoenix, AZ 85063. Owners of Honda Gold Wing motorcycles organized for mutual benefit, such as recreation, safety, and information exchange. Sponsors competitions and bestows awards. Publications: Directory, *Wing World Magazine,* and related materials.

Harley Owners' Group. PO Box 653. 3700 W. Juneau, Milwaukee, WI 53208. Owners of Harley-Davidson motorcycles organized for mutual benefit, such as recreation, motorcycle rental, and information exchange. Maintains museum and bestows awards. Publications: *Hogtales* newsletter, and related materials.

Rider Club. 29901 Agoura Road, Agoura Hills, CA 91301. Promotes motorcycle touring. Sponsors competitions. Publication: *Rider Magazine.*

Wheelchair Motorcycle Association. 101 Torrey Street, Brockton, MA 02401. Handicapped persons confined to wheelchairs interested in rediscovering the outdoors. Researches, develops, and tests off-road vehicles for quadriplegics and other severely handicapped persons. Publication: *Climb for Independence.*

Women on Wheels. PO Box 5147, Topeka, KS 66605. Women motorcyclists united to gain recognition from the motorcycle industry concerning the needs of females. Publications: *Women on Wheels Magazine,* and membership directory.

Women's International Motorcycle Association. 360 E. Main Street, Waterloo, NY 13165. Women interested in international motorcycle competition. Conducts competitions and bestows awards. Publication: *WIMA News.*

Movies and the VCR

TEENAGERS AND YOUNG ADULTS comprise the majority of moviegoers. As a result, most movies slated for theater viewing are aimed at that segment of the population. The older set is more likely to rent video movies. This poses a problem for producers who desire a video revival of their films made for the younger theater audience. This accounts for the fact that some films aimed at the older population don't do well in the theaters, but enjoy financial success in the video market. The expansion in home video watching has caused increased viewer interest in films. The unexpected result is that home viewers are now attending the theater more often. As the anticipated increase in the average age of the population takes place, and older patrons frequent the theaters, their needs will have to be considered more carefully by movie producers.

Renting videos is the only way people have of seeing films that appeal to a small segment of the population. Because of their limited appeal, such videos may not be stocked by local stores. Those who live in remote areas have an optional way to obtain off-beat videos. Mail-order video organizations will mail videos that you select from their catalogs. You will usually have three days to view the video before returning it in the special mailer provided. Most special interest associations also have videos available for loan or purchase by their members.

As TV networks insert more commercial breaks into programmed movies, the public will be more inclined to turn to rental videos when they want to see an old favorite again without interruption. In the meantime, there is a trend toward showing old movies in certain theaters in many communities. The theaters continue to fight back.

History

Watching motion pictures has been a favorite pastime for ninety years. Thomas A. Edison introduced a fifteen second peep-show device called a kinetoscope in 1894. He would be amazed to see what has developed since. It became possible to project moving pictures on a screen with Thomas Armat's vitascope in 1896. Presentation time jumped to a full minute. The vitascope made an interesting diversion when played between vaudeville acts. The first real narrative film was *The Great Train Robbery,* shown in 1903. This eight-minute feature launched the motion picture industry.

Presentations of early black and white movies were accompanied by on-screen subtitles and mood music, usually furnished by piano. Sound effects were sometimes added manually using various devices. A way needed to be found to add music and sound effects to the performance without the piano player. At first a phonograph was tried, but it was found difficult to link and synchronize it with the picture. In addition, the sound wasn't loud enough to reach the back rows. With the invention of Lee De Forest's radio tube, the needed sound amplification became available. De Forest provided another breakthrough in 1923 when he found a way to record a sound track directly on film. By 1930, silent films were a thing of the past; talkies were in.

Color pictures were introduced in 1922, but quality problems resulted in slow acceptance. Good results were finally demonstrated in 1939 with the landmark film, *Gone With the Wind.*

Soon after World War II, television appeared and began to draw audiences away from theaters. The theater industry fought back in 1952 with the introduction of wide screens and stereo sound systems. What was becoming a disaster for theater owners turned out to be a boon to motion picture production companies. Hundreds of new films were needed to fill time on the growing number of TV channels. The studios sold existing films and used their facilities to produce new films and programs for TV.

Another assault on the movie theaters began in 1969 in the form of the videocassette recorder (VCR). Home viewers could record TV movies for later viewing or rent videocassettes (videos) from video rental stores. Films produced for viewing in theaters took on a second life as rental videos. Once again theater owners fought back, subdividing theaters into multiple units, each showing different movie titles to please most every taste.

Advanced Television Systems

Major changes are occurring in the television industry. Research and development have produced high resolution digital television with movie-like quality. By converting the TV picture to a digital mode, we can now narrow the TV signal band width, making it possible to send more channels on a cable network. In addition, new fiber optic cables have almost no limit to band width capability. The combination of these factors permits the transmission of many more channels. The possibility of as many as 400 cable channels will have TV broadcasters scrambling to find programming material to fill the new channels. So, much of the off-beat, limited-appeal material now furnished on video tape may be programmed on cable.

The digital revolution may help theater owners, at least in the short run. Direct broadcast satellites can be used to beam the latest digitized movies to theaters. The movie house will process the signals and show the movie on its screen. Once again the balance between home viewing and theater attendance may be restored.

Bibliography

REFERENCE BOOKS

Ebert, Roger. *Roger Ebert's Movie Home Companion.* Kansas City, MO: Andrews, McMeel & Parker, 1992. Full length reviews of films on cassette. Includes cast list and rating.

Everson, William K. *The Hollywood Western.* New York: Citadel, 1992. Traces the ninety-year history of western films.

Hay, Peter. *MGM: When the Lion Roars.* Atlanta, GA: Turner, 1991. A definitive look at the history of the MGM movie studio. Well illustrated with photographs, posters, lobby cards, magazine covers, and other memorabilia from significant movies.

Kael, Pauline. *5001 Nights at the Movies.* Rev. ed. New York: Holt, 1991. Informative reviews of a range of movies covering more than fifty years. Includes both American and foreign films. No video information is provided.

Lloyd, Ann, ed. *Movies of the Thirties.* London: Orbis, 1983. Covers an important decade in movie history. Best films are described and illustrated.

Maltin, Leonard, ed. *Leonard Maltin's TV Movies and Video Guide: 1993 Edition.* New York: New American Library, 1992. Brief reviews of more than 18,000 films, both good and bad. Listings include ratings and identify films that are available on videocassette.

Quinlan, David. *Quinlan's Illustrated Directory of Film Comedy Actors.* New York: Holt, 1992. Profiles the careers of nearly 300 movie comedy stars.

Vermilye, Jerry. *The Films of the Twenties.* Secaucus, NJ: Citadel, 1985. Reviews of selected films of the twenties, well illustrated with photos of famous motion picture figures of the period. Credits are listed for both production staff and actors.

———. *More Films of the Thirties.* New York: Citadel, 1989. Reviews of selected films of the thirties, profusely illustrated with photos of famous motion picture figures of the period. Credits are listed for both production staff and actors.

PERIODICALS

Adult Video News. 8600 West Chester Pike, Suite 300, Upper Darby, PA 19082.

American Classic Screen. American Classic Screen, Box 7150, Shawnee Mission, KS 66207.

Big Reel. Empire Publishers, 3130 U.S. 220, Madison, NC 27025. (Film buff forum.)

Black Film Review. Sojourner Productions, 2025 I Street, NW, Suite 213, Washington, DC 20006.

Bowker's Complete Video Directory, 3 vols. R. R Bowker, 121 Chanlon Road, New Providence, NJ 07974. (Library reference—contains 75,000 videos.)

Catalog of Captioned Films For the Deaf. Associations for Education of the Deaf, Special Materials Project, c/o Association Builder Contra., 4061 Powder Mill Road, Beltsville, MD 20705–3149.

Coming Attractions. Star Video Entertainment LP, 550 Grand Street, Jersey City, NJ 07302–4112. (New videocassette releases.)

Facets Features. Facets Multimedia, 1517 W. Fullerton Avenue, Chicago, IL 60614. (International films and video, including foreign, independent, and classic.)

Fiesta En Video. 331 Jaffry Road, Peterborough, NH 03458. (Available video movies in Spanish.)

Film Comment. Film Society of Lincoln Center., 70 Lincoln Center Plaza, New York, NY 10023. (Film criticism and history.)

Film Quarterly. University of California Press, Journals Division, Berkeley, CA 94720. (Experimental, documentary, and special interest films.)

Film Threat Video Guide. Film Threat Video, 2805 W. Magnolia, Burbank, CA 91505. (The new and unusual on video.)

The Motion Picture Guide Annual. Baseline-CineBooks, R. R Bowker, Distributer, 121 Chanlon Road, Box 31, New Providence, NJ 07974. (Library reference—detailed reviews of domestic and foreign features released in the U.S. during the previous year).

Movie Collectors World. Arena Publishers, Box 309, Fraser, MI 48026.

Movie Marketplace. World Publishers Co., 990 Grove St., Evanston, IL 60201–4370. (Video listings available for direct purchase.)

Orbit Video. Orbit Publishers, 8330 Boone Boulevard, Suite 600, Vienna, VA 22180. (Reviews of video releases.)

Parent's Guide to Children's Video. 2601 Ocean Park Boulevard, Suite 200, Santa Monica, CA 90405. (Reviews videos for ages 3–12.)

Take One: The Video Entertainment Newspaper. Falcon Publications, 1601 Broadway, Box 1028, Little Rock, AR 72203. (New movies on videocassette each month.)

Video Event. Connell Communications, 331 Jaffry Road, Peterborough, NH 03458. (Reviews of video releases.)

Video Magazine. Reese Communications, 460 W. 34th Street, New York, NY 10001.

Video Source Book. Gale Research, Dept. 77748, Detroit, MI 48226. (Library reference—contains 125,000 videotapes and discs.)

ASSOCIATIONS

American Film Institute. John F. Kennedy Center for the Performing Arts, Washington, DC 20566. Dedicated to preserving and developing the nation's resources in film and video. Goals are to catalog and preserve films and bring outstanding films to public attention through the American Film Institute in the Kennedy Center. Maintains exhibition services to produce touring film series, and conducts TV and video services to develop new audiences for the video arts. Publications: *American Film,* and *Catalog of Motion Pictures Produced in the United States.*

American Film and Video Association. PO Box 48659, 8050 Millawake, Niles, IL 60714. Those interested in 16mm film and video. Maintains information library, bestows awards. Publications: Evaluations of films, videos, and books on audiovisual education. Also publishes a bulletin, and related material.

Anthology Film Archives. 32–34 2nd Avenue, New York, NY 10003. Maintains research facilities open to scholars and the public. Facilities include visual and written research library, nightly public screening of films in the collection, and presentation of video works.

Film Advisory Board. 1727½ N. Sycamore, Hollywood, CA 90028. Previews and evaluates films and promotes better entertainment in motion pictures and video. Bestows awards. Publications: Film, TV, and video listings, and reviews.

Hollywood Studio Collectors Club. 3960 Laurel Canyon Boulevard, Suite 450, Studio City, CA 91614. Movie memorabilia collectors and film buffs. Conducts research on motion picture history and maintains biographical archives on the movie industry. Publication: *Hollywood Studio Magazine.*

National Center for Film and Video Preservation. c/o American Film Institute, 2021 N. Western Avenue, Los Angeles, CA 90027. Coordinates American film and TV preservation activities by locating, and preserving films and TV programs for inclusion in the AFI collection at the Library of Congress. Publications: *AFI Catalog of Feature Films,* and related material.

Old Time Western Film Club. c/o Milo Holt, PO Box 142, Siler City, NC 27344. Fans of old time western films. Maintains museum, library, and hall of fame. Publication: Newsletter.

Sons of the Desert. PO Box 8341, Universal City, CA 91608. Stan Laurel and Oliver Hardy fans. Maintains biographical archives and bestows awards. Publications: *Pratfall,* and a journal.

Music, Appreciation

THE MORE WE KNOW about an activity, the more likely we are to appreciate the contributions of an expert in the field. This is especially true of the arts. Those who have learned to play a musical instrument will be intrigued by the performance of a master musician. Music is all around us today. Modern sound systems communicate most of the colorful nuances of sound to our ears. But we must learn to listen. Obtaining an understanding of what to expect adds to the thrill of anticipation. When we see a live musical performance, the combination of sight, sound, and feel of the music has a great impact.

A famous radio personality used to say, "Unbutton your ears dear children and I will tell you a story." We can only add, unbutton your senses to the wonderful world of music.

The Elements of Music

A musical composition owes its character to the mix of certain elements, emphasized to varying degrees in all music. The elements are rhythm, melody, harmony, color, and form.

Rhythm regulates the flow of music. It creates the regularity or irregularity of the beat. Rhythm contributes to the establishment of musical measures, phrases, and to the entire composition.

Melody is a series of tones sounded one after another to make a succession of pitches.

Harmony is the simultaneous sound of two or more tones. They may originate from combinations of voices, instruments, or both. As Benjamin Franklin wrote, "An agreeable succession of sounds is called a melody, and only the coexistence of agreeable sounds harmony."

Musical color is the sum of the factors that make up a composer's or a performer's style. It is influenced by the choice of instruments used. That choice may be determined by the time and place the composition originated.

Musical form consists of a variety of patterns. The pattern structure is based upon repetition and contrast—unity and variety. A three-part or ternary form contains a musical idea, or phrase, followed by a contrasting idea, and then returns to the first. It may be expressed as A–B–A. Often the first phrase is repeated—A–A–B–A. Such units of phrases can then be built into a larger formation with like, or dissimilar, phrase structure.

Categories of Musical Composition

A sonata is a musical composition for any single instrument, or more commonly, for any such instrument and the piano.

The first movement of a sonata consists of three sections. The first section is the exposition, or statement, that sets forth two opposing keys and their respective themes. The second, development, section wanders through a series of keys, building up tension against the return home. The third, recapitulation, section returns to the first section, restating the first and second themes more or less in their original form. The second movement is usually slow and contemplative. The third movement is of a lively nature. While the first movement usually adheres to the sonata form, the form of subsequent movements can vary significantly.

The history of the sonata as a three-part concept dates back to the time of Bach.

The symphony may be considered a sonata for orchestra, following sonata-form in the first movement, but free to follow other forms in subsequent movements. Most symphonies consist of four movements. The symphonic format solidified during the time of Haydn and Mozart. It is the primary form for large-scale orchestral music.

Simply stated, the concerto provides solo display of one, or as many as three instruments in collaboration with the orchestra. The first movement is usually in sonata form, the second slow in tempo, and the third is a lively movement called a rondo.

Chamber music is for an ensemble of instruments, each playing its own part. This differs from an orchestra where identical parts are played by groups of players. One of the most often featured groups is the string quartet.

A suite is an instrumental composition in which various sections or movements, most frequently of a dance-like character, are combined in free succession. The suite is of baroque origin and connotes a series of dances, all written in the same key, with each dance representative of a different national style.

An anthem is a choral composition, with or without accompaniment. Once mainly religious, now it may also be nationalistic, as in a national anthem.

A cantata is a vocal composition consisting of arias (solos), recitatives (spoken parts), ensembles, and choruses. Originally it was used primarily for church music. This form was used extensively by Bach.

The madrigal is an unaccompanied song, usually for two or three voices. It is very free and unstructured. The madrigal dates back to the thirteenth century.

The Mass is a most solemn form of worship in the Roman Catholic Church. The High Mass has been celebrated with choral compositions down through the ages.

The motet originally was a composition for an unaccompanied choir with a sacred text. During seven centuries of evolution it retained the sacred Latin text, but the option of an instrumental accompaniment was added.

An opera is a large staged work which is sung, or mostly sung, by soloists and ensembles, with an instrumental accompaniment ranging from chamber music to orchestras.

The Evolution of Music as an Art Form

Historians like to classify music according to time periods that have been assigned to art. We see references to music of the baroque, classic, or impressionist eras. This is brought about by the close relationship between music, art, architecture, mathematics, the political climate, and various style characteristics they have in common.

Plato said, "The introduction of a new kind of music must be shunned as imperiling the whole state, since styles of music are never disturbed without affecting the most important political institutions." Sound familiar?

Greek mathematician Pythagoras demonstrated that simple numerical ratios produce all the intervals necessary to create a musical scale. But it wasn't until the eleventh century that the Benedictine monk Guido d'Arezzo perfected a four line staff in which both lines and spaces were used to assign notes.

In the following discussion we'll look at some important contributors to the advancement of music, and at the era in which they began significant work. Many were

active beyond the era. Some changed their style in subsequent eras to accommodate new thinking.

Baroque Era

The term baroque was used to mean something bizarre. In music it implies fundamental transformation. And, with no apology to Plato, music was changed during this period.

Johann Sebastian Bach (1685–1750) started his career as a church organist and was associated with church music for most of his life. Bach drew from the works of others and whatever he touched he brought to its ultimate development. There was no facet of music, except the opera, that he did not enrich. A prolific composer and a virtuoso organist, he also had a sense of humor. When complimented on his playing he responded, "There is nothing remarkable about it. All you have to do is hit the right notes at the right time and the instrument plays itself."

Bach was almost forgotten soon after his death. It wasn't until 1829, when Felix Mendelssohn directed a performance of one of Bach's works, that his genius came again to the world's attention.

George Frederick Handel (1685–1759) was the son of a surgeon who opposed his interest in music. Handel would secretly practice on a small harpsichord located in his garret. After the death of his father, he settled in Hamburg and began to write operas. He traveled to Italy and eventually moved to England, where he became the most popular and successful composer in the country.

Handel wrote forty operas, famous oratorios, and concertos. Although he became completely blind seven years before his death, he continued to write music, play the organ, and conduct performances.

Classic Period

Music of this period was based upon accepted conventions of form. The musical language formulated previously enabled classical composers to give free reign to their imagination and to build on earlier musical structures, such as balance and symmetry.

Ludwig van Beethoven (1770–1827) was taught to play the harpsichord by his father. While in Vienna at age seventeen he met and impressed Mozart, who predicted a great future in music for the boy. Later he was given lessons by Haydn. Beethoven's early compositions used Haydn's and Mozart's work as models. In time his own technique began to emerge as he developed slow emotional movements and sudden forceful changes in style. He contributed significantly to the growth of the symphony, sonata, concerto, and string quartet. Beethoven began to lose his hearing at the age of thirty and was completely deaf in the last years of his life. During that period he composed great music that he never heard.

Joseph Haydn (1732–1809) studied violin and harpsichord as a youth. His further development in a choir school was abruptly terminated when his voice broke at seventeen. Most of his working career involved the direction of orchestras at the palaces of noblemen. During this period he wrote music for the string quartet, symphonies, oratorios, and an anthem which became the Austrian National Anthem. Haydn is credited with making notable advances in harmonic writing and orchestration. Haydn and Mozart were close friends.

Wolfgang Amadeus Mozart (1756–1791) was a child prodigy. His violinist father recognized Mozart's talents, and music lessons were begun at the age of four. He wrote sonatas, symphonies, and an opera by the time he was fourteen. As a child he was welcomed and acclaimed by Europe's royal courts. As Mozart matured, the novelty wore off, and he lived much of his life in poverty. He is considered a master of technique and a musical genius. Despite acclaim for such notable operas as *The Marriage of Figaro* and *Don Giovanni,* his financial problems continued and he was buried in a pauper's grave.

Romantic Era

This period brought a diversity of forms and styles to music as well as art. Composers tended to prefer instrumental music to vocal music.

Johannes Brahms (1833–1897) showed great promise very early in life. While still a boy he arranged music for small local bands. He gave his first concert at fourteen. His work was influenced by his fondness for the works of Beethoven and Schumann. He wrote fine chamber music, piano music, and more than 200 songs; the latter no doubt resulting from his love of folk songs and dances.

Frederic François Chopin (1810–1849) began piano lessons at eight. His second teacher, Joseph Elsner, is credited with allowing Chopin to develop a free personal style. Chopin's primary contribution is the writing of exceptional works for the piano. Born in Poland, he moved to Paris where he enjoyed considerable success.

Antonin Dvorak (1841–1904) completed a thorough musical education and played the viola and organ for an orchestra in Prague. He wrote a symphony and an opera. Dvorak achieved fame through his next orchestral work, "Slavonic Dances." In 1892 he came to New York to direct the National Conservatory. While in the United States he wrote a successful symphony and other works before retiring to his native land in 1895. He is noted for his richly melodic music.

Franz Liszt (1811–1886) studied piano in Vienna. He established his career in Paris, developing his talents to the point that he was recognized as the premier pianist of the day. Liszt originated the public solo piano recital as we know it today. He directed orchestral and operatic performances. His prodigious output of musical composition included a thousand works in virtually every form.

Gustav Mahler (1860–1911) studied music in Vienna. After graduation he served as the conductor for a series of prestigious opera companies in Europe and the United States. During this period he wrote symphonies, songs for voice and orchestra, and voice and piano. His symphonies were large and profound. They were not well received at the time.

Felix Mendelssohn (1809–1847) started composing music at the age of seven in Germany. He wrote his first symphony and a comic opera at fifteen. He introduced the public to the works of Bach, restoring that composer to his rightful position. Mendelssohn conducted orchestras, served in the court of the King of Prussia, and later taught music. During this period he wrote symphonies, an orchestral suite, concertos, oratorios, and other piano works.

Franz Schubert (1797–1828) taught school children and wrote music. During his eighteenth year alone he wrote two symphonies, five operas, two Masses, and almost 150 songs. He abandoned the teaching profession and although his works were neither published nor performed, he kept writing. A successful concert featured his works just two years before his death. Much of Schubert's work lay forgotten for years before being rediscovered. His work emphasizes beautiful melody.

Robert Schumann (1810–1856) gave up the study of law to concentrate on music. He suffered a temporary paralysis of the hand while practicing piano. Schumann then turned to composition. Inspired by a happy marriage, he produced some beautiful love songs. Other subsequent work included symphonies and chamber music. He is noted for his piano compositions.

Peter Ilich Tchaikovsky (1840–1893) completed his studies for law and pursued that career while beginning the study of music. Upon graduation from the music conservatory, he accepted a professorship at the Moscow Music Conservatory. Subsequent compositions proved interesting to a wealthy patroness, Mme. von Meck. She provided the financial security he needed to concentrate on his greatest works. He is noted for symphonies, the melodies often derived from Russian folk songs.

Giuseppe Verdi (1813–1901) completed his studies in music and took a job as conductor of an orchestra. During this time he wrote his first successful opera—the first of many. Verdi then refrained from operatic composition for sixteen years. Shortly before his death he enjoyed an additional productive period and composed several notable operas. He is considered to be the most famous opera composer of his generation.

Richard Wagner (1813–1883) saw his first symphony performed in 1833. He wrote a series of operas during a turbulent life. Gambling and rejection of his work caused financial difficulties. He was forced to live in exile following the threat of imprisonment for revolutionary activities. During his twelve-year exile he formulated new ideas for operatic composition that resulted in the production of music dramas that made him famous. Wagner was pardoned in 1860 and returned to a productive and successful career. He changed the course of operatic art.

Nationalist Era

Aaron Copland (1900–1990) studied music in the United States and France. After several minor preliminary pieces he wrote his first symphony, introduced in 1925. The success of the symphony led to commissions for additional compositions. Copland received a series of awards for his work, assuring his financial security. In the late 1930s he made an effort to simplify his style. He is noted for a variety of popular works including symphonies, music for children, music for movies, and ballet.

Johann Strauss II (1825–1899) studied violin in Vienna. He began his career as a musical conductor at a casino in 1844. Strauss composed waltzes during this period, but his best were written after 1864. Subsequently he wrote several operettas. He is noted for his compositions of popular music.

Impressionist Era

Bela Bartok (1881–1945) started composing at nine. After completing musical studies he taught piano, acquiring a professorship in 1907. Bartok's music is the product of a variety of influences. He undertook an intensive study of Hungarian folk music, uncovering several thousand such melodies. Bartok's work reflected the primitive aspects of the folk music he discovered. It wasn't very popular at the time. He was more than an impressionist. His admiration for Bach and Beethoven caused him to employ a unity of form and material that was inspired by the spirit, but did not imitate the methods, of these composers. In 1940 he moved to the United States and wrote a series of concertos in a simplified style that was well received. Recognition of his genius came soon after his death.

Claude Debussy (1862–1918) completed his musical studies and acquired a position as a pianist. He wrote several cantatas before settling in Paris. Debussy was influenced by his contemporaries in the arts who wished to promote an impressionist movement in France. Success came quickly as he wrote works for the orchestra, piano, and for voice. He is noted for founding the impressionist school of music.

Maurice Ravel (1875–1937) studied at the Paris Conservatory. By 1905 he had written several distinguished works for piano. At the outset of World War I he was accepted as the foremost living composer in France. He is noted for his interest in many styles. They include Spanish song, satire, the Viennese waltz, fantasy, and impressionism.

Expressionist Era

Arnold Schoenberg (1874–1951) studied music in Vienna. He started his musical career as a conductor for a cabaret orchestra in Berlin. His early compositions evolved from a Romantic style to an arbitrary style that was based on twelve definite tones. Radical for the time, his approach was slow to gain acceptance. He is noted for having conceived the most revolutionary changes in music. His works included compositions for piano, strings, and orchestra.

Igor Stravinsky (1882–1971) completed his musical education with two years of study with Rimsky-Korsakov. His first orchestral works were a success. Stravinsky's next commissions and assignments involved music for ballet. His style included dissonance and multiple rhythms, which were somewhat unique for their time.

During his career Stravinsky moved from Russia to Switzerland, then Paris, and finally to the United States. While in Paris he was influenced to adopt a simpler, more formal style. He is noted for his compositions for symphony, opera, ballet, and a Mass.

Early American

Stephen Collins Foster (1826–1864) began to write music as a young boy. He wrote over 200 songs, including the lyrics for most of them. Unlike many great composers, he had little musical training. Foster wished to be known as the best writer of black minstrel songs, and many of his compositions were inspired by southern life and melodies heard at Negro church services. It is surprising that he visited the south only once.

George Gershwin (1898–1937) took music lessons in New York City. Most of his teachers tried to persuade him to stay with the classics, but George wanted to write popular music from the beginning. He earned his living as a pianist in a music publishing house. One of his first songs was published in 1916. Gershwin's work consisted of songs, musical comedies, piano concertos and an opera. His musical innovation made a vital and self-respecting art out of the popular song, by bringing to it the harmonic, rhythmic, and melodic resources of serious music.

John Philip Sousa (1854–1932) began violin lessons when he was ten, followed by study of musical theory and composition. His early years were spent in civilian orchestras, the Marine Band, and as director of a band in a comedy theater house. This background led to a varied and distinguished body of work. He wrote ten comic operas, three novels, and his autobiography. Most important, however, were his marches. They resulted in his international acclaim and the title, "March King." His skill in composition and arrangement contributed significantly to the stature of the Marine Band in Washington during the twelve years he served as director.

Ragtime

Ragtime was introduced in the 1890s. The name derived from the ragged timing of the upper notes played with a simultaneous steady bass beat. This placing of musical accents on beats not normally accented is called syncopation. The technique, as applied to ragtime, has roots in the rhythms brought to America by African slaves. It is also found in the work of other early composers. John Philip Sousa used the principle well before the popularity of ragtime.

Scott Joplin (1868–1917) played a key role in the elevation of ragtime music to its status as a respectable musical form during the early 1900s. Before Joplin's time, ragtime was played only in saloons and brothels. Joplin rose from humble beginnings and achieved national prominence through persistent dedication to his music and a high level of creative talent.

Ferdinand "Jelly Roll" Morton (1885–1941) published many piano rags starting in 1918. He recorded the story of his life for the Library of Congress, with musical illustrations at the piano.

Thomas "Fats" Waller (1904–1943) composed his first rag at the age of fifteen. Many of his 400 compositions were piano rags.

Blues

The blues are a form of Afro-American folk music in solo singing. The form consists of a sorrowful, lamenting strain, often combined with an undertone of humor.

William Christopher Handy (1873–1958) was particularly associated with the rise of the blues as a type of popular music. He wrote "Memphis Blues" and "St. Louis Blues."

Many great composers also popularized the blues as a type of popular song, including Irving Berlin, George Gershwin, and Jerome Kern.

Jazz

Jazz made its appearance about 1916. It is characterized by sounding treble notes out of time with the bass beat. Players improvise freely, interacting with both complementary and contrasting rhythms.

Louis "Satchmo" Armstrong (1900–1971) was a notable exponent of jazz. His long and illustrious career was highlighted by international tours made on behalf of the U.S. State Department to promote international goodwill. He possessed a natural talent and good humor that endeared him to fans the world over.

Edward Kennedy "Duke" Ellington (1899–1974) was playing jazz almost ten years before the musical style became popular. His highly successful career spanned half a century. Duke was acclaimed internationally as the greatest jazz musician.

Dixieland jazz has its roots in the New Orleans area. Some Dixieland groups were composed of players who would go on to lead their own bands. One notable band leader was Earnest Loring "Red" Nichols (1905–1965), who occasionally employed sidemen Jimmy Dorsey, Benny Goodman, Eddie Lang, Miff Mole, and Joe Venuti.

The 1930s saw the emergence of swing and the Big Band era. Swing is a simple type of jazz that has a strong rhythmic and unvarying bass, with a melody improvised above with embellishments.

There were many fine musical groups during the Big Band era. Admirers of the music of the period can enjoy the works of Count Basie, Bunny Berigan, Les Brown, Cab Calloway, Benny Carter, Larry Clinton, Bob Crosby, Jimmy Dorsey, Tommy Dorsey, Duke Ellington, Benny Goodman, Glen Gray, Lionel Hampton, Horace Heidt, Woody Herman, Harry James, Hal Kemp, Gene Krupa, Kay Kyser, Guy Lombardo, Jimmie Lunceford, Ray McKinley, Glenn Miller, Ray Noble, Red Norvo, Artie Shaw, Charlie Spivak, Jack Teagarden, Claude Thornhill, Chick Webb, and Paul Whiteman.

In bebop or bop jazz, the rhythm was carried on the cymbal, with only the occasional use of the bass drum. The string bass also carried rhythm as well as melody. Bop is the manner in which notes are phrased and accented. Every other note is accented.

Musicians associated with the development of bop include Thelonius Monk, Charlie "Bird" Parker, and John Birks "Dizzy" Gillespie.

By the end of the 1940s bop had run its course and a cooling-off period began. A chamber-music type of cool jazz evolved, utilizing brass, saxophones, bass, piano, and drum. Trumpet player Miles Davis, arranger Gil Evans, and saxophonist Gerry Mulligan helped define the new direction in jazz.

A reaction to cool jazz began in the late 1950s. The trend was back to a more primitive folk-rooted jazz combined with blues and gospel style. Musicians involved with the movement included saxophonists Stan Getz, John Coltrane, and Sonny Rollins.

Rock and Roll and Rap

During the 1950s there were three distinct music classifications in addition to the classics. The first was Rhythm and Blues, consisting of rhythm and gospel, jazz, and blues. The second was the so-called popular, or Pop, listing. The third was Country and Western.

When gospel, jazz, and rhythm and blues were combined with country and western, rock and roll began. Chuck Berry was one of the early figures in rock and roll.

Another integration of music classifications soon occurred when Elvis Presley came on the scene combining rock and roll with country and western. The result was called rockabilly. It lasted from about 1956 to 1958.

Rock and roll, or rock, has gone through many stages, keeping pace with the times. The Beatles introduced their sound in 1964.

Folk music merged with rock during a period of Vietnam War protest. This was followed by soul music combining gospel, blues, country, and rock.

During the 1970s rock divided into soft and hard rock. Soft rock featured disco dance music combining Latin music with rock and rhythm and blues. Hard rock featured loud, distorted, and primal sounds called heavy metal, and the still more violent punk rock.

Another form of rock called raggae came to the United States from Jamaica. The music has roots in political protest in its country of origin.

Rock was joined by rap in the mid 1980s. Rap is a sort of chant, characterized by rapid rhyming speech keeping time with a strong beat background. It is used by some as a form of protest.

Old Favorites Endure

When jazz was at its peak, lovers of classical music feared that it would replace the classics in the hearts of many. The classics survived. As modern musical styles take syncopation, overwhelming electronic amplification and strident sounds to the limit, radio stations featuring nostalgic music of the past find increasing popularity. Once again we find that music styles are diverse enough to satisfy everyone, though Plato would be aghast.

Bibliography

REFERENCE BOOKS

Chase, Gilbert. *America's Music: From the Pilgrims to the Present.* 2nd ed. New York: McGraw-Hill, 1966. A far-reaching chronicle of American music.

Collier, James Lincoln. *Duke Ellington.* New York: Macmillan, 1991. The life of a composer and band leader at the forefront of jazz.

Ewen, David. *The Home Book of Musical Knowledge.* Englewood Cliffs, NJ: Prentice-Hall, 1954. Musical history, terminology, personalities, and masterworks.

Goldberg, Joe. *Jazz Masters of the 50s.* New York: Macmillan, 1965. Discussion of the work of twelve prominent jazz musicians.

Grout, Donald J., and Claude V. Palisca. *A History of Western Music,* 4th ed. New York: Norton, 1988. Chronological presentation of the development of western music within western culture.

Haas, Karl. *Inside Music: How to Understand, Listen to, and Enjoy Good Music.* New York: Doubleday, 1984. Excellent overview of music theory, instruments, and music in the flow of history.

Hanmer, Trudy J. *An Album of Rock and Roll.* New York: Watts, 1988. Chronicles rock and roll from the early 1950s through the 1980s.

Howard, John Tasker. *Our American Music: A Comprehensive History from 1620 to the Present.* 4th ed. New York: Crowell, 1965. Detailed account ranging from music of the American Indian to twentieth-century composers.

Jones, Max. *Talking Jazz.* New York: Norton, 1988. A collection of interviews of jazz greats made over a forty-year period by a man who became editor of *Jazz Music* magazine.

Machlis, Joseph. *The Enjoyment of Music,* 4th ed. New York: Norton, 1977. Possibly the most widely read music-appreciation text in the English language.

———. *Introduction to Contemporary Music.* New York: Norton, 1961. A survey of twentieth-century composers and their music. Emphasis on classical works.

Panassie, Hugues. *Louis Armstrong.* New York: Scribner's, 1971. The life of Louis Armstrong by a friend who is a French music critic.

Preston, Katherine. *Scott Joplin: Composer.* New York: Chelsea House, 1988. The life of the composer who first made ragtime respectable.

Rosenstiel, Leonie, ed. *Shirmer History of Music.* New York: Schirmer Books, 1982. Survey of western hemisphere music from medieval chant to the twentieth century.

Sanford, Herb. *Tommy and Jimmy: The Dorsey Years.* New Rochelle, NY: Arlington House, 1972. Biography of the Dorsey brothers. Emphasis on their careers in the music business.

Shaw, Arnold. *The Jazz Age: Popular Music in the 1920s.* New York: Oxford University Press, 1987. Documents a period when black and white music came together in the form of jazz.

Simon, George T. *The Big Bands.* Rev. ed. New York: Collier Books, 1974. A report on the big bands during their greatest years—1935–1946.

———. *Glenn Miller and His Orchestra.* New York: Crowell, 1974. A biography featuring Glenn Miller's musical career.

———. *Simon Says: The Sights and Sounds of the Swing Era 1935–1955.* New Rochelle, NY: Arlington House, 1971. The best writing of George T. Simon selected from *Metronome* magazine.

Tanenhaus, Sam. *Louis Armstrong: Musician.* New York: Chelsea House, 1989. The life and times of one of America's most beloved entertainers.

PERIODICALS

Bam: The California Music Magazine. Bam Publications, 3470 Buskirk Avenue, Pleasant Hill, CA 94523. (Pop.)

Beats Magazine. The Wiz, 1300 Federal Boulevard, Carteret, NJ 07008. (All Genre.)

Bluegrass Unlimited. Bluegrass Unlimited, Box 111, Broad Run, VA 22014. (Bluegrass.)

Boston Symphony Orchestra Program. Boston Symphony Orchestra, Program Office, Symphony Hall, Boston, MA 02115. (Symphony.)

Circus. Circus Enterprises, 3 W. 18th Street, New York, NY 10011. (Pop, Rock.)

Country America. Meredith, 1716 Locust Street, Des Moines, IA 50309–3023 (Country.)

Down Beat. Maher Publications, 180 W. Park Avenue, Elmhurst, IL 60126. (Contemporary.)

Jazz Times. Jazz Times, 7961 Eastern Avenue, Suite 303, Silver Spring, MD 20910–4898. (Jazz.)

Jazziz. Jazziz Magazine, 3620 NW 43rd Street, Suite D, Gainsville, FL 32606. (All Genre.)

Metallix. Pilot Communications, 831 Federal Road, Box 804, Brookfield, CT 06804. (Heavy Metal, Rock.)

Opera News. Metropolitan Opera Guild, 70 Lincoln Center Plaza, New York, NY 10023. (Opera.)

Opera Quarterly. Duke University Press, Box 6697, College Station, Durham, NC 27708. (Opera.)

Rockbill. Rave Communications, c/o E.M.C.T., 24 Richmond Hill Avenue, Suite 8, Stamford, CT 06901–3600. (Pop, Rock.)

Rolling Stone. Straight Arrow Publishers, 1290 Avenue of the Americas, New York, NY 10104 (Pop, Rock.)

Wavelength. Box 15667, New Orleans, LA 70175. (Jazz.)

ASSOCIATIONS

American Music Center. 30 W. 26th Street, Suite 1001, New York, NY 10010–2011. Appointed official U.S. Information Center for American Music by National Music Council. Maintains information center and library. Bestows awards. Publications: Newsletter, directory, and catalogs.

American Music Scholarship Association. 1030 Carew Tower, Cincinnati, OH 45202. Sponsors World Piano Competition, bestows awards, coordinates music festivals and recitals. Publications: Newsletters.

Big Band Academy of America. c/o Milton Gerald Bernhart, Kelly Travel Service, 6565 W. Sunset Boulevard, Suite 516, Los Angeles, CA 90028. Promotes big band music by seeking to increase public awareness of the big band sound, bring attention to new bands, and assist these groups in becoming better known. Maintains library, sponsors big band concerts, and bestows awards. Publications: *The Bandstand,* and *That Was This, Then Is Now.*

Classical Music Lovers' Exchange. Box 31, Pelham, NY 10803. Seeks to unite classical music lovers to share musical interests and friendship. Publications: Membership list and newsletter.

Country Music Foundation. 4 Music Square E., Nashville, TN 37203. Operates Country Music Hall of Fame. Maintains library of 200,000 recordings, and sponsors educational programs. Operates CMF Records, a re-issue record label of historically important recordings. Publication: *Journal of Country Music.*

International Bluegrass Music Association. 326 S. Elizabeth Street, Owensboro, KY 42301. Serves the bluegrass music industry. Maintains speakers' bureau and conducts a seminar. Publications: *Bluegrass Radio News, International Bluegrass,* and a newsletter.

Jazz World Society. c/o Jan A. Byrczek, PO Box 777, Times Square Station, New York, NY 10108. Operates library of records, books, and photographs. Organizes competitions, bestows awards, offers educational programs, and a placement service. Maintains hall of fame. Publications: *Jazz World,* and several directories.

National Federation of Music Clubs. 1336 N. Delaware Street, Indianapolis, IN 46202. Local and state music associations. Offers scholarships, commissions symphonic works, assists opera companies, and conducts auditions. Publications: *Junior Keynotes,* and *Music Clubs Magazine.*

Rhythm and Blues Rock and Roll Society. PO Box 1949, New Haven, CT 06501. Sponsors concerts, conducts workshops, sponsors a musical radio program, and bestows awards. Operates a library. Publications: *Big Beat,* and bulletin.

Music, Listening

LOOKING OUT OVER A BEAUTIFUL landscape, we can casually examine each feature—perhaps even feel a light breeze on the skin. When an orchestra performs in an auditorium, the listener hears subtle instrumental sounds and feels the full power of the brass and percussion instruments. However, unlike the tranquil landscape scene, a great deal happens in a piece of music that the unskilled listener does not hear. There is little time to perceive and examine the individual elements of the piece. Musical recordings allow us the opportunity to study the piece in detail. We can play the music again. Repeated listening contributes to an appreciation and understanding of music.

When a favorite composition is played, the listener can anticipate the upcoming musical passages, and enjoy them more fully. If the listener has learned to identify the sounds of individual instruments, and has an understanding of the skills being demonstrated by the performing artists, the music will be enjoyed on an intellectual, as well as a sensory level. Listening skills can be refined by learning to hear basic elements of musical expression. Learning the complex details of music is an ongoing process; the rewards are well worth the effort. Music appeals to the ear and the mind, to the senses and the intelligence.

Unfortunately, our society provides incentives to consciously ignore music. We tend to "tune out" constant background, or elevator music. It is said that if you become aware of the background music played throughout a motion picture presentation, the producers have failed in their attempt to create the mood. We are not supposed to notice the soft music during a love scene, the nervous fidgeting of the violins building suspense in a thriller, or the lively, bubbly music that accompanies a happy ending. At the other extreme, patrons of rock concerts or symphonies focus intently on music in a controlled environment.

To properly reproduce music in the home, a listener should attempt to simulate the environment in which the recording was made. Some users may wish to eliminate distractions, control sound absorption, and locate speakers to permit optimum sound reproduction. Others may only want soft, pleasing background music for relaxation, or to accompany quiet conversation.

In the following discussion we'll examine the current state of the art in sound equipment.

Equipment

The simplest sound system consists of a radio with a single speaker. The sound is monophonic, it comes from a single direction. We have no way of knowing that when the song was recorded, the drummer was on the left and the singer stood on the right.

When the same song is recorded with two widely separated microphones, and the recording is heard from two speakers, we perceive the separation of the drummer and singer. We sense a three dimensional effect. The system is called stereophonic sound. Many radio stations broadcast music in a stereo mode, allowing the listener to experience the advantages of the original stereo recordings.

A radio provides two basic functions. It selects, or tunes, one radio station from the many available. This is done by the tuner section. The selected station signal is then amplified (strengthened) enough to power a speaker. The amplified signal causes the speaker to vibrate to move air to produce sound waves that can be heard. The speaker is a reproducer. It reproduces the sound.

In more complex systems, the radio is replaced with separate components. A tuner module is placed in a separate cabinet. The tuner is connected to a preamplifier in another cabinet. The preamplifier brings the weak radio signal up to about one volt. It is connected to a power amplifier that increases the signal strength sufficiently to drive powerful speakers. Such speakers are used in large rooms or anywhere high sound levels are required. The tuner, preamplifier, and amplifier modules are available separately as above, or combined in various ways.

In the above examples, a tuner or radio served as the music source. Other musical sources include an analog record player or a digital compact disk (CD) player.

An analog audio component (record player), or recording medium (record, tape), is one that operates with signals whose wave forms are directly analogous to the sounds they represent. The wave forms are continuous. A digital audio component, or recording medium, operates with signals in a pattern representing numbers. A normal (analog) sound is converted to digital form (strings of ones and zeros) on a CD record. The CD record player converts the digital form back to analog form to be heard on a speaker. The reason for such conversion will be found below.

Over the years sound recording media have evolved from the gramophone cylinders to records. The record players were designed to spin the records at 78 revolutions per minute, then 45, and then long playing (LP) vinyl records turning at 33⅓ rpm.

Many music enthusiasts have large collections of LP records. Some of this music has not been recorded on CDs or tapes. Although the stock of LP record players is not very large in audio stores, they are still readily available, including some sophisticated designs costing thousands of dollars.

An LP record has a continuous irregularly shaped groove that stores music. A special cartridge, located on the end of the tone arm, rides in the groove. It converts the mechanical energy it obtains from the irregularities in the groove to electrical energy that produces the sound. The problem with such a system is that the record groove becomes worn by the action of the cartridge.

Compact disk players are designed to handle records that are about 4¾ inches in diameter. The records have continuous tracks, instead of grooves, spaced so closely that their total length of 2½ to 7 miles fits on the record. One LP groove width would accommodate about sixty CD tracks. The CD tracks are made up of a series of pits. A laser beam scans these pits and reflects the encoded digital data back into an optical sensor. The signal is converted to a continuous analog wave form and amplified on its way to speakers. There are several advantages to the process. First, the record is played by means of a laser light beam, hence no record wear. Second, the information stored on the record is simply a series of binary numbers, each of which represents and describes the music as it existed for $1/44,100$ of a second, assuring accurate sound reproduction. Third, the binary code is not affected by noise or distortion.

Another music source is the audio tape deck. This device records musical sounds on magnetic tape, and then plays it back when required. The tape itself is a plastic film with a metallic coating. When recording, the tape is moved past an electromagnetic tape record head. An incoming musical signal continuously changes the magnetic field of the tape head. The variations in the magnetic field magnetize the metal particles on the tape to record the signal.

While playing back the process is reversed. The magnetic field on the tape varies the field on the playback head creating an electronic signal that is fed to the speakers. Although this is an analog process, the sound quality is equal to or better than most vinyl LPs. Most music audio tapes are contained in small cassettes to ease handling and storage.

The laser disk is another form of digital record. It is about the same size as an LP. The laser disk did not achieve the popularity of the cassette tape or CD due to its high cost. Some upscale CD players are now capable of also playing the laser disks, creating a modest increase in their popularity.

The next phase in audio recording sources will likely be the digital compact cassette (DCC), or digital audio tape (DAT). Advance marketing claims are that the sound quality will equal that of the CD. This process has been in development for years. It will require special tape playing equipment, but the equipment will also play current analog tape cassettes. Still another competitor in the audio market is the miniature compact disk.

Two other radio-oriented digital technologies are just around the corner. Within the next decade there is little doubt that traditional AM and FM stations will become obsolete. The Federal Communications Commission is completing the testing of various all-digital transmission systems with crystal-clear, interference-free fidelity. Secondly, licenses are being granted to initiate broadcasting from high-powered satellites that will deliver quality sound to your home or car, no matter where you are in the U.S.

The advent of digital recording has reduced the noise and distortion inherent in analog recording. This has increased the dynamic range of speakers. Speakers now have to be able to faithfully reproduce this expanded dynamic range. The very quietest of musical sounds, even the silence before music begins, is not masked by the tape noise that has been present on analog tapes. At the other end, the loudest sounds are also more faithfully reproduced loading the speaker. This places greater demands on present and future speaker design.

Recordings

As the availability of new LP records begins to slow, the number of audiophiles (music lovers) searching painstakingly through stacks of old LPs in flea markets is on the increase. Used records and tape stores are found in most cities. Collectors band together in associations and read specialty magazines. Record companies release old recordings once again for a new generation of music lovers. Publishers print extensive annual discographies listing recordings currently available. A sampling of these sources is included in the following bibliography.

Bibliography

REFERENCE BOOKS

Clifford, Martin. *The Complete Compact Disk Player.* Englewood Cliffs, NJ: Prentice Hall, 1987. In-depth book on compact disk players. Includes basic theory, maintenance, and servicing data.

Drucker, David. *Billboard's Complete Book of Audio: How to Choose, Buy, and Use a Stereo Hi-Fi System.* New York: Billboard Books, 1991. Useful text for the beginning stereo buyer confused by the technical language used in popular stereo magazines.

Haas, Karl. *Inside Music: How to Understand, Listen to, and Enjoy Good Music.* New York: Doubleday, 1984. Suggestions for building a classical record library.

Ivey, Donald. *Sound Pleasure: A Prelude to Active Listening.* 2nd ed. New York: Schirmer Books, 1985. Examines the elements of music in a wide range of contexts.

Kerman, Joseph. *Listen.* New York: Worth, 1972. Overview of the elements of music. Includes a recording to complement the text.

Mattfeld, Julius. *Variety Music Cavalcade 1620–1969: A Chronology of Vocal and Instrumental Music Popular in the United States.* 3rd ed. Englewood Cliffs, NJ: Prentice Hall, 1971. Listings of songs accompanied by historical narrative.

Wink, Richard L., and Lois G. Williams. *Invitation to Listening: An Introduction to Music.* 2nd ed. Boston: Houghton Mifflin, 1976. Explains the elements of musical sound. Good coverage of musical instruments.

PERIODICALS

American Record Guide. Record Guide Productions, 4412 Braddock Street, Cincinnati, OH 45204. (Classical recordings.)

Audio. Hachette Magazines, 1633 Broadway, New York, NY 10019. (Audio equipment and recordings.)

CD Review. Connell Communications, Forest Road, Hancock, NH 03449. (Recordings and equipment.)

Fanfare. Fanfare, 273 Woodland Street, Tenafly, NJ 07670. (Record collectors.)

Goldmine. Krause Publications, 700 E. State Street, Iola, WI 54990. (Record collectors.)

Home and Studio Recording. Music Maker Publications, 21601 Devonshire Street, Suite 212, Chatsworth, CA 91311. (Recording equipment.)

Record Exchanger. Vintage Records, Box 6144, Orange, CA 92667. (Vintage records.)

Schwann Opus. Schwann Publications, 440 Cerrillos Road, Suite C, Sante Fe, NM 87501. (Recordings Guide-classical.)

Schwann Spectrum. Schwann Publications, 440 Cerrillos Road, Suite C, Santa Fe, NM 87501. (Recordings guide-nonclassical.)

Stereophile. Box 5529, Santa Fe, NM 87502. (Stereo Hi-Fi.)

Stereo Review. Hachette Magazines, 1633 Broadway, New York, NY 10019. (Audio equipment and recordings.)

Stereo Review's Stereo Buyers' Guide. Hachette Magazines, 1633 Broadway, New York, NY 10019. (Stereo equipment.)

ASSOCIATIONS

Antique Phonograph Collectors Club. 502 E. 17th Street, Brooklyn, NY 11226. Collectors, libraries, and historical societies. Facilitates communication among collectors of antique phonographs and records. Publications: *Antique Phonograph Monthly, Edison Phonograph,* and related books and materials.

Collectors Record Club. 1206 Decatur Street, New Orleans, LA 70116. Persons interested in authentic jazz and big band music. Publications: *Jazz Beat,* newsletter, and catalogs.

Institute of the American Musical. 121 N. Detroit Street, Los Angeles, CA 90036. Maintains large collection of recordings, sheet music, and other memorabilia dating back to 1890s. Library open to qualified scholars by appointment.

International Association of Jazz Record Collectors. c/o Shirley L. Klett, 127 Briercliff Lane, Bel Air, MD 21014. Collectors of jazz records from twenty-two countries. Provides information exchange for collectors. Issues recordings of big bands. Publications: Journal, directory, and discographical information.

Musical Heritage Society. State Highway 35, Ocean, NJ 07712. Mail order clearinghouse for classical music recordings.

National Sheet Music Society. 1597 Fair Park Avenue, Los Angeles, CA 90041. Songwriters and sheet music collectors. Conducts research and educational programs. Publications: *The Song Sheet,* and a directory.

Ragtime Society. PO Box 520, Sta A, Toronto, ON, Canada M5H 1W7. Produces recordings of both old and new ragtime music, available to members.

Record Collectors Club. 5129 Joe Bond Trail, Murfreesboro, TN 37129. Business that buys and sells old and rare records, especially country and western. Provides collectors with referrals to other record outlets.

Remember That Song. 5623 N 64th Avenue, Glendale AZ 85301. Those interested in the history of music from 1850 to the 1940s. Publication: *Remember That Song.*

Music, Performance

IN THE FOLLOWING DISCUSSION we'll consider the characteristics of a selection of musical instruments. Most instruments are designed to fill certain roles in a musical ensemble. A few, by virtue of their wide tonal range and flexibility, also lend themselves to solo performance. Musical instruments, like the human voice, are classified according to their pitch range.

Classes of Voice

The high notes played on a flute or piccolo are said to have a high pitch. A foghorn produces movements in the air that we perceive as a low-pitched sound. Pitch is determined by the speed, or frequency, at which an object vibrates. The vibrating object may be a violin string, or simply the column of air found inside a flute. The human vocal cords vibrate by means of the wind supplied by our lungs. Instruments and human voices vary in their pitch ranges. The various classes of voice are described below in descending order of pitch.

The female soprano voice is the highest range. It is divided into three subranges. The coloratura has the most flexibility. A dramatic soprano has a full, powerful voice. The lyric soprano possesses a lighter singing voice.

The female mezzo-soprano (half-soprano) has a lower pitch, and the alto, or contralto, has a lower, rich, range of pitch. The mezzo-soprano, contralto, and most voices to follow, are subdivided into dramatic and lyric classes as above.

The male tenor voice is the highest masculine voice. It is lower than the feminine alto. The male baritone, and still lower bass voices, are the lowest pitched classes. The bass has a full, deep, rich, and resonant sound.

Musical instruments have evolved from the sounds found in the human voice, and their pitch ranges are counterparts to the soprano through bass voices described above.

Musical Dimensions and Instruments

Let's look at some elements of music and their relationship with musical instruments.

Rhythm regulates the flow of music. Most percussion instruments set the rhythm. They are used to keep time and provide both color and emphasis in the orchestra. In the absence of a percussion instrument, other instruments that have the capacity to provide both rhythm and melody can be substituted. The piano or string bass fit that description.

Melody is defined as a group of tones sounded one after another. The string section usually serves that function in an orchestra. Woodwinds or the brass section may carry melody in a dance or marching band.

Harmony is the simultaneous sound of two or more tones. Just as an alto singer performs close harmony with a soprano, the viola provides harmony to the violin in a string quartet.

Musical color, or timbre, can be influenced by the combination of instruments used. The predominance of brass instruments included in the playing of a Sousa march, or the strings used in a Straus waltz, contribute to the color of the performance. One of the characteristics of vibration is that an object vibrates at several frequencies simultaneously. When a string vibrates along its full length, it also vibrates at harmonic frequencies, set up at one half its length, one fourth, and so on. The sounds, or overtones, generated by the harmonic frequencies may be barely audible, but they contribute to the timbre of an instrument.

We have seen that various families of instruments influence the sound of a musical composition. Identification of instruments that make up the families follows.

Brasses

The French horn, shown in Figure 1, has a long air tube describing a circular path around a plumber's nightmare of valves and secondary air paths. It is distinguished by a

Figure 1

The French Horn. The sound produced by the vibration of the musician's lips sets off a resonating air column within the tube leading to the flared bell at the end. When the musician fingers the valves, the different length tube routes to the bell's end change the tone produced by the horn.

large bell at the end. Sound is produced by vibration of the musician's lips, which sets off a resonating air column within the tube. This is typical of all brass instruments. The French horn has an alto pitch range that is very wide.

The trombone has a long air tube having a variable length to change its pitch. A portion of the tube slides within the main body of the instrument. The sound is primarily in the tenor range. The trombone's ability to slide through a range of tones lends color to both jazz ensembles and orchestras. Trombones are also made in the bass range. B flat-F trombones have an F attachment consisting of a coil of extra tubing. A rotary valve connects this attachment to the main tube, lowering the pitch of the instrument.

The trumpet is the highest pitched instrument in the brass family. It has a narrow tonal range, but retains its clear, penetrating sound when played either loud or soft. The trumpet is used in a variety of musical ensembles.

The tuba has the lowest pitch of the brasses. It's comparable to the string double-bass. The tuba's powerful deep sound can provide rhythm or melody to the orchestra. It requires good lungs to supply the air necessary to sustain notes.

Keyboard

The organ has changed considerably from the tenth century instrument that required two players and numerous manual air pumps to operate hundreds of pipes. The individual pipes were shaped like a whistle. The air passing through the pipe escaped through the mouth, producing sound. Another type of pipe had a metal reed at the bottom to produce the sound. Although some air-operated church and theater organs may still be found, modern units depend on electronics to generate the tones called for when a key is depressed.

The piano has a very wide range of pitches. It is well suited for both solo and support performance. Sound is produced when keys are depressed, causing hammers to strike strings. The strings may be positioned horizontally as in a grand piano, or vertically as in an upright. The piano is one of the most popular instruments due to its adaptability to various musical ensembles.

Percussion

Drums are used to provide rhythmic support for an orchestra. The timpani drum has a bowl-shaped body with calf-skin stretched over the top. The tone can be changed within a limited range by means of a foot pedal. Usually several such drums are employed, each with a different tonal range. Timpani are played with two sticks. The stick heads are made with different materials to achieve a variety of tonal effects.

The bass drum has a cylindrical body with heads stretched over both ends. Its pitch is said to be indefinite; it doesn't vary. The bass drum is usually played with a heavy stick having a felt-padded knob at its end.

The snare drum is a small drum played on its upper end with two sticks. The lower head has strings (snares) of gut or silk stretched taut against its surface. The vibration of the lower head against the snares produces the brilliant sound peculiar to this drum.

Some percussion instruments produce a variety of pitches. The chimes feature tubes of varying lengths that are struck with mallets. The xylophone consists of hardwood bars of varying lengths with tube resonators located below to amplify the sound. Similar instruments include the glockenspiel and the marimba. The glockenspiel utilizes metal bars with or without resonator tubes.

Rhythm patterns are augmented by a wide variety of other noise makers such as gongs, cymbals, castanets, tambourines, and the triangle.

Strings

The banjo is very popular in the United States. It consists of a drum-shaped body covered with parchment on top. The banjo has from five to nine strings passing over a bridge and a long neck. It is commonly strummed or plucked with the fingers while playing folk tunes.

The cello is normally used to provide a bass foundation for harmony. It often carries the melody. Its construction is similar to a violin, although somewhat larger. It has a support pin at the bottom that rests on the floor. The strings may be played with a bow or plucked.

The double bass, or bass, is the lowest in range of the string section. Popular in both classic and jazz music, the strings may be either bowed or plucked. Like the cello, it is supported by a pin at the bottom. Often teamed with the cello, it furnishes basic support to the entire orchestra.

The guitar has a fretted finger board. Its strings are plucked with the fingers or a plectrum (pick). It is effective in company with other stringed instruments, or when used for vocal accompaniment. The guitar is popular internationally, used for both classical and popular music. Variations include gut or steel strings, and various forms of electronic amplification.

The harp is one of the earliest instruments. Strings are stretched across a frame that is shaped to accommodate their varying lengths. The sound is soft and melodious. Harp strings are plucked by one or both hands. Used primarily in large orchestras, it is sometimes played solo in settings such as upscale restaurants.

The viola is somewhat larger than the violin, and is lower in range. It is the alto member of the string family. The viola is effective when carrying the melody or filling in the harmony. The strings may be bowed or plucked. It has wide application in the orchestra and for chamber music.

The violin is the soprano member of the string family. It is the highest pitched of the string instruments, with an extremely wide range of pitch and timbre. The violin possesses a singing tone, close to that of a human voice. Its strings are both bowed and plucked. It is used extensively in orchestras to provide both melody and harmony.

Woodwinds

The bassoon is the masculine baritone voice of the woodwind section. A larger version, the contrabassoon, provides the bass voice. These instruments have a wide tonal range, and are capable of wide jumps in pitch from one note to the next. This is often exploited with humorous results. Sound is produced by blowing against a double reed. The tube, or air path, of a contrabassoon is over sixteen feet long. The tube is folded back on itself four times to make it less unwieldy.

The clarinet is a versatile instrument, capable of solo work with the orchestra. Sound is produced by blowing against a single reed. It is relatively high pitched, with a wide tonal range, providing soprano or alto sounds. The very popular clarinet is also made in a lower pitched version called a bass clarinet. It is shaped like a thin-bodied saxophone.

The flute is a small high-pitched instrument. Sound is produced by blowing across an opening, creating a vibrating air column within. It is used to play melody in the soprano pitch range. The flute is noted for its clear sound. A smaller version, the piccolo, has the highest pitch of all instruments.

The oboe is a high-pitched instrument with a somewhat nasal tone. Sound is produced by blowing against a double reed. It lends itself to solo work, carrying the melody. The English horn is a medium-pitched version in the alto or tenor range.

The saxophone is made in many sizes to accommodate pitch ranges from soprano to bass. Sound is produced by blowing against a single reed. The tone is a combination of that expected from horns and woodwinds. At home in an orchestra or a jazz ensemble, its popularity is a credit to Adolphe Sax, its inventor.

Computers in Music

Advances in electronics, and the widespread use of personal computers, have resulted in the development of computer generated music. In 1983 industry established a communication standard to connect differently manufactured musical electronic devices. It is called the Musical Instrument Digital Interface, or MIDI.

A MIDI keyboard is connected to a MIDI interface module that is connected to a common personal computer. The personal computer is supplied with a musical software program to process the information. The computer can be connected to a pair of speakers, and/or a stereo radio, or recording tape, or a printer.

The keyboard is played like a piano and the resulting music sounds can sound like a piano. It may also sound like any other instrument or groups of instruments, such as a saxophone or a big orchestra with brass and strings.

The individual instrument voices have been recorded a note at a time, and became part of the software in the computer. The notes are selected by the computer when a key on the MIDI keyboard is depressed. The speed of key pressure and release determines the sound of the note as it would on a piano. The finest musical instruments are recorded for use by the computer, so the effect is extraordinary.

If the user wishes to compose a piece of music, the computer can be set up to draw the notes on a musical staff when the keyboard is played. The sheet music thus generated on the computer screen can then be printed on a common computer paper printer.

The average price of a quality MIDI keyboard, MIDI interface, and computer music program is about $1,650. This assumes you have a personal computer and stereo radio. Of course, more sophisticated units are available costing much more.

An alternative to the MIDI keyboard/computer arrangement is also available. A keyboard unit that generates its own musical signals is connected directly to a stereo radio. The sound quality is not as good, and the equipment doesn't provide many features of the system described above, but the unit costs less than $200.

Which Instrument Shall I Play?

We have seen that some instruments lend themselves to solo performance, while others are intended for a supporting role.

If you plan to play only for personal pleasure, select an instrument that can carry the melody. That's why pianos and guitars are so popular. If you enjoy the classics, a violin may be the answer. You may want to join others in some chamber music.

If you haven't had experience with the instrument of your choice, consider renting with the option to buy. You may have second thoughts regarding your first choice. It is especially convenient when the instrument supplier can also provide lessons. If a music store can't supply lessons, your choice of instrument may be limited by the skills of local teachers.

Bibliography

REFERENCE BOOKS

Bartlett, Harry R. *Guide to Teaching Percussion.* 3rd ed. Dubuque, IA: Brown, 1978. Textbook style coverage of more than fifty percussion instruments.

Burmeister, Ellen. *Keyboard Sight Reading.* Mountain View, CA: Mayfield, 1991. How to improve the ability to read and play sheet music for the keyboard.

Gat, Jozsef. *The Technique of Piano Playing.* 4th ed. London: Collet's, 1974. Detailed analysis and recommendations regarding piano playing technique. Emphasis on posture and fingering.

Kozak, Donald P. *A Guide to Computer Music: An Introductory Resource.* Peabody, MA: Sound Management Productions, 1988. An introduction to the musical instrument digital interface. Controling music with a computer-based music workstation.

Lamb, Norman. *Guide to Teaching Strings.* 5th ed. Dubuque, IA: Brown, 1990. A detailed overview of string instruments. Covers history, maintenance, accessories, and playing techniques.

Sandberg, Larry. *The Acoustic Guitar Guide: Everything You Need to Know to Buy and Maintain a New or Used Guitar.* Pennington, NJ: A Cappella Books, 1991. Focus is on the instrument itself, not on learning to play.

Saucier, Gene A. *Woodwinds: Fundamental Performance Techniques.* New York: Schirmer Books, 1981. Teaching text for woodwind instruments. Covers maintenance, teaching, and playing techniques. Provides bibliographic source information.

Turetzky, Bertram. *The Contemporary Contrabass.* Rev. ed. Berkeley, CA: University of California Press, 1989. How to achieve various effects with the contrabass. Emphasis on playing techniques.

Westphal, Frederick W. *Guide to Teaching Woodwinds.* 4th ed. Dubuque, IA: Brown, 1985. A detailed overview of woodwind instruments. Covers maintenance and playing techniques.

Winter, James H. *The Brass Instruments: Performance and Instructional Techniques.* 2nd ed. Boston: Allyn & Bacon, 1969. General discussion of instruments and playing techniques. Provides routine studies and exercises.

PERIODICALS

American Organist. American Guild of Organists, 475 Riverside Drive, Suite 1260, New York, NY 10115. (Organ.)

Bass Player. G P I Publishers, 20085 Stevens Creek, Cupertino, CA 95014. (Electric and String Bass.)

Brass Player's Guide. Robert King Music Sales, Shovel Shop Square, 28 Main Street, Building 15, N. Easton, MA 02356–1499. (Brass.)

Electronic Musician. Act III Publishers, 6400 Hollis, Suite 12, Emeryville, CA 94608. (Computers and Electronics in Music.)

First Bass. First Bass International, 33 Essex Street, Hackensack, NJ 07601. (Electric and Acoustic Bass.)

Guitar for the Practicing Musician. Cherry Lane Music, 10 Midland Avenue, Port Chester, NY 10573. (Guitar.)

Guitar Player. G P I Publishers, 20085 Stevens Creek, Cupertino, CA 95014. (Guitar.)

Harmonizer. Society for the Preservation and Encouragement of Barbershop Quartet Singing in America, 6315 Third Avenue, Kenosha, WI 53143–5199. (Singing.)

Keyboard. G P I Publishers, 20085 Stevens Creek, Cupertino, CA 95014. (All Keyboard.)

Modern Drummer. Modern Drummer Publishers, 870 Pompton Avenue, Cedar Grove, NJ 07009. (Percussionist.)

Sheet Music Magazine: Standard Piano-Guitar Edition. Sheet Music Magazine, 223 Katonah Avenue, Katonah, NY 10536. (Piano and Guitar.)

Singing News. Singing News, Box 2810, Boone, NC 28607–2810. (Gospel Music.)

ASSOCIATIONS

Amateur Chamber Music Players. 545 8th Avenue, 9th Floor, New York, NY 10018. Amateur and professional musicians who play chamber music as a hobby. Maintains library. Publications: Newsletter, directory, and books on chamber music.

American Federation of Pueri Cantores. 5445 11th Avene N, St Petersburg, FL 33710. Children in Roman Catholic church choirs. Publications: Newsletters and brochure.

Drum Corps International. PO Box 548, Lombard, IL 60148–0548. Drum and bugle corps. Establishes rules and regulations, sponsors clinics and seminars, and produces events. Maintains hall of fame. Publication: *DCI Today.*

Gospel Music Workshop of America. 3908 W. Warren Street, Detroit, MI 48208. Individuals interested in gospel music. Offers musical instruction in performance and composition. Publication: Bulletin.

North American Brass Band Association. c/o Bert Wiley, Secretary, PO Box 2438, Cullowhee, NC 28723. Fosters the establishment and development of adult amateur British-type brass bands. Sponsors competitions, holds workshops. Publication: *Brass Band Bridge.*

Percussive Arts Society. PO Box 25, Lawton, OK 73502. Sponsors competitions in percussion music. Maintains museum and presents hall of fame award. Conducts education and research programs. Publications: *Percussion News,* and *Percussion Notes.*

Society for the Preservation and Encouragement of Barbershop Quartet Singing in America. 6315 Third Avenue, Kenosha, WI 53143–5199. Men interested in barbershop quartet singing. Conducts annual competition. Provides scholarships and maintains library of old songs. Publications: *Harmonizer,* barbershop arrangements and songbooks.

Sweet Adelines International. PO Box 470168, Tulsa, OK 74147. Women interested in barbershop harmony singing. Teaches and trains members in singing four-part harmony. Maintains speakers bureau. Operates in ten countries. Publication: *Pitch Pipe.*

Note: There are many additional associations devoted to specific musical instruments listed in the *Encyclopedia of Associations,* available in libraries.

Photography

WOULDN'T IT BE WONDERFUL if photography existed a thousand or more years ago? Historians and scientists would have so much more information. Thanks to photography we can see exactly what our parents looked like before we were born. With well over seventy-five million of us out there clicking our shutters, there is obviously a strong attraction to the photographic arts. Photography has become an integral part of family life, weddings and travel. It has brought us in touch with the world through motion pictures and such magazines as *National Geographic* and *Life*. It reached a true art form in the hands of masters such as Ansel Adams. Taking photographs tends to make us more sensitive to the beauty of the world around us. Photographers stop and look at things that others pass by.

History

When light enters a dark room through a small hole, an inverted image of the outdoor scene is projected into the room. The image may be seen by placing a piece of oiled paper or ground glass at the proper distance from the hole. This phenomena was known as early as the fourth century B.C. by Aristotle. During the 1500s the principle was applied to a light-tight box with a pin-hole in the front to admit light, and a viewing screen at the rear made of ground glass or parchment. By 1570 the pinhole was replaced by a simple lens that produced a brighter image. The box was called a camera obscura. Artists used it as an aid to the sketching of scenes. Joseph Nicephore Niepce, a Frenchman, became the world's first photographer in 1827. He used an adaptation of the camera obscura to project an image onto a crude photo plate coated with bitumen. He recorded the view outside his window with an exposure lasting eight hours. Many experimenters worked to improve the process using various chemicals to improve

sensitivity and fixing agents to preserve image. Louis Da Guerre sensitized a silvered plate, exposed the picture, developed it in mercury vapor, and fixed it with hypo sulfite of soda. His Daguerreotype process was a sensation when it was introduced in 1839. In 1888 George Eastman manufactured his first compact roll-film camera and called it the Kodak. This product was largely responsible for the spread of photography. The photographer was able to take 100 pictures on a roll of film, after which the camera was returned to Kodak for processing. The photos and reloaded camera were then returned to the user. This was followed by the famous Brownie box camera, and later a compact camera with a folding bellows.

We have seen a constant development and refinement of films and cameras during the twentieth century, based on the foundations laid by the early experimenters. Films are much more sensitive, allowing faster shutter speeds that freeze motion. Color films have been introduced. Advances in optical design have resulted in superior lenses at reasonable cost. Significant electronic developments permit automatic focusing, film advance, integration of flash illumination, and other more complex refinements and applications we'll discuss further on.

How Cameras Work

A modern camera is basically a camera obscura. It is an enclosed container with a lens in the front to admit light, and a film held in place at the back to record the patterns of light that form the image projected there by the lens. There are two types of light seen by the camera—light reflected from the surface of the subject, and light radiated by an object such as a light bulb or the sun.

The amount of light that a lens allows to pass can be varied on medium to high priced cameras by changing the size of a hole (aperture), in a partition (diaphragm), usually behind the lens. In some cameras the hole is a slit in a moveable opaque curtain (focal plane shutter) located near the film.

The intervals of aperture opening are called *f* stops or *f* numbers. The largest opening permits the maximum amount of light to enter, perhaps *f*-1.4 on a quality lens. The next stop, *f*-2 cuts the amount of light by a half. It is said to be one stop slower than *f*-1.4. A typical camera may have six or seven such stops.

The length of time (exposure time) is varied by a shutter device that opens, lets light through, and closes very quickly. Shutter speed may typically be varied from one second or more to as fast as $1/1000$ second or less. For cameras equipped with a focal plane shutter, the slitted-curtain speed is varied to achieve the required exposure time.

Another adjustment on medium priced cameras allows you to obtain maximum sharpness of your subject. This is called bringing the subject into focus. The camera is focused by moving the lens away from, or closer to, the film. The lens-to-film distance (focal length) will vary depending on the distance from lens to the subject being photographed. Technically, the focal length of a given lens is the distance between a certain location in the lens and the film in the camera, when the lens is focused at infinity. Once you have adjusted the focus, the setting of the *f*-number and shutter speed is what most of the mystery of photography is all about. If you decrease the *f*-number and simultaneously shorten the exposure time by choosing a faster shutter speed, you can obtain the same light exposure to the film that you had with the previous setting. However, this manipulation of *f*-number (aperture) and shutter speed will adjust the depth of field. The distance between the near and far limits of good focus define the depth of field for a given setting. You can bring things into focus closer and at greater distance at the same time by choosing a larger *f*-number and a longer shutter opening time. The reverse is also true, shortening the depth of field. By keeping the depth of field short when taking a portrait, your background is intentionally blurred and will not detract from the subject.

The above discussion describes the primary "controls" found on a camera. Expensive cameras will feature many more.

When a camera shutter is opened, light from the subject acts on an emulsion coating of the film that contains a light-sensitive material. The light triggers a chemical change in the material. At this point the film has an invisible image, called a latent image. When the film is treated with chemicals to develop it, the subject image becomes visible.

Variations in lighting conditions such as reflectivity or direction of the light source sometimes make exposure control setting difficult. The built-in light meters found in some cameras can be misled when facing into the sun or when distribution of light and dark areas in the scene varies from the average situation the meter is designed to react to. More about this later. Experienced photographers learn to recognize difficult lighting conditions and compensate by bracketing exposures. This is accomplished by taking additional shots with more and less exposure time than recommended by the light meter reading.

Composing a Picture

Our eyes view a scene with great flexibility. They constantly change focus as objects are noted both near and far. Details in light and dark areas are seen without difficulty. Scientific studies have shown that our eyes dart from one object to another, the direction of sight often tracing a path around the perimeter of an object of interest. The camera frames a limited part of the scene. We are free to examine details on the printed photograph that our eyes may have missed. However, we must take into account the limitations of depth of field and acceptable light contrast.

Try to achieve balance as you frame a subject in your viewfinder. The position of the subject, and the way the shapes being photographed lead the eye to areas you wish to emphasize, are important to good composition. It has been found useful to divide the frame into thirds, both horizontally and vertically. The subject is then positioned at one of the four points where the lines dividing the thirds intersect. Where there is only one subject such as a person located in an otherwise vacant setting, the subject may be moved toward the center a little. In this case it is often advisable to have the person face slightly toward the center.

The eye can be drawn toward a subject of interest by framing it with contrasting shapes in the scene. For example, a beautiful lake framed between trees with overhanging limbs; Or a distant farmhouse with a road or path leading from the foreground to the house.

When a scene contains extreme contrasts in brightness, some compromise is required. When we use a light meter to determine the exposure for such a scene, it will measure the average brightness of the entire scene. Photographer Ansel Adams proposed a solution to this problem. In his zone system, he assigns values to brightness or tone levels found in a scene. The zone levels range from 0 to Roman numeral X; where 0 is the absolute darkest part of the scene, as when photographing the side of a cliff containing a cave; VI is the lighter midtones of a scene, as found with shadows on snow in a sunlit scene; and X is the absolute brightest part of the scene, as found when a light source such as the sun is included in the scene. By using these guidelines when analyzing the content of a frame, photographers can estimate how much to compensate for their meter readings to best capture important features of the scene. Details of this system can be found in Fred Picker's book, *Zone VI Workshop,* or *The Complete Kodak Book of Photography.*

Getting Started

Read a basic book on photography from your library or camera store. This will help you match a camera to your needs. The simplest of cameras is capable of award-winning photographs. A more refined camera design eases the picture taking process, but in itself does not make an excellent photograph. The beginner should consider a compact 35-mm camera for early work. The automatic types allow you to concentrate on composition and become familiar with camera handling. As you gain experience and go on to more expensive specialized equipment, the compact will still be found useful as a lightweight travel companion. Color slide films require the expense of a projector for comfortable viewing so you may wish to use films designed for making prints. Film sensitivity or speed is rated with an ISO number. ISO 400 is a very high speed film that is useful in a wide range of lighting situations.

Equipment

Cameras are available costing from under ten dollars to ten thousand dollars. Some popular camera types follow.

One Time Use Cameras. These revert back to the days of George Eastman and his camera that was sent back to the factory for reload. They have plastic lenses and internal parts usually housed in a cardboard case. They use fast color print film. When the pictures have been taken, the camera is given to a film processor who develops the pictures and returns the camera to the manufacturer. Many types are available including ones with wide angle lenses and one with a telephoto lens.

Fully Automatic 35-mm Compact Camera. These are small lightweight cameras with many electronic control functions built in. They are portable and easy to use, but much more sophisticated than a basic fixed focus camera. They are not as flexible as the standard 35mm single lens reflex. Lenses are not usually interchangeable and a separate viewfinder is used.

Single-Lens Reflex 35-mm Camera. An internal movable mirror allows you to view your subject through the camera lens before shooting. The lens is removable on the more expensive types permitting the replacement of the normal lens with another giving a wider field of view or greater enlargement of distant objects. This is the standard camera used by most experienced amateurs.

Twin-Lens Reflex Camera. An upper lens focuses the subject on a ground glass screen viewed by looking down at the top of the camera. A lower lens transmits the picture

to the film as in any other camera. This camera usually makes a 2¼-by-2¼ inch negative picture on the film. It's not as commonly used in recent years, but is still available.

Medium Format Camera. Most can be fitted with interchangeable film backs that enable use of 120 size film or instant films. They have multiple viewfinder options, interchangeable lenses, and many accessories. Intended primarily for professional use, they are very expensive. An example is the Hasselblad camera that was taken to the moon.

Experienced amateurs may wish to develop their own film and print enlargements of the pictures. The type and cost of such equipment depends upon whether black and white or color photos will be developed. A typical black and white setup will include an enlarger, developing tank for film, trays to process prints, measuring graduate to mix chemicals, thermometer, and other minor items.

Color processing requires closer temperature control and more processing stages. The enlarger must have a special color head that can vary the levels of the yellow, cyan, and magenta colors. An inexpensive processing drum for prints is also useful. The rest of the equipment is the same as for black and white processing. It's best to consult with an experienced photo shop operator when selecting this equipment.

Advanced Systems

Automatic cameras make full use of the latest developments in computer systems. Some higher priced cameras offer predictive autofocus. The system takes several successive distance readings of a moving subject, and uses its computer to calculate the subject's speed and direction, and predict its exact location at the moment of exposure.

A photo compact disk system allows sound, graphics, and text to be recorded with photographic-quality images on photo CD disks. The photo CD system allows users to get 35-mm negatives and slides inexpensively scanned by photofinishers onto photo CD disks that can be played back on TV sets using special CD players. The photo CD system images can also be accessed from a personal computer (PC), displayed on the PC screen, and integrated with other PC documents.

A KODAK digital camera system consists of a special camera back attached to a 35-mm Nikon camera. The camera takes pictures in the normal fashion and the camera system electronically captures digital images that are instantly available for transmission. The high quality images can be fed into a computer through a modem and phone lines, and to another computer at a remote location. Photojournalists working anywhere in the world can transmit a photo back to their newsroom in less than four minutes. The applications for police work and science would seem to be endless.

The Apple QuickTake 100 is another digital camera. It's a one-piece unit. Its pictures are loaded into a Macintosh computer for viewing and/or integration with text in word-processing programs.

Bibliography

REFERENCE BOOKS

Adams, Ansel. *The Camera.* Boston: Little, Brown, 1980. Visualization. Cameras, lenses, meters, accessories, special purpose equipment and techniques.

———. *The Negative.* Boston: Little, Brown, 1981. The zone system, lights, film exposure, filters, darkroom processes, equipment, and procedures.

———. *The Print.* Boston: Little, Brown, 1983. Printing materials, printing and enlarging, processing, and finishing.

Dickey, Thomas, and Don Earnest. *The Complete Kodak Book of Photography.* New York: Crown, 1986. Broad coverage of still photography. Taking pictures, developing, and printing.

Grimm, Tom. *The Basic Darkroom Book: A Complete Guide to Processing and Printing Color and Black-and-White Photographs.* Rev. ed. New York: NAL Books, 1986. Darkroom processing.

Hedgecoe, John. *The Book of Photography: How to See and Take Better Pictures.* New York: Knopf, 1984. Photographic history. How the camera works, how to take better pictures, processing, and choosing equipment.

KODAK Guide to 35mm Photography. 6th ed. Rochester, NY: Eastman Kodak, 1989. Broad coverage including camera handling, films, lenses, composition, filters, and close-up photography.

Picker, Fred. *Zone VI Workshop.* New York: Watson-Guptill, 1974. Film exposure, zone system, processing, and equipment.

Platt, Richard. *The Photographer's Idea Book.* New York: Watson-Guptill, 1985. Broad coverage of composition and photographic technique. Well illustrated with a variety of subjects.

Schaub, George. *The Amphoto Book of Film: A Complete Guide to Current Photographic Films.* New York: Watson-Guptill, 1991. Color, black and white, and instant films.

Stroebel, Leslie et al. *Basic Photographic Materials and Processes.* Stoneham, MA: Butterworth, 1990. College-level text on the physics, optics, and chemistry of photography.

Additional current photographic books on specific subjects are available from your local photo store, or publishers such as H. P. Books, PO Box 5367, Tucson, AZ 85703; (Learn Photography Series), and Consumer/ Professional and Finishing Markets, Eastman Kodak Co., Rochester, NY 14650. (Kodak Workshop series.)

PERIODICALS

Camera and Darkroom Photography. Larry Flynt Publications, 9171 Wilshire Boulevard, Suite 300, Beverly Hills, CA 90210.

Darkroom and Creative Camera Techniques. Preston Publications, 7800 N. Merrimac Avenue, Niles, IL 60714.

Petersen's Photographic. Petersen Publishers, 8490 Sunset Boulevard, Los Angeles, CA 90069.

Popular Photography. Hachette Magazines, 1633 Broadway, New York, NY 10019.

ASSOCIATIONS

American Photographic Historical Society. 1150 Avenue of the Americas, New York, NY 10036. Historians, collectors, curators, and authors. Maintains library, and bestows awards. Publications: Newsletter and *Photographica* magazine.

American Society of Camera Collectors. 4918 Alcove Avenue, North Hollywood, CA 91607. Amateur and professional photographers, antique camera collectors, restorers, and those interested in photo history.

Friends of Photography. c/o Ansel Adams Center, 250 Fourth Street, San Francisco, CA 94103. Supports serious, creative photography. Sponsors exhibitions, workshops, and seminars. Bestows awards. Publications: *Friends of Photography-Untitled,* and newsletter.

International Kodak Historical Society. PO Box 21, Flourtown, PA 19031. Persons interested in the history of photography. Publication: Journal.

International Photographic Historical Organization. PO Box 16074, San Francisco, CA 94116. Individuals interested in studying photographic history and collecting photographic artifacts.

National Stereoscopic Association. PO Box 14801, Columbus, OH 43214. Those interested in history as recorded by the stereo photographer, and present day uses of three dimensional photographic equipment. Maintains library, sponsors competitions, and bestows awards. Publication: *Stereo World* magazine.

Photographic Society of America. 3000 United Founders Boulevard, Suite 103, Oklahoma City, OK 73112. Amateur and professional photographers. Sponsors competitions, presents awards, provides instruction and other technical services. Publication: *PSA Journal.*

Stereo Photographers, Collectors and Enthusiasts Club. PO Box 2368, Culver City, CA 90231. Furthers interest in the subject. Maintains library. Publications: *3-D Catalog,* and *The World of 3-D: A Practical Guide to Stereo Photography.*

Underwater Photographic Society. PO Box 2401, Culver City, CA 90231. Certified scuba divers, amateur and professional underwater photographers. Promotes underwater photography, sponsors competitions, and bestows awards. Publication: Newsletter.

Physical Fitness

FITNESS IS THE ABILITY to perform work with a minimum of effort. Your physical fitness is dependent upon the condition of the various systems that enable the body to function. The cardiovascular system is composed of the heart, lungs, and the blood vessels and airways that serve to couple them together.

Muscles are attached to our bony skeletal structure by means of tendons. When muscles contract and shorten, they pull on the tendons to move a bone in a given direction around its end joint.

Your ability to use these systems effectively is somewhat dependent upon heredity. Your genes will determine your height, bone structure, and to some extent, your weight.

Cardiovascular System

In the lungs, oxygen from the air diffuses across thin-walled membranes into tiny blood vessels, called capillaries. The oxygen combines with blood hemoglobin and travels to the heart. The heart pumps the oxygen-rich blood to all the body's organs. The arteries that carry the blood to muscles branch into small capillaries. Oxygen in diffused from the capillaries into muscle cells where it is used as fuel for the energy of contraction. Waste products from the process diffuse out of the muscle into capillaries, and proceed to the heart by means of veins. The heart pumps the waste-laden blood to the lungs and liver. The lungs exhale carbon dioxide, the waste product of aerobic exercise. The liver processes lactic acid, the waste product of anaerobic exercise. The liver converts the lactic acid into glycogen, which is later converted to simple sugar.

When you exercise for short periods your muscles are driven by anaerobic enzymes that don't require oxygen. These enzymes are used up in about two minutes of maximum use. Muscles then require aerobic enzymes when used for longer periods, and those enzymes use oxygen for metabolism. Once sufficient oxygen reaches the muscles you can continue with your exercise. Breathlessness during exercise is produced when your muscles demand more oxygen than your heart and circulation can deliver.

The Aging Process

The ability to process oxygen during exercise varies with age. The ability peaks in your twenties and then declines. Regular exercise slows the oxygen processing decline considerably.

With aging, muscular strength and mass declines, flexibility of ligaments and joints decreases, bones lose calcium, and fat content of the body increases. You can slow these changes by means of physical activity.

Endurance training increases heart and lung capacities, lowers blood pressure, and decreases body fat. Muscles become stronger and reaction time is improved. The body adapts to accommodate the increased demands placed on it by appropriate exercise programs.

Determine Your Fitness Level

What is your current fitness level? You have to know in order to plan a safe and practical fitness program. Our society has become less labor-intensive and more dependent on cars for transportation. This has resulted in a sedentary way of life that has had an impact on the fitness of all ages.

You can make a preliminary self-assessment by attempting the calisthenics described in Dr. Harvey B. Simon's book, *The Athlete Within.* Less than so many push-ups is poor, more is moderate, and still more is good; and so on for touching toes, sit-ups, etc. But suppose you have an undetected problem such as high blood pressure. Since your fitness program will be placing stress on various parts of the body, there will be an element of risk involved.

The safest approach is to have an accurate medical assessment made. You'll have a clear picture of where you are at the start and will be able to chart progress toward better fitness levels. Cardiovascular fitness can be measured by means of a stress test. The test includes measurement of heart rate and blood pressure as you exercise on a treadmill or other such device. Measurements can also be made of the maximum oxygen uptake under these conditions.

Exercise

When we run, swim, or ride a bike, we are experiencing dynamic or isotonic exercise. Muscle fibers contract and muscle tension remains constant. Blood vessels widen and blood pressure increases slightly. Heart rate increases significantly. Isotonic exercise builds muscle endurance and efficient blood circulation.

When we lift weights, shovel snow, or do push-ups, we are doing static, high resistance, or isometric exercise. Muscle fibers contract and muscle tension increases. Blood vessels narrow and blood pressure increases significantly. Heart rate increases slightly. High resistance exercise builds muscular strength and power.

Our overall objectives are to not only increase strength and endurance, but also improve flexibility, reaction time, and coordination. These elements of fitness can be improved by sports participation preceded by suitable warm-up and stretching exercises.

An exercise program should include a warm-up period to gradually achieve the aerobic state described above. Stretch muscles slowly, minimizing rapid bouncing movements. Before maximum effort can be attained, a muscle must be warmed-up through the repetition of a movement that is less demanding than the muscle is capable of handling. The heart rate is gradually increased.

The periods of exercise need not be excessively long to be effective. Muscular strength and growth are more dependent on the amount of muscular force you use during exercise. Climbing hills builds more muscle than slow walking.

The body should be allowed sufficient recovery time between workouts. Three exercise periods per week spaced at least a day apart provide adequate results. When your fitness level reaches a plateau, and fails to improve, it's time for a seven to ten day layoff to rest and recuperate.

Exercise increases strength by creating a need for growth. It makes demands on the body that can't easily be met by its existing muscular development. Muscles grow as a result, including the heart muscle. Scientific tests reveal that growth spurts occur within periods as short as ten minutes. Further, the growth happens during rest periods over thirty hours after the muscle stimulation occurs.

Bones constantly change in response to stress and use. Activity increases the mineral content and strength. Cartilage is found on the ends of bones where it provides a slippery surface and shock absorption. Cartilage contains water, which is partially squeezed out during exercise. The water returns when the joint is at rest. Cartilage gets its nutrients from the joint fluid that flows in and out. Inactivity leads to thinning of joint cartilage and to osteoarthritis.

There seems to be but one conclusion regarding the exercise of our bodies. We either use them or lose their capabilities.

Most fitness books state that you need to have your heart rate up to its working level for a period of time to achieve the benefits of aerobic effects. They set a target rate at somewhere between 60 and 85 percent of your maximum heart rate. Formulas are given that take into account the reduced maximum heart rate experienced with age. These recommended targets can't take your present fitness level into account. They may be too high if you have high blood pressure or other cardiovascular problems. They may not be high enough to provide the proper challenge to a superbly fit athlete. Let you physician help set a target heart rate appropriate for you.

Exercise Equipment

Exercise machines make it possible for you to get fit in the privacy of your home.

Stationary bikes are designed to allow you to sit and pedal, turning a wheel having a variable resistance. By adjusting the braking action on the wheel, you vary the amount of work it takes to peddle. Boredom can be a factor, but music or TV can provide a distraction.

Treadmills allow you to walk or run indoors. Some depend on your stride to move the belt. Others are motorized; and most can be inclined to simulate training on hills.

Cross-country ski machines have simulated skis that rest on rollers. Handles attached to cables simulate ski poles. As you perform the exaggerated striding action of the sport, you condition both arms and legs. The aerobic benefits are varied by adjusting the resistance independently for arms or legs.

Rowing machines have handles simulating oars. They provide exercise to your shoulders, arms, back, and legs. The resistance to the pulling action is variable.

Rope jumping is an aerobic activity that can provide high-level cardiovascular conditioning. It also develops coordination and balance.

Barbells have been used effectively in weight training since the turn of the century. However, they do have some limitations. A barbell works a muscle harder in some positions than others. When the arms are positioned out in front horizontally, the muscles are being taxed. When the arms are positioned vertically overhead, the barbell is supported with minimal muscular action.

Multi-purpose home gyms vary considerably in utility and cost. To provide the most effective conditioning, a well-designed unit should work a muscle during all stages of a given movement. Any movement of a body part should produce a resistance against that body part. While a few home units meet this requirement to some extent, the more expensive units found in fitness centers have the ability to work specific body parts separately and effectively.

Sports

Sports are a form of preventative medicine. They relieve stress and fight depression, obesity, and cardiovascular disease.

Some sports provide aerobic benefits with minimal physical risk. Walking, running, swimming, rowing, biking, cross-country skiing, skating, and aerobic dance are examples of aerobic sports that can be enjoyed in moderation by beginners and by people of all ages.

Golf and bowling also can be enjoyed at all ages, but rank low in aerobic benefits.

Many competitive team sports provide significant aerobic benefits. Some of the highest ranking include basketball, fencing, touch football, gymnastics, hockey, martial arts, skating, down hill skiing, and soccer. See separate sections in this text for more details of these sports.

Bibliography

REFERENCE BOOKS

Cluff, Sheila, with Eva Shaw. *Sheila Cluff's Aerobic Body Contouring: The New Low-Impact Exercise Program for the Ageless Body.* Emmaus, PA: Rodale, 1987. A total fitness program with emphasis on calisthenics with wrist weights.

Darden, Ellington. *The Nautilus Bodybuilding Book.* Rev. ed. Chicago: Contemporary Books, 1986. How to train correctly and achieve maximum gains from workouts. Emphasis on Nautilus exercise equipment.

de Varona, Donna, and Barry Tarshis. *Donna de Varona's Hydro-Aerobics.* New York: Ballantine Books, 1986. A series of aerobic exercises done using the natural resistance of water.

Ilg, Steve. *The Outdoor Athlete: Total Training for Outdoor Performance.* Evergreen, CO: Cordillera, 1987. Explores physical training, nutrition, and mental training as related to sports.

Macchia, Donald Dean. *Weight Lifting and Bodybuilding: Total Fitness for Men and Women.* Chicago: Nelson-Hall, 1987. The information that a successful weight lifter needs to improve skills.

Mangi, Richard, Peter Jokl, and O. William Dayton. *Sports Fitness and Training.* New York: Pantheon Books, 1987. A comprehensive training guide. Emphasis on relationship to popular sports.

Prudden, Bonnie. *Bonnie Prudden's After Fifty Fitness Guide.* New York: Villard Books, 1986. Comprehensive coverage of fitness and exercise. Includes discussion of myotherapy treatment for pain.

Sawyer, Phyllis, and Pat Thornton. *Aerobic Dancing: A Step at a Time.* Chicago: Contemporary Books, 1981. Discusses general health, cardiovascular fitness, and regular exercise.

Simmons, Richard. *Reach for Fitness: A Special Book of Exercises for the Physically Challenged.* New York: Warner Books, 1986. Emphasis on stretching and calisthenics for children and adults who are physically challenged.

———. *Richard Simmons' Better Body Book.* New York: Warner Books, 1983. Exercise programs for all levels of fitness. Emphasis on stretching and calisthenics.

Simon, Harvey B., and Steven R. Levisohn. *The Athlete Within: A Personal Guide to Total Fitness.* Boston: Little, Brown, 1987. Information on exercise, nutrition, and stress management.

Wolf, Michael D. *Nautilus Fitness for Women.* Chicago: Contemporary Books, 1983. Assists women in gaining a better understanding of Nautilus equipment and in attaining positive results from their training.

PERIODICALS

American Fitness. Aerobics and Fitness Association of America, 15250 Ventura Boulevard, Suite 310, Sherman Oaks, CA 91403.

Fitness in America. National Sporting Goods Association, 1699 Wall Street, Mt. Prospect, IL 60056–5780. (Analysis of adult participation in seven fitness activities.)

Vim & Vigor. McMurry Publishers, 8805 N. 23rd Avenue, No. 11, Phoenix, AZ 85021.

Walking Magazine. Walking, 9–11 Harcourt Street, Boston, MA 02116.

Weightlifting U.S.A. U.S. Weightlifting Federation, 1750 E. Boulder Street, Colorado Springs, CO 80909.

ASSOCIATIONS

Aerobics and Fitness Association of America. 15250 Ventura Boulevard, Suite 310, Sherman Oaks, CA 91403. Fitness professionals and enthusiasts, and sports enthusiasts. Establishes competition standards, produces educational videotapes. Publication: *American Fitness.*

American Fitness Association. PO Box 401, Durango, CO 81301. Conducts research and educational activities in the field of aerobic exercise. Tests exercise products. Publications: *American Fitness Association* newsletter, and *Aerobic Dance.*

American Fitness Association. 6285 E. Spring Street, No. 404, Long Beach, CA 90808. Professionals and interested individuals. Promotes interest, involvement, and education in health and fitness. Sponsors seminars and competitions. Endorses athletic events and sports-related tours. Maintains hall of fame and bestows awards. Publications: Journal, directory, and related materials.

United States Water Fitness Association. PO Box 3279, Boynton Beach, FL 33424. Promotes water aerobics and deep water exercise. Maintains library and bestows awards. Publications: *National Aquatics Exchange Newsletter,* and *National Water Fitness Newsletter.*

U.S. Powerlifting Federation. PO Box 389, Roy, UT 84067. Amateur powerlifters. Sponsors clinics, seminars, and a sports medicine program. Bestows awards. Coordinates the competition of foreign athletes in the U.S. and sanctions Special Olympics powerlifting meets. Maintains hall of fame.

Racquetball

RACQUETBALL IS A COURT SPORT played with a racquet and a soft rubber ball.

The game utilizes a standard handball court that is forty feet long, twenty feet wide, and twenty feet high. The end walls are identified as the front and back wall. A line is marked on the floor twenty feet from the back wall. It defines the back court and is called the short line. Another line, called the service line, is marked twenty-five feet from the back wall. It defines the front court. A receiving line is marked five feet back of the short line. The area between the short line and the receiving line is the safety zone.

The game uses virtually the same rules as handball. The server has two chances to make a legal serve. Standing behind the service line, he/she serves the ball by bouncing it to the floor, and on the first bounce the ball is struck by the server's racquet so that it hits the front wall and on the rebound hits the floor, either with or without touching one of the side walls. If it hits the back wall first, hits in front of the short line, or hits more than one side wall, the serve is illegal. After the serve, the players alternate striking the ball.

The opponent must strike the ball with his/her racquet either on the fly after passing the receiving line, or after the first bounce and before the ball touches the floor for the second time. The opponent must return the ball to the front wall either directly or after touching one or both side walls, the back wall or the ceiling, or any combination of these surfaces. A returned ball may not touch the floor before touching the front wall. An opponent's failure to return a ball in the prescribed manner results in a point for the server.

The objective is to win each series of shots exchanged (volley) by returning the ball so the opponent is unable to keep the ball in play. Only the server gains points. If the server fails to return the ball, or makes two illegal serves, the opponent takes over the serve. The side first scoring fifteen points wins the game. A match is won by the first side winning two games. In the event each side wins one game, the tie breaker game is played to eleven points.

You don't have to be an experienced player to enjoy racquetball. The twenty by twenty foot front wall is a relatively easy target for the beginner. Pace of the games depends on the condition and skill of the players. However, owing to the rate of speed that the ball returns, and the number of directions from which it can come, making a good return can be a challenge. Eye protection is important in this sport. The ball can leave a welt when it strikes you, and eye contact would be serious.

The sport requires considerable stamina. Players should prepare their bodies by engaging in suitable calisthenics, pregame warm-up, and stretching exercises.

History

Handball is the oldest forerunner to racquetball. The game of Fives, later called handball, originated in Ireland during the tenth century. Irish immigrant Phil Casey settled in Brooklyn, New York about 1882. He built a handball court and recruited immigrant players to popularize the game in the United States. Handball players use all walls, floor, and ceiling during play. No net is used.

Squash was introduced to the United States from England in the 1880s. The game uses a smaller enclosure than handball, but shares the rules that permit use of the walls in play. No net is used.

Paddleball is a combination of tennis and handball developed in the 1920s by Earl Riskey of the University of Michigan. A net is used on a court much smaller than that used for tennis.

The game of racquetball was created in the late 1940s by Joseph G. Sobek, a tennis and squash teaching professional. He decided that paddleball might be improved by substituting a strung racquet for the wooden paddle normally used. Sobek called the game paddle-rackets. Robert W. Kendler, founder and first president of the International Racquetball Association (later the U.S. Racquetball Association) and the National Racquetball Club, is given credit for standardizing the game. It is a marriage of paddleball, handball and squash.

Equipment

The uniform consists of a shirt, shorts, and socks that are white or of a bright color. Warm-up up pants and shirts may be substituted.

A flat-soled shoe such as those made for tennis or basketball allows quick movements in all directions.

The racquet maximum dimensions are: head length—eleven inches, width—nine inches; handle—seven inches; total length and width of the racquet—twenty-seven inches. The racquet must include a thong for attachment to the player's wrist. Frame material is optional; string material can be gut, monofilament, nylon, or metal.

The ball is 2.25 inches in diameter. Weight is 1.4 ounces. When dropped from 100 inches at 70–74 degrees F., it shall bounce 68 to 72 inches.

Some players prefer to play using leather gloves to keep sweaty hands from reducing their grip on the racquet.

Strategy

Grip the racquet as if you were shaking hands with it. Hold it square to the intended line of flight of the ball. As you change from a backhand stroke to a forehand stroke, rotate the racquet slightly to maintain the proper angle to the line of flight.

After hitting the ball, assume a crouched ready position. Hold the racquet level with your chest, ready to start your backswing. Face the side on which you expect to hit the ball. Bend your knees and keep your weight on the back foot. Stand in central court, about four feet behind the short line. Control of the center court is one of the keys to winning at racquetball.

When you are about to hit the ball, move to a location that will permit racquet contact at about knee height. Position yourself sideways to the line of flight of the ball, weight on back foot, and the racquet back ready to strike. Keep your eye on the ball and aim your shot low (kill shot) to minimize the time your opponent will have to retrieve it. Concentrate on choosing the spot to aim your return. At contact with the ball, move your weight forward, and follow through.

The lob is a floating shot, aimed high on the front wall, that should go over your opponent's head, forcing him/her

to go into the back court. Aimed high enough, the lob bounces off the front wall to the ceiling (ceiling ball) and ends up in the back court.

Hit a pass shot so it rebounds from the front wall waist high and goes deep into the back court without touching a side wall. Position yourself between the ball and your opponent. If the opponent is at center court, and you are to his/her left, have the ball pass to your left.

When your opponent aims a kill shot low to the front wall, and you are near the front wall, hit the ball softly to a still lower point on the front wall (drop shot), leaving him/her little time to recover and return the shot.

With experience, a player can hit the ball with a glancing stroke imparting spin, or English, on the ball. Done occasionally, you gain the element of surprise when the ball doesn't fly in a normal trajectory.

With practice you can make use of the walls to cause the ball to travel in unexpected directions. Examples include: the front wall, side wall, opposite side wall, to floor shot; or the side wall, front wall, opposite side wall, to floor shot. The objective is to make the ball land out of the reach of your opponent.

Handball

Although the game of racquetball has taken over many handball courts, the game of handball continues to have a strong following.

The two games share the same court dimensions and most of the same rules. Handball players strike a smaller ball with gloved hands. The player first scoring twenty-one points wins the game. A match consists of two games of twenty-one points each with an eleven-point tie-breaker if the first two games are split.

In the United States, national Amateur Athletic Union handball championships were started in 1919, national YMCA championships in 1925, and the national Jewish Welfare Board championships in the late 1940s. The official regulatory agency for the game, the United States Handball Association, has held national championships at the collegiate level since 1953.

The first world four-wall handball championship was held in New York in 1964. The United States won over Australia, Ireland, and Mexico.

The handball uniform consists of shirt, shorts, socks, and shoes. Color is optional, but unusual patterns affecting the opponents view of the ball may not be worn.

Handball gloves must be light in color, form fitting and made of a soft material or leather. The fingers of the gloves may not be webbed, connected, or removed.

The ball is $1\frac{7}{8}$ inches in diameter. Weight is 2.3 ounces. When dropped from 70 inches at 68 degrees F., it shall bounce 46 to 50 inches.

Since handball players expend so much energy, gloves and clothing must be changed when their perspiration moistens the ball.

From ready position to kill shots and pass shots, handball strategy is the same as that described for racquetball.

Bibliography

REFERENCE BOOKS

Brumfield, Charles, and Jeffrey Bairstow. *Off the Wall: Championship Racquetball for the Ardent Amateur.* New York: Dial, 1978. The rules, the serves, the tricks and strategies of serious competitive play.

Hogan, Marty, and Charlie Brumfield. *Marty Hogan's Power Racquetball.* Chicago: Contemporary Books, 1978. Coverage of equipment, conditioning, and techniques.

Kittleson, Stan. *Racquetball Steps to Success.* Champaign, IL: Leisure, 1992. Step-by-step instruction, and drills.

Reznik, John W. *Racquetball.* New York: Sterling, 1979. The equipment, shots, strategy, and conditioning for play.

Sauser, Jean, and Arthur Shay. *Inside Racquetball for Women.* Chicago: Contemporary Books, 1977. An instruction book that illustrates the most common errors made by students of racquetball, followed by photos of the correct techniques.

Shay, Arthur, with Chuck Leve. *Winning Racquetball.* Chicago: Contemporary Books, 1976. A comprehensive illustrated guide, showing how to advance from beginner to winning competitor.

Shay, Arthur, and Terry Fancher. *40 Common Errors in Racquetball and How to Correct Them.* Chicago: Contemporary Books, 1978. Photographic essay of problem situations and the correct response.

Strandemo, Steve, with Bill Bruns. *Strategic Racquetball.* New York: Pocket Books, 1985. Well illustrated coverage of specific shots and techniques.

Sylvis, James. *Racquetball for Everyone: Technique and Strategy.* Englewood Cliffs, NJ: Prentice-Hall, 1985. How to practice, control game tempo, and exercise.

Wright, Shannon, with Steve Keeley. *The Women's Book of Racquetball.* Chicago: Contemporary Books, 1980. Definitive overview of the game, with emphasis on women's participation.

Yessis, Michael. *Handball: Exploring Sports Series.* Rev. ed. Dubuque, IA: Brown, 1984. Techniques and strategy of handball.

PERIODICAL

Handball. U.S. Handball Association, 2333 N. Tucson Boulevard, Tucson, AZ 85716.

ASSOCIATIONS

American Amateur Racquetball Association. 815 N. Weber, Suite 101, Colorado Springs, CO 80903. Racquetball players and enthusiasts. Conducts racquetball events including annual national and international tournaments. Maintains hall of fame, and children's services. Sponsors competitions, presents awards, and scholarships. Affiliated with the United States Olympic Committee. Publication: *Official AARA Rules.*

International Racquetball Federation. 815 N. Weber, Suite 101, Colorado Springs, CO 80903–2947. International sports federations representing over fourteen million members. Helps coordinate the efforts and activities of organizations promoting racquetball, serves as a clearinghouse for coaching aids, rules, literature, films, and research materials. Trains and certifies officials. Maintains a hall of fame, and museum. Sponsors competitions and bestows awards.

National Racquetball Association of the Deaf. 7532 Tarpley Drive, Rockville, MD 20855. Hearing impaired athletes. Promotes fellowship and the development of members' athletic skills through the game of racquetball. Publication: *NRAD Newsletter.*

United States Handball Association. 930 North Benton Avenue, Tucson, AZ 85711. Establishes rules, sponsors tournaments, and promotes handball as an intercollegiate activity. Supports games and tournaments for youngsters. Maintains hall of fame. Publication: *Handball* magazine.

Radio, Amateur

AMATEUR RADIO OPERATORS communicate with one another using special radio bands assigned for their use. At one time or another, most of us have become so involved in the message coming over our radio or television that we have felt the urge to talk back to the person speaking. Amateurs, called hams, have this opportunity to talk with other amateurs because they share a common interest in radio and electronics.

While on the air, they also tend to make repeat contacts with other hams having similar secondary hobbies. What easier way to seek information, an opinion, or discuss a problem than to simply turn on the transmitter, tune the ham band and say "CQ," which is the recognized code for inviting anyone listening to have an exchange of conversation? With over 450 thousand hams in the United States, someone is sure to be listening. In this hobby you may speak with people from all walks of life and from around the world. People like a famous United States senator, or the nun who relays emergency calls for help from foreign countries each afternoon, or a nervous teenager struggling to become better at sending the dots and dashes of the Morse code.

Experienced telegraph operators were critical of the "ham fisted" way early amateurs pounded their code sending keys. This may be the origin of the expression ham operator. Hams always seem to be there in times of emergency, expediting communications when normal facilities have broken down. Explorers on polar expeditions have been known to depend on a network of amateur radio operators.

History

In 1895 Guglielmo Marconi transmitted signals through the air for two miles on Salisbury Plain in England and practical radio was born. Soon many experimenters were transmitting signals at various frequencies and power levels. Congress passed the Radio Act of 1912 to bring some order out of the developing chaos. At the time commercial and military stations received priority regarding frequency assignment. Frequencies shorter than 200 meters were considered useless, and were given to amateurs and other noncommercial interests.

It didn't take long for hams to organize and take advantage of the "useless" frequency assignment. The American Radio Relay League (ARRL) was founded in 1914. Since broadcast range was limited, hams would pick up messages from the original sender and rebroadcast them (relay them) along to the intended distant recipient. By 1916 there were over 6,000 licensed amateur stations.

Many of these hobbyists served with distinction as radio operators during World War I. In 1925 the ARRL cooperated with the U.S. Navy in tests designed to demonstrate the possibility of using short waves for long distance communications with ships at sea. Amateur radio experienced rapid growth after this period, taking advantage of, and contributing to, the advancement of the science.

In this day of super miniaturized integrated circuits hams find it more difficult to build their equipment from discarded components as they did in the golden age of radio, but many are still doing it and finding ways to advance the state of the art. People whose main interests lie in the communication aspect of the hobby need not be put off by concerns about building equipment. Excellent ready-built radio gear is available and costs are being reduced by advances in electronics.

Radio Waves and Their Reception

When a ham operator presses a sending key to send code or speaks into a microphone, the signal is processed by an electronic unit called a transmitter. It is then fed to an antenna and broadcast in the form of radio waves.

When a radio signal is transmitted, the waves travel along the surface of the earth and also through the upper atmosphere. The part of the wave that travels along the ground loses energy quickly and travels relatively short distances. The part that radiates upward (the sky wave) strikes the ionosphere. The ionosphere consists of four layers of ionized particles that blanket the earth between forty and 250 miles above the surface. When high frequency (HF) sky waves strike one of these ionized layers they bounce back toward the earth. If the signal is strong enough it may then bounce or skip off of the earth's surface and continue in this manner for many miles.

Radio signals go through a cycle or beat. The number of beats in a given length of time is called it's frequency. When waves occur at high frequency in a given length of time, they become shorter than those used on the regular broadcast band that we listen to for our news and music. Hence the name "shortwave" to describe high frequency broadcast bands.

Very high frequency (VHF) and ultra high frequency (UHF) waves travel in a line-of-sight fashion. They are much less likely to skip as HF waves do. They can skip when certain weather conditions exist in a lower atmospheric layer called the troposphere. The more reliable skip that contributes to HF distance transmission can't be depended on for VHF and UHF, but we will see how earth satellites are used to relay these signals to solve that problem.

Radio receivers are designed with certain qualities or characteristics that are balanced against one another. Let's review these characteristics that enable a radio to meet specific requirements.

Fidelity is the accuracy of reproduction of the original sound. Most of the highs, lows, and presence of the original are maintained in high fidelity. Fidelity is obtained by admitting a wide signal band through the radio for amplification.

Selectivity is the ability to pick up a single radio station from among a group of stations with closely spaced frequencies. Also, the ability to reject those adjacent stations. It is obtained by admitting a narrow signal band through the radio for amplification, sacrificing fidelity.

Sensitivity is the ability to receive distant stations. It is obtained by using a high degree of amplification within the radio after the signal is received. As sensitivity is increased, selectivity must be as well or closely spaced distant stations would both be heard.

In a radio designed for amateur radio, selectivity and sensitivity are emphasized at the expense of fidelity. These radios are called communications receivers. Figure 1 illustrates this type of receiver used by amateurs. Some units, called transceivers, combine the features of a transmitter and a receiver. To minimize the band width used in amateur applications, many use transmitters that cut off one side of the normal band width. This is called single side band broadcasting.

Figure 1

A typical communications receiver used by amateur radio operators and shortwave listeners.

Activities and Procedures

Special interest groups of hams have been formed to share their enjoyment of hobbies, associations, similar occupations and other interests. The ARRL publishes a directory each year listing time and radio frequency information for hundreds of such amateur radio networks.

Hams enjoy the challenge of achieving long distance contacts using their equipment. A ham who shows proof of having contacted (worked) all states qualifies for a WAS certificate. Proof of a contact is sought for and provided when the person contacted sends a postcard to the sender with date, time and other details of the contact specified. These are called QSL cards. They are eagerly collected by DX operators (hams who seek long distance contacts). The ARRL lists 323 active countries in the world. At the time of writing thirty-nine hams from around the world have contacted all 323.

International Q signals have been established to minimize Morse code transmissions. Examples include QTH meaning "my location is," QSL "Can you acknowledge receipt?" and QRM "your transmission is being interfered with."

Sophisticated approaches are taken in the never-ending quest for long distance operation. We saw that early hams relayed messages through other hams to achieve long distance contacts. Today various forms of repeater stations are also used. The repeater receives the signal, may change its frequency, amplify it, and send it along its way. This is especially useful when VHF signals with their straight "line-of-sight" paths are used.

A series of earth satellites has been constructed by hams and launched into orbit through the cooperation of various space agencies. The number of orbital satellite carrying amateur radio (OSCAR) satellites has reached thirteen at the time of writing. OSCAR 13 receives the signal from earth and transmits it back affording a high level skip to the signal. For example if the satellite was over the mid-Atlantic Ocean, a transmitter in the United States could contact it, and the satellite could relay the signal to a receiver in Europe. Thus the satellite helps the sender's signal reach destinations over the horizon. The Russians launched a pair of repeaters on a COSMOS navigation satellite in 1991 that is also free for use by all of the earth's radio amateurs. The repeaters are called RS–12 and 13.

Skillful amateurs with a computer tracking program for aiming purposes use a much higher satellite to advantage. They bounce their signals off of the moon.

A new and fast growing mode of operation is called packet radio. In this method of operation the sender types a message into a personal computer. The computer language is fed to a unit called a terminal node controller (TNC) that organizes and controls the message (groups the data into packets to be sent in short bursts). The message then proceeds to a modem (MOdulator DEModulator) unit that transforms it into a signal that is acceptable to a radio transmitter. The transmitter then broadcasts the message to a listener's receiver.

At the receiving end, the signal passes through a radio receiver, a modem, a TNC and into a computer. It then can be read on the computer screen and/or printed on a printer attached to the computer.

Amateurs are rapidly expanding the capabilities of packet radio. Pictures or drawings can be converted to signals using a scanning device and communicated in the same way as text. A weak signal from a small transmitter can be relayed by a repeater station that can be instructed to rebroadcast it with more power and/or on a different frequency. If instructed to do so, the message can be repeated by satellite and sent anywhere in the world. This system will be of great benefit to the deaf amateur.

Television broadcasting requires a very broad band of frequencies to transmit a signal. This is a luxury not available to amateurs. To avoid the problem, hams transmit television signals by a slow scan method that utilizes a much narrower band, but takes longer to transmit a complete picture. Perhaps amateurs will take advantage of new methods of digital compression being applied to images by the TV industry. See "Movies and the VCR" elsewhere in this book.

Getting Started

To get started in amateur radio, write to the ARRL and ask for information. The league coordinates the hobby in the United States. You may also wish to contact your local radio club for more information. Radio parts stores can often help you locate a club. To operate on radio frequencies set aside for hams, you must have a license. To obtain a license you are required to pass a test of your ability to send and receive Morse code and answer questions about radio theory. As you become more proficient, you may take advanced tests that qualify you for higher ratings, permitting additional privileges such as a greater selection of frequencies upon which to operate.

In 1991 a new Federal Communications Commission (FCC) ruling became effective regarding the licensing requirements for the entry-level technician license amateur rating. The requirement to demonstrate the ability to send and receive Morse code at a rate of five words-per-minute was removed. The radio theory test remains. This step was taken to encourage individuals to join the ranks of radio amateurs, expanding the pool of people knowledgeable in the field of electronics who would go on to become technicians, engineers, and scientists.

Equipment

Equipment selection is dependent upon the space available for your operations and the money you can afford to spend. If space is limited, a beginner can start operations with a transceiver, a CW key (to send Morse code), and a microphone. These components can often be used when you upgrade to a higher class license by adding a high-power amplifier and other accessories. The key to future use is careful, informed selection of the basic components. Research equipment in magazines and seek advice from experienced hams.

Start-up costs can be reduced by buying used equipment. The element of risk in this approach can be reduced by buying radio gear from a reputable dealer who services equipment before offering it for sale. Avoid obsolete items dating before the introduction of modern solid-state radios. Again, seek experienced advice, preferably from those who have owned the type of equipment being considered.

Unless a beginning ham has had considerable experience in electronics it would be best to postpone the building of equipment. It would be difficult for the novice to provide the quality workmanship and to deal with the complexity found in modern transmitters and receivers. Reserve early construction attempts for support equipment and accessories.

Detailed advice on equipment selection can be found in the book, *Now You're Talking,* published by the ARRL.

Relationships and Interfaces

Amateur radio has a well-deserved reputation for public service. Voluntary communications service and loans of equipment are provided during international emergencies.

Hams spend hours of their time on the air relaying messages from servicemen overseas. Other examples are reported in the press on a regular basis.

Hams promote international goodwill and understanding through their extensive contacts and conversations with foreign nationals.

Amateur radio operators interface with many disciplines, scientific and otherwise. They use computers to calculate communications satellite locations, and many other factors influencing their operations. The computer interface is an integral part of packet operations.

Some hams have become involved with radio astronomy, capturing electromagnetic wave information from the heavens.

Weather-watch networks are being studied to communicate instant meteorological data from many locations. Information such as the temperature, wind direction and velocity, and data from a rain gauge can be collected, automatically fed into a transmitter, and accessed from a remote location.

Hams enjoy experimentation. If there is something new in electronics, hams will find applications for it and the public will benefit.

Other Radio-Related Pastimes

Radio equipment is also used in applications where licensing isn't required. Some hobbyists simply listen, others choose to limit their communications to short distances.

Shortwave Listening

In the early days of radio, listeners tuned across the broadcast band carefully to pull in distant stations. It was exciting to hear a station hundreds of miles away. Some transmitters used to broadcast at much higher power than today to help compensate for the relatively crude receivers of the day.

On shortwave bands it was, and still is, possible to hear commercial radio stations from around the world. All it takes is a radio capable of shortwave reception, a good antenna, and the knowledge of where to tune in the stations you want to hear. Books such as *Passport to World Band Radio* and *The Complete Shortwave Listener's Handbook* will help you choose a radio and find the stations. An endless variety of programming awaits the shortwave listener—foreign stations that direct broadcasts to America, public service stations that broadcast weather and other vital data, plus a vast selection of foreign broadcasts that include programs of music and information on the cultures and customs of other countries, as well as news

reports that give the listener first-hand reports on developing situations from a foreign country's point of view.

Shortwave listening is an excellent hobby for a shut-in. Some listeners enjoy identifying stations in different countries and writing them indicating what they heard and when. Commercial stations will usually respond with a collectible QSL card, just as amateur radio operators do.

Citizens Band Radio

Although not a part of the amateur radio service, citizens band radio operation often sparks an interest in acquiring an amateur license in order to enjoy activities limited to hams. The citizens band radio service (CB) exists for short-distance low-power, personal and business communication only. Licenses are not required for CB operators and call signs are not assigned. CB users may operate from base (fixed) stations or from mobile equipment. The service is useful for local communications, especially in times of emergency.

Bibliography

REFERENCE BOOKS

American Radio Relay League. *ARRL Antenna Book.* 16th ed. Newington, CT: American Radio Relay League, 1991. Antenna fundamentals, design, and construction.

———. *ARRL Operating Manual.* Newington, CT: American Radio Relay League, 1987. How to make the best use of your station.

———. *ARRL 1992 Handbook.* 68th ed. Newington, CT: American Radio Relay League, 1991. Comprehensive source of amateur radio reference material.

———. *Now You're Talking: Discover the World of Ham Radio.* Newington, CT: American Radio Relay League, 1991. Everything you need to know to earn your first radio license, select equipment, and get on the air.

Bennett, Hank, and Harry L. Helms. *The Complete Shortwave Listener's Handbook.* 3rd ed. Blue Ridge Summit, PA: TAB Books, 1986. Information from all over the world on the latest developments in shortwave listening technology, clubs, associations, practices, and stations.

Helms, Harry L. *Shortwave Listening Guidebook.* San Diego, CA: High Text, 1991. Comprehensive overview of shortwave listening from an author who has extensive experience in the hobby.

Locher, R. C. Jr. *Complete DX'er.* 2nd ed. Deerfield, IL: Idiom, 1989. Guidance for long distance ham operation.

Long, Mark, Bonnie Crystal, and Jeffrey Keating. *The World of C.B. Radio.* 3rd ed. Summertown, TN: Book, 1987. Covers all aspects of CB radio including getting on the air, buying a new rig, and other equipment. Provides American and British frequency charts.

Magne, Lawrence, ed. *Passport to World Band Radio,* 1993. Penn's Park, PA: International Broadcasting Services, 1992. Similar to a TV guide for world band radios. How to get started in shortwave listening, what's on, and reviews of the best equipment.

Mayo, Jonathan L. *The Packet Radio Handbook.* 2nd ed. Blue Ridge Summit, PA: Tab Books, 1989. Definitive guide to amateur packet operation.

Orr, William. *All About VHF Amateur Radio.* Lake Bluff, IL: Radio, 1991. Includes antennas, repeaters, and OSCAR satellites.

———. *Radio Handbook.* 23rd ed. Carmel, IN: Sams, 1987. Overview of radio communication. In depth study of basic components used in radio.

Radio Amateur Callbook, 1992: Radio Amateurs of North America. Vol. 70, No. 1. New York: Watson-Guptill, 1992. Listings of call signs of licensed hams in North America.

Radio Amateur Callbook, 1992: Radio Amateurs of the World. Vol. 70, No. 1. New York: Watson-Guptill, 1992. Listings of call signs of licensed hams worldwide.

West, Gordon. *Technician Class New No-Code: Element 2 and 3A.* Richardson, TX: Master, 1991. What you need to know to become a technician class ham. Test questions and answers.

PERIODICALS

C B Radio—S9. Cowan Publishers, 14 Vanderventer Avenue, Port Washington, NY 11050.

CQ; The Radio Amateur's Journal. CQ Communications, 76 North Broadway, Hicksville, NY 11801.

Popular Communications. CQ Communications, 76 North Broadway, Hicksville, NY 11801.

QST. American Radio Relay League, 225 Main Street, Newington, CT 06111.

73 Amateur Radio Today. Wayne Greene Enterprises, Forest Road, Hancock, NH 03449.

Shortwave Directory. Grove Enterprises, Box 98, Brasstown, NC 28902.

SWL. American Shortwave Listeners Club, 16182 Ballad Lane, Huntington Beach, CA 92649–2204.

ASSOCIATIONS

American CB Radio Association. 3478 Main Street, Hartford, CT 06120. CB radio enthusiasts. Encourages proper and courteous use of CB airways. Publications: Handbook, newsletter.

American Radio Relay League. 225 Main Street, Newington, CT 06111. Licensed hams in the United States and Canada. Maintains museum, operates an experimental equipment laboratory. Serves as secretariat for the International Amateur Radio Union. Publications: QST, and numerous publications useful to all levels of amateur radio operators and experimenters.

American Shortwave Listeners Club. 16182 Ballad Lane, Huntington Beach, CA 92649–2204. Hobbyists interested in listening to shortwave radio broadcasts. Holds contests for members, bestows awards, maintains library, and conducts research programs. Publications: *SWL, Equipment Survey,* and *Proper Reporting Guide.*

International Amateur Radio Union. PO Box 310905, Newington, CT 06131–0905. Federation of national amateur radio societies. Encourages agreements among national societies, promotes amateur radio, and furthers international goodwill.

International Handicappers' Net. PO Box 1185, Ashland, OR 97520. Handicapped, licensed radio amateurs. Promotes international fellowship and helps members to enter the worldwide fraternity of amateur radio operators. Makes referrals for specialized equipment. Publications: Bulletin, and newsletter.

North American Shortwave Association. 45 Wildflower Road, Levittown, PA 19057. Hobbyists interested in listening to shortwave radio broadcasts. Provides a means for exchanging information and ideas. Publication: *The Journal.*

Quarter Century Wireless Association. c/o Ted Heithecker, 159 E. 16th Street, Eugene, OR 97401. Hams throughout the world who were licensed for operation at least twenty-five years ago. Seeks to use the knowledge and experience of members for the benefit of all radio amateurs. Provides scholarship awards. Has museum, library, and hall of fame. Publications: *Hotline Report,* and *News.*

Radio Amateur Satellite Corporation. PO Box 27, Washington, DC 20044. Licensed amateur radio operators and others interested in communicating through AMSAT's series of satellites. Participates in data collection, extensive modification, fabrication, spacecraft design, testing, licensing, and launching arrangements for satellite projects throughout the world. Publication: *AMSAT Journal.*

Railroads and Railfans

FEW HOBBYISTS ARE AS DEDICATED as railfans. Their interests range from hands-on restoration of rolling stock to riding and photographing the equipment of their favorite railroad. Older fans still remember their first sight of a steam locomotive. The senses where overwhelmed with the sight and sound of escaping steam and the chuffing roar of the smokestack and the rhythmic ringing of the bell as the fire breathing monster pulled away from the station. The scene is still repeated for younger fans at the many tourist railways in operation. Today's generation is more likely to be exposed to the day-to-day operation of diesel powered equipment. The sheer size of growling locomotives and the distant haunting wail of the whistle at a crossing is still impressive.

History

Freight movement and passenger travel in America at the beginning of the nineteenth century were confined to horse drawn wagons, river boats and canal barges. When the Erie Canal was completed in 1825, it linked the Hudson River at Albany, New York to Lake Erie at Buffalo. This waterway permitted commerce to flow more easily from the Port of New York to the nation's interior. Other port cities, such as Philadelphia and Baltimore, took note of these developments. In many cases it was impractical to build canals to the west from eastern ports, so plans were laid to use the recently developed steam locomotive to create land links to the Ohio River. The Baltimore and Ohio railroad began operations in 1830. The ancestor of the Pennsylvania Railroad, the Main Line of Public Works, was chartered in 1828. It was a system of railroads and canals. Soon railroads were built inland from Boston and Charleston, South Carolina. Most railroads of the period were built in short sections, facilitating trade between populated areas. Most railroads had equipment and track gauge (distance between rails) that was not standardized. One line would start out with an odd gauge, and others nearby had to match it.

Gradually the short railroad lines were joined and new track was added until the first transcontinental line to California was completed in 1869. During the early development of the rail system, most northern states settled on a standard gauge of 4′8½″. This was based on the gauge used in England, which in turn was very near the wheel gauge of ancient Roman chariots. Southern states had standardized on a five foot gauge. The difference was relatively unimportant until after the Civil War, when commerce resumed between the north and south and standardization became desirable. The southern railroads gradually converted to the standard gauge, and the conversion was completed in 1886. In June of that year, the Louisville and Nashville completed the astounding feat of narrowing two thousand miles of track in a single day. Railroad building accelerated during this period with operating track mileage reaching 192,556 by 1900. Industrial and railroad empires were being built, and small railroad companies were acquired and merged into huge systems. The railroads were taken over by the Federal government, and placed under the jurisdiction of the United States Railroad Administration (USRA), during World War I to assure total control during the war effort. The USRA established a set of standardized locomotive design specifications during that period, which were adhered to through 1944.

During the depression of the early 1930s, the railroad giants fell on hard times, and many declared bankruptcy. The government again nationalized the railroads during World War II. After the war, the competition from trucks, buses, and the airlines caused many of the major railroads to merge to remain competitive. In 1980 the government deregulated the railroads, allowing them to raise prices to certain prescribed levels. Since passenger traffic was less profitable than freight hauling, passenger trains were being eliminated on many routes, except for the heavily-used commuter trains servicing the largest cities. As the situation continued to deteriorate, it became evident that the country couldn't rely solely on highways and the airlines for domestic travel needs. To solve the problem, the government formed the National Railroad Passenger Corporation, which developed Amtrak. Amtrack serves as a contractor, buying service from the nineteen railroads over which it runs passenger trains. Since the beginning of Amtrak service in 1971, railroad ridership has gradually increased. Although government subsidies have been required to keep fares competitive, the need for such funding has gradually decreased and plans are for the railroads to be totally self-sufficient by the end of the century.

As large railroads merge, small short lines are being incorporated to take advantage of markets that have become available. Among the new enterprises are groups studying the feasibility of using the new high speed trains for inter city and commuter service. Speeds over 150 mph are being achieved abroad. Looking into the not-too-distant future, a Maglev (magnetically levitated) system promises to increase speeds further. The system employs superconducting magnets and linear synchronous motors to suspend the train above the track and propel it. The Japanese achieved speeds of 248.5 mph with the system in 1987.

Railfan Activities

The brief historical account above covers the background that produced the railfan. Some railfan associations are advocate groups for train travel. They promote greater utilization of railroad lines and lobby for the introduction of new passenger facilities. Examples of such associations are the National Association of Railroad Passengers and the Ohio Association of Railroad Passengers.

Other groups exist to research the history of early railroads and perpetuate their memory. They collect old photographs and artifacts. Two of the largest groups are the National Railway Historical Society and the Railway and Locomotive Historical Society.

Another important sector of the hobby is made up of the volunteers who restore, maintain and operate historical equipment. Many railroad museums and other railroad-related tourist attractions couldn't exist without them. The skills that can be learned and applied to this work are diverse. Examples include: woodworking, metal smithing, heavy construction, organizing public events, developing interpretive displays, and writing press releases. Some organizations of this type include the Association of Railway Museums, the San Diego Railroad Museum, and the Steamtown Volunteer Association.

Most railfan organizations sponsor rail excursions to railroad shops and yards and other historic sites, as well as trackside and photographer's trips. Fan trips often feature steam locomotives or other antique rolling stock. Photographic opportunities are provided when trains are positioned in historical settings or run by photographers for action shots.

Tourist Railroads and Museums

During the 1950s the railroads turned to diesel locomotives and modernized their rolling stock. Enterprising groups and individuals bought some of the outmoded equipment in order to preserve railroad history. Although some equipment has been placed on static display in museums, much of it is still seeing active service on tourist railroads. This is a very expensive undertaking that usually involves appealing for public or governmental financial support. It requires many skilled employees to run a short line tourist railroad, and some of those skills are slowly becoming lost arts. Troubleshooting an ailing steam locomotive is not a job for amateurs. Fortunately for railfans, dedicated people are preserving antique railroad equipment and keeping it in running order. In George H. Drury's *Guide to Tourist Railroads and Railroad Museums,* Kalmbach Books identifies over 250 such railroad attractions in North America.

Worldwide Train Travel

Statistics in *Jane's World Railways* show a steady increase in railroad passenger travel in most heavily populated areas of the world. Train travelers enjoy significant discounts in Europe by purchasing rail passes. These passes can be purchased for periods of time ranging from fifteen days to three months. Some types allow unlimited travel; others impose minor restrictions. Similar passes are available in Canada and Australia. Such passes are available on the United States' Amtrak system, but are sold only outside North America. Citizens of the U.S. or Canada are not eligible to buy them.

Bibliography

REFERENCE BOOKS

Allen, Geoffrey Freeman, ed. *Jane's World Railways 1991–92.* 33rd ed. Coulsdon, U. K.: Jane's, 1991. Extensive data on the world's railroads.

Baken, Lenore. *Camp Europe by Train.* 5th ed. Bellevue, WA: Ariel, 1988. Ties train routes to the camping facilities available in all major European cities. Maps and detailed how-to information.

Drury, George H. *Guide to Tourist Railroads and Railroad Museums.* Milwaukee, WI: Kalmbach Books, 1988. A directory of over 250 railroad attractions in North America.

———. *The Historical Guide to North American Railroads.* Milwaukee, WI: Kalmbach Books, 1985. Histories, figures, and features of more than 160 railroads abandoned or merged since 1930.

Frayn, Michael, et al. *Great Railway Journeys of the World.* New York: Dutton, 1982. Lighthearted, detailed accounts of train trips in many countries. Originally commissioned by the BBC for a television series.

Hubbard, Freeman. *Encyclopedia of North American Railroading: 150 Years of Railroading in the United States and Canada.* New York: McGraw-Hill, 1981. Includes histories of major railroad lines and biographies of key figures in railroading.

Lewis, Edward A. *American Short Line Railway Guide.* 3rd ed. Milwaukee, WI: Kalmbach Books, 1986. Provides facts, figures, and detailed locomotive rosters of over four hundred U.S. short lines.

Maiken, Peter T. *Night Trains: The Pullman System in the Golden Years of American Rail Travel.* Chicago: Lakme, 1989. Explores Pullman scheduling, examining first class rail travel in America as an entire system during the period from 1920 to 1955.

Turpin, Kathryn M., and Marvin L. Saltzman. *Euraill Guide: How To Travel Europe and All The World By Train.* 22nd ed. Malibu, CA: Eurail Guide Annual, 1992. Covers worldwide train passes, schedules, and tourist attraction information.

Wood, Katie, and George McDonald. *Europe By Train: The Complete Guide to Inter Railing.* New York: Harper, 1992. Information for the traveler including getting there, accommodations, what to take, and more.

PERIODICALS

Car and Locomotive Cyclopedia. Simmons-Boardman Publishers, 1809 Capitol Avenue, Omaha, NE 10014.

Extra 2200 South. Doug Cummings, Box 8110–820, Blaine, WA 98230.

High Speed Rail-Maglev Yearbook. High Speed Rail Maglev Association, 206 Valley Court, Suite 800, Pittsburg, PA 15237.

Locomotive & Railway Preservation. Box 246, Richmond, VT 05477.

Pacific Rail News. Interurban Press, Box 6128, Glendale, CA 91225.

Passenger Train Journal. Interurban Press, Box 6128, Glendale, CA 91225.

Railfan and Railroad. Carstens Publications, Box 700, Newton, NJ 07860.

Railway Age. Simmons-Boardman Publishers, 345 Hudson Street, New York, NY 10014.

Railway Passenger Car Annual. R P C Publications, Box 296, Godfrey, IL 62035.

Steam Passenger Service Directory. Great Eastern Publishers, Box 599, Richmond, VT 05477.

Trains. Kalmbach Publications, Box 1612, Waukesha, WI 53187–1612.

ASSOCIATIONS

Association of Railway Museums. PO Box 3311, City of Industry, CA 91744–0311. Museums. Publications: *Report to You,* and related material.

Central Electric Railfans' Association. PO Box 503, Chicago, IL 60690. Those interested in all types of electric railways. Conducts inspection trips. Publications: Books on electric railway history.

Mid-Continent Railway Historical Society. PO Box 55, North Freedom, WI 53951. Preserves railroad equipment from the 1885–1915 era. Restores rolling stock and operates a steam passenger train. Publications; *Mid-Continent Rail Heritage Series, Mid-Continent Railway Gazette,* and related material.

Midwest Railway Historical Society. 533 W. Glencoe, Palatine, IL 60067. Conducts study of American railroads. Data dating to 1850.

National Association of Railroad Passengers. 900 2nd Street NE, Suite 308, Washington, DC 20002. Those wishing to expand railroad service. Publication: *NARP News.*

National Railway Historical Society. PO Box 58153, Philadelphia, PA 19102–8153. Preserves historical information and sponsors railfan trips. Publications: *National Railway Bulletin,* and related material.

North Coast Railroad Historical Society. 4897 Corduroy Road, Mentor, OH 44060–1216. Those interested in preservation and restoration of railroads documents and artifacts. Conducts field trips.

Pacific Railroad Society. PO Box 80726, San Marino, CA 91118–8726. Preserves railroad history, equipment, and artifacts. Maintains ten railroad passenger cars. Conducts excursions. Publications: *Wheel Clicks,* and related materials.

Railroad Enthusiasts. 102 Dean Road, Brookline, MA 02146–4212. Railfans, photographers, model builders, and railroad employees. Sponsors rail excursions and trips. Publication: *RRE Journal.*

Railway and Locomotive Historical Society. PO Box 1418, Westford, MA 01886. Preserves railroad documents and records. Publications: *Railroad History,* and newsletter.

San Diego Railroad Museum. 1050 Kettner Boulevard, San Diego, CA 92101. Engaged in the preservation, restoration, and operation of steam and diesel locomotives on eight miles of track. Offers private railway excursions in Mexico and the U.S. Publication: *Report.*

Society of Freight Car Historians. PO Box 2480, Monrovia, CA 91017. Railfans, historians, and modelers. Publications: *Freight Cars Journal, Freight Cars Journal Monograph, Journal of Container-Transport,* and *Journal of Railway Tank Cars.*

Steamtown Volunteer Association. 150 S. Washington Avenue, Scranton, PA 18503–2079. Supports the Steamtown National Historic Site, a museum of equipment, operating trains, and functioning repair facilities. Publication: *Steamtown Newsletter.*

Three Rivers Narrow Gauge Historical Society. RD 2, 16A Walker Road, Canonsburg, PA 15317. Promotes the study of narrow gauge railroads. Publications: *Light Iron and Short Ties,* and related materials.

Transport Museum Association. 3015 Barrett Station Road, St. Louis, MO 63122. Museum housing more than 140 locomotives and assorted rolling stock, and other transportation vehicles. Publications: *Transport Museum-News and Views,* and related materials.

Note: There are additional associations devoted to specific railroad lines listed in the *Encyclopedia of Associations,* available in libraries.

Sewing

HOME SEWING HAS DECLINED because of low priced imported clothing and the reduced free time available with both spouses working. However, for many reasons sewing continues to appeal to a large segment of the population. You can choose the fabric type, color, and design for your garment. You can adjust patterns to compensate if your figure deviates from standard sizes. You can try out design ideas or make repairs if you are creative. You can alter newly purchased items to compensate for weight changes, or to accommodate children's growth. Sewing is a pastime that affords satisfaction, convenience, and cost saving.

Sewing Area

The ideal place to sew is a separate room where work can be left in place when it's time to stop. The area should have plenty of natural light, space for a layout table, sewing machine, ironing board, and closet space to hang projects in process. Since most homes don't have such ideal facilities, let's look at alternatives. A ping-pong table makes an excellent layout table. New plastic garbage cans make excellent material storage bins. A piece of plywood placed over two garbage cans also makes a satisfactory layout surface. The plywood can double as a bed board or be stored under a bed. Lightweight folding picnic tables are another alternative. You can make a work surface from half of a flush door to provide a table for your sewing machine. Save space by hinging it to fold down from inside a closet. Design temporary arrangements such as these for quick set-up or you will be reluctant to go to the trouble of preparing to sew.

Tools and Equipment

Good quality tools last longer. Choose the best you can afford as you find a need for them. The following list identifies the basic tools required for sewing.

1. Inexpensive full length mirror to see how pieces fit.
2. A dress form to simulate the torso shape—for trial fitting patterns and assembling garments.
3. Bent-handled dressmaker's shears—for cutting fabric.
4. Pinking shears—to finish fabric edges.
5. Small sewing scissors—for fine cutting.
6. Seam ripper—for quickly removing sewn seams.
7. Quality yardstick.
8. Cloth or fiberglass flexible tape measure with metal tips.
9. Sewing gauge—a six-inch ruler with a sliding indicator.
10. Curved ruler or French curve—to redraw curved pattern lines after adjustments have been made.
11. Transparent straight-edge ruler—to draw straight lines on patterns. Specialized examples have slots used to draw parallel lines.
12. Drafting triangle—to check fabric grain squareness and make lines perpendicular to other lines on patterns.
13. Pattern marking pencil—to mark flimsy tissue patterns.
14. Special marking pen—to make lines on fabric that fade away in time.

15. Tracing wheel and tracing paper—for pressing the wheel against the paper and moving it along to create a line on fabric.
16. Tailor's chalk for marking fabrics.
17. Miscellaneous pins and needles.
18. Needle threader for inserting thread into the eye of a needle.

Measurements and Fit

Take body measurements at the bust, waist, and hips. Compare these measurements to those given on a standard size chart provided on the pattern envelope or in the pattern catalog. Choose the pattern size whose charted measurements most closely match yours. The pattern size may not be the same as your ready-to-wear size.

The measurements given on the size chart are body measurements. The pattern will be somewhat larger so that the garment will be large enough for you to move. The extra allowance is called "wearing ease." Some clothing designs will have extra material to create a certain effect, or to emphasize or conceal aspects of the figure. This additional allowance is called "design ease."

While design ease can be effective in helping conceal minor figure concerns, informed selection of designs, patterns, and colors will go even further in helping you look your best. Loose fitting designs can cover a thick waist. Horizontal pattern lines emphasize width, but when placed well below the waist, they can make the upper body appear longer. Vertical lines make a person look taller and thinner. Dark colors reduce apparent figure size.

Commercial Patterns

Pattern envelopes provide a wealth of information to the buyer. A drawing or photo shows what the finished garment will look like. Charts help you pick the right pattern size. Fabric types are suggested and required yardage noted. Additional items (notions) required for the project, such as zippers, are listed.

Sewing patterns are provided for each piece of material that makes up a garment. Many patterns are designed to be used for more than one standard size. These multiple-sized patterns are useful when the wearer requires one size for the upper part of the body and another for the lower part. Some patterns are adjustable. Instructions and separate cutting lines are furnished on the pattern for modifications to accommodate specific body contour variations such as broad shoulders. Most patterns will show a double line where major alterations, like length changes, are to be made.

Patterns will show a long grain line with arrows at each end. The grain in fabric refers to the lengthwise and crosswise threads. The lengthwise threads are warp threads. The crosswise threads are weft threads. The grain line on a pattern indicates the desired path for the warp threads. They are usually thicker. They lie parallel to the selvage (border). Since grain direction is important in the finished garment, it must be considered when pinning the pattern to the material. Check to see that the warp and weft threads are at right angles to one another. Pull the cloth and iron it to achieve this condition. If you are using a plaid or figured material, you must match the design where the pieces join. Considering the foregoing, and the cutting layout shown in the pattern instruction guide, pin the pattern to your material.

A dotted line is usually used on patterns to indicate the seam line along which adjacent pieces are sewn. Symbols such as triangles are shown along the seam to locate joining points for positioning the adjacent pieces. Placement lines will also be found to indicate locations of items such as pockets or buttons.

Commercial patterns accommodate a wide variety of sewing instruction needs. For example, a pattern for a crocheted garment may include complete step-by-step crochet instructions, starting with how to make basic crochet stitches.

Basic Fitting Shell

If you plan to sew much of your own clothing it pays to make your own master garment, called a fitting shell. Carefully make all the necessary adjustments to a commercial pattern to achieve a custom fit. Make the shell from a firmly woven medium-weight fabric such as muslin. Then use the shell to create your own master, permanent pattern. When you buy a commercial pattern in the future for a new garment design, it is easy to compare it to your master pattern and make your required adjustments.

Some people disassemble a favorite worn garment to use as a pattern for a new replacement. This method can also be used to combine features of several garments.

Materials

Buy quality fabrics; it makes sewing easier. Firmly woven or knitted fabrics do not ravel or require extra work on seam treatments. Fabrics such as broadcloth, flannel, and poplin are easy to sew. Slippery fabrics or deep pile fabrics require special care and sometimes special tools.

Pick a color that coordinates well with your hair and skin color. When choosing fabric consider where you will wear the garment and in what temperatures. Other factors in the choice may be flexibility of the weave, ability to retain color or remain wrinkle-free.

Fabrics that have not been preshrunk must be washed and shrunk before sewing. Iron both the fabric and the paper pattern to eliminate wrinkles that would distort the final garment shape if removed at a later stage.

Construction Techniques

Cut the fabric using the pattern as a guide. Cut notches in edges at the positioning marks, and transfer other markings before separating the pattern from the material. Assemble the pieces with pins, then use large basting stitches to facilitate later removal. Try the garment on for fit and make any additional adjustments required. You should be able to move without any restriction. Sit, bend, walk, and move your arms to evaluate how the garment feels.

Make a trial run on a scrap piece of material to test sewing machine adjustments. Finish the seams by machine stitching, install buttons, zippers, and any decorative touches. Adjust and sew hems and give a final pressing.

Tailoring

Most sewing techniques apply to tailoring. The primary differences involve the addition of linings and interfacings. Interfacings are secondary fabrics added to help a garment retain its shape in areas such as collars and lapels. Attach the interfacing to the inner surfaces of the garment using padstitching. The interface material is padstitched to the fabric forming the external part of the garment by catching only a few threads of the outer fabric with the needle. The stitching is not visible from the outside. An alternative method of attachment makes use of fusible interfacing. This material has a resin coating on one side. Heat it with an iron to fuse it in place.

Linings are usually sewn into tailored garments, such as jackets, to allow them to slide easily over other garments.

When dealing with expensive fabrics, make test garments similar to the fitting shell discussed above. Make the test garment from an inexpensive firmly woven fabric in a weight similar to the garment fabric.

Bibliography

REFERENCE BOOKS

Argent, Jeanne. *The Complete Step-by-Step Guide to Home Sewing.* Radnor, PA: Chilton, 1990. How-to information for home sewing. Emphasis on nonclothing items, from curtains to upholstery.

Bensussen, Rusty. *Making Patterns from Finished Clothes.* New York: Sterling, 1985. Details the method of creating sewing patterns from existing garments.

Benton, Kitty. *Sewing Classic Clothes for Children.* New York: Hearst Books, 1981. Details for making clothing, a teddy bear, and other accessories.

Jackson, Carole. *Color for Men.* New York: Ballantine Books, 1984. Choosing the right colors for clothing to complement the colors of your skin, hair, and eyes.

Locke, Sue. *Learn to Make Children's Clothes.* Pittstown, NJ: Main Street, 1987. Sewing basics, and wardrobes for pre-school children.

Maehren, Bernice, and Susan Meyers. eds. *Singer—Tailoring.* Minnetonka, MN: DeCosse, 1988. Tailoring techniques, fabric selection, tools and stitches for handwork, and construction methods.

Meyers, Susan, and Bernice Maehren. eds. *Singer—The Perfect Fit.* Minnetonka, MN: DeCosse, 1987. How patterns are sized, figure size chart, and guidelines for pattern adjustments.

Moore, Helen. ed. *Vogue—Easy Sewing.* New York: Harper & Row, 1985. Requirements for the sewing area, figure analysis, tools, patterns, and sewing techniques.

———. *Vogue—Fitting: The Book of Fitting Techniques, Adjustments and Alterations.* New York: Harper & Row, 1987. Fitting fundamentals, from pattern to basting the garment.

Ruggieri, Lorraine. *The Woman's Day Book of No-Pattern Sewing.* New York: Fawcett Columbine, 1981. Sewing basics, selecting fabrics, and many projects using very simple pattern outlines.

Vogue Patterns Editors. *The Vogue/Butterick Step-by-Step Guide to Sewing Techniques.* New York: Prentice Hall, 1989. Detailed, illustrated information about specific sewing techniques.

PERIODICALS

McCall's Needlework and Crafts. P J S Publications, News Plaza, Box 1790, Peoria, IL 61614.

Sew Beautiful. Martha Pullen, 518 Madison Street, Huntsville, AL 35801.

Sew It Seams. Sew It Seems, 333 11th Place, Kirkland, WA 98033.

Sew News. P J S Publications, News Plaza, Box 1790, Peoria, IL 61614.

Threads. Taunton Press, 63 S. Main Street, Box 355, Newtown, CT 06470–5506.

ASSOCIATION

American Sewing Guild. PO Box 8476, Medford, OR 97504. Home sewers and people interested in sewing. Provides information through lectures, demonstrations, classes, seminars, and fashion shows. Encourages the development of workshop groups. Publications: Local chapters publish newsletters.

Silkscreen Printing

A STENCIL IS A THIN SHEET of material perforated or cut through in such a way that when ink, paint, or other marking or etching agents are applied to the sheet, patterns form on a surface beneath the sheet.

Decorators apply paint to walls through stencils to create attractive border designs.

The silkscreen process originated when stencils were applied to a fabric screen to hold them in position. On the screen, nonimage areas were blocked out with a stencil and ink was forced through the image areas with a squeegee to produce a print.

History

The Chinese have used stencils to decorate fabrics for centuries. Stencils are used to paint letters and numbers on crates for shipment. Such characters have a common characteristic. They have small bars or ties across the letter or number. For example, the bars on the letter *O* hold the center in position. Artists in twelfth century Japan used an improved stencil in their work. They glued hair across the loose and floppy parts of their stencils, keeping everything in position. By the late 1800s European workers used woven silk to hold and position their stencils. Although Englishman Samuel Simon patented the use of silk as a background material in 1907, the use of the process was somewhat limited. It wasn't until the 1930s that it caught on in the United States. The use of the process increased dramatically once artists and printers became aware of the method and its potential.

Applications

The screen process is perhaps the most versatile of commercial printing methods. Almost any surface of any shape or size can be printed. Applications of the process are virtually everywhere we look. The lettering on a ball point pen is printed by the screen process. The decorative pattern on a drinking glass, dinner plate, T shirt or bumper sticker is added by the method. If the piece to be decorated is too large to screen directly, the design is placed on material that can then be applied to the piece. Pictures are screened onto adhesive-backed material and applied to huge billboards. Patterns are screened onto wallpapers and fabrics that are many yards long.

If the piece to be decorated has a complex surface, or is too fragile for normal screen processing, decals can serve to transfer the image. Clear lacquer is screened onto a special paper backing. This is followed by screening successive coats of color, defining the image. Then another clear lacquer coat may be added. In use, the paper is soaked off and the decal is slid in place. The decal method is also used to transfer glaze patterns to pottery before it is fired.

A coating called a resist is screened onto electronic circuit boards where the circuit belongs. The copper-clad board is then etched with acid, removing the unwanted copper, but leaving the resist-protected circuit intact. A TV screen has a pattern of phosphor dots on its inner surface. This material is sometimes applied by the screen process. We find that many materials can be applied to different types of surfaces, creating the need for special formulations of inks, paints, and other coatings.

The silk screen process emerged from its purely commercial applications into a flexible art form during the 1930s. The opportunities for a hobbyist to use it for decoration, pictures, posters, and other artistic projects are limited only by one's imagination.

Basic Equipment and Procedures

Hobbyists will find that silk screen printing can be accomplished with a minimum amount of equipment. To get started, you will only need a screen-printing frame (Figure 1), a squeegee, and a place to dry the prints.

The screen is a wooden or metal frame used to hold a stretched fabric. The fabrics most often used are silk, polyester, nylon or metal wire. The mesh count of a fabric is the number of threads per inch of fabric. A mesh number is assigned that indicates both mesh count and fabric strength. The letter X after the number indicates the fabric strength. The more Xs, the stronger the fabric. For example, a silk fabric with a mesh number of 8XX indicates that it has a mesh count of 86, and the double X rating makes its strength in the appropriate range for screen-process work. Mesh number 8 silk is good for coarse work, 12 for general purpose work, and 14 or higher for detailed illustrations.

Screens are easy to construct using wooden frames and 12XX mesh silk or dacron. However, in most large cities it can be just as cost-effective to order one ready-made from a supplier of materials to the screen-process trade. Art and hobby store suppliers may charge more.

The screen frame is hinged to a flat base board. The base is at least as large as the screen. You fasten the paper to be printed on the base. Let's suppose you are going to print a simple pattern on the piece of paper. A paper or film template is prepared with the pattern cut out to leave holes in the shape of the desired design. The template is attached to the top of the screen. You lower the screen until it either touches the paper or is positioned just above it. Pour or scoop a quantity of ink onto the top of the screen above the template, and use a squeegee to force it through the screen and onto the paper below. Mask off the area between the

edges of the template and the inside edge of the frame or ink will flow through the screen and onto the paper in that area. After pulling the squeegee across the screen once, lift the screen and remove your print from the base.

The squeegee consists of a hard rubber blade held in a wooden handle. For most general printing on flat surfaces, the blade will have a simple rectangular cross section.

The tusche and glue method is another approach to screen masking. Tusche is a greasy, black substance made from waxes, oils, and soap. The glue is soluble in water, but not in the solvents to be used on the tusche.

Sketch your design on paper and place it under the screen. Then trace the outlines of the image areas on the screen with a soft pencil. Next, apply tusche to the screen image areas with a brush or lettering pen. Tusche crayons and pencils are available for detail work. Squeegee the glue over the tusche image and the entire screen area. When the glue is thoroughly dry, turpentine or kerosene is used to remove the tusche from the image areas. The solvent will dissolve the tusche. Since the tusche filled the screen mesh, it will come off together with the glue that was over it. The remaining glue will still adhere to the fabric mesh, forming the stencil or mask needed for printing the design.

Multicolor Printing

When your pattern is printed in several colors, you must modify your template, or screen, to mask all areas that are not to receive the color being applied. Suppose you wish to print a picture of a blue star surrounded by a yellow

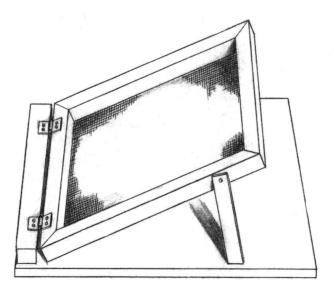

Figure 1
A simple printing frame used in the silkscreen process. The stencil is applied to the screen. The sheet of material to be printed is placed beneath. The frame is lowered, and ink is squeegeed through the screen to produce the image.

background. You would block out the star, ink your screen with yellow ink, and print the background. Allow it to dry. Block out the background and remove the mask or blocking material from the star. Re-ink your screen with blue ink, and print the star. Blocking out can be accomplished with tape, paper, hide glue, lacquer, and commercial water-soluble block-outs. Suitable solvents must be used to remove the blocked-out areas as required.

Photographic Stencils

With the introduction of photographic stencils the process becomes more complex, challenging and rewarding.

The first step in making a photographic screen process plate (photographic stencil) is to create a photographic film positive. This can be done from a photographic film negative by exposing a piece of photo-sensitive film to light coming through the negative in much the same way that you would make a paper photographic print.

Other ways to create a positive image on film include exposing the film to light using a silhouette mask cut from opaque paper, or by using opaque India ink images on translucent paper. Another approach is to hand-cut a pattern into masking film and use the masking film to create the positive.

Once you have the positive film, you can use it to print a photo-transfer film. During exposure, the transfer film gelatin hardens in areas not protected by dark, or image areas on the positive film. In the image areas the gelatin remains soft and is easily washed away after exposure is completed. The transfer film gelatin is attached to the screen and its film backing is peeled away, leaving the hard gelatin as the mask for your ink printing process.

Another approach is to coat the silk fabric screen with photo emulsion. Expose it to light through the film positive and wash away the unexposed emulsion as above.

When the desired image is a photograph containing various shades of gray, the gelatin is exposed through a halftone screen, resulting in an image composed of dots. The inked screen print will also be composed of dots, simulating gray areas.

You must consider the relationship of the silk screen fabric mesh to the number of lines (of dots) per inch of the halftone screen. If the silk screen is too coarse, the dots will wash out.

Inks, Solvents and Paper

Ink types are chosen to be compatible with the surface to be printed. In turn, the stencil material and solvents used must be compatible with the ink.

Poster inks may be either oil-base or water-base. Both will work well on paper or cardboard. The water-base type affords the convenience of water clean-up. Mineral spirits will be required for the oil-base type.

Oil-base enamel inks can be used on a broader range of materials including glass and metal. Mineral spirits is the usual thinner.

Lacquer inks also can be used on many materials, including the painting of decals. Clean-up with lacquer thinner.

Special textile inks are also sold in both water and oil-base.

Many other inks are formulated to accommodate the properties of the surface being printed.

Other silk screen printing compounds are made to deposit ceramic glaze, etch surfaces, add adhesive, or conduct electricity.

Paper is classified according to weight. The weight designation is based on five hundred sheets of a basic size of a particular type of paper. Basic sheet size varies with the type of paper. Five hundred sheets of 17 × 22 inch 16-pound bond paper weigh 16 pounds. In another example, five hundred sheets of 22½ × 28½ inch 80-pound Bristol card stock weigh 80 pounds.

Safety

Most screen-process safety precautions concern the chemicals used during the process. Work in a well-ventilated area and protect yourself from the exhaust fumes of solvents, inks, and acids. Wear eye protection. Don't smoke when handling the above materials or when near where they are stored. Store flammable materials such as solvents in appropriate explosive-proof containers.

Bibliography

REFERENCE BOOKS

Banzhaf, Robert A. *Screen Process Printing*. Mission Hills, CA: Glencoe, 1983. Overall coverage of the process, written in textbook style by a college professor who deals with the subject.

Biegeleisen, J. I., and Max Arthur Cohn. *Silk Screen Techniques*. Rev. ed. New York: Dover, 1958. Discusses the origin and development of the process. Covers basic principles, equipment, and various methods of producing silk screen prints.

Gardner, Andrew B. *The Artist's Silkscreen Manual*. New York: Grossett & Dunlap/ Perigee Books, 1976. Coverage of basic equipment and processes. Emphasis on problem identification and solutions.

Swerdlow, Robert M. *The Step-by-Step Guide to Screen-Process Printing*. Englewood Cliffs, NJ: Prentice Hall, 1985. In-depth coverage of the process, including commercial equipment. Written in textbook style by a college professor who deals with the subject.

Termini, Maria. *Silkscreening.* Englewood Cliffs, NJ: Prentice-Hall, 1978. Comprehensive coverage of the silk screen process. Describes the development of the process, visual effects, equipment, inks, and various methods.

PERIODICALS

Screen Printing. S T Publications, 407 Gilbert Avenue, Cincinnati, OH 45202.

Screen Printing Network. Virgo Publishers, 4141 N. Scottsdale Road, No. 316, Scottsdale, AZ 85251.

Screen Printing Today. Virgo Publishers, 4141 N. Scottsdale Road, No. 316, Scottsdale, AZ 85251.

ASSOCIATIONS

Screen Printing Association International. 10015 Main Street, Fairfax, VA 22031. Organizes study tours, holds seminars, and bestows awards. Publications: *The Tabloid,* and *Technical Guidebook of the Screen Printing Industry.* Also publishes studies, surveys, newsletters, and related material.

Screen Printing Technical Foundation. 10015 Main Street, Fairfax, VA 22031. Conducts technical research and hands-on training programs. Sponsors educational programs and prepares educational materials. Provides scholarships, grants, and other forms of assistance to students, teachers, and educational institutions interested in screen printing. Maintains library. Publications: *Measurement and Conversion Guide for Screen Printing,* and research updates.

Skating, Ice

ICE SKATING IS A FAMILY SPORT that appeals to all ages. It's a pleasant way to engage in aerobic exercise, with you controlling the effort and the time spent. The sport develops coordination and improves posture. Skating on a beautiful pond in a setting designed by Norman Rockwell may appeal to some, but many prefer the hospitable temperatures of the hundreds of indoor ice rinks scattered across the country.

A skater can develop faster and enjoy the sport more by taking classes. Skating instruction follows two general pathways. The majority of skaters, those primarily interested in recreation and team competition, will benefit from classes conducted by the Ice Skating Institute of America (ISIA). Skaters with an interest in figure skating competition leading to International and Olympic competition, should enroll in classes conducted by clubs associated with the United States Figure Skating Association (USFSA).

History

The earliest known skates were found bound to the skeleton of a Stone Age man in Holland. They were made of horse bone ground to a flat surface. In his oft-quoted *Description of London,* William Stephanides wrote in 1180: "Some tie bones to their feet and under their heels; and shoving themselves by a little picked staff, do slide swiftly as a bird flieth in the air or an arrow out of a cross-bow." Skates were used as a means of transportation in early times, and the use of a push pole was common.

The course of history could have been changed in 1791 had not Napoleon Bonaparte narrowly escaped drowning when skating on the fort moat at Auxerre. It was not unusual for royalty to enjoy skating during this period.

In 1396 St. Lydwina of Schiedam fell and broke a rib while skating. A hundred years later she gained fame when featured in a Dutch wood carving that was printed. This led to her becoming known as the patron saint of skaters.

An American named Jackson Haines is known as the "father of figure skating." A ballet master, Haines combined dance movements with his skating. After winning the American championship, he left for a tour of Europe in 1865. His style of skating was not appreciated at first because it varied so much from current styles. In Vienna he was an instantaneous success, and there he taught the Viennese to waltz on ice. The international style of skating was born, forming the basis for the evolution of modern figure skating as we know it.

Recreational Skating

The first steps onto the ice can be somewhat intimidating. Most people are concerned about looking foolish and falling. You will find yourself in the company of others who feel, or have felt, the same way. Simply hold the barrier rail around the outside edge of the rink with one hand, and practice small steps with your skates. If (when) you fall, relax as you feel yourself going and the unplanned contact with the ice will cause less damage. Avoid putting too much weight on your wrists in catching yourself. Landing on your backside is a good option, especially if you can roll on to it smoothly. Wear gloves to protect your hands.

When you feel comfortable leaving the barrier rail, it's time to practice skating forwards. Stand with the feet about twelve inches apart and pointing straight ahead. Bend the knees slightly. Turn the left skate out at about forty-five degrees and lean the ankle in slightly; use the inside edge of the skate to push off and obtain forward motion. You will glide along on the right skate. Transferring your weight to the right foot, bring the left skate forward pointing straight ahead, put weight on it; then repeat the process by turning your right skate out and pushing off with it. The secret of balance lies in keeping the knees slightly bent and the body in an upright position.

To stop, place your weight on one skate, position the other skate behind it at right angles, in a T formation. Drag the rear skate lightly while keeping your weight on the forward skate.

Build on these elementary first moves by learning to skate backwards, then attempt some simple figures, and learn to skate with a partner. Practice jumps without skates on soft carpeting. Skating is an extension of dance. Confidence will come with practice. ISIA training programs will help meet your recreational skating goals. Their advanced programs can lead to a career in professional skating.

Skating Competition

The United States Figure Skating Association (USFSA) was founded in 1921. The USFSA is affiliated with the International Skating Union and the United States Olympic Committee. The USFSA has a series of tests that are tailored to the various divisions of figure skating competition. A U.S. skater must pass these tests to compete in national championships. The skater is unlikely to be picked for a world championship team or an Olympic team unless he or she has placed among the first three in the national championships.

The USFSA testing programs are discussed in the descriptions of figure skating divisions that follow.

School Figures

Compulsory school figures (or simply figures) are skated in the form of two precise circles touching one another in the form of a figure 8, and as three such circles touching in a similar manner. The figures to be judged are selected from a pool of over eighty possibilities. The selection is announced to the participating skaters shortly before the competition. Judges score the accuracy of the figure inscribed on the ice, and the way the figure is skated. Figures are performed using techniques such as turns, changes of skate blade edge, and loops. At different points around the circles the skater is required to turn from skating forward to backward, or vice versa. Loops are smaller circles skated within the main figures. They tend to be difficult for beginners to master.

In the USFSA program a skater first passes twelve incremental tests to show proficiency in basic skating. The next phase of testing specifies nine figure tests. Those who pass all nine tests are figure gold medalists.

Free Skating

Singles free skating competitors perform their own special program to music. It must be varied and should include dance steps, jumps, and spins. The jumps consist of leaps off the ice and from a half turn to triple turns in the air. Even somersaults in the air have been included in free skating performances. Competitions are judged for content and performance. Many jumps and other skating movements are named after the individual who first used them in competition. The Axel jump was originated by nineteenth century skater Axel Paulson. Another popular jump, the Salchow, was invented by Swedish champion Ulrich Salchow.

There are six tests in the USFSA free skating test program. These demanding tests examine technique with final judgment based on technical merit and artistic expression.

Pair Skating

A pair skating program is similar to the singles program in content and construction. Of course, the addition of a partner introduces the opportunity to display artistic interaction between the two skaters. Such moves include lifts, throws, and spins, taking full advantage of the accompanying music. In lifts, the man lifts the woman and holds her in the air in a hand-to-hand or hand-to-body hold.

There are four USFSA pairs tests judged on technical merit and artistic expression.

Ice Dancing

There are two divisions in ice dancing. The compulsory dance competition is based on approximately nineteen internationally recognized dances. The dances are skated to a predetermined pattern.

The free dance is similar to pair skating with limitations to reduce the gymnastic aspects, and stress the artistics. Lift height and spin revolutions are limited, and partner separation time and distance are kept short. It is the free dance, with its individualized programs and music, that is normally seen when viewing televised competitions.

The USFSA compulsory dance test program includes seven tests with judgment based on dance rhythm and excellence of execution. Two additional tests on free dance emphasize the artistic aspect of the program.

Speed Skating

The official track for world championship speed skating measures 400 meters. It is shaped like a horse race track (circular ends connected by straight sections). Two competitors race at a time on the two lane course. During the race the skaters change lanes at a prescribed section of the track to avoid giving one the inside lane advantage. World championship competitions are held at distances of 500, 1,500, 5,000, and 10,000 meters for men, and 500, 1,000, 3,000, and 5,000 meters for women.

Competitive speed skaters require extensive training to build strength and stamina. The leg stroke is most effective when the body is bent well forward, with the weight concentrated over the hips. Avoid body sway or weaving during the leg stroke to minimize loss of momentum. Only the last few feet of the stroke curve slightly outward as the skate leaves the ice.

Equipment

Each category of skating places different requirements on skate design. Ice hockey players require a rugged skate that can stand up to the rough and tumble activity of the sport. Speed skaters benefit from an extra long blade that gives them more contact with the ice to withstand the powerful stroke of their legs without slipping.

A typical skate design suitable for use in figure skating is shown in Figure 1. Note that the blade curves from front to back, facilitating skating in a curved path. Saw tooth rakes at the front assist landing and take-off during jumps. They also help the skater perform spins. The blade also has a hollow groove running along its length. When the skater tilts the skate during figures the sharp edge on the side of the blade digs into the ice and prevents skidding sideways.

Skates require periodic sharpening to maintain their sharp edges. Time between sharpening can be lengthened by using a pair of skate guards to protect the blades when walking to and from the ice.

Recreational skaters can be flexible about clothing provided that it is warm and loose fitting. Clothing that can find its way between skates and the ice can be dangerous, so avoid wearing scarves or long pant legs.

Figure 1

Typical skate design. Note the saw-tooth rakes at the front to assist in jumps and spins, and the hollow groove at the bottom of the blade, seen in the front end view.

Bibliography

REFERENCE BOOKS

Bass Howard. *Let's Go Skating.* New York: St. Martin's, 1974. Covers the technique, history, and activities of skating. Detailed information on the many aspects of the sport.

De Leeuw, Dianne, with Steve Lehrman. *Figure Skating.* New York: Atheneum, 1978. Covers skating history, equipment, clothing, and the various moves used in competition.

Dolan, Edward F. *The Complete Beginner's Guide to Ice Skating.* Garden City, NY: Doubleday, 1974. Covers equipment, the basic moves of ice skating, and the more complex moves used in competition.

Ogilvie, Robert S. *Competitive Figure Skating: A Parent's Guide.* New York: Harper & Row, 1985. A book for the parent who wants to guide his or her child intelligently through basic training and early competition in figure skating, freestyle, pair skating, or ice dancing.

Petkevich, John Misha. *Figure Skating: Championship Techniques.* New York: Sports Illustrated, 1989. Selecting equipment, and detailed, illustrated instructions on how to perform the basics as well as advanced spins, jumps, and more.

———. *The Skater's Handbook.* New York: Scribner's, 1984. How to select and care for equipment. How to structure a training program and choose a coach.

Whedon, Julia. *The Fine Art of Ice Skating: An Illustrated History and Portfolio of Stars.* New York: Abrams, 1988. An illustrated history of ice skating.

PERIODICAL

Skating. United States Figure Skating Association, 20 First Street, Colorado Springs, CO 80906.

ASSOCIATIONS

Amateur Speedskating Union of the United States. 1033 Shady Lane, Glen Ellyn, IL 60137. Individuals interested in ice speed skating competition. Conducts seminars, training programs, and Speed Skating Hall of Fame. Publications: Directory, *The Racing Blade* newsletter, and related materials.

Ice Skating Institute of America. 355 W. Dundee Road, Buffalo Grove, IL 60089–3500. Ice rink owners and managers, suppliers, skaters, and ice skating instructors. Provides recreational ice skater class and testing programs in various figure skating categories as well as hockey and speed skating. Sponsors Ice Skating Hall of Fame. Publications: Newsletter, competition and testing standards, and *Recreational Ice Skating* magazine.

Professional Skaters Guild of America. PO Box 5904, Rochester, MN 55903. Professional ice skaters engaged in the teaching and coaching of ice skating. Sponsors competitions, bestows awards, and conducts seminars. Publications: *Professional Skater,* and related materials.

United States Figure Skating Association. 20 1st Street, Colorado Springs, CO 80906. National governing body for amateur figure skating in the U.S. Establishes rules and determines the amateur status of figure skaters. Bestows awards and maintains World Figure Skating Hall of Fame and Museum. Publications: *Skating Journal,* and a rulebook.

Skiing

SKIING IS A FAMILY SPORT that offers a lifetime of healthy exercise, personal challenge, and freedom of movement in outdoor settings. Skiers can choose their own pathway, unconfined to court or rink. The sport offers enough diversity to stimulate and hold the interest of people of all ages. Mature skiers can participate at their own pace and share their enthusiasm with younger generations.

Physical fitness is important to skiing because it reduces the chances of injury on the slopes and it makes the basic skiing maneuvers easier. As with any sport requiring unaccustomed physical effort, you should have a physical checkup from your doctor before you begin training. If you enjoy a certain amount of physical work as part of your lifestyle, you have a good start in preparing your body for skiing. If you participate in other sports that develop your cardiovascular system, even better. Your aim is to train with the same effort you'll ski with. Hiking, running, biking, and lifting weights are all helpful.

Skiing exercises the whole body. The legs must be strong enough to guide the skis and upper body strength is needed to manipulate the ski poles, especially in cross-country skiing and uphill climbing.

Before you begin skiing, do a few warm-up and stretching exercises. They relax muscles stiff with the cold and improve circulation. Stop skiing when fatigue sets in. Your judgment isn't as sharp and your muscles are less able to respond to stress without injury.

Safe skiing requires planning and preparation. Wear several layers of light clothing. Remove layers as you warm up to avoid sweating. Damp clothing doesn't afford much protection from the cold. It is very important to replace liquids during exercise. Take a supply of water with you on long outings. Avoid alcoholic drinks; they reduce resistance to the cold.

History

In an Oslo, Norway ski museum there is a 2,500 year-old ski shaped remarkably like a modern ski. Swedish and Norwegian skiers shuffled along on skis as you would ride a scooter. They would glide on a long ski and pump with the other leg that wore a shorter ski covered with fur to give it traction.

During the last half of the nineteenth century, Scandinavians brought skiing to the United States. In both California and New England skiing took a foothold that has continued to this day. Now there are more than a thousand ski areas in the United States and Canada. People have skied for almost 5,000 years, but it has only been practiced as a sport for the past century. Farmers in Norway's Telemark Valley held impromptu cross-country races and jumping contests in the early 1800s. For years afterwards, these Nordic events dominated the ski scene. Although downhill racing was done by California miners during the 1850s, downhill and slalom contests didn't achieve widespread popularity until the next century. The first Alpine world's championships were held in 1931, and these events were added to the Olympic games in 1936. An American woman won an Olympic medal in skiing before the men when Gretchen Frazer won in 1948. Billy Kidd and Jimmy Huega won in 1964. Since then Bill Johnson, Phil Mahre, and Tommy Moe have won Olympic skiing medals.

Forms of Skiing and Their Related Equipment

Certain basic positions and movements are common to most types of skiing. After clamping on your skis, put your hands through the straps of your ski poles and grasp the handles. Assume the ski stance by bending the knees and moving the hips forward to place weight over the balls of the feet. Hold the body erect and head up so you can see well ahead. Position the arms forward with elbows slightly bent and the ski poles pointed to the rear. The skis should be parallel to one another. This position provides a balanced starting point for other movements.

When you are ready to move forward you can move as you would when walking, moving each arm with the opposite leg, and sliding one ski forward. At the same time your forward arm positions the ski pole ahead and into the snow. The forward arm presses down and back to push you forward. The alternate advance and push of the poles, in combination with the forward stride of alternating legs, maintains forward movement.

An alternative method of moving forward makes use of the double pole push. In this method you allow your body to lower as you push with both poles at the same time. This method reduces the effort required of your arms. After the stroke, the body is straightened, the poles are moved ahead and planted, and the next stroke is begun.

After attaining sustained movement on a slope without poling, assume the balanced stance for stability.

To stop, skiers must increase the drag between their skis and the snow. One way to do this is to spread the legs and angle the skis to form a snowplow or wedge. The front ski tips are held close together and the tails apart. At the same time the knees are bent inward slightly to raise the outer edges of the skis. The wider the angle, the more drag and a quicker stop. The snowplow can be used to slow and control downhill movement by holding the skis at a narrow angle and distributing body weight equally on both skis.

The most direct path down a hill is the fall line. Schussing is the unchecked movement down the fall line with skis held parallel. If the incline is steep, a skier may prefer to ski across the slope, changing direction in a zig-zag pattern to slow the descent.

Several techniques are used to make turns. In the snowplow turn, the skier transfers weight to push against one ski to turn toward the opposite ski. In the stem turn the skier holds one ski parallel to the direction of movement and pushes the rear of the other out to form a half snowplow. During the turns the body should continue to face down the fall line.

Falling is an inevitable part of skiing. When possible, relax and sit down toward the uphill side of your skis. If you sit back on the skis you will gain speed as though riding a toboggan. Hold your ski poles behind you and swing your skis around below you at right angles to the fall line. Keep your arms up and forward to protect hands and wrists. During an uncontrolled fall, where you tumble head over heels (an eggbeater), your ski bindings are designed to release and your skis should come off.

Cross-Country Skiing

Modern cross-country (x-c) skiers slide their skis in an exaggerated walking motion and use their arms to push themselves along with ski poles. The total body gets the benefit of exercise and the eyes are treated to the beauty of a snow covered landscape. All this at much lower prices than you must pay for ski lifts and the use of specially prepared slopes.

Most x-c skis are wider at the tip (front or shovel) and tail (rear) than at the waist (under the boot binding area). This feature facilitates making turns. Generally narrower than downhill skis, x-c skis vary in width to accommodate different applications and types of snow. X-c racing skis are very narrow, about 45mm at the waist. They are very light skis designed for racing on fast well prepared tracks. The normal touring ski measures about 54mm at the waist. Their width makes them more stable and easier to learn on because they have less tendency to tip sideways. Beginners are advised to start with touring skis.

When a ski is set on a surface (the ground or snow), it rests on the front and back running surfaces. The waist is raised above the surface a predetermined distance. This arched shape of the lower ski surface is the bottom camber. The cambered surface almost touches the snow when a skier stands with equal weight on both skis. When most body weight is placed on only one ski, the whole bottom running surface touches the snow surface.

X-c skiers often travel over slight upgrades. An ideal ski should have a base treated to grip the snow when the ski is pressed backward and downward, while not hindering forward glide. This has been accomplished by placing a strip of mohair under the cambered waist area of the ski. When the skier places most body weight on a single ski in the walking motion, the cambered area is depressed and the mohair makes contact and grips the snow. The direction of the grain of the material is such that it slides easily in the forward direction.

Modern x-c skis often have plastic running surfaces. Just as the teeth of a file grip and remove wood in only one direction, plastic ski bottoms are designed with a pattern of indentations into the ski bases to grip in one direction, reducing backward slippage. The patterns chosen may resemble fish scales or a herringbone shape.

For the hardy x-c uphill skier, a system of skins (strips of plastic material) can be temporarily attached to the entire ski bottoms, allowing the skier to plod up steep grades. It's the ancient Scandinavian idea of the fur on a ski revisited.

X-c ski bindings grip the ski boot, providing good directional control of the ski. At the same time, they allow the heel to rise during the walking motion encountered in x-c skiing.

X-c tour-races are held for clubs or the general public (citizen races). Most follow locally established rules, but national championship or Olympic tryout races follow rules established by the United States Skiing Association.

Always travel in groups of three or more on cross-country tours. If a member of the party is injured, one can stay with the injured person while the other goes for help.

Night skiing has become popular at some resorts. Be especially alert for fallen trees and objects hidden under the snow during periods of reduced visibility.

X-c skiing develops basic skills and the coordination required for downhill skiing.

Downhill Skiing

Downhill skis are made in a bewildering array of sizes, types, and materials. Long skis are faster and give a smoother ride, but are harder to turn. The opposite is true of short skis. Soft skis follow irregular ground contours more readily and are easier to turn, but tend to flutter. Stiff skis bridge over irregular terrain better, but are inclined to be harder to turn. The average skier needs a ski design combining the ability to turn easily with a good edge grip, and a ski that allows moving freely at different speeds on soft snow and hard trails. In view of the foregoing, a beginner should consider buying from a dealer who knows how to match the proper equipment to the buyer's needs.

Downhill (Alpine) skiing competitions include downhill racing and slalom racing. Downhill racing is a speed contest where skiers can exceed 90 mph. The course is designed to provide challenge in the form of turns and jumps and mandatory gates consisting of sets of flags. The vertical drop in the course is 800 to 1,000m for men and 500 to 700m for women. Crash helmets must be worn and straw bales or nets line the course where falls are most likely to occur.

Slalom downhill racing is done between a series of flags on poles set in positions that define single and multiple gates. The course should allow a fluent run, but test the widest variety of ski technique, including changes of direction with very different radii. A gate consists of two poles set from 4 to 6m apart. The vertical drop of a slalom course is 180 to 220m for men and 130 to 180m for women.

Giant slalom racing is done on a course that features 4 to 8m gates, and greater distance between gates. The vertical drop is 250 to 400m for men and 250 to 350 for women. The combination of the greater drop and gate spacing allows the racers to attain faster speeds, but the course layout still affords the challenge of the required turns.

Ski Jumping

Competitive ski jumping is highly specialized and is pursued by a relatively few advanced skiers. Competitors must undergo intensive and lengthy training. The jumps are made from specially constructed jumping hills that vary in height according to the length of the jumps. A 70m hill is considered normal. A hill over 90m is used for a separate competition called ski flying. Ski jumpers land on a downward slope that transitions into a gradual upward curve. If the jumper passes over the normal landing point on the downward slope (at 70m for a 70m hill), and past a critical point just before the upward slope, the landing impact is severe and dangerous. When competitors begin to reach distances close to the critical point, judges will start the jumpers farther down the ski hill to reduce the distance in flight.

Snowboarding: Another Alternative

A snowboard looks like a very wide, short (150 to 180cm) ski. The rider's feet face to one side of the board. Over two thirds of the riders prefer to face to the right with the left foot leading (regular foot). The rest face left (goofy foot—a surfing term). The feet are fastened to the board with bindings similar to those found on skis, except that most don't provide the quick release feature found on skis. One foot is positioned at or near the waist of the board; the other about half way back toward the tail. No ski poles are used.

With the feet secured in place and relatively close together, the snowboarder must develop a good sense of balance. The skill develops quickly, but the first sessions can be bruising. Young skateboarders make the transition to snowboarding with ease. Their terminology is finding its way into the sport. Skiers may shuss, but snowboarders "shred" the hill. A high jump into the air is "big air," higher still is "nuclear air."

Turns are accomplished by shifting weight from one foot to the other and by concentrating the pressure on heels or toes. Keep the knees bent. When making a turn keep your weight inside the curved path you are taking. Keep your balance with outstretched arms, but don't drag the low hand on the snow in a turn (patting the dog); it's bad form.

Ski resorts were slow to accept snowboarding at first, but the sport, sometimes called snow surfing, has become very popular.

Bibliography

REFERENCE BOOKS

Bartelski, Konrad, with Robin Neillands. *Learn Downhill Skiing in a Weekend.* New York: Knopf, 1992. An illustrated handbook covering pertinent information about downhill skiing.

Caldwell, John. *Cross-Country Skiing Today.* Brattleboro, VT: Greene, 1977. Comprehensive coverage of cross-country skiing by a longtime advocate.

Crawford-Currie, Ronald. *Cross Country Skiing*. New York: Van Nostrand Reinhold, 1982. Overview of equipment, technique, and touring. Includes review of famous cross-country races.

Gamma, Karl. *The Handbook of Skiing*. New York: Knopf, 1981. A guide to skiing skills and techniques. Covers downhill and cross-country. Includes identification of principal ski areas around the world.

Heller, Mark, and Doug Godlington, eds. *The Complete Skiing Handbook*. New York: Mayflower Books, 1979. A comprehensive, illustrated guide to equipment selection, training, downhill skiing, and cross-country skiing.

Jonas, Bob, and Seth Masia. *Ski Magazine's Total Skiing*. New York: Putnam's Sons, 1987. A comprehensive illustrated guide to Alpine and cross-country skiing including citizen racing.

Killy, Jean-Claude, with Mike Halstead. *Situation Skiing*. Garden City, NY: Doubleday, 1978. Comprehensive guide to preparation and training, with emphasis on downhill techniques under varying conditions.

Shelton, Peter. *The Snow Skier's Bible*. New York: Doubleday, 1991. An introduction to Alpine and cross-country skiing with advice for both novice and experienced skier.

Yacenda, John. *High Performance Skiing: How to Become a Better Alpine Skier*. Champaign, IL: Leisure, 1987. Emphasis on downhill skiing training, techniques, and problem solving.

PERIODICALS

Ski. Times Mirror Magazines, 2 Park Avenue, New York, NY 10016.

Ski America. Ski America Enterprises, 370 Wahconah Street, Box 1140, Pittsfield, MA 01202–1140.

Ski X-C. Rodale Press, 33 E. Minor Street, Emmaus, PA 18098.

Skier's Pocket Guide. Pocket Guide Publications, 8630 Delmar, Suite 215, St. Louis, MO 63124.

Skiing. Times Mirror Magazines, 2 Park Avenue, New York, NY 10016.

Snow Country. 5520 Park Avenue, Box 395, Trumbull, CT 06611–0395.

Snowboarder. Surfer Publications, Box 1028, Dana Point, CA 92629.

ASSOCIATIONS

American Ski Association. P.O. Box 480067, Denver, CO 80248. Recreational skiers. Provides members with travel and ski area discounts. Publication: *American Skier*.

National Handicapped Sports. 451 Hungerford Drive, Suite 100, Rockville, MD 20850. Promotes sports and recreation opportunities for individuals with physical disabilities. Provides direct services to people with mobility impairments. Offers and sanctions recreational programs including learn-to-ski clinics, and competitive Alpine and Nordic skiing. Sponsors teams, bestows awards, and maintains hall of fame. Publications: *Handicapped Sport Report, Nationals* magazine, and related materials.

National Ski Patrol System. Ski Patrol Building, Suite 100, 133 S. Van Gordon Street, Lakewood, CO 80228. Promotes ski safety at ski areas. Assists governmental agencies in cold weather disasters and in rescue attempts. Bestows awards. Publication: *Ski Patrol Magazine*.

Pacific Northwest Ski Association. 640 NW Gilman Boulevard, Suite 104, Issaquah, WA 98027. Sponsors competitions. Bestows awards, grants, and scholarships to qualified ski racers.

Seventy Plus Ski Club. c/o Lloyd T. Lambert, 104 East Side Drive, Ballston Lake, NY 12019. Active downhill skiers 70-years-old and older. Sponsors competitions and bestows awards. Operates museum and hall of fame. Publication: Newsletter.

Ski for Light. 1455 W. Lake Street, Minneapolis, MN 55408. Assists interested groups in conducting x-c skiing programs for the visually impaired and other physically disabled people. Operates ski library and bestows awards. Publication: *Ski for Light Bulletin*.

Student Ski Association. 26 Sagamore Road, Seekonk, MA 02771. Membership entitles college and graduate students to reduced rates at 150 ski areas. Publications: *Poor Howard's Guide to Skiing,* and *Student Skier*.

U.S. Association for Blind Athletes. 33 N. Institute Street, Colorado Springs, CO 80903. Aims to develop individual independence through athletic competition. Works with other international organizations. Promotes competitions for Alpine and Nordic skiing and other sports such as swimming and wrestling. Publications: Directory, rulebook, and related materials

United States Skiing. PO Box 100, Park City, UT 84060. Chartered as the official governing body for skiing in the U.S. by the International Ski Federation and the U.S. Olympic Committee. Administers competitions, maintains hall of fame, and maintains numerous committees. Publications: Directory, and *Ski Racing*.

Worldloppet. PO Box 911, Hayward, WI 54863. Cross-country skiers who attempt to complete a series of eleven long-distance ski races throughout Europe and North America, a total of 632 kilometers. Publications: *Worldloppet Brochure,* and directory of European x-c ski race sites.

Snowmobiles

DURING THE WINTER, snow covers Canada and about half of the continental United States. Where there is snow, there are snowmobiles. They travel swiftly into once-hostile environments previously negotiated only on snowshoes. Snowmobiles have replaced sled dogs for both Eskimos and the Canadian Mounted Police. The dog teams are now primarily reserved for the sport of racing.

An expedition headed by Ralph Plaisted reached the North Pole by snowmobile in 1968. Others who put snowmobiles to practical use in their daily lives include country doctors, farmers, forest rangers, police, telephone line repairers, and trappers.

Snowmobiles have a wide range of recreational applications. Those who ice fish use them to quickly reach remote fishing spots and tow their shelters into place. Sports enthusiasts race them, play games, and use them to reach remote locations to camp, hunt, skate, ski, and take nature photographs. Snow resort areas sponsor guided tours, or safaris for snowmobilers. Many resorts rent snowmobiles and provide instruction in their use. Some clubs conduct point-to-point cruises for members, and feature a hot-meal picnic while en route.

When cruising with a snowmobile in remote wilderness areas, be especially sensitive to the environment. Nature can be fragile in winter. Observe local regulations and restrictions. Snowmobile clubs usually obtain landowners' permission to cross their property as they lay out trails for the season. The United States Forest Service marks and maintains snowmobile trails in some national forests. Some national parks and state parks also accommodate snowmobilers. Contact the appropriate agency about trail locations before you go. Many of the states, as well as the provinces of Canada furnish maps of marked snowmobile trails.

History

Mechanized sleds were originally designed for utilitarian use when roads were impassable by other means of trans-portation. Many home-built rigs were put together using automobile engines, sleds, and toboggans. A kit was marketed to convert the Model T Ford (1909–1927) to snow travel. Tracks were fitted to the back wheels and two skis replaced the front wheels. While these vehicles were intended for delivering mail and general work around the farm, it wasn't long before the owners used them for some friendly competition. Historical records show that Bill Neu won a race with Harold Hanson on a frozen Wisconsin lake in 1926.

Mechanized snow vehicles evolved along two paths. One group featured large enclosed units with caterpillar treads on each side. E. M. Tucker's Sno-Cat is an example of this type. The second group was pioneered by inventors such as Carl J. Eliason who, in 1927, patented a snow vehicle with a toboggan-like base with two steerable skis in front. A gasoline motor powered a wide belt-like tread located in the center of the rear half of the toboggan. The tread was pressed into the snow to drive the vehicle. The operator sat astride the seat located behind a windshield. Although crude by today's standards, all of the primary elements of a modern snowmobile were in place.

J. Armand Bombardier produced large commercial snowmobiles in 1936, but it wasn't until 1959 that he produced lightweight recreational snowmobiles—the now-famous Ski-Doos. Another pioneering team, Allan Hetteen and David Johnson, produced their first small, two-passenger Polaris snowmobile in 1954.

Snowmobile Types

Today, most snowmobiles have two skis in front, steered with a handlebar. Moving to the rear, a cowled motor drives a transmission that drives the track that propels the vehicle. The driver sits behind a windshield astride an elongated seat that extends to the rear of the vehicle. The feet are placed on ledges that resemble running boards located on each side. Some models accommodate a passenger behind the driver. A belt-like track is located under the seat. The driver controls vehicle speed by rotating a throttle on the right handlebar. The brakes are controlled on the left handlebar.

As snowmobiles continue to evolve, they become more specialized. Variables include: Size, weight, power, track width and length, cleats used on the track for traction, and passenger carrying capacity. A heavy, high-powered unit may be fine for commercial use, but wouldn't be suitable for light recreational use. It would be harder to get on and off of a trailer, for example. It's best to try out several snowmobile types by renting before you buy one. Some users always rent, preferring to leave maintenance and storage to others. Most users prefer a middle-sized machine. The tracks average about fifteen inches wide and 121 inches long.

Other Equipment

Passengers, sporting gear, or working gear may be carried in various types of sleds towed behind snowmobiles. The sleds range from special factory-built units to cutters, sleighs, and even toboggans.

Snowmobiles are usually carried to distant activity sites on special low flat-bed trailers that are towed behind a car or truck. Some trailers require loading ramps, others tilt to facilitate loading.

A variety of after-market accessories are available including: Snowmobile cover, speedometer, tachometer, electric starter, special suspension items, camping items, wheel conversions, spare parts kits, and saddlebags.

Clothing for the Snowmobiler

Snowmobile drivers and their passengers don't exercise sufficiently to generate body heat as skaters and skiers do. In addition, they are subjected to wind-chill factors that make it difficult to conserve body heat. Special clothing has been designed to enable snowmobilers to enjoy their sport in comfort. Either one- or two-piece insulated suits are available that are wind resistant and water repellent. Helmets, goggles, and high, lined boots, together with gloves complete the outer wear. Quilted and thermal underwear, wool socks, and heavy knit sweaters are worn under the insulated suit.

Driving Techniques

It's a good idea to take a ride as a passenger before trying to drive a snowmobile. The forces that act on the body will be experienced and the driver's response can be observed. When the snowmobile moves forward, the track covers a certain area of snow mixed with air. The weight of the machine and driver compresses the snow and trapped air so that the machine actually floats along on the compressed air. To change direction, turn the handlebars to point the skis in the direction you wish to go and lean your body into the turn to put pressure on the inside ski. When going uphill, stand on the side ledges and lean forward (Figure 1). This action places downward pressure on the skis, maintaining steering control.

Figure 1
Proper driver position when driving uphill. Moving weight forward maintains ski contact with the snow.

When riding across the slope of a hill, lean into the uphill side. If the amount of lean is too much, or too little, one side of the track will receive less pressure, allowing the air in the snow to escape from that side, and the machine will dig in and bog down. When running in deep snow it's best to sustain speed so that air under the track doesn't have time to bleed away and allow the snowmobile to sink deeper into the snow.

When riding on ice, the compressed air factor does not apply, but new problems come into play. If a turn is made too abruptly, the snowmobile is likely to skid sideways. Brakes are also less effective despite the action of the track cleats digging into the ice.

Snowmobiles are driven and raced on grass or hay fields that have been mowed. By adding wheels to the skis, they can even function on sand.

Snowmobile safety depends on proper driver training and being continually alert to potentially hazardous obstructions partially hidden by snow—especially at night. It's best to travel with a companion having a second snowmobile, in case of motor failure or accident. If you must travel alone, be sure to inform others about your planned destination and time of return. Read other precautions furnished with your equipment. For distant travel in remote areas take along a survival kit that includes at least: A first-aid kit, tools, compass, matches, candles, signaling devices, blanket, food, and snowshoes.

Bibliography

REFERENCE BOOKS

Malo, John W. *Snowmobiling: The Guide.* New York: Macmillan, 1971. An overview of snowmobiling. Describes the equipment, history, and both recreational and commercial applications.

Thomas, James L. *Safe Snowmobiling: Fun Without Damage.* New York: Sterling, 1971. Explores snowmobile uses, accessories, and racing.

Tuite, James J. *Snowmobiles and Snowmobiling.* New York: Cowles, 1969. An overview of the sport. Emphasis on location of trails and legislation affecting operation.

Wimer, Sally. *The Snowmobiler's Companion.* New York: Scribner's, 1973. Advice on buying and maintaining a snowmobile. Discusses safety, racing, and the impact on the ecology.

PERIODICALS

Hummer Trail and Touring Guide. Royal Printing, 112 Market Street, Sun Prairie, WI 53590.

Michigan Snowmobiler. Box 417, E. Jordan, MI 49727–0417.

Race and Rally. Snowmobiler Publications, Box 993, Alexandria, MN 56308.

Snow Goer. Ehlert Publications, 601 Lakeshore Parkway, Suite 600, Minnetonka, MN 55305–5215.

Snowmobile. Ehlert Publications, 601 Lakeshore Parkway, Suite 600, Minnetonka, MN 55305–5215.

Snowmobile West Magazine. Harris Publishers, 520 Park Avenue, Idaho Falls, ID 83402.

Wisconsin Snowmobile News. 112 Market Street, Sun Prairie, WI 53590.

ASSOCIATIONS

Antique Snowmobile Club of America. 1675/67 Golf Course Boulevard, Independence, IA 50644. Persons owning antique snowmobiles. Sponsors competitions and bestows awards. Publications: Bulletin, and *Iron Dog Tracks.*

Superior Shore Systems. Route 3, Box 1024, National Mine, MI 49865. Recreational and competitive snowmobilers and downhill skiers. Promotes improved performance and standards in winter sports. Publication: Newsletter.

Soccer

THE OBJECT OF THE GAME is to advance the ball into an opponent's goal, using any part of the body except the hands and arms.

A soccer team is composed of eleven players. One goalkeeper and ten field players. The basic field positions are forwards, midfielders and defenders.

How the Game is Played

A game is begun with a kickoff from the center of the midfield line. The offensive team takes a free kick to start. The defending team must be ten yards or more from the ball and on their side of the midfield line. The ball must travel one full revolution after the kick and the kicker cannot touch it again until another player has done so.

The ball is controlled and moved primarily with the feet. Kicking is done with different parts of the foot as the situation warrants. The ball may be passed from one player to another by kicking while on the run. It is dribbled by a player making a series of short kicks to move the ball while running down the field. When a player passes to another, the receiver stops the ball by using the head, body, legs or feet. A player may move the ball by butting it with the head—the forehead is the best. This is called a header.

Soccer is played on a field laid out as shown in Figure 1.

There are a few exceptions to the law banning the use of the hands. (Rules are called laws in soccer.) The goal-keeper is allowed to defend the goal and throw the ball back into play with the hands. Another exception occurs when the ball crosses a touch line or goal line. Play is restarted by a member of the side that did not touch the ball last. The ball is thrown into the field of play with both hands above the head from the position where the ball crossed the line.

Free kicks are awarded for fouls or violations of rules. A direct free kick is allowed for such major fouls as kicking, pushing, tripping, holding, striking, or jumping at an opponent. A direct free kick is taken from the penalty spot inside the penalty area. The kicker is the only player other than the goalkeeper allowed inside the penalty area prior to the kick. An indirect free kick is allowed for less serious fouls such as illegally using the body to impede an opponent from playing the ball or charging the goalkeeper within the penalty area. On an indirect free kick, a goal cannot be scored until after the ball has touched another player.

When a ball passes over the defending team's goal line, and was last touched by an attacking player, and a goal was not scored, an indirect kick is taken by the defending team from the goal area nearest to where the ball crossed the line.

When a ball passes over the defending team's goal line, and is last touched by a defending player, and a goal was not scored, an attacking team player kicks from the corner of the field nearest to where the ball crossed the line.

When a referee wants to officially warn a player that misconduct has been noted, the referee will hold up a yellow card. Further misconduct by the player warrants a red card and ejection from the match.

The laws state that soccer matches, "shall be two equal periods of forty-five minutes unless otherwise agreed upon." Youth leagues often play shorter games, as short as fifty minutes total length for players under ten years of age. Leagues vary in their use of overtime when a tie score exists at the end of regulation play. In most championship contests overtime periods are employed.

Only two major law changes have been made since the beginning of the twentieth century. They are an offside law and a substitution law.

The offside law provides that an attacking player (A), is offside if (A) receives a forward pass from a fellow attacker (B), while (A) is in the defender's half of the field with fewer than two defenders between (A) and the goal line. Defenders will sometimes use this law to their advantage by quickly moving a defender toward the attackers to

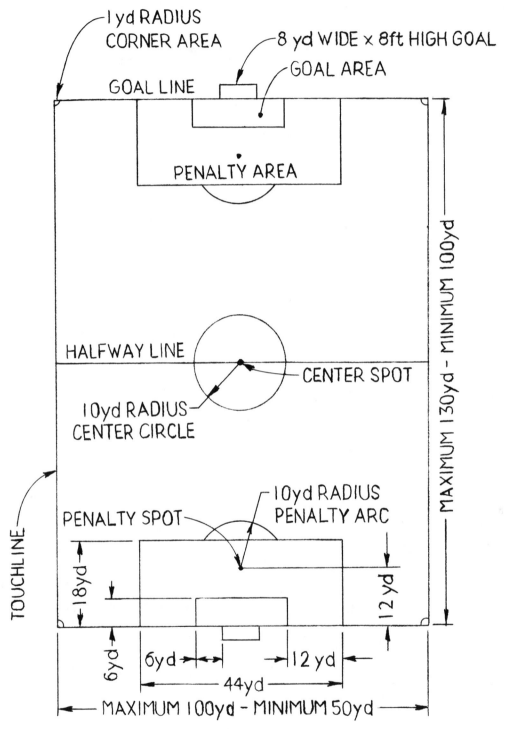

Figure 1
Soccer playing field layout.

reduce the number of defenders below the limit and prevent the attackers from making a pass. This law was passed to prevent attackers from grouping around the goal and taking unfair advantage of the goalkeeper. It is one of the most controversial and difficult to enforce laws in the game.

The substitute law provides that any two players may be substituted during a match. In the past only the original eleven players were allowed to play. If a player was injured the team played with fewer players. In youth and collegiate leagues there are no limits on substitutions.

History

The game of soccer has evolved from similar games played for centuries. The Chinese kicked a ball around over 2,000 years ago in a game called Tsu Chu. The Romans kicked an inflated animal bladder to a goal in a game called Harpastum. They played the game in England during their occupation of that country. The Romans used both hands and feet in their game, so it wasn't totally similar to soccer.

In 1843 Cambridge University in England formulated a set of rules governing its own games. These rules changed as they were adopted by a growing number of schools and associations. Few rule changes have been found necessary since the beginning of the twentieth century.

Before 1900 soccer was played in the United States almost entirely by immigrants who brought it from their native lands. Various ethnic groups played among themselves, largely unnoticed by the general population.

Organized soccer in eastern universities such as Princeton, Harvard, and Rutgers was placed under the sponsorship of the National Collegiate Athletic Association in 1905.

The game has had a long history in the United States, but had not achieved the popularity found in the rest of the world, where the number of fans is estimated to be over one billion. Now participation in soccer is growing rapidly in the United States. National organizations have facilitated a dramatic increase in participation and interest, particularly among the young. Although professional soccer in the United States had a slow start in the 1960s, today's young players will be strong supporters in the future, assuring rapid growth of the game.

World cup soccer competition is a source of fierce national pride and emotion to players and citizens of the competing countries. Game results often receive headline coverage in newspapers.

Equipment

The soccer ball is a leather-covered, inflated rubber bladder 27 to 28 inches in circumference, weighing 14 to 16 ounces. Smaller balls are used for youth teams.

Shoes are usually studded for use on grass fields. Studs are not used on artificial grass surfaces or indoor hard surfaces.

Uniforms consist of a shirt, shorts, socks and shoes.

Protective gear may include shin guards and an athletic supporter. The goalkeeper may also include padded shorts, and special gloves.

Strategy

The eleven player team of forwards, midfielders and defenders can be distributed in a number of formations, and their descriptive names change accordingly.

A 4–3–3 formation indicates (reading from backs toward center field) four defenders: a right and left fullback with a stopper at center and a sweeper who ranges back and fourth behind them. Three midfielders: left, right and center. Three forwards: left and right wingers and a striker at the center. Strikers are usually selected for their scoring skills.

Other formations include the 4–4–2, 4–2–4, and other combinations. In modern play any formation is simply a flexible framework from which all-round players move to attack when their team has the ball and all defend when they don't.

The defending player uses several methods to resist an attacking player. Blocking is permitted by moving slowly in front of the ball handler. In a one-on-one situation the defender will attempt to be positioned between the attacker and the goal at all times. This is called marking an attacker. The defender may attempt to tackle an attacker. In soccer, tackling is defined as stripping the ball away from the ball carrier. This may be done with fancy footwork, sometimes combined with a certain amount of shoulder contact, provided the ball is touched first in the process.

Some part if the ball carrier's body should be positioned between the ball and a defender.

Fitness

The President's Council on Physical Fitness calls soccer "one of the best all-around activities for the development of physical fitness, sportsmanship, teamwork, and all the other intrinsic values of sports competition."

Bibliography

REFERENCE BOOKS

Aschermann, Kurt, and Jim San Marco. *Coaching Kids to Play Soccer.* New York: Simon & Schuster, 1987. Coaching six- to sixteen-year olds, rules, safety, and teaching.

Athletic Institute. *Youth League Soccer Coaching and Playing.* North Palm Beach, FL: Athletic Institute, 1988. Coaching youth leagues, tips, and techniques.

Coerver, Wiel. *Soccer Fundamentals for Players and Coaches.* Englewood Cliffs, NJ: Prentice Hall, 1986. Game techniques, well illustrated.

Hargreaves, Alan. *Skills and Strategies for Coaching Soccer.* Chicago: Leisure, 1989. Broad game coverage, emphasis on coaching methods.

Herbst, Dan. *Sports Illustrated Soccer: The Complete Player.* New York: NAL/Dutton, 1988. Overview of the game, techniques, drills, and illustrations.

Waiters, Tony. *Coaching Youth Soccer.* Dobbs Ferry, NY: Sheridan; London: Black, 1991. Practice drills described by an international coach.

PERIODICALS

Soccer America. Berling Communications, Box 23704, Oakland, CA 94623.

Soccer Digest. Century Publishers, 990 Grove Street, Evanston, IL 60201–4370.

Soccer Jr. Triplepoint, 27 Unquowa Road, Fairfield, CT 06430.

Soccer Rulebook. National Federation of State High School Associations, 11724 NW Plaza Circle, Box 20626, Kansas City, MO 64195.

Soccer U.S.A. 11999 Katy Freeway, Suite 460, Houston, TX 77079.

ASSOCIATIONS

American Youth Soccer Organization. 5403 W. 138th Street, PO Box 5045, Hawthorne, CA 90250. Dedicated to youth soccer. Publications: Handbook and newsletters.

Intercollegiate Soccer Association of America. 1821 Sunny Drive, St. Louis, MO 63122. Promotes college soccer, bestows awards. Affiliated with National Collegiate Athletic Association, U.S. Olympic committee, and U.S. Soccer Federation.

National Soccer League. 4534 N. Lincoln Avenue, Chicago, IL 60625. Amateur soccer clubs. Sponsors international games and maintains hall of fame. Affiliated with U.S. Soccer Federation.

Soccer Association for Youth. 4903 Vine Street, Cincinnati, OH 45217. Forms leagues and schedules games for children aged six to eighteen, prescribes rules and regulations, and bestows awards. Publications: Rulebook, directory, guides, and newsletter.

United States Soccer Federation. 1801–1811 S. Prairie Avenue, Chicago, IL 60616. Promotes soccer with clubs, leagues, schools, and associations. Affiliated with American Youth Soccer Organization, Armed Forces Sports Committee, Intercollegiate Soccer Association of America, National Federation of State High School Associations, National Soccer Coaches Association of America, Soccer Association for Youth, Soccer Industry Council of America, and Special Olympics. Publications: *FIFA Laws of the Game, USSF Official Administrative Rulebook,* and other news publications.

United States Youth Soccer Association. 2050 N. Plano Road, Suite 100, Richardson, TX 75082. Players aged five to nineteen. Sponsors competitions and bestows awards. Affiliated with the International Federation of Association Football. Publications: Newspaper, directory, handbooks, and pamphlets.

Stained Glass

WHEN THE SUN STREAMS through a stained glass window we see color at the peak of its intensity. Many feel there is a degree of secrecy and mystery surrounding the creation of such beautiful transparent artwork. We have come a long way since artisans hid the secrets of their craft. Books, classes and videotapes bring the details of stained glass techniques to anyone who has the desire to learn them. Once involved, the hobbyist will view the depth, vibrancy and glow of this fascinating material with a heightened awareness and respect.

How Stained Glass is Made

Stained glass is made from silica sand containing about one percent iron, soda ash, limestone and borax. Metallic oxides are added to the mix to obtain the color. Sulphur or cadmium is used to produce yellows, dichrome for green, copper and cobalt for blue, and selenium or gold salts for red and orange. The gold content accounts for the higher prices placed on red glass.

In early times a glassblower would gather some molten glass on the end of a blowpipe, blow it into a ball, and shape it into an elongated cylinder. As it cooled the glassblower would cut off the ends, split it lengthwise and reheat it in an oven causing it to flatten into a sheet. The resulting material, called antique glass, is still produced this way in limited quantities in France, Germany, England and the United States. It may contain small trapped air bubbles and will often vary somewhat in thickness.

Most modern glass is machine rolled glass. Clear glass scrap is recycled by grinding it into fine pieces. Oxides are added for color and the resulting mix, called cullet, is melted. The molten glass is poured onto the flat bed of a machine and rolled into a flat sheet. The hot glass is placed in an annealing oven to cool slowly. The machine rollers may be embossed to impart a texture to the glass.

The variation in rates of expansion of the oxides used for coloration causes internal stresses in the glass. After cooling, glass remains slightly liquid. When very old windows are measured they are found to be thicker at the bottom than at the top. The combination of built-in stresses, variable thickness and surface texture results in a material that is sometimes unpredictable to cut.

A third type of stained glass is called slab glass. It is produced by pouring the molten glass mix into molds. The final product is much thicker than antique or machine rolled glass.

Dimension, Texture and Color

Stock sheets of machine-made glass may be as large as 32 × 84 inches. Antique glass sizes are much smaller. Mail order houses that supply the amateur and semi-professional sell smaller cut sizes for either type. Typical examples range from 8 × 12 to 16 × 24 inches. Machine rolled glass averages one-eighth inch thick. Slab glass is molded in 8 × 12 and 8 × 8 inch sizes. It is usually about one-inch thick, but may be obtained up to two inches in thickness.

Machine rolled glass is produced with various surface textures. Granite glass has a rough texture on one side. Hammered glass has small round smooth bumps on the back surface. Flemish glass has random deep channels. Crackle glass results when antique glass is briefly dipped in water during processing, producing random fracture lines. Glue chip glass has an appearance similar to frost on a window pane. It is made by coating the glass with animal hide glue and slowly baking until the glue peels off, chipping the surface.

Machine-made transparent colored glass is called cathedral glass. One side is smooth, the other usually textured. Cathedral is most often found in one color. Machine-made semi-opaque glass of milky or marbleized appearance is called opalescent glass. This type is harder than the cathedral type. It is usually smooth on both sides, but may have some texture. Opalescent glass may be one color; often is two colors, one of which is usually white; or occasionally is three colors.

Origins of the Craft

Glass objects have been discovered in Egypt and Babylonia dating from 3000 B.C. The Romans found ways to improve and color glass. It is thought that the popular use of colored ceramic tiles to create mosaics on floors led to the use of colored glass fragments to create wall mosaics. Early church windows consisted of plain glass pieces that were let into holes in stone, marble or wooden frames. Further evolution led to colored glass made into patterns inspired by the illuminated church manuscripts. Lead was eventually used to frame the glass, possibly as early as the fourth century A.D.

In the early 1100s a German monk called Theophilus wrote a treatise called "The Various Arts." It outlined techniques of leaded stained glass window making and fired painting that are remarkably similar to methods used today.

Design Considerations

A stained glass pattern is composed of colored glass pieces surrounded by leaded lines. The leaded outline contributes to the overall design and provides structural strength. The lines should be positioned so they don't distract from the design intent and so they result in glass shapes that are practical to cut. When cutting a piece of glass you will usually start at one edge and continue the cut to another edge of the piece. Sharp right angle turns in the middle of a piece would not be possible, but a well placed lead line crossing the cut at the required sharp turn would create the desired result. Lead line widths can be varied in a design to emphasize certain features. Don't use glass pieces so small or narrow that they will be covered by the lead.

Tools and Equipment

Special pattern shears may be used to cut out paper glass patterns. More about their design later.

Your glass cutter should be fitted with a carbide wheel. The average hardware store cutter has a steel wheel which will soon dull when used on stained glass, particularly opalescent glass. If a dry wheel cutter is used, dipping it in kerosene before making a cut will greatly prolong wheel life. A better approach is to purchase a cutter with an oil reservoir in the handle. Oil is fed to the cutter continuously

during the cut. Scented lamp oil (kerosene) makes a good clean-smelling lubricant.

Diamond bladed band saws can be substituted for a glass cutter for volume work.

When breaking a small piece of glass along a scored line a breaking pliers is clamped on the smaller side while holding the other side by hand. A quick up and out movement of the pliers snaps the glass.

When excess glass is left beyond the scored pattern line, it can be nibbled away with the serrated jaws of a grozing pliers.

A running pliers has a curved jaw design that is positioned at the end of a scored line. The curved jaw exerts equal pressure on each side of the score until it breaks cleanly and safely. It is especially useful when used on narrow pieces that do not afford space to grip the piece with the hand.

Motorized glass grinders are available to smooth glass edges after cutting.

Lead nipper pliers are used to cut lead strips to length.

A 100 watt soldering iron is required for most stained glass work. The better units have a temperature control built-in that maintains a constant soldering temperature.

Horseshoe nails may be used to hold glass pieces in position while soldering. Their flat sided cross section provides a wider contact surface against the glass, minimizing breakage.

Kilns (ovens) are used to heat and soften glass to obtain contoured shapes. They are also used to fuse glass pieces together. Small electric-powered units are available to hobbyists.

Procedures

You may choose to work from an existing pattern or create an original design. Let's use a simple flat design assembled with lead strips, called came, as an example. Came is an Old English word meaning string or length. The lead lines are drawn on paper and pieces are numbered and coded to indicate color.

A piece of plywood makes a good work surface for the job. Attach the paper pattern (called a cartoon) to the plywood. Use small finish nails to attach thin, straight, wooden laths along the left side and bottom edges of the pattern.

The lead came used will come in strips about six feet long. It will have a U shaped cross section for use along the outside edges of the pattern and an H section for use between pieces of glass. Came is made of pure lead and is very flexible. The two sides of the H shape are called faces. The cross bar between faces is called the heart.

Cut out individual glass piece patterns from a copy of the cartoon. This is done by cutting the cartoon with the pattern shears. It removes a one-sixteenth inch strip of paper along the pattern line. You may substitute two single edge razor blades taped to each side of a one sixteenth inch thick spacer. Since the glass pieces will fit into the slots of the U and H shaped came, this allowance must be made for the thickness of the heart of the came. Cut glass pieces to match the paper pattern. This can be facilitated by attaching the paper piece pattern to the glass with spray adhesive.

Glass "cutting" actually involves scoring the smoothest side of the glass with the glass cutter. Pressure is then exerted to cause the glass to fracture along the scored line. The glass may be tapped along the scored line from beneath with the cutter handle to initiate the fracture. The glass may be held with the scored line along a table edge and the overhanging edge pressed down to make the break. Another method is to grasp the glass with one hand on each side of the scribed line, thumbs on top and knuckles together below. Roll the thumbs apart and down, keeping the fingers clear of the glass edges.

If the edges of the piece need touching up for a perfect fit, grind the edges with a motorized grinder. With experience, grinding will be minimized.

Cut and fit the came around the first piece and continue this process working up and to the right, holding pieces in place with the special nails as you go. When the cutting and fitting is complete, brighten the came joints with fine steel wool to eliminate oxide and add a small amount of liquid flux to the joints. Using solid core, one-eighth inch diameter, 60/40 solder (60 percent tin, 40 percent lead), solder all joints.

Copper Foil Process

Let's now take the same project done with copper foil. This process is said to have originated with Louis Comfort Tiffany, son of the famous jeweler, noted stained glass designer, and manufacturer. During modern times a very thin strip of copper foil, with an adhesive applied to one side, is wrapped around the edges of each piece of glass. It covers the edge and folds over on the top and bottom of each glass piece edge to form a C cross section of copper. In this process the pieces must nest tightly together, so little allowance is made on the pattern for foil thickness. When the pieces have all been fitted in place, flux the copper joints and run a solder bead around the entire copper framework. Turn the entire glass project over and repeat the process on the other side. The copper foil method is very popular for making stained glass pictures and lamp shades. The shades are assembled over special forms.

Slab Glass Process

Working with slab glass involves entirely different cutting techniques. A T shaped piece of metal is firmly fastened to the workbench upside down (with the stem of the tee pointed up). The tip of the stem is ground to form a nine to twelve inch long chisel-like edge. An alternate design uses a vertical wedge with an edge perhaps three inches long. The wedge is embedded in lead for stability. The piece of glass is scored with the glass cutter then brought briskly down onto the chisel edge, aligned with the scored line. The glass will snap apart. If much work is done with slab glass, a motorized lapidary saw can be used in the same manner as a table saw. The pieces may then be chipped (faceted) along their edges to better reflect sunlight. The pieces are positioned in a shallow box and epoxy or cement is poured into the joints to form the completed panel.

Special Techniques

The surface of stained glass may be altered in several ways to achieve special effects.

Sandblasting removes material leaving a frosted image. A special contact paper, called a resist, protects areas that are to remain untouched. Three dimensional effects are achieved by stage blasting, exposing certain areas to one, two or more successive blasts.

Another sandblasting process involves the use of flashed glass. This glass has one or more layers of color over a thicker clear base. When a patterned resist is placed on the flashed side, sandblasting removes the exposed flashed color revealing the clear base in the desired pattern.

Acid etching is done using a similar resist technique as with sandblasting. An acid etching cream does the work of material removal.

Glass painting is best done with a special paint. The paint is made from powdered glass mixed with oxides in powdered form that give it the desired color. Mixed with water, it is painted on the stained glass, which is then fired to melt the paint into the surface permanently. This process is used to obtain more subtle effects than lead lines would provide. It might be applied to delineate the veins in a leaf or to paint a face on a flesh colored piece of glass.

Stained Glass Projects

Projects are only limited by your imagination. Some popular ones include:

Boxes	Pictures
Candle Chimneys	Room Dividers
Fireplace Screens	Sun Catchers
Jewelry	Terrariums
Kaleidoscopes	Wall Decorations
Lampshades	Windows
Mobiles	

Bibliography

REFERENCE BOOKS

Gick, Terri L. *Sandblasting, Etching and Other Glass Treatments.* Laguna Hills, CA: Gick, 1980. Materials, techniques including engraving and beveling.

Isenberg, Anita, and Seymour Isenberg. *How to Work in Stained Glass.* Radnor, PA: Chilton Books, 1972. General coverage, design, tools, and techniques.

———. *Stained Glass: Advanced Techniques and Projects.* Radnor, PA: Chilton Books, 1976. Tools, techniques, lamps, painting, and projects.

Isenberg, Anita, Seymour Isenberg, and Richard Millard. *Stained Glass Painting: Basic Techniques of the Craft.* Radnor, PA: Chilton Books, 1979. Extensive coverage of glass painting techniques.

O'Brien, Vincent. *Techniques of Stained Glass: Leaded, Faceted, and Laminated Glass.* New York: Van Nostrand Reinhold, 1977. Emphasis on slab glass, laminated glass, and working with came.

Quagliata, Narcissus. *Stained Glass from Mind to Light.* San Francisco: Mattole, 1976. Techniques, heavily illustrated.

Scobey, Joan M. *Stained Glass Traditions and Techniques.* New York: Dial, 1979. History, techniques, and projects.

PERIODICALS

Glass Art Society Journal. Glass Art Society, 1305 Fourth Avenue, Suite 711, Seattle, WA 98101–2401.

Glass Patterns Quarterly. 8300 Hidden Valley Road, PO Box 131, Westport, KY 40077.

Glass Workshop. Stained Glass Club, 8 Frasco Lane, Norwood, NJ 07648–2407.

Professional Stained Glass. Edge Publishing Group, Tonetta Lake Road, RR 6, Box 69, Brewster, NY 10509.

Stained Glass. Stained Glass Association of America, 6 SW 2nd Street, Suite 6, Lee's Summit, MO 64063–2348.

ASSOCIATION

Stained Glass Association of America. PO Box 22642, Kansas City, MO 64113. Professionals and student associates. Seeks to advance the craft. Assembles exhibits, sponsors apprentice program, loans instructional videotapes, and holds competitions. Publishes *Kaleidoscope,* and *Stained Glass.*

Stamps, Collecting

STAMP COLLECTING HOLDS a fascination for over ten percent of all Americans. There are almost a half million different stamps cataloged, and each has a story to tell. With stamps, one can trace the history of nations over the past one hundred years, and see the faces of their leaders in science and politics. A nation's stamps record the rise and fall of colonialism, as well as the accumulation, division, and renaming of lands. Collectors learn the names given to currencies, and see economies rise and fall as stamp denominations change. Stamp collecting supplements the young collector's formal schooling, and contributes to a well-rounded education.

Most young people begin by collecting stamps of all countries. While it's impossible to collect them all, this is a good way to become familiar with the various aspects of the hobby. Most collectors identify favorite countries or topics and specialize as experience is gained. The cost of an individual stamp can range from pennies to thousands of dollars, which allows everyone access to a hobby enjoyed by schoolchildren and sophisticated philatelists (stamp collectors) such as Franklin D. Roosevelt.

A beginner can purchase inexpensive batches of stamps in mixtures, or all different packets. The mixtures contain duplicates and are therefore less expensive. Most stamps will be found still attached to the corner of an envelope, and you are quite unlikely to find a rare stamp in the batch. They make excellent space fillers in an album, and enable the collector to become familiar with stamp identification. The number of stamps sold in packets ranges from 100 to 50,000. Young people should limit the packet size to about 3,000. Adults may wish to choose about 5,000. Packets are sold as all-world, single country, by topic, by years, etc. As noted earlier, expect quality to be average, unless stated otherwise. Packets containing all new U.S. stamps issued during the past year are available at post offices.

Advanced collectors furnish dealers with their want list, identifying stamps they would like dealers to hold for them if they come across any.

Some dealers and countries' postal systems will accept a cash deposit against future shipments to you of new stamp issues. You specify areas of interest such as topicals, blocks, or other criteria.

Most large dealers will go to great lengths to establish you as a customer for their stamp approval service. After determining your special collecting interests, the dealer mails groups of stamps for your consideration. You select what you want to buy, and mail the rest back with payment for what you keep. Stamp periodicals contain many such dealer listings, together with their loss-leader offers to get you to subscribe.

Certain hobbies that involve communications are natural companions to stamp collecting. Amateur radio operators, computer information services, and pen pal organizations all have special interest groups that bring distant like-minded enthusiasts together—an excellent way to find stamp trading partners. Stamps are usually traded on the basis of their catalog value. Since some of the best stamp catalogs are large multi-volume publications, you may wish to refer to them at your local library.

Embassies, both foreign and our own, are also possible contact sources. Be aware however, stamps are usually most expensive in the country that issues them.

History

The first United States postage stamps were distributed July 1, 1847, seven years after Great Britain issued its first adhesive postage stamp. Before 1847, Americans paid a postmaster to mail a letter. The postmaster had to mark the amount of postage collected and the city of origin on the envelope. The first stamp-printed postal cards were issued in 1873. The first air mail service was established in May, 1918. The first stamped envelopes were printed in 1953.

Specialization

We have seen that almost a half million different stamps have been produced. No one can expect to collect them all. As a first world-wide album begins to fill, a collector will begin to develop preferences. Such preferences will be influenced by an interest in the chosen specialty, the availability of the special stamps, purchase cost, and potential for future sale.

Specialization by Country or Topic

Single country collections can vary considerably in size. If you choose one or more newly independent nations, you can easily collect every issue made at relatively low cost. If you choose a more popular single country collection such as Great Britain and its colonies, availability and expense of early issues must be taken into account.

Many enthusiasts collect all stamps related to a single topic. The American Topical Association publishes handbooks and checklists of stamps issued that relate to a specific subject. There are currently more than 320 different subject checklists. Most hobbyists will find it easy to combine philately with their other hobby interests.

Definitives and Commemoratives

Some regular stamps of each denomination continue to be issued over a long period of time at post offices. These are termed definitive stamps. Others, called commemorative stamps, are designed to honor a person (only after death in the case of U.S. stamps), or subject. They are intended to be issued for a limited time period. A citizen or group wishing to propose a topic for a new stamp can write to the Citizens' Stamp Advisory Committee, suggesting a person, animal, historical event, sport, or other subject for consideration. The committee makes recommendations to the postmaster general, who must approve the suggestion before design work is begun on the stamp.

A popular way to collect commemoratives is by means of the first day cover. Sometime before a commemorative stamp is issued, private companies have beautifully engraved envelopes designed and produced for sale to collectors. A city related to the subject of the stamp is designated to be first to issue the stamp for public use. The collector self-addresses one or more of the special envelopes, and mails them to the first-day-issue postmaster, together with a money order for the amount of postage required to return the envelopes. The postmaster will affix the new stamp to each envelope, cancel them with a special die and mail them back to the sender. First day covers make attractive collectibles, but due to their popularity, they usually appreciate little in value.

Panes

Many enthusiasts collect entire panes of stamps, or significant portions of a pane, as new designs are issued. Each plate used to print panes of stamps is assigned a number. The number is printed on the margin of the pane at a corner, outside of the stamp perforations. Where several plates are required for multi-colored stamps, more than one plate number will appear. Collectors collect a block of corner stamps (usually four) that are attached to the margin bearing the plate number. This is called plate number block collecting.

Occasionally panes of stamps are printed with two or more different stamps next to one another. They are said to occupy se-tenant positions. The number of probabilities of different corner position arrangements in this case can make plate number block collecting expensive. This has resulted in the practice of collecting single stamps that are positioned adjacent to each plate number.

When two adjacent stamps of one design in the same pane are positioned so that one is upside down in relation to the other, they are said to be tête-bêche. While this may occur because of an error in plate making, some European stamps are intentionally printed in this manner.

The list of special collectible stamps and covers (envelopes) is long. Some other popular items include: Christmas stamps, postal cards, stamped envelopes, stamps containing errors, revenue stamps, and special cancellation collections.

Manufacture

Stamp paper falls into two broad categories: wove and laid. Wove paper is made by depositing ground cellulose fibers onto a fine wire screen (early wove paper was deposited on a felt surface). Laid paper is produced when the fibers are deposited on a screen consisting of closely spaced parallel wires with cross wires at wider intervals. The screen and fiber pulp are passed through rollers when the pulp is almost dry, flattening the pulp and forming paper. Watermarked paper is produced by adding a raised design on the rollers, which is pressed into the paper during manufacture. A watermark can be seen by holding the paper to the light. The paper is thinner where the lines forming the design have been impressed.

Stamps have been printed using different processes: The engraved process, in which the lines to be reproduced are cut into the surface of a plate and inked, the surface is wiped clean, and paper under pressure is forced down into the cut (engraved) lines that receive the ink. The typography process, in which the lines to be printed are raised above the surface and inked. The photogravure process, in which lines are photographed through a screen on a sensitive film covering the plate, and then etched into it as in engraving. The lithographic process in which the lines to be reproduced are drawn on a metal plate with an oily ink that attracts the oily ink used to reproduce the line. The rest of the plate is covered by an acid fluid that repels the oily ink used in printing. The embossed process, in which the design is sunk into a metal die. Printing is done against a yielding platen, such as linoleum. The platen is forced into the depression of the die, thus forming the design on the paper in relief.

Early stamps were cut from a sheet (pane) of stamps with a pair of scissors or knife. Subsequent issues included perforations between individual stamps to facilitate separation. Most perforations are a series of holes. Some countries employ a series of slits. Such stamps are referred to as "roulette."

Gum is the glue on the back of a stamp. It's applied before the stamp sheets are perforated. A variety of glues have been used over the years, ranging from a potato, wheat, and acacia concoction used on the first adhesive stamps to the current mild tasting formulas. Some stamps were issued with no adhesive. The condition of the gum is a factor in determining a stamp's value.

Some stamps are coated, or marked, with a luminescent ink, which is visible under ultra violet light. This tagging process is used to expedite mail handling. The luminescence triggers electronic machinery used for sorting or canceling letters.

Stamps are sometimes overprinted with a mark or inscription that was not part of the original design. Two common examples are the requirement to change a stamp's value, or to add a notation indicating a change in government.

When a stamped letter is mailed, postal employees cancel the stamp. The inked imprint used to indicate cancellation may take the form of a circular date stamp which has the date of cancellation appearing inside the circle. Cancellation markings indicate the stamp has been used, usually lowering its value to collectors. Certain unusual or historically significant cancellations can increase the stamp's worth. Some small countries in need of capital cancel whole panes (sheets) of stamps that are never used in a postal system. These precancelled stamps are intended for sale to stamp collectors.

The primary picture or design printed on a stamp is called a vignette. If the stamp contains a printed border around the vignette, the border is called a frame. A margin is the unprinted area outside the vignette or frame.

Scott Publishing Company is the recognized source of standard stamp catalogs in the United States. Each different stamp is assigned a Scott catalog number, which will be found referenced in almost all price lists and auction literature.

Condition and Grade

Few individuals are more meticulous about the condition of their collected items than stamp collectors. In view of this, it's ironic that there is no formal, enforced grading system for postage stamps. Books often define a stamp's grade in terms of its manufacturing defects and its condition. Grade and condition influence value and the price you can expect to pay for a stamp. Factors that increase the value of a stamp include exceptionally wide margins, particularly fresh color, and the presence of selvage (the paper attached outside the stamps on a pane). Factors that decrease value include: no gum, or evidence of regumming, a hinge remnant, a straight unperforated edge on an otherwise perforated stamp, irregular perforations, a missing piece, tear, surface scuff, thin spot, crease, color modification, oxidation, stain, or evidence of repairs such as reperforation.

Grading terms you may encounter include: superb, very fine, fine-very fine, fine, good, poor, bad, or damaged. *Superb* is defined as perfect in every respect. It will be lightly canceled, if used. *Fine* is described as: a somewhat uneven margin, perforations don't cut into frame, a few short perforations are allowed but none are missing, no paper defects, and some heavy hinge marks are allowed on gum. Fine stamps may be heavily canceled when used, but the design isn't obliterated. Fine is the best most ordinary mortals can afford when buying older stamps. The *fine-very fine* grade has been used in stamp illustrations in *Scott's Standard Postage Stamp Catalog*. Stamps graded *good* are found in packets and mixtures, which are stamps purchased in bulk from dealers. They may be far off center, heavily canceled but not obliterated, lightly creased; but no tears or excessive thin spots are allowed.

Tools

Stamps absorb acids, grease, and moisture when in contact with skin. This causes stains and accumulation of dirt. They should be held and manipulated with stamp tongs, a tweezer-like device with flat surfaces on the gripping inside of the tips.

A perforation gauge is used to check perforation spacing on the edges of stamps. Perforation gauge numbers are based on the number of holes on two centimeters of the length of a stamp's side. The gauge device has a group of different gauge spacings shown on its surface with the corresponding gauge number printed alongside. A stamp is held over the illustrated gauge spacings to find a match, and the number is noted. Some otherwise identical stamps have had different perforation spacings over time. The perforation gauge is used to distinguish which perforation type, and time period, the stamp belongs to. It's also used to detect fake or repaired stamps.

Some stamps and stamped envelopes were made with watermarked paper. Occasionally, otherwise identical stamps will be found that were produced both with and without watermarks. Sometimes the value of a stamp is significantly different if one of the two conditions is rare. To detect a watermark, a stamp is placed face down in a small black glass or plastic watermark tray. When a small amount of watermarking fluid is applied to the stamp; the watermark will show up as an image darker than the rest of the stamp. Watermarking fluids are quick-drying organic compounds that are harmless to most stamps, even with gum on the back.

A magnifying glass is useful to see and appreciate the fine details of an engraved design. Its use isn't essential unless you are looking for minor defects when purchasing expensive specimens.

Handling and Storage

Most beginners will find, collect, or purchase stamps still affixed to envelopes or other paper. They are separated by soaking in a pan of water. Soak only long enough to dissolve the gum. You may handle the stamps with the fingers while wet to avoid rust stains from tongs, but use tongs after the stamps are dry. Stamps produced with aniline dye may lose some color and stain adjacent stamps. In a like manner, various papers can contaminate the soaking water, so it's best to treat separately stamps on darker colored papers.

Stamps are usually stored in albums. They offer the convenience of compact storage and individual spaces for specific stamps, with an illustration of the specific stamp printed in the space. You match up your stamp with the illustration and fix it into place. If you are dealing with average quality used stamps, the stamp is attached with a hinge. Hinges are small pieces of semitransparent paper coated with a special peelable gum. You fold the paper a third of the way down with the gummed side out. Moisten the short side and attach to the back of the stamp. The fold is positioned at the top of the stamp just below the perforations. Then, moisten the bottom half of the long side of the hinge and place the stamp neatly in its space in the album. However, if the stamp is moved a number of times, each hinge removal peels away a bit of the back of the stamp. This is called thinning. When hinges are applied to new stamps whose gum is intact, the stamp's value can be reduced by ten percent. The solution is to use a plastic mount, typically a clear mini-envelope to house an individual stamp. The mount is affixed to the album space.

Stamp albums are designed to house one or more countries, or a variety of other specialized stamp collections. Young people may want to start with an album with 10,000 to 20,000 spaces. A 25,000 to 40,000 space album is more suitable for an adult. Remember, if you outgrow the smaller album, you have to transfer all those stamps to the next larger album. Advanced albums by Minkus or Scott will hold almost every stamp ever issued.

There are many options for stamp storage. One popular style is the stock book. It often has loose leaf pages of clear plastic with pockets to hold the stamps. The stock book is especially useful to house a topical collection for which printed albums are not made.

Avoid stamp contact with moist air that will cause the stamps to adhere to albums or mounts. Moisture will also promote mold growth.

Investing and Selling

When selling any product, the margin of profit is determined by supply and demand. We have seen that many millions of Americans are stamp collectors. They have an inexhaustible supply of new stamps available to them from the U.S. Postal Service. Collectors have built up a significant backlog of recently issued stamps. When collections to be sold consist of recent (post World War II) unused stamps, the profit from a sale can be little or none.

When collections consist of average quality, used, worldwide stamps, their value is minimal. A dealer will make a greater profit selling packets than trying to resell material purchased from a collector.

An experienced collector/investor who is well aware of catalog values, market cycles, and trends will invest in stamps in short supply (minimum issue), having a well-deserved reputation as being desirable, and showing a consistent appreciation in value. The stamps will be held long enough to allow market trends to rise sufficiently to sell at a required profit. Such stamps will usually be expensive. They should be authenticated by a leading dealer and a certificate of authentication should be obtained before purchase. One way to evaluate a rare stamp being offered for sale is to ask several dealers what they would pay for the stamp if you had it to sell to them. Expect a dealer's offer to buy to be about fifty percent of a proper selling price. A dealer usually makes such a mark-up to cover costs of doing business. This emphasizes the need to hold investment stamps until their value increases significantly.

Bibliography

REFERENCE BOOKS

Cummings, William W., ed. *Scott 1994 Standard Postage Stamp Catalog.* 5v., Sidney, OH: Scott, 1993. This annual catalog is used by collectors and the industry to identify stamps, obtain benchmark information relative to current value, and to note other special characteristics that relate to each stamp. The introduction contains basic information about stamps, currency conversion tables, and more.

Hobson, Burton. *Getting Started in Stamp Collecting.* Rev. ed. New York: Sterling, 1982. Comprehensive coverage of the hobby for the beginning collector. Emphasis on United States and topical stamps.

Krause, Barry. *Advanced Stamp Collecting.* Crozet, VA: Betterway, 1990. Covers rare stamps, neglected specialties, fakes, societies, museums, auctions, dealers, and dealer types.

———. *Collecting Stamps for Pleasure and Profit.* White Hall, VA: Betterway, 1988. Concise overview of collecting. Covers tools, stamp manufacture and condition, with special emphasis on buying, selling, and investment. Useful bibliographic information on societies and foreign postal agencies.

———. *Stamp Collecting: An Illustrated Guide and Handbook for Adult Collectors.* White Hall, VA: Betterway, 1989. Starting out in stamps, where to find them, categories, defects, investing, and more.

Villiard, Paul. *Collecting Stamps.* New York: New American Library, 1974. Somewhat dated, but wide-ranging and informative in its treatment of the hobby of stamp collecting.

PERIODICALS

American Philatelist. American Philatelic Society, Box 8000 State College, PA 16803.

Linn's Stamp News. Amos Press, Box 29, Sidney, OH 45365.

Postal Service Guide to U.S. Stamps. U.S. Postal Service, 475 L'Enfant Plaza SW., Washington, DC 20260–6757.

Scott Stamp Monthly. Scott Publishers, 911 Vandemark Road, Box 828, Sidney, OH 45365.

Stamp Collector. Box 10, Albany, OR 97321.

Stamps. American Publisher, 85 Canisteo Street, Hornell, NY 14843.

ASSOCIATIONS

American Airmail Society. PO Box 110, Mineola, NY 11501. Collectors of airmail stamps and covers. Sponsors competitions, bestows awards, and maintains hall of fame. Publications: *Airpost Journal,* and related material.

American First Day Cover Society. PO Box 3355, Poughkeepsie, NY 12603. Collectors of first day covers. Sponsors competitions and bestows awards. Publication: *First Days.*

American Philatelic Society. 100 Oakwood Avenue, PO Box 8000, State College, PA 16803. Stamp collectors. Operates library, maintains hall of fame, and provides correspondence courses. Publications: *American Philatelist,* and related materials.

American Topical Association. PO Box 630, Johnstown, PA 15907. Those specializing in the collection of stamps by subject matter, includes members in ninety countries. Maintains sales service for exchange of member's stamps, and a language translation service. Bestows awards. Publications: *Topical Time,* and related material.

Benjamin Franklin Stamp Club. 475 L'Enfant Plaza SW, Room 4485E, Washington, DC 20260–6757. A division of the U.S. Postal Service through which local groups work to promote interest in stamp collecting by children. Sponsors competitions and bestows awards. Publications: *Stamp Fun/Leader Future,* and *Treasury of Stamps Album.*

Citizens' Stamp Advisory Committee. U.S. Postal Service Headquarters, 475 L'Enfant Plaza SW, Washington, DC 20260–6757. Advisory committee appointed by the postmaster general to screen citizens' suggestions for issuance of commemorative stamps, and make recommendations.

Cover Collectors Circuit Club. c/o Allan J. Bagnall, RD 1, Box 1025, New Freedom, PA 17349. Stamp and philatelic cover collectors. Exchanges information through correspondence among collectors.

Junior Philatelists of America. PO Box 557, Boalsburg, PA 16827. Stamp collectors under age nineteen in eleven countries. Encourages stamp collecting among youth. Operates pen pal and stamp exchange services. Bestows awards. Publications: *Philatelic Observer,* and related material.

National Association of Precancel Collectors. 5121 Park Boulevard, Wildwood, NJ 08260–0121. Those interested in the collection of stamps that are canceled before being postally used. Maintains museum and library. Publications: *Precancel Stamp Collector,* and related materials.

U.S. Philatelic Classics Society. Briarwood, Lisbon, MA 21765. Philatelists and postal historians interested in issues of U.S. postage stamps and the postal history of the period 1847–1893, and in the preceding stampless period. Presents awards to those who have provided significant contributions to research. Publications: *Chatter, Chronicle of U.S. Classical Postal Issues,* and related material.

Note: There are additional associations devoted to specific stamp areas of interest listed in the *Encyclopedia of Associations,* available in libraries.

Surfing

SINCE THE EARLY 1900s a growing number of people have experienced the thrill of riding awesome and powerful ocean waves as they rush to the shore. Like the bronc-busting cowboys of the old west, they have developed the equipment and techniques needed to tame the waves. But like those wild horses, the ocean can be unpredictable, and it will bite the surfer unschooled in its ways.

How Waves Create Surf

To understand the sport of surfing, we must first understand the "playing field." Waves are created by the wind. Waves formed by wind and ocean storms grow into patterns called seas. The waves, or swells, become a series of long, regular undulations. Waves from different sources that have similar characteristics tend to catch up to one another and begin to "train," moving at relatively the same speed. When a group of training swells finally break on a sloping shore, surfers call it a set. They usually travel in sets of from three to seven. Although the wave shape moves through the ocean, the water itself moves forward very little. The action is similar to waves in a field of grain, where the grain itself remains in the same location.

As the waves reach the shore they feel drag from the bottom and they begin to slow. This causes them to squeeze closer together, the wave length shortens, and the back of the wave catches up to the front squeezing the wave up higher. The top of the wave usually tumbles forward when water depth equals 1⅓ the wave's height. A six foot wave will break in eight feet of water. Depending on a wave's size and the shape of the ocean floor, the swell will grow steeper until the crest rises sharply, peaks forming a lip, and the lip rolls forward (breaks) trapping air that forms whitewater as it roars to the shore as surf. If the ocean floor is relatively flat, the wave will not break all along the shore

at once, but will spill over at one location and the spill will spread gradually across the wave. This type of wave is best for surfers, affording the longest ride. If the ocean floor has a steep slope the spilling action occurs abruptly across the shore line. This type of wave is called a plunger. Mastering such a wave offers a challenge to surfers.

Trains of swells originating in the Southern Hemisphere reach the beaches of Hawaii during the summer. Swells originating in the northwest Pacific pound Hawaii's northern beaches during the winter. The steep bottom there causes the formation of huge waves that attract surfers from around the world.

There are several nationwide telephone services that provide surf reports of wave, wind, weather, and other information useful to surfers. Armed with this knowledge, the surfer sets out to get to a starting point far enough from shore to begin a ride.

A surfer lies, or kneels, on the surfboard and paddles out through the surf, ducking under, and through, breaking waves until undulating swells are reached. A wave is selected and the surfer paddles hard toward shore to reach a position just past the peak of the wave. Rising to the knees, and then standing erect, the surfer slides down the front of the wave and continues to do so for perhaps a quarter of a mile. If heading straight for the shore, the surfer is surfing "straight off."

An oblique path can be taken that carries the surfer across the wave, increasing the speed traveled. By timing turns carefully, a surfer can cut across the face of the wave at the instant the lip of the wave falls forward, forming a hollow tunnel of water that surfers call a tube. The surfer glides through the tube and is propelled out the end of it by the air pressure build-up caused by the collapse of the tube.

An experienced surfer can turn by leaning or concentrating body weight to the left or right side of the board, and slow down, or stall, by stepping back on the board. Forward speed can be increased by stepping forward on the board, but care must be taken not to make the nose of the board dig into the wave and cause the surfer to pearl. To pearl is to dive forward into the water like a pearl diver. Experienced surfers wear a line called a leash between them and their surfboard so they won't be separated in the event of a spill.

A surfer who executes the most radical controlled maneuvers in the most critical section of the biggest and/or best waves, for the longest functional distance, wins in competition. The surfer must know how to pick the right wave and move with style and skill.

See the bibliography for associations and periodicals that promote and publicize competitions. Surfers dating back to Duke Kahanamoku have looked forward to the day when surfing would be considered for Olympic competition. There is a possibility that it will happen in 1996.

History

Hawaiians had been surfing for about a thousand years before Captain James Cook showed up in 1778. Natives lying prone on surfboards paddled out to Cook's ship to see the "trees moving on the sea." The European sailors were equally intrigued with the native's ability to swim. Swimming for pleasure had been discontinued in Europe since about 500 A.D. because people thought it caused the spread of diseases such as the plague. The sailors were further impressed when the natives surfed to shore standing on their surfboards.

Hawaiian natives of all ages and social status enjoyed surfing. When the surf was up, all other activity stopped and everyone headed for the beach. The Hawaiian natives were also somewhat unique in their love of gambling. They placed bets on surfing competition that included their worldly possessions and even their freedom or their lives. One social aspect of surfing involved the sexes. If a lady caught a wave being surfed by a man, it indicated her interest in him, often resulting in some dalliance on the beach.

The Hawaiians didn't have a written language during this period. Past events were communicated verbally in the form of chants. Foreign settlers, followed by missionaries, taught the natives to read and write. The missionaries took a dim view of the carousing associated with surfing, and the sport began to decline. By 1900, most surfboards had been cut down into school desks and benches.

Before Cook's arrival, natives were surfing at other Pacific locations, such as Easter Island, New Zealand, and especially Tahiti. However, Hawaiian surfing was much further advanced, probably due to the ideal wave conditions enjoyed there. The west coast of Africa was an exception to the Pacific monopoly on surfing before the nineteenth century. Natives along the coast of Senegal, the Ivory Coast, and Ghana also mastered the art of surfing standing erect on their boards.

Twentieth-Century Growth

During the nineteenth century few Caucasians learned to surf. Some famous personalities such as writers Mark Twain and Jack London tried, with limited success. In the early 1900s the sport began a slow comeback. George Freeth, an Irish-Hawaiian, and Alexander Hume Ford played major roles in the revival. Freeth brought surfing to the mainland, and Ford, a mainlander, conducted classes at Waikiki. The most famous of all surfers of the day was Duke Kuhanamoku, the father of surfing. He was an Olympic champion swimmer in 1912. Duke was joined by Native American, Jim Thorpe at that Olympics. Jim won on land, and Duke on the water that year.

Duke demonstrated swimming and surfing techniques across mainland America after the Olympics, popularizing the sport. He did the same for Australia in 1915. The Australians revived the sport in New Zealand in the 1930s. From these beginnings, surfing spread throughout British Commonwealth countries. The origin of surfing in France is unique in that the French studied drawings of surfboards, read about techniques, and taught themselves to surf.

Inspired by Duke Kuhanamoku, Tom Blake organized the Pacific Coast Surfriding Championships in 1928. When Blake tried to duplicate a long board he had seen in a Hawaiian museum, it was too heavy. He drilled the board full of holes, plugged the holes and came up with a light surfboard that enabled him to win competitions. Blake's hollow surfboard idea was resisted at first, but soon set the pattern for ever lighter surfboards to come.

Surfing activity increased dramatically in the United States after World War II. Innovators such as surfboard developers Bob Simmons, Joe Quigg, Matt Kivlin, and Hobie Alter kept pace with the demands created by new surfing techniques.

Surfboard Evolution

Early Hawaiian boards were of two general types. Long boards, called Olo, were reserved for use by the chieftain class. A typical Olo was eighteen feet long, two feet wide and five inches thick. They were made from wiliwili, a light buoyant wood. Olo boards could catch a swell long before it reached the shore, affording a long ride. They were stable in big surf. Their disadvantages were that they were difficult to paddle out through the surf, and they were hard to turn. Shorter boards, called alaia, were used by both commoners and chiefs. They were, by far, the most common. Alaias were about seven feet long, eighteen inches wide, and an inch thick. They were usually made from koa, a mahogany-like wood. Their size compares favorably with modern boards. They were very maneuverable.

Tom Blake experimented with hollow redwood Olo-style boards. Others experimented with balsa boards with redwood edges, and laminated pine and redwood combinations.

After World War II Bob Simmons built boards of balsa wood covered with fiberglass and sealed with plastic resin. By the mid 1950s, polyurethane plastic foam replaced the balsa. The fiberglass covered plastic foam construction is still popular today. Experiments are in progress with carbon fiber and graphite materials, but high costs are a limiting factor.

As short-board surfers began to maneuver across waves, they found that their boards tended to skid sideways. Both Blake and Simmons experimented with an aft-mounted fin, or skeg, which solved the stability problem. Some modern boards have two or three fins to accommodate the more radical turning movements common today.

Board design changes continue to accelerate, enabling surfers to perform maneuvers in ways that would amaze the early Polynesians.

Windsurfing

During 1966 surfer Hoyle Schweitzer and sailor Jim Drake developed the idea of placing a sail on a surfboard. The idea may, or may not, have been thought of before, but they designed and built the first workable unit in 1967. Production was started and the new sport gained rapid acceptance.

The equipment consists of a surfboard, a mast, a boom, a small retracting keel (daggerboard) and fin (skeg). See Figure 1. The combination of parts (sailboard) is unique in that the combined mast, sail, and boom (rig) pivots freely at the point the mast base meets the surfboard. The surfer moves the rig by holding onto the boom.

The surfer mounts the assembled sailboard in shallow water with the wind directed at one side of the board. The rig is lying horizontal in the water at the time. The rig is raised to a vertical position by pulling hand over hand on an uphaul rope. The sail is allowed to flap in the breeze at right angles to the board. In this condition the sailboard is not propelled by the wind. It is called the secure position. The secure position can be assumed at any time you find yourself in trouble and wish to stop.

The rig is manipulated to control speed and direction. If the flapping rig is pulled parallel with the board and its mast is leaned toward the back of the board the sailboard will turn into the wind. The speed of the turn is determined by how far and how fast the mast is tipped back. You can turn the front of the board away from the wind by leaning the rig toward the front of the board. When you are ready to sail away, you tip the mast into the wind until it feels balanced, and gradually rotate the rig until the sail begins to fill with wind. At the same time, holding onto the boom, lean your body into the wind to counteract the force of the wind on the sail. You will sail along, keeping the mast tipped into the wind.

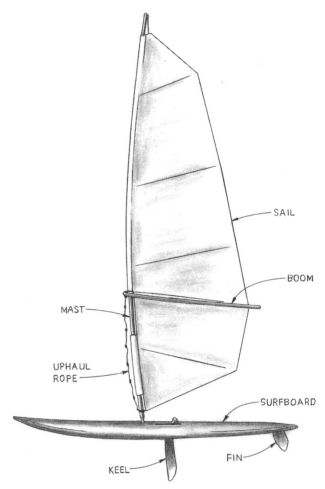

Figure 1

Sailboard used for windsurfing. The mast pivots freely at the point the mast base meets the surfboard. The surfer stands on the surfboard and manipulates the sail by exerting pressure on the boom.

As with a sailboat, the sailboard must be sailed upwind in a zig-zag course called tacking. You cannot sail directly into the wind. If you sail as close to upwind as possible, you are sailing close hauled. Sailing at right angles to the wind is called sailing a beam reach.

Wind Force

Windsurfers must be keenly aware of the force of the wind. The force is specified in units of the Beaufort scale. A force 0 wind has a velocity of less than one knot. It is considered calm. At force 1—water ripples, and the wind is at one to three knots. At force 2—there are small wavelets, and the wind is at four to six knots. At force 4—whitecaps form, small branches move, and a moderate breeze blows at eleven to sixteen knots. In the early stages of learning to windsurf, avoid winds over force 4. Windsurfing is not a sport for weak swimmers.

Special Purpose Windsurf Boards

Experienced windsurfers use short, light boards called wave boards, to jump from waves and do somersaults with their craft. Some competitions are based on the ability to do acrobatic maneuvers of the above type. Other boards, called slalom boards are designed to do well in a form of racing that follows a zig-zag course around buoys. Most of these specialty boards are fitted with footstraps to enable the surfer to stay with the board during radical maneuvers.

Windsurfing became an Olympic sport in 1984.

Bibliography

REFERENCE BOOKS

Coutts, James. *Start Windsurfing Right!* Newport, RI: U.S. Yacht Racing Union, 1991. Covers equipment, techniques, rules of sailing, and the weather.

Finney, Ben R., and James D. Houston. *Surfing: The Sport of Hawaiian Kings.* Rutland, VT: Tuttle, 1966. Slightly dated, but good overview of the sport with emphasis on history.

Gadd, Mike, John Boothroyd, and Ann Durrell. *The Book of Windsurfing: A Guide to Freesailing Techniques.* Toronto: Van Nostrand Reinhold, 1980. How to rig and launch, basic maneuvers, and sailing in high wind.

Grissim, John. *Pure Stoke.* New York: Harper & Row, 1982. Surfboard coverage describing activities in the lives of individual surfers.

Jones, Phil. *Learn Windsurfing in a Weekend.* New York: Knopf, 1992. Well illustrated book about the basics of getting started.

Lueras, Leonard. *Surfing: The Ultimate Pleasure.* New York: Workman, 1984. Overview of surfing and windsurfing including activities, surf films, music, and foreign surfing locations. Emphasis on history.

Stickl, Niko, and Michael Garff. *Windsurfing Technique.* New York: Hearst Books, 1982. Emphasis on windsurfing techniques, racing, and trick sailing.

Taylor, Glenn. *Windsurfing: The Complete Guide.* Rev. ed. New York: McGraw-Hill, 1980. An overview of windsurfing written by the man who started the first windsurfing school in 1974.

Waltze, Mike, with Phil Berman. *Performance Windsurfing with Mike Waltze.* New York: Norton, 1985. Rigging and tuning windsurfing equipment. Detailed description of advanced techniques such as jibing, jumping, and sailing in surf.

Wardlaw, Lee. *Cowabunga: The Complete Book of Surfing.* New York: Avon Books, 1991. Overview of surfing including selecting equipment, techniques, surfing locations, history, and a bibliography of schools, literature and related material.

PERIODICALS

Surf Report. Box 1028, Dana Point, CA 92629. (Surfing conditions.)

Surfer. Surfer Publications, 33046 Calle Aviador, San Juan Capistrano, CA 92675.

The Surfer's Journal. 1050 Calle Cordillera, Unit 106, San Clemente, CA 92672.

Surfing. Western Empire Publications, 950 Calle Amanecer, Suite C, Box 3010, San Clemente, CA 92672.

Wind Surf. 621 Stone Canyon Road, Los Angeles, CA 90077–2924.

Windsurfing. World Publications, 330 W. Canton, Box 2456, Winter Park, FL 32790.

ASSOCIATIONS

Association of Surfing Professionals. PO Box 309, Huntington Beach, CA 92648. Governing body of professional surfing worldwide. Sponsors world surfing tour, bestows awards. Publications: *ASP Guide,* and *ASP Newsletter.*

Eastern Surfing Association. PO Box 582, Ocean City, MD 21842. Promotes surfing through amateur competitions. Sponsors ecology education and scholarship aid programs. Bestows awards, sponsors hall of fame. Publications: *Eastern Waves.*

Hawaii Surfing Association. c/o Anthony Guerrero, 3415 Paty Drive, Honolulu, HI 96822–1444. Individuals who have entered at least one surfing meet. Conducts meets and seminars. Maintains Surfers Hall of Fame.

International Windsurfer Class Association. 2030 E. Gladwick Street, Compton, CA 90220. Sailors of windsurfer sailboards. Promotes racing, provides race committee assistance, and holds seminars. Publications: *Windsurfer Class Yearbook,* and *Windsurfer News.*

National Scholastic Surfing Association. PO Box 495, Huntington Beach, CA 92648. Students grades six to college and others interested in surfing. Promotes high school and college team competitions. Awards scholarships and maintains a national team training camp. Publication: *Surflines.*

United States Surfing Federation. 7104 Island Village Drive, Long Beach CA 90803. Acts as national governing body for amateur surfing in the U.S. Conducts national championships and selects team for international competition. Operates hall of fame.

United States Windsurfing Association. PO Box 978, Hood River, OR 97031. Racers and recreational sailors. Issues sailing numbers for events and sanctions competitions. Publications: *USWA Event Guidelines, USWA News,* and related material.

Swimming

PEOPLE OF ALL AGES enjoy the healthful, lifetime sport of swimming. It's a low impact, aerobic activity that exercises more muscle groups than any other sport. Knowing how to swim well is a matter of survival for those who spend time in, on, or around the water. Good recreational swimmers can participate, with a greater degree of safety, in a wide range of water sports, such as boating, scuba and skin diving, spear fishing, springboard diving, surfing, synchronized swimming, water polo, water skiing, and windsurfing. Physical fitness and flexibility are helpful when taking swimming lessons. They will help you develop your swimming skills much faster. A preclass physical checkup is advised. See the "Physical Fitness" section in this text for more information.

History

Swimming was popular in ancient Greece and Rome. It was often used in training warriors. Swimming declined sharply during the Middle Ages due to concern that outdoor bathing may be linked to the epidemics so common at the time. Recreational swimming and associated competition resumed in the last half of the nineteenth century. It was included in the 1896 Olympic Games. Diving events were added in 1904, and women's swimming and diving in 1912.

General Concepts

While swimming, you move forward when you pull water from in front of you with your arms, and push it behind you. Just as a boat's propeller pushes a boat from the rear, leg action also contributes to propulsion. Any portion of a leg kick that extends above the water's surface is wasted; it doesn't move water. While swimming, you expend the least energy when your body creates the least drag. You can lower drag by presenting the smallest possible profile to the flow of water. This occurs when the body is in a horizontal attitude, and the limbs are positioned to form a streamlined contour. Frictional drag is reduced by wearing a smooth, snug fitting swimsuit. Competitive swimmers reduce surface friction by wearing racing bathing caps, and shaving body hair.

Breathing is synchronized with the swimming stroke. Timing is such that one inhales when the face is above water, and exhales under water. Breath control is practiced until it becomes automatic.

Getting Started

As with any sport requiring a sudden burst of energy, it's best to do some simple warm-up and stretching exercises before entering the water, particularly if the water is cool. Push-ups, sit-ups, or jogging in place, together with exercises that gently stretch arm, leg, and body muscles are all useful.

Instructors will usually begin by having a student enter a pool and, while standing with the head above water, practice bobbing the head below water. This allows the student to become accustomed to water in the face, and to practice breath control. The next step is learning to float on the water with minimum help from hand and arm movements. This may be done using the kick board or other floatation device.

Some people are unable to remain totally horizontal on the surface without floatation aids. Since the legs are heavier than the water they displace, they tend to sink first. This is avoided while in motion, as the legs contribute to propulsion. Many swimming clubs teach a semi-floating procedure called drownproofing, first developed in 1963 by Fred Lanoue. It permits lengthy stays in water using a minimum of energy. With this method, you float with the body in a vertical position, take a breath, and slowly sink below the surface. The air in the lungs causes a slow rise to the surface, partly exposing the head. Extend arms out horizontally, and position one leg forward, the other back. Gently bring arms down and legs together. Exhale slowly through the nose as you rise. Once the mouth is above water, take a breath. Let yourself sink, and as the head goes under, give a slight downward push with the arms to slow descent. Rest underwater until you wish to breathe, then repeat the above. This method takes advantage of breath control skills and the fact that you have overcome the anxiety of having your head underwater. It should first be attempted under the supervision of a competent instructor. The above method with additional variations is illustrated in Hank Ketels' and Jack McDowell's book, *Sports Illustrated Scuba Diving: Underwater Adventuring.*

Basic Swimming Strokes

As your instruction continues, you will learn the following four basic swimming strokes used in competition.

Freestyle or Crawl

While maintaining a continuous up-and-down kicking action with alternate legs, the arms alternate between a working and recovery stage. In the working stage, the fingertips of one hand enter the water from above the surface in line with the shoulder, and the arm continues to move forward under water until fully extended. It then sweeps downward. Next, with elbow flexed, it moves inward under the body, still moving aft. It then sweeps up toward the surface. The power of the stroke involves pressing down and back during the first third of the stroke, pulling during mid-stroke, and pushing through and back during the final third. In the recovery stage, the elbow is bent as the arm comes out of the water and the forearm circles quickly out and around until it points toward the place of entry. During the stroke, the fingers and thumb are held close together. The legs are held fairly straight while being alternately moved up and down so that in both the up kick and the down kick there will be a backward push against the water with the lower part of each leg and foot. The more fully the ankle can be extended, the greater the surface area of the foot comes into play against the water. The number of kicks per complete arm cycle is usually either two or six (one or three with each foot). The body alternately rolls down on the side of the arm performing the working stroke stage. At that time the head rolls with the body and the face is momentarily out of the water. You inhale at that point. As you roll in the opposite direction your face is temporarily underwater and, during that period, you exhale. One breath is usually taken for each full stroke (right and left arm).

Backstroke

The backstroke is done with the body positioned face up. As with the freestyle stroke, the arms move alternately. In the working stage, the arm is fully extended behind and the hand enters the water, little finger first, in line with the shoulder. The body rolls toward the working arm, and the hand moves downward and outward. Once past the shoulder its action changes from a pull to a push with the elbow flexed, and begins to move toward the surface. It then begins a second down sweep ending low with the arm fully extended forward. At this point the body rolls toward the opposite arm pulling the working arm out of the water, with the hand emerging thumb-first. In the recovery stage, the arm is held straight and rotated through a vertical position to the point at which it enters the water in the working stage. Competitive swimmers do six to eight leg kicks per arm stroke cycle.

Breaststroke

The arm stroke begins with both arms stretched fully forward. The head is tilted back so you're looking forward. The hips are held high, and the swimmer is totally under water. The arms sweep out and back with the palms of the hands tilted at forty-five degrees, little fingers leading the sweep. After the hands move apart a few feet, the elbows begin to bend and strong, propulsive downsweep occurs. When the elbows and hands have come back almost as far as the shoulder, the hands sweep in toward one another, and slightly up. This action lifts your upper body and head out of the water, affording the opportunity to inhale. Inhale on every stroke. When your hands come together under your chin, they are quickly stretched forward as you sink into a brief glide and the beginning of another stroke cycle. Exhale while submerged. The frog-like kick is begun by bending the knees fully—heels to the body. This occurs as your hands stretch forward. The knees are rotated outward and the feet kick out and back to full extension, and are moved briskly together. After the kick, the body glides for a very brief time, forming a straight line from hands to pointed toes.

Butterfly Stroke

The butterfly stroke is characterized by a simultaneous up and down action of both legs, creating a dolphin-like undulating motion. Arm and leg motion raises the upper body and head above the water, allowing both arms to recover and be brought forward over the water. The arm-stroke begins with the arms stretched fully forward, hips held high, and the swimmer is totally submerged. The arms sweep out and back during the rise of the hips. The elbows bend and a strong downsweep begins. During this time the back is arched and the feet extend briefly above the water. The hands sweep down, inward, upward, and backward under the body. The legs are simultaneously kicked downward. The hands and elbows are brought out of the water and the arms are swung around to a forward position where they enter the water to begin another stroke.

Dives and Turns

Most swimming competitions are begun with the swimmer diving into the water. Prime consideration is given to a smooth entry and an underwater glide that quickly transitions into the first swimming stroke. Just before a typical racing start, the swimmer stands with the feet close to the edge of the pool, or starting block, and the toes curled over the edge. The body is bent forward with the hands also curled over the edge. At the start signal, the legs are bent and the arms swing forward, the head tilts back and an entry point is picked on the water surface. You push off with the legs and feet, moving out horizontally. The head is brought down between the arms and the hips are flexed. The arms are extended fully as the hands enter the water. A streamlined, fully extended body is maintained during the underwater glide. Begin kicking as the glide begins to slow. During the process, the least water resistance will occur if your entire body passes through the point in the water first entered by your hands.

In a typical racing turn, the swimmer strokes to a point close to the wall, does a forward underwater somersault or flip, stopping rotation with the feet against the wall, and pushes off in the direction from which he/she came. The flip is begun by bending at the hips, head tilted forward, arms at the sides. As the body tucks under, the feet rotate up out of the water and against the wall. During this forward rotation, the swimmer begins to twist the body so that when pushing off from the wall, a face down attitude is quickly assumed. As the swimmer leaves the wall, he/she should assume a totally streamlined shape while making a brief glide before resuming the swimming stroke. These movements are all accomplished underwater except for the brief time when the swimmer's feet emerge during the forward rotation.

Competition

After basic swimming skills have been mastered many enjoy competitive swimming in their own age class and against others at a comparable skill level. Swimming clubs exist at high schools, colleges, the "Y's," and other similar civic and industrial organization's pools. For adults over nineteen years of age, the U.S. Masters Swimming organization offers a comprehensive swimming program including competition.

Equipment

Although a minimum of equipment is needed for swimming, some additional items afford protection from pool chemicals, or act as training aids during the learning process.

Swimwear for efficient swimming (as opposed to attracting the opposite sex) is designed to allow free movement and create minimum drag through the water. For women, a high neckline promotes streamlined water flow. Lycra, or a Lycra cotton mix is the most common material. Dark colors avoid transparency when wet.

Goggles are useful to protect the eyes from the chlorine found in most pool water. Some swimmers also use nose clips and ear plugs to protect against infection or chlorine irritation. Do not use ear plugs when skin diving however; water pressure will press them into the ear canal.

Kick boards of various sizes are held in the hands to provide buoyant support while concentrating on the development of your kicking motion. They are also used to support the stomach or legs during other drills. Kick boards are made of a buoyant material such as Styrofoam.

Flippers or swim fins extend the surface area of the feet, affording added propulsion when the legs are moved. Their use also promotes ankle flexibility, important to efficient leg strokes done with or without fins.

A pull-buoy is a buoyant device placed between the legs to support them while concentrating on the development of your arm strokes. It's often used in conjunction with a small inner tube placed around the ankles to further support them while restricting movement of the legs.

Hand paddles are small, often rectangular, flat devices that are attached to the palm of the hand. They are used to increase the surface area of the palm, making it more difficult to pull through the water. This strengthens the shoulder, chest, and back muscles.

Bibliography

REFERENCE BOOKS

Brems, Marianne. *Swimming: Going for Strength and Stamina.* Chicago: Contemporary Books, 1988. Contains training advice, suggested workouts, and detailed step-by-step coverage of stroke techniques.

Clevenger, Cynthia. *Infant Swimming.* New York: St. Martin's, 1986. A water play method for teaching your child to swim. Covers the age to begin teaching, medical and safety considerations, and how to choose a class.

Davies, Sharron. *Learn to Swim in a Weekend.* New York: Knopf, 1992. A handbook covering a highly structured program that shows the novice how to master the fundamental skills of swimming.

Elkington, Helen, and Jane Chamberlain. *Synchronised Swimming.* North Pomfret, VT: David & Charles, 1986. Covers the principles, strokes, routines, and training relating to synchronized swimming.

Ketels, Hank, and Jack McDowell. *Sports Illustrated Scuba Diving: Underwater Adventuring.* New York: Sports Illustrated, 1988. Illustrates several concepts of survival in the water called drownproofing.

Schubert, Mark. *Sports Illustrated Competitive Swimming: Techniques for Champions.* New York: Sports Illustrated, 1990. Comprehensive coverage of competitive swimming. Covers dry-land exercises, nutrition, and detailed descriptions of stroke techniques.

PERIODICALS

Swim Fashion Quarterly. Virgo Publishers, 4141 N. Scottsdale Road, Suite 316, Scottsdale, AZ 85251.

Swim Magazine. Sports Publications, Box 45497, Los Angeles, CA 90045.

Swimming Technique. Sports Publications, Box 45497, Los Angeles, CA 90045.

Swimming World. Sports Publications, Box 45497, Los Angeles, CA 90045.

Swimsuit International. Swimsuit Publishers, 801 Second Avenue, New York, NY 10017.

Synchro Swimming. U.S. Synchronized Swimming, 201 S. Capitol Avenue, Suite 510, Indianapolis, IN 46225. (Synchronized swimming.)

ASSOCIATIONS

International Swimming Hall of Fame. 1 Hall of Fame Drive, Ft. Lauderdale, FL 33316. Those in twenty-three countries interested in supporting the museum. Honors and supports swimming activities. Sponsors competitions. Publication: *International Hall of Fame News.*

Polar Bear Club-U.S.A.. 376 Naughton Avenue, Staten Island, NY 10305. A group that swims in the Atlantic Ocean weekly during the winter.

United States Diving. Pan American Plaza, 201 S. Capitol Avenue, Suite 430, Indianapolis, IN 46225. Professionals and interested individuals promoting diving as a sport. Conducts diving programs at all levels of ability. Publications: Magazine, and related materials.

United States Masters Swimming. 2 Peters Avenue, Rutland, MA 01543. Adults aged nineteen years and older interested in swimming for fun, fitness, and competition. Sponsors competitions, bestows award, and maintains library. Publications: *Places to Swim in the United States, USMS Rule Book,* and related material.

United States Swimming. 1750 E. Boulder Street, Colorado Springs, CO 80909. National governing body for competitive amateur swimming. Selects teams for international competitions. Conducts programs, sponsors competitions, and bestows awards. Publications: *Lanelines, National Qualifier, U.S. Swimming News, U.S. Swimming Volunteer,* and related material.

United States Synchronized Swimming. Pan American Plaza, 201 S. Capitol, Suite 510, Indianapolis, IN 46225. Those interested in developing and improving synchronized swimming programs. Conducts competitions, maintains hall of fame, and provides education and training. Publications: *Synchro-USA News,* and related material.

Tennis

TWO OPPOSING PLAYERS or two pairs of players use rackets to hit a ball over a net on a rectangular court. Points are awarded to a player or team when the opponent fails to return the ball within the rules of the game. The court is laid out as shown in Figure 1.

How the Game is Played

To start play the server tosses the ball up and hits it with the racket, sending it over the net to the opponent. The ball must clear the net and land on the diagonally opposite half of the opponent's service court before passing the service line. The server has committed a fault if this fails to happen. If a second fault is committed, the opponent gets a point.

The opponent may return the ball to any portion of the server's court within applicable sidelines. If the opponent fails to do so, the server gets a point. If the opponent returns successfully, play continues until one player either misses the opponent's court, hits the net or allows the ball to bounce more than once in his/her court.

A game is completed when one player wins at least four points, providing the point spread with the opponent is at least two points. So, if the game were tied at three to three, a player must win two consecutive points to win the game. A score of 15 is awarded for the first point, 30 for the second, 40 for the third and game for the fourth point. The server's score is stated first. A score of 30—love means that the server has two points and the opponent none. Love derives from the French word *l'oeuf* for egg. When a tie score of 40—40 is reached it is called deuce.

A set is completed when one side wins six games. However, if a tie exists at five games, one player must win two consecutive games to win a set. Tie breaking methods such as "sudden death," eliminating the two game margin requirement, are often employed. In major tournaments a match usually consists of three out of five sets for men and two out of three for women.

History

Some historians trace the origins of tennis to *jeu de paume* (game of the palm) first played in France as early as 1300 A.D. The ball was batted by hand over a solid three foot tall structure. Soon a paddle, then a racket, was used. The solid structure was later replaced by a net. The name tennis may have derived from *tenez,* a French word meaning to begin play—a word often used by the French when playing the game.

In 1874 British Major Walter Wingfield patented the game sphairistike, a name later changed to lawn tennis. Wingfield published the game's first book of rules.

Tennis spread to the United States in the 1870s. In 1881 the first official U.S. championship was held at Newport, Rhode Island under the auspices of the U.S. National Lawn Tennis Association. That organization became the U.S. Tennis Association in 1975.

Equipment

A tennis ball is between $2\frac{1}{2}$ and $2\frac{5}{8}$ inches in diameter. It weighs between 2 and $2\frac{1}{16}$ ounces. Balls may be white or yellow.

Racket specifications remained undefined until 1981. Currently rackets must not be more than 32 inches long and $12\frac{1}{2}$ inches wide. The strung hitting surface is limited to $15\frac{1}{2}$ inches long and $11\frac{1}{2}$ inches wide. The distance between strings must not be less than one-fourth inch nor more than one-half inch.

Strategy

Good tennis players study and practice basic tennis strokes. Very good players know how to combine the strokes to take advantage of the element of surprise.

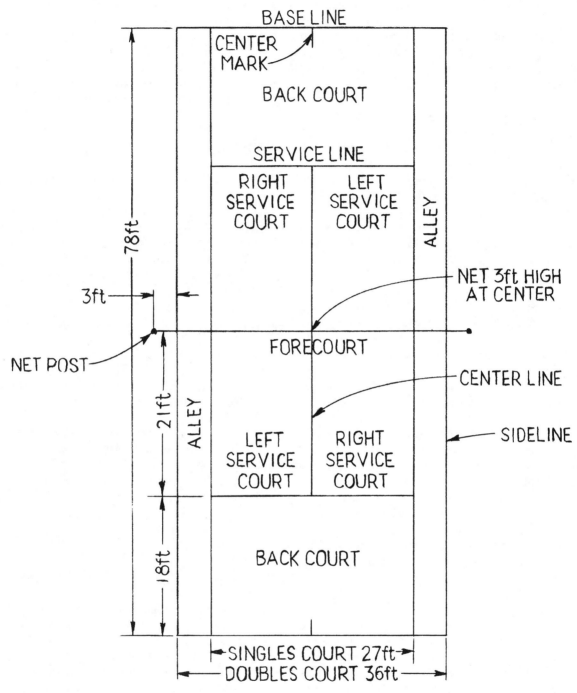

Figure 1
Tennis court layout.

Play begins with the serve. The server tosses the ball overhead and hits it across the net in a manner that will be difficult for the receiver to return. Players new to the game should emphasize getting a high percentage of their serves into the receiver's court. As experience is gained the player will be able to employ techniques such as: hitting the ball forcefully to reduce the opponents reaction time, causing the ball to bounce in an awkward location, and imparting a spin to the ball causing an unexpected flight path.

The serve return may be an offensive move in which the player attacks the bouncing ball with a hard-hitting drive, at the same time moving forward to hit the next ball that comes over the net before it bounces. That is called a volley. Volleying from the forecourt and close to the net gives the player a wider choice of target locations when hitting the ball. It can be returned closer to the net or at a sharper angle to left or right. A chipped return may be employed. The chip imparts a short underspin flight to the ball that may be directed at the opponent's feet, or far from the opponent, going by the opponent in what is called a passing shot.

The serve return may be a defensive move where the player blocks the ball with the racket and hits with a short stroke to return the ball. Another method is to hit the ball high and deep into the opponent's court. This is called a lob. It gives the lobbing player time to move forward into volleying position for the next return. Strokes taken after a ball bounces are called ground strokes.

Players move about the court to position themselves to the right or left of the oncoming ball. A right handed player hits a ball coming to his right with a forehand stroke. As the ball approaches, a pivot is made, turning to the right until the left shoulder aims at the ball. This movement takes the racket back with the body. On the forward swing the body uncoils and the racket is swung forward to strike the ball out in front of the body.

When the ball approaches to the left a backhand stroke is used. The player pivots to the left and the right shoulder is aimed at the ball, the racket arm is taken back then moves forward as the body uncoils striking the ball out in front of the body.

Consistency is of prime importance in tennis. Consistency is attained through practice, both on and off the court. One universally accepted practice drill involves hitting the ball against a wall and attempting to keep the volley going as long as possible. You can chalk one or more target points on the wall and try to hit them during the volley to improve your accuracy.

Find players a bit better than yourself to play with. This will motivate you to continue to strive for improvement.

Doubles

Doubles is a game between two pairs of tennis players. After the serve the full thirty-six foot width of the court is used, which includes the alleys on each side. In general, each team member is responsible for activity on one side of the court. During a serve the server is positioned behind the baseline as with singles. The serve must be placed within the receiver's service court area. The receiver is usually behind the base line, diagonally opposite the server. The server's partner takes a position in the service court, on his/her side of the court. This forward position is most advantageous for handling the return from the receiver. The receiver's partner also takes a position in the service court area.

Doubles play requires close coordination between team members. Each member must instinctively know who will play a ball coming down the center line. On occasion, by prearranged signal, a team member will cross over to a partner's side to volley a shot at the opposition. This is called poaching. During the serve, the server's partner may occasionally take a position at the net on the same side as the server to confuse the opposition. This type of irregular activity takes careful coordination between partners.

Fitness

The sport of tennis stresses the player physically, especially when playing singles, since you move around the court more. It is easier to "get up to speed" in tennis for those who have been physically active. It ranks high as a conditioner. Tennis is a lifetime sport. Practiced in moderation it can be played well into maturity. Senior players employ experience to offset reduced agility.

Bibliography

REFERENCE BOOKS

Braden, Vic, and Bill Bruns. *Vic Braden's Tennis for the Future.* Boston: Little, Brown, 1980. Explanation of techniques and drills.

———. *Vic Braden's Quick Fixes: Expert Cures for Common Tennis Problems.* Boston: Little, Brown, 1990. Cures for problem areas.

Brown, Jim. *Tennis Steps to Success.* Champaign, IL: Leisure, 1989. Emphasis on practice drills.

Conners, Jimmy, with Robert J. La Marche. *Jimmy Conners: How to Play Tougher Tennis.* Trumble, CT: Golf Digest/Tennis, 1986. How to play tennis better, by one of the game's top players, well illustrated.

Douglas, Paul. *Learn Tennis in a Weekend.* New York: Knopf, 1991. Compact, no-nonsense overview.

Gallwey, W. Timothy. *Inner Tennis: Playing the Game.* New York: Random House, 1976. Insights into the mental aspects of tennis.

Petro, Sharon. *The Tennis Drill Book.* Champaign, IL: Leisure, 1986. Tips on drilling, practice, warm-up, and conditioning.

Ralston, Dennis, with Steve Flink and Bud Freeman. *Dennis Ralston's Tennis Workbook.* Englewood Cliffs, NJ: Prentice Hall, 1987. Instruction, illustrations, progress checklists from a professional coach.

Singleton, Skip. *Intelligent Doubles: A Sensible Approach to Better Doubles Play.* Crozet, VA: Betterway, 1989. Fundamentals of tennis doubles.

Tantalo, Victor. *U.S.A. Tennis Course.* Orlando, FL: U.S.A., 1986. Simplified explanation of techniques.

Van der Meer, Dennis. *Dennis Van der Meer's Complete Book of Tennis.* Ottawa, IL: Jameson Books, 1986. Techniques, instruction, and drills by a professional who teaches pros.

PERIODICALS

Racquet. Heather and Pine International, 42 W. 38th Street, Suite 1202, New York, NY 10018.

Tennis. 5520 Park Avenue, Box 395, Trumbull, CT 06611–0395.

Tennis Buyers Guide. 5520 Park Avenue, Box 395, Trumbull, CT 06611–0395.

Tennis Week. 124 E. 40th Street, Suite 1101, New York, NY 10016.

Tennis Northeast; Tennis South; Tennis West; Texas Tennis. Regional Sports Publications, Box 50405, Henderson, NV 89016–0405..

ASSOCIATIONS

American Tennis Association. PO Box 3277, Silver Spring, MD 20918–9998. Promotes tennis among blacks. Publication: *Black Tennis Magazine.*

International Tennis Hall of Fame. 100 Park Avenue, 10th Floor, New York, NY 10017. Supports training programs, conducts amateur and professional competitions. Publication: *Hall of Fame News.*

National Senior Women's Tennis Association. 1696 W. Calimjrna, No. B, Fresno, CA 93711. Women over thirty. Sponsors competitions. Publication: Newsletter.

People-to-People Tennis Committee. PO Box 2650, La Jolla, CA 92038. Seeks to further international relations through tennis. Organizes local teams from various countries to play one another to promote goodwill. Publication: *Annual Announcement.*

Peter Burwash International Special Tennis Programs. 2203 Timberloch Place, Suite 126, The Woodlands, TX 77380. Offers special tennis instruction to blind, deaf, retarded persons, wheelchair athletes, and prison inmates. Operates speakers' bureau.

United States Tennis Association. 1212 Avenue of the Americas, New York, NY 10036. Sanctions tournaments, sponsors programs, and maintains library. Affiliated with International Tennis Federation. Publications: *Yearbook, Tennis Championships Magazine, Tennis U.S.A., Official Encyclopedia of Tennis,* clinic kits, and rules manuals.

USTA National Junior Tennis League. 70 Red Oak Lane, White Plains, NY 10604. Novice tennis participation program of the United States Tennis Association. Publications: Newsletter, and program guide.

Wheelchair Tennis Players Association. 940 Calle Amanecer, Suite B, San Clemente, CA 92672. Individuals with a physical disability that precludes participation in nonhandicapped tennis. Publications: *Two Bounce News,* and newsletter.

Theater

THEATER, AS WE KNOW IT, evolved in Greece from ancient religious ceremonies. The earliest plays were made up of sequences of choral odes interrupted by elements of speech for actors. The Greeks held contests for the best play and for the best actor. Natural delivery and expression were praised by critics and overacting was scorned. Three dramatic styles emerged—tragedy, comedy, and a burlesque-like play called satyr.

Roman drama also featured tragedy and comedy, gradually expanding to include pantomime and other entertainment forms. Roman theater became commercialized, tasteless and bawdy. This was to be the downfall of theater in Rome, as Christianity struggled with and overcame paganism.

Production of a Play

In modern times the actor is assisted in the creation of illusion by a staff of specialists:

It is the producer who selects the plays; engages the actors, director, composer, orchestra, and technical staff; who acquires the playhouse; who raises and spends the show's finances. The producer is the link between the artists and the audience.

The director is responsible for the casting of a play and the conduct of rehearsals. The director supervises the timing and other activities on the stage. As the interpreter of the writer's text to the players and the audience, the director must integrate performance, script, lighting, and decor into a harmony of style and unity of theatrical effect.

Although the actor is supported by many creative and talented persons, the success of a play depends on the quality of the actor's performance. Acting is the most appreciated and least understood of the arts. The actor must have the ability to react to imaginary stimuli, feel the emotions of the character being played, and speak in a manner most natural to the circumstances created by the plot.

Learning the Acting Craft

Many actors learn their craft on the hundreds of university stages. Others get their first acting exposure in high school and go on to gain further experience in community theaters.

When acting methods are discussed, the work of Konstantin Stanislavski is often mentioned. He noted the level of inspiration that great actors displayed on stage, and tried to capture it in a form that could help both the beginner and experienced actor. Without minimizing the value of voice, speech, and body training, he tried to find ways to develop the actor's concentration, belief, and imagination. The actor's appearance on stage must be a continuation of the circumstances that have previously taken place. The senses are trained so the actor is able to see, hear, taste, smell, and relate to the many objects that compose the imaginary situation. The actor learns to look beneath the lines to find the meaning of the play.

Stanislavski's theories influenced the teaching methods of the Strasberg Actor's Studio, attended in the 1950s by many prominent American actors. An actor's task is to interpret life. To do that, actors must be careful observers of people—their mannerisms, and their body language.

Amateur actors enjoy attending professional theatrical performances. They can relate to the skill and craftsmanship displayed on the stage. However, their greatest reward is to actually perform.

Forms of Amateur Presentation

Here we will discuss amateur participation in a few of the most popular theatrical forms, together with the historical background of these forms.

Community Theater

Modern acting began in Italy at the time of the Renaissance. In about 1545 a type of improvised comedy, called commedia del l'arte, was performed by groups of traveling players. Up to this time, acting was an amateur occupation. The actor was confined to illustrating the words of a playwright by means of gesture and oratory. In commedia del l'arte, the actor used only an outline and improvised the play. This required the performance of a professional actor who could create the imagery and illusion required.

Books are available that provide guidance in preparing for the presentation of a play. They usually cover such things as play choice, casting, stage behavior, projection, props, costumes, discussion of theatrical terms, rehearsal, study methods, and self discipline. Become familiar with this material well before the date of your big production.

It is advisable to choose an experienced director who can make the most appropriate play selection and act as the aesthetic organizer of the play.

Many skills are needed to present a quality production. Designers, carpenters, painters, costume makers, and musicians are all given an opportunity to showcase their talents.

Actors must develop the capability to think on their feet, to improvise when things go wrong. Students of acting sometimes are given a set of circumstances that require making up lines to fit the situation. They must interact with one another and continue a dialog. Improvisation can be an interesting pastime for amateurs. Philip Bernardi's book *Improvisation Starters* provides useful information about this valuable technique.

Actors are required to speak clearly and project their voices to the audience. Some amateur actors enjoy the practice of reading plays aloud. Each member in a group is given a copy of the script and assigned a part to read. Your library has books of suitable plays, such as Marshall Cassady's, *An Introduction to Modern One-Act Plays*.

Comedy

Success with humor hinges on your ability to recognize and appreciate something funny. Choose material appropriate for your audience and style of presentation. It also helps to be a keen observer of life and keep informed about current events.

The funniest jokes are those in which we are carefully led to expect one thing and are then surprised by another at the last instant. This manipulation of two ideas is expressed in many formats:

Satire is distortion by exaggeration, quoting facts out of context, attributing obviously false motives, or trying to make isolated instances seem typical. It's entertainment through criticism. Brevity is desirable. Funny, we never thought of the evening news as satire before!

A pun is a play on words. It takes advantage of multiple meanings for words, or words that sound the same. Examples range from Henny Youngman's "Take my wife—please," to Norm Crosby, the master of this format, who said, "An ounce of perversion is worth a pound of cure."

Visualization and imagery are used, creating a mental picture in the listener's mind by using descriptive words, then creating amusement by the sudden distortion of that image. Myron Cohen has enhanced this format by the skillful use of dialect. Rich Little's humor is also amplified using his voice to impersonate famous people.

Some use objects as props to speed audience visualization. Gallagher uses a car door attached to a tricycle to create a humorous image, and his "sledgeomatic" to smash vegetables has brought many laughs—and cleaning bills. Jonathan Winters has used different hats to complement ad lib routines. Other examples include the costumes worn by Carol Burnett, Red Skelton, and many other famous performers.

Exaggeration involves taking a thought or idea beyond realistic bounds. When Johnny Carson quipped, "It was so cold that—." The audience couldn't wait to respond with, "How cold was it?" This was followed by outrageous exaggeration.

Some use the effect of shock by attacking authority, or create humor at the expense of others. Many comedians confuse the nervous laughter of an audience to their barrage of four-letter words as general public acceptance. More skillful comedians, such as Don Rickles, take the shock format to its limit and enjoy success.

Additional joke formats involve implication, idea reversal, insult (such as the "roasts" of personalities), and many other combinations of the above.

Comedy is thought to be older than recorded history. It's known that comedies were performed in Athens during the spring festival of Dionysus, god of wine, intoxication, and fertility. The first was presented in 486 B.C. Three top writers of the period were Aristophanes, Eupolis, and Cratinus. Performances were judged and prizes were awarded for best comedy. Aristophanes won four firsts and three seconds during this time without an Oscar or Emmy to show for it. Eleven of his plays still survive. Historians refer to this period as Athenian Old Comedy. Aristophanes' work was characterized by invective, indecency, free political criticism, imagination, fresh wit, and satire.

A transition to the period of Middle Comedy took place early in the fourth century B.C. Best writers were Antiphanes and Alexis. Little survives of this period, but plays appeared to feature social satire and parody.

The New Comedy period began around 320 B.C. with the writings of Diphilus, Philemon, and Menander. It was the work of Menander that was most admired. He wrote 105 plays of which only one survives; however portions of many others have been found. Menander wrote fictional accounts of ordinary people. Sort of the situation comedy writer of his time. His themes and story lines have been copied down through the ages.

Roman comedy was amusing, reflective, and sometimes moral. The writer Plautus borrowed from Greek New Comedy and in turn the Broadway musical, *A Funny Thing*

Happened on the Way to the Forum borrowed heavily from Plautus' comedies. He used jokes, puns, and obscenity in his writings.

After the fall of Rome the theater was replaced by traveling performers. Theater returned during the Middle Ages to celebrate Christian festivals. It had a strong religious and moral theme at this time that gave way to a less restrictive format by the late Middle Ages.

The fools and jesters of the Middle Ages were the vanguard of today's clowns and comedians. The jesters played to a limited elite audience. Today successful comedy depends upon an enlightened audience, familiar with social rules and current events. The comedian can use this material to satirize, distort, and poke fun.

When we see comedians performing on national television, we often forget that the quality of their performance reflects training and years of practice. Even clubs like the Improv, which features beginners, still expect some degree of experience and polish.

One way to get a start is to volunteer to give an after-dinner speech. If you do, remember to tell your second-best joke at or near the beginning of your performance, and save your best for last. Leave them laughing.

Magic

Magic is an old art form. Early Egyptian records from 3000 B.C. describe a magic show given for the Pharaoh. Even the Bible in Exodus chapter seven describes a contest between Moses and the Pharaoh's magicians. American Indians practiced magic before the white man arrived.

Before the sixteenth century, books on magic described the feat, but not the method used to create the illusion. Since then, how-to information has been more available. One of the outstanding collections of books on magic was owned by famous escape artist and magician, Houdini. He accumulated thousands of books on magic, spiritualism, and all aspects of the occult. His collection also included stage illusions, and hundreds of locks, manacles, and chains.

Magician's organizations require that members keep their methods secret—except to other magicians. This code of secrecy keeps audiences baffled and interested. Magic devices may be purchased to enliven your performance. Check your telephone yellow pages or subscribe to magic magazines for sources.

Good magicians spend much time in practice so their acts go smoothly. The key to a successful magic act is misdirection. Direct your gaze where you want the audience to look—away from your hands. Misdirection is also achieved by interesting or funny conversation. That's why magic is often presented in combination with comedy or ventriloquism.

Many stage-struck young people use magic as a way to get into show business.

Ventriloquism

As with magic, ventriloquism relies upon misdirection and illusion. This form of illusion is based upon the principle that when the source of a sound is the same distance from each of your ears, you can't pinpoint the source. Try it with a blindfold; you'll be convinced. So ventriloquists don't really "throw" their voices. They simply adopt a second voice different from their normal one and practice creating words with minimum lip movement. The second voice is produced by moving the diaphragm to push air through the voice box to create sounds. The sound is brought to the front of the mouth to generate reasonably clear sounding words. Some sounds are almost impossible to make without moving the lips. In these cases, alternate sounds are substituted that sound similar.

By using a dummy and manipulating its mouth, eyes, and head, the ventriloquist can create the illusion of another live person if the dummy's movements are coordinated carefully with the dialog. It also aids in focusing audience attention away from the ventriloquist's mouth. The ventriloquist must create a character with its own realistic and expressive movement. This takes close observation of the movements of people, and much practice.

By skillful use of a good script the audience is led to respond to the dummy as a person. Good technique holds the attention of the audience and becomes a powerful communication tool. This has been known and used since ancient times. It's especially useful in the education of the young.

A note about the spelling of theater. The alternate spelling, theatre, is of French origin, derived from the Latin theatrum, or Greek theatron. The alternate form will be found in the bibliography where referenced material uses that spelling.

Bibliography

REFERENCE BOOKS

Allen, Steve, with Jane Wollman. *How to be Funny.* New York: McGraw-Hill, 1987. How you can develop your natural gift for humor.

Bernardi, Philip. *Improvisation Starters: A Collection of 900 Improvisation Situations for the Theater.* White Hall, VA: Betterway, 1992. Fresh ideas for setting up improvisational situations.

Bordman, Gerald. *The Concise Oxford Companion to American Theatre.* New York: Oxford University, 1987. A listing of plays, individuals, and places that are prominent in the theater.

Cassady, Marshall. *An Introduction to Modern One-Act Plays.* Lincolnwood, IL: National Textbook, 1991. A collection of short play scripts useful for reading practice by groups. Includes thought-provoking questions after each play.

Christopher, Milbourne. *Houdini: The Untold Story*. New York: Crowell, 1969. The dramatic life of the world's most famous magician and escape artist.

Fitzsimons, Raymund. *Death and the Magician: The Mystery of Houdini*. New York: Atheneum, 1981. A biography of Houdini.

Geen, Michael. *Theatrical Costume and the Amateur Stage*. Boston: Plays, 1968. A commonsense approach to the making, altering, and storing of theatrical costumes.

Gillette, A. S., and J. Michael Gillette. *Stage Scenery: Its Construction and Rigging*. 3rd ed. New York: Harper Collins, 1981. Covers the construction of theater settings, from organization of personnel to painting the finished product. Written for use by nonprofessional personnel.

Gillette, J. Michael. *Theatrical Design and Production*. Palo Alto, CA: Mayfield, 1987. Broad-ranging coverage of the activities attended to by a producer. Includes organization, design, fabrication and the painting of sets, lighting, and costumes.

Griffiths, Trevor R., ed. *Practical Theater: How to Stage Your Own Production*. Secaucus, NJ: Chartwell Books, 1982. A concise overview of producing, directing, and acting a play. Written at a level useful to an inexperienced amateur group.

Hoggett, Chris. *Stage Crafts*. New York: St. Martin's, 1975. Emphasis on design, construction, and decoration for the stage.

Hutton, Darryl. *Ventriloquism*. New York: Sterling, 1975. Instructions and practice drills for performing ventriloquism.

James, Thurston. *The Theater Props Handbook*. White Hall, VA: Betterway, 1987. A comprehensive guide to theater properties, materials, and construction.

Kalter, Joanmarie. *Actors on Acting*. New York: Sterling, 1979. Interviews with ten prominent contemporary actors about their craft.

Kernodle, George R. *The Theatre in History*. Fayetteville, AR: University of Arkansas, 1989. Examines the development of the theater. Discussion of theater's primitive origins, its artistic shaping through the ages, its stagecraft, and its cultural relationships.

Mulholland, John. *Magic of the World*. New York: Scribners, 1965. A book of magic feats from countries all around the world. Step-by-step instructions are given for performing magic feats.

Thorndike, Ashley H. *Shakespeare's Theater*. New York: Macmillan, 1961. Chronicles the history of Shakespearean epoch in England.

PERIODICALS

Comedy USA Newswire. Laughs Unlimited, Box 20214, New York, NY 10028–0051.

Linking Ring. International Brotherhood of Magicians, c/o Phillip R. Willmarth, 348 S. Wishire Lane, Arlington Heights, IL 60004.

M-U-M Magazine. Society of American Magicians, P.O. Box 510260, St. Louis, MO 63151.

Studies in American Drama, 1945–Present. Ohio State University Press, 1070 Carmack Road, Columbus, OH 43210. (Theater history, dramatic influences, and technique. Reviews.)

TCI. Theatre Crafts International, 135 Fifth Avenue, New York, NY 10010–7193. (All aspects of performing arts including lighting, sound, and set and costume design.)

Theater. Yale University, School of Drama, Yale Repertory Theatre, 222 York Street, New Haven, CT 06520. (Reviews, interviews, full text of a new play in each issue.)

Theater Week. That New Magazine, 28 W. 25th Street, 4th Floor, New York, NY 10010. (Broadway and regional.)

Theatre Journal. Johns Hopkins University Press, Journals Publishing Div., 701 W. 40th Street, Suite 275, Baltimore, MD 21211. (Topics in the study and teaching of theater.)

TYA Today. International Association of Theatre for Children and Young People, United States Center, c/o Theatre Service, Box 15282, Evansville, IN 47716–0282. (Promotes professional theater for young audiences.)

ASSOCIATIONS

American Association of Community Theatre. c/o L. Ross Rowland, 8209 N. Costa Mesa Drive, Muncie, IN 47303. Organizations and individuals involved with community theater. Maintains placement service and bestows awards. Publications: *Spotlight*, and related materials.

American Humor Studies Association. c/o David Sloane, University of New Haven, West Haven, CT 06516. Professional humorists and general readers. Encourages study of American humor. Publications: *American Humor: An Interdisciplinary Newsletter*, and *Studies in American Humor*.

The Association of Comedy Artists. PO Box 1796, New York, NY 10025. Comedians, comedy buffs, and other interested individuals. Sponsors Comedy Arts Institute, which offers classes in improvisation, stand-up comedy, and related subjects. Maintains hall of fame, bestows awards.

International Brotherhood of Magicians. 103 N. Main Street, PO Box 89, Bluffton, OH 45817. Professionals and other interested individuals. Seeks to advance the art of magic. Publication: *The Linking Ring*.

International Save the Pun Foundation. PO Box 5040, Station A, Toronto, ON, Canada M5W 1N4. People who enjoy word play. Sponsors competitions, bestows awards. Publications: Annual report: *The 10 Best-Stressed Puns of the Year*, and *The Pundit*.

North American Association of Ventriloquists. 800 W. Littleton Boulevard, PO Box 420, Littleton, CO 80160. Amateur and professional ventriloquists and puppeteers. Assists members in solving problems, locating supplies, and obtaining instruction. Publications: *Newsy Vents*, and newsletter.

Society of American Magicians. PO Box 510260, St. Louis, MO 63151. Promotes interest in magic as a hobby or profession. Maintains hall of fame and sponsors competitions. Publication: *M-U-M Magazine*.

Travel

TRAVEL PROVIDES RELAXATION and enjoyment —two key benefits of any hobby. Travel broadens our outlook by exposing us to the lives and environments of other people. It helps us better understand differing points of view. We can bring this knowledge home and put it to good use. A writer can gather material for a book, or a photographer can build a photo file. Some students study overseas to obtain specialized education and sharpen their foreign language skills.

We travel to satisfy our curiosity about the other side of the mountain, or sea. Perhaps to enjoy the awesome vistas of the Grand Canyon or the color of New England's leaves in the fall. We are refreshed by a change in the climate, scenery, or the people we meet. Many try out great golf courses, participate in hiking expeditions, or go surfing.

People visit historical sites and museums to learn more about their country's past. They may experience the thrill of being allowed to touch the Liberty Bell, or to see Plymouth Rock. Aspiring scientists will long remember a trip to a space center or planetarium.

Whether it's a trip to Disneyland just for the fun of it, or to Las Vegas or Atlantic City to donate some money to the needy casinos, Americans love to travel. They consider it a significant part of the enjoyment of a vacation. Although there are many reasons people travel, over half of the trips are made to visit friends and family. Whatever the reason for your trip, it will be more enjoyable if you plan carefully before you start.

Research and Planning

When contemplating long trips involving considerable expense, check your local library for travel literature. You will find travel guides for almost any country you may wish to visit. Information found in these guides will help make the most of your time away from home. Publishers specializing in travel guides include Birnbaum, Fielding,

Fisher, Fodor, Frommer, and Passport Books. They furnish hundreds of books dedicated to specific countries or areas. Most are updated annually.

Once you have scanned the available literature and determined which will be most useful, you may want to visit your bookstore to buy a personal copy of a travel guide, atlas, or other reference material.

Another way to gather information about your destination is to write to foreign embassies or state tourist bureaus. They want to sell you on their location, so they are generally very cooperative. Once again, the reference department of your library is your best source for this information.

Sometimes your hobby or pastime can be used effectively to gather information while on a trip. For example, a photographer can stop at local photo shops to inquire about the routes that will provide the best photographic opportunities. You may experience unexpected benefits by tying hobbies in with travel. One American couple found memorable contacts and experiences at a square dance club in Japan.

The tourist who can be flexible regarding travel timing has a cost advantage. For example, January is the slowest month of the year for travel. Prices for transportation and accommodations are lower during the winter months in northern areas.

When tours and cruises are not fully booked, the remaining openings are offered at reduced cost. There are companies that make it their business to keep informed of these opportunities and pass the information along to subscribers of their service.

Travel Agencies

After you have decided on your destination and completed your preliminary research, you may want to consult a travel agent. Unless you cause the agent last minute expenses such as long distance phone calls, the service is usually free to you. Subcontractors normally pay the agency a percentage of the cost of your trip. Subcontracting travel wholesalers and carriers may supply whole package tours or separate elements of a trip such as hotels or air travel. A good agency has a carefully screened portfolio of such vendors. A poor agency may be more concerned with the size of its rebate from the vendor than your repeat business. Even the best agencies with a time-tested vendor list sometimes have problems. Even the most reliable subcontractors have been known to go bankrupt.

Agencies can help in many ways. They can save you money because they buy tickets and blocks of hotel rooms at reduced rates. By buying in volume in advance, they also get the best facilities. Because they are big customers for the hotels and other services, the quality of service is likely to be better. Travel agents have to be informed about all aspects of travel including data on destinations, language and currency problems, schedules, visas, inoculations, insurance, and reservations.

When dealing with a travel agency, it is important to give the agent a clear understanding of your interests and desires for the trip. You may want a cruise ship that stops at ports that cater to tourists and has a casino on board. Another person may want a sailing vessel headed for a remote archaeological dig. Make your requirements known and ask questions. On long plane trips you may find that you can include stops of interest along the way without added expense.

The American Society of Travel Agents (ASTA) is the largest association of travel agents in North America. ASTA conducts basic courses, designed for new agency employees, in subjects related to travel.

The Institute of Certified Travel Agents (ICTA) started as a committee of ASTA interested in setting up an advanced training system for travel agents. The ICTA system stipulates that after a two- or three-year course and five years of agency employment, a person can be designated a Certified Travel Counselor (CTC). If you see CTC after your agent's name, the agent has had the advanced training.

Sponsorship and Specialized Tours

A money-saving method of working with agencies involves being a group sponsor. A sponsor provides a list of prospective travelers to the agency. Travelers must be going to the same place at the same time. In return, you get to go along free if the group is large enough. The agency may get a free airline ticket for a group of about fifteen, or a free hotel room for a group of about twenty-five, and will often pass these along to you.

Package tours with free time at the destination appeal to many. They provide time for you to pursue your own interests after you arrive. Clubs and associations sometimes engage agencies to provide package trips to stimulate interest in their organization and increase membership.

The murder mystery tour is gaining in popularity. A group of actors stage a make-believe killing. The travelers play detective to try to identify the murderer. This kind of tour has been made available on the Orient Express train, the Queen Elizabeth II ocean liner, and at some hotels.

Museums and educational institutions conduct group tours, often related to specific fields of interest. With this type of tour you travel with others having similar interests, and get the services of a tour guide who is expert in the field being studied or observed.

Modes of Travel

The typical approach to a vacation for many Americans is to drive the family car. If your traveling party consists of more than one driver, consider alternating drivers periodically. You will see more, travel relaxed, and arrive less fatigued.

If your plans include touring by car, see your auto club. If you aren't a member, it may pay to join for the maps and campsite information a club can provide. An international driver's license is needed when driving in some countries. In others, you may be asked to go to the local bureau and have them issue a special permit. Your auto club can furnish details on the international license.

There are associations that plan extensive trips for trailer caravans. Enduring friendships are made on these long trips as the "covered wagons pull into a circle for the night." If you plan to tow a trailer, you will need a substantial vehicle for the job. It's best to rent a travel trailer for your first trip or two to be sure you like this sort of activity. Travel trailers represent a considerable investment.

At least one manufacturer converts large buses into luxury motor homes. At the other extreme, small motor homes are made that can be used at the national network of campsites and many other remote locations. For those who travel by highway extensively, they offer a combination of compact size and comfort. Truck campers offer a lower cost alternative to the motor home, but living space is somewhat restricted.

Bus tours and charter services provide a carefree travel style. Relieved of map reading and driving tensions, the traveler is free to enjoy the scenery. Tours give a feeling of security to many who would be unable to travel otherwise. Many foreign tours include bus travel as part of the package. This can be an advantage where language barriers are a problem.

Passenger train travel has increased in the United States since the federal government formed the National Railroad Passenger Corporation, which developed Amtrak. Amtrak serves as a contractor, buying service from the nineteen railroads over which it runs passenger trains. As Amtrak introduces new equipment, and planning goes forward on high speed train projects, it's likely that rail travel will be the preferred method of travel for some applications. Those who spend prolonged periods in different parts of the country already enjoy the car-train feature, where passengers transport their car on the train with them, carried in attached freight cars.

Many countries make rail passes available. Passengers buy a pass for a given length of time, and travel extensively during that period without further charges for fares. Additional charges are sometimes levied for reservations or sleeping car service. Innovations such as this have contributed to an increase in passenger train travel worldwide. See the section in this text entitled "Railroads and Railfans" for more information on trains.

A walking tour is an interesting way to get a first-hand look at a large city. You can plan your own tours using a city map. Find your hotel or other starting point and locate points of interest and major streets with respect to your home base. Plan a series of short walks with your starting point as the hub. Go over the plan with a hotel clerk or other knowledgeable person to ensure that you include local points of interest and avoid any unsafe areas. Travel guidebooks list commercial walking tours available in most large cities.

The airliner has almost completely replaced the ocean liner, but the cruise ship is alive and well. Your travel agent can furnish information about scheduled cruises. The agent can also find special cruise opportunities. A long distance cruise ship sometimes completes its tour at a location far from its home port. The trip back to the starting point is called a repositioning voyage. You can obtain lower cost passage on these repositioning trips. Another interesting variation is travel by a passenger-carrying ocean freighter or cargoliner (up to twelve passengers), or combination cargo-passenger ship (over twelve). Passenger cabins on some modern freighters compare favorably with first-class accommodations on an ocean liner, and often at half the cost. However, they do have irregular sailing schedules. For more information see *Ford's Freighter Travel Guide*.

When time is limited, air travel comes to the rescue. Choosing the least expensive way of getting there is tricky business. Air fares vary by season, day of the week, time of the day, and the airline chosen. The longer the trip and the more competitive the route, the more variation in cost. Shop around if you can be flexible about departure times. Costs to fly from different airports vary. If you live within driving distance of more than one airport, compare the fares from each. Book your flight in advance for the lowest fare.

Because of no-shows, airlines sometimes intentionally overbook flights. If too many are booked, a passenger may be bumped from the flight and have to take a later plane. To compensate a person taking the later flight, some airlines provide the passenger who volunteers to be bumped with an additional free ticket that can be used at a later date.

Travelers over sixty-two years of age can purchase coupon books of four or eight tickets at reduced rates.

There are some minor restrictions on usage, but the program affords significant savings.

Accommodations

Use travel guides and tour books such as those furnished to members by the American Automobile Association to choose hotels and motels. Associations stake their reputations on the quality of the accommodations they list. It isn't usually necessary to stay at luxury hotels to obtain clean rooms and good service.

When booking rooms always ask for the lowest available rate. Most hotels and motels offer discounts to members of various associations such as auto clubs, certain corporations, and senior citizen organizations.

If you would like to get away from the pressures of modern life, consider a short vacation at a country inn. See the most recent publication of *Country Inns and Back Roads* for more information.

Another option for travel abroad, and increasingly available in the United States, is the bed and breakfast. In this arrangement, you book accommodations in a private home. You are served breakfast as part of the lodging arrangement. Rooms are usually booked in advance by a reservation service. The American Bed and Breakfast Association and the National Bed and Breakfast Association publish listings of accommodations that are available.

Hosteling began in Europe in 1909. It grew out of a movement by a German schoolteacher to allow his students inexpensive travel. At first schools were used for overnight lodging. The idea spread rapidly throughout Europe. In 1934 the American Youth Hostels (AYH) organization was formed. It maintains about 250 hostels in the United States. It is one of about fifty affiliates of the International Youth Hostel Federation. The AYH sponsors bicycling, hiking, skiing, sailing, canoeing, and motor trips in the United States and abroad. Some members are youths as old as ninety-four!

Hostels usually provide a bed and mattress in a dormitory setting. Cooking facilities are often available. You must provide sheets or a sleeping bag and food. Hostelers travel at a slower pace so they hear, smell and feel a country, instead of just looking at it. Surprisingly, hostels can be found in major cities such as New York or Paris.

To become familiar with foreign currency, determine the rate of exchange at a bank. One way to control impulse buying is to refer to a wallet-sized currency conversion card. You can make one showing the foreign equivalent of each dollar through ten dollars, and by tens through 100. This can be done quickly using a pocket calculator. When you see an item that you can't do without, pull out your card to see what it would cost at home. You may find you can do without it.

Another solution to inexpensive travel accommodations is a stay at a college or university. Hundreds of them in the United States and overseas offer guest lodgings at low rates when school is out.

There are several senior citizen hostel programs linked to education. In the Elderhostel program students room and board at a college. See the section in this text entitled "Continuing Education" for details. The University of New Hampshire also has a program for those over fifty called Interhostel. It operates in about a dozen European countries.

A more complex accommodation arrangement is the practice of home exchanging. Here people trade homes for a designated period of time. Houses, duplexes, apartments, bungalows, cabins, or even single bedrooms can be exchanged in trades involving one or more parties. Associations exist that put interested people in touch to arrange for trades. Thousands of people exchange their homes every year in most states and between many foreign countries. See James Dearing's book *Home Exchanging: A Complete Sourcebook for Travelers at Home or Abroad.*

Bibliography

REFERENCE BOOKS

Bree, Loris G. *Best Low Cost Things to See and Do.* Saint Paul, MN: MarLor, 1988. Interesting attractions listed by state for the United States, and by province for Canada. Emphasis on having fun and adventure without spending a lot of money.

Dearing, James. *Home Exchanging: A Complete Sourcebook For Travelers at Home or Abroad.* Charlotte, NC: East Woods, 1986. Explains the philosophy of home exchanging and walks the reader through the how-to process.

Frayn, Michael, et al. *Great Railway Journeys of the World.* New York: Dutton, 1982. Describes seven railway adventures in various parts of the world.

Heilman, Joan Rattner. *Unbelievably Good Deals and Great Adventures That You Absolutely Can't Get Unless You're Over 50.* 4th ed. Chicago: Contemporary Books, 1992. Discounts for seniors with emphasis on travel.

Herring, Charlanne Fields. *The Cruise Answer Book.* 2nd ed. Bedford, MA: Mills and Sanderson, 1988. Overview of cruises including planning, the ports, and the ships.

Howard, Judith. *Ford's Freighter Travel Guide and Waterways of the World.* 68th ed. Northridge, CA: Fords Travel, 1986. Overview of available cargo ship cruising.

International Youth Federation Staff. *International Youth Hostel Handbook.* Vol. 1, *Europe and Mediterranean.* Vol. 2, *Africa, America, Asia and Australia.* New York: Harper Collins, 1991.

Rundback, Betty. *Bed and Breakfast U.S.A. 1992.* New York: NAL-Dutton, 1992. A comprehensive guide to over one thousand bed and breakfast establishments.

Savage, Peter. *The Safe Travel Book: A Guide for the International Traveler.* Lexington, MA: Lexington Books, 1988. Broad coverage of safety considerations regarding accommodations, travel, and activities.

Simony, Maggy, ed. *The Traveler's Reading Guide: Ready-Made Reading Lists for the Armchair Traveler.* Rev. ed. New York: Facts on File, 1987. Suggested readings about places around the world. A good reference to materials that will enable one to become familiar with an intended destination.

Simpson, Norman, and Jerry Levitin. *Country Inns and Back Roads: North America.* New York: Harper Collins, 1991. Describes a selection of inns in North America.

Webster, Susan. *Group Travel Operating Procedures.* 2nd ed. New York: Van Nostrand Reinhold, 1993. Describes the methods and advantages of group travel.

Weinreb, Risa. *The Adventure Vacation Catalog.* New York: Simon and Schuster, 1984. All the details of more than six hundred vacations worldwide. This catalog links many hobby activities to travel.

Wood, Katie, and George McDonald. *Europe by Train, 1992: A Comprehensive, Economy Minded Guide to Train Travel in 26 Countries.* New York: Harper Collins, 1992. Coverage of the European railroad system.

PERIODICALS

Bed and Breakfast North America. Betsy Ross Publications, 24406 S. Ribbonwood Drive, Sun Lakes, AZ 85248.

Bed and Breakfast USA. Penguin Books, USA, 375 Hudson Street, New York, NY 10014.

Inn Business Review Newsletter. Norman Strasma Publications, 105 E. Court Street, Box 1789, Kankakee, IL 60901. (Inn, Bed and Breakfast.)

Tours! National Tour Marketing, 546 E. Main Street, Lexington, KY 40508. (Escorted group tours.)

Tours and Resorts. World Publishers, 990 Grove Street, Evanston, IL 60201.

Trailblazer. Thousand Trails, 12301 N.E. 10th Place, Bellevue, WA 98005. (RV, Resort camping.)

Travel and Leisure. American Express Publishers, 1120 Avenue of the Americas, New York, NY 10036.

Travel Holiday. Travel Publications, 28 W. 23rd Street, New York, NY 10010.

Travel 50 and Beyond. Vacation Publications, 2411 Fountain View, Houston, TX 77057. (Senior travelers.)

TravLtips. Box 188, Flushing, NY 11358. (Freighter and other unusual cruises.)

Vacations. Vacation Publications, 2411 Fountain View, Suite 201, Houston, TX 77057.

ASSOCIATIONS

American Bed and Breakfast Association. 10800 Midlothian Turnpike, Richmond, VA 23235–4700. Publications: *B & B*

Traveller: Bed and Breakfast TravelClub Newsletter, Treasury of Bed and Breakfast.

American Society of Travel Agents. 1101 King Street, Alexandria, VA 22314.

American Youth Hostels. PO Box 37613, Washington, DC 20013–7613. Maintains two hundred hostels in the U.S. Belongs to a network of over 5,300 hostels in fifty-nine countries. Publications: *AYH Discovery Tours, Hostelling in North America,* and *Knapsack.*

Elderhostel. 75 Federal Street, 3rd Floor, Boston, MA 02110. A network of over 1,600 educational institutions in forty countries. Offers short-term residential academic programs for adults over sixty and their younger spouses or companions. Publication: *Elderhostel Catalog.*

Family Motor Coach Association. 8291 Clough Pike, Cincinnati, OH 45244. Owners of motor homes. Publication: *Family Motor Coaching.*

Freighter Travel Club of America. 3524 Harts Lake Road, Roy, WA 98580. Individuals with an interest in traveling by passenger-carrying, ocean-going freighters. Publication: *Freighter Travel News.*

Good Sam Recreational Vehicle Club. Box 500, 29901 Agoura Road, Agoura Hills, CA 91301. Recreational vehicle enthusiasts who act as "Good Samaritans" on the road by helping members in distress. Publications: *Highways, RV Campground and Services Directory.*

Institute of Certified Travel Agents. 148 Linden Street, PO Box 812059, Wellesley, MA 02181–0012.

Interhostel. University of New Hampshire, 6 Garrison Ave., Durham, NH 03824. Adults over fifty study a particular region of the world under the auspices of the University of New Hampshire and participating institutions overseas. Publication: Catalog.

International Cruise Passengers Association. 1521 Alton Road, Suite 350, Miami Beach, FL 33139–3301. Cruise passengers and ship enthusiasts in thirty-six countries. Provides rating information on cruise ships. Advises disabled regarding access and suitability of ships. Publications: *Cruise Digest Reports, Berlitz Complete Handbook to Cruising.*

Mountain Travel-Sobek. 6420 Fairmount Avenue, El Cerrito, CA 94530. Those interested in adventure travel. Sponsors international exploration trips. Publications: *Adventure Book, Crocodile.*

National Bed-and-Breakfast Association. PO Box 332, Norwalk, CT 06852. Publication: *Bed and Breakfast Guide for the U.S., Canada, and the Caribbean.*

Underwater Sports

SPORT DIVERS ENJOY THEIR PASTIME in a silent, often breathtakingly beautiful world. They explore and photograph marine life, search the sea floor for shipwrecks and artifacts, spear fish, and collect other forms of seafood. Divers do these things and more, while swimming freely and remaining weightless as an astronaut in space. Here, we'll look at two popular forms of sport diving: skin diving and scuba diving. But first, let's take a closer look at the medium divers enter seeking adventure.

The Marine Environment

We walk about on land, unmindful of the "sea" of air pressing on our bodies, accustomed to the effects that the atmosphere has on our senses of sight and sound. As we immerse ourselves in the denser sea of water, we must get used to a new set of circumstances. Water filters light and the colors seen by a diver. Under average conditions, red, yellow, and orange have been filtered out at thirty feet below the surface. Below fifty-two feet only blues and greens can normally be seen. However, when artificial light is used, the brilliant colors of deep water marine life can be seen and photographed. Sound travels four times faster in water than air, but most of its energy is quickly scattered and absorbed. Water is a good conductor of heat. This results in body heat loss at a rate twenty-five times faster than in air. As the sun warms surface water, a sharply defined temperature change occurs at a level called a thermocline. Water below that level may be considerably colder than above. When a diver descends through a thermocline, the colder water can cause cramps and greater air consumption.

The Greek physicist Archimedes stated that an object will float if it displaces an amount of water that weighs more than the object. Since the displaced water often weighs more than the diver, the diver tends to be buoyant and to rise to the surface. This is overcome by carrying an amount of weight that will allow the diver to remain at a desired level. This condition is called neutral buoyancy.

Water pressure increases with depth. As a skin diver descends, pressure increases, squeezing body parts having air-filled cavities such as lungs and sinuses. Below water, scuba divers will be breathing air several times as dense as on the surface. Inhaling the dense air involves effort. The overall impact of pressure limits most sport diving to a depth of about one-hundred feet.

Other factors in the marine environment that affect divers center around water movement. Tides, currents, waves, and surf all pose conditions that divers must learn to deal with. They must not allow tides to carry them too far from shore, or allow waves to dislodge face masks or other gear. Each beach has unique characteristics that impose conditions that affect a diver's plan.

Hazards Imposed by Sea Creatures

The sharp edges of barnacles found on solid objects and the sharp edges of corals forming tropical reefs can cause cuts that may become infected. Beautiful cone shaped snails usually found in tropical Pacific waters can inflict serious stings. Sea urchins, found in temperate sea waters around the world, are covered with pointed spines that can produce a painful puncture in human flesh. Jellyfish have a semi-transparent dome structure with fringes of short tentacles hanging from its edges. The touch of a tentacle produces a burning sting. A large jellyfish measures nine inches across. In the Atlantic, a member of the same family, the Portuguese man-of-war, measures as much as twelve inches across and has tentacles as long as ninety feet; in the Pacific, the tentacles are about half that. It also inflicts a painful sting. Divers can avoid injury from such stings by wearing a full wet suit. Moray eels bite and many sea snakes inflict poisonous bites. The sting ray, a flat, winged-

319

like fish with a pointed tail, will usually employ its barbed tail to sting you only if it's stepped on. Venomous fish are usually found only in tropical waters. Sharks are to be avoided, especially in the larger sizes.

Skin Diving

Skin diving is a form of breath-hold diving that has been practiced for centuries. Fifteenth century prints show divers in action, in war, or performing salvage work. Notables as diverse as Leonardo da Vinci and Benjamin Franklin toyed with the idea of swim fins. Leonardo even made sketches of a proposed snorkel.

Equipment

Minimum equipment for the modern skin diver consists of the following: A face mask having a large tempered glass lens set in a soft rubber body. It's held in place by a broad rubber strap around the back of the head. Masks are available with prescription lenses for those with poor eyesight. Some feature one-way valves used to purge water that accumulates inside. Some designs also allow the nose to be pinched to equalize pressure in the ears when required.

A snorkel is a breathing device consisting of a J-shaped tube about twelve inches long, with a mouthpiece on the short end. In use, the long end extends up beyond the water surface as you swim face-down below the surface. The tube should have a large enough bore to allow easy breathing. It's attached to the face mask to prevent loss.

Swim fins that look like an elongated duck foot are worn on the feet. They may have an adjustable strap that is worn around the heel, or the heel may be fully enclosed.

The following additional useful equipment may be used by the skin diver.

Wet Suit. We have seen that body heat loss occurs in water. This can be uncomfortable in even relatively warm water. A wet suit is made of a foam synthetic rubber material. The suit allows a thin layer of water to lie between it and your skin. The water is warmed by your skin, and the air cells in the suit material act as insulation to retain the heat.

Weight belts. These are usually made of lead weights housed in a belt to be worn around the waist. The number of weights can be varied to suit conditions. A quick-release buckle is furnished to permit quick removal in emergency situations. Weight belts are worn to allow the diver to achieve neutral buoyancy (remain at a constant level in the water).

Buoyancy Compensator Vests (BCVs). These are worn around the back and shoulders, extending forward over the chest, and reaching from neck to waist. They are used in conjunction with weight belts to achieve buoyancy control. BCVs may be inflated orally, by CO_2 cartridge, or when

scuba diving, by tank air. Although not a life jacket, it can be used as a personal flotation device when resting on the surface. We'll return to BCVs during the discussion of scuba diving.

Diver's knife. This is worn in a sheath on the inside of one leg, below the knee. It's for freeing yourself from underwater entanglements. The multipurpose blade has a sharp, smooth edge and a serrated edge. The latter for cutting rope. Most divers' knives have a metal end on the handle for pounding or tapping metal surfaces to signal a buddy.

Procedures

As with all forms of diving, skin diving is not a solo sport. You should dive with a buddy and maintain contact during a dive. There are times when water will seep into your face mask or enter the end of the snorkel. It's best to practice clearing this equipment of water in a controlled environment, such as a swimming pool, before entering open water. When water enters the face mask, tilt your head back, press the top of the mask against your forehead, and exhale through your nose. The water will be forced out at the bottom of the mask. If the mask is equipped with a purge valve, tilt your head forward and exhale through your nose. When you dive below the surface, water will enter the snorkel. As you rise to the surface, look up and exhale slowly through the mouth. Air will be trapped in the snorkel and you can inhale at the surface. If you need to look down as you rise, wait until you reach the surface, and blow the water out rapidly, then inhale.

Conserve energy while swimming with fins. A slow, firm, flutter kick will be adequate. Fins have a tendency to trip you while walking forward on land. It's best to shuffle sideways or backwards while going to and from the water. When suiting up, don the weight belt last. This will minimize tangling with other gear if it has to be dropped quickly in an emergency.

Experienced skin divers are best equipped to begin courses in scuba diving.

Scuba Diving

Self-contained underwater breathing apparatus systems enable a diver to breathe air from a tank carried below the water's surface. Credit goes to Frenchmen Benoit Rouquayrol and Auguste Denayrouze for the earliest development of the concept in 1865. They used a compressed air container carried on the diver's back that was connected through a form of pressure regulator to the diver's mouthpiece. Technology available at the time limited container pressure to less than five-hundred pounds per square inch, so tank air had to be supplied through a hose connected to an air pump on the surface. True self-containment hadn't arrived. In 1926 Frenchman Yves Le Prieur was able to eliminate the hose to the surface when a tank air pressure of 1,500 pounds per square inch could be attained. The diver used a hand operated valve to regulate the flow of air as needed. In the early 1940s three Frenchmen, Georges Comheines, Jacques Cousteau, and Émile Gagnan carried out experiments that included connecting a Rouquayrol-Denayrouze regulator to a Le Prieur high-pressure tank. The result was patented as the Aqua-Lung. Refinements to the exhaust system were made in 1943, and the system was first marketed commercially in 1946.

Equipment

In addition to the equipment described above for skin diving, the scuba diver usually wears a BCV fitted with a backpack that accommodates mounting the air tank on the back. Air tanks are available made from steel or aluminum. Aluminum has the advantages of lighter weight and corrosion resistance. Most used steel tanks hold 71.2 cubic feet of air at 2,250 pounds per square inch, and the aluminum eighty cubic feet at 3,000 pounds per square inch.

The air supply system consists of the tank with a valve which, when opened, allows air to flow to the regulator. A regulator consists of a mouthpiece, a hose, and usually two pressure-reducing stages. The first stage reduces the high tank pressure to about 130 pounds per square inch. The second stage uses a disk-shaped unit on the mouthpiece that houses the mechanism to give a diver a breath of air when wanted, at a pressure balanced with that of the surrounding water, regardless of depth. This is called an open-circuit system because the breath is exhaled directly into the water.

The following additional equipment may be carried by the well-equipped scuba diver:

A pressure gauge is used to monitor the tank pressure level. This enables the diver to determine the air supply remaining and when it's necessary to begin an ascent to the surface. Waterproof watches and bottom timers also help the diver keep informed of the passage of time. Divers use more air in a given period as they go deeper. Dive timers have been developed that give a visual reading of minutes of air remaining for any depth. Some computer units keep track of depth and available air, warn of the need for a decompression dive, and advise of the depth at which to decompress. Depth gauges are useful in locations that permit a diver to venture below the limitations of the scuba equipment.

A diver can become disoriented in dark or murky water. Compasses are useful in such cases to find one's way back to the point of entry. Waterproof lights are also useful, especially to photographers.

When divers plan to cover significant distances under water they may use propulsion vehicles. These electrically powered units pull the diver along in the water. Surface floats are also used to conserve energy by allowing the diver to rest on them between dives. They can be as basic as an inner tube.

Scuba Procedures and Physical Effects

Learn to swim well, and build up your endurance before beginning scuba lessons.

When ready to enter the water the air valve should be turned on and the regulator should be in the mouth. When entering the water from a boat or dock, take a large step forward over the edge with one leg, and enter the water with legs apart. Hold the face mask in place with one hand as you enter the water. Bring the legs together as they enter the water to keep your head above the water. Other accepted methods include tumbling into the water, either forward or backward, while holding the face mask in place. Entry from a beach is best done holding a buddy's hand and backing through the surf.

Use your snorkel if you swim from the point of entry to the dive location. When ready to dive, place the regulator in your mouth, exhale through the mouthpiece, and begin breathing. Release the air in your BCV and you will descend. During descent, water pressure will rise, creating an external pressure on eardrums, sinuses, and lungs. Internal pressures must equalize as you descend. If discomfort is felt, blow some air into your BCV, ascend a few feet and hold until equalization takes place. Squeeze on eardrums will occur if the eustachian tube is congested or blocked. Sinus squeeze is also felt when sinuses are congested. Lung squeeze is accommodated by the air regulator response. As you approach thirty-three feet the pressure will reduce the air cells in your wet suit, reducing your buoyancy. Add air to your BCV to slow and control descent. Reaching your desired depth, adjust your BCV to achieve neutral buoyancy; check your buddy's location, move along together side by side, maintaining visual contact. Further communication between diving partners is done by hand signals, an underwater slate, hand squeezing, or by whistle. A buddy-line may be used in waters having limited visibility. This is a short, unfastened line that is held by both divers.

At a depth of thirty-three feet the density of gas is doubled and its volume is decreased by half. At sixty-six feet the density of your air supply is tripled and its volume is cut to one third. Nitrogen makes up about 80 percent of the air we breathe. When air pressure is increased, body tissue and the blood start to become saturated with nitrogen. This is not a problem at moderate depths with short dive lengths, but at over thirty-three feet, dive duration has some limitations. Current dive tables prescribe a time limit of two-hundred minutes at forty feet, forty minutes at eighty feet, and twenty-five minutes at one-hundred feet. (These tables are revised periodically, as scientists learn more about the subject.) Beyond these so-called no-decompression limits, a diver must pause during ascent at a prescribed schedule to allow the nitrogen gas to escape and be removed from the body. Failure to do so can cause decompression sickness, commonly known as the bends.

If a diver's air supply fails, scuba divers are trained to employ a buddy-breathing system. Partners alternately breathe from one diver's regulator, passing it back and forth while ascending to the surface. Another emergency measure is the swimming ascent. When your air supply becomes unexpectedly exhausted, adjust buoyancy by dropping your weight belt if no other means is available; keep your regulator in your mouth and slowly exhale as you swim to the surface. As you ascend you may get a small amount of air from your tank as the air inside expands. Remain calm and do not hold your breath during the ascent. It can cause an air embolism. Ascending from a depth of only thirty-three feet, the air in your lungs doubles in volume. If you hold your breath, air can't escape and it will be forced into the bloodstream where it can be carried to the brain. Proceed slowly during a normal ascent, allowing time for pressure equalization to occur. Look up and slowly rotate your body to detect any obstructions such as boats that may lie above.

Leave the water with caution. Before climbing on a boat, hand your fins and other loose gear to someone on deck. If exiting onto a beach, inflate your BCV enough to assure positive buoyancy, time your passage through surf between waves, and crawl forward on hands and knees when you hit the beach.

We have seen that controlled, uncongested breathing and a clear-headed, calm approach are required. This means a minimum of tobacco, and no alcohol or drugs.

Training

Take a comprehensive course in recreational scuba training that includes academic study and in-water skills. The brief discussion above only provides an introduction to the subject. Qualified diving schools provide certification at many levels. Examples include: open water scuba diver, specialty diver, advanced diver, and instructor. Take a course in first aid and lifesaving if your scuba course doesn't cover these subjects. A basic knowledge of weather forecasting is also useful when planning a trip out over open water. Diving trips will be more meaningful and interesting if you acquire some knowledge of marine biology.

Related Underwater Activity

Aside from the general underwater sight-seeing, one of the most popular diving activities is underwater photography.

Diving magazines such as *Discover Diving* often feature articles on the subject. Underwater photographic championship competitions are sponsored by a number of related industries.

Underwater fishing is done with spears and spear guns, but prepare for a ride if you spear a big one. National contests are held in spearfishing, and winners compete in world championships. Perhaps less adventurous, but pleasing to those who love seafood, is the collecting of lobsters and abalone.

Treasure and artifact hunting have held a fascination since man began to skin dive centuries ago. There are a lot of sites within sport-diving depth, but many are protected by local governments and historical groups. Restrictions vary, so check with local authorities first. Research into the sites of shipwrecks may begin with the archives of the U.S. Coast Guard, the U.S. Library of Congress, or local newspapers. It's an interesting prospect.

Bibliography

REFERENCE BOOKS

Clark, John R. *Snorkeling: A Complete Guide to the Underwater Experience.* Englewood Cliffs, NJ: Prentice-Hall, 1985. Covers snorkeling techniques and equipment, sea life, and photographic techniques.

Frame, Sandy. *Diver's Almanac: Guide to the West Coast from Baja California to British Columbia.* Rev. ed. Costa Mesa, CA: HDL, 1986. Describes locations of specific sites, attractions, dive shop locations, and facilities. Discusses techniques, diet, and conditioning.

Griffiths, Tom. *Sport Scuba Diving: In Depth.* Princeton, NJ: Princeton, 1985. Textbook on scuba diving covering equipment, diving techniques, planning, and marine life.

Ketels, Hank, and Jack McDowell. *Sports Illustrated Scuba Diving: Underwater Adventuring.* New York: Sports Illustrated, 1988. Comprehensive, well illustrated book on the subject including equipment selection, training, and techniques.

Vallintine, Reg. *Learn Scuba Diving in a Weekend.* New York, Knopf, 1993. Concise coverage of the sport including equipment, snorkeling, scuba diving, and an introduction to sea creatures to avoid.

PERIODICALS

Scuba Times. Poseidon Publishing, Box 2409, Pensacola, FL 32513–2409.

Scubapro Diving and Snorkeling. Aqua-Field Publishers, 66 W. Gilbert Street, Shrewsbury, NJ 07702.

Skin Diver Magazine. Petersen Publications, 8490 Sunset Boulevard, Los Angeles, CA 90069.

ASSOCIATIONS

The Cousteau Society. 870 Greenbriar Circle, Suite 402, Chesapeake, VA 23320. Environmental education organization. Organizes Project Ocean Search field trip to study marine ecosystems. Publications: *Calypso Log, Dolphin Log,* and related material.

Handicapped Scuba Association. 7172 W. Stanford Avenue, Littleton, CO 80123. Seeks to advance and promote scuba diving among the handicapped. Maintains training agency for handicapped divers, and instructors of the handicapped. Conducts diving vacations. Publications: *Getting Down Scuba News,* and *Instructor Training Manual.*

Institute of Diving. 17314 U.S. Hwy 98, Panama City Beach, FL 32413. Professional and sport divers, and interested individuals. Acts for the advancement of knowledge related to human-oriented activity in the undersea environment. Maintains library and museum. Publications: *Institute of Diving Newsletter,* and diving journal.

National Association of Underwater Instructors. PO Box 14650, Montclair, CA 91763. Certified instructors of underwater diving. Offers training and certification programs. Maintains library, sponsors competitions, and bestows awards. Publications: *The Journal of Underwater Education,* and related textbooks.

Professional Association of Diving Instructors. 1251 E. Dyer Road, No. 100, Santa Ana, CA 92705. Educates and certifies scuba instructors. Offers courses in diving specialties. Sanctions training courses in eighty-seven countries. Publications: *Dive Traveler, Undersea Quarterly,* and related materials.

Underwater Society of America. PO Box 628, Daly City, CA 94017. Those who participate in and support underwater sports. Interested in advancement of underwater exploration, engineering, and science. Sponsors competitions in skin diving, scuba diving, and other underwater sports. Maintains hall of fame, and bestows awards and scholarships. Publications: *Outlines: Underwater Sports, Visibility,* and related materials.

Volleyball

TWO OPPOSING TEAMS OF PLAYERS use their hands and arms to hit a ball over a net on a rectangular court. Points are awarded to the serving team when the receiving team fails to return the ball within the rules of the game. If the serving team fails to return a ball, the receiving team earns a side-out (the right to serve), no points.

The court is laid out as shown in Figure 1. Six players on each team are positioned as shown in Figure 2 on page 326.

How the Game is Played

To start play, the right back player (server) tosses the ball up and hits it with a hand or arm, sending it over the net and into the opponents' court. If the receiving team fails to return the ball, the serving team gets a point. If the server hits the ball into the net, a side-out occurs. The first team to score fifteen points wins the game as long as there is at least a two-point lead. If two teams are tied at fourteen to fourteen, play continues until one team has a two-point margin of victory.

During a rally, the ball is considered out of play when it touches the ground or goes out of bounds. When a ball is returned softly over the net, it's called a free ball. Teams try to avoid returning the ball softly, because it allows the opponents time to set up an aggressive return.

The following is a typical sequence of events during play: The server hits the ball over the net, where a receiver (digger) deflects the ball to a team member (setter) who relays the ball to another team member positioned close to the net who then may hit the ball forcibly over the net (spike the ball) between opposing players, or gently tip it over, close to the net. On the other side of the net, the sequence is repeated—dig, set, and attack. Other players (blockers) try to prevent the ball from coming over the net by jumping up with arms raised to deflect the ball back into the opponents' court. The ball may be contacted only three times during play on one side of the net. A blocker's contact isn't counted. The ball can't come to rest during the contacts. Both situations constitute a foul.

Following a side-out, and before the next serve, each player on the serving team rotates one position clockwise. Under international rules, a team is allowed to make six individual substitutions in a game (one entry per player). A team is allowed two 30-second time-outs per game. Since team members rotate positions and transition from the serving mode to the receiving mode in seconds, it can be seen that individual players must master the skills of several of the roles described above.

Failure to comply with certain additional restrictions placed on play action can result in a foul. They include: Only players in the front zone (court) may block or attack. Back zone players may only attack from the three meter line that separates zones. Players must be in their correct relative rotational position and zone during the serve, but they may change position during play immediately after the serve. This allows players with particular skills to quickly move into new positions where their skills are most effective, as a digger for a blocker, for example. A served ball may not touch the net or go out of bounds without being touched by the opponent. A player must not touch the net. The ball must not touch the ground. A team must not be out of rotation. A player must not make two consecutive contacts with the ball (except during digging or blocking). The team that commits the foul either loses the right to serve or loses a point.

History

The game was originated in 1895 by American William G. Morgan, a physical education director of a YMCA in Holyoke, Massachusetts. The game of mintonette was developed to provide recreation and relaxation for businessmen who found the then-new game of basketball too

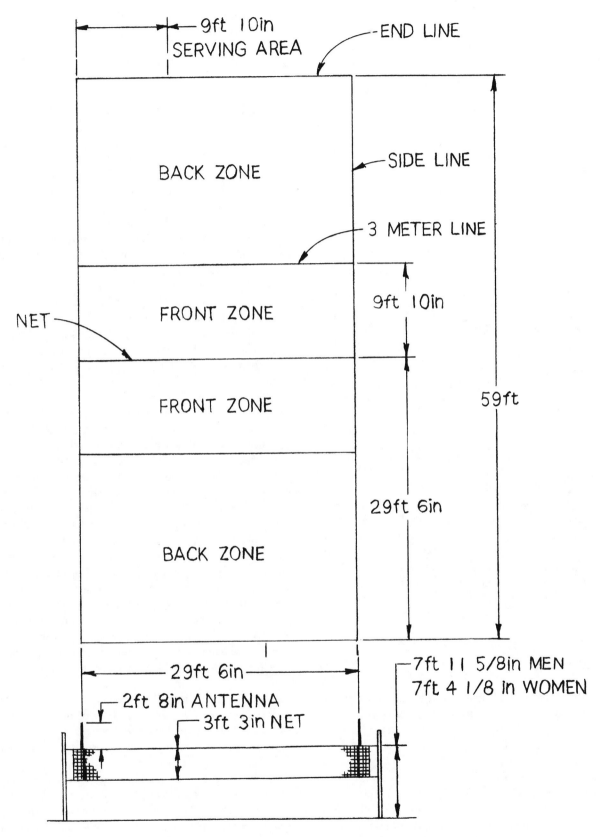

Figure 1
Volleyball playing court layout.

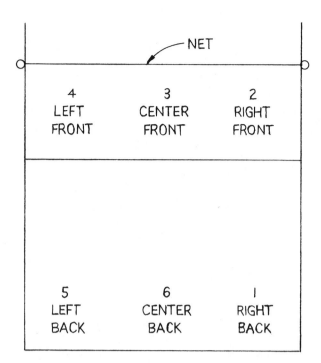

Figure 2

Nominal player positions. Players must be in their correct relative positions during the serve, but they may change positions during play, immediately after the serve.

vigorous. It's evident that they couldn't imagine the fiercely contested volleyball games of today. The name was changed to volleyball when it was noted that the men volleyed the ball back and forth over the net. The first game of volleyball was played on July 7, 1896 at Springfield College. American soldiers played the game overseas in World Wars I and II, helping to spread its popularity around the world. The first world championships were held in Prague, Czechoslovakia in 1949. It was accepted as an approved sport for Olympic competition in 1957, and was included in the 1964 games.

Equipment

The net is 39 inches wide and 32 feet long. A vertical two inch wide strip of tape is positioned on each side of the net over the corresponding sidelines. An antenna is placed on the outside of each of the two tapes to mark the vertical side limits of the court.

The ball is made of pieces of uniform material, usually leather or vinyl. It's light colored. The ball measures 25 to 27 inches in circumference. It weighs 9 to 10 ounces, and is inflated to a pressure of 5.5 to 6.5 pounds per square inch.

Shoes should be light, and provide good shock absorption to accommodate the continual jumping and twisting motions experienced during the game.

Most teams wear long sleeved jerseys and brief short pants to permit free movement.

Knee pads are worn for protection during frequent knee contact with the floor during play.

Player Roles and Associated Skills

Most servers use the overhead float serve. It imparts no spin to the ball. The ball is tossed up about two feet above eye level. Contact is made in the middle of the ball with the heel of the hand. The wrist remains stiff. Advanced players may impart a spin to the ball with the top spin overhand. A forward spin is placed on the ball as it is tossed about four or five feet above eye level. Contact is made below the center of the ball with the heel of the hand, then a rapid wrist snap is used to provide whole-hand contact. The top spin overhand requires careful execution for success, but yields more points when done correctly. Another high-skill serve is the jump serve. The server tosses the ball forward and up, strides forward and jumps, striking the ball while airborne, as when spiking a ball. It gets points, but is also cause for errors. Beginning players often use a simple underhand serve, but this is not practical for competition due to its slow movement.

Diggers are often the first team members to play the ball after it comes over the net. They stand in a ready position with knees flexed, body bent forward with shoulders ahead of the knees, head up with eyes following the ball. When a ball approaches, the arms are fully extended forward, elbows in, hands clasped together with thumbs down. They attempt to make ball contact with both arms simultaneously at a point between the elbows and the wrists. They must move reflexively to a position that will permit such contact before the ball reaches the floor. Forward movement is often accompanied by a sprawl or dive with the arms and legs cushioning the fall. Side movement involves a foot shuffle, hop, or body roll into position. Balls approaching above the head may be taken on the bottom of the arms, held above the head. A digger's primary goal is to deflect the ball to a target position in front of a setter. If this is not possible, the digger may direct a ball back over the net.

Setters are the volleyball equivalent of a football quarterback. They direct much of the flow of the play. They receive the ball with the hands held close together, fingers spread and cupped, forming a sort of basket to trap the ball. It must be relayed in one fluid motion to an attacker who is in the best position to get the ball over the net effectively. This is often done by the attacker hitting a set ball from above the level of the net into an opponents' court at a location where the opponent is most vulnerable (a spike). The setter must aim the ball where the attacker will be at the time of the spike. The attacker begins the jump as the ball leaves the setter's hand. The setter will try to disguise an intended pass to catch the opposing team unaware. In certain play strategies, teams will consist of more than one setter and/or more than one attacker. All must coordinate their movements.

A spiker (attacker) takes three or four steps, jumps and hits the ball, imparting top spin, presenting opponents with any speed on the ball from a gentle open handed tip to a hard, driving, shot.

Blockers attempt to either stop the ball from coming over the net, or deflect the ball to a position that is playable by other team members. They scan the opponents' developing play to see where the ball is coming from. They assume a ready position with knees bent and hands sometimes raised in front to shoulder level. From this position they can quickly leap straight up, arms fully raised to intercept the ball. Blockers often coordinate their efforts as they work in pairs, or sometimes threes. This grouping is accomplished by following the opponents' play and ranging from side to side to meet an oncoming ball.

Strategy

Even though the court appears small it's very difficult for six players to cover all of it. A player has a very limited time to react and move to meet a speeding ball. It has been found that even a well-trained team can only cover about two-thirds of the court. To compensate, player formations are devised based on probability. Players with specific skills are positioned where they will be most useful. A backup digger behind a pair of blockers, for example. If the ball gets through the blockers, the digger can save the ball.

In the broadest sense, teams are made up of setters and hitters while on offense. Certain team compositions have proven their worth over time. They are identified by signifying the number of hitters, followed by the number of setters. A 4–2 team composition has four hitters and two setters. Two of the hitters and one setter are placed in the front row at all times. The 4–2 has the advantage of simplicity. There's always a skilled setter to feed the two hitters up front. But, because of their function, setters make weak blockers, and they will be positioned at the front center where most blocking is required. Also, since there are only two front row hitters, the attack patterns become predictable. Once the most popular composition, the 4–2 has lost favor to other compositions.

The 6–2 composition is composed of six hitters, two of which also act as setters. In each rotation, the back row setter comes up to the net (after the ball has been served) and all three front row hitters are free to attack.

The 5–1 composition is composed of five attacking hitters and one skilled setting specialist. The setter doesn't have to master spiking or digging skills. The setter is in charge and doesn't have to coordinate setting activities with another setter.

As players are rotated and substituted, an important element of team strategy is team balance. At the start of a game the coach is required to furnish a team lineup, as in baseball. As play progresses, the six substitutes enter the game. The original lineup, and changes brought about by substitution, should maintain a balance of physical and mental skills. If one of two adjacent blockers jumps higher than the other, opponent hitters will always hit over the weak jumper, rendering the weak jumper ineffective. If a hitter/spiker at right front is significantly less skilled than the hitter/spiker at left front, opponents will play percentages and favor blocker coverage of the strong spiker. Experienced players (and inexperienced players) should be distributed evenly on the court so that opponents can't concentrate their hits on certain weak areas of the court.

Fitness

The sport of volleyball stresses players physically. It's easier to "get up to speed" in volleyball for those who have been physically active. It ranks high as a conditioner. Obtain a physical checkup before active participation. See the section in this text on "Physical Fitness" for more information.

Game Variations

The above coverage of volleyball describes formal, competitive play. The game is often played by children with the net lowered to compensate for their height. The number of players may also be varied for recreational volleyball, sometimes incorporating a third row of players on each team.

Beach volleyball is usually played with two, sometimes four, players on each team. The length of sustained play for a point (rally) tends to be shorter than with six-person teams, because each player has so much more court to cover, court size being essentially the same. The only other significant differences are that the playing surface is sand, there are no attack lines, and the serve can be made from any area along the end lines. Professional beach volleyball is rapidly gaining popularity across the country. Winning players are well compensated by tournament sponsors, who are beginning to show more games on television. A game with basically the same rules as beach volleyball is played on a grass surface.

Bibliography

REFERENCE BOOKS

Banachowski, Andy. *Power Volleyball: The Woman's Game.* North Palm Beach, FL: Athletic Institute, 1983. A brief account of the skills required for volleyball. Includes practice drills.

Beal, Doug, et al. *Volleyball Coaching Tips for the 90s.* 2nd ed. Evanston, IL: Sports Group, 1991. Provides tips on various elements of the game including conditioning, playing offense and defense, and practice drills.

Bertucci, Bob, ed. *The AVCA Volleyball Handbook.* Grand Rapids, MI: Masters, 1987. The official handbook of the American Volleyball Coaches' Association. Covers everything from fundamentals to the physical and psychological aspects of the game. Portions written by eighteen volleyball authorities.

Scates, Allen E. *Winning Volleyball.* 3rd ed. Dubuque, IA: Brown, 1989. Covers the fundamentals of serving, passing, setting, attacking, and blocking. Discusses systems of play for offense and defense, and volleyball for children.

Selinger, Arie, and Joan Ackermann-Blount. *Arie Selinger's Power Volleyball.* New York: St. Martin's, 1986. Comprehensive coverage of the sport. Covers rules and skills, player's roles, components of the game, strategies, training, and preparation.

Stevenson, Jon, and Raymond Obstfeld. *Hot Sand: The Beach Volleyball Handbook.* Irvine, CA: Windmill, 1989. Contains the rules of three related organizations, and interviews held with notable players and tournament directors.

Viera, Barbara L., and Bonnie Jill Ferguson. *Volleyball: Steps to Success.* Champaign, IL: Leisure, 1989. Describes the various skills required, and the systems of play for offense and defense.

PERIODICALS

USA Volleyball. Hagen Marketing and Communications, Box 9008, Rapid City, SD 57709–9008.

Volleyball. AVCOM Publications, 21700 Oxnard Street, Suite 1600, Woodland Hills, CA 91367.

Volleyball Monthly. Straight Down, 1880 Santa Barbara Street, Suite F, San Luis Obispo, CA 93401.

Volleyball USA. USA Volleyball, 3595 E. Fountain Boulevard, Suite 1–2, Colorado Springs, CO 80910–1740.

ASSOCIATIONS

American Deaf Volleyball Association. c/o Farley Warshaw, 300 Roxborough Street, Rochester, NY 14619. National amateur volleyball organizations, coaches, and players. Seeks to provide camps, programs, and training for hearing impaired children and adults. Sponsors U.S. volleyball teams in international competition. Publication: *ADVBA.*

American Volleyball Coaches Association. 122 2nd Avenue, Suite 201, San Mateo, CA 94401. Professional coaches. Conducts educational and research programs, sponsors competitions, and bestows awards. Publications: *American Volleyball, Coaching Volleyball, Power Tips,* and related material.

United States Volleyball Association. 3595 E. Fountain Boulevard, Colorado Springs, CO 80910–1740. National governing body for the sport of volleyball. Sponsors Olympic teams. Publications: *Volleyball USA,* and related material.

Volunteering

THE PROBLEMS THAT CONFRONT our country and the world have been, and will continue to be, met by millions of volunteers and selfless individual Americans. Recent polls indicate at least half of the population engages in volunteer work. The democratic form of government that we enjoy depends upon the participation of its citizens. We'll look here at ways we can use our free time to help others help themselves.

History of Volunteerism in America

In 1776 volunteers met to write our constitutional documents. During the colonial period when minimal taxation couldn't support the hiring of civic employees, most of the work was done by volunteers. When the government couldn't or wouldn't act, the do-it-yourself spirit of the people asserted itself. Construction projects weren't limited to barn-raisings for neighbors or house building for new members of the community. Groups also built and maintained school houses, public buildings, and roads.

Following Benjamin Franklin's lead in Philadelphia in 1731, groups throughout the colonies established libraries by means of voluntary contributions and organizational effort. Even today this spirit is seen in "Friends of the Library" organizations that raise funds for book purchases and volunteer their time and services. Volunteer fire companies, so prevalent today in rural areas, trace their origins to colonial times as well.

Law enforcement was also a cooperative effort with the town constable serving during the day and volunteers rotating the night watch. In true Hollywood Western fashion, the constable would organize a posse when the occasion warranted. Once again, today's local "neighborhood watch" activity reflects the past. Frontier citizens volunteered to accept the above duties and more. Other examples include serving as town officials and members of the local militia.

The origins of social services in the United States are rooted in a combination of governmental and private voluntary action. Government help was provided for by the enactment of a body of law called the "Poor Law" modeled after similar laws in England. The Poor Laws provided meager last resort help in a dire emergency.

During the nineteenth century most volunteers were women from middle- and upper-class families. Because this segment of the population seldom worked at paid jobs, they were able to allocate some of their time to volunteer work.

In recent years we have seen increasing volunteerism by both working men and women to meet the more complex needs of modern society.

Local and Global Needs

It's self-evident that those who most need help and guidance with problems involving hunger, illiteracy, and substance abuse are least able to pay for that help. These problems are international in scope. Today volunteer agencies are working to provide relief from such adversities at home and abroad. Growing numbers of emerging democracies are asking for assistance in their efforts to establish appropriate governmental and business practices. The private sector is helping to supply skilled advisors in the face of tight national budgets. While it's impossible for even the wealthiest nations to meet the needs of all of their own people, well-coordinated programs staffed by volunteers make limited funds go further.

The network of volunteer agencies and programs is mind-boggling. They overlap, duplicate, and exist at many levels. Each has its own interest(s). In the following discussion we'll look at a selection of volunteer agencies, and how to locate them.

The Network of Agencies

There are several ways you can find volunteer agencies at the local level. Many phone books carry a heading "Community Service Numbers" in their table of contents. Under that heading, look for an organization called Voluntary Action Center (VAC), or a similar title. These VACs can supply a list of local opportunities for volunteers. Most VACs are affiliated with the National Volunteer Center or the United Way. Either agency can help if no local VAC is available.

If you are interested in a religious orientation to your work, consult with your religious leaders. Service clubs such as the Lions or Kiwanis can help where your interests match their specialties. Consult a college or university for internships. Your employer may be involved with social work and welcome your voluntary services. You can get specific questions answered about federal volunteer agencies by contacting the office of your local member of Congress. Don't overlook other organizations such as your local Salvation Army or the American Red Cross; they need volunteers too.

Your public library may have reference books such as: The *Encyclopedia of Associations,* or *Volunteer!: The Comprehensive Guide to Voluntary Service in the U.S. and Abroad,* or *Volunteerism, the Directory of Organizations, Training, Programs, and Publications.* These reference books provide a broad overview of volunteer opportunities at the local, national, and international levels. At the county level check the Welfare Department and any Park District Office.

There is an increased emphasis on the use of volunteers at all levels of government. Examples at the national level include the following:

The Land Grant University Extension System trains master gardeners capable of responding to questions from the public concerning insects, weeds, plants, and plant diseases. The supervising agent of the extension service reviews the master gardener's recommendations.

The Department of Defense trains young volunteers to aid medical personnel in military and civilian hospitals. The DOD also considers joint military-civilian use of defense installations.

The Small Business Administration created the Service Corps of Retired Executives (SCORE). SCORE helps new business people over the rough spots providing advice and counsel.

Those interested in aviation have a long history of cooperating with the government. The use of airplanes to carry mail was instigated in 1911 by volunteer sportsmen pilots and off-duty commercial pilots flying free of charge until the postal service became convinced of the advantages. That same spirit is alive today in the Civil Air Patrol (CAP), the civilian auxiliary of the United States Air Force. About 60,000 volunteers take part in the program.

They have become famous for air search and rescue missions, flying four out of every five hours flown in such missions, directed by the Air Force. The CAP also maintains a nationwide network of shortwave radio stations as a backup to state and local civil defense communications.

ACTION, The National Volunteer Agency, coordinates efforts with other federal agencies and develops both public and private support for volunteer activities in the United States. ACTION's programs for volunteers include:

Foster Grandparent Program—links older persons with children having special needs.

Retired Senior Volunteer Program—provides volunteer opportunities for retired persons.

Senior Companion Program—links older persons with adults having special needs.

Volunteers in Service to America—uses volunteers to work and live in low-income areas to address local problems.

In America there is a large body of voluntary nongovernment, noncommercial organizations. This group is sometimes referred to as the "third sector"—after government and business. Since 1980 the primary representative of the third sector has been a nonprofit coalition of seven hundred corporate, foundation, and voluntary organization members called the Independent Sector (IS). The IS voluntary organizations represent a myriad of interests, more than twenty separate and distinct causes, including: agriculture, arts and culture, communications, conservation, consumer groups, educational entities, health and medical rehabilitation, labor unions, minority rights, public policy, social welfare, and trade associations. Examples of diverse organizations represented by the IS are the following: American Cancer Society, Boy Scouts of America, Boys Clubs of America, Catholic Charities USA, Ducks Unlimited, Evangelical Lutheran Church in America, Ford Foundation, GE Foundation, Habitat for Humanity, United Way of America, YMCA of the USA, and the National Volunteer Center. The IS organization's mission is to create a national forum capable of encouraging the giving, volunteering, and not-for-profit initiative that helps the public serve people, communities, and causes. It represents the third sector's interests in governmental decision making.

A brief description of some of the many volunteer organizations follows.

Habitat for Humanity International. This Christian organization uses volunteers to build and rehabilitate houses. Low-income potential homeowners work with other volunteers during construction, and later help with other projects. The homeowner is furnished with a small no-interest mortgage for the completed home.

Special Olympics. A program of sports training and athletic competition for mentally retarded people. Over a million members participate in games held in sixty-one countries. The program depends upon volunteer participation.

Both the government and the private sector reach out internationally. The following are just a few of many worthy organizations:

Peace Corps. A 6,000 member program serving in eighty-six countries to help people meet trained manpower needs. Volunteers usually serve for two years.

United Nations Volunteers. An international organization based on the Peace Corps and similar groups. Volunteers are recruited from all UN member nations and serve in projects such as the World Food Organization. Many Americans who become UN volunteers are former Peace Corps volunteers.

Citizens Democracy Corps. A private nonprofit organization dedicated to mobilizing U.S. private sector resources to assist the countries of Central and Eastern Europe and the Commonwealth of Independent States in the transition to democratic institutions.

YMCA International Program Services. Participants include YMCAs, local community groups, academic institutions, and government agencies. Promotes overseas experiences to help develop world-minded citizens. Sponsors International Youth Exchange Program.

Most of these sources will be glad to have your help, but take the time to find the match that will be best for you. In that way, you are more likely to enjoy the work and stick with the project, and that will benefit all concerned.

Why Volunteer?

Each of us is unique in that we are a product of our environment and life experiences. These determine our values and attitudes, which in turn establish the reasons we volunteer. Some of these reasons apply to all age groups and can be summarized as the enjoyment of doing something useful and the unselfish concern for the welfare of others. A more detailed look at the reasons we volunteer includes:

Increased self worth—desire to feel needed.

Interest in the program.

Work for a cause that helps a friend.

Religious reasons.

Broaden experience.

Patriotism and sense of civic duty.

Meeting people.

Appreciation for the problems of others.

Youthful volunteers' reasons center about learning and developing awareness. Examples include:

Internships—working at a job without pay to gain experience and a job reference for future job applications.

Career exploration—seeing if your chosen field is right for you.

Academic credit—earning credit for course equivalency from some schools and colleges that offer it.

Social awareness—getting to know your community and local government better.

Leadership development.

The worker and the homemaker have another set of priorities:

Achieve professional and personal growth.

Use talents and skills not used at work, and develop new skills.

Increase and reinforce skills used on current job.

Create an identity separate from work.

Break up the regular routine.

The senior citizen or retiree needs to remain active for physical and mental health. The following reasons to volunteer apply:

Desire for self-fulfillment; feel useful, needed.

Be involved with the community; spread your knowledge and interests to friends and neighbors.

Be with people and make new friends; have an active social life.

Learn new roles and applications for existing skills.

Obtain intellectual stimulation.

Take on hard-to-fill assignments because of having flexible working hours.

The total monetary value of American volunteer services is more than $64 billion a year. Those over sixty-five years of age contribute over $36 billion worth of volunteer labor annually, and their percentage of the population is predicted to increase.

Qualifications and Expectations

As a volunteer you will use the experience gained from your education, your job, and your hobbies. Volunteer agencies have noted certain qualities that are common to the best volunteers. They are committed to the project, take the initiative, and work without close supervision. When things go wrong they can tolerate change and compromise, or possess the creativity to start a new approach. In remote assignments, particularly in foreign lands, they have the ability to adapt, tolerate loneliness, and keep a sense of humor.

You have a right to expect certain things from a volunteer organization. Your assignment should match your skills and provide a reasonable degree of challenge. The organization should provide specialized training, job familiarization, and continuing communication. Many projects require repetitive activity. If your assignment is lengthy, the organization should provide an opportunity to take on added responsibility.

Before committing yourself to an assignment, visit the program site to be sure you understand what is expected. Satisfy yourself that you believe in the cause and the way the program is run. If a visit is not practical, talk with others who have participated in the program.

Applying for Assignment

When possible, try to choose volunteer work that complements your other activities. This provides variety and helps to avoid burn-out. Apply for an assignment with an inquiry letter. Include a resume so that the volunteer agency can match your qualifications with its requirements. Don't let any disability that you may have deter you, but describe it fully to help in your proper placement. Include age, work experience, and education. Extend the courtesy of return postage on a self-addressed envelope.

To qualify for your voluntary service, the organization served must be nonprofit.

Bibliography

REFERENCE BOOKS

Burek, Deborah M., ed. *Encyclopedia of Associations.* 27th ed. Detroit: Gale Research, 1992. Extensive coverage of associations in the United States.

Carroll, Andrew. *Volunteer USA.* New York: Fawcett Columbine, 1991. A comprehensive guide to worthy causes that need you—from AIDS to the environment to illiteracy—where to find them, and how you can help.

Chambré, Susan Maizel. *Good Deeds in Old Age: Volunteering by the New Leisure Class.* Lexington, MA: Lexington Books, 1987. A study of the impact of volunteering on older people.

Gilbert, Sara. *Lend a Hand: The How, Where, and Why of Volunteering.* New York: Morrow, 1988. Emphasis on the younger volunteer. Lists more than one hundred organizations seeking volunteers, arranged by various categories of activity.

Kipps, Harriet Clyde, ed. *Volunteerism: The Directory of Organizations, Training, Programs and Publications.* 3rd ed. New

Providence, NJ: Bowker, 1991. Comprehensive coverage of all levels of volunteer work.

O'Connell, Brian. *America's Voluntary Spirit: A Book of Readings.* New York: The Foundation Center, 1983. Forty-five selected examples of the voluntary sector's strength and variety in history.

O'Connell, Brian, and Ann Brown O'Connell. *Volunteers in Action.* New York: The Foundation Center, 1989. Describes diverse roles volunteers play to help others and make a difference in their lives.

Weitsman, Madeline. *The Peace Corps.* New York: Chelsea, 1989. The history and contributions of the Peace Corps. Explains training practices and provides examples of the accomplishments of individual volunteers.

PERIODICALS

Earthwatch. 680 Mt. Auburn St., Box 403N, Watertown, MA 02272.

Partners in Education. National Association of Partners in Education, 209 Madison Street, Suite 401, Alexandria, VA 22314. (School volunteers).

Volunteer! Council on International Educational Exchange, 205 E. 42nd Street, New York, NY 10017.

Volunteerism. R.R. Bowker, 121 Chanlon Road, New Providence, NJ 07974.

ASSOCIATIONS

Citizens Democracy Corps. 2021 K Street, NW, Suite 215, Washington, DC 20006. A private nonprofit organization dedicated to mobilizing U.S. private sector resources to assist the countries of Central and Eastern Europe and the Commonwealth of Independent States in the transition to democratic institutions and free market economies. Skilled volunteers work with institutions in countries requesting assistance.

Civil Air Patrol. Bldg. 714, Maxwell AFB, AL 36112–5572. Civilian volunteer auxiliary of the United States Air Force. Publications: *Civil Air Patrol News, Quarterly Public Affairs,* and related materials.

Council on International Educational Exchange. 205 E. 42nd Street, New York, NY 10017. Provides voluntary service opportunities for American students in Western and Eastern Europe. Sponsors a variety of work camps for American and non-American youth in the United States. Publications: *Volunteer,* and related materials.

Earthwatch. 680 Mt. Auburn Street, Box 403, Watertown, MA 02272. Volunteer team members support, physically and financially, ongoing scientific research projects in most disciplines of the sciences, in exchange for being able to work as research assistants for a 2- or 3-week period. Publications: *Earthcorps—Our Daily Planet,* and *Earthwatch* magazine.

Foster Grandparents Program. 1100 Vermont Avenue NW, 6th Fl., Washington, DC 20525. Members, aged sixty and over, provide one-on-one assistance to children with special or exceptional needs. Publication: *Foster Grandparents Program Directory.*

Habitat for Humanity International. 121 Habitat Street, Americus, GA 31709–3498. Ecumenical Christian ministry devoted to providing low-cost, nonprofit housing in partnership with low-income people throughout the world. Extensive use of volunteers. Sponsors over one-hundred projects in twenty-nine countries. Publications: *Habitat World,* and related materials.

Independent Sector. 1828 L Street, NW, Suite 1200, Washington, DC 20036. Purposes are to preserve and enhance our national tradition of giving, volunteering and not-for-profit initiative.

Peace Corps of the United States. 1990 K Street NW, Washington, DC 20526. Seeks to promote world peace and friendship and help people in other countries meet trained manpower needs. Serves eighty-six countries.

Points of Light Foundation. 1737 H Street NW, Washington, DC 20006. Seeks to encourage more Americans to become volunteers. Assists communities in improving the effectiveness of their volunteer activities. Maintains a network of four-hundred affiliated volunteer centers. Publications: *Volnet, Voluntary Action Leadership, Volunteering,* and related materials.

Retired Senior Volunteer Program. 1100 Vermont Avenue NW, Washington, DC 20525. Volunteers, aged sixty and over, performing a wide variety of community services including meal delivery service for those unable to leave their homes, work with schools, health care, and rehabilitation.

Senior Companion Program. Washington Urban League, 2900 Newton Street, NE, Washington, DC 20018. Volunteers, aged sixty and over, who establish a one-to-one relationship with other older persons, particularly the frail elderly in their homes, in an effort to delay or prevent institutionalization.

Service Corps of Retired Executives Association. 409 3rd Street, SW, Suite 5900, Washington, DC 20024. Volunteer program in which business people provide free management assistance to those starting or having problems with, a small business. Publications: *The Savant,* and *Handbook for Counselors.*

Special Olympics International. 1350 New York Avenue, NW, Suite 500, Washington, DC 20005. Seeks to contribute to the physical, social, and psychological development of the mentally retarded through sports training and athletic competition. Games are conducted in sixty-one countries.

United Nations Volunteers. Palais des Nations, CH–1211 Geneva 10, Switzerland. Adult volunteer-specialists from 110 countries working for economic and social progress in 116 developing nations. Publication: *Serving Abroad with UNV,* and related materials.

United Way of America. 701 N. Fairfax Street, Alexandria, VA 22314. Administers staff and volunteer department training through the National Academy for Voluntarism. Conducts competitions and presents Alexis de Tocqueville Society Award to honor outstanding volunteer leaders.

Volunteers in Service to America. 1100 Vermont Avenue NW, Suite 8100, Washington, DC 20525. Individuals committed to improving the self-sufficiency of low-income communities. Volunteers must be at least eighteen years old.

YMCA International Program Services. 356 W. 34th Street, Suite 320, New York, NY 10001. Promotes overseas experiences both for U.S. and foreign young adults to help develop world-minded citizens and foster cultural understanding.

Walking, Jogging, and Running

WALKING IS A SAFE, relaxing form of exercise. It's an activity that helps people of all ages to maintain fitness and health. As we increase walking speed to a jog, it becomes difficult to maintain ground contact with both feet, and we become airborne at some parts of the movement cycle. This more rapid movement increases the heart rate and places other stresses on the body. Over time, these stresses cause the body to adapt by increasing lung capacity, muscular strength, and cardiovascular fitness. When we increase our speed from a jog to a run, additional health benefits will be experienced, provided we follow a proper training program to avoid overexertion and injury.

Legs or arms move when a muscle contracts and pulls them in a given direction. A second, opposing muscle must relax to allow movement to occur. If the second muscle doesn't relax completely the first muscle must use more energy to overcome it. In an ideal situation, the first muscle starts the motion and lets the leg or arm swing under its own momentum. This is called a ballistic stroke. We all experience learning situations where a movement is slow and tentative due to uncertainty, and tension exists between opposing muscles throughout the range of motion. As confidence increases, short ballistic muscle contractions are employed to achieve the desired movement, using less energy. The second muscle acts to slow, stop and reverse movement as required. These principles are applied when a walker or runner moves in a relaxed manner, increasing endurance considerably.

People vary in their ability to adapt to long periods of running, due to the fiber content of their muscles. Muscles are composed of slow twitch (ST) and fast twitch (FT) fibers. ST fibers take longer to reach peak tension (pulling power), but have good endurance and fatigue slowly. FT fibers take a shorter time to reach peak tension, but have poor endurance. A runner whose ST fibers dominate is best suited for long distance endurance events. Where FT fibers dominate, the runner will do best in explosive sprinting events.

Walking or running requires energy, which is obtained from the food we eat. Carbohydrates are the main source of energy during hard exercise. Runners will eat a diet high in pastas and bread for several days before a race.

See your doctor for a medical checkup and a stress test before beginning a jogging or running program. The stress test will reveal any hidden problems and determine your level of fitness. This gives you a starting baseline that will enable you to measure your improvement.

When your training sessions require that you walk or run on a road, it's best to use the left side, facing traffic. Yield to oncoming cars because the driver may not be able to move over due to approaching traffic. If you use the roads at night, wear light colored clothing incorporating some reflective material. Keep in mind that drivers will only see your reflective material if their lights strike it first.

Walking for Fitness and Pleasure

Walking is a moderate path to exercise for fitness. When done at a natural pace it doesn't tend to overstrain the body. However, walking does have the advantage that you can gradually increase the pace or carry more weight to obtain a desired level of conditioning.

At least one foot is on the ground at all times while walking. At each step you land on the heel and roll forward to push off with the toes. Little stress is placed on the body structure. Your body will tend to lean forward when walking fast or when walking for a long time. This shortens your stride and causes fatigue and back pain. Assume an erect posture with shoulders back and relaxed.

Walking is a basic conditioner and supplement to other exercise, especially for running and sports requiring leg strength, such as basketball, soccer, or skiing. Injured runners find brisk walking helps to maintain fitness during recovery periods.

Begin walking sessions at a slow pace. This warm-up period increases the blood supply to the muscles, raising their temperature and making them more pliable, which allows them to stretch. Flexibility can also be improved by including some stretching exercises before starting a brisk walk.

A gradual cooling down period with stretching also helps the heart and blood vessels to return to normal. The reason to stretch and relax muscles becomes apparent when we recall that walking or running involves a prolonged series of muscular contractions. Regular walking for exercise need not be a boring experience. A pleasant Sunday afternoon stroll over open country or through wooded areas provides health benefits for both mind and body. Even the one mile per hour pace of a stroll has the effect of a limbering-up exercise.

The average everyday walker moves at a three mile per hour pace. Hiking or taking walking tours at this pace is another way to mix pleasure with exercise and work off excess calories during vacations.

As you gain strength and endurance, adjust your walking to increase fitness levels. Hikers can increase walking speed and distance, or carry weight in the form of a backpack. Additional stress can be applied by walking up hills or along sandy beaches. The foot-dragging effect produced by sand is also experienced by walking in snow. It is important to raise stress levels gradually over a period of time. We'll talk about warning signs of overexertion when we discuss running.

Walking shoes should fit comfortably, with room for the toes to move, spread, and expand. They should have a flexible sole and upper. The sole should be cushioned to avoid blistering. Adequate support should be given to the heel and arch. This includes adequate lateral support to the heel. The shoes should be lightweight and allow some air circulation. The capacity to "breathe" helps the feet remain drier.

Special walking socks are available that absorb moisture and have extra padding on the heel and foot for cushioning.

Walkers keep their toenails trimmed to avoid bruising. Blisters can be reduced by liberal application of Vaseline to the foot and especially between the toes.

Wear layers of clothing in cool weather and remove outer layers as required to reduce sweating.

Race Walking

Race walking techniques take walking as close as possible to running, without leaving the ground. Competitors must comply with strict rules regarding movement. The front foot must touch the ground before the rear foot is lifted and the leg must be fully locked at the knee in the support phase of the stride. The stride is made as long as possible by rotating the hip forward and down. Each stride is begun with a straight leg to achieve maximum pulling power and avoid walking with bent knees (creeping). Creeping is cause for disqualification, as is lifting. Lifting is a springing motion involving high shoulders and high arm action. Placing the forward foot on the ground before raising the rear foot helps prevent lifting. Lifting can also be prevented by pulling with the leg to move forward rather than pushing off with the rear foot. The sport requires considerable training to build up the stamina needed for competition.

Jogging

It becomes difficult to maintain ground contact with both feet as speed is increased from the level of race walking. You tend to become airborne at some part of the movement cycle. You are then jogging, which is nothing more than a slow run. During jogging or running, a runner actually rises above the normal body height. As the forward foot strikes the ground a jolting action results that can cause discomfort or injury if done without proper preconditioning. Many joggers experience problems when enthusiasm overcomes better judgment regarding the distance traveled during workouts. A novice should limit jogging to no more than two or three miles a day, alternating jogging days with rest days.

Jogging shoe requirements are similar to those described for walking shoes. Make sure the shoe provides proper cushioning for the heel.

Running

As running increases our speed to the threshold of physical pain and potential injury, it's time to ask—why run? The answers are as varied as the people who participate. Some common responses are that running provides a sense of physical well-being, a sense of achievement and self discipline, mental relaxation, or the thrill of competition.

We know that running places stress on our bodies. Your body adapts to stress that is repeated often enough for conditioning to take place. It's a good plan to begin conditioning for running by doing some preventive exercises. Running subjects the lower back and knees to stress. Exercises that condition the lower back include bent leg sit-ups, and others that gently stretch back muscles. Exercises for the legs include the leg lift. This is done from a sitting position on a chair. Place weights on the feet and alternately straighten each knee. Another exercise strengthens shin muscles. Sit on a chair and cross one leg. Push down on the toes as you pull up with your foot. Strengthening these muscles reduces the likelihood of the painful strain called shin splints.

When running, only one foot is on the ground at any time and the pushoff from that foot is so strong that the body is launched into the air with both feet off the ground. Running is a kind of bounding action.

If you plan to take up running, get a physical checkup as described earlier. Begin each running session with a gradual warmup. Start to run in a style that feels natural. Keep your body straight, your head up, and lean slightly forward. Don't exaggerate arm motion. Run with elbows bent but not held against the chest. Your hands should be relaxed to avoid tension in other parts of the body. Each foot should strike the ground at the heel and roll forward, finally pushing off with the toes. Breathe naturally; faster movement often requires breathing through the mouth. The key to efficient running is to run with a smooth, relaxed motion.

Hot temperatures are a threat to runners. When you move a muscle about two-thirds of your food energy generates heat. Your blood carries this excess heat to the skin surface where evaporation of perspiration cools the blood, which returns to the body core. If the day is very hot this system becomes overloaded and body temperatures can rise to dangerous levels. When this begins to happen— slow down. Drink plenty of water to replace the fluids lost from perspiring. Replace lost minerals, particularly potassium, by eating foods such as bananas and vegetables. During the cool-down phase, keep moving to permit maximum evaporation of sweat to lower body temperature.

During cold-weather running, your muscles are colder and tighter. Without a proper warmup period cold muscles are subject to strain. If the heat generated by running doesn't offset the cold, your body core temperature drops and hypothermia sets in.

Runners require rest periods of a day or so after a session of hard training. If you feel sluggish after a warmup period, don't push yourself. While training, balance your stress loads. Run hard enough to build but not so hard that you tear down.

When fatigue accumulates you get an out-of-sorts feeling. You become ill-tempered and impatient. Routine tasks seem difficult. Other signs of fatigue include—pain in joints and muscles, trouble falling asleep, more subject to colds, continual thirst resulting from dehydration, and a tired feeling after sleep. Additional physical warning signs are higher morning pulse rate than normal, sudden weight loss, labored breathing during mild training, dizziness or nausea, and swollen glands in the neck, groin, or underarms.

Long-term overtraining may require weeks of recovery time.

Advanced Training

Your approach to training will be determined by the type of event you plan to run. For a short race you will stress speed training, while a marathon will require strength, pace judgment, and mental endurance.

Competition runners build up their training over a given time cycle in order to reach peak performance at the time of a race. Various training schemes are described below.

Interval training involves a series of speed runs over a set distance in a fixed time with a set recovery jog between each fast stretch. Training is gradually made more intensive by increasing the time, distance, or number of fast runs.

Repetition training utilizes a series of fewer, but longer, speed runs than interval training. The runs are separated by walking or complete rest instead of jogging.

Long, slow distance training is characterized by long, nearly painless, daily tours of the countryside at a pace of seven or eight miles per hour. Surprisingly, this relatively slow training pace enables runners to achieve the much higher speeds needed during competition.

In the Fartlek system, which originated in Sweden, the runner sets the pace. There are no set distances to run fast. The pace may vary from sprinting to a normal race pace, and there is no set time for the recovery jog between fast surges. The runner speeds up when ready to go again. This method is not recommended for inexperienced runners without guidance from a coach.

Racing

Races are run over a variety of distances ranging from 800 meter (m) sprints to ultra-marathons covering as many as 1,300 miles. We'll take a closer look at two popular race types; the 10,000m (6.2 miles) race, and the marathon.

The 10,000m, or 10k race covers about the same distance a runner travels during an average thirty to sixty minute training session. To finish the distance in thirty minutes the runner would have to run 12.4 miles per hour. In sixty minutes the speed would be only 6.2 miles per hour. The challenge of the 10k lies in running the distance faster than a normal training pace, but not too fast. Training for the 10k can be as simple as slightly increasing the pace of one or two training runs each week for about eight weeks. Little or no attention need be paid to long runs, because normal daily training usually supplies all the length required for the 10k. The 10k is short enough to permit quick recovery, allowing the runner to participate in other races in as soon as one week.

The marathon is a twenty-six mile, 385 yard long race. For most runners it's a survival test run slower than normal training pace. Your training program should include long runs, fast runs, and easy runs. Runs must be long enough to cope with the race distance, fast enough to handle its pace, and easy enough to recover between the long and fast work. In a typical training plan, the long runs are taken every other week. Gradually increase their length until they reach the time you expect to take to complete the marathon. Between long runs, run shorter fast runs. Experienced runners pace themselves early in a marathon. This enables them to push on somewhat faster in the last half of the race.

The marathon is a grueling event and your body takes time to recover. Training sessions should be limited to easy running for a month or more after the race. Training for long distance running, such as the marathon, should be undertaken with experienced guidance, which may be found at a running club.

Bibliography

REFERENCE BOOKS

Alford, Jim. *Complete Guide to Running.* New York: Sterling, 1985. Covers the training, tactics, and equipment necessary to compete in running events from 800m to ultra-distance.

Clayton, Derek. *Running to the Top.* Mountain View, CA: Anderson World, 1980. How to achieve goals in running by a former world record holder in the marathon.

Fixx, James F. *The Complete Book of Running.* New York: Random House, 1977. Covers the many facets of the running life. It tells you when, where, how much, what effect, and why.

Joyner, Steven Christopher. *The Joy of Walking: More Than Just An Exercise.* White Hall, VA: Betterway, 1992. Walking basics. Covers exercises, equipment, and diet.

Lawrence, Allan, and Mark Scheid. *Running and Racing After 35.* Boston: Little, Brown, 1990. Training schedules, stretching and strength improvement, and related information designed to bring the mature runner to competitive performance levels.

Lebow, Fred, and Gloria Averbuch. *The New York Road Runners Club Complete Book of Running.* New York: Random House, 1992. Covers training techniques, psychology of running, equipment, and diet.

Martin, David E., and Peter N. Coe. *Training Distance Runners.* Champaign, IL: Leisure, 1991. Integrates scientific knowledge about how the body adapts to training with practical principles for designing training programs for middle- and long-distance runners.

Nelson, Cordner. *Runner's World Advanced Running Book.* Mountain View, CA: Anderson World Books, 1983. Covers physiology, interval training, race strategy. Overall emphasis on training.

Rodgers, Bill, and Priscilla Welch. *Masters Running and Racing.* Emmaus, PA: Rodale, 1991. Advice for runners over forty about how to train, run smarter, run faster, and avoid injury.

Schubert, John. *Running: A Celebration of the Sport and the World's Best Places to Enjoy It.* New York: Fodor's Sports, 1992. Provides advice on training, safety, equipment, and health. Includes list of significant international runs.

Schwartz, Leonard. *Heavy Hands: The Ultimate Exercise.* New York: Warner Books, 1982. An exercise system with emphasis on upper body development using hand weights. Covers relationship to walking and running.

Sheehan, George. *George Sheehan on Running to Win: How to Achieve the Physical, Mental, and Spiritual Victories of Running.* Emmaus, PA: Rodale, 1992. Covers training, techniques, adapting to surroundings, and diet.

Wood, Robert S. *Dayhiker: Walking For Fitness, Fun, and Adventure.* Berkeley, CA: Ten Speed, 1991. Describes various types of walk. Covers techniques, locations, weather, first aid, and diet.

Yanker, Gary D. *Rockport's Complete Book of Exercise Walking.* Chicago: Contemporary Books, 1983. Covers the biomechanics and techniques of walking. Provides advice on building an exercise program and selecting walking equipment.

Yanker, Gary, and Carol Tarlow. *America's Greatest Walks: A Traveler's Guide to 100 Scenic Adventures.* Reading, MA: Addison-Wesley, 1986. Suggested walks throughout the U.S. Information regarding facilities and surroundings.

PERIODICALS

Runner's World. Rodale Press, 33 E. Minor Street, Emmaus, PA 18098.

Running Journal. Carolina Runner, Box 157, Greeneville, TN 37744.

Running Times. Air Age Fitness, Route 7, 251 Danbury Road, Wilton, CT 06897.

Walking! Journal. Walking Journal, c/o Walkways Center, Box 1335, Concord, NH 03302–1335.

Walking Magazine. Walking, 9–11 Harcourt Street, Boston, MA 02116.

ASSOCIATIONS

Achilles Track Club. 1 Times Square, 10th Floor, New York, NY 10036. Disabled runners. To encourage people with all types of disabilities to participate in running. No previous athletic experience necessary. Affiliated with New York Road Runners Club.

American Medical Athletic Association. PO Box 4704, North Hollywood, CA 91617. Encourages endurance sports among physicians and their patients. Sponsors marathons. Also known as American Medical Joggers Association.

American Running and Fitness Association. 9310 Old Georgetown Road, Bethesda, MD 20814. Promotes running and other aerobic activities. Maintains library and conducts educational programs. Publications: *Running and FitNews,* and related materials.

The Athletics Congress of the U.S.A. 200 Jenkins Court, 610 Old York Road, Jenkintown, PA 19046–2627. Serves as the national governing body for track and field, long distance running, and race walking. Arranges international competition for U.S. athletes, and organizes national championships. Provides clinics and training camps. Codifies and enforces athletic rules. Bestows awards and operates hall of fame. Publications: *American Athletics, Athletics Record, Track Technique* magazine, and related material.

Fifty-Plus Fitness Association. PO Box D, Stanford, CA 94309. Men and women aged fifty years and older who run and walk regularly. Circulates newsletters as a means of exchanging information and stimulating interest in all aspects of fifty-plus exercise. Publication: *Fifty-Plus Bulletin.*

International Association of Triathlon Clubs. PO Box 6480, Yorkville Station, New York, NY 10128. Triathlon clubs in thirty countries. Encourages physical fitness through participation in races consisting of three phases—swimming, bicycling, and running. Assists in the establishment of triathlon clubs, provides race information to member clubs. Publications: *Tri-ing Times,* and related material.

National Organization of Mall Walkers. PO Box 191, Hermann, MO 65041. Sponsors walking events and sports and fitness promotional programs. Bestows awards. Publication: *Heart and Sole Newsletter.*

New York Road Runners Club. 9 E. 89th Street, New York, NY 10128. Sponsors 150 races throughout the year, including the New York City Marathon. Conducts classes, clinics, and maintains library. Publications: *New York Running News* magazine, and a newsletter.

Road Runners Club of America. c/o Henley Gibble, 629 S. Washington Street, Alexandria, VA 22314. Sponsors championships and other races on the road, track, and cross-country. Originated a program of fun runs for men, women, and children. Certifies road courses, maintains hall of fame, and bestows awards. Publications: *Footnotes,* and a handbook.

Society of Saunterers, International. 2461 Whitehouse Trail, Gaylord, MI 49735. Promotes walking. Publication: *The Saunterer.*

Triathlon Federation/U.S.A. 3595 E. Fountain Boulevard, Colorado Springs, CO 80910. Coordinates state, regional, and international championships. Designates U.S. Ironman Qualifiers. Conducts seminars. Publications: *Triathlon Times* newsletter, manuals, and a competition guide.

Water Skiing

WATER SKIERS ARE PULLED across the water fast enough to allow them to skim over the surface. Their skis form an inclined surface, raised at the forward edge, that planes on the top of the water. Water skiing is closely related to other pastimes covered in this book: the skier requires an adequately powerful and reliable boat; techniques and moves are similar to downhill skiing and ski jumping; skiboarding shares techniques with surfing and snowboarding; and skiers spend part of their time swimming. Water skiing has come a long way since Ralph Samuelson made his first successful attempt in 1922 on Minnesota's Lake Penn.

Basic water skiing is done on two skis. The first step in becoming a water skier is to learn to "ski on two." Details of the methods are beyond the scope of this work, but let's look at what it takes to get up and running on your skis. Facing the tow boat, put the skis on your feet while floating in the water. The tow boat pilot will idle forward to pull the towline taut. You assume a crouched position with knees drawn up to your chest, skis parallel and their front tips extending above the water. As the boat moves forward, you will be drawn to the surface still in a semi-crouched position, with arms held straight. Keep head erect, and gradually straighten your legs, maintaining some flexure to cushion uneven pressure exerted on them by waves or boat wakes. Don't yield to the temptation to bend your arms and pull on the rope. It will move you forward and cause your skis to dig in, causing you to fall forward.

To change direction, rotate your skis and tilt your shoulders in the direction you wish to go. Lean back during the direction change maneuver.

Combination skis (combos) are useful beginners' skis. Besides the normal foot binding on each ski, one of the skis has a second foot binding located behind the normal location. As your skills increase, you will want to learn to maneuver on one ski. This is where the second foot binding comes in. Most people will be comfortable with their left foot in the forward binding. Some will prefer the right foot

forward. Water skiers have adopted the surfer term for the latter position. It's called the "goofy-foot" stance. Single ski operation (skiing on one) provides the added mobility desired for slalom skiing. In slalom skiing, the tow boat is guided in a straight line between two rows of buoys, and the skier follows a zig-zag course around other buoys set farther away from the path of the boat. As a skier becomes adept at this form of skiing and begins to compete, the next step is to purchase a specially designed slalom ski. Slalom skis should be selected to match the style of the skier. There is a trade-off between stability and maneuverability. The combo style ski provides stability for the beginner. The advanced slalom ski sacrifices some qualities to obtain others. More on this below.

Equipment

Skiers require a tow boat with an adequate speed range to compensate for the surface drag of the skis, the skiers weight, and other factors.

Minimum speed requirements increase as the bottom surface area of the ski decreases. Faster speeds are also required for heavier skiers. A 160-pound adult will water ski on two skis at an average of about twenty-five mph. When performing slalom maneuvers with one ski, the speed goes up to about thirty mph. When performing tricks on the wider trick skis, the speed requirements drop to the fifteen mph range. Very wide skiboards, similar to small surfboards, are used at speeds ranging from ten mph to forty mph, depending on the application. With all of the variables due to skier weight, skier activity at any given moment, and the skis being used, it is apparent that the ski boat pilot must be very familiar with the sport in order to properly time speed changes.

An observer is usually carried as a second member of the boat's crew. The observer watches the skier at all times and communicates the skier's needs to the pilot.

Instant communication between the skier and the tow boat pilot is essential during the fast-paced activity associated with water skiing. Verbal signals are possible when motor noise levels are low during start-up. They are chosen to minimize similarity to words with different meanings. To signal the pilot to move away to straighten the towline, say "take up slack." To begin rapid acceleration to lift you to the water's surface, say "hit it." Once up and moving, hand signals come into play. Some examples include: Thumbs up means speed up. Thumbs down, slow down. The okay signal, with thumb and forefinger forming an O means speed is okay. A slicing motion across the neck means cut the engine. When a fall occurs, one or more arms are waved over the head to signal you're okay.

As the tow boat moves through the water it leaves a V-shaped wake in its path. The wake is like a small wave. The wave's shape is determined by the shape of the boat's hull, boat speed, and other variables in the propulsion system. Skiers like the smooth wake formed by V-hulled boats. They steer their skis through and over the wake as a challenge and to use it as a launching point to make jumps. Skiboarders ride the wake as they would a wave while surfing.

The tow boat is fitted with an attach point for the towline. On boats used in competition the attach point is often located at the top of a pylon placed at the middle of the boat. A standard towline is seventy feet long with a five foot handle bridle, for a full length of seventy-five feet. Special towlines are used for slalom competition where line lengths are shortened in increments to speed directional changes. These lines have loops at designated points along the line to facilitate reattachment at the pylon.

Skis are usually designed for a particular aspect of the sport. Let's look at some design elements and see how they affect performance.

Ski bottoms are usually scooped out along their length. A narrow (width) recess provides stability. A shallow (depth) recess allows easier turns. The bottom lengthwise edges may have a chamfer (bevel), or may be rounded (radiused). A large bevel increases stability, but causes more drag. A rounded edge rolls sideways more easily. The shape, as viewed from above, makes a difference. Skis that are narrow at the front will turn more sharply, but offer less forward support to a skier who prefers smooth gradual turns. Other variables in ski design include the amount of curvature seen when viewed from the side (rocker), the amount of stiffness built into the ski (flex), and the shape of the fin.

All skiers should wear a personal flotation device. These Coast Guard-approved life jackets for skiers should fit snugly, and have large armholes to permit free arm movement.

Water dissipates body heat quickly. If you plan to ski for long periods, even in temperate waters, consider the purchase of a wet suit. These neoprene rubber suits are made in many styles. Skiers often choose a design that exposes their lower arms, and lower legs. Water ski jumpers wear a special wet suit with extra padding and extra flotation built-in to eliminate the need for a personal flotation device. They also wear special helmets.

All water skiers benefit from the use of ski gloves. They prevent blisters caused by gripping the towline handle.

Other Skiing-Related Activities

Tow boats are used to pull hobbyists over the water on everything from inner tubes to their bare feet. A few examples follow.

Tubes and Kneeboards

A skier's balance must be maintained when standing on skis while moving across the water. Although not considered especially good form, the closer one's body is to the water (keeping a low center of gravity), the easier it is to maintain balance. For this reason children and beginners enjoy being towed on devices such as truck inner tubes and kneeboards, where their low center of gravity provides a stable ride. The truck inner tubes have been replaced by specially designed tubes with hand holds. Kneeboards look like a small surfboard. The skier kneels on the board and attaches a strap over the thighs to prevent slipping off the board. The kneeboard is steered by leaning in the direction you wish to go. In the hands of advanced riders, tricks are performed such as rotating the board front to back, or all the way around (360 degrees) while under tow.

Freestyle Skiing

Hotdogging, or freestyle skiing, involves jumping, somersaults and other tricks performed on special skis. The trick skis are wider, shorter, and built tougher to withstand the high impact placed on them.

Professional water ski jumpers remain airborne for more than two-hundred feet. Boat speed is carefully regulated in competition, since it contributes to the distance traveled during the jump. Thirty-five mph is typical for professional men; however, the course the skier travels in the approach to a jump imparts a whipping action that propels the skier to speeds over seventy mph. Skis for jumping are very specialized and expensive. The sport should be learned from a qualified coach.

Barefoot Skiing

Barefoot skiing is another sport best left to advanced skiers and professionals. Since you are using your feet as skis, the surface area in contact with the water is relatively small. This means that boat speeds in the thirty-six to forty-four mph range are required. If your toes happen to dig in, you hit the water long before you have time to think about it. You will have plenty of time afterwards to nurse the bruises. The start can be accomplished from a moving kneeboard, a single ski, or with practice, from water without any other aids.

Kite Skiing

Kite skiing involves the towing of a skier suspended below a large kite. As boat speed is increased, the kite becomes airborne. Altitude is maintained by the speed of the boat. The skier has some lateral control by shifting weight to one side, as with hang gliding.

Skiboarding

A skiboard is similar to a small surfboard. Some designs include a fin underneath at the rear for stability, as with a surfboard. Skiboarding is much like snowboarding. When tow boat speeds are limited to ten mph, the sensation is like that of surfing. Skiers can ride the wake wave at that speed. Boat speed must be increased to about twenty mph for wake crossing and slalom patterns. At boat speeds of about forty mph, the skiboard acts like a water ski. Aside from the much wider configuration, the skiboard differs from the slalom ski in that the foot bindings are positioned at right angles to the ski, as opposed to facing forward. This means that steering control is accomplished by use of heel or toe pressure. When you push down with your toes, the board will go in the direction your toes are pointing. Another unique aspect is the concept of frontside and backside movement. As you cross the wake in the direction you are facing, you make a frontside crossing. When you cross in the other direction, you are backing across it.

Safety

Water skiing is a sport that abruptly places stress on the body at the start of the activity. It's advisable to do stretching and warm-up exercises before beginning, in order to ease the transition. When fatigue sets in, stop for a rest. Never ski tired; it slows your reaction time, increasing the chance of injury.

Beginners should learn to swim, and get into reasonably fit condition before beginning training with a competent instructor.

Bibliography

REFERENCE BOOKS

Duvall, Camille, with Nancy Crowell. *Camille Duvall's Instructional Guide to Water Skiing.* New York: Simon & Schuster, 1992. Comprehensive coverage of water skiing. Well illustrated, detailed instruction. Emphasis on slalom skiing.

Klarich, Tony. *Hot Dog Slalom Skiing: An Illustrated Guide to Over Thirty Amazing Maneuvers.* Winter Park, FL: World, 1988. Well illustrated, step-by-step instructions for performing freestyle maneuvers on water skis. Includes boat driving tips.

Robertson, Jo. *Boating Watersports: The Ultimate Get-Started Guide to Towing Fun.* Winter Park, FL: World, 1990. An overview of the various forms of water skiing. Covers equipment and techniques.

PERIODICALS

Water Ski. World Publications, 330 W. Canton Avenue, Box 2456, Winter Park, FL 32789–3195.

Water Skier. American Water Ski Association, 799 Overlook Drive, Winter Haven, FL 33884.

ASSOCIATIONS

American Barefoot Club. c/o American Water Ski Association, 799 Overlook Drive, Winter Haven, FL 33884. Enthusiasts of barefoot water skiing. Establishes rules and regulations for tournaments, bestows award.

American Water Ski Association. 799 Overlook Drive, Winter Haven, FL 33884. Promotes competitive and recreational water skiing. Establishes rules for competition, and conducts training programs for instructors and officials. Maintains hall of fame and library. Bestows awards. Publishes *Water Skier,* and related materials.

Weather Forecasting

WEATHER INFORMATION IS USEFUL to almost any outdoor hobbyist. Inclement weather can be life threatening to flyers, sailors, or those who frequent remote high altitude locations such as backpackers, hunters, or skiers. Professional weather forecasts are most accurate for stormy weather conditions that tend to extend over broad areas. When overall fair weather conditions are reported, one must consider local factors that modify the general forecast. At noon on a sunny day, a south facing slope may be ten or more degrees warmer than a north facing slope. On a clear calm night, the temperature in a low lying area may be twenty degrees colder than on a nearby slope. Windchill effects from a mild breeze or the cooling down caused by a cold fog can easily reduce body temperatures, producing hypothermia when the temperatures are in the fifties. A weatherwise person will enjoy the outdoors in greater comfort and safety.

Weather Basics

Since the earth is tilted at 23.5 degrees to its year-long path around the sun, the upper and lower hemispheres take turns tilting toward the sun. This produces the seasons with their varying temperatures. The tropical areas near the equator are least affected, still getting the largest share of the sun's energy. The high temperatures and high humidity reduce air pressure around the equator. Around the poles, the low temperatures and low humidity increase pressure. Air movement in the form of wind moves from high pressure areas to low pressure areas. Wind might be expected to blow in a straight line to the south if it weren't for the fact that the earth rotates from west to east under the winds. The rotation causes the winds to flow in a curved path with respect to the earth's surface. The motion is called the Coriolis Effect. As the air over land at the equator becomes heated it rises and spreads its heat energy toward the poles. Equatorial air over the sea carries water vapor toward the poles. As it approaches cooler air the water vapor condenses and becomes rain.

The above generalized air mass movements are diverted by major land masses and the oceans in between. The air splits up into pressure cells around which the air moves. Low pressure cells create strong circular air movements called cyclones. High pressure cells create light circular winds called anticyclones. The Coriolis Effect produces counterclockwise air movement in cyclones in the Northern Hemisphere. Anticyclonic air moves clockwise.

A front is the boundary between two air masses having different characteristics. The primary difference is their relative temperature. Other differences include dew point, barometric pressure, wind direction, and wind velocity. Although the difference in temperature of the air masses may not be large, when the cooler mass advances it is termed a cold front. An advancing warm mass is called a warm front. When a strong cold front encounters a warm air mass it forces its way under the warm air rapidly driving the warm air up to higher altitudes where it is cooled and clouds are formed. The clouds often produce thunderstorms. If a warm front predominates, the warmer of the two air masses is lighter, so as they come together it will slide over the cooler air creating a boundary with a gentle slope. As the warm air continues to rise, it too will create clouds and precipitation in the form of rain, snow, sleet or freezing rain. When cold and warm air masses meet and are of relatively equal strength, a stationary front is created. Widespread clouds can form on both sides of the boundary. The front may dissipate or resolve itself into an active front. Another type of front, called an occluded front, occurs when cold, warm and cool air come in conflict, forming boundaries above ground as well as at the surface.

The principal source of our rain and wind is the extratropical cyclone. In the Northern Hemisphere, this is a traveling system of winds rotating counterclockwise around a center of low barometric pressure and containing a warm front and a cold front. The sharp contrasts of temperature and wind that are present often generate low pressure areas with counterclockwise winds swirling in towards the center. As the air moves inward, it replaces air being sucked upward and outward from the center of the low. This upward motion produces clouds and rain as the air cools and reaches saturation.

Air has its ups and downs for other reasons too. On a sunny day, air heated by contact with the hot ground rises. The upward movements of air are called thermals. If the air contains sufficient water vapor, the cooling caused by the expansion of the rising air will reach a point where condensation occurs and a cloud is formed. The added heat energy provided by the condensing water vapor can push the air still higher, triggering precipitation. The local rising thermals are balanced by a broad slow-moving downward flow of cool air. An exception to the slow downward flow occurs when very dry air either enters the area under a thunderstorm or already exists there. Evaporating rain cools the dry air causing it to plunge rapidly toward the ground, creating what is termed a microburst. These violent downdrafts are a safety hazard to aircraft, especially when flying close to the ground.

The temperature at which the water vapor present in air produces saturation, and condenses into a visible cloud, is called the dewpoint. When the air temperature and the dewpoint temperature coincide, fog or other forms of a cloud can develop. When air becomes saturated the water vapor is attracted to cloud condensation nuclei. The nuclei are primarily tiny particles of salt or dust. Salt particles enter the atmosphere from the sea due to wave action and the bursting of bubbles. Clay particles resulting from erosion also serve as nuclei. When gaseous water molecules accumulate about the nuclei, condensation takes place, creating a cloud droplet. The droplets join together, or coalesce, to form raindrops. Under certain conditions the droplets form ice crystals that can become snow, hail, or sleet. A falling raindrop takes on a shape similar to the head of a mushroom, as opposed to the streamlined shape often depicted coming from a faucet. The particles in the air, so important to the formation of water droplets, scatter sunlight to form the white rays seen radiating outward from a cloud, particularly when the sun is at a low angle. They are termed crepuscular rays. Blue skies are also caused by the scattering of light. White light coming from the sun is composed of all the colors of the rainbow. Air molecules are the right size to scatter blue and violet light wavelengths, the remaining colors continue on to the surface.

Cloud Types

Clouds provide visible evidence of weather conditions. Sailors have known this in a general way for hundreds of years. In 1802 a cloud classification system was developed by an amateur observer, and presented to a small club of London-

ers. Englishman Luke Howard felt that there must be a cause-effect relationship taking place in the atmosphere to produce the many forms of clouds. He noted that there were three basic shapes of clouds: Heaps of separated cloud masses with flat bottoms and cauliflower tops that he named cumulus (heap). Clouds in uniform layers such as a low fog or a heavy haze not touching the ground were assigned the name stratus (layer). Wispy curls like mare's tails were called cirrus (curl). Another category was set aside for clouds that generated precipitation—nimbus (rain). The cloud categories are subdivided further to identify the altitude at which they are found: Low clouds up to 8,000 feet, medium clouds from 8,000 to 20,000 feet, and high clouds found over the 20,000-foot level. Howard's work is considered a classic in the history of science. German poet and scientist Johann Wolfgang Goethe was so impressed with Howard's work that he dedicated four nature poems to the pioneer in meteorology. In the following discussion individual cloud types will be described together with their significance regarding weather forecasting.

Low level clouds consist of the following:

Stratocumulus (Sc). Forms in layers or patches of rolls or waves. It is usually accompanied by chopy winds. Usually not associated with rain, but mist or drizzle is possible.

Nimbostratus (Ns). A low, dense, and dark cloud layer that usually produces steady rain or snow. Ragged in appearance, it usually evolves from altostratus which lies above.

Cumulus (Cu). This heap-type fair-weather cloud is white and fluffy. It forms at the top of a thermal current. This cloud type is a favorite of both full-scale and model glider pilots who take advantage of this updraft marker.

Stratus (St). A uniform layer of low fog, or heavy haze. Frequently forms below nimbostratus, and sometimes produces sprinkles or drizzle.

Cumulonimbus (Cb). Formed from cumulus clouds, they build up vertically and form thunderheads full of turbulence, violent updrafts, lightning, and hail. Their bases are low and tops often reach above 30,000 feet.

Medium level clouds consist of the following:

Altostratus (As). A dense, grayish sheet, similar to cirrostratus, but heavier and lower. It usually produces rain or snow.

Altocumulus (Ac). Pronounced puffy globules, ripples, or bands of cloud often called a "mackerel sky." It indicates brewing storm conditions.

High level clouds consist of the following:

Cirrus (Ci). Thin wispy clouds often called mare's tails. They are the highest clouds of all, and consist of ice crystals. They often come from the anvil-shaped tops of thunderheads. When formed as long narrow bands, they are associated with low pressure and can signal weather deterioration. When they are light and thin they usually indicate fair weather.

Cirrostratus (Cs). A thin layer of high haze made up of ice crystals that often produce a halo around the sun or moon. They usually indicate bad weather in twenty-four to thirty-six hours.

Cirrocumulus (Cc). Small, high altitude clouds with a fine grain or ripple pattern of white masses or blobs. They also have a mackerel sky appearance that signals changing weather patterns, including stormy weather.

The sky is often filled with combinations of the above cloud types, making accurate predictions difficult. An observer should practice combining the information gathered from weather reports with the indications presented by local cloud formations.

Courses in the study of weather forecasting are available by correspondence, and various continuing education sources such as university evening classes. Boaters can contact their local United States Power Squadron or United States Coast Guard Auxiliary to determine the availability of special classes. Aircraft pilots receive classes in meteorology through flight training schools.

Weather History

When the astronauts saw earth's thin layer of atmosphere from their space vehicles, they were in awe at how fragile and vulnerable it appeared. Scientists conducting research on the history of our atmosphere and weather are finding long-term variations in the climate. The challenge is to identify the causes of past changes. Precipitation in Antarctica has built up layers of ice as much as three miles thick. The ice contains the recorded history of climate, human activity, and global change. It contains ash from an 1883 volcanic eruption, lead from 1950s automobile exhaust, and radioactive waste from 1960s nuclear tests. To study the ice, scientists collect samples with a drilling rig much like a small version of an oil drill. A hollow shaft follows the drill head into the ice, and an ice core is extracted. The core is then refrigerated and transported to a laboratory for study. The ice from some cores dates back 200,000 years. It has been found that carbon dioxide and oxygen isotope data give firm evidence that when carbon dioxide in the atmosphere increases, temperature does too.

Study of such cores has revealed that 25,000 years ago and again at 65,000 years ago earth's average temperature declined to ten degrees C. colder than it is today. About 140,000 years ago the earth's average temperature peaked at two degrees warmer than today, and stayed near the same level as it is today for about 20,000 years.

Geologists and paleontologists provide other climate indicators. Ancient sedimentary rocks have ripples caused by wave action. Sedimentary rocks that were formed in lakes on land masses contain pollen grains that were deposited in layers of clay in the past. Their age and distribution indicate periods of favorable weather for plant growth. Fossil sea creatures help define early ocean locations and the extent of their coverage. Fossil plants and animals define early land masses. Botanists study tree rings to pinpoint years of drought or high rainfall. With inputs such as the above, meteorologists can deduce continental shapes, temperatures, moisture precipitation, and other factors that determined weather patterns in the past. As we have seen, weather forecasting on a daily basis is a highly complex process. However, knowledge of historical trends assists in the preparation of long-range weather forecasting.

Equipment

A starter set of instruments for an amateur weather watcher includes the following:

Thermometer. Used to measure air temperature. It should have both Fahrenheit and Celsius scales because both types of units will be encountered in meteorology. A six-type maximum-minimum thermometer has sliding iron indicators that record the extremes of temperature encountered during a given period of time. Varieties of digital thermometers are also available.

Rain gauge. A simple calibrated open-topped vessel for catching rain to determine the amount of rainfall.

Barometer. Used to measure atmospheric pressure. A single reading is less important than a series of readings over time that indicates trends.

Wind sock or weather vane. Used to determine wind direction.

Anemometer. Used to measure wind speed. Often made with a set of spinning cups that catch the wind. The wind speed usually registers indoors on an electrical dial.

Psychrometer or Hygrometer. Instruments used to measure humidity. A sling psychrometer consists of two thermometers, one is a standard thermometer arrangement having a dry bulb at the base of the mercury column. The other thermometer is fitted with a sock covering its bulb. The instrument is whirled around to cause rapid evaporation of the liquid on the wet bulb, lowering its temperature. Both thermometers are then read and standard tables are used to determine relative and other humidity readings. Dial hygrometers are also available that may be somewhat less accurate.

Weather Information

National Weather Service and Other Sources

The National Weather Service provides observations, general forecasts, and special forecasts such as river level and general thunderstorm and tornado forecasting. This data is supplied to local weather service offices who produce basic public forecasts, aviation forecasts, and marine forecasts. The data is used as a starting point by private forecasting firms, and local TV weather reports.

The National Weather Service makes use of data collected by weather balloons from about five hundred worldwide locations, from satellite photographs, specially equipped aircraft, radar, and other equipment.

Pilots access weather data from flight service stations by telephone. A timely source is the A.M. weather telecast on the PBS television network, broadcast Monday through Friday mornings. A useful portable weather source is a special low-frequency radio with which you can listen to the transcribed weather broadcast on the 150 to 400 kHz band. For the dedicated weather watcher, there are numerous private industry sources that supply information on a pay for information received, or contract pay basis. Various forms of up-to-date weather charts are provided by FAX machine. The beginning forecaster will find daily newspaper weather charts useful.

Weather Charts

The weather information gathered from many locations is presented on maps in a way that weather forecasters (meteorologists) and knowledgeable users can interpret overall weather conditions. By viewing several such maps, or charts, at known time intervals, weather trends can be seen to develop. The cluster of symbols shown in Figure 1 represents the information that may be received from a single weather station and presented at the station's location on the map. It was taken from an example furnished in Elbert S. Maloney's book, *Piloting: Seamanship and Small Boat Handling*. While a detailed review of the information presented is beyond the scope of this work, we'll look at several significant pieces of the information. The black circle at the center represents a completely cloud-covered sky. If the cloud cover is less, more of the

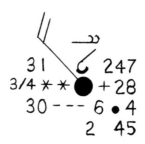

Figure 1

This group of numbers and symbols represents the weather picture at a specific weather station. All, or part of, the data shown appear on weather maps at the various station locations. See text for interpretation of the coded information.

circle's disk is shown as white. The "flag," that looks like a musical note angling off to the left, shows that the wind is coming from the northwest. The number and shape of the lines depicting the flag indicate wind speed. The two "tails" on the flag shown indicate a wind speed of twenty-one to twenty-five mph. The number 247 represents a barometric pressure of 1024.7 milibars, the initial 9 or 10 is omitted. A meteorologist draws lines (isobars) connecting the stations having the same barometric pressure. The resulting pattern reveals the locations of highs and lows. The direction that the various flags point reveals the total wind pattern. These patterns enable trained personnel to locate fronts, and they are drawn on the chart. We have seen the importance of fronts as sources of precipitation and storms. Cold fronts are drawn with a series of triangles forming a sawtooth pattern on one side indicating the direction the front is moving. Warm fronts are shown with a series of half circles on one side to indicate their direction of motion. The data selected for inclusion on a weather chart are determined by the requirements of the user. For example, pilots find charts showing wind flow information at flight altitudes very important.

Bibliography

REFERENCE BOOKS

Atkinson, B. W., and Alan Gadd. *Weather*. New York: Weidenfeld and Nicolson, 1987. A well-illustrated guide to basic meteorology in pocket book format.

Day, John A., and Vincent J. Schaefer. *Peterson First Guide to Clouds and Weather*. Boston: Houghton Mifflin, 1991. A brief illustrated pocket guide to the atmosphere.

Gallant, Roy A. *Earth's Changing Climate*. New York: Four Winds, 1979. Covers the earth's climate with emphasis on its history.

Goldsack, Paul John. *Weatherwise: Practical Weather Lore for Sailors and Outdoor People*. North Pomfret, VT: David and Charles, 1986. An investigation of old weather lore, sayings, and rhymes including conclusions relative to their accuracy and reliability in forecasting.

Ludlum, David M. *The American Weather Book.* Boston: Houghton Mifflin, 1982. Covers significant weather events in history.

————. *The Audubon Society Field Guide to North American Weather.* New York: Knopf, 1991. A comprehensive well illustrated pocket guide to the understanding of weather phenomena and forecasting.

Maloney, Elbert S. *Chapman Piloting, Seamanship and Small Boat Handling.* 60th ed. New York: Hearst Marine Books, 1991. First written by Charles F. Chapman at the request of Franklin D. Roosevelt in 1922, this book has been continually updated over the years. It provides comprehensive coverage of boating information, including a chapter on weather and the yachtsman.

Mitchell-Christie, Frank. *Practical Weather Forecasting.* Woodbury, NY: Barron's, 1978. A brief summary of weather forecasting basics.

Reifsnyder, William E. *Weathering the Wilderness: The Sierra Club Guide to Practical Meteorology.* San Francisco: Sierra Club Books, 1980. An introduction to meteorology with emphasis on the climate patterns in selected areas of the United States.

Schaefer, Vincent J., and John A. Day. *A Field Guide to the Atmosphere.* Boston: Houghton Mifflin, 1981. Part of the Peterson field guide series. A useful pocket guide to the weather with emphasis on cloud identification and interpretation. Contains interesting coverage of snow crystal photography.

TAB-Aero Staff. *AIM/FAR 1992: Airman's Information Manual/ Federal Aviation Regulations.* Blue Ridge Summit, PA: TAB Aero, 1992. A compilation of federal aviation regulations. Includes a section on meteorology for pilots.

Williams, Jack. *The Weather Book.* New York: Random House, 1992. A comprehensive weather guide from the people who developed the *USA Today*'s newspaper weather page.

PERIODICALS

Local Climatological Data. U.S. National Climatic Data Center, Federal Building, MC–02, Asheville, NC 28801–2696.

Mariners Weather Log. U.S. National Oceanographic Data Center, NOAA–NESDIS, E–OC2, Universal Bldg. 1, Room 415, 1825 Connecticut Avenue, NW, Washington, DC 20235.

Weatherwise. Heldref Publications, 1319 Eighteenth Street, NW, Washington, DC 20036–1802.

ASSOCIATIONS

American Meteorological Society. 45 Beacon Street, Boston, MA 02108. Meteorological professionals and interested individuals. Develops and disseminates information on the atmospheric and related oceanic and hydrospheric sciences. Provides educational materials, guidance and scholarships. Sponsors workshops and bestows awards. Publications: *AMS Newsletter, Bulletin of the American Meteorological Society, Journal of Applied Meteorology, Journal of Atmospheric and Oceanic Technology, Journal of the Atmospheric Sciences, Journal of Climate, Journal of Physical Oceanography, Meteorological and Geastrophysical Abstracts, Monthly Weather Review, Weather and Forecasting,* and related material.

Association of American Weather Observers. PO Box 455, Belvidere, IL 61008. Observer networks, school weather clubs, professional and amateur meteorologists. Seeks to facilitate communication and cooperation among enthusiasts. Bestows awards, and scholarship. Publications: *American Weather Observer,* and related material.

Woodworking

OR THOUSANDS OF YEARS man has shaped needed objects from wood, an easily worked and readily available raw material. Flint knives were once used to cut and scrape the wood to make weapons and other implements. Primitive tribes made canoes by using a controlled fire to hollow a log. Modern individuals engrave wood using controlled lasers to instantaneously burn material away, creating intricate shapes. Some tools evolve; others are reinvented. Tools are an important link between ourselves and the workpiece. They serve as extensions of a worker's skillful hands. Properly designed tools feel right and minimize work effort when applied to the task for which they were intended.

Working with wood is a satisfying, rewarding and challenging experience. Woodworkers enjoy the sight of beautiful grain patterns, the aroma of freshly cut wood and the smooth feel of a properly worked surface. It can be challenging in that the material sometimes seems to have a mind of its own. The wood can warp, shrink, or have swirling grain that surprises the unwary worker by binding a saw or causing a hand plane to catch and break out chips.

General Procedures

All woodworking projects follow a similar sequence of events. Let's use a simple bench as an example. First locate a measured drawing of the bench or develop a plan yourself. Such drawings can be found in woodworking magazines or books.

Next procure the necessary materials. Lumber yards are fine for common woods such as pine or oak, but you may have to go to a specialty supplier to locate walnut, cherry or mahogany needed for furniture or cabinetmaking projects. These sources also stock a wider range of sizes, from very thin wood used for veneering to thick pieces used to carve an ornate chair leg or to turn a bowl. If supplies can't be found locally, try mail-order houses. You'll find their advertisements in woodworking magazines.

With the drawing as a guide, lay out the pattern of each piece on the wood. A tape rule will most likely be used for measuring distances and lines will be drawn along the blade of a combination square or carpenter's square to guide saw cuts. (See Figure 1.) The line will be scribed with an awl or simply drawn with a pencil. As the old adage goes, "Measure twice, cut once." Doing so will prevent a lot of waste.

In view of the characteristics of wood, it is best to cut out pieces as you need them in the sequence of assembly. If the long piece needed for the bench top is spoiled while cutting, you may be able to cut smaller pieces such as the legs from it and turn to another piece for the top.

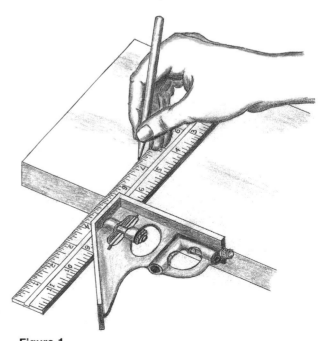

Figure 1

Using a combination square to lay out a line perpendicular to the edge of a piece of wood.

The sequence of cutting operations on each piece should be considered. Leave extra stock on a part requiring final trim at assembly. Drill holes before assembly in areas that will be inaccessible later. You may need to drill undersized holes for nails used to assemble hardwood to avoid splitting. This is best done when the pieces are in position for assembly. Even the most experienced woodworkers sometimes find themselves "painted into a corner" when they fail to notice the requirements of assembly sequence.

Begin cutting out parts using a crosscut saw to make cuts across the grain and a rip saw to cut with the grain. A coping saw is used when abrupt changes are required in the path of the cut. Other tools that may be required include a hand plane to smooth the saw cuts and a chisel to remove wood from slots. A brace or hand drill is used to make holes for fasteners.

Assembly is accomplished by using carpenter's glue and nails or screws. When using screws, use a screwdriver of appropriate size. The tip should be the same width as the screw slot to avoid slipping off and damaging the part or the screw head.

After assembly give the bench a final sanding and apply the finish. One of the least understood of all tools is sandpaper. Charts are often found on the back of sandpaper packages that enable the user to make a suitable selection of sandpaper type and grade for the material being sanded. The least expensive type is usually aluminum oxide. When working with unfinished wood you will find garnet paper to be longer lasting and perhaps cheaper in the long run. Waterproof silicon carbide paper is often used when a fine finish is required. The ultra fine grades can be used with soapy water on finished surfaces to achieve a hand rubbed finish, requiring only a final buffing.

Hand Tool Selection

The beginning woodworker is advised to invest in hand tools first to keep start-up costs low. You will find them useful in combination with power tools on future projects.

A useful starter set of hand tools will be found below. Buy tools as you need them, and buy the best you can afford. Good tools will often last a lifetime.

1. Claw hammer with curved claw for general purpose use.
2. Screw drivers for slotted head and Phillips head screws.
3. Crosscut saw—11- or 12-point.
4. Rip saw—5½- to 7-point.
5. Coping saw.
6. Power saber saw (may substitute for item 5).
7. Jack or smoothing plane (Figure 2).
8. Block plane.
9. Combination square.

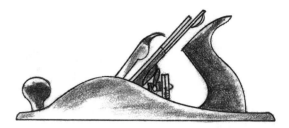

Figure 2
Jack Plane

10. Tape measure—¾ inch wide and 12 to 16 feet long.
11. Brace with auger bits.
12. Hand drill
13. Power hand drill—⅜ inch chuck (may substitute for items 11 and 12).
14. Chisels—set of straight-sided, heavy duty, in the ¼, ½, ¾ and one-inch sizes.
15. C-Clamps.
16. Handscrew clamps (Jorgensen clamps). (See Figure 3.)

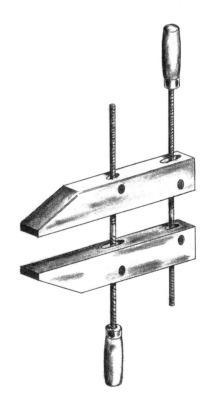

Figure 3
Handscrew Clamp

Advanced Techniques

Increasingly complex projects can be undertaken as techniques are mastered. Suppose the next project is a chest of drawers. Once again we begin with a plan, using it as a guide to accumulate the required materials.

In this case construction begins with the frame that holds the drawers. This is called the carcase. Portions of the carcase that are not exposed to view are often made of less expensive woods such as poplar or pine.

The carcase must be built square and to close dimensional tolerances so that drawers will fit and operate freely. Two pieces are said to be square with one another when they meet at right angles, or ninety degrees. Assemblies are sometimes measured diagonally across corners each way to determine squareness. A carcase or drawer is square when the dimensions are equal.

A cabinetmaker or carpenter may choose to either hide or emphasize the joints in a chest. The horizontal drawer supports may be made with a tongue that fits into a groove in the vertical end pieces, hiding the joint and affording added strength. In an Early American style chest, the tongue or tenon of a mortise and tenon joint may extend through an end piece and be pinned with several dowels visible from the front. A perfect fit in such a joint testifies to the craftsmanship of the cabinetmaker. Careful examination of a fine piece of furniture will reveal tongue and groove joints, lapped joints, and dovetail joints. More intricate joints of these types are used to achieve a desired result. It may be to provide rigidity, afford more gluing surface for greater strength, allow for expansion and contraction or simply to contribute to the aesthetics of the design. A good woodworking text will illustrate many such joints and explain the methods used to create them. No matter how complex the joint, it is prepared one cut at a time. It is a case of measure, scribe and cut until the desired shape is achieved. The worker will often use a back saw for fine work of this type. It has a metal stiffener fastened to the back side of the blade. A typical backsaw will have fourteen points or more. Saws having such fine teeth cut more slowly, but leave a smoother cut. A back saw may be used to cut the dovetail joints found at the corners of drawers in fine furniture. Back saws are often used in conjunction with a miter box or other guide to assure accuracy of the cut.

Drawers are built last to custom-fit the carcase. Again drawer bottoms, sides and backs are usually made with less expensive wood.

Power Tools

The foregoing description has focused on the use of hand tools. They can be used in combination with hand power tools or the entire job can be accomplished with large stationary power tools if they are available. Square accurate cuts are easier to make using fences and guides furnished with power tools to position the workpiece. Special jigs can also be built to hold pieces or guide tools to ensure accurate, repetitive cuts. Such jigs expand the capabilities of a woodworking power tool. Many provide for safer tool operation. Books that include jigs for the band saw, drill press and router will be found in the bibliography.

Discussion of some useful hand power tools follows.

Power hand drills are manufactured in an exceptionally wide range of sizes, quality and durability. A good first choice for general use is one with a three-eighths inch chuck capacity in the medium price range. When doing outdoor work away from a power source a three-eighths inch battery operated drill makes a good second unit. The battery type eliminates the electrical shock hazard caused by a short circuit in the drill. You must still avoid drilling into other electrical wiring.

Power hand sanders are commonly found in the belt, pad and palm types. Belt sanders are used for rapid stock removal over large surfaces. The pad sander is sized to make efficient use of standard sandpaper sheets. The smaller palm sander fits in the palm of one hand, uses square sandpaper sheets and sands close to nearby vertical surfaces on three sides.

Saber saws are usually rated by their motor horsepower. A one-fourth horsepower unit fills most general purpose needs.

Hand circular saws are rated by blade diameter and motor horsepower in a wide range of sizes. The seven or 7¼ inch blade models are suitable for most work. Larger models can be heavy.

In its simplest form a router is an electric motor with a bit (a shaped cutter) attached to the shaft. It is guided along a workpiece by hand. The bit has a shank or stem that fits into a collet or chuck on the end of the motor shaft. Routers are rated by motor horsepower and size of bit shank they will accommodate. Selection will depend upon the intended use. A medium duty one horsepower unit capable of accepting one-fourth inch diameter bit shanks is suitable for most work. Routers are very versatile tools. They can produce decorative molded edges, make recesses for hinges, trim laminates and perform many other specialized functions.

Tool catalogs feature many accessories that can be used with hand power tools. Two accessories that can be used as tool guides are especially applicable to circular saws, saber saws and routers. One is an aluminum triangle with a flange on one edge. It is intended to replace a try square. By placing the flange against the workpiece the edge will guide a saw to make a ninety degree cut. The other is a clamping bar that can be attached to sheets of plywood or other large work. It will also guide the tools for a straight cut.

Discussion of large power tools is beyond the scope of this book. The most common tools of this type found in home workshops include scroll saws, table saws, radial arm saws, band saws, drill presses, jointers, planers, belt and disk sanders and lathes. Combination power tools such as the *Shopsmith* and other multi-purpose units provide maximum utilization of valuable shop space. On some combination units set-up time required when changing for one mode to another may take longer than using separate tools. Get sound advice on costly power tool purchases.

Operating safety measures are normally included in the manuals supplied with tools. Take the time to read these instructions and follow them. Wear eye protection equipment and avoid loose clothing or jewelry near moving machinery. Learn suitable sharpening methods and keep tools sharp. The extra effort required to force any dull tool through material often spoils the workpiece and can result in personal injury.

The Workshop

An ideal workshop would have a solid workbench equipped with a woodworking vise, good lighting and plenty of working and storage space and a pair of saw-horses. Unfortunately, most of us don't have the luxury of such a shop. One alternative is the use of a commercially available folding workstation. Select one that is sturdy, has a good clamping capacity for the workpiece and affords a comfortable working height. They have the advantage that they can be easily moved to the job location.

If working space is available, and your level of woodworking activity warrants the financial outlay, you will want to buy or build a workbench. Since commercial woodworking bench prices start at $250 and go much higher, you may want to build one yourself. Plans for workbenches and sawhorses will be found in most woodworking books.

If possible attend woodworking classes to get hands-on experience. You will learn subtle techniques like extending your index finger along the side of a handsaw handle to obtain better control of the saw, cocking a wood plane to one side of the direction of travel to obtain a shearing cutting action, and how to hold a hammer properly. You will learn to avoid forming unsafe tool handling habits and to select the right tool for the job. The instructor will demonstrate how to get the most out of the tools available to you. You will learn two important things: to pay close attention to detail, and that only your best work is good enough.

Most home woodworkers depend upon popular woodworking magazines as a source of ideas for projects. Simple projects such as toys, wall shelves and footstools soon provide the confidence to tackle more complex undertakings. Woodworking is a very practical hobby because it has so many applications. Many enjoy building furniture, cabinetmaking, carpentry or boatbuilding. Some develop an interest in woodcarving. It can be applied to furniture or used to create art objects. Family needs and desires soon play a part in project selection.

Antique Tools

Recent surveys have shown there is a growing trend of appreciation for the past. Interest is increasing in restoring houses, cars and tools. Early woodworkers took great pride in owning the best tools they could afford. Since before recorded history, tools were made with care, lavishly decorated and often served the needs of many generations.

In colonial times American woodworkers imported cases of assorted molding plane cutters from England and crafted wooden plane stocks to match the irons. Later some American craftsmen specialized in making tools as a trade. Most were still made of wood. During the latter half of the nineteenth century American iron tools were developed to the point that they found a market in America and worldwide.

A review of antique tool catalogs reveals that many hand tools were discontinued in the 1940s. Those that remain are more utilitarian. They have shed most of their decoration and fine finishes.

Some furniture and cabinetmakers prefer to continue to use those discontinued hand tools. They feel they have more precise control of them than when using power tools. In some cases where a woodworker chooses to do an operation by hand, such as planing a fancy molding, an old tool is the practical choice. If you only have an occasional need to produce moldings or molded edges, a large expensive power tool is not an economical alternative. For planing flat surfaces, old Bailey planes with wooden bodies and metal adjustment mechanisms offer the best of both worlds. The wooden bodies work with less friction and the metal mechanisms provide easy adjustment.

With the passage of time old tools in good condition are becoming scarce, and collectible, not to mention expensive. An outstanding display of antique tools can be seen at the Shelburne Museum in Vermont.

Early tools can be seen in action on Roy Underhill's PBS-TV program, "The Woodwright's Shop." By way of contrast the use of modern large tools is demonstrated by Norm Abram on his PBS-TV show, "The New Yankee Workshop."

Bibliography

REFERENCE BOOKS

Abram, Norm. *Classics from the New Yankee Workshop*. Boston: Little, Brown, 1990. A selection of projects demonstrating tools and techniques.

————. *The New Yankee Workshop*. Boston: Little, Brown 1989. Setting up shop, a selection of projects demonstrating tools and techniques.

Barlow, Ronald S. *The Antique Tool Collector's Guide to Value*. 3rd ed. El Cajon, CA: Windmill, 1991. Over 5,000 items described and priced. Includes historical information on inventors and manufacturers.

Birchard, John. *Make Your Own Handcrafted Doors and Windows.* New York: Sterling, 1988. Setting up shop, using hand and power tools, applications, and techniques.

Burk, Bruce. *Game Bird Carving.* Hampton, NJ: New Win, 1988. Detailed coverage of bird carving, tools, painting, and anatomy.

Butz, Richard. *How to Carve Wood: A Book of Projects and Techniques.* Newtown CT: Taunton, 1984. Tools, design, chip carving, relief carving, and architectural carving.

Cliffe, Roger W. *Woodworker's Handbook.* New York: Sterling, 1990. General text. Design, material selection, and tools.

DeCristoforo, R. J. *The Band Saw Book with 20 Projects.* Blue Ridge Summit, PA: Tab Books, 1989. Detailed coverage of band saw techniques, projects, jigs, and fixtures.

———. *The Drill Press Book.* Blue Ridge Summit, PA: Tab Books, 1991. Drill press tools, jigs, accessories, and techniques.

Dunbar, Michael. *Restoring, Tuning and Using Classic Woodworking Tools.* New York: Sterling, 1989. Buying guidelines. Restoring, planes, chisels, saws, braces, and bits.

Feirer, John L. *Furniture and Cabinet Making: A Complete How-to by America's Foremost Expert on Woodworking.* Mission Hills, CA: Macmillan, 1983. History, styles, design, tools, construction, and finishing.

Jackson, Albert, David Day and Simon Jennings. *The Complete Manual of Woodworking.* New York: Knopf, 1989. General text. Materials, tools, joints, and hardware.

Klenke, William W. *The Art of Wood Turning.* New York: American Craft Council, 1983. Materials, tools, and techniques.

Krenov, James. *The Fine Art of Cabinetmaking.* New York: Simon and Schuster, 1984. Advanced cabinetmaking, tools, materials, and techniques.

Proudfoot, Christopher, and Phillip Walker. *Woodworking Tools: Christie's Collectors Guides.* Rutland, VT: Tuttle, 1984. Authoritative guide to tool collecting, with auction prices.

Schiff, David, and Kenneth S. Burton, Jr. *The Woodworker's Guide to Making and Using Jigs, Fixtures and Setups.* Emmaus, PA: Rodale, 1992. Innovative jig and fixture designs to extend the capabilities of your tools. Emphasis on power tools.

Spence, William P., and L. Duane Griffiths. *The Woodworker's Illustrated Benchtop Reference.* Blue Ridge Summit, PA: Tab Books, 1989. General text; design, materials, tools, and hardware. Includes both furniture and cabinet construction.

Spielman, Patrick. *Router Jigs and Techniques.* New York: Sterling, 1988. Detailed coverage of router types and techniques, jigs, and fixtures.

———. *Scroll Saw Handbook.* New York: Sterling, 1986. History, scroll saw types, techniques, and projects.

Walter, John. *Antique and Collectible Stanley Tools: A Guide to Identity and Value.* Akron, OH: Tool Merchant, 1990. Comprehensive coverage of Stanley hand tools, dates of manufacture, and price guide.

Watson, Aldren A. *Country Furniture.* New York: Crowell, 1974. History, wood properties, tools, and methods.

———. *Hand Tools: Their Ways and Workings.* New York: Norton, 1982. Detailed coverage of hand tool techniques, well illustrated.

Wildung, Frank H. *Woodworking Tools at Shelburne Museum.* Shelburne, VT: Shelburne Museum, 1957. Photographs of unique antique tools in the collection.

Note: Additional reference books on specific tools or woodworking processes are published by The Taunton Press (*Fine Woodworking On* series); Sterling Publishing; and TAB Books.

PERIODICALS

American Woodworker. Rodale Press, 33 E. Minor Street, Emmaus, PA 18098.

Fine Woodworking. Taunton Press, 63 S. Main Street, Box 5506, Newtown, CT 06470–5506.

Popular Mechanics. Hearst Magazines, Popular Mechanics, 224 W. 57th Street, New York, NY 10019.

Popular Woodworking. EGW Publishers, 1041 Shary Circle, Concord, CA 94518.

Wood. Meredith Corp., 1716 Locust Street, Des Moines, IA 50336.

Woodsmith. Woodsmith Publishers, 2200 Grand Avenue, Des Moines, IA 50312–5306.

The Woodworker's Journal. Madrigal Publishers, 517 Litchfield Road, PO Box 1629, New Milford, CT 06776.

Workbench, KC Publishing, 700 W. 74th Street, Suite 310, Kansas City, MO 64112.

ASSOCIATIONS

Affiliated Woodcarvers Ltd. PO Box 10408, Bettendorf, IA 52722. Woodcarvers and others interested in collecting and promoting woodcarving.

American Association of Woodturners. 667 Harriet Avenue, Shoreview, MN 55126. Amateur and professional woodturners. Provides educational and organizational leadership in the art of woodturning. Publication: *American Woodturner.*

Center for Wooden Boats. 1010 Valley Street, Seattle, WA 98109. Maritime historians, crafts people, sailors and others with an interest in preserving traditional wooden watercraft. Offers introductory instruction in boat building and master classes for experts. Publication: Newsletter.

Marquetry Society of America. c/o Allan E. Fitchett, 32–34 153rd Street, Flushing, NY 11354. Persons interested in cutting and joining together different types and colors of wood to create pictures or designs.

National Woodcarvers Association. 7424 Miami Avenue, Cincinnati, OH 45243. Members interested in wood carving. Publication: *Chip Chats* magazine.

Woodworking Association of North America. PO Box 706, Route 3 and Cummings Hill Road, Plymouth, NH 03264. Members engaged in woodworking. Promotes woodworking as a hobby and an occupation. Publication: *International Woodworking Quarterly* magazine.

Wrestling

THOUSANDS OF YOUNG PEOPLE participate in amateur wrestling in high schools and colleges. Some participate in Amateur Athletic Union Junior Olympic Program competitions, and in the ultimate wrestling challenge, the Olympics. Professional wrestling has degenerated into a form of entertainment put on by actors. Although the pros get most of the media coverage, the amateur sport offers exciting demonstrations of skill, strength, and stamina without a predetermined winner.

The object of the sport is straightforward. The wrestler attacks an opponent and attempts to move the opponent's shoulders to the mat for a very brief period. The premise is simple, but making it happen has been the object of research and training for centuries. So many moves and countermoves have been developed that it's impossible to know them all. Success in wrestling requires a high degree of commitment and discipline.

History

The earliest artifact showing any form of athletics is a Sumerian bronze statuette of two wrestlers. It was made about 3000 B.C. Hundreds of scenes on the walls of the temple-tombs of Beni Hasan near the Nile River in Egypt depict most of the wrestling holds and falls known and used today. Wrestling was a highly developed sport more than 5,000 years ago. Wrestling was first featured in the eighteenth Olympiad, in about 704 B.C. Modern Olympics feature both freestyle and Greco-Roman competitions. Both styles are discussed below.

Early American pioneers engaged in a rough form of freestyle wrestling. There is evidence that the sport was enjoyed by all levels of society. George Washington is known to have participated, and at the age of twenty-one, Abraham Lincoln was recognized as wrestling champion of his county.

The first collegiate wrestling conference originated in 1904, when the Eastern Intercollegiate Wrestling Conference was formed.

Competition Styles and Rules

The two basic styles of modern wrestling are freestyle and Greco-Roman. The primary difference between the two is that Greco-Roman competitors may attack only from the waist up. In freestyle, a wrestler may attack most any part of the opponent's body, subject to certain rules against inflicting bodily harm. Two forms of competition are held. In dual meets, two teams compete matching a wrestler from each team in each of several weight classes. In tournament competition several teams or several wrestlers enter each weight class. Teams may or may not be represented.

Weight Classes

Wrestlers compete in weight classes established for specific age categories. Since weight is such an important factor in the sport, the permissible weight range in a given weight class is quite narrow for some age groups. This leads some competitors to adjust their eating habits to qualify for a desired weight class competition. According to the International Amateur Wrestling Federation (FILA) rules of international wrestling, the senior (open) category starts with class 1, allowing a maximum of 105.5 pounds and ranges up to class 10, allowing a weight of up to 286 pounds.

Conduct of a Match

When a match is to begin, the referee calls the two wrestlers to the center of the mat and inspects them to assure that their person and attire meet the FILA rules. The competitors shake hands and return to their corners. At the sound of the referee's whistle, they approach one another and immediately begin to wrestle.

In American Athletic Union (AAU) competition, bouts consist of two periods. For ages seventeen to thirty-four, there are two 3-minute periods separated by a 60 second rest. For ages thirty-four and older, there are two 2-minute periods with a 30 second rest.

The wrestling mat, used for world championships and international events, is divided by concentric circles. The central wrestling area is defined by a 22.9 foot diameter circle. A passivity zone exists between a 22.9 foot circle and a 29.5 foot diameter circle. A protection area lies outward from the 29.5 foot circle for another 3.9 to 4.9 feet.

During a wrestling period, a bout will be stopped and resumed standing in the middle of the mat under certain circumstances. Examples include: If one foot touches the protection area, if a move ends in the protection area, if the wrestlers leave the mat, if wrestling in the zone isn't continuous, if a hold begun on the ground ends on the protection area, if a wrestler with back exposed (position of danger—see below) slides from the mat to the protection area, or if the shoulder or neck of the wrestler touches the protection area.

During a wrestling period, a bout will be stopped and resumed in the middle of the mat where the attacked wrestler is dominated by the opponent when the two go out of bounds, through the zone and onto the protection area. Examples include: A wrestler touches the protection area with the head while flat on the back, on the mat, under control, or if the active wrestler requests ground wrestling following a caution for passivity on the opponent.

When restarting a bout on the ground (referee's position), the dominated wrestler assumes a hands and knees kneeling position. The dominant wrestler places one hand on the opponent's elbow and the other hand around the opponent's waist. An alternative method may be used where the dominant wrestler places both hands on the opponent's back with thumbs touching.

A "position of danger" occurs whenever the line of the wrestler's back, or the line of the wrestler's shoulders, faces the mat vertically or parallel, forming an angle of less than ninety degrees, and the wrestler resists a fall with the upper part of the body. Back exposure (danger) ceases as soon as the wrestler breaks the vertical line of ninety degrees, with the chest and stomach turned toward the mat.

A takedown occurs when a wrestler brings the opponent to the mat from a standing position and gets control.

Earning Points

Wrestlers earn points for certain moves and holds. A "grand technique" hold or move occurs if it: forces the opponent to completely lose ground contact, controls the opponent, results in the opponent traveling through the air at "great amplitude or height," and returns the opponent to the ground directly in a position of immediate danger. If the result is immediate danger, the score is 4 points. If the result brings no immediate danger, 2 points. If the grand technique is executed from the ground, 5 points.

Examples of other moves that earn points:

One point is scored for bringing an opponent to the mat with no back exposure; for moving from underneath to the upper position in control; for applying a correct hold without causing the opponent's head or shoulder to touch the mat; or for the wrestler whose opponent flees the mat.

Two points are scored when an opponent rolls from side to side to form a bridge using elbows or shoulders.

Three points are scored for a standing throw of small amplitude that directly takes the opponent's back to danger; for holds where the opponent is lifted from the mat, with a throw of small amplitude, even if the attacker has one or two knees on the mat, provided the opponent's back is immediately placed in danger.

A fall has occurred when both shoulders of a wrestler simultaneously touch the mat when the opponent is in control for a count of one second in college competition, or two seconds in high school competition.

The bout ends when a fall or technical superiority (15 points) is established, when one of the two wrestlers is eliminated or disqualified, when there is an injury, or when the time allowed for wrestling expires.

Restricted Actions

Modern wrestling moves prohibit stalling techniques (passivity), but at the same time protect wrestlers from intentional bodily harm. A few examples of restrictions placed upon competitors include the following actions that are forbidden:

Pulling of hair, ears, or genitals; pinching, biting, or twisting fingers, toes; or other twisting capable of hurting.

Punching, kicking, head butting, strangle, push, or the application of holds that may endanger life.

Walking on an opponent's feet, touching the face between the eyebrows and the line of the mouth, or grabbing the sole of an opponent's foot.

Certain holds that create conditions such as those listed above.

Fitness and Equipment

A wrestler requires hours of training and conditioning before it's safe to commit to the brief period spent in competition. Calisthenics, road-work, and weight lifting under the supervision of a qualified coach build the strength and stamina needed to compete. Don't participate without a physician's permission.

Personal wrestling equipment consists of wrestling shoes, sweat socks, tights and shorts, supporter, athletic shirt, and wrestling helmet.

Strategy

We have seen that the number of possible wrestling moves and countermoves is extensive. In the early 1970s, coaches of the U.S. Wrestling Federation (now USA Wrestling) worked to define skill areas that have broad application to the sport. They identified a list of seven basic skills. Much has been written about the subject, and details will be found in books listed in the bibliography below. Here, we'll look at a brief outline of those seven basic skills.

Stance. Look ahead with the head up. Keep hands in front of the body, elbows near hips. Keep the hips below the head and shoulders when possible, even when wrestling on the mat. Keep knees bent and shoulder width apart.

Motion. Keep feet, hips, and upper body in motion. This presents a more difficult target for the opponent, and helps the attacker set up maneuvers.

Changing Levels. Change levels by lowering or raising hips, not head or shoulders.

Penetration. Drive the hips into and through an opponent, keeping your stance as you penetrate. Driving your weight in and over your knee puts pressure into your opponent.

Lifting. An opponent is most vulnerable when the opponent loses contact with the mat. Lift with the hips and squeeze with the arms.

Arch and Turn. When placed in a position of danger, with the back towards the mat, support your body on two feet and one shoulder, and raise your hips to form an arch. Encircle the opponent with your arms and pull tight. Thrust your hips into the opponent to raise him from the mat, and at the same time turn your body to tumble your opponent over onto his back.

Back Step. Step back with one foot as you turn from a position facing the opponent. Rotate on both feet while holding the opponent in an armlock or headlock. This places you in a position to pull the opponent over your back in a throw to the mat.

Some additional basic skills have since been identified, but they are often variations or combinations of the seven basic skills listed.

Bibliography

REFERENCE BOOKS

Combs, Steve, with Chuck Frank. *Winning Wrestling.* Chicago: Contemporary Books, 1980. Covers the seven basic skills and a number of holds and countermoves against such holds.

Hellickson, Russ, with Andrew Baggot. *An Instructional Guide to Amateur Wrestling.* New York: Perigee, 1987. Comprehensive coverage of wrestling that supplements the basic skills with techniques used to achieve various objectives such as takedowns and escapes.

Johnson, Dennis A. *Wrestling Drill Book.* Champaign, IL: Leisure, 1991. A book of wrestling practice drills emphasizing the seven basic skills.

Mood, Dale, et al. *Sports and Recreational Activities,* 9th ed. St. Louis, MO: Times/Mirror/Mosby, 1987. Contains an overview of wrestling with emphasis on holds and moves.

Rookie Coaches Wrestling Guide. Champaign, IL: Leisure, 1992. Advice and counsel for the first-time wrestling coach. Covers conditioning and practice drills.

Umbach, Arnold, and Warren Johnson. *Wrestling.* Rev. ed. Dubuque, IA: Brown, 1984. Covers history, various moves, equipment, and training.

White, Jess R., ed. *Sports Rules Encyclopedia.* 2nd ed. Champaign, IL: Leisure, 1990. Includes the International Amateur Wrestling Federation Rules of International Wrestling Greco-Roman and freestyle including AAU/USA Junior Olympic Program Rules.

PERIODICALS

USA Wrestler. 225 S. Academy Boulevard, Colorado Springs, CO 80910.

Wrestling Manual and Case Book. National Federation of State High School Associations, 11724 NW Plaza Circle, Box 20626, Kansas City, MO 64195–0626.

Wrestling Rulebook. National Federation of State High School Associations, 11724 NW Plaza Circle, Box 20626, Kansas City, MO 64195–0626.

Wrestling U.S.A. Magazine. 1924 Baxter Drive, Bozeman, MT 59715.

ASSOCIATIONS

Amateur Athletic Union of the United States. 3400 W. 86th Street, PO Box 68207, Indianapolis, IN 46268. Sports associations. Sponsors AAU/ USA Junior Olympic Games, which includes competition in fifteen sports, AAU Youth Sports Program, and the Presidential Sports Award. Maintains library and hall of fame. Publications: *Info AAU,* newsmagazine, and related materials.

National Wrestling Coaches Association. c/o Les Anderson, Iowa State University, 10 State Gym, Ames, IA 50011. Coaches and officials connected with amateur wrestling. Bestows awards and helps maintain hall of fame. Publication: *Amateur Wrestling News.*

U.S.A. Wrestling. 225 S. Academy Boulevard, Colorado Springs, CO 80910. Amateur wrestlers, coaches, and others interested in amateur wrestling. Serves as national governing body and member of U.S. Olympic Committee. Conducts clinics, maintains National Wrestling Hall of Fame, museum, and library. Bestows awards. Publications: *USA Wrestler, Link,* and related materials.

Writing

MOST WRITING FALLS INTO one of two categories. Writers of good fiction produce imaginative stories using word-pictures to create images in the mind of the reader. The second category, nonfiction for lack of a better term, deals primarily with factual explanations of ideas and concepts. A successful nonfiction writer will also use an imaginative and creative writing style to hold the interest of the reader.

Some representative fiction genres (types) include action/adventure, fantasy, horror, mystery, romance, science fiction, suspense/thriller, and western. Over half of the books sold are romance novels, written in over ten sub-categories. Quality novels are popular.

Poetry is another form of imaginative writing that requires the creative use of language. While some may win a mate with poetry, it generally has little commercial sales appeal.

Nonfiction categories include advertising materials, biographies, how-to books and articles, magazine articles, newsletters, newspaper fillers, research papers, technical specifications, and video scripts. Writing short newspaper fillers is a good beginner's activity. How-to material enjoys a large market due to widespread need for this type of information.

Some creative people find that writing satisfies a deeply felt need for self-expression. Many who enjoy letter writing engage in correspondence with friends and distant pen pals. The study of effective writing can be an enjoyable and challenging activity that leads to refined communication skills. These skills will add clarity and credibility to job-related writing. The student may also wish to write for pleasure, and if this leads to selling the work, that's just icing on the cake. Due to the popularity of writing as a pastime, publishers receive many manuscripts, so they can afford to be very selective. Translation—don't be too quick to quit your day job.

Preliminary Preparation

The development of adequate writing skills requires far more study and preparation than most other pastimes. Ideally, a writer should supplement standard English courses with creative writing courses, workshops, and extensive reading of material relating to the genre of writing being contemplated. During training sessions contact will be made with others having similar goals and interests. This often results in the opportunity to join workshop groups that provide mutual support, encouragement, and useful criticism. You will learn by listening to what others do, and by the mistakes they make.

Expand your vocabulary while reading by consulting a dictionary as you come across unfamiliar words. Playing word games like scrabble and working crossword puzzles also help to learn new words. Listen carefully while associating with others who communicate well, and listen to quality radio and television programs.

Writer's magazines list numerous specialized courses and workshops to further development and creativity. They also announce many contests intended to identify deserving new talent. These competitions provide a challenge to do your best work, and help to focus your efforts to improve your writing.

As your skills develop, study specialized texts, such as those in the bibliography, that cover the finer points of writing in a chosen genre.

Research

Writing requires research. It starts when you conduct research to pick a genre and select an interesting and salable subject within the genre.

To write realistic fiction, an author will research all aspects of the era and location being featured. The environment in which the story is set should be communicated to the reader. Clothing styles, transportation methods, vocabulary used, and many other aspects must be appropriate for the time and place.

Nonfiction should provide factual and useful information to the reader. Writing in nonfiction categories demands the accuracy made possible through careful research.

Writing ideas for all genres come from memory, observation, and imagination, all related to experience. These factors must be supplemented and confirmed through research. Thorough research includes confirmation from more than one source. Original sources are best, especially for a book such as a biography. A good place to start your search is the local library, where you will find reference books, magazines, newspapers, biographies, clipping files, and a wealth of other sources.

Reference books include encyclopedias, almanacs, fact books, and guides to other sources of information. The *Readers' Guide to Periodical Literature* is a compilation of information found in magazines. It has listings of topics, directing the user to the article of interest. The *Subject Guide to Books in Print* enables a writer to establish whether current books are available on a given subject, and what competition may exist for a contemplated book project.

Industrial libraries feature material related to their products. Although intended for private use, some firms will respond to requests for specific information.

See the "History and Research" section in this text for additional information about the use of university libraries and historical society libraries. Also, see the "Computers, Personal" section in this text for information relating to the access of data bases. This service is sometimes available through your library for a fee.

The Writing Process

After selecting your genre and subject and updating your knowledge through research, do two more things before you start. First, determine if there is a market for your project should you want to sell it. Does it fill a need? Second, formulate your writing approach to reach the intended reader.

When starting a new project, a sculptor often models the subject in clay first because it is easy to work with. It becomes the basic form from which the end product can be developed. When planning a book, your clay is the chapter outline. You can develop and accumulate notes for each chapter in individual folders or envelopes. Use these notes to refresh your memory and stimulate the thought process during your actual writing. The same approach applies to shorter projects where paragraphs receive the same preparation as chapters.

Write your first draft of each chapter without undue concern for sentence structure, spelling, or neatness. It's your "sloppy copy." Once the basic ideas are in place, later rewrites will be much easier.

Make your work clear, concise, and easy to read. Use a thesaurus if necessary to avoid repetitive use of words. Don't try to use big words to impress the reader. Vary sentence length, use punctuation properly, and keep paragraphs down to one element of the subject.

Equipment

A hobbyist needs only a pencil and paper to get started. However, a dedicated writer will find some of the following equipment indispensable for the more complex projects.

A personal computer with word processing software will speed work and facilitate rewrites. Most software includes a spelling checker, automatic hyphenation, and a built-in thesaurus.

Eliminate painstaking typing chores by connecting a printer to the computer. Your words are your product, and the more they look like fine printing, the better impression they will make. Early printers created letters from a grouping of dots (dot matrix). Reading their output can be hard on the eyes. Consider a mid-scale printer that produces good quality copy.

You can connect a modem between your computer and a telephone line to permit access to information data bases. This arrangement allows you to do research at your convenience, twenty-four hours a day.

A cassette tape recorder is useful if you expect to interview people or record other information. If the recorder has a remote jack, you can attach a transcriber foot pedal to it, making it easier to type the recorded conversation.

Selling Your Work

A surprising number of writers don't adequately research the publishers they select. Few large publishing houses will consider the work of an unpublished author without an agent. In addition, few agents will consider handling the work of an unpublished author. Fortunately, publishers of writer's magazines sift through thousands of publishers in the United States and identify the publishing houses most likely to review a beginner's proposal.

Most publishers specialize in a limited number of genres. If you send your book proposal about archeological research to a publisher specializing in woodworking you are wasting your time and that of the publisher. The first step in selecting a publisher is to study an annual publication such as the *Writer's Market*. The detailed information provided includes the type of work that each publisher is seeking. Select one or more publishers that need your material and prepare your query letter or proposal.

A query letter is a brief, but detailed letter written to interest an editor in your manuscript. Fiction is sometimes queried, but the majority of fiction editors will want to see a synopsis and sample chapters. Most fiction editors don't like to make a final decision until they see the complete manuscript.

Most editors of nonfiction prefer to be queried. The query may be followed by a book proposal, which includes information regarding the marketability of the book. As a minimum, your proposal should do the following:

1. Describe the subject and scope of the work.
2. Identify similar works and explain how yours differs.
3. Identify target audience and any secondary audience.
4. Provide annotated table of contents.
5. Estimate manuscript length and time required to complete.
6. List illustrations required.
7. State how text will be transmitted (computer disk, paper copy).
8. Include resume of your experience, stressing your unique qualifications for writing the work.
9. Include one or two sample chapters.

Publishers may choose to reject your proposal for a number of reasons, many of which have no relationship to the quality of your proposal. They don't need additional projects at the time. They have a similar work under contract. The market for the work isn't very large. The subject matter may be outdated before the work comes out. There are many other such reasons.

Just under one percent of unsolicited, first time authors' books are published; so prepare yourself for rejection. Unless you have sent your proposal to at least twenty-five publishers, you haven't given your book the chance it needs to get published.

With persistence, you can join the thousands who have sold their first book, magazine article, or other work. It's a challenging pastime.

Bibliography

REFERENCE BOOKS

Balkin, Richard. *How to Understand and Negotiate a Book Contract or Magazine Agreement.* Cincinnati, OH: Writer's Digest Books, 1985. Takes the mystery out of the legal terms in writing contracts.

Burack, Sylvia K., ed. *How to Write and Sell Mystery Fiction.* Boston: Writer, 1990. Twenty-one authors offer advice on crime fiction writing.

Evans, Glen, ed. *The Complete Guide to Writing Non-Fiction.* Cincinnati, OH: Writer's Digest Books, 1983. Written by the American Society of Journalists and Authors. Explains the essentials of the writing craft, and tells how to find and sell to a variety of markets.

Horowitz, Lois. *Knowing Where to Look: The Ultimate Guide to Research.* Cincinnati, OH: Writer's Digest Books, 1984. How to use everything from libraries to U.S. embassies, newspapers to videotext systems—and which sources are most likely to have what you need.

Hull, Raymond. *How to Write "How-To" Books and Articles.* Cincinnati, OH: Writer's Digest Books, 1981. Step-by-step workbook showing how to write and sell the how-to genre.

Kirby, David. *Writing Poetry.* Boston: Writer, 1989. The writing of all types of poems. Outlines basic rules, form, rhyme, and meter.

Larson, Michael. *How to Write a Book Proposal.* Cincinnati, OH: Writer's Digest Books, 1985. A literary agent explains each step in writing a nonfiction book proposal.

Millward, Celia. *Handbook for Writers.* 2nd ed. New York: Holt, Rinehart & Winston, 1983. Covers grammar, punctuation, rhetoric, and research.

Naylor, Phyllis Reynolds. *The Craft of Writing a Novel.* Boston: Writer, 1989. Step-by-step discussion of the techniques required for writing novels.

Perry, Carol Rosenblum. *The Fine Art of Technical Writing.* Hillsboro, OR: Blue Heron, 1991. Covers writing style and grammar for all types of nonfiction.

Provost, Gary. *Beyond Style: Mastering the Finer Points of Writing.* Cincinnati, OH: Writer's Digest Books, 1988. Covers writing aspects such as pace, imagery, credibility, and tension. Applies to fiction and nonfiction.

Rockwell, F. A. *How to Write Non-Fiction that Sells.* Chicago: Contemporary Books, 1975. Covers a variety of nonfiction genres. Explores information sources and techniques.

Strunk, William, Jr., and E. B. White. *Elements of Style.* 3rd ed. New York: Macmillan, 1979. A brief, important book about writing style that has stood the test of time.

University of Chicago Press. *The Chicago Manual of Style.* 14th ed. Chicago: University of Chicago Press, 1993. The definitive book on writing style.

Whitney, Phyllis A. *Guide to Fiction Writing.* 2nd ed. Boston: Writer, 1988. Techniques for writing fiction. How to sell novels and stories.

Yolen, Jane. *Guide to Writing for Children.* Boston: Writer, 1989. Gives specific, practical advice for juvenile writing.

PERIODICALS

American Poetry Review. World Poetry, 1721 Walnut Street, Philadelphia, PA 19103.

Ideals. Ideals Publishers, 565 Marriott Drive, Box 14800, Nashville, TN 37214. (Poetry.)

Poets and Writers Magazine. Poets and Writers, 72 Spring Street, New York, NY 10012.

World of Poetry. 11419 Cronridge Drive, Suite 10, Owings Mills, MD 21117–6216.

Writer. Writer, 120 Boylston Street, Boston, MA 02116.

Writer's Digest. F & W Publications, 1507 Dana Avenue, Cincinnati, OH 45207.

Writer's Journal, Minnesota Ink, 27 Empire Drive, St. Paul, MN 55103–1861.

Writer's Market, F & W Publications, 1507 Dana Avenue, Cincinnati, OH 45207.

Writer's NW, Media Weavers, 24450 NW Hanson Road, Hillsboro, OR 97124.

ASSOCIATIONS

Academy of American Poets. 584 Broadway, Suite 1208, New York, NY 10012. Encourages the production of American poetry. Bestows awards. Publications: *Booklist,* and *Poetry Pilot.*

American Poetry Association. 250–A Potrero Street, PO Box 1803, Santa Cruz, CA 95061. Encourages interest in poetry. Sponsors contests. Publication: *American Poetry Anthology.*

American Society of Journalists and Authors. 1501 Broadway, Suite 302, New York, NY 10036. Freelance writers of nonfiction magazine articles and books. Operates or sponsors services benefiting members. Presents awards. Publications: Membership directory, newsletter, and several books on nonfiction writing.

Associated Writing Programs. Old Dominion University, 1411 W. 49th Street, Norfolk VA 23529–0079. Writers, students and teachers in writing programs, editors, publishers, and creative and professional writers. Helps writers get published and find jobs. Operates placement service, and sponsors competitions. Publications: *AWP Chronicle, Official Guide to Writing Programs,* and related material.

Federation of International Poetry Associations. PO Box 579, Santa Claus, IN 47579. Operates under the auspices of the United Nations Educational, Scientific and Cultural Organization. Unites and represents diverse societies and groups of professional poets of all nations. Presents honors and maintains library. Publications: *New Muses,* and a monograph series.

International Women's Writing Guild. Box 810, Gracie Station, New York, NY 10028. Women writers in twenty-four countries. Facilitates manuscript submissions to literary agents. Conducts workshops and bestows Artist of Life Award. Publication: Newsletter.

Mystery Writers of America. 17 E. 47th Street, 6th Floor, New York, NY 10017. Professional mystery-crime writers. Unpublished writers are affiliate members. Publishers and agents are associate members. Provides workshop and sponsors awards. Publications: *Anthology, MWA Directory, Mystery Writers Annual,* and newsletter.

National Federation of State Poetry Societies. c/o Wanda Blaisdell, 2664 Shemrock, Ogden, VT 84403. Sponsors annual national poetry contest. State groups conduct workshops and seminars. Publications: *Prize Poems,* and newsletter.

Romance Writers of America. 13700 Veterans Memorial Drive, Suite 315, Houston, TX 77014. Supports beginning, intermediate, and advanced romance writers. Conducts workshops and individual manuscript consultations. Sponsors competitions and bestows awards. Publications: *Romance Writers Report,* and an advisory letter.

Library Classification Identification of Subjects Covered in This Book

LIBRARY BOOKS ARE IDENTIFIED, cataloged and shelved according to their classification numbers. These numbers are usually displayed on the ends of library shelves. For your convenience, the following explanation of the classification system has been prepared to help you find the shelving containing books you wish to browse.

This book's primary subjects are listed, together with their library classification identification. Each subject title is followed by the Dewey number and the Library of Congress (LC) classification. The LC is shown in parenthesis.[1]

The Dewey Decimal Classification (Dewey Number) system is used by 95 percent of all public and school libraries, and 25 percent of all college and university libraries. The class number is composed of three numbers followed by a period and additional numbers as required to narrow the identification of a subject.

The Library of Congress classification system is used by large libraries that require a more expandable classification system. The LC meets this need by using letters as well as numbers to provide class identification. The LC classification notation begins with one capital letter for a main class and two or three capital letters for subclasses. Within each main class or subclass integers 1–9999 are used for subdivisions. Decimal extensions of the integers are used where there are no available integers for new subjects. After the first set of letters and numerals, another set follows. This is called a Cutter number. It's always preceded by a period.

Both classification systems are frequently updated to accommodate the rapid expansion of knowledge and printed information.

---

1. Classification Reference Sources:
  Melvil Dewey, *Dewey Decimal Classification and Relative Index,* 4 v., 20th ed. (Albany, NY: Forest Press, 1989).
  Subject Headings, 3 v., 14th ed. (Washington, DC: Library of Congress Office for Subject Cataloging Policy), published annually.

Aircraft: 387.73-aircraft, 629.132521-piloting of, (TL670–TL723).
Anthropology: 301, (GN).
Antiques: 745.1-antiques, 749.1-antique furniture, (NK).
Archaeology: 930.1-archaeology, (CC-general, GN700–GN890-prehistoric antiquities).
Archery: 799.32, (GV1185–GV1189).
Astronomy: 520-astronomy, 520.92-astronomers, 522.2-astronomical instruments, 523-specific celestial bodies, (QB).
Automobiles: 388.342-automobiles, 629.28-repair of, 796.7-sports, (TL1–TL445).

Baseball: 796.357, (GV862–GV881).
Basketball: 796.323, (GV885).
Bicycles: 388.3472-bicycles, 629.28472-riding, (GV1040–GV1058).
Billiards: 794.72, (GV891-billiards, GV891–GV899-billiards, pocket).
Bird Watching: 598.07234, (QL60).
Birds: 598, (QL671–QL699).
Birds, caged: 636.686, (SF512).
Boats: 623.82, (GV771–GV836.15).
Bowling: 794.6, (GV901–GV909).
Boxing: 796.83, (GV1115–GV1137).

Camping: 796.54, (GV191.68–GV198.9).
Carpentry: 694, (TH5601–TH5695).
Cats: 636.8, (SF441–SF449).
Ceramics: 738.1-ceramics, 666.6-pottery, (NK3700–NK4695-ceramics, TT919–TT924-pottery).
Coins: 332.4042-coins, 737.4-numismatics, (CJ1–CJ4625-coins, CJ-numismatics, general).
Collectibles: 790.132, (AM200–AM501).
Computers: 004-data processing, 004.16-personal computer, (QA76.9.C64-computer literacy).
Cooking: 641.5, (TX643–TX840).
Crochet: 677.662-crochet fabrics, 746.434-crocheting, (TT820–TT825).

Skiing: 796.93, (GV854.9).
Skin Diving: 797.23, (GV840.S78).
Snooker: 794.735, (GV900.S6).
Snowboarding: 796.93, (GV857.S57).
Snowmobiles: 796.94, (GV857.S6).
Soccer: 796.334, (GV943–GV944).
Softball: 796.3578, (GV881).
Stained Glass: 748.5, (NK5300–NK5410).
Stamps: 769.56, (HE6187–HE6230).
Surfing: 797.32, (GV840.S8–GV840.S82).
Swimming: 797.21, (GV837–GV838).

Tailoring: 646.4, (TT570–TT630).
Tennis: 796.342, (GV990–GV1005).

Theater: 792, (PN2000–PN3299).
Travel: 910, (G149–G180).

Volleyball: 796.325, (GV1015–GV1015.57).
Volunteering: 361.37, (HN49.V64).

Walking: 613.7176, (GV1071).
Water skiing: 797.35, (GV840.S5).
Weather forecasting: 551.5–551.6, (QC995).
Windsurfing: 797.33, (GV811.63.W56).
Woodworking: 684.08, (TT180–TT203.5).
Wrestling: 796.812, (GV1195–GV1196).
Writing: 808, (PN101–PN249).

Subject Index